Danish Towns during Absolutism
Urbanisation and Urban Life 1660-1848

In the series *Danske Bystudier* (Danish Urban Studies), the following titles have been published:

Middelalderbyen (2004)
Den klassiske købstad (2005)
Den moderne by (2006)
All these books have English summaries.

Front Cover:
The town of Vejle ca. 1800
Painting, Vejle Byhistoriske Arkiv og Stadsarkiv

Inner Front Cover:
The Kingdom of Denmark, Norway, Schleswig-Holstein, and southern Sweden (belonging to Denmark before 1660). The frontier between the two duchies Schleswig (in north) and Holstein (in south) was a few kilometres south of the towns Husum and Schleswig.

Danish Urban Studies, 4

Danish Towns during Absolutism

Urbanisation and Urban Life 1660-1848

Edited by
Søren Bitsch Christensen & Jørgen Mikkelsen

The Danish Centre for Urban History

Aarhus University Press

Danish Towns during Absolutism. Urbanisation and Urban Life 1660-1848

Danske Bystudier (Danish Urban Studies), 4

© The authors and Aarhus University Press 2008

Cover and layout: Jørgen Sparre

Font: Indigo Antiqua

Paper: Arctic Volume

Printed by: Narayana Press, Denmark

ISBN: 978 87 7934 152 4

Aarhus University Press

Langelandsgade 177

DK-8200 Aarhus N

www.unipress.dk

Published in cooperation with

The Danish Centre for Urban History

www.byhistorie.dk

The Danish Centre for Urban History was founded in 2001

by Den Gamle By, National Open Air Museum of Urban History and Culture,

and The Institute of History and Area Studies, University of Aarhus

Published with grants from

The Danish Research Council for the Humanities

The Aarhus University Research Foundation

Augustinus Fonden

Hielmstierne-Rosencroneske Stiftelse

Konsul George Jorck og Hustru Emma Jorck's Fond

Farumgaard-Fonden

Carlsen-Langes Legatstiftelse

Ruth og Finn Riis-Hansens Familiefond

Contents

Søren Bitsch Christensen
Jørgen Mikkelsen

Preface

All too often Denmark has been conspicuous by its absence from international urban historical literature, and the main reason for this was the lack of literature published in an international language about Danish urban development. The principal aim of this book, therefore, is to rectify this situation by presenting – in English – recent significant research on Denmark's urban development.

This book marks the culmination of two research ventures undertaken by The Danish Centre for Urban History on the basis of grants from the The Danish Research Council for the Humanities.

The first venture was a researchers' network called 'Byens rum og det rummelige bysamfund i historisk perspektiv' (Urban space and urban community in a historical perspective), that in 2003 and 2004 involved a number of seminars with Danish and International researchers. Many of the books' articles are related to this network. However, the editors' contributions were written partially as a part of the research programme called 'Urban kultur og urbane netværk under enevælden 1660-1848' (Urban culture and urban networks during Absolutism, 1660-1848), that took place 2005-2007.

The anthology examines the development of the urban system and urban life in Denmark during the age of Absolutism, 1660-1848. The years of Absolutism were marked by a general crisis for the Danish urban community, mainly caused by the devastating effects of the warfare of the seventeenth century. But some towns stood out with positive development, first and foremost Copenhagen which flourished in its function as the centre of the Absolutist regime. The book traces both the roots of the urban crisis and the regional and temporal variations. Many articles provide an overview of urbanisation in both the Kingdom of Denmark and the Duchy of Schleswig, while other articles focus on the economic, social, and cultural urban functions.

The 'Introduction' gives a deeper presentation of the editorial principles of the book, and in this regard we wish to mention that a glossary is included at the back of the book to guide foreign readers through the Danish vocabulary. A map of the most important places dealt with in the book is found on the inner front cover, while more specified maps are to be found in many of the articles. Multimedia companions to some of the articles are published on the Centre's homepage www.byhistorie.dk.

Danish Towns during Absolutism. Urbanisation and Urban Life 1660-1848 is published as Volume 4 in the series *Danske Bystudier* (Danish Urban Studies), and while the previous books are in Danish, they contain English summaries.

Sincere thanks to Maeve Drewsen, MA, for language revision and translation of many of the articles, and to Lisbeth Skjernov, MA, for her assistance with illustrations, the drawing of maps, etc.

Last, but not least, our deep gratitude to the many Foundations that have kindly supported the project financially and thus made the publication of this book possible.

Søren Bitsch Christensen
Jørgen Mikkelsen

Introduction

Denmark during Absolutism – a conglomerate state

Today, Denmark is a small country with a population that is much more homogeneous than that of most other European countries.[1] In contrast, 200-300 years ago, Denmark was a medium-sized conglomerate state consisting of a number of relatively comparable geographical units, linked strongly or loosely, but differing quite a lot from each other, not just in regard to their landscape and commerce, but also in regard to language and culture, as well as social, judicial, administrative and political structures.[2] Specifically there were two Kingdoms, Denmark and Norway, and two Duchies, Schleswig and Holstein. Furthermore the state was composed of three North-Atlantic territories, Iceland, the Faroes and Greenland, which had all been colonised by Norwegians in the early Middle Ages and considered since then as dependencies of Norway. Finally, there were a few small colonies in India, West Africa and the West Indies, which had been acquired in the period 1620-1733.[3]

The Danish Kingdom – or 'the core area of Denmark' as some historians like to call it – covered the Jutland peninsula north of Kongeåen, the islands of Funen, Zealand, Lolland, Falster, and Bornholm, as well as numerous small islands. In addition, the regions of Scania, Halland and Blekinge, east of Øresund, belonged to the Kingdom until 1658 when these areas were ceded to Sweden after a war. Afterwards Denmark attempted to regain these regions several times, but in vain. The Norwegian Kingdom was acquired by the Danish Crown through inheritance in 1380 and continued to be under the Danish King until 1814 when Norway entered into a union with Sweden instead. On the other hand, the North-Atlantic territories remained under Denmark after 1814. However, Iceland became an independent state in 1944. The overseas colonies were sold in the years from 1845 to 1917.

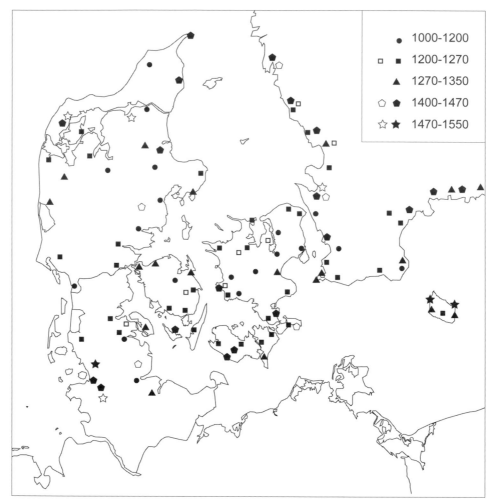

FIG. 1.

Towns established in Denmark and the Duchy of Schleswig 1000-1550, according to Anders Andrén.

Politically, and with regard to administration, Schleswig and Holstein were by far the most complicated parts of the conglomerate state. In 1459-1460 both Duchies passed to the Danish King, who on the same occasion promised that the two territories should remain forever together and undivided. In 1544, however, both Duchies were divided between three of the King's sons, and during the following 150 years or more, there were many bitter conflicts between their descendants. A solution to these problems was first achieved when the Danish King in 1721 became Duke of the entire Schleswig and, in the course of the following 50 years or so, of almost the whole of Holstein.[4] However, during the rise of nationalism after 1830 new conflicts arose about the constitutional status of the two Duchies. These brought about two wars in 1848-1850 and 1864, and the second war resulted in both Schleswig and Holstein being incorporated in Prussia. After a referendum in 1920, the northern part of Schleswig was 're-united' with Denmark.

When working with the history of Danish towns in earlier times, it is important to remember that the state was comprised of much greater areas than present-day Denmark. Nevertheless, in this book, we will chiefly concentrate on conditions in the Kingdom of Denmark during the Age of Absolutism. However, most of the articles to a greater or lesser extent also involve other parts of the monarchy, and a single article even takes its point of departure completely outside the Kingdom. In addition, many of the writers put their contributions into a wider European context.

But before we look more closely at the various articles, we will present some fundamental concepts and two 'framework' stories that can form the background for the rest of the book. The first is about the development of the Danish town system from the Middle Ages until the present, while the second is about Danish Absolutism in theory and practice, including the way administration functioned in the towns.

The concept of towns

In the Absolutist period 1660-1848, practically all towns in the Kingdom of Denmark were so-called *købstæder* (singular: *købstad*), meaning 'places in which to buy'. We have chosen to translate this term to market town(s). The total area of a market town consisted of the built-up area called the town ground and, outside this, the town fields. The jurisdiction of the town covered the entire area while the customs barrier between the country and the town was often just outside the town ground. The crucial social stratification was between burghers and non-burghers. Being a burgher was normally a precondition for having an independent business and for participation in a town's political and administrative life. And, in order to be admitted as a burgher, it was necessary to get a trade licence from the municipal administration.[5] Until 1848 burghers formally constituted the third rank in society, coming after the two ranks that, in principle, were tax exempt – the nobility and clergy, but the burghers were always considered to be higher than the peasant class, who did not have any privileges at all. Economically and socially, however, only a very few burghers were on a par with the owners of private estates,[6] and very few burghers achieved top posts in society on a national level before ca. 1800.

There was no real inclusive town legislation during the period of Absolutism, but in 1683 most of the still valid general regulations about the towns' judicial and economic conditions were included in *Danske Lov* ('Statute of the Danes', the codified statute book). Besides these regulations, a large part of town legislation was written into the privileges and municipal charters of the individual market towns. The market town privileges meant that they had their own administration and constituted independent jurisdictions – in this regard, incidentally, like many estates.[7] As special tax areas they were exempt from many of the state taxes that were imposed on rural districts; in return, the bulk of the consumption taxes, *accise* or *konsumtion* (excise) duties, which existed in the period 1671-1852, were levied only in the market towns. But the most important thing was that, until the freedom of trade legislation of 1857 (which came into force five years later), the market towns had the monopoly on conducting most forms of commerce, trade, shipping and other 'burgher business'. However, there were some exceptions to the rule. For example, the right to perform a number of basic trades in the villages was confirmed in 1558, and this right was not changed afterwards. On the whole, Absolutism did not make any fundamental changes in these conditions, even though a number of adjustments were made towards the end of the period that allowed larger commercial activities in the country.[8]

The urban system in the Danish Kingdom before the 17th century[9]

In international urban history research of recent decades, the central place theory and the network model have come to prevail as the most used theoretical tools for undertaking analyses of the urban system of a country or a region. The central place theory is based on the role of the towns as service organs for the rural population, functioning as selling and buying places for material products, as well as supplying various non-material services such as education, religious services and the administration of justice. The main task of the model is to describe the extent and nature of the services of the individual towns in specific areas so that, on this basis, a stratified hierarchy of towns can be set up. The greater the number of commercial and administrative functions a town had, the higher its position in the 'pyramid'. But the size of the population is naturally also an important criterion when setting up the hierarchy – and in practice often the most important.

While the central place model is suitable for studying the relationship between neighbouring towns, the network model focuses on long-distance connections. It deals in particular with towns that are strongly trade oriented, which often have greater contact with distant trading towns than with the closest towns in its hinterland. These 'network towns' in many cases will therefore have experienced a course of trading cycles different from the neighbouring towns. However the network model can be used not only for analyses of goods supply, but also to study the flow of non-material elements, for instance information. The model lays stress on the so-called gateways, i.e. nodal points connecting two regions through the exchange of goods or other services.

The two models can be regarded as complementary and several scholars, among them Paul M. Hohenberg and Lynn H. Lees, have indeed also pointed out that a more finely differentiated description of developments in a town or region is often obtained by combining the two models. For example it can sometimes be seen that a town, which at one time had extensive trade and shipping, later – when international trading routes changed – finds a new role as an administrative and service centre in the region in question.[10] Both models can also be used with advantage to illuminate urban development in the Danish Kingdom, but they do not have equal weight in all periods. In general, it must be said that the central place model is most relevant. This is connected with the fact that right up until 1870 the rural population constituted at least 75 % of the whole population of Denmark, and that the demands of the rural inhabitants were therefore of crucial importance for the vast majority of the towns. For its part, the network model is of particular interest because the long Danish coastline gave the Danish towns numerous opportunities for shipping contacts abroad and with other parts of the monarchy – and because Denmark ever since the Middle Ages has benefited from its central location on one of North Europe's most important trading routes, namely the route between the Baltic States and Western Europe. The Danish historian, Knud J.V. Jespersen, also plainly characterised the geographical location of Denmark as a gateway. At the same time, he declared – perhaps a little pointedly – that the Danish conglomerate state in the early modern period was only held together by the sovereignty of the Danish Crown and regular shipping between the different parts of the monarchy.[11]

A characteristic feature of the Danish urban landscape before ca. 1850 was that the majority of the towns had been granted full market town privileges by the Crown. For most of them, this happened at a very early stage in the life of the town. Indeed in many cases, the privileges were very probably the decisive reason that an actual town, and not just a small village or fishing hamlet, emerged at all in the place in question.[12] As early as in the 13th and 14th centuries, there are traces of a tendency towards commercially regulative town legislation, but it was not until the 15th century that this became a reality. From then on, it thus became commonplace to allot market towns a zone of a fixed radius subject to trade restrictions, within which the town in question had the monopoly on conducting burgher trade and business with peasants. At the same time, a start was made on strengthening the economy of the market towns, for instance by prohibiting harbours outside the towns and by moving certain fairs from rural parishes to the towns. The Swedish archaeologist Anders Andrén believes that the background for the development of this 'mercantile dominance' was that the state had considerable fiscal interests in concentrating business and trade in as few places as possible.[13] The allocation of the protective zones, however, became in the course of time the subject of a large number of conflicts between neighbouring towns, with each trying to use its privileges to promote the town's financial interests. And many small market towns would undoubtedly have failed to survive as towns if they had been unable to adhere to the principles of 'mercantile dominance'. It thus appears that the strong formal structures bear a considerable part of the responsibility for the fact that the urban system has been far more stable in Denmark than in many other countries.[14]

Apart from a few towns that can trace their origin back to the 9th-11th centuries,[15] Denmark experienced its first real urbanisation wave between 1000 and 1200, when 17 towns were established in the Kingdom (and two in Schleswig-Holstein), cf. fig. 1.[16] These were fairly equally distributed across the country and seem to have mainly served as administrative, religious and military centres for the Crown – the latter achieving strong control over the whole country during these two centuries – as well as for the newly established church. The next wave of urbanisation – from 1200 to 1350 – was completely different. During these years, no fewer than 57 new market towns saw the light of day in the Kingdom (as well as six in Schleswig-Holstein). These towns were oriented towards the coasts to a much greater extent than their predecessors. This should be viewed as indicating that economic motives underlay the establishment of these towns. One of the most important reasons was the general growth in population. It is presumed that the population of Denmark increased from about 500,000 to 1.5 million between 1050 and 1250.[17] That is why 1,600-1,700 new permanent villages were also established in this period. Furthermore, it seems that ecclesiastical and secular landowners were increasingly able to produce a surplus of agricultural products to be exchanged with other products at a central place.[18]

The Black Death in the years around 1350, and frequent epidemics in the subsequent decades resulted in a definite break in the urbanisation of the country, similar to the situation in many other countries. Today, however, there is a growing consensus that there was already an agrarian crisis twenty to thirty years before the pandemic plague. Numerous farms and entire villages became deserted in the 14th and 15th centuries, and not even a single market town was founded between 1350 and 1400. The formation of towns recommenced, however, in the first half of the 15th century, but to a much lesser extent than in the 13th century. And the new towns were mainly situated in the peripheral regions of the Kingdom, whereas the need for towns in the central parts of the country seems to have been already met. It is also interesting that most of the new towns were and remained *Minderstädte*: they never managed to make their mark, and several of them later lost their privileges.[19]

The Late Middle Ages were characterised by a clear recovery in the North German and Baltic trade, and the Danish towns too benefited from this, as close commercial relations were developed between them and several Hanseatic towns, especially Lübeck. Many Hanseatic merchants also settled in Denmark to conduct trade there. Danish historian Bjørn Poulsen argues that the Danish towns at that time became part of a larger urban hierarchy centred on Lübeck.[20] However this is only true in economic respects. As far as political life was concerned, Copenhagen became the definite centre of Denmark in the 15th century when 'the travelling monarchy' was increasingly replaced by a stationary central administration based in Copenhagen. But economically too, Copenhagen became more prominent and from about 1500 onwards, this applied also for Malmö, Copenhagen's neighbouring town east of the Øresund. This is a clear reflection of the growing importance of Øresund as a 'commercial link' between Eastern and Western Europe. A third town that benefited from this was Elsinore, which is probably Denmark's most prominent example of a gateway city, and which in 1429 was chosen as the collection point for a new levy, the Sound Dues. The town has a very small natural hinterland, but for long periods it was one of the country's largest and richest towns on account of its international contacts.

But in West Denmark too, connections abroad resulted in new urban expansion at the end of the Middle Ages. There was a growing demand from North Germany and the Netherlands for Danish oxen, and this involved Schleswig, Jutland and Funen. This trade must be regarded as one of the most important driving forces underlying the economic differentiation among the West Danish towns, which can be observed at this time. The most dominant town, with regard to both the cattle trade and other economic activities was Ribe, with Aalborg following closely after. It is very significant that Ribe merchants in 1480 were given permission to make purchases all over Jutland, i.e. far outside the 1-4 miles (7½ – 30 km) that was normally a town's legal trading radius. Twelve years later the other Jutland towns were also given the right to purchase all over the province, but this had only limited practical consequences, since very few of the towns had the capacity to carry on trade in a larger area.

The urban system in the Danish Kingdom from the 17th century until ca. 1850

In his work on the urbanisation of Europe from 1500 to 1800, Jan de Vries divides this epoch into three phases. The period from about 1500 to 1600/50 was generally characterised by population growth in the towns. After that there was a rather long period with highly selective growth, the capitals and certain other large towns showed signs of definite progress, while smaller towns stagnated or declined. Finally, general progress occurred again between 1750 and 1800, but then the growth was relatively stronger in the smaller towns.[21] De Vries' phases also largely apply in Denmark. Thus, in all probability the population generally grew in the 16th century, especially in the towns that benefited from the growing demand for oxen and grain from the Netherlands and other West European countries – these towns serving as gateways between the Danish rural districts and cities abroad. The major change in market conditions for the Danish towns has traditionally been associated with the wars between Denmark and Sweden in 1657-1660, as many towns suffered greatly from plundering and destruction. Some research results indicate, however, that as early as the 1630s and 1640s some of the towns were showing signs of crisis, and in this connection a rapidly increasing burden of taxation, due to increased military expenses, is mentioned as the most important factor.[22] According to this view the wars in the 1650s merely exacerbated a decline that was already underway. And the decline was made worse by a diminishing demand for Danish agricultural products in Western Europe in the second half of the 17th century.

The Danish towns underwent a prolonged period of crisis. Thus a comparison of the population figures in the country's first town census in 1672, with figures from the first national census in 1769, shows a general growth of approximately 10 % in the provincial towns of the Kingdom, while only a very few towns experienced significantly greater growth in this 100-year period.[23] The population of Copenhagen, however, grew from about 41,500 inhabitants in 1672 to about 80,000 in 1769, and the capital's share of the overall urban population in the kingdom grew from 37 % to 50 % during this time. The population growth of Copenhagen should be seen in relation to a substantial expansion of the army and the navy, which were largely concentrated in the capital, a considerable growth in the royal household as well as central administration, and the growing number of service trades required by the public sector.[24] So Copenhagen experienced the same development as many other capital cities in the same period. The growth rate of Copenhagen increased at the end of the 18th century, and the 1801 census showed that the capital now had approximately 100,000 inhabitants. In the same years, however, the Danish provincial towns also entered a new period of growth: from 1787 to 1801 alone, the population grew by about 10 %. At the same time Danish agriculture was subjected to sweeping agrarian reforms aimed at commercialising the peasant class through a significant increase in cultivated acreage and grain production. This of course stimulated the role of towns as purchasers of surplus agricultural products and suppliers of goods to the peasants.

In his article in this volume, Ole Degn gives an impression of the urban hierarchy in the middle of the 17th century, or at approximately the time when Denmark ceded all provinces east of Øresund. By weighing information from a large number of sets of economic and administrative data from ca. 1630 to 1675 and combining these with the population figures from the 1672 census, he has placed the towns at four different levels: the capital, the provincial centres, the regional centres and the local centres. Degn's map p. 102 also gives a good impression of the great regional differences with regard to the density of market towns. While the islands east of the Great Belt had a considerable concentration of towns, towns were thinly scattered in North- Mid- and West-Jutland. In addition, there were only very few large towns in this part of the country. This is a clear reflection of the fact that this region had extensive moorland areas and a very modest rural population. The need for the functions of a central place was therefore much less than in the rest of the country.

Fig. 2 gives a sense of the relative size of the towns in the kingdom at the time of the 1801 census, and since a corresponding census was carried out in Schleswig and Holstein two years later, the towns in these regions have also been included on the map. Apart from Copenhagen, no town in the Danish Kingdom at the time had

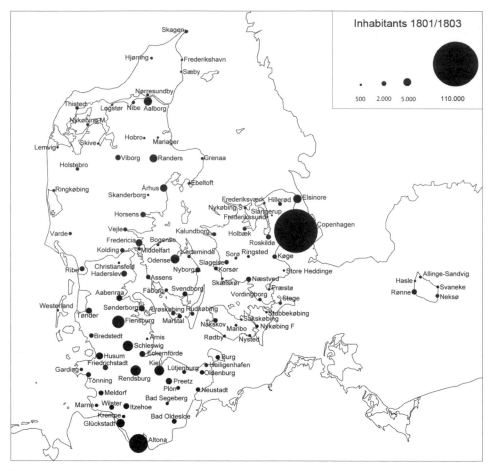

F<small>IG.</small> 2.

The population figures of the towns in the Danish Kingdom 1801 and the Duchies of Schleswig and Holstein 1803.

more than 6,000 inhabitants, and nearly half of them had only 250-1,000 inhabitants. However, by including other parts of the monarchy, the urban hierarchy has a more harmonious configuration. The reason is that in the Duchies and in Norway there were several towns with between 7,500 and ca. 13,000 inhabitants and these were thus placed between the capital and the largest provincial towns in the Danish Kingdom. It is unlikely that this distribution pattern is completely accidental.[25] In any case, it seems sensible to regard the two Kingdoms and the two Duchies as one integral and rather well integrated urban system in the 18th and beginning of the 19th century. The production sectors in the different areas supplemented each other quite well; Denmark in particular was a large supplier of grain to Norway, while

Norway supplied Denmark – which had little raw material and few forests – with iron and timber, and in addition with fish. The mercantilist policy during much of the 18th century underpinned this trade with customs barriers and import prohibitions. Thus Denmark actually had a monopoly on supplying the southern and most densely populated part of Norway with grain from 1735 to 1788. With reference to Immanuel Wallerstein's centre-periphery thesis, Niels Steensgaard has called this a Danish-Norwegian imperial sub-system within the European world economy.[26] The relinquishment of Norway in 1814 resulted in a considerable reduction in these trade relations in the following two decades. On the other hand, the Danish towns became much more involved in trade with West Europe, especially England, during the following decades.

The many towns established in the Middle Ages were still sufficient to service the Danish rural districts in the early modern period; indeed, in some regions it is no exaggeration to say there were almost too many towns. From time to time proposals came from various local government officials to divest certain towns, with very modest trade activities, of their town privileges. This happened in only a very few cases however – such as in 1809 when Slangerup in Northern Zealand had to relinquish its privileges to the neighbouring settlement of Frederikssund, which managed rather better because of its situation on a watercourse. On the other hand, new town privileges were also issued to some towns between the 16th and the 18th centuries. Almost without exception, however, these towns had special, but usually very few, functions. This was the case for instance with Hillerød, Sorø and Hirschholm. Hillerød was a castle town, while Sorø's main function in the 17th and 18th centuries was to service an academy for young noblemen, and Hirschholm was the seat of a new royal palace. It is striking that the state played an essential role in the establishment of these towns. In these respects Denmark followed a general tendency in Northern Europe in the early modern period. On the other hand, Denmark differed from many other countries in the sense that proto-industry resulted in the rise of only a very few urban settlements, and none of these achieved market town privileges before 1900.[27]

Of greater general interest are probably the towns that emerged for military purposes in the 17th century. During the very tense security situation between 1610 and 1680, when Denmark became involved in a total of six wars, the structure of the Danish fortifications was revised. Formerly, most towns had a modest stronghold or rampart. At this time, however, the government concentrated on fortifying relatively few places, especially at the frontiers and at the most important ferry stations. On the other hand these fortifications were larger than their predecessors – to be better able to deal with the improved artillery. Most of the fortified towns were founded in the Middle Ages, but there were also some new towns among them. However, only very few of the newly established military towns were successful in the long run. One of these was Fredericia in Eastern Jutland, founded by King Frederik III in 1650. The fortress in this town was supposed to offer protection to Danish troops who had to use the narrow sea passage between Jutland and Funen. To entice inhabitants to the town, it was given extensive economic privileges, and in 1682 these were supplemented with the right to asylum for debtors and foreign killers, as well as with the right to freedom of religion. The town thus became a place of refuge for Jews, Catholics and Calvinists (including many immigrants from France), and they came to play an important role in the history of the town. Parallels may be drawn with contemporary *Exulantenstädte* (towns characterised by immigrating refugees) in other places in Europe, especially in the German Empire.[28]

The military policy of the Absolutist regime also influenced the urban system in another way. Military considerations played a crucial role after 1661 when the central authorities decided to concentrate all foreign trade in the Kingdom in a handful of towns – the so-called 'staples' – just as Sweden had done earlier in the 17th century.[29] Copenhagen and Fredericia were chosen for this, as well as the two fortified towns of Nyborg and Korsør, which guarded the important ferry route across the Great Belt. Six years later, Nakskov, the principal town on the island of Lolland and one of the most important fortified towns in South-Eastern Denmark, received the same right. The staples were granted various economic privileges, but at the same time were obliged always to have a considerable stock of goods. Townsmen were supposed to be able to purchase these goods at a reasonable price in the respective parts of the country. But a subsidiary motive for this was undoubtedly to acquire enough goods to support the army should a new war break out. However, apart from Copenhagen, the towns selected were all relatively small and economically weak, so they were completely unable to enforce the provisions of the staple legislation. In 1682, it was therefore decided to expand the number of staples to 26 market towns, which were probably those towns that carried on some sort of foreign trade. But this arrangement did not function as intended either, so in 1689 the staple legislation was replaced by a regulation stipulating that all market towns were allowed to trade with foreign countries provided this was done with domestic ships.

Apart from the military motives, the staple legislation was certainly aimed at encouraging a more hierarchical and advanced urban system. In contrast to another institutional influence – the privileged trading districts – it nevertheless had only a very modest effect on the urban system. The principal reason for this was the very limited foreign trade carried out by the towns and the rest of the Danish Kingdom after the crisis of the 17th century.

The urban system in the Danish Kingdom after ca. 1850

It was not until about 1840 that the Danish urban population began to increase more rapidly than the rural population, and since then the proportion of urban residents has been constantly increasing.[30] Between 1870 and 1890 alone, the proportion increased from 25 % to 35 % and at the beginning of the First World War, it was up to 50 %. Today ca. 85 % of Danes live in urban areas. The number of towns also rose considerably, due to both proper urbanisation and changes of the administrative or statistical town concepts (see fig. 3).

Industrialisation is one of the crucial factors underlying this development. From the start, Copenhagen was the country's industrial centre, but the provincial towns came on well in the second half of the 19th century (see fig. 4). Of greatest significance in the location of early industry in the provinces was proximity to the sea, as well as the possibility of relatively inexpensive rail-haulage between the town and the immediate surrounding area. This was because Denmark's foreign trade at the end of the 19th century was based on the export of refined agricultural products and the import of additives for agriculture, as well as industrial raw materials for use in industry based on the home market. These circumstances benefited the largest, oldest market towns, which were precisely the ports with solid *umland* functions. Consequently these towns had a significant first mover advantage, which made it difficult for many other towns to make an impression. Indeed a clearer stratification of the town hierarchy can also be observed: the regional centres further distanced themselves from the smaller towns. This is most noticeable in Eastern Jutland, where previously there had been some competition for the role of most dominant town; after the middle of the 19th century, however, Aarhus became the undisputed centre of the region. The significant infrastructural developments, including the construction of railways and major improvements to roads and ports seem to be the most important reasons for this development.

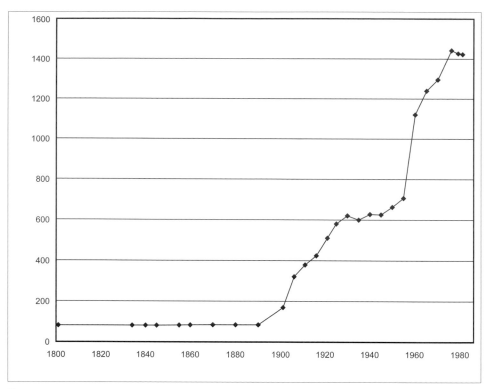

FIG. 3.

The number of Danish towns and urban settlements according to the official statistics, 1801-1981.

The infrastructural improvements and economic growth also resulted however in a boom for certain new towns. The most pronounced example is Esbjerg, which was established in 1868 as a port at the end of the railway-line from Copenhagen to the westernmost part of Jutland. At the very beginning of the 20th century, Esbjerg became the most important town for the export of agricultural products (especially to England), and in addition it became one of Denmark's largest fishing towns with accompanying industries. That is why, only 33 years after its foundation, this specific gateway city had advanced to a position as the ninth largest city in Denmark with around 13,000 inhabitants. Another upcoming new town was the former village of Herning in the central part of Jutland. This region experienced a boom after most of the moors were transformed into arable land in the second half of the 19th century. Herning concentrated on industry and in the 20th century became famous for its textile factories, which carried on the old, local tradition of cottage industries.

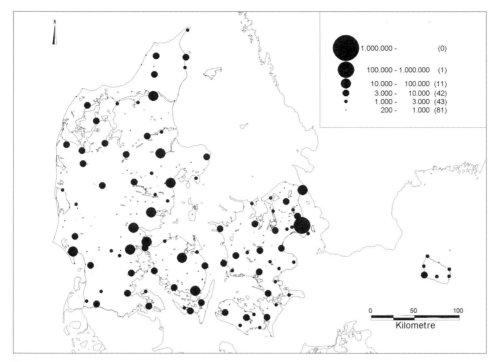

FIG. 4.

The size of the Danish towns, 1901.

The circle's size indicates the town's size. In the signature explanation the interval that the individual circles cover can be seen, while the figure in parentheses after each category gives the number of towns in the category.

Herning was just one of the numerous villages all over the country that, because of improved infrastructures, developed into new central places in the last decades of the 19th century. During these years a secondary urban landscape was created consisting of small rural towns, typically with a railway station and a limited number of industries able to service the immediate rural areas. One of the preconditions for this development was the Trade Act of 1857, which (as mentioned earlier in this Introduction) repealed the prohibition on trade in the countryside, albeit with certain limitations. However, the vast majority of the small rural towns remained quite small. Even today most of them have less than 3,000 inhabitants, while only a few have more than 10,000. By comparison, only nine of the 81 towns, which were formerly privileged as *købstæder*, have less than 3,000 inhabitants today. Of these towns, 46 have more than 10,000 inhabitants and 17 more than 30,000. Yet Denmark still has only four cities with more than 100,000 inhabitants; apart from Copenhagen they are the old provincial centres of Aarhus, Odense and Aalborg. And with the increasing centralisation of Danish urban development which has taken place since ca. 1980, there is reason to believe that there will be further differentiation between the large and small towns in the future.

However Danish urban history also has exceptions to the rule, in that the towns which at one time achieved status as large regional centres continue to be important. Ribe is the best example of this: with a population today of ca. 8,000 it has until the recent local government reforms been an important administrative centre. It was one of the dominant trading towns in Jutland from the early Middle Ages until around 1620, but was dealt a devastating blow in the 17th century, especially because of the declining oxen trade and the havoc and destruction during the wars with Sweden. Afterwards foreign buyers and enterprising shipmasters from the islands in the Wadden Sea and along the west coast of Jutland took over a considerable part of the foreign trade that had previously been conducted by Ribe merchants. And in 1864 the town lost a large part of its closest hinterland which then came under Prussian rule.

The new town of Esbjerg is now the main city and administrative centre of the large new Southwest Jutland municipality.

Administration of the Danish Kingdom and its market towns during Absolutism

But let us return to the Absolutist epoch, which is the focus of this book. This period began when King Frederik III in 1660 exploited a critical political situation to effect a *coup d'état*, which meant a drastic reduction of the influence hitherto exercised by the nobility. And it ended in 1848 when King Frederik VII voluntarily gave up his power under the impact of the political unrest that had just spread to Copenhagen from a number of other European cities. In the following year, a new democratic constitution was written. It is not however only for the sake of keeping to the cut-off years in national politics that we have chosen to end the book in the middle of the 19th century: as mentioned, in several ways the time around 1850 also marks a clear break in centuries-old urban development.

Lex Regia (in Danish: *Kongeloven*) of 1665 constituted the legal foundation for Danish Absolutism, and formally it made the Danish King the most powerful monarch in Europe.[31] *Lex Regia* meant that the King was above the law and he had the supreme legislative, executive and judgemental power. His only obligations were to profess the Lutheran faith, to maintain Protestantism as the official religion, to ensure that the Kingdoms were not divided, and to refrain from diminishing his own power by changing *Lex Regia*.[32] In practice, of course, the King could not personally make all the necessary decisions himself. But several of the Absolute Kings – particularly the first three (1660-1730) – actually made persistent efforts to do this and often handed over only the most routine transactions to their officials.[33] Gradually as the number of cases grew however, it became increasingly necessary to delegate executive tasks *ad mandatum regis* (i.e. on behalf of the King). In the second half of the 18th century, the picture changed completely as Denmark was ruled by two passive kings; the first had no interest in administration and the other was unable to cope with the task on account of mental illness. Central bureaucracy then gained the opportunity to take independent initiatives, not just with regard to administration, but also with regard to initiatives of a political nature.[34] The political developments were rather unstable in most of the 18th century, but at the same time there was considerable consolidation of central administration, which experienced both growth and increasing specialisation.

In the first years of Absolutism, there were only a very few central authorities, namely:

- *Danske Kancelli* (the Danish Chancellery), which was in charge of civilian domestic administration in Denmark, Norway and the North-Atlantic territories.
- *Tyske Kancelli* (the German Chancellery), which dealt with relations to foreign countries and the administration of the Duchies.[35]
- *Rentekammeret* (for a time called *Statkammerkollegiet*), which was in charge of the financial administration in the whole monarchy, but in practice was primarily an auditing and controlling organ.
- *Krigskollegiet* and *Admiralitetskollegiet*, which formed the central administration for the army and navy respectively.[36]

After 1730 a number of new administrative bodies came into being, especially in the economic field, and more stress was laid on regulation of the economy to increase state revenue. One of the new authorities was *Kommercekollegiet* which saw the light of day in 1735 and had special responsibility for domestic and foreign trade, production of raw materials and the growth of industrial activities.[37] This department came to play a very central role during the mercantilist 'golden age' in the middle of the 18th century. Just as important was *Generaltoldkammeret*, which was established in 1760 and among other things had the job of supervising the collection of customs duties and taxes and supervising the administration of the Danish tropical colonies. During approximately the first 100 years of the Absolutist period there were numerous restructurings of the military sector, which at that time made up a very large part of the total administration. For both the army and the navy this ended with all personnel, command, mustering and provision matters being put under one central authority. For the army this was *Generalkrigsdirektoriet*, later called *Generalitets- og Kommissariatskollegiet*, while the supreme authority for the navy was called *Admiralitets- og Generalkommissariatskollegiet*.

At the same time as central administration grew, officials here also became considerably more professional, as greater importance was attached to fixed administration procedures, uniformity in the way matters were dealt with, and objectively motivated recruitment of employees.[38] The introduction of a law degree in 1736 probably played a role in this connection, even though many decades passed before the legal profession set an appreciable mark on the personnel profile of central administration.[39] Several scholars have also noted that during the period from ca. 1730 to 1800 a gradual but pronounced change occurred in civil servants' self-perception and feeling of loyalty. From primarily having considered themselves as servants of the King, they began to regard themselves rather as servants of the state and society.[40] It is tempting to see this development in the light of the much more unobtrusive role of the later Kings, but it is more important to be aware of the foreign models. For instance historian Ole Feldbæk notes that in the middle of the 18th century, Frederik II of Prussia declared that the Prince was the first servant of the state. Feldbæk also points out that the leading Danish officials and politicians at the end of the 18th century considered happy subjects to be the primary goal of Absolutism. That is why they considered it important to listen to the opinions expressed in the media of the time, and many scholars actually characterise the decades after 1770 as 'opinion-driven Absolutism'. At the beginning of the 19th century, Denmark again had a King who took the authority of the Absolute King quite seriously. But this did not have any significant consequences for the ethics of office that were developed in central administration in the 18th century.

Compared with most other European countries at the time, quite a strong state power was constructed during Danish Absolutism, and this was probably also what was felt in Copenhagen, where central authorities frequently interfered in municipal affairs. This was particularly the case in the decades after 1770 when, for instance, detailed rules were given for the administration of the economy of the capital city and the administration of trust funds. In addition, daily administration was increasingly being carried out by permanent commissions, which consisted partly of citizens of the city and partly of officials from the civil and military central administration.[41]

The situation was somewhat different in the provincial areas of the Kingdom. Here Absolutism could often experience difficulty in imposing its will because of the lack of resources. In the individual rural parishes, the clergy were for instance the only real officials, and in time they were indeed burdened with a flood of administrative jobs, especially concerning reports to the central authorities.[42] The other 'key workers' were the *amtmænd* (chief administrative officers) who each supervised an *amt* (loosely: county). After 1671, seven of these functioned moreover as *stiftamtmænd*,[43] a post that included supervision of the market towns in the diocese in question, whereas the other *amtmænd* had the job of concentrating on the rural districts. The post of *amtmand* was introduced in 1662 to replace the *lensmænd* (noble holders of fiefs). However the two posts are not fully comparable. The *lensmænd* had an important military function, being responsible for the arming of the citizens, and they were also in charge of state tax collection and the administration of Crown estates. The *amtmænd* were relieved of these duties,[44] but on the other hand they were quickly given a wide range of control and reporting tasks, and they had to communicate the decisions made by the central authorities to the inhabitants in their districts. In short, they were the local representatives of the state – or, as a leading official phrased it in the middle of the 18th century, 'the eyes of the departments'. During the 18th century, central administration also involved the *amtmænd* to an ever-greater extent in obtaining evaluations both in more general matters such as preliminary legislative work, and in very specific matters concerning the replies to applications and inquiries.[45]

Absolutism also used a number of private actors in order to make local administration function. For instance, until well into the 18th century, it was commonplace to put the collection of customs duties and taxes out to tender. In addition, private estate owners were put in charge of all tax collection on their estates in 1662, and from 1701 they were also obliged to supply a certain number of farm hands for military service. In many cases, the area of the estate was also a separate jurisdiction where the estate owner was responsible for the appointment of the judge. All these conditions have caused Birgit Løgstrup to characterise administration in the rural districts during approximately the first 125 years of the Absolutist period as 'the leased-out state',[46] and the phrase gives meaning particularly when one remembers that about two-thirds of the land in Denmark was owned by private estate owners at the beginning of the 18th century. This 'state within a state' situation underwent however a fundamental change in the period around 1800 when the state authorities took over the levying and collection of taxes and a large proportion of the country's copyholders bought out their copyhold.

With regard to the market towns too, there was a considerable degree of independent administration in earlier times, even though the Danish towns never had the degree of independence that characterised many German towns. However, tendencies towards increasing state control of market town administration can be seen during the 17th century. After 1660 for instance, it was an unalterable demand that the King appointed all mayors, aldermen, town clerks and *byfogeder* (the town judges and police chiefs). Previously, members of the municipal corporation had been self-elective, though from the 16th century it was usual for the *lensmænd* to confirm these appointments.[47] Of much greater significance, however, was the fact that an ordinance from 1682 directed the towns to make a drastic reduction in the number of mayoral and alderman posts. In 30 of a total of 62 market towns, all municipal functions from that time on were delegated to the *byfoged*.[48] This significant decision was the implementation of a commission report from the previous year. The commission had been charged with the task of producing suggestions to improve the economic condition of the towns, and pointed out among other things that the revenue basis was not great enough for the number of officials in many of the small towns. Indeed, the ordinance about the reduction of the local apparatus of official posts also laid down that, in the future, members of the corporation and the *byfogeder* should be chosen from among 'the best and wealthiest citizens, who have paid tax [to the town] for a long time and know best the condition of the town'. This implied that it was important that the officials had other income as well (as had also been the case until then when the posts had been mainly filled by merchants from the town). The income from the official posts was in fact extremely variable. For instance, it was a share of certain taxes to the town as well as perquisites from various acts of the Court. In many places though the officials also had a certain part of the town fields at their disposal.[49]

Although the reduction in the number of officials meant that the pay of the remaining officials could be improved, several examples are known from the following decades that a mayor or *byfoged* performed doubtful or directly illegal official actions in order to remedy personal financial difficulties.[50] This should probably be seen as one of the weightiest motives for the responsible authorities encouraging more accumulation of posts[51] in market towns. This was typically done by a person

S. B. CHRISTENSEN & J. MIKKELSEN

taking over an extra post when the holder of it died or left the town. For example, it could be the post of town clerk, postmaster, or head of an institution for old people and invalids in the town in question, but it was also commonplace for the *byfoged* to combine his role of judge and policing functions in the town with the corresponding functions in the surrounding rural districts. Likewise, many mayoral and alderman-posts were lost when a vacancy arose, and in 1787 there were mayors left in only 19 of the market towns of the Kingdom. On the other hand, *byfogeder* increasingly became full-time officials, and it probably became more usual too for them to appoint assistants. Even though such appointments were made at their own expense, there is no doubt that the income basis for *byfogeder* was generally greatly improved at the end of the 18th century, which helped to make the posts more attractive. In the same period, members of the legal profession also began to find favour when appointments to the post of *byfoged* were being made. At the start however, almost all of these lawyers had only what approximates a Bachelor Degree, but after 1800, the vast majority had a Masters Degree in law, and from 1821 on, it was actually a condition of appointment to the post of *byfoged* that the person had such a degree. Nevertheless, it can be shown that the central authorities – in any case until around 1800 – attached great importance to local knowledge and practical administrative experience when they appointed a new *byfoged*.[52]

The accumulation of posts after 1782 meant, however, that it became more difficult to keep a check on the possible abuse of power by the remaining official or officials. This was one of the reasons that several *stiftamtmænd* introduced permanent citizen committees from 1720 on – the so-called *eligerede borgere* – in a number of market towns. In some places, the institution was introduced directly on account of corruption on the part of a corporation or a *byfoged*, and/or because there were intense conflicts between the leadership of the town and the citizens.[53] The *stiftamtmand* wanted to use the members of the committee as a source of information and as assistants in the supervision of the town officials. Nevertheless, as time went by these citizen committees seem generally to have been of most benefit to the local officials. As representatives of the citizens, the committees could act as useful partners in hearings in many contexts. A study of the administration in Aarhus also shows that the municipal corporation in this town was inclined to delegate difficult tasks such as road surveying to the committee.[54] During the 18th century, in addition, it was very commonplace to let the committees audit the town accounts. So in 1787 when a rescript was sent out stating that in future each town should prepare an annual budget, it was only natural that it was demanded that the *eligerede borgere* should also be involved in this work. The rescript indicated that such a citizen committee should be introduced in the few towns that did not already have one. In 1797, a new rescript was issued ensuring the town citizens considerable influence on who should have a seat on these committees, which typically had six members. The next big step towards a modern elected municipal council was an ordinance of 1837, which replaced the *eligerede borgere* with *borgerrepræsentanter* (delegates of the citizens). The ordinance laid down that in each town 5-18 men should be elected among the citizens and that at regular meetings with the corporation these delegates should discuss important municipal affairs. In cases of disagreement between the two parties, the *amtmand* had to make a decision.

The *eligerede borgere* however were far from being the only permanent committee that existed in the market towns during Absolutism. For instance the poor inspectorate administered the poor relief system in the town from 1708 on, and this consisted of a member of the corporation as well as a clergyman and two citizens. Later a number of commissions were set up which also had representatives from both the town leadership and citizens. Apart from the poor commissions (which replaced the poor inspectorates), there were commissions for the billeting of soldiers, the port administration, the school system and supervision of private building.[55]

There were a number of minor officials in market town administration who did certain municipal tasks for a small emolument and, as well as this, attended to their work as tradesmen, day labourers, farming or the like. These were, for instance, watchmen, town-hall attendants and field custodians, who looked after the joint cultivation of the town fields ensuring this was done with as little friction as possible. But there were also a number of tasks that were done as a civic duty. These were carried out by the town citizens, who each had a turn for 1-2 years – normally without getting any fee. Among these was, for instance, the job of preparing the annual assessment list for the town taxes and the *kæmner* assignment. The *kæmner* administered 'the town coffers'. He collected all the town taxes and made payments according to the instructions of the municipal corporation or the *byfoged*. At the end of his term, he had to prepare accounts of all the transactions. Helle Linde's study of town administration in a number of market towns on Zealand around 1750 shows, however, that these officials in a number of cases handed over the paperwork to the town clerk or another professional scribe. Moreover, the *kæmner* of the 18th century had no obligation to take measures against the transactions of the corporation and seemingly never did so.[56]

It was not until 1773 that *Rentekammeret* demanded that the market towns send in their accounts for scrutiny. This can be regarded as one of the first attempts on the part of the central authorities to become involved in the internal administration of the towns. Until then, the towns were left to themselves to a great extent as long as the state got the customs duties, taxes and excise it was due, and that otherwise nothing went on in the towns that could threaten the national interest. As a reflection of the prevailing indifference in *Danske Kancelli* in the middle of the 18th century, it can be mentioned that enquiries from the towns to the Chancellery with regard to disagreements between the citizens and local officials were generally referred to decisions in the law courts – 'so the King can be spared such petty things', as was plainly stated on one occasion. This attitude could naturally cause irritation out in the town communities, because it could be expensive to conduct a case in court.[57]

On the other hand, there are – in any case after ca. 1720 – many examples that the *stiftamtmænd* took their role of supervision of the market towns fairly seriously, even though there probably were great individual variations in these efforts. On the basis of detailed studies of selected towns during the period 1730-1760, however, Helle Linde warns against overrating the significance of the *stiftamtmænd*. It is true that they made decisions in many cases, especially in the legal system and in church, school and poor relief cases, but Linde believes that generally they were reluctant to interfere directly in the internal situations in the towns. The *stiftamtmænd* considered their primary task to be that of finding a solution to the local conflicts submitted to them. But as long as no complaints were forthcoming, they did not as a rule make any great effort to ensure that the decisions made were also implemented. Linde therefore concludes that the local authorities and inhabitants in the middle of the 18th century had the chance to make and implement even very far-reaching decisions without interference from the responsible authorities – as long as there was local agreement about them.[58] On the other hand, she believes that, by and large, the citizens in the towns had no possibility of influencing political decisions at a higher level in the 18th century.

Nevertheless, it must be added that 18th century *stiftamtmænd* had great influence in central administration, where their advice and evaluations were often followed, for instance in questions about the appointment of officials and various economic conditions.[59] A number of cases are also known of a *stiftamtmand* in practice acting as an advocate of a town's interests with regard to central administration, and in this way he could come into conflict with the *amtmand* who supervised the surrounding rural districts. This type of friction was part of the background for implementing a reform in 1793, by which the *stiftamtmænd* handed over their supervisory tasks with regard to the towns to the *amtmænd*, who thus had responsibility for all rural parishes and market towns in the same region.[60] The reform meant a considerable reduction of the average distance between the *amtmand*'s residence and the individual market town – and probably also a generally closer supervision of conditions in the towns. On the part of central administration too, there was an increase in the supervision of and interest in the internal affairs of the market towns during late Absolutism.

Articles in the book

The main purpose of this book is to give people who cannot read Danish an introduction to many important aspects of the history of Danish towns during the period of Absolutism. We therefore invited a number of scholars who have each studied problem complexes within these subject areas – and in several cases have even written one or more treatises or monographs on the subject in question. At the same time, we have endeavoured to cover all the most important aspects of the economic, social and cultural history of the towns. The greatest problems concerned the field of culture, where there is a great lack of synthesising literature.[61] On the other hand, there are many research results within certain parts of the cultural sector. Incidentally, it is characteristic of Danish urban history research in recent years that very few scholars regard themselves as urban historians in the real sense, but rather as scholars of culture, business historians, military experts, historians of ideas, or something completely different, but from these perspectives, they often make considerable contributions to a broader understanding of the life of towns. A typical example of this is Jens Henrik Koudal's research concerning the institution of the town musician, which throws light on Absolutism's privilege-society and the guild system. The anthology clearly reflects this inter-disciplinary approach to urban history, as only about half of the contributors primarily consider themselves urban historians.

The articles can be grouped according to different thematic, typological, geographical and chronological criteria. With regard to themes, most of them are limited to a definite economic or social sector, but there are also several articles that cross over different sectors. An example is Søren Bitsch Christensen's work on Danish towns as economic agents in the urban system ca. 1600-1850 – an article that examines how the individual towns exploited their respective privileges to maintain their position in relation to each other in the struggle for the hinterland. Another example is Ole Degn's article about the background for, and the effects of, the prolonged market town crisis, which set in during the 17th century.

With regard to typology, one can differentiate between overview articles that give a general characterisation of the most important features of the period within the subject in question without dwelling particularly on individual towns, and articles that to a greater extent focus on structures, phenomena, and conditions in particular towns, but put these into a larger context. The first-mentioned category includes Anders Monrad Møller's article about shipping and harbour administration, Thomas Bloch Ravn's work about craft guilds and their culture, and Christian Larsen's article about the towns' grammar schools and national schools. The second group includes Karsten Skjold Petersen's article about garrison towns and life in garrisons (where by far the largest garrison town in the country, Copenhagen, naturally plays an important role) and Henrik Harnow's account of the early contours of the Danish manufacturing towns (which contains a description of two of the oldest – and very different – manufacturing towns, Frederiksværk and Silkeborg). But the most pronounced example of the case-study form is Trine Locht Elkjær's article, which, by means of a comparative analysis of farming and animal husbandry in three market towns Aarhus, Randers and Skanderborg, gives an impression of similarities and differences in the towns' farming – a subject that is far too often overlooked in studies of town economy in earlier times.

The majority of the articles concentrate on the Danish Kingdom, but many also involve other parts of the monarchy. This is the case for instance in the articles by Christian Larsen, Anders Monrad Møller, Jens Henrik Koudal and Karsten Skjold Petersen, but it is most marked in Juliane Engelhardt's article about the patriotic societies. These societies, which were some of the most important among the many associations that sprang up in the Danish towns and rural districts at the end of the 18th century and beginning of the 19th century, took a great number of concrete initiatives to promote the common good. Two of the most important subjects of interest were children's education and activating the poor. This last subject is also touched on in two articles about social services. Peter Henningsen has written about the poor relief system in Copenhagen, while Jørgen Mikkelsen has dealt with the situation in the provincial towns in the Danish Kingdom and the Duchy of Schleswig. The two articles show that there were many parallel features in the various parts of the monarchy with regard to the attitude to poverty, but there were also several significant differences, especially as regards legislation.

Finally the anthology has two articles, which are particularly defined by their geographical boundaries. In his essay, 'Copenhagen – the capital of an empire', Michael Bregnsbro asks why Copenhagen today is so disproportionately large in relation to the rest of Denmark, and answers by describing the role of the capital in the conglomerate state or empire of former times. Lars Henningsen on the other hand concentrates on the towns in Schleswig. His article describes the role of the individual towns in the urban system of the Duchy ca. 1700-1850, and he gives an account of the towns' shipping, commerce, trade, industry and local administration. The article can therefore be regarded as a parallel study to several of the other articles that describe the subjects in question with regard to the Kingdom of Denmark.

Most of the articles cover all or most of the period of Absolutism. In some cases, the nature of the subject has necessitated limiting the period described to some few decades. On the other hand, a couple of the writers have chosen to take the presentation back to the Middle Ages or the years of the Renaissance to put developments during Absolutism into a broader perspective. The article on the school system begins for example with church and school legislation that was implemented immediately after the Protestant Reformation in 1536; this legislation had indeed crucial significance for the operation of the towns' school system until well into the 18th century.

BIBLIOGRAPHY

Andrén, Anders 1985. *Den urbana scenen. Städer och samhälle i det medeltida Danmark.* Malmö: Gleerup.

Andrén, Anders 1994. 'State and Towns in the Middle Ages. The Scandinavian Experience'. In: Charles Tilly & Wim P. Blockmans, *Cities and the Rise of States in Europe, A.D. 1000 to 1800.* Boulder, San Francisco and Oxford: Westview Press, pp. 128-49.

Becker-Christensen, Henrik 1976. 'Stabelstadspolitikken 1658-1689'. *Erhvervshistorisk Årbog 1975,* pp. 90-105.

Boje, Per & Ole Hyldtoft 1977. 'Økonomiske, geografiske og demografiske aspekter'. In: Grethe Authén Blom (ed.), *Industrialiseringens første fase. Urbaniseringsprossessen i Norden.* Vol. 3. Oslo: Universitetsforlaget, pp. 178-244.

Bøgh, Anders 1999. 'Samfundet'. In: Else Roesdahl (ed.), *Dagligliv i Danmarks middelalder – en arkæologisk kulturhistorie.* Copenhagen: Gyldendal, pp. 24-53.

Christensen, Søren Bitsch & Jørgen Mikkelsen 2006. 'The Danish urban system pre-1800: a survey of recent research results'. *Urban History,* Vol. 33, 3, pp. 484-510.

De Vries, Jan 1984. *European Urbanization 1500-1800.* London: Methuen.

Degn, Ole 1977. 'De nylagte byer og byudviklingen i Danmark 1600-1800'. In: Grethe Authén Blom (ed.), *De anlagte steder på 1600-1700 tallet. Urbaniseringsprossessen i Norden.* Vol. 2. Oslo: Universitetsforlaget, pp. 9-48.

Eliassen, Finn-Einar 2006. 'Småbyenes storhetstid, ca. 1500-1830'. In: Knut Helle et al., *Norsk byhistorie. Urbanisering gjennom 1300 år.* Oslo: Pax Forlag, pp. 143-245.

Eliassen, Finn-Einar 1995. 'The mainstays of the urban fringe: Norwegian small towns 1500-1800'. In: Peter Clark (ed.), *Small towns in early modern Europe.* Cambridge: Cambridge University Press, pp. 22-49.

Engberg, Jens 2005. *Magten og kulturen. Dansk kulturpolitik 1750-1900.* Vol. I-III. Copenhagen: Gads Forlag.

Feldbæk, Ole 1990. *Den lange fred 1700-1800. Gyldendal og Politikens Danmarkshistorie.* Vol. 9. Copenhagen: Gyldendal & Politiken.

Feldbæk, Ole 2000. 'Vækst og reformer – Dansk forvaltning 1720-1814'. In: Leon Jespersen, E. Ladewig Petersen, Ditlev Tamm (eds.), *Dansk Forvaltningshistorie I. Fra middelalderen til 1901. Stat, Forvaltning og Samfund.* Copenhagen: Jurist- og Økonomforbundets Forlag, pp. 227-340.

Gustafsson, Harald 1998. 'The conglomerate State'. *Scandinavian Journal of History,* pp. 189-213.

Hohenberg, Paul M. & Lynn Hollen Lees 1985/1995. *The making of urban Europe 1000-1950.* (2nd edn.: *The making of urban Europe 1000-1994*). Cambridge, Massachusetts & London: Harvard University Press.

Ilsøe, Grethe 1978. *Vejen til embede. En undersøgelse af udnævnelserne til kgl. retsbetjent- og magistratsembede 1735-65.* Aarhus: Universitetsforlaget i Aarhus.

Jespersen, Knud J.V. 2004. *A History of Denmark.* Houndsmills & New York: Palgrave Macmillan.

Jørgensen, Harald 1985. *Lokaladministrationen i Danmark. Oprindelse og historisk udvikling indtil 1970. En oversigt.* (Administrationshistoriske studier, 11). Copenhagen: Rigsarkivet & G.E.C. Gads Forlag.

Knittler, Herbert 2000. *Die europäische Stadt in der Frühen Neuzeit.* Vienna and Munich: Verlag für Geschichte und Politik & R. Oldenbourg Verlag.

Knudsen, Pernille Ulla 2001. *Lovkyndighed og vederhæftighed, sjællandske byfogeder 1682-1801.* Copenhagen: Jurist- og Økonomforbundets Forlag.

Knudsen, Tim 1995. *Dansk statsbygning.* Copenhagen: Jurist- og Økonomforbundets Forlag.

Ladewig Petersen, E. et al. 1984. *De fede år. Odense 1559-1660.* (A volume in: Tage Kaarsted (ed.), *Odense bys historie,* Vol. I-X. Odense: Odense Kommune, 1978-88).

Lilja, Sven 2000. *Tjuvehål och stolta städer. Urbaniseringens kronologi och geografi i Sverige (med Finland) ca 1570-tal till 1810-tal.* (Studier i stads- och kommunhistoria, 20). Stockholm: Stads- och kommunhistoriska institutet.

Lind, Gunner 2000. 'Den heroiske tid? Administrationen under den tidlige enevælde 1660-1720'. In: Leon Jespersen, E. Ladewig Petersen, Ditlev Tamm (eds.), *Dansk Forvaltningshistorie I. Fra middelalderen til 1901. Stat, Forvaltning og Samfund.* Copenhagen: Jurist- og Økonomforbundets Forlag, pp. 159-226.

Linde, Helle 1991. 'Købstadsadministration'. In: Erik Alstrup, Poul Erik Olsen (eds.), *Dansk kulturhistorisk Opslagsværk*, Vol. I. Copenhagen: Dansk Historisk Fællesforening.

Linde, Helle 1982. 'Købstadsadministrationen i Danmark'. In: Birgitta Ericsson (ed.), *Stadsadministrationen i Norden på 1700-talet.* Oslo, Bergen & Tromsø: Universitetsforlaget, pp. 11-78.

Linde, Helle 1978. *Magistrat og borger. Købstadstyret på Sjælland omkring 1750 med særlig hensyntagen til forholdene i Helsingør, Roskilde, Næstved og Holbæk.* Aarhus: Universitetsforlaget i Aarhus.

Løgstrup, Birgit 1985. 'Den bortforpagtede statsmagt. Godsejeren som offentlig administrator i det 18. århundrede'. *Bol og By*, No. 1, pp. 21-58.

Løgstrup, Birgit 2004. 'Enevælden og konglomeratstaten – et forsøg på en helhedsopfattelse af Danmarkshistorien i tidlig moderne tid'. *Historie,* pp. 253-301.

Løgstrup, Birgit 1984. 'The Landowner as Public Administrator: The Danish Model'. *Scandinavian Journal of History*, Vol. 9, No. 4, pp. 283-312.

Mikkelsen, Jørgen 2003. 'Europæisk byudvikling ca. 1500-1800. En oversigt over nyere forskning'. *1066 – Tidsskrift for historie*, No. 2, pp. 24-38.

Mikkelsen, Jørgen 1990. "Her er et uroeligt og ulydigt Folck'. Forholdet mellem stiftamtmand, byfoged og befolkning i Skælskør i årene 1749-1752'. In: Tommy P. Christensen et al. (eds.), *Slægter – Skjolde – Steder. Festskrift til Knud Prange 6. juni 1990.* Odense: Odense Universitetsforlag, pp. 197-212.

Mikkelsen, Jørgen 1994. 'Sjællandske markeder 1775-1800'. *Historie*, pp. 1-39.

Munch, P. 1900. *Købstadstyrelsen i Danmark fra Kristian IV's Tid til Enevældens Ophør (1619-1848).* Vol. I-II. Copenhagen: Det nordiske Forlag. (Repr. 1977).

Nørr, Erik 1981. *Præst og Administrator. Sognepræstens funktioner i lokalforvaltningen på landet fra 1800 til 1841.* (Administrationshistoriske studier, 4). Copenhagen: Rigsarkivet & G.E.C. Gads Forlag.

Paludan, Helge 1996. 'Bispestaden'. In: Ib Gejl (ed.), *Århus – Byens historie.* Vol. 1. Aarhus: Århus Byhistoriske Udvalg, pp. 121-240.

Pedersen, Karl Peder 1998. *Enevældens amtmænd. Danske amtmænds rolle og funktion i enevældens forvaltning 1660-1848.* Copenhagen: Jurist- og Økonomforbundets Forlag.

Poulsen, Bjørn 2004. 'Tilbagegang og vækst i senmiddelalderens danske by'. In: Søren Bitsch Christensen (ed.), *Middelalderbyen.* (Danske Bystudier, 1). Aarhus: Aarhus Universitetsforlag, pp. 191-248.

Rasmussen, Carsten Porskrog 2006. 'The Duchy of Schleswig – political status and identities'. In: Harald Gustafsson, Hanne Sanders (eds.), *Vid gränsen. Integration och identitet i det förnationella Norden.* (Centrum för Danmarksstudier, 10). Göteborg & Stockholm: Makadam, pp. 180-203.

Steensgaard, Niels 1996. 'Slotsholmen og verdenshavet. Kan adelsvældens og enevældens Danmark placeres i det kapitalistiske verdenssystem?'. In: Hans Jeppesen et al. (eds.), *Søfart – Politik – Identitet, tilegnet Ole Feldbæk*. (Handels- og Søfartsmuseet på Kronborg, Søhistoriske Skrifter, XIX). Copenhagen: Falcon, pp. 81-91.

Thestrup, Anna 1964. *Eligerede borgere i Århus 1740-1837*. Aarhus: Universitetsforlaget i Århus.

Villadsen, Kjeld 1976. *Pest, skatter og priser. Befolkningsudviklingen i Køge 1629-72*. Copenhagen: Lokalhistorisk Afdeling.

NOTES

1 Cf. Jespersen 2004, who, in his overview of some of the most important features of Danish history after ca. 1500, attaches great importance to the evolution of a special propensity for consensus, compromise and uniformity. His account is inspired by the characterisation in 1992 of the Danes by the English Ambassador, James Mellon, as 'a Tribe' (pp. 5-7).

2 The term conglomerate state is taken from geology where a conglomerate stone is made up of clearly defined elements that differ in relation to each other and in relation to the mass that binds them together. The term has been used in recent Nordic history accounts of the early modern period, especially by the Swedish historian Harald Gustafsson. The Danish conglomerate state is described for instance in Løgstrup 2004, where the argument is that the Absolute monarchy made considerable efforts to develop a unitary state (with greater uniformity in legislation, tax collection systems etc.), but for various political and practical reasons, it proved impossible to effectuate the process at the desired speed.

3 Cf. the more detailed description in Michael Bregnsbo's article.

4 A short clear introduction to the complicated political and legal conditions in Schleswig and partly in Holstein too is in Rasmussen 2006, which also contains a discussion of Schleswig-Holstein identity.

5 Munch 1900 (1977), I, p. 91.

6 In the 18th century there were about 700 estates in the Kingdom of Denmark. Cf. Feldbæk 1990, p. 41.

7 Market towns stopped being independent jurisdictions in 1919, while they were independent municipalities right up to 1970.

8 Cf. Søren Bitsch Christensen's article.

9 A more extensive account of this development with examples is in Christensen and Mikkelsen 2006.

10 Hohenberg & Lees 1985/1995, pp. 47-73. Note in particular the exemplary comparison of the characteristics of the two models, p. 65.

11 Jespersen 2004, pp. 1 and 4. Incidentally it is worth noting that Norwegian urban development – in contrast to the Danish – must be mainly explained by the network model. A very large number of the coastal towns in West and South Norway arose in the 16th -18th centuries as a result of the increasing Western European demand for Norwegian wood and other

raw materials. See for instance Eliassen 1995, pp. 22-49. With regard to Norwegian urban history in general in the period ca. 1500-1830, see Eliassen 2006.

12 In this too, there are clear differences between Denmark and Norway. The towns that emerged along the Norwegian coast after 1500 typically got trading rights first when they had achieved a certain economic importance. And at first these were just so-called *ladested* rights, i.e. the right to load and unload goods to and from other parts of the monarchy and to export timber cargoes abroad. But the inhabitants often exerted pressure to get full market town privileges, and this also had positive results in a number of cases. Actually limited trading rights were also given to individual settlements in the Danish Kingdom between 1500 and 1800; for example some fishing hamlets in North-West Jutland got the right to trade with South Norway. Schleswig and Holstein differed from the rest of the monarchy with the existence of the so-called *flækker* (in German: Flecken). These settlements were subject to the courts of the counties or ducal provinces, but they had their own local authorities and the right to carry on trade and crafts, cf. Lars Henningsen's article.

13 Andrén 1994, p. 141. The article, which gives an excellent overview of the different phases of Scandinavian urban development in the Middle Ages, can be regarded both as a summary and a further development of the main views in Andrén 1985.

14 See more details in Søren Bitsch Christensen's article.

15 The three oldest, Ribe, Aarhus and Hedeby, all seem to have been typical gateways in the Viking era, as they had important functions as nodal points for the exchange of luxury goods between different towns and regions in Northern Europe.

16 In the figures for the establishment of towns in the Middle Ages, there are also towns from the Danish regions east of the Øresund.

17 Bøgh 1999, p. 24.

18 Paludan 1996, p. 145. Andrén 1985, p. 255.

19 This is consistent with the conclusions in Lilja 2000, in which the author shows that towns established in periods of crisis generally did poorly, which is related to the fact that the towns that appeared later were often squeezed in between older towns and had less access to natural resources.

20 Poulsen 2004, p. 194.

21 De Vries 1984, pp. 253 ff.

22 Ladewig Petersen 1984, pp. 113, 262, 274, 429. Villadsen 1976, pp. 66 ff. Cf. Ole Degn's article.

23 Degn 1977, pp. 9-48 (especially p. 11).

24 There is more detail about this in Michael Bregnsbo's article.

25 In international urban history and urban geography research, many studies have been made since the 1940s of the distribution of towns according to size in selected countries and regions. One of the tools used most often is the so-called rank-size-distribution graphs, which in a double-logarithm diagram show the population at a certain time for every single town in the hierarchy, as the towns are placed in numerical order according to their size. If the graph

describes an approximately straight line from the top left-hand corner to the bottom right-hand corner (which means that the urban system contains a few large, a greater number of medium-sized, and an even greater number of small towns), this is in the opinion of many scholars an indication that the system was quite well integrated i.e. that there was a lot of contact between the towns and that the respective strong points of the different towns were being used rationally through specialisation. See for instance de Vries, pp. 49 ff. and 85 ff. and Mikkelsen 2003, p. 28.

26 Steensgaard 1996, pp. 81-91. Cf. Anders Monrad Møller's article.

27 Cf. Henrik Harnow's article.

28 Cf. Knittler 2000, pp. 71-74. Fredericia's right to grant asylum was not abolished until 1821.

29 Becker-Christensen 1976, pp. 90-105.

30 A good overview of urbanisation ca. 1840-1914 can be found in Boje & Hyldtoft 1977.

31 In practice, Absolutism was in force for the whole monarchy, but formally it was not the case in the Duchies, cf. Lind 2000, p. 162.

32 Feldbæk 1990, p. 108.

33 Lind 2000, pp. 207 ff. (especially 208).

34 Feldbæk 2000, p. 332.

35 While the Absolutist regime made great efforts to make administration in Denmark and Norway the same, Schleswig and Holstein were allowed in many ways to keep or develop a different administrative structure. This was allowed in order to respect different political interests in the Duchies, cf. Feldbæk 2000, p. 238. With regard to the special local and regional administration in Schleswig, see Lars Henningsen's article.

36 Lind 2000, pp. 167ff. Lind also mentions another central authority *Statskollegiet*, which in the years 1660-1676 acted as a form of a unifying superstructure. In addition, he notes that *Danske Kancelli* was in charge of relations with some specific countries until 1676. See too Feldbæk 2000, pp. 247 ff.

37 However such a department had already existed at the end of the 17th century and from 1704 to 1731, but the primary task of these two authorities was to promote trade in Copenhagen and they are regarded today as belonging partly to central administration and partly to the administration of Copenhagen Municipality. See too Feldbæk 2000, pp. 258 ff.

38 Feldbæk 1990, p. 127. Feldbæk 2000, p. 332. Knudsen 1995, pp. 122 and 136.

39 After 1773, the legal profession had priority for top positions in central administration and after 1814 they almost had a monopoly on these. Cf. Knudsen 1995, pp. 121-122.

40 Feldbæk 2000, p. 242. Cf. Knudsen 1995, p. 121. Interestingly enough, this change in attitude can also be seen at the local level. In a study of applications for the positions of the *byfoged* in individual towns, Pernille Ulla Knudsen could for instance show a shift in the argumentation of the applicants. At the beginning of the 18th century, they often described themselves as the King's loyal subjects. Later they attached more importance to the fact that they wished to

serve their native country and the town where they applied for the post. See Knudsen 2001, p. 225.

41 Feldbæk 2000, p. 261-63 and 296-98.

42 Nørr 1981 contains a thorough introduction to the clergyman's tasks in the first half of the 19th century, especially with regard to school matters and poor relief. For instance there is a survey (pp. 416-419) of the 104 different types of certificates that the clergyman was obliged to issue for the use of other authorities and private citizens.

43 Individual *stiftamtmænd*, though, handled only this post, cf. Jørgensen 1985, p. 89. Harald Jørgensen gives an excellent overview of the content of the posts of *amt-* and *stiftamtmænd*. A more detailed account is found in Pedersen 1998.

44 The administration of Crown lands was transferred to another new group of officials, *amtsforvalterne*.

45 Pedersen 1998, p. 391.

46 Løgstrup 1985, pp. 21-58. Løgstrup 1984, pp. 283-312.

47 Linde 1991, pp. 517-18.

48 Munch I, 1900 (1977), pp. 205-25, contains a complete list of all types of officials in all market towns in selected years between 1682 and 1847. From 1682, information about a single market town is missing.

49 Munch I, 1900 (1977), pp. 84 f. On the officials' share of the town fields, see Trine Locht Elkjær's article.

50 A very glaring example is described in Mikkelsen 1990, pp. 197-212. See too Knudsen 2001, pp. 142 ff.

51 The term is used instead of 'combination of posts' because there continued to be two independent posts, and indeed in some cases they were also handled by two people at a later time.

52 Knudsen 2001, pp. 221, 224 and 381 f. Cf. Ilsøe 1978, who documents that very great importance was attached to practical administrative experience in the appointment of alderman and *byfoged* posts in the years 1735-65 (pp. 88 and 118).

53 Linde 1978, pp. 66 ff. Thestrup 1964, p. 26. Mikkelsen 1990, pp. 200 ff.

54 Thestrup 1964, p. 53.

55 The billeting commissions also included an officer, while the town clergyman (or men) had seats in the poor commission and the school commission. There are more details about the commissions in the articles by Christian Larsen, Jørgen Mikkelsen, Anders Monrad Møller and Karsten Skjold Petersen.

56 Linde 1978, pp. 54 ff., especially pp. 62-64.

57 Linde 1978, p. 99. Linde 1982, pp. 39 and 63.

58 Linde 1982, pp. 38, 51 and 63. Linde 1978, p. 102. Gunner Lind is in agreement with these views in his evaluation of administration in the Kingdom during early Absolutism (1660-1720): 'Through the steps on the official ladder, a significant shift could occur between the Crown command and local reality, provided that there was local agreement about it'. (Lind 2000, p. 211).

59 Cf. for instance Knudsen 2001, pp. 122 ff. and Mikkelsen 1994, pp. 28 ff. (on cases regarding the introduction of fairs).

60 Pedersen 1998, pp. 241 ff. and 279 ff. The reform was implemented when a post became vacant. Several *stiftamtmænd* therefore continued their tasks as heretofore for many years after 1793.

61 However, Engberg 2005 can be mentioned, which contains a wealth of detailed analyses and synthesising considerations about Danish cultural policy 1750-1900.

Søren Bitsch Christensen

Danish towns as economic agents in the market town system, ca. 1600-1850

The market town system

This article is about how the Danish towns functioned as economic agents in relation to the countryside and how trade and other commercial activity was conducted within the urban hierarchy. By the term economic agents is meant that the towns served the rural sector and mediated the flow of goods, information and services to and from the network of cities and between this network and the countryside. In theory, and even partly in practice, Danish towns exercised a very strong dominance over trade with rural products. Even the nobility, who held many exclusive rights to trade, most often chose to channel their sales and purchases through the towns.

The majority of towns were located on the coast with relatively easy access to both the sea and the surrounding rural area. This alone indicates that the primary function of most Danish towns was a combination of being service centres in the central place sense and being part of the network between towns.[1] The period ca. 1600-1800 was a time marked by stagnation as regards the number of towns and their functional specialisation. A few new towns were established, but these were predominantly administrative centres, and, except for a handful of small maritime settlements, they did not originate in any commercial expansion or innovation. The bulk of towns remained greatly dependent on interaction with the countryside and the exchange of primary goods. However, around 1800 a number of factors gave rise to a loosening of the strict division of labour between town and country. One outcome of this was a more dynamic and flexible urban hierarchy.

The article utilises an institutional framework. In doing so it challenges the prevailing view that the function of the towns can best be described as what might be called the 'natural market town system'. According to this view the basis of existence for the market towns was the natural resources of their immediate rural hinterland. Instead, the article makes the point that the inflexible urban hierarchy was also the result of the set of legal rights that regulated commercial activity between town and countryside and between the towns. I therefore propose the term the 'legal market town system' as a better hypothesis. In its simplest form this means the set of rights that directed the production surplus of the peasants and to some degree that of the nobility to the markets and merchants in the nearest town. In a more advanced form the legal market town system, however, also means that some towns were favoured in terms of larger privileged trading districts at the expense of other towns.

The view that the concept of a 'legal market town system' should replace 'the natural market town system' draws on the works of S.R. Epstein. In an analysis of European urbanisation 1300-1800, Epstein points out that urbanisation as a whole was less than optimal, because European towns were not inhabited to their full potential and there was a weak correlation between urban ratios and economic performances. In his explanation of this imperfect economic interaction between town and country, Epstein bases his theory on the classic service-centre thesis – that the towns were economic agents in relation to the countryside – but in connection with recent institutional economic theory, he also involves the towns' economic rights and their capacity to mediate market signals optimally. His conclusion is that the main force behind the extent of urbanisation in a 'typical' West and Central European country between the 14th century and industrialisation was the extent of the towns' legal compulsory measures and territorial influence as these had been handed down from the Middle Ages.[2] The explanation is that the more legal compulsory measures and rights enjoyed by the towns in a country in relation to the countryside, the greater the basis for trade, crafts and industry being concentrated in the towns.

The natural centre?

Let us first look at the reality of what I call 'the natural market town system'. Looking at a map of the location of Danish market towns ca. 1200-1800, there is seemingly an almost perfectly balanced geographical distribution of towns with approximately equally sized surrounding areas. According to Jørgen Elsøe Jensen, the location of the towns in the country from the 13th century was in itself evidence of a commercialised society, which, within the bounds of nature, was organised in order to be able to collect and re-sell the farmers' crops as well as possible.[3] In 1947, historian Vil-

SØREN BITSCH CHRISTENSEN

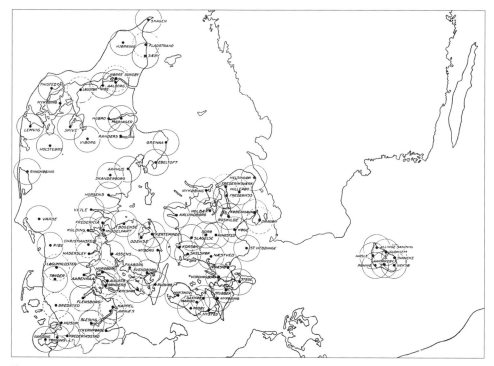

FIG. 1.

The 'natural market town system' in which the market towns are maintained primarily by the resources of the surrounding area. The map shows the market towns and the Schleswig-Holstein 'flecken' around 1680. The circles mark a radius of 15 km, which is believed to have been the average maximum return-travel distance in one day for a peasant with a wagon.

helm Lorenzen had a map drawn of the Danish market towns on which he gave a circle with a radius of two Danish miles (1 Danish mile = 7.5 km) as the towns' natural hinterland (fig. 1).[4] On closer inspection, however, the idea that natural geographical conditions determined the towns' equally sized surroundings proves to be too simple. A number of towns thus lie closer than 30 km to each other, and some parts of the country had a low density of towns.[5]

The thesis that the size and resources of a market town were determined by the resources of the surrounding area can be relatively easily tested statistically on the basis of censuses for the countryside and towns as well as tax assessments of agricultural production capacity, the so-called *hartkorn* assessments. Calculations made by Jeppe Klok Due on the basis of the 1845 census and *hartkorn* figures for 1844 show that there was no statistical correlation between the size of the towns and the production capacity of the surrounding area, nor between the population of the towns and that of the surrounding area. The statistical correlation is so poor that there are no grounds to imagine that it had previously been better.[6]

Nature has not been equally kind to all towns. It is well known that ships have had to shelter from the wind, but who thinks about farmers who could risk having to stay on the hills above the towns lying in the valleys on the coast, waiting until the roads dried so that they could drive on them at all? In Aabenraa in the 1760s, they had to put a mechanical device on the wagon wheels in order to manoeuvre the wagons down to the town.[7] Poor harbour conditions could turn a regional trade pattern upside down, as when Ringkøbing harbour in West Jutland became unusable at the beginning of the 18th century, and the farmers therefore had to undertake the 6-10 miles (approximately 45-75 km) journey to the harbour at Hjerting.[8] In 1735 in Næstved on Zealand trade in the town was on the point of being stopped by poor navigation conditions and the town merchants had to ship their goods from neighbouring towns.[9] In 1825 Denmark's largest fjord, Limfjord, became opened to the west when the sea broke through the narrow coastal strip, and at one fell swoop, trading conditions for the towns of the region were turned upside down. Many other examples of how nature has affected conditions in the market towns could be named.

Practically all farmers drove or walked to the market town. The sailing farmers – we must surmise – used their vessels chiefly to sail to places further away – to Norway and Copenhagen and the northern German areas in particular, and to a lesser extent to Hamburg and the Elbe. Travelling over land was a slow business – in Denmark as everywhere else. Denmark has no mountains or large rivers, but even so, there were large impassable areas earlier. Central Jutland was covered by moors and in several places bogs got in the way of traffic. People had to sail between the different parts of the country, although this did not make communication slower. If people were out in the geographical periphery, they could be forced to communicate with smoke signals, as a buyer on the island of Samsø suggested to his employer in the town of Kalundborg on the mainland in 1839.[10]

So once again we must ask: How natural was it really that the closest town should be the natural market for a farmer?

SØREN BITSCH CHRISTENSEN

The town system and trade conditions

During the 17th and 18th centuries and until the beginning of industrialisation in the middle of the 19th century, the Danish town system was extraordinarily stable. In any case this is true if one just counts the number of towns and estimates the urban population ratio for the period ca. 1620-1855. The urban ratio swung between ca. 20 and 25 % and during Absolutism 1660-1848 it was almost completely unchanged. Wars, structural crisis conditions in agriculture during most of the 18th century and subsequent reforms of cultivation methods and land ownership changed the urban population ratio only by a few percentage points. What can be the cause?

TABLE 1.

The urban ratio in the Kingdom of Denmark ca. 1620-1855.

	Ca. 1620-40	Ca. 1672	1769	1801	1855
Urban ratio	Ca. 25	Ca. 20	20	21	22,4
Number of towns	54	64+6	67+4	67+5	70+5

Note: The Danish possessions east of Øresund before 1660 have been omitted.

(+) = existing towns which later got market town or other town charters. For the year 1855 however, towns that got a town charter before 1900 are only included if the population in their parish exceeded 200 in 1855.

Sources: Ole Degn's article in this book. C.W. Matthiessen 1985, p. 19.

The urban stagnation after the Middle Ages gave Denmark a completely new character in relation to the European town system. In the 13th century, the country had been one of the most urbanised countries outside the large urban centres, the Netherlands and Italy. Denmark had by and large the towns that were needed for a long time, even though there was also an urban expansion after about 1440.[11] The many early towns can of course explain why growth in the Danish urban population after the year 1600 could not keep pace with the general European increase: The towns' share of the population of Europe 1500-1800 increased from ca. 8-9 to ca. 12 %,[12] and in Northern and Western Europe, the towns increased even further, from ca. 6 to 15 %.[13] The Danish urban ratio was still high, but this does not alter the fact that it was stagnant.

The urban stagnation from the middle of the 17th century was also obvious in two other ways. First, there were only a few large towns with advanced and special-ised functions. Examples are Elsinore, where the Sound Dues were paid, and Aalborg with a large export trade in fish and agricultural products. Within the borders of the Kingdom, the bulk of towns consisted mainly of a group of medium-sized towns and small towns that had little specialisation. The European commercial revolution of the 17th and 18th centuries did not affect the number of Danish towns. On the other hand, Copenhagen as capital of the realm grew steadily throughout the period and pulled the town system of the Kingdom increasingly in the direction of a primate urban system.

Swedish historian Sven Lilja has made the most consistent analyses of the Nor-dic town systems. On this basis, he can place Denmark and the rest of the Nordic countries in relation to each other and in relation to the rest of Europe with more certainty than previously. During the 18th century, Sweden-Finland had a stronger development towards urban integration than Denmark-Norway. Here the process was the opposite of the Swedish-Finnish experience and was towards weaker inte-gration, which can be attributed to the fact that the Danish-Norwegian system tilted even more towards an over-dimensioned capital city. Nevertheless, both town sys-tems were quite well integrated according to the European standard of the time, and cannot therefore be called under-developed.[14] Lilja analyses the Danish Kingdom together with Norway, but not Schleswig and Holstein, and in this way, important parts of the *de facto* town system are omitted. Norway, Schleswig and Holstein had precisely the medium-sized towns lacking in the Kingdom. Trade on the Atlantic and exchange of goods between east and west through Øresund were primarily the concern of these towns, while the broad majority of Danish towns – especially after ca. 1680 – were relegated to the supply of goods internally in the Kingdom and trade with Norway.

The second way that stagnation in the town system could be seen was in the geo-graphical distribution of town economy. If the proportions of the total town taxes of the market towns in three selected periods are compared, before, during and after Absolutism (1596-1621, ca. 1760-1774 and 1864), two conspicuous elements are ap-parent. First, the almost 300 years were characterised, as mentioned, by an increas-ing primate urban system: Copenhagen, which from 1596 to 1621 paid a little less in tax than all the other towns on Zealand together, could collect about five times as much as these towns in town gate duty after the middle of the 18th century, and in 1864 was directed to pay more than 10 times as much as the rest of the Zealand towns in war tax. The second obvious element was a striking stability on a general regional level in the distribution of the economic resources between the towns in Jutland and on Funen, Zealand-Møn and Lolland-Falster.[15]

The stagnation in establishing towns and lack of change in the distribution of geographical pivotal areas were not completely synonymous with lack of differentiation or shifts in the existing Danish town system. A survey of town gate duty per civilian inhabitant in the 1760s gives an insight into the urban hierarchy, as the town gate duty in many respects was a turnover tax on the consumption of basic foodstuffs and necessities. It shows that there was a moderate correlation between the size of the towns and their turnovers, so that larger towns tended to have a bigger turnover per capita than smaller towns. The towns that Ole Degn in his article in this book characterises as the national centre (Copenhagen) and as regional centres (Aalborg, Aarhus, Viborg, Ribe, Odense, Elsinore, Nykøbing Falster and Nakskov) had generally higher turnovers per capita, but even so, around a dozen other towns were in line with them.

Furthermore, within each region some towns came to contribute more to the regions' tax burden and others fell back. Most marked was the decline of Ribe, the most southern town in Jutland. From a position as the country's leading town for the export of oxen, the town was hit around 1620 by the rising dominance of the Netherlands in this trade as well as by deteriorating port facilities. Aalborg also faced a decline in the early years of the 19th century due to growing decentralisation of the urban economy in the region and the loss of nearby Norway in 1814 and, hence, the loss of a secure market. There were losers in the other regions as well. Køge on the east coast of Zealand lost ground in the export trade to Copenhagen and the Netherlands in the 17th and 18th centuries, and on the islands of Lolland and Falster the towns became more equal, with older dominating centres (Nakskov and Nykøbing) losing primacy.

On the whole, however, there was no significant regional re-distribution of the urban resources. In a macro-perspective, the Danish urban system was characterised by relatively many and equal market towns as well as by a standstill in terms of the relative importance of the urban sector to the countryside and the distribution of the urban population between the regions. It seems unquestionable that some towns were able to use legal rights to enforce economic dominance upon other towns, while at the same time the market towns as a whole used the urban charters to concentrate the lion's share of trade, shipping and craftsmanship in the towns.

What did the relatively inflexible urban system and the high number of towns mean for economic interaction between town and country? Ole Degn has argued that the short distances between the towns led to the creation of regional town hierarchies in which a leading centre dominated the sub-centres by a combination of better natural access to the sea and the main roads, economic power, and legal rights.[16] Is it possible to make a sharper distinction between these factors?

Institutional development prior to 1600

In a Danish-Swedish connection, Bjørn Poulsen and Anders Andrén have discussed the content of the medieval market towns' progressive, but never complete, takeover of commercial activities in the countryside. Andrén concluded that the towns gained a 'mercantile dominion' 1200-1350,[17] while Poulsen subsequently raised the question of whether this power relationship existed between town and country in general or had a more refined form in which the countryside was divided among particular towns as regular trade districts. He called this latter type of dominion 'a legal dominion'. He did not find this until ca. 1400 because the towns' trade until then was effectively curtailed by small landing sites in the countryside run by peasants and fishermen, foreign merchants operating outside the towns, commercially active peasants and rural markets. After 1400, commercial activities in the countryside were to a larger extent suppressed and the trade monopoly of the market towns as specified in their charters became more effective.[18] The term 'legal dominion' implies an artificial power relationship sustained by privileges that ran counter to the economic reality. This reality was that the land-owning nobility had overwhelming economic superiority – and despite a more meritocratic policy by the kings of Absolutism, this was never really changed – and that entrepreneurial peasants were less than willing to accept the towns' dominance.

The progressive concentration of commercial life in the market towns is compatible with the economic advantages of urban concentration according to classical land use theories and service centre theories. One can also argue that Poulsen's finding of economic or market rationality among (some of) the peasants of the Middle Ages makes these theories even more plausible, as central place theorists right from von Thünen to Christaller have operated with the existence of free and unrestrained peasants acting on the basis of the commercialisation of the countryside as a necessary condition for their theories.[19] The question is only what the increasing power of the market towns did to the commercialisation of the Danish countryside after ca. 1400.

Rivals to the towns – the estate owners and the peasants

Before we look more closely at the market towns, it is thus necessary to understand the economic rights of town citizens in relation to the other social groups.

During the 16th century, the Crown confirmed the policy it had started in the 15th century: as a starting point, advanced commercial activities were to be handed over to merchants in the market towns; harbours outside the jurisdiction of the market towns must not be used; trade and other business had to be done within the town gates. In 1623, the limits for trade in small goods in the countryside were also tightened, as by far the largest part of this was handed over to tax-paying town citizens, who at the same time were to live and have their business in the town. Peddlers in the countryside were prohibited, except in connection with seasonal fairs. Concurrently with the urban crisis becoming established during the 17th century (cf. Ole Degn's article), it became increasingly important for the towns to maintain the rights of the urban sector, and on the occasion of the accession of King Frederik III in 1648, several towns sent in a number of petitions which caused the King to write an open letter in 1649 formulating his economic market town policy: illegal merchandising, *forprang* (trading outside the town gates and outside the fixed market hours) and shipping at illegal harbours were as hitherto prohibited.[20]

This could suggest that the towns were inordinately favoured, but there were two exceptions that undermined their trading position. The most important was that the nobility retained its right 'to utilise his own property as well as possible and to sell it to whom he wishes' – as written in a royal *reces* (body of laws) in 1558. The estate owners could bypass the nearest market town and sell their goods wherever they wished and could even ship their cargo from any point on the coastline. However, the nobility and other estate owners had not at any time the right to sell basic commodities such as salt, cloth, and hops in the villages. Still, their trading rights made substantial inroads into the markets of the towns. Prior to 1660 the nobility even gained almost exclusive rights to the profitable trade in oxen. After a prolonged process that gradually curtailed the rights of merchants, the situation after ca. 1630 was that merchants were only allowed to buy oxen from peasants at the fairs. Their only legitimate sale of oxen was restricted to the stable-fed oxen that they could feed with their own fodder or that had been fattened in the stables of the King or the nobility. To begin with, the merchants could partly compensate for the loss of market share by engaging in the transport of the oxen to the German and Dutch markets, but even this opportunity was lost when first the oxen exports from the leading town of Ribe were being shipped on foreign ships from the 1630s and later when buyers from the Netherlands and Schleswig-Holstein took over this trade. However, the trade in oxen – which used to be the primary export article – dwindled, beginning in the 1630s and 1640s, due to warfare and the reorientation of international trading routes. In our context it should be remembered that the oxen trade had resulted in great capital accumulation in the 16th and 17th centuries from which both the nobility and some of the towns profited, the latter despite the diminution of their trading rights.

The peasants were also given a number of trading rights. Laws from the 16th century gave them the right to purchase seed and other articles necessary for the 'maintenance of the household', which also included the right to buy building timber and firewood in ports outside the towns. All of these rights – both the peasants' and the estate owners' – were codified in *Danske Lov* of 1683 and in 18th century laws. However peasants in several parts of the country retained older rights to export their own products by sea – see below.

In the period after 1660 the situation was that local trade was conducted on the basis of the general trading policy, the privileges and charters of the individual towns and local exceptions, which together described the rights of each town and social-economic group in this field.

The trading rights of the market towns

So, what was left for the towns? In accordance with the thesis of S.R. Epstein, the medieval statutes were normative even after 1660. This is true both for the above-mentioned general trading laws regulating the rights of towns, nobility and peasants and for the individual rights of the towns. One provision deserves special interest. As a result of a clash between a number of large towns and Ribe about Ribe's comprehensive rights to trade within the trading districts of other towns, it was stipulated in 1541/42 that all towns in Jutland were free to engage in all kinds of trade with any nobleman and clergyman, regardless of their location. Only trade with peasants was limited to the market town that kept the license to trade in the district in question.

There were various ways in which a market town could get a fixed trading district. Fundamental was the right to force peasants to sell their goods in the towns. This was often – as described above – a matter of general legislation, but if the towns in the eyes of the state administration did not provide sufficient buying power to sustain this, the towns could well be ordered to provide 'good prices' and 'reasonable supply'. This was repeated several times and with special zeal in the first decades of the 17th century. No less than 10 towns got – or regained – their first regular weekly market day as late as in the 17th century, and this was due to pressure from the King. The most important way for a town to obtain a trading district of its own, however, was to be given a privileged district of a certain size, either with a strict radius of typically two Danish miles (15 km) or a certain area, typically one *herred* (the lowest legal district) or more. Another way was to take over markets and fairs held in the countryside and have them transferred to the town. A third way was to gain supremacy over countryside ports or to have them closed. A fourth way was to gain the monopoly on the sale of certain articles within an area (fig. 2).

Approximately 80 such regulations (the transfer of ports is not included) can be documented for the period 1354 to ca. 1800. To this should be added some general provisions. In 1681 the brewing of beer in inns was prohibited within a radius of two miles of market towns, and in the 1730s the towns in Schleswig-Holstein were generally protected by trading zones (see Lars N. Henningsen's article). However, where no provisions are known to have existed in a certain town, fig. 2 still shows a two-mile protection zone. Evidence suggests that at least some of these towns believed they had such a zone, even though this is not documented. On the map, these two-mile radii are shown without a date.

I will not discuss in great length this distribution of trade rights, as it was primarily in place prior to 1660. Suffice to state a few characteristics: There is a slight tendency to a 'neighbour' effect as the granting of a privileged trade district to one town was often soon followed by the desire of the surrounding towns to obtain one as well. To give one example, we can take Jutland. The spread of protected trade areas began to a greater extent in the southern part of Jutland in the latter half of the 15th century, presumably due to the presence of many foreign merchants in that area and the King's preferential treatment of Ribe, the leading oxen trade town. Another wave began in the northern part of Jutland from the 1460s to 1552 as most of the towns here wanted to protect themselves from the dominance of the leading town in the region, Aalborg, as well as from Ribe. Clearly the larger towns came first (1494-1505) and the smaller ones after (1515-1552).

Funen was divided almost equally between the towns in the 15th and 16th centuries while at the same time some of the towns facing the German coast had to accept that the peasantry in Southern Funen retained old rights to ship homemade products. It seems that the towns on the islands of Zealand, Lolland, Falster and Møn in general were given protected trade areas later and with a less precise content than the towns in Jutland at least. This was probably due to two factors. First of all, the rising economic importance of Copenhagen apparently meant that less concern was shown for the other towns in the region. Secondly, more attention was paid to defining the general trading rights of the peasants in the aftermath of the decline of the Scania Fairs around 1500, which had played a substantial role in the peasants' economy, and less attention was paid to the rights of each individual town. Furthermore, there was a certain association between poorer protection of a market town and a strong peasantry in terms of engagement in long-distance trade. This was the case with the islands of Langeland and Ærø where the peasants kept up old traditions for active trade with the German coastline and towns, much to the detriment of the two towns on the islands, Rudkøbing and Ærøskøbing. And this was also the situation on the islands of Lolland, Falster and Møn where the peasants were never quite stripped of their old rights to ship their own products, although in the latter half of the 16th century these were restricted to certain articles at certain times of the year.

Fig. 2 clearly shows that despite all these efforts the result was a division of trade districts that was both incomplete and self-contradictory. Some areas were not even covered (the white parishes on the map), not only in the sparsely populated parts of Central Jutland but also elsewhere. Confusingly, a large number of parishes were forced to trade in more than one market town (the grey parishes), first of all in the most urbanised parts of the east coast of Jutland, Western Funen and Central and Eastern Zealand, Lolland and Falster. A little group of parishes were even subordinated to such contested and unsettled trade regulations that it cannot be established which town they were formally forced to trade in (the lilac parishes). One might focus on all of these cases and say that such an incomplete 'market town system' was irrelevant. But one can also – as I will – pay attention to the hundreds of parishes that were clearly and explicitly bonded to a specific market town – either because they belonged to a certain *len* or *herred* (i.e. administrative and legal districts)

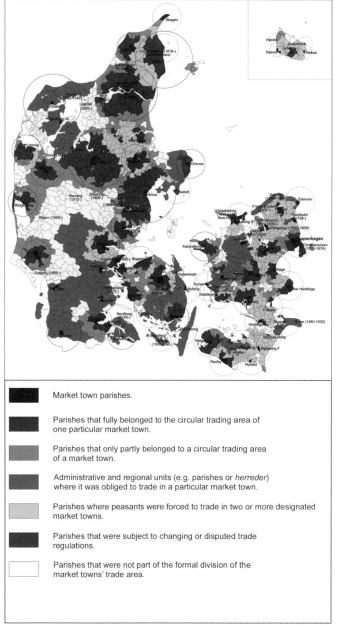

FIG. 2.

The 'legal market town system'. The map shows the formal division of the market towns' trade districts ca. 1450-1800. The basic idea of the map is that all market towns had a trade radius of two Danish miles (15 km), which was the common contemporary belief. The circles illustrate these two-mile radii unless other regulations are known to have existed. For example, Aalborg, Aarhus and other large towns were given a four-mile radius. The system has been modified taking into account all known regulations of the trade districts.

■	Market town parishes.
■	Parishes that fully belonged to the circular trading area of one particular market town.
■	Parishes that only partly belonged to a circular trading area of a market town.
■	Administrative and regional units (e.g. parishes or *herreder*) where it was obliged to trade in a particular market town.
■	Parishes where peasants were forced to trade in two or more designated market towns.
■	Parishes that were subject to changing or disputed trade regulations.
□	Parishes that were not part of the formal division of the market towns' trade area.

or because they fell within only one trading district (the red, the pink and the orange parishes).

DANISH TOWNS AS ECONOMIC AGENTS   *57*

The relevance of the protected trade areas – two examples

To support the view that this *institutional* framework was an active and decisive force in determining the flow of goods, one can also point to the fact that an – uncountable – number of legal procedures were the result of conflicting interest. About twelve such cases were brought to the High Courts prior to 1660 according to the published records and six more cases are found in the published ordinances 1558-1660. More typically, the controversies never reached the national level, but were negotiated on the local level.

I will give two examples. One is from Aalborg, the regional centre of Northern Jutland, while the other is from Varde, a small town on the west coast of Jutland, near Ribe and Germany.[21]

Aalborg is located inside Limfjord, which was the area in the Kingdom that from the middle of the 15th century was the subject of most judicial controversies about trading districts. In 1449 Aalborg, together with Viborg, Nykøbing and Lemvig were designated as the only four legal ports on the fjord where foreign merchants could call. A decisive geographical factor in this was the difficult navigation in Limfjord, which in practice made Aalborg the transhipment port for nearly all through-traffic of goods. In 1462 the town was given the monopoly on buying up oxen, hides, skin, and other merchandise in a radius of 4 miles (30 km) of the town (fig. 3). The town became the centre for a greatly increasing trade in herring and oxen, and a feature of the late 15th century and 16th century privileges of the town is the fact that the greatest trading problem was the illegal purchase of herring, especially in the non-chartered urban settlement of Nibe, but also in other towns on the fjord. In 1459 the townsmen in Nykøbing had got the right to buy salt and engage in fishing all over Limfjord, whereas foreigners could only call at Aalborg. But in 1516 Aalborg and the small non-chartered urban settlement of Løgstør got the monopoly on salting herring. Nykøbing is not mentioned, but in practice, this meant that some of the rights from 1459 were taken from the town. However, in 1553 this town again received the right to salt herring. Parallel with this, other elements in Aalborg's commercial rights were pushed further out. First, Nibe's seasonal fair was moved to Aalborg about 1490, and subsequently in 1505 Aalborg's shoemakers got a monopoly on the production of shoes within three miles (21.5 km) of the market town. However, Aalborg did not succeed in depriving Nibe of the right to salt herring – apart from the period 1516-1518 – and Nibe continued to hold markets, which until 1699 were illegal. In 1554, it was also determined that all ships in Limfjord had to call at Aalborg.

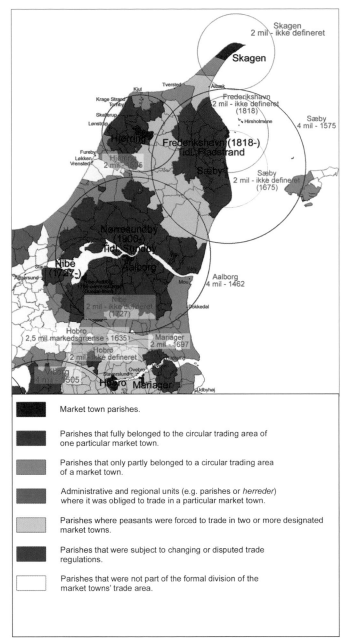

FIG. 3.
The 'legal market town system' in Northern Jutland, ca. 1450-1800.
'2 mil — ikke defineret' means '2 miles customary, not legal pratice'.

Market town parishes.

Parishes that fully belonged to the circular trading area of one particular market town.

Parishes that only partly belonged to a circular trading area of a market town.

Administrative and regional units (e.g. parishes or *herreder*) where it was obliged to trade in a particular market town.

Parishes where peasants were forced to trade in two or more designated market towns.

Parishes that were subject to changing or disputed trade regulations.

Parishes that were not part of the formal division of the market towns' trade area.

In general, the legal division of trade within the Limfjord region meant that Aalborg appropriated most of the trade transported by sea, while the dominance of the town was not so pronounced on land as on the water. At the end of the 16th century, Aalborg can be seen entering into 'strategic alliances' with other market towns and urban settlements. In 1590, citizens from Hjørring and Aalborg were put on an equal footing in each other's towns as regards trading. Løgstør came into the spotlight in 1598 when the town was accused of conducting mercantile business, which led to the decision that the town traders in future had to take out a trading licence in Aalborg, Viborg or other market towns. Similarly, market towns outside the region also had to secure royal privileges to maintain a position beside Aalborg. Thus Aarhus and Randers in 1553 got a royal judgement that they could hold various sales of goods at some times of the year in the small fishing settlements on Limfjord. In 1618 the citizens of the market town of Skive got permission to brew and sell beer in the nearest neighbouring fishing settlements and harbours on condition that this did not develop into inn-keeping proper. Of the other market towns located on Limfjord, Thisted was for some time the best positioned with a trading district of a 4-mile radius from 1524, which meant that the town's trading district overlapped that of Aalborg. The large district was due to the fact that for a short time the town had become important for the Crown in a clash with the local bishop. Aalborg crushed this opponent in 1619 by getting the King's decision that the town merchants could trade in Thisted's district, and similarly, a nascent market in Sundby just opposite Aalborg on the other side of Limfjord was partially stopped in 1639 and 1648.

In 1655 the citizens of Aalborg got the definitive right to trade freely everywhere on Limfjord with their ships, small craft and barges, both for themselves and their servants. This time the right was given in return for the town building naval ships for the King. The 1655 privilege is known to have been decisive in several conflicts with the neighbouring towns, Skive, Thisted and Lemvig. In 1693 the people of Aalborg got yet another golden privilege in the form of a prohibition on anyone, except themselves, trading in the fishing settlements within the town's privileged district. But after this, the other towns won some territory. In 1699 everyone was allowed to sail to Nibe with barrels and salt and take herring back, and the people of Nibe could export their fish to Denmark and Norway. Afterwards, in 1727, the town received a market town charter probably influenced by a boom in herring fishery. There were thus changes in the legal distribution of trading districts right up to the 18th century. In 1759 Skive succeeded in pushing the boundary of the town's statutory trading district further out, when the privilege was extended from the original two miles to apply to the peninsula of Salling to the north of the town. In practice, the size of the trading district was thereby doubled. Since Aalborg could still invoke the 1655 decisions, and since Nibe too had become a market town in 1727, thereby

SØREN BITSCH CHRISTENSEN

having some claim to a trading district, the whole situation was becoming critical. In 1752, the very small town of Løgstør also got certain shipping rights. In 1769, at the request of Nibe, an arrangement was agreed between Nibe and Aalborg which the parties themselves considered binding. The boundary was drawn more or less centrally between the towns, and a formal division of districts was made between Nibe and Løgstør in the opposite direction. The competition for privileges lasting

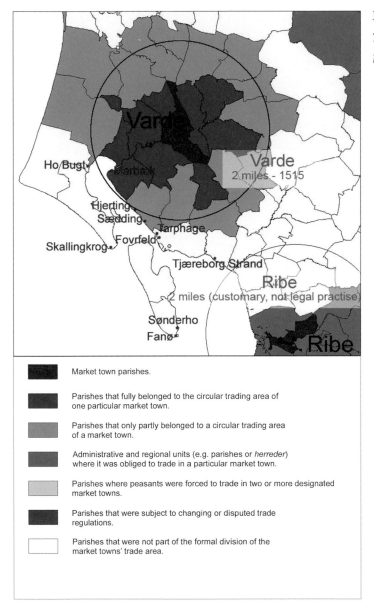

FIG. 4.
The trade privileges of
Varde, ca. 1515-1800.

Market town parishes.

Parishes that fully belonged to the circular trading area of one particular market town.

Parishes that only partly belonged to a circular trading area of a market town.

Administrative and regional units (e.g. parishes or *herreder*) where it was obliged to trade in a particular market town.

Parishes where peasants were forced to trade in two or more designated market towns.

Parishes that were subject to changing or disputed trade regulations.

Parishes that were not part of the formal division of the market towns' trade area.

almost 400 years can first be said to have ended when all the market towns on Lim-fjord became customs posts in 1841.

Varde's basic problem was that it was difficult for ships to sail right into the town, and that is why competing non-chartered urban settlements arose that attracted trade with the fishermen and peasants in the neighbourhood. In 1515 the town had got a protected area with a radius of two miles, and in addition the town got permission to arrest buyers who operated within a distance of two miles of the town and on the coast (fig. 4). The trading conditions around Varde give exceptionally good evidence about how an effort was made to organise trade with the radius as reference. With re-gard to the town it is recounted for instance in 1688 that trading peasants and farm-ers made calculations so that they could settle right outside the two-mile boundary. Many years of conflict with the surrounding islands and coastal communities ended with several of these getting the right in 1685-1689 to conduct shipping and export fish and 'other agricultural products' both domestically and to other countries. In this way, Varde lost its maritime hinterland and in 1692 lost its customs post to the coastal community of Hjerting. However there was a small victory in 1688 when the town had its land-based district extended so this reached half-way to Ribe and Ring-købing.

The corn trade – examples from 1761/62

After the decline of the trade in oxen in the 17th century, trade in corn was the most important item of trade in the Kingdom during Absolutism, both in exports and do-mestic trade. Therefore it was also the trade in corn more than any other commodity that determined the nature of the economic exchange between the countryside and town, even though other commodities could regionally be of greater importance.

As mentioned, corn could be sold by estate owners and clergymen without regard to the privileges of the market towns. The question can therefore be asked about whether this led to the towns being played off against each other and thus creating or maintaining a competitive situation between them.

I have quantified the volume of the corn trade on the basis of a number of re-ports from estate owners, clergymen, shippers and merchants about their trade in rye and oats in 1761/62. The reports were obtained by the state authorities in order to get a broad view of the supply situation in the Kingdom, which was being mili-tarily threatened by Russia. The material is noteworthy, but not as representative

1	(458)
2	(99)
3	(10)
4	(3)

Fɪɢ. 5.

The map shows how many market towns each parish (almost entirely represented by estate owners in the material) in the Kingdom of Denmark sold rye and oats to. No records exist from the parishes marked with the brightest colour.

as could be wished, nor is it without bias. Questions were asked only about rye and oats, which means that parts of the country where other cereals were cultivated are under-represented in the material. This is the case primarily for Lolland-Falster and parts of Zealand. Not all the reports have been preserved. The respondents themselves had to give information about their circumstances but the answers were subsequently still subject to inspection.[22] In all, reports could be gathered from 896 parishes (out of a total of about 1,100) with information from 1,855 people (608 estates, 559 merchants, 643 clergymen, 35 shippers and 10 'others') giving information about 2,165 corn-trade transactions with a stated volume of 185,162 barrels of corn.[23] In this context, it is best to use the information to map the trade relations of the parishes to the market towns, in other words their 'activity spheres'.[24] These show that the vast majority of the rural parishes are registered with relations to only one town (80 %). If Copenhagen is taken out of the analysis, 403 parishes had sold rye and oats to one market town, 67 to two towns, four to three towns, and three to four towns. The results are shown in fig. 5.

The nature of the material does not permit reaching conclusions that are too far-reaching. But it is acceptable to present the main outline of the distribution of trade districts:[25]

Northern Jutland was a dynamic region with clear Aalborg dominance, while several of the smaller towns had still retained a trading district that was approximately circular. According to the material, the smallest towns were without any real trading district (it should be noted here that peasants' trade is not included in the material). These conditions reflect Aalborg's legal dominance on the coasts of Limfjord and the legal position of precedence of the market towns of Skive, Viborg and Hobro in the hinterland behind the coastline. Finally, a number of small shipping communities facing the North Sea had seized the hinterland trade from the surrounding market towns with a view to export to Norway.

In this regard, *West Jutland* does not seem to have been a particularly dynamic region, only Varde stepped out of its limiting framework and seems on the whole to have been the region's leading town for trade in corn. This was largely due to a single merchant who visited remote parishes so he could fill a special order from a royal agent who wanted the corn shipped from Horsens on the east coast. But this was a one-off transaction. Lemvig, Holstebro and Ringkøbing maintained trading districts that were approximately circular, but the information is scanty and corn cultivation played a smaller role in this region than anywhere else in the Kingdom.

East Jutland seems to have been a typical balanced region where the trade districts of the relatively large towns followed the legal division of the trade districts quite closely. There was no completely dominant centre, but if one had to point out such a centre, it

SØREN BITSCH CHRISTENSEN

would have to be Aarhus, because, in accordance with the privileges, the trading district of the town was the largest geographically and after all the most extensive. However it is more pertinent to say that the top layer consisted of five towns all characterised by the fact that they had to share many parishes with other towns: Aarhus (13 out of 37 parishes) Randers (11/35), Grenaa (6/20), Ebeltoft (7/16) and Horsens (9/28). In this area, which also had very productive corn cultivation, there was strong competition between the towns. Towards the south – Kolding, Fredericia and Vejle – the material is not good enough to give a precise assessment. The relationship between the three towns is nevertheless a good example of the significance of institutional and geographic conditions. In a report in 1735, the recorder in Vejle stated that the peasants drove right through the town to sell their corn in Fredericia – at that time just an 80-year-old garrison town – in order to take advantage of that town's reduced town gate duty. In 1762 the mayor of Vejle reported that the poor supply to the town was because bad roads surrounded the town, and later in the century, in 1793, it is known that export of corn had been completely taken over by out-of-town merchants and shippers. In 1452 Kolding had been granted the monopoly on all trade within the then Koldinghus *Len* (Fief), and even though this provision was not repeated later, the Crown gave the town protection several times, undoubtedly prompted by the presence of a royal castle. Studies have shown that in the 1750s, the town had a trading district that, by and large, was identical with the old 1452 provision.[26]

The trading pattern on *Funen* was marked by trading zones of almost equal size, though in a few places this was broken by purchases made by shippers from the countryside (fig. 6). A trading structure had been created where all towns had to share many parishes with other towns. This is a good reflection of both geographical and institutional circumstances, as the towns on Funen are evenly distributed and no town was particularly favoured in the legal sense. However there were two leading towns. One of them was the largest town, Odense; the other was Svendborg. If one looks at fig. 6, this is a surprising appraisal. Actually no reports from Svendborg or its closest hinterland have been preserved; on the other hand no merchant from other towns reported purchases in Svendborg's zone, which extended all the way to just south of Odense.[27]

A true metropolis springs into view when we look at *Zealand* (fig. 7). Copenhagen was the completely dominating centre of consumption in the country, a giant that put nearly all the towns on Zealand and Lolland-Falster into the shade. The material shows it sharing 50 parishes with other towns. In normal circumstances, sales at the

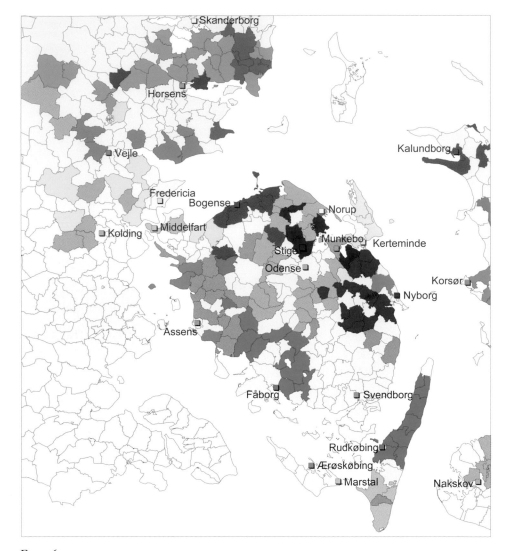

Fig. 6.

The corn trade districts on Funen, 1761/62.

The map shows the dominating market towns in relation to each parish. Note: Data from many parishes are missing. Market towns not on the map:

- ■ Copenhagen
- ■ Varde
- ■ Aarhus

market places brought corn to Copenhagen, as the wholesalers in the capital did not do much trade in corn. For example, in October 1772 they had only 100 barrels of wheat in stock.[28] Only a very few wholesalers took part in the supply of corn to the inhab-

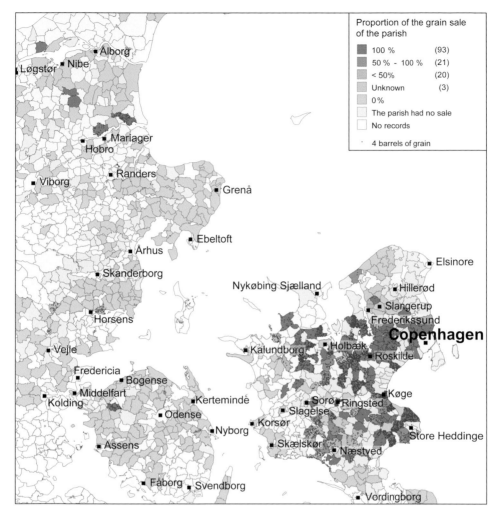

FIG. 7.

The corn trade district of Copenhagen, 1761/62.

itants of the city.[29] However they became involved in the corn trade when the state needed special supplies from the Baltic countries to supply Norway, the royal storerooms, or – as in 1761/62 – the army.[30] In these situations, the wholesalers activated their trading connections; in any case their ships were often at the end of the Baltic Sea with groceries. In 1761/62 it was a case of a combination, in that the King had entrusted a large part of army supplies to selected wholesalers while the material gives information about supplies to the market places. The stated distribution of purchasing groups was: 'the market'[31] 35 %, merchants 18 % (though not for consumption in the town but for the army), 'citizens' 15 %, bakers 14 %, and 'unknown' 17 %.

However there were limits to Copenhagen's purchasing zone. The most important limit went in a line east of Kalundborg, and Western Zealand was left more or less in peace. Fig. 7 shows there was also a boundary south of Næstved. Both of these boundaries must be assumed to have been real boundaries for the rye and oats trade – but since barley was the most important cash crop in these areas, a certain amount of trade with Copenhagen is probably concealed. A few of the larger towns on Zealand maintained their own small trading districts or even expanded into other towns' trading districts. This applies primarily to Korsør, which had taken over the area Korsør-Slagelse-Sorø-Næstved-Skælskør-Korsør.[32] But Køge, too, had invaded the zone of neighbouring towns at Store Heddinge and Ringsted, and Vordingborg and Stege had a protected turnover, incidentally in keeping with the privileges of these towns. The losers were towns such as Nykøbing, Skælskør, Hillerød, Sorø, Ringsted etc. Nearly all these towns indeed report that there is no trade in rye and oats.[33]

As mentioned, *Lolland* and *Falster* are inadequately covered in the material. But a picture emerges of a very homogeneous region with equally sized towns, typical local centres with locally limited centrality. In general, this is in accordance with the privileges of the towns.

The material has also documented a widespread practice of sellers and buyers making a prior agreement about delivery of fixed amounts at predetermined prices to ensure a stable turnover. In the material from 1761/62, the information about these agreements must be considered as being the minimum of what actually occurred. Nevertheless, 33 % of the corn sold by the estates is stated as having been sold in this way and 15 % of the clergymen's. It is clear that the agreements were most used in the districts where competition was strongest: Funen, East Jutland and South-West Zealand. The extensive use of such contracts shows very clearly what costs were incurred in gaining commercial security and market information. To improve co-ordination between producer and consumer, the merchants of the market towns were willing to forego the optimal speculation in profitable changes of prices and market opportunities.

In broad outline, the flow of goods to the towns from the estates and clergymen in the country followed the guidelines that were laid down in the legal trading district regulations. If one excludes single dominating towns such as Copenhagen, Aalborg and partly Aarhus and Odense, the trade structure was rather decentralised. There was something for almost every large town, but not very much for many of the smaller towns (perhaps their figures would have been relatively higher if the peasants' own trade in corn had been included in the material). Before we anticipate a conclusion about the nature of the market town system in the middle of the 18th century, there are grounds to see if conditions were different for products other than corn.

Peddlers and peasant traders

In 1735 answers to eight questions came to the central authority from all the market towns and nearly all *amter* (counties, administrative districts). These questions had been formulated by *Kommercekollegiet* (the central authority in matters regarding commerce and industry) about the economic situation in rural areas and towns. The answers constitute a quite unique source because of their synchronicity: they are contemporary and thematically congruent, and they are motivated – such is how we must understand them – by a general need to explain and bring all discrepancies to light. The reports have recently been published on The Danish Centre for Urban History's homepage.

A large number of comments on the situation of the towns in relation to trading districts were made as answers to the questions. It is not possible to go into detail here with these extensive reports, and I will limit myself to deal thematically with the towns' perception of prohibited trade in the countryside. At that time, the two terms *forprang* and *landprang* were used indiscriminately about illegal economic activity in peasant society, but the statements can still be sorted so some main groups of illegal activity stand out:

- Rural artisans doing what is actually town craftsmanship. This seemed to be generally widespread all over the country and I will ignore it in this connection.
- People from outside the local area making illegal retail sales in rural areas.
- Peasants' illegal sales, both direct sale and onward sale.
- Competing economic 'centres' such as manors, rectories and inns.

In general it can be stated that the local authorities in the towns and their opposite numbers in rural areas were well aware of the law and took their arguments from that. They were very clear that they operated in a privilege-regulated economic system. The illegal buying and selling in the countryside was therefore considered to be an infringement of time-honoured rights and good economic order. As such, it was a problem noted by almost all market towns, but the problem had different regionally determined forms.

The Zealand towns complained most persistently and in most detail about rural tradesmen and peddlers. There were also accusations about merchants from the market towns, smallholders, innkeepers and ferrymen. From Roskilde, close to Copenhagen, it is reported for example 'that now the peasant in the country, in inns and other places, both can buy his heavy goods such as salted herring, tobacco, salt, iron, train oil, wooden shoes, hops, small goods and the like and there sell most of his corn as well as honey, wax, candles and skins etc.' Something similar is indicated from Holbæk. Most of the purchased goods were undoubtedly sold in Copenhagen, but when merchants from the towns also went out to the country to buy goods it can just as well be because the commercial dominance of Copenhagen had cut them off from a large part of the daily turnover. A picture thus emerges showing that the economic division of labour between town and country on Zealand was ruled less by a desire to concentrate sales in all market towns than a wish to generate enough economic activity to keep the supply lines to Copenhagen open.

The greatest limitations in the trade of the Kingdom's towns with their closest trading district were found in a southern belt from Ribe in South Jutland over Southern Funen to the islands of Langeland, Lolland and Falster, but in different forms. In South Jutland, it was seemingly the peasants themselves who disregarded the market town legislation and traded retail goods – small wares and larger goods – almost freely as both buyers and sellers. Peasants in the same role were found on Zealand. But on the south-facing islands mentioned, it was generally outside actors, in particular shippers from the Schleswig island of Ærø, who exploited holes in the tariff legislation to deprive the towns of trade, incidentally trade in corn too.

The more definitely defined division of trading districts in Northern Jutland did not have correspondingly fixed positions for the peasants. In North-Western Jutland and the western part of Limfjord, a number of outside actors (shippers from the coast) operated in the peasant community and took over some of the export of heavy goods. In East and Mid-Jutland on the other hand, the peasants followed the rules for the sale of heavy goods to a greater extent, but bought small goods on a large scale from travelling peddlers.

SØREN BITSCH CHRISTENSEN

The market town system – a characterisation

How can we characterise the market town system in the middle of the 18th century, seen through the material used about the formal division of trading districts, the corn trade and the trade of the market towns in 1735?

There was no question of an equally distributed supply of corn to all towns, and many small towns did not have any significant corn trade with estates and clergymen. The situation was different for the medium-sized and large market towns. If one excludes single dominant towns such as Copenhagen and Aalborg, and to a lesser degree, Aarhus and Odense, the trade structure among these was, as mentioned, rather decentralised. This is consistent with the legal town system having a tendency to favour those towns with a large formal trading district. Conversely, it was also part of the legal market town system that peasants in some parts of the country had various commercial rights; this was typically the case for peasants on large islands with and without market towns. An analysis of the formal division of trading districts shows that the towns were aware of their rights – both the general and the particular – and used them in a continuous campaign to maintain the trading district assigned to them. In several towns, the formal trading district was identical with an administrative or judicial area, and in these cases it was an advantage for the towns that a decree in 1639 introduced compulsory registration of peasants' debts to merchants.[34] In this way, the local merchants got better access to information about their trading district from the public announcements on the *thingsteads*, while it was more difficult for other merchants to obtain the same certain knowledge.

The 'natural market town system', in which all goods were taken to the nearest town, was far from reality. Apart from the divergences from this 'rule', which were due to the formal division of trading districts, there was also, as documented in 1735, an undergrowth of economic activity with small goods and everyday necessities which did not follow the path from peasant to the nearest town, indeed it does not seem to have been subject to the formal division of trading districts at all. It is impossible to quantify the extent of the commercial activity that the towns complained about in 1735 with travelling peddlers, trading in inns etc. But other activities that bypassed the nearest town can be estimated with a certain precision. This is the case for goods such as fish, various proto-industries and trade in cattle, pigs, lambs and grain.

Fishery

Coastal fishery in the 18[35] century was only a faint reflection of the large-scale fishing operation of earlier centuries.[35] In the words of Maibritt Bager, there was 'a massive deficit of fish' in Denmark in the second half of the 18th century. As the main consumer, Copenhagen could get only a fraction of its consumption from Denmark. On a countrywide basis, it has been conservatively estimated that Danish fish amounted to 1/5 of the total consumption of herring. Incidentally, the herring catch was largely included in the privileges of the towns. That is why fishery was not a threat to the market town system even though it could be important locally.

Proto-industry and rural production culture in Jutland

According to Epstein, proto-industry was one of the economic activities for which the towns considered it important to secure legal rights. In Denmark, proto-industry had nothing like the same economic significance as in many other West European countries, but it belongs in this context (cf. Henrik Harnow's article).

West Jutland was the centre for the production of black pots, which could have great importance locally. In the overall economic picture, however, they were not important, and the value of their exports was only a few thousand *rigsdaler* in the 1760s.[36]

Another rural production in Jutland was *hosebinding* (knitted woollen socks). In Central Jutland, sock knitting was an alternative peasant trade, where only a certain part of the sales went through market towns merchants. The largest earnings were transferred to Copenhagen. It was a two-piece organisation. Local salesmen were middle-men between the peasants and the Copenhagen wholesalers. The raw material, wool, was also provided bypassing the towns' merchants and was supplied from large parts of Jutland and Funen, most often at the market in the town of Holstebro. The Copenhagen wholesalers themselves also supplied wool to the knitters.[37] It was a growing business in the 18th century. In the 1760s, a topographical work estimated the value at 16,000-20,000 *rigsdaler*, but as early as the 1780s, the Copenhagen wholesalers' guild themselves valued the total Jutland export to Copenhagen, Norway and Hamburg at 100,000-150,000 *rigsdaler*, and of this 50,000 *rigsdaler* to Copenhagen alone.[38]

A third Jutland production was the lace industry in Tønder and to a lesser extent in Aabenraa and Haderslev, all three Schleswig towns. Much of this production was within 'the natural market town system' – as part of the exchange between the country and the closest town – but its extent alone suggests that the three towns must also have siphoned off resources from the hinterland of other towns. In 1780 alone, there were 12,000 lace-makers. The industry was organised in the way that merchants supplied the lace-makers with thread and patterns, after which they worked on credit while the merchants sold the wares themselves or through peddlers.[39]

A fourth production was linen weaving. This was a traditional rural occupation. In 1838 there were 27,882 looms in the Kingdom.[40] The main concentration was in Aalborg, Hjørring and Thisted *amter* and in areas near Randers and Ribe. But what had been the situation earlier? In both Aalborg and Ribe, linen weaving was organised as a putting-out system so that the town merchants supplied the flax from the Baltic countries and sold on the finished product. But this was because flax could not be grown there. In the area between Vejle and Viborg, the land was more suitable for flax growing, and therefore the merchants' role there was limited more to selling on a *Kaufsystem*.[41] In 1761, the total Danish consumption of linen was estimated to amount to 1 million *rigsdaler* a year, and a significant portion of this was traded. Large amounts of linen went from the Randers and Aarhus region to Norway. On the basis of customs material, the value of the exported linen can be cautiously estimated to be ca. 80,000 *rigsdaler* around 1770. This can then be compared with the value of the wooden shoes from the Silkeborg area, which were exported through Aarhus, namely 4,550 *rigsdaler* in 1745.

Animal and dairy products

Proto-industrial businesses were thus concentrated in Jutland. The same was true for the cattle trade, although this was much smaller in the 18th century than in the good times. At that time only the nobility had the right to export cattle. The Jutland estate owners were the people responsible for sales to foreign buyers. In 1768 exports abroad amounted to 7,000-8,000 animals at a value of 140,000-160,000 *rigsdaler*. However the large amount of smuggling over the river Kongeåen (the border between the Kingdom and Schleswig) has not been taken into account in this amount. The other large market was Copenhagen. From 1760 to 1765, the annual import of live cattle to the capital is assessed at 7,477 bullocks, 1,409 cows and 5,224 calves to a value of ca. 130,000-162,000 *rigsdaler*. This traffic came primarily from the Zealand estates.

Copenhagen was also the centre of a large supply district for slaughtered animals, smoked meat and live lambs. This trade was not market town regulated either, but was in the hands of the Zealand estates and peasants, with a small input from other parts of the country. The meat came in through the town gates and the harbour. For the period 1760-1765 this import can be estimated at 370,516 *rigsdaler* annually.

Dairy products were of course not only supplied to Copenhagen from the peasants who lived around the town, but also from estates in Jutland, on Funen and Zealand and from the Duchies. The annual supply of butter 1760-1765 can be valued at 32,150 *rigsdaler*. The annual supply of cheese to Copenhagen 1763-1771 had a value of 2,000 *rigsdaler* from Jutland, 500 *rigsdaler* from Funen and 20,000 *rigsdaler* from Zealand.[42]

Corn

Practically all the corn that went to Copenhagen bypassed the closest market town and hence undermined 'the natural market town system'. This happened too with the estates' corn purchase from other estates, clergymen and peasants. In addition, some estates – but not as many as one might think – exported their corn themselves and a number of shipper communities were also exporters. I have been able to document these trading patterns for rye and oats 1761/1762. The shipper communities' export was a minimum of 5,785 barrels from Stige on Funen and the shippers on the west coast of Jutland. The estates' own export of rye and oats was also ca. 5,000 barrels. But there are ways to get the other grain types included in the calculations. It is known from other sources that the peasants on Samsø exported ca. 5,000 barrels of all sorts to Norway annually. Copenhagen's total corn import in 1760 was 249,000 barrels and it is known that estates on Lolland-Falster exported ca. 7,000 barrels of wheat to other countries. With a unit price of 1½ *rigsdaler* per barrel, it can be conservatively estimated that corn for 431,800 *rigsdaler*, or rather half a million *rigsdaler*, was traded outside 'the natural market town system'.

All goods

One can thus cautiously estimate that domestic goods to a value of at least 1.7 million and probably ca. 2 million *rigsdaler* were traded outside 'the natural market town system'. This corresponded to 28½ *rigsdaler* per market town citizen. Or for that matter, the equivalent of every person in the rural area bypassing the nearest market town and sending 3 *rigsdaler* to Copenhagen, Norway, a completely different town, or abroad. Smuggling cannot be estimated for good reasons, and the same is true of sales at the seasonal fairs in the countryside and in the towns. The relations between town and country thus did not reflect the decisive victory for the towns' 'mercantile dominion', even though it could probably be called a relative victory.

Institutional reforms of the corn trade

In the last decades of the 18th century, Danish agriculture went through great changes that in Danish history are lumped together under the term 'the reform period'. The reforms resulted in agriculture becoming commercialised to a much greater degree than previously, and the nucleus of future agriculture became an almost fixed number of medium-sized farms owned by the farmers themselves. It is clear that this change had to have significance for relations between town and country.

The European price increase for corn in the second half of the 18th century also happened in Denmark. From 1730 to about 1772, corn prices were increasing gradually in spite of repeated price falls, 1772-1784 prices fell or were unchanged, but from 1784 an unbroken and dramatic price rise started which lasted until the war years of 1807-1814, in some cases until 1819.[43] The extensive reforms of Danish agriculture from ca. 1780 thus took place against a background of higher corn prices.

Agricultural reforms are not the focus in this context, but rather the initiatives taken in the 1780s and 1790s to modernise trade and, with that, the town sector. They were initiatives which were believed to be a direct extension of the reforms of agriculture.

Since 1735 Denmark had a monopoly on supplying the Kingdom of Denmark and the southern – and most densely populated – part of Norway with corn.[44] With time, this corn monopoly was subjected to many adjustments, and in the public debate – as far as it was allowed – it was vehemently criticised. The great famine years in the beginning of the 1770s sparked off a discussion of the effects of the monopoly on prices, production and the relationship between the two countries and between the urban and rural sectors. It was beyond question that the monopoly benefited the largest producers, the estate owners. A few debaters spoke directly about the effects of the monopoly on the relationship between town and country, but the situation of the towns was only debated as a subject in itself as an exception. The towns were drawn into the debate more as a symptom of the problems, especially when they were affected by the high prices caused by the monopoly and the repeated years of failed crops. Or by the low prices that held sway in the years with good harvests, when the Danish merchants could not adapt quickly enough from the protected domestic market to sales on the international market. The debate was thus very general, as the corn monopoly was considered to be the mainstay of the general economic organisation of society and the corn trade policy was considered to be a guideline for the extent of the right of free enterprise and the intervention of society in the economy. Several of the debaters revealed knowledge of the leading European economic theoretical discussion, but even though most of them agreed to emphasise agriculture as the primary creator of growth, it cannot be described as a breakthrough for French physiocratism. In the first instance, the debate namely resulted in a body of laws which at the same time tried to modernise and direct a cameralist type of state interventionism, show respect for the physiocratic idea of integrated corn markets as a necessary precondition for stable supplies and steady prices, and create the framework for a certain degree of free trade inspired by early liberalist ideas.[45] At the same time, there was an almost definitive showdown with the mercantile belief in the value of state manufactures as a real alternative to agriculture and private trade.

The complex body of corn legislation was started with the ordinance of 26 May 1788, which allowed the free import of corn on payment of a small duty, the free export of corn without duty and the establishment of bonded warehouses in port towns. In addition, a large state corn silo was established. In 1791, the peasants' corn tax to the royal coffers was replaced with a money tax in return for the state putting its corn requirements out to public tender. And finally, in the same year, corn could be traded according to weight and not volume.

It took many decades before these changes were completely implemented but they were all of fundamental importance for the sale of goods and for the nature of town trade. On the theoretical level, the ordinances are in accordance with economic institutional theory. This theory points out the importance of the actual forms of the exchange of goods and indicates that economic growth and the optimal economic incentive structure are dependent on conditions such as low transaction costs, a high level of market transparency and market feed back, learning processes and accurate assessment of the value of goods.[46]

These conditions played a major role in the Danish corn debate. The incentive

SØREN BITSCH CHRISTENSEN

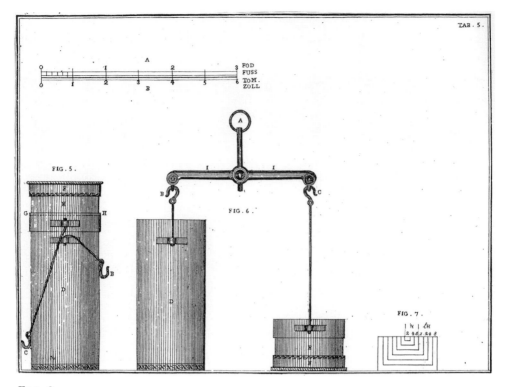

FIG. 8.

The introduction of trade in corn by weight rather than by the generally used barrel meant that corn was to a greater extent priced according to quality. The corn could then be traded on the basis of samples, and this meant that merchants in large towns could more easily take over the corn trade in smaller towns. Instrument maker P.A. Thiele designed the first corn weigher developed in Denmark in 1821 modelled on the so-called Dutch weights. The picture shows the corn weight of the famous designer O.J. Winstrup from 1824. When folded it was only 13 cm long.

to produce clean grain was believed – correctly – to have been reduced by the secure sale to the domestic market before 1788. For several decades a central element in the debate was that Danish corn was not as pure and dry as corn from the Baltic countries. The governmental corn warehouse with storing and drying facilities was set up to deal with this. The vision was that the corn from the warehouse, after being brought up to a certain standard, could be used as an investment object through the issuing of a sort of bank note with corn as security. As the final consequence, this could change the whole character of urban corn trade, as the trade would be lifted up from a commodity trade to a capitalist exchange trade.

Next after the change from being copyholders to being peasant farmers, the transformation of the corn tax into a money tax was the single most important change in the peasants' market relations and an important step towards the commercialisation of the rural society.[47] Equally important was the open tendering for the supply of corn to the state. The state administration summarised the intention as follows: 'the corn trade in the provinces will be revoked and the peasant will get an incentive to grow better corn products as these are getting higher prices than poor corn.'[48]

Of the corn trade laws, the permission in 1791 to trade corn by weight took the longest time to become fully realised. State agencies and quasi-state agencies such as *Det kongelige danske Landhusholdningsselskab* (The Royal Danish Society of Agriculture) and *Grosserer-Societetet* (The Society of Copenhagen Wholesale Dealers) debated for several decades whether the permission should be changed into an order. The Crown took a great step forward in this respect in 1818 when a certain weight was prescribed for the corn to be supplied by the winners of the open tendering process. In 1830 *Grosserer-Societetet* stated that corn in the export trade was traded almost exclusively on the basis of weight. Only in the very first years did the governmental corn warehouse function as a true state corn bank and it was dismantled in the 1830s when private merchants rented the facilities. However, this did not mean the end of the dissemination of corn trade technology, only that it was taken over by the private sector in the form of privately owned winnowers and drying machines promoted by *Det kongelige danske Landhusholdningsselskab* in particular. In the 1830s and 1840s this spread of technology was completed so that all regions and major towns had the basic equipment necessary to conduct a modern corn trade.

All this might perhaps seem to be of little relevance to the issue of this article. However, the changes in the institutional framework of the corn trade paved the way for the emergence of the dynamic and hierarchical urban hierarchy of the 19th century. The main reason was that corn could now be traded independently of its physical presence. And, apart from relatively few cases in the 18th century when Copenhagen merchants, as royal agents, had purchased corn from large areas, this was new and would eventually open the door to a merchant elite exercising a real market dominance.

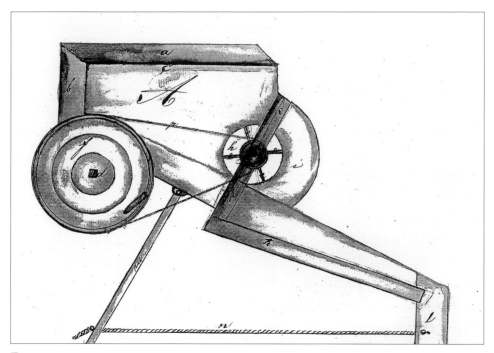

FIG. 9.

Hans Rasmussen's winnowing machine, 1823, length 1.9 m, height 1.25 m. Winnowing machines have two functions – they blow dust and chaff away from the grain by means of a wind wheel, and they separate the grain from the chaff and dust by letting the grain fall through several riddles, usually while the machine is mechanically shaken. In Denmark winnowing machines became popular ca. 1820-1840. The biggest supplier to the private market was Hans Rasmussen, a sexton and school teacher from the Funen town of Assens. In 1817 he established a handicraft school for poor children who were brought up to do 'industrial work'. Up to 1840, he produced more than 600 winnowing machines of various types.

The urban network of corn merchants

A town hierarchy implies that assets are moved from one town to another. Within the corn trade in the Kingdom of Denmark, such commerce was very limited for a long time. An assessment of the total corn exports in 1793, shows that only about 34,000 barrels of corn were shipped from one town on behalf of a merchant from another town – equivalent to ca. 18 % of total exports.[49] To this should be added transport over land to Copenhagen of the goods mentioned on page 74.

However, three factors speeded up trade between towns: the state corn-tendering system, the crisis policy during the great fall in prices 1819-1828, and the rising demand for Danish corn from abroad, which started in the 1790s and culminated in

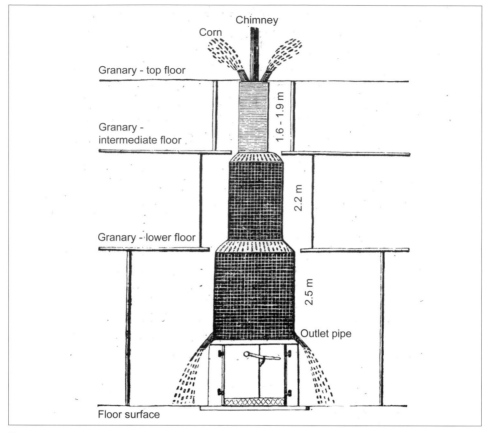

FIG. 10.

Grain-drying apparatus from Stralsund, copied by Hans Rasmussen in Assens, c. 1838. The machine could dry 90-100 barrels of rye in 24 hours at 45 degrees Celsius. It was 6.3 m high and was to be installed so that it went through several grain lofts. The heat from the boiler at the bottom rose through cylinders in an internal chimney. Around the chimney a wire net cylinder was constructed. The net cylinder was double and the grain was sifted down between the two nets and was dried by the heat. The leading merchants in Copenhagen and the provinces in the 1830s used the grain-drier. It was a crucial prerequisite for the export of Danish grain to England and Hamburg.

the period 1828-1875, which in the Danish context is simply called 'the great corn-sale period'.

The tendering process was implemented for the first time in 1791.[50] By far the largest part was put out to tender in quantities of 500 barrels of corn to be supplied to the garrisons in the provinces and in Norway. Since this was a significant amount for the time, the medium-sized and large corn merchants were favoured. In the first three years, 150,000 barrels of corn were bought by tender. Merchants from 23 towns won the contracts. Merchants from four towns alone supplied 100,000 barrels. The towns were Randers, Copenhagen, Aalborg and Korsør, while the remaining contracts were equally divided among the other towns. The largest order went to the merchant family Hansen from Randers with a total of more than 35,000 barrels. By way of comparison, the largest exporter of corn in the provinces had exported only a little over 8,000 barrels in 1793. During the years 1799-1803, the tenders can again be assessed. By then drastic changes had occurred in relation to about 10 years earlier. Copenhagen wholesalers now supplied almost 178,000 barrels out a total of ca. 293,000 barrels. What had happened was that several of the largest Copenhagen commercial firms, by drawing on their experience – and earnings – from the profitable international corn market during the European war years, were able to win a large share of the domestic Danish market. Among other things, they made use of commission agents in the provinces. After the relinquishment of Norway in 1814, the Danish garrisons were smaller and the state tendering system was correspondingly reduced, in 1840 for example to ca. 36,000 barrels. The Copenhagen commercial firms at that time still won over half of the tenders.

This hierarchical structure would become even more obvious. To support the depressed Danish agriculture during the period of great price falls from 1819 to 1828, the state from 1820 to 1828 directed the peasants to sell it large amounts of corn at fixed prices, formally considered as an exceptional tax paid in the form of corn.[51] In this way, a total of just fewer than two million barrels of corn ended by being channelled through the state and further on to the private market. In the first years, efforts were made to let a few selected Copenhagen commercial firms be responsible for the re-sale, and then several provincial merchants were admitted to the negotiations, until, in the final years, it was decided to concentrate on storing the corn in Copenhagen and letting the Copenhagen wholesalers gradually buy the corn. The result can be seen in Table 2.

TABLE 2.

The largest dealers in the tax corn 1820-1828.[52]

Blach's Widow & Co	*Copenhagen*	*223,779 barrels*
F. Tutein & Co	*Copenhagen*	*167,450*
Agent Suhr	*Nyborg*	*117,471*
I.P. Suhr & Son	*Copenhagen*	*102,085*
Hambro & Son	*Copenhagen*	*87,746*
Frölich & Co	*Copenhagen*	*74,513*
Lütken's Widow & Co	*Copenhagen*	*46,227*
Brs. Tutein & Co	*Copenhagen*	*44,009*
Merchant S.W. Bruun	*Assens*	*41,946*
Merchant Enevoldsen	*Ribe*	*25,576*
Merchant H. Ree & Co	*Randers*	*24,938*
Merchant Theil	*Korsør*	*24,705*
Merchant Smith	*Holbæk*	*19,950*
Merchant Krøyer	*Maribo*	*18,195*
Merchant Clausen	*Nakskov*	*17,423*

Note: Due to lack of source evidence, the figures are not complete.

The concentration of the corn trade in a small number of towns, however, was not due only to the state taxation policy. It was also caused by the development of business forms and by foreign demand.

From the 1730s until ca. 1840, exports of Danish corn increased steadily from ca. 300,000 barrels to 1.2 million barrels (without deduction of imported corn), interrupted by exceptional circumstances such as years with poor harvests and outbreaks of war. In the 18th century, almost all the corn exports of the Kingdom of Denmark went to Norway, except during the period of 1793-1804 when the French revolution and the greater corn production meant that exports to other countries were larger than exports to Norway. After ca. 1820, exports to Norway were stable while exports to other countries – especially to England – were increasing. The breakthrough came in the period 1843-1847 when the average annual exports increased dramatically to almost 1.9 million barrels of corn.[53] Measured by weight, the increase however was even greater. The weight of a barrel of rye increased by about 11 % from 1790 to 1850, and barley by as much as about 20 % from 1800 to 1850, when corn in the same period was better cultivated, winnowed, and cleaner.[54]

Trade during the corn-sale period was organised very differently from during the 17th and 18th century, and that led to economic concentration. Technological investments were substantially larger. In the 1830s and 1840s, granaries with modern facilities became common in the towns that had the most corn trade and among individual estate owners. The total capacity in these modern granaries can be estimated at ca. 939,000 barrels at the beginning of the 1840s.[55] The French historian Fernand Braudel attributed a decisive role to the emergence of advanced warehouses in the evolution from the simple market to the capitalist market.[56] A warehouse – in this case a granary or a corn silo – serves many purposes. The greater storage capacity gives the opportunity for sales that are large enough to cover investments in the machines for drying and winnowing corn that are a prerequisite for improving the keeping qualities and standardisation of the corn. In this way corn can be sold as a speculative item on the basis of certain classifications. Previously, provincial merchants had space for only a limited quantity of corn in their granaries and therefore had to sell a large part of their corn continuously (the widespread use of contracts agreed in advance can be seen as an effort to solve the great problems on the corn market of obtaining stable and plentiful supplies of good-quality corn). However, corn silos also made the market more exclusive and more difficult to penetrate for other merchants. These circumstances were also reflected in the town hierarchy.

Town hierarchy ca. 1820-1850

The town hierarchy now became even more obvious in the corn trade. Danish historian Per Boje's studies of the period 1820-1845 show that the largest towns had taken over a disproportionately large share of the trade in their regions. In Jutland, Aalborg, Aarhus, Horsens and Randers had ca. 21 % of the town population in that province, but had appropriated 47-69 % of corn exports. On Zealand, Lolland and Falster, the largest trading towns, Maribo (and the nearby port of Bandholm), Kalundborg, Nysted, Skælskør, Nakskov and Holbæk (and the port of Rørvig) had ca. 43 % of the town population in their regions, but between 63 % and 68 % of corn exports.[57] As Per Boje points out, this hierarchy was brought about by the widespread use of commission trade as early as 1820. Typically, commission trade meant that the shipping was done at the expense of the seller. However there were also cases where commercial companies in Denmark and abroad gave orders in various forms directly to Danish provincial merchants.

Per Boje's studies show that the concentration of the corn trade in the largest towns was accompanied by similar tendencies for the other export goods in the period ca. 1820-1843. Exports of butter, skins, hides, meat and bacon were mainly from Jutland. There was a clear geographic pattern, so that the customs posts of Hjerting and Ringkøbing dominated the export of animal products from the Jutland west coast, while Randers dominated in East Jutland. The towns on Funen were – as always – the most equal, while the towns on Zealand, Lolland and Falster to a very great extent concentrated their exports around grain production and direct sales to Copenhagen. Copenhagen though continuously had 15-25 % of the exports of animal products.[58] This regional specialisation of the export of animal products reflected differences in the geography of the provinces, but the tendency to the dominance of individual towns was also a clear sign of a more pronounced trade hierarchy.

Towns' purchases of goods from other towns also showed large movements in the period, but nothing weakened Copenhagen's position. According to Per Boje, throughout the whole period 1817-1847, Copenhagen was the biggest supplier of goods to the towns in the provinces, with the exception of West Jutland which had close trading relationships with Altona and Hamburg. Several of the smaller East Jutland and Funen towns took advantage of the short sea routes and received substantial supplies from Flensburg and Lübeck. On Zealand, Copenhagen was completely dominant, while Lübeck had considerable exports to Lolland and Falster, although in no way could it compare with Copenhagen. The importance of Copenhagen as a trade centre remained unweakened. In West Jutland, Hamburg was the most important supplier of credit and goods until the Danish-German war of 1864, but in the rest of the country Copenhagen dominated, and both in 1840 and 1870 nearly twice as many people were occupied within the trading sector as in the rest of the country together.[59]

Undermining of the market town privileges

Just like most other European countries, Denmark was subjected to gradual liberalisation and deregulation of economic life after the 1790s. Some of these changes can be ascribed to the need to feed the growing population and the desire to create

SØREN BITSCH CHRISTENSEN

economic turnover in areas that were distant from the towns, while others can best be explained as the result of an ideological endorsement of liberalism and as adaptation to increasing international demand. The result was an extension of commercial activities in the countryside and a gradual undermining of the trading privileges of the towns.[60]

After ca. 1830 in Jutland, for example, several permits were given for trade in the countryside in areas that were far from the towns. The goods still had to be obtained in the towns. However, there was another line of development that was a much greater threat to the town privileges: in the 1790s peasants and pork butchers on Zealand were allowed to purchase foodstuffs in the countryside in order to sell them in Copenhagen. In 1815, the right to trade with the peasants in their homes was extended to be valid for the whole country. Only buyers who acted on behalf of the town merchants were allowed to trade in the countryside, if sales were not made in Copenhagen. In 1818, it was further clarified that the law also implied that merchants could trade freely in other towns. For several years at the end of the 1820s, a fierce discussion raged about whether merchants could transfer their trading rights in the countryside to authorised peasants. The opponents took their stand on the excellence of the old privilege system. They feared that further liberalisation would result in trade being concentrated among individual merchants, and that the goods would be taken away from the daily market trade, resulting in the ruin of the small towns. In several towns, the traders made voluntary agreements not to use hawkers in the countryside. The supporters held that freedom of trade was absolutely crucial for Denmark's position in international economy. In 1828 the High Court decided that merchants could let peasants make purchases on their behalf. In 1845, the permission that everyone could purchase peasants' products in the countryside and sell these in Copenhagen was extended to the rest of the country. However this did not mean that the town privileges were abolished. All goods still had to be brought to the town and sold on from there. In 1856, people who were not town citizens were able to set up as hawkers in the countryside at a distance of one mile from the towns, but these hawkers had to buy their foreign goods in the towns also.

All this did not abolish the old circles and other protected trading districts. It just meant that they were worth much less than previously. When first the financially strong merchants and their hawkers, and then the peasants at their own risk, had bought what there were of goods in the hinterland, there was not much left to fight about. The census in 1840 thus showed that there were no fewer than 1,100 traders in the countryside, of whom the vast majority were small shopkeepers, while others traded in livestock or homemade stockings and woollen products.[61]

The final consequence was taken in 1857 when the democratic government (democracy had been established in 1848/49) decided to abolish the privileges of the market town guilds and the last remnants of the towns' monopoly on business and trades with effect from 1862. These businesses then became deregulated, although some consideration was shown for the towns by stating that certain businesses must not be practised within a distance of 1½ miles (11.3 km), and no trade within half a mile of a town. When these limits were completely abolished in 1920, the last remnants of the market towns' legal dominance also disappeared.

Communication and financial infrastructure

If towns are regarded as economic agents that serve the surrounding area and mediate the flow of goods and services to and from the network of cities, it is important to see how these functions were eased or constrained by the modes of communication. In this context, one can say that the primary function of communication was to provide the towns with rapid exchange of money and physical goods in terms of credit facilities and transport, and give fast and trustworthy information about prices and other market conditions.

One would think that 'the legal market town system' gave little impulse to a smooth and stable flow of information about prices since the towns were almost guaranteed a certain outlet. However, knowing that this system gradually weakened around the early years of the 19th century and especially towards the middle of the century, it could also be expected that it became more important that the preconditions for a flow of information were in place, for instance that roads, port facilities, postal services etc. were adequate.

Of general importance for urban trade on the local level was the introduction of a town gate duty in 1657 and then again in 1660. After some irregularities, the duty was reorganised in 1671, after which it was in force all over the country. To a certain degree the duty was a codification of older *accise* duties, but it also had to be paid in ca. seven non-market town settlements or settlements with a disputed legal status. After 1686 the term *accise* was used for a duty on incoming ships.[62] The town gate duty was levied upon the importation of basic foodstuffs and other products from the countryside and it is reasonable to think that it meant higher taxation of the

SØREN BITSCH CHRISTENSEN

turnover than earlier taxes, although this has not been thoroughly examined.[63] On the other hand, the literature is full of examples of the time-consuming and, for the peasants, even socially depraving effects of being examined by townspeople prior to paying the gate duty. The gate duty was removed in 1850-1852.

On a higher – even national – level, urban trade depended on the postal and financial services functioning well and on the physical infrastructure.

The Royal Mail introduced the so-called double system on the important route from Copenhagen to Hamburg in 1694.[64] With this, there were two departures with horsemen and one departure with mail coach each week. The route on horseback could be done in 51 hours, under the most favourable conditions; on the other hand, the mail coach with passengers, parcels and money took 6-7 days. The route between Copenhagen and Hamburg ran through the middle of Zealand and Funen, but the southern islands of Lolland and Falster and most of Jutland were connected to the route by mounted post. In Jutland, the mounted post could cover the route from Aalborg in the north, over the important eastern market towns, to Haderslev in Schleswig in the south, in 26-40 hours. It was not until 1750 that there were mail-coach routes from south to north in Jutland (Haderslev-Aalborg, 1794 to Frederikshavn). The Jutland west coast had only mounted post. In 1694 the Royal Mail also got the monopoly on letters, which of course could be easily infringed, and indeed it was. The finest route network for parcel post in the realm, however, was developed in Holstein after 1714, after which the towns of the region got flexible communication with both Hamburg and Lübeck. After the end of the Napoleonic wars, the postal service got a few new primary routes, especially around Copenhagen, and more post offices proper were opened in Northern Jutland. But the most important progress was due to the private coachmen's routes, stagecoaches, from 1829, and especially the more intensive use of the post routes. In 1834, 72,000 private parcels were sent in the Kingdom, in 1844, 182,000. In the same period, the number of letters increased from ca. 2.1 million to over 3 million. The increase came mainly after 1830 when the introduction of speedy stagecoaches also improved the conveyance of passengers. On the other hand, railways did not have much importance before 1850 – the first route in the realm was built in 1844 between Altona and Kiel; the next between Copenhagen and Roskilde in 1847, and this was extended to Korsør in 1856, so there was a connection between Copenhagen and the primary ferry town from Zealand to Funen. A rail network mainly constructed by Peto, Brassey & Betts in the 1860s, covered Jutland.

By all accounts, there was no increase in the speed of transport on the roads – and thus no speedier communication – until the last quarter of the 18th century.[65] From 1764 until 1861 a network of main roads was built in Denmark, based on the French chaussé technique. Before that, the roads were so bad that they were in themselves an obstacle to trade. In 1790 a large estate on Zealand had to accept that their peasants paid their rent in corn because the roads were so bad that the peasants could not get to the towns to sell their corn there, nor were they certain of a decent price.[66] The new main roads were built out from Copenhagen, but an ordinance in 1793 supplemented with a revision in 1841 got the extension of roads in the rest of the country underway. War and economic crises meant however that the country's remotest areas (seen from Copenhagen!) first acquired main roads at a very late stage, i.e. Lolland, Falster, Funen and – as the last – the most northerly part of Jutland. The main road network was undoubtedly favourable to the towns as it connected the town centres. At first it is unlikely that the network of roads was built to transport goods over long distances, rather it was to promote the turnover of people and post in inns, staging posts and hotels.[67] Transactions between country and town were only to a limited extent done by means of the new main roads; here the small roads were more important. These were greatly improved after the introduction of local self-government around 1840.

In the 1830s and 1840s, the electric telegraph became of practical significance as a channel of information. A Danish state line was laid from Elsinore over Copenhagen, Korsør, Fredericia and further to Hamburg in 1854, and then in 1855 with a line to Sweden, and in 1860 to England.

The harbours seem to have been a greater problem in the 18th century than in the 17th century. Ships became larger, but since the largest ships generally only moored in Copenhagen's excellent harbour because of the reduction in foreign trade, this cannot explain the many repeated complaints about bad harbour conditions. The explanation is more probably that the economically difficult years after the end of the Great Nordic War in 1720 made the local authorities postpone maintenance until better times.[68] In 1742 and 1774 the majority of town harbours were characterised as being in a state of disrepair.[69] A national harbour plan from 1798 resulted in the improvement of harbours with deeper channels, jetties and quays, especially between 1820 and 1860.[70] In the 1840s and 1850s steamships became important in regular and ferry service, while they still had a marginal position in the merchant fleet.

Trade was financed until about 1830 almost without proper credit institutions.

The most important credit was given in the form of bills of exchange and ordinary business debt.[71] Hamburg played a significant role in this as supplier of the so-called banco bills of exchange, but the Danish National Bank got a firm grasp on the Danish credit market in the 1830s. The first market town savings bank was founded in Odense in 1816, and before 1829 there were savings banks in 12 towns, including Copenhagen. These savings banks though had very limited outward-looking financial activity.[72] From 1840 to 1870, the number of savings banks grew from 21 to 168; however, most of these were in the country areas. The first real bank of discount or commercial bank was Fyns Disconto Kasse in Odense from 1846. In four years, from 1854 to 1857, commercial banks were opened in 13 other provincial towns. In 1857, Privatbanken in Copenhagen was established and this bank introduced both the current account and the interest bearing account.[73]

As mentioned, the domestic circulation of goods was helped by the elimination of the town gate duty in 1851/52 and the Free Trade Act in 1857 (coming into effect in 1862). The free-trade inspired Tariff Act of 1863 smoothed the way for the foreign circulation of goods.

The greatest improvement of the commercial infrastructure in the period 1660-1850 thus occurred in the decades after ca. 1820. Of course this is not surprising. It corresponds with the result put forward by historian Ole Hyldtoft, in that he calculated the so-called 'residual factor' as the most important growth factor after 1820. The residual factor is part of the explanation for empirical productivity growth in an economy. It is that part of growth that cannot be ascribed to capital, land or workforce accumulation and is sometimes referred to as 'technology'.[74]

Conclusion

This article started with conjecture about why the urban ratio in Denmark remained almost unchanged from 1620-1855, though with a small decline in the period 1620-1672 and a small increase in the first half of the 19th century. With inspiration from an institutional model for the relationship between town and country, the article therefore focused on the formal framework in which the towns acted as economic agents serving the surrounding area and mediating the flow of goods and services to and from the network of cities. Danish urban researchers in various contexts have repeated that, as a starting point, the size and function of towns were the result of the resources of their surrounding areas, and that transport-economic reasons determined in principle that the towns had equally sized surrounding areas. This view was called 'the natural market town system'. But the view could not bear closer scrutiny. Firstly, a correlation analysis could repudiate the existence of such a connection. Secondly, it was shown that the market towns got their economic strength largely from special privileges and stipulations about trading districts. In accordance with S.R. Epstein's thesis, the situation was that these privileges – even though the most important dated from the Middle Ages and the 16th century – continued to be guidelines for the struggle of the towns to secure for themselves protected trading districts right up until around 1800. The mercantile and legal dominion of the market towns was thus far from being a natural condition.

Studies of the corn trade and commercial activities in the countryside in the first six decades of the 18th century showed that apart from individual dominant towns such as Copenhagen and Aalborg and to a lesser extent Aarhus and Odense, the trade structure among these was very decentralised. However, several of the smaller towns had in reality only a limited trading district, which they often had to share with other towns. In a general way, this is consistent with the relative strengths introduced by 'the legal market town system'. Conversely, it was also part of 'the legal market town system' that peasants in some parts of the country had various commercial rights.

From the end of the 18th century the supply of goods to the towns was increasingly liberalised. For the corn trade, reforms of the trading methods were initiated and the royal supply system with competitive tendering was introduced. Together with the growing foreign demand for Danish agricultural products this resulted in a clearer urban hierarchy as some towns were able to exploit the expansion of trade to take over the trading districts of smaller towns, possibly in cooperation with local merchants.

Banks, savings banks, credit institutions and other financial institutions also broke with the traditional town-trading district pattern during the period 1820-1860. They really created town hierarchies with top-bottom relations, something which Danish historians have not however studied in any great depth. The improved means of communication – first the post routes at the end of the 17th century, then main roads and harbours ca. 1790-1850, and after that railways, telegraph and steamships – increased the pace of the flow of information and took better care of trade secrets. This improved effective commerce and put the automatic exchange of goods between town and country under further pressure.

BIBLIOGRAPHY

Andersen, Bent Schiermer 1986. 'Mejeri eller staldgård? En studie i dansk hovedgårdsdrift i det 18. århundrede'. *Bol og By* 1986. Vol. 2, pp. 75-114.

Andrén, Anders 1985. *Den urbana scenen: städer och samhälle i det medeltida Danmark*. (Acta archaeologica Lundensia, Series in 8°,13). Malmö.

Bager, Maibritt 1998. 'Dansk fiskeri i 1771'. *Sjæklen, Årbog for Fiskeri og Søfartsmuseet*, pp. 43-50.

Boje, Per 1977. *Danske provinskøbmænds vareomsætning og kapitalforhold 1815-1847*. Aarhus: Jysk Selskab for Historie.

Braudel, Fernand 1992. *Civilization and capitalism, 15th-18th century*. Vol. 2. *The wheels of commerce*. Berkeley: University of California Press.

Bruus, Michael 2005. 'Købstadshavnene og byvæksten 1798-1868'. In: Søren Bitsch Christensen (ed.), *Den klassiske købstad*. (Danske Bystudier, 2). Aarhus: Aarhus Universitetsforlag, pp. 199-256.

Carter, Harold 1976. *The Study of Urban Geography*. 2nd edn. London: Edward Arnold.

Christensen, Ole H. (ed.) 1982. *Storlandbrug under omformning. Uddrag af danske godsforvalterbreve 1784-1792*. Copenhagen: Landbohistorisk Selskab.

Christensen, Søren Bitsch 2001. Monopol, marked og magasiner. Dansk kornhandel og kornpolitik 1730-1850 – med hovedvægt på reformårene. Unpublished PhD thesis. Aarhus: University of Aarhus.

Christensen, Søren Bitsch 2005a. 'Det naturlige midtpunkt? Købstædernes økonomiske centralitet ca. 1450-1800'. In: Søren Bitsch Christensen (ed.), *Den klassiske købstad*. (Danske Bystudier, 2). Aarhus: Aarhus Universitetsforlag, pp. 47-136.

Christensen, Søren Bitsch 2005b. 'En karakteristik af den klassiske købstad og dens historiografi'. In: Søren Bitsch Christensen (ed.), *Den klassiske købstad*. (Danske Bystudier, 2). Aarhus: Aarhus Universitetsforlag, pp. 11-46.

Christensen, Søren Bitsch 2006a. 'Den private kornhandel i anden halvdel af 1700-tallet'. *Erhvervshistorisk Årbog*, vol. 55, pp. 44-90.

Christensen, Søren Bitsch 2006b. 'Købstadsystemet og oplandets bygder ca. 1450-1800'. In: Per Grau Møller et al. (eds.), *Bygder – regionale variationer i det danske landbrug*. Odense: Landbohistorisk Selskab, pp. 77-103.

Christensen, Søren Bitsch 2006c. 'The Baltic Buffer: Danish Corn Trade in the Second Half of the Eighteenth Century'. In: Stefan Kroll & Kersten Krüger (eds.), *Städtesystem und Urbanisierung im Ostseeraum in der frühen Neuzeit. Urbane Lebensräume und Historische Informationssysteme. Beiträge des wissenschaflichen Kolloquiums in Rostock vom 15. und 16. November 2004*. Berlin: LIT VERLAG, pp. 9-30.

Degn, Ole 1977. 'De nylagte byer og byudviklingen i Danmark 1600-1800'. In: Grethe Authén Blom (ed.), *De anlagte steder på 1600-1700-tallet*. (Urbaniseringsprosessen i Norden, 2. Det XVII. nordiske historikermøte). Oslo: Universititetsforlaget, pp. 9-48.

Degn, Ole 1981. *Rig og fattig i Ribe. Økonomiske og sociale forhold i Ribe-samfundet 1560-1660*. Vol. 1-2. Aarhus: Aarhus Universitetsforlag.

Epstein, S.R. (ed.) 2001. *Town and Country in Europe, 1300-1800*. Cambridge: Cambridge University Press.

Feldbæk, Ole 1997. *Storhandelens tid 1720-1814. Dansk søfarts historie*. Vol. 3. Copenhagen: Gyldendal.

Guldberg, Mette 1999. *Jydepotter fra Varde-egnen. Produktion og handel ca. 1650-1850*. Kerteminde: Landbohistorisk Selskab.

Hansen, V. 1987. 'Jysk trikotage. Fra Æ Bindstouw til storindustri'. *Bol og By* 1987. Vol. 1, pp. 102-28.

Herstad, John 2000. *I helstatens grep: kornmonopolet 1735-88*. Oslo: Tano Aschehoug.

Hohenberg, Paul M. & Lynn Hollen Lees 1995. *The making of modern Europe 1000-1994*. Cambridge: Harvard University Press.

Hornby, Ove, & Erik Oxenbøll 1982. 'Proto-Industrialisation before Industrialisation? The Danish Case'. *The Scandinavian Economic History Review* 1982, vol. 1, pp. 3-34.

Hyldtoft, Ole 1999. *Danmarks økonomiske historie 1840-1910*. Aarhus: Systime A/S.

Jensen, Jørgen Elsøe 2002. 'Forandring og funktion – danske middelalderbyer i et markedsøkonomisk landskab'. In: Helge Gamrath (ed.), *Fra tid til anden. Historiske og historiografiske afhandlinger*. Aalborg: Institut for Historie, Internationale Studier og Samfundsforhold, Aalborg Universitet, pp. 105-40.

Johansen, Hans Chr. 1968. *Dansk økonomisk politik i årene efter 1784*. Vol. 1. Aarhus: Aarhus Universitetsforlag.

Jørgensen, J.O. Bro 1943. *Industriens Historie i Danmark 1730-1820*. Vol. 2. Copenhagen.

Jørgensen, Steffen Elmer 2005. 'Byerne og hovedlandevejsnettet 1761-1910'. In: Søren Bitsch Christensen (ed.), *Den klassiske købstad*. (Danske Bystudier, 2). Aarhus: Aarhus Universitetsforlag, pp. 173-78.

Lorenzen, Vilhelm 1947. *Vore Byer. Studier i Bybygning I. Den middelalderlige By og dens begyndende Afvikling 1536-1600*. Copenhagen: G.E.C. Gad.

Lilja, Sven 2005. 'Urbaniseringens dynamik och funktioner. Vad kan studiet av urbana system tillföra urbaniseringshistorien? Norden och Östersjöområdet i fokus'. *Heimen. Lokalhistorisk tidsskrift*. Vol. 1, pp. 25-48.

Matthiessen, Christian Wichmann 1985. *Danske byers vækst*. (Atlas over Danmark, serie II, 3). Copenhagen: Det Kongelige Danske Geografiske Selskab.

Mikkelsen, Jørgen 1993. 'Korn, købmænd og kreditter. Om kornhandel og kornpriser i Sydvestsjælland ca. 1740-1807'. *Fortid og Nutid* 1993, pp. 177-212.

Møller, Anders Monrad 1981. *Fra galeoth til galease. Studier i den kongerigske provins søfart i det 18. århundrede*. Esbjerg: Fiskeri- og Søfartsmuseet.

Møller, Anders Monrad 1992. *Postrytter, dagvogn og fodpost. P&Ts historie 1711-1850*. Copenhagen: Post- og Telegrafvæsenet.

Møller, Anders Monrad 1991. 'Omsætnings- og forbrugsafgifter'. In: Erik Alstrup & Poul Erik Olsen (eds.), *Dansk kulturhistorisk Opslagsværk*. Vol. 2. Copenhagen: Dansk Historisk Fællesforening, pp. 662-65.

Mørkegaard, Ole 1993. *Søen, slægten og hjemstavnen: en undersøgelse af livsformer på åbenråegnen 1700-1900*. (Etnologiske Studier, 2). Copenhagen: Museum Tusculanum.

Nielsen, Helge & Victor Thalbitzer 1976. *Skatter og Skatteforvaltning i ældre Tider*. Copenhagen: Selskabet for Udgivelse af Kilder til Dansk Historie.

North, Douglass C. 1990. *Institutions, institutional change and economic performance*. Cambridge: Cambridge University Press.

Petersen, E. Ladewig et.al. 1984. *De fede år. Odense 1559-1660*. (Odense bys historie, 2). Odense: Odense Kommune.

Poulsen, Bjørn 1988. *Land, by, marked: to økonomiske landskaber i 1400-tallets Slesvig*. Flensburg: Studieafdelingen ved Dansk Centralbibliotek for Sydslesvig.

Poulsen, Bjørn 1994. 'Land og by i senmiddelalderen'. In: Per Ingesman & Jens Villiam Jensen (eds.), *Danmark i Senmiddelalderen*. Aarhus: Aarhus Universitetsforlag, pp. 196-220.

Poulsen, Bjørn 2001. 'Tilbagegang og vækst i senmiddelalderens danske by'. In: Søren Bitsch Christensen (ed.), *Middelalderbyen*. (Danske Bystudier, 2). Aarhus: Aarhus Universitetsforlag, pp. 191-248.

Rawert, Ole Jørgen 1850 (1992). *Kongeriget Danmarks industrielle Forhold. Fotografisk genoptryk ved Niels Peter Stilling*. Copenhagen: Arbejder-, Håndværker- og Industrimuseet.

Smith, Otto 1935. *Næstved 1135-1935*. Næstved: Næstved Byråd.

Svendsen, Knud Erik & Svend Aage Hansen 1968. *Dansk pengehistorie 1700-1914*. Vol. 1. Copenhagen: Danmark Nationalbank.

Thestrup, Poul 1971. *The standard of living in Copenhagen 1730-1800. Some methods of measurement*. (Københavns Universitet. Institut for Økonomisk Historie, 5). Copenhagen.

Wittendorff, Alex 1973. *Alvej og kongevej. Studier i samfærdselsforhold og vejenes topografi i det 16. og 17. århundrede*. Copenhagen: Akademisk Forlag.

Vries, Jan de 1984. *European Urbanization 1500-1800*. London: Methuen.

www.byhistorie.dk/1735

NOTES

1   Cf. Hohenberg & Lees 1995, pp. 47-73. The authors propose a 'dual perspective' on the towns as being dependent both on the resources of the immediate surrounding area as in the service center theory, and on the contacts between towns independently of their rural hinterland.

2   Epstein 2001, especially pp. 9-13.

3   Jensen 2002, p. 110 and generally.

4   Lorenzen 1947, p. 18.

5   It should be mentioned that Lorenzen pointed out these circumstances too. Op. cit.

6   Calculations made at the Danish Centre for Urban History. According to the central place theory, the towns' surrounding areas are best described as a hexagonal pattern with the towns in the middle of each of their hexagons. As can be seen from fig. 1, this was far from being the case in the Kingdom of Denmark. Instead, a model approximating it can be made by draw-

ing Voronoi polygons around each town. This implies that the sides of the polygon are determined by the mid-point between it and the neighbouring town, so that all localities within the single polygon lie closest to the town in the centre of the polygon. The correlation analysis is then made between the population of the towns and the population in the single polygons.

7   Mørkegaard 1993, p. 170.

8   Se www.byhistorie.dk/1735, report from Rinkøbing.

9   www.byhistorie.dk/1735, the corporation's report.

10 Christensen 1999, p. 10.

11 Poulsen 2001.

12 Hohenberg & Lees 1995, p. 84 f.

13 de Vries 1984, p. 88.

14 Lilja 2002.

15 Christensen 2005b, pp. 17-24. In Jutland as a whole, however, there was a significant shift from west to east, which can be explained solely by the decline in the taxable capacity of Ribe. The towns on Bornholm are not found in the oldest material.

16 Degn 1977, pp. 28 f.

17 Andrén 1985, pp. 108 ff.

18 Poulsen 1994, pp. 212 f.

19 Carter 1976, pp. 72 f.

20 Christensen 2005a, pp. 52-59.

21 Op. cit. pp. 61-75.

22 The estate owners and clergy were in this way asked what they had sold of this season's corn, and to whom, what contracts and agreements they had made for the remaining corn, and how much corn they would use in their own operations. They also had to give information about their present stock. The merchants did not have to give information about their earlier corn purchases, but only about their stocks and agreements made. In cases where there were discrepancies between the information from the buyer and seller, an average is used.

23 Christensen 2001, pp. 5-11. Same author 2006a, pp. 45 f.

24 Poulsen 1988, pp. 212 ff., with reference to Rudolf Häpke and Börje Hanssen.

25 Christensen 2005a, pp. 62-114.

26 Studies done by Søren Poder, cf. Christensen 2006b, pp. 85 f.

27 The town had the most shipping traffic on Funen until the end of the 1790s when Nyborg had most. Møller 1981, pp. 129-131 with the underlying tables.

28 Christensen 2001, pp. 414-26.

29 In 1789 a survey showed that out of 31 wholesalers, there were only a couple who kept corn in stock, while another few had sold out. Ryberg & Co. had sold 1,600 barrels of rye to the people of the town and still had 1,000 barrels of barley in reserve. Christensen 2001, p. 520.

30 Christensen 2006c, p. 16.

31 Information about sales at markets is only available from the sellers; the figures are therefore certainly too small.

32 Mikkelsen comes to the same result. Mikkelsen 1993, p. 208. His material probably does greater justice to Skælskør than the above, cf. p. 192.

33 With Nykøbing in the north-western corner of Zealand, it was different: the small town of Rørvig at the entrance to Isefjord was the shipping port for the towns of Nykøbing, Roskilde, Frederikssund and Holbæk, and the fishermen here could pick up corn to trade in Elsinore and Copenhagen and some for themselves. Again the material distorts reality, because in normal years there were many ships from Norway to Rørvig, which then brought corn back with them, most probably directly from the estates in the area. But this trade was forbidden in the spring of 1762 when there was a prohibition on exports. Møller 1981, p. 81.

34 Petersen 1984; cf. Degn 1981, 1, pp. 280-83.

35 Bager 1998.

36 Guldberg 1999, pp. 144-63.

37 Bro Jørgensen 1943, p. 43.

38 Hornby & Oxenbøll 1982, p. 27. Hansen 1987, pp. 115 f.

39 Rawert 1850 (1992), p. 619.

40 Hornby & Oxenbøll 1982, p. 12.

41 Op. cit. p. 21, with references.

42 A more detailed explanation for these calculations can be found in Christensen 2006b. The underlying information about quantities and prices can be found in Andersen 1986 and Thestrup 1971.

43 Christensen 2001, p. 132.

44 The most recent studies of this are Herstad 2000 and Christensen 2001.

45 Christensen 2001, pp. 464-97.

46 A central work is North 1990.

47 Johansen 1968, p. 326.

48 Statement by *Finanskollegiet* 1791. Christensen 2001, pp. 512 f.

49 Christensen 2006a, pp. 73 f.

50 Christensen 2001, pp. 545-52.

51 Op. cit. pp. 701-12.

52 Op. cit. p. 710.

53 Christensen 2001, pp. 160-63. Boje 1977, p. 62.

54 Christensen 2001, pp. 165-69.

55 Op. cit. pp. 727-29.

56 Braudel 1992, pp. 81 ff.

57 Boje 1977, pp. 78-100.

58 Op. cit. pp. 70-79.

59 Hyldtoft 1999, pp. 85 f.

60 Boje 1977, pp. 247-74.

61 Hyldtoft 1999, p. 83.

62 Møller 1991, p. 662.

63 Nielsen & Thalbitzer 1976, pp. 15-17.

64 Møller 1992, pp. 22 f., 50-52, 232-55.

65 Wittendorff 1973, p. 162.

66 Christensen 1982, p. 82.

67 Jørgensen 2005, p. 187.

68 Feldbæk 1997, p. 186.

69 Bruus 2005, pp. 201 f.

70 Op. cit. pp. 225-30.

71 Svendsen & Hansen 1968, p. 21.

72 Op. cit. pp. 187 f.

73 Hyldtoft 1999, pp. 96-102. Svendsen & Hansen 1968, p. 266.

74 Hyldtoft 1999, pp. 14-17, 290.

Town development and urban population in the Danish Kingdom, ca. 1620-1680 – From prosperity to crisis

The development 1620-1680[1]

In the last years of his reign King Christian IV (1577-1648) could look back on the results of an urban and military policy by which in the course of approximately 40 years, from 1599 to 1638, he had founded five new towns in the Kingdom of Denmark. These were the fortified towns of Kristianopel in Blekinge, Ny Varberg in Halland, Kristianstad in Scania and Christianshavn and Sorø on Zealand. These could be added to about 80 chartered towns (*købstæder* in Danish) that already existed in the Kingdom at the time of his accession in 1596.[2] Other towns were also founded in the Duchies and in Norway, but we shall concern ourselves here with the Kingdom alone.

An important factor for the development of the towns was that in 1650 King Frederik III established on the coast of Lillebælt in Jutland the chartered town and fortress Frederiksodde, which from 1664 was named Fredericia. Thanks to its special privileges, among these exemptions from tax for 50 years, it developed rather unusually for the time. In 1672 it had nearly 1,600 inhabitants and was twelfth in size among the Danish towns. Of less importance was the fact that in 1655 Frederikssund was granted privileges as a chartered town; but it did not become large. After this, more than half a century elapsed before changes were seen in the hierarchy of towns.

It would seem that from the end of the 16th century the towns had experienced some progress. But in the years around 1620 a recession started, which was further aggravated during the following forty years. The foreign policy of King Christian IV and the rivalry between Denmark and Sweden played a crucial role here. In 1625, in an attempt to secure his dominant position in relation to the advancing Sweden, Christian IV joined in the Thirty Years' War and started a war against the German Emperor Ferdinand II. After his defeat by General Tilly in the battle at Lutter am Barenberge

Fig. 1.

Most important localities in the article.

in August 1626, Jutland was occupied by enemy troops and was plundered until peace came in 1629. As yet another result of the Danish-Swedish rivalry, in December 1643 the Swedes started a war against Denmark and, in the so-called Thorstensson War, Jutland was again occupied by enemy troops and looted, and this time the Eastern Danish provinces of Scania, Halland and Blekinge were also occupied. The war and the occupation lasted until 1645 and weakened yet again the economy of the towns and affected the population figures. Conditions greatly deteriorated again in 1657 when Frederik III started a war against Sweden resulting in the occupation of most of Denmark during two wars 1657-1658 and 1658-1660. The country was pillaged and houses burnt down, not only by the Swedish troops but also by the Brandenburg and Polish troops who came to the rescue of Denmark. The peace in 1660 meant that Denmark lost the Scanian provinces, and with them a third of the Danish towns and town populations were lost. But the troubles of this era had not yet ended. In order to recover Scania, a fruitless war followed – the Scanian War – from 1675-1679. However, it did not result in the occupation of Denmark, but huge taxation followed.[3]

Accurate population figures are not known before the censuses from the second half of the 18th century. But a still extant count of the town population in 1672 presumably gives almost accurate population figures at that time. These again can be compared with results from the counting based on the tax lists, which make it possible to get an impression of the development of the town population in the period 1620-1680.

The town system ca. 1672

On the basis of the count from 1672, and considering a number of factors, an overview of the Danish town system at that time can be obtained. Besides the capital Copenhagen, Denmark had 62 chartered towns after 18 chartered towns in the Scanian provinces had been lost in 1660. The towns can be ranked in relation to each other on the basis of the population figures. Of the 57 towns where the population figures are known, only 22 had more than 1,000 inhabitants and no less than 12 had fewer than 500.[4] Only the dominating capital city had more than 5,000 inhabitants. With about 41,000 inhabitants Copenhagen alone equalled the population of the 49 smallest towns. The largest towns after the capital were Aalborg, Elsinore, Odense and Aarhus with 4,181, 4,033, 3,808, 3,474 inhabitants respectively. Small towns were a dominant feature of the Danish townscape.

With population figures of only 272, 343 and 343 the three smallest chartered towns were surpassed by many of the small villages.[5] It may be presumed that these three chartered towns had between 55 and 70 gårde (houses with adjoining buildings and a yard) and houses, as an average of five inhabitants per residence seems to have been the norm in the period. This means that 29 villages with 55-70 properties were on a level with the smallest chartered towns as regards population figures. In addition about 20 villages were larger than the small chartered towns, the largest, Store Magleby near Copenhagen, with 117 farms presumably on a level with chartered town number 18. But even though the large villages resembled towns, they were without the privileges and functions of the chartered towns; they remained villages.

The comparatively large number of towns, which Denmark had as early as in the Middle Ages meant that town density in several regions of the country was remarkable. Only a few towns were situated so that they could have a trade area without competition within a radius of 20 kilometres, a day's journey for a primitive peasant cart travelling on bad roads. Only the towns of Aalborg, Varde, Ringkøbing and Ystad (then Ysted) had such a trade area. The trade areas of Ringkøbing and Ystad were limited by the fact that they were situated on the coast. All the other towns were in the situation that the trade area of other towns limited their trade area. Towns such as Roskilde, Køge and Maribo had their trade area limited by no fewer than four neighbouring towns. However, Northern, Western and Central Jutland was little urbanised and towns such as Hjørring, Sæby, Viborg and Ribe had almost ideal trade areas, but for some of them the areas were limited by their location on the coast.

The town density resulted in keen competition between the towns and meant great variation in the opportunities for merchants and tradesmen to do business in the trade area. In addition the quality of the farmland played a role, giving variations in population density. There was a great difference between areas with fertile farmland such as Lolland and Falster and parts of Zealand, Funen and East Jutland, and that of the poor farmland of North and West Jutland with many moors and areas difficult to cultivate.

An important background for the town system and the differences in the size of the towns was their role as central places, with functions in trade, crafts and administration.[6] An important basis was the population in the trade area within the radius of 20 km, which was the customer base for the merchants and tradesmen of the towns, in addition to the population of the towns themselves. Figures for the rural population in the parishes are not known further back than from the census in 1769. But an impression of the situation can be found in the figures for farms and houses known from the land register made in the year 1688.[7]

Here considerable differences between the regions are seen because of variations in the fertility of the land and thus the population density, and because of restrictions of the trade area caused by neighbouring towns. For the largest chartered towns, Aalborg, Odense and Aarhus, farm figures of 1,200-1,700 are found. For Elsinore, however, the figure is only 465, so that the size of the population of this town is presumably explained by the role of the town in connection with the levying of the Sound Toll. For the 27 smallest towns, farm figures of 350-900 are seen in the trade area.

However, the small towns of Nykøbing Mors, Lemvig, Skive and Hjørring had farm figures of 1,100-1,200, while Holbæk had 1,300.

With regard to the administrative situation, towns were clearly at different levels. The functions connected with the provincial court, diocese and county administration were, with a few exceptions, located in the large towns, cf. fig. 2. These towns too were among the oldest towns, which presumably was largely the background for their rank in the hierarchy. The connection between town age and population size is very clear. In the four towns established before the year 1000 the average population figure in 1672 was 2,854, as seen in Table 1. The figures for the towns founded in the following centuries are gradually falling until the pattern is broken by the towns founded in the 16th and 17th centuries, i.e., Hillerød, founded in 1654 near the royal castle Frederiksborg, and the much privileged fortress town of Fredericia, founded in 1650.[8]

TABLE 1.

The Danish towns in 1672 grouped according to age, with indication of important functions.

Period of foundation	Number of towns	Population average	Diocesan seat	County seat	Provincial court	Guilds 1550-1700	
						Number	Per town
-1000	4	2,854	4	4	1	43	11
1000-1099	5	2,291	2	3	2	41	8
1100-1199	6	1,184		4		18	3
1200-1299	23	886		15		73	3
1300-1399	4	652		4		1	
1400-1499	8	595		3		3	
1500-1599	2	979		3	1	2	
1600-1672	2	1,060		1		4	2
Total	54		6	37	4	185	3.4

The 54 towns are only some of the 62 towns in 1672. Figures for the population in the other towns are lacking, cf. note 13.

Source: Degn 2002, p. 13.

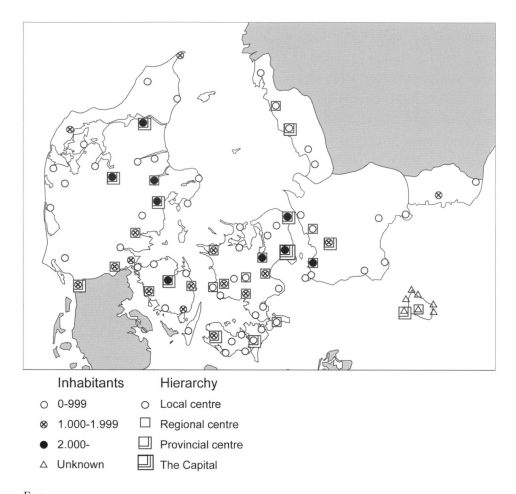

Inhabitants

- ○ 0-999
- ⊗ 1.000-1.999
- ● 2.000-
- △ Unknown

Hierarchy

- ○ Local centre
- ▢ Regional centre
- ▢ Provincial centre
- ▢ The Capital

Fig. 2.

The market towns in Denmark 1672 and the Sound provinces 1655.

On fig. 2, which is based on Walter Christaller's central place model from the 1930s, the towns are placed on three levels. However Copenhagen is placed on a level alone at the top. The towns on the three levels are designated as provincial centres, regional centres and local centres. In every province, the islands, or large parts of Zealand and Jutland, a town is considered to be dominant, in terms of population or as an administrative and economic centre. Correspondingly some towns are considered to be dominant in smaller territories, and finally, between these, are the many small towns. The larger towns here could be seen as centres not just in the smaller trade area but also in a larger trade area in which some small towns were located.

Administrative functions, as well as economic conditions, led to considerable inertia in the economy of the towns, and help to explain the difficulties for the urban policy of the government. This policy was not backed by essential changes in technical and economic development which would raise the level of productivity.

The technical development of that time, the low level of productivity and the comparatively low level of trade connected with this meant that most of the towns had to be rather small. Around 1670, however, Denmark presumably had an urban population rate of approximately 20 %. Seen against the background of the economic development of Danish society, this was a high percentage and even more so if it is considered against a Nordic background where Norway and Sweden had urban population percentages of perhaps the half. As a consequence there was keen competition, both between the merchants and tradesmen in the town itself and between the towns. Incessant complaints about competition are to be found.

The urban population in 1672

Extant tax lists are a prerequisite for an estimation of the urban population figure in this pre-statistical era. For the period from 1620 to 1680 quite a number of tax lists from many towns are found in the city archives, so it should be possible on the basis of these to make some, as yet uncertain, estimates of the urban population and trend.[9] The use of tax lists gives some problems, however, even if there is an indication of the connection between the figures for taxpayers and the urban population on the basis of comparisons with the above-mentioned population figures from 1672. The tax lists not only change in structure during the period; but considerable differences are also seen from town to town.

The tax lists from the period ca. 1620-1650 are simple lists mentioning the taxpayers: the so-called *skatskillingslister* (lists based on valuations in *skilling*) have valuations from 0 or 1 *skilling* up to 320. However, some have valuations in *sletdaler*, *mark* and *skilling*. As in later cases the taxpayers were presumably identical with the heads of households, and their share of the tax burden is expressed in a number of *skilling* corresponding to the proportion with which each was taxed. The total of the valuations was divided into the imposed tax and through this was found the multiple to be used for tax.

Some of the tax lists from the time after 1660 are a little different. Often they are written with the actual tax and in the tax lists in the form of *skatskillingslister* there are curiously low figures, as in Aalborg in 1672 where there are figures of 1/6 and 1/3 *album*, which are only 1/18 and 1/9 *skilling*. In Ribe there was a large difference between the highest valuations in the 16th century of up to 480 *skilling* and the highest valuation in 1682 of 26 *skilling*. The valuations had really been reduced and this of course meant that the multiple had to be increased correspondingly, six times, ten times etc. The changes resulted in an equalisation of the taxpayers and are presumably a sign of an impoverishment of the well-to-do classes.

To understand the calculations in the following, the known figures for the urban population in 1672 have to be examined. These figures have been given only as totals for each of the chartered towns in previous research, but as can be seen from Appendix Table 1, the original material also has figures for households ('families') and for children under six years of age.[10] It is thus partly possible to see what lies behind the totals.

Consequently the figures seem to have been based on real counting, maybe in a similar way to the Kolding list from about 1692 mentioned below. The figures have also been judged as probable.[11] It should be possible to study the background for the making of the lists from the correspondence in the city archives.

With the urban population figures from 1672 we should have the basis for an estimate of the total population that year. At the census in 1769, the first for Denmark as a whole, the country had an urban population percentage of 20, at the censuses in 1787 and 1801 this was 21 %. Considering the long recession in the cities in the decades before 1660, in general, and the impoverishment both of the towns and of the countryside caused particularly by the wars in the 1650s – the latter being an important element in urban economy – it is not relevant to imagine an urban population percentage of more than 20 % in 1660 or 1672.

This is inconsistent with Aksel Lassen's calculations in a study from 1965.[12] On the basis of church registers, reports from the dioceses etc., he calculated the population figure for the Kingdom of Denmark for the time after the devastation in the wars 1657-1660 and a plague in 1659 at 430,000. With an annual population growth, calculated by him, of 3,600 in the following years, the population in 1672 should then be about 473,000. With a total urban population of about 108,000[13] in 1672 the percentage of urban population would then be 23 %, which is unlikely. On the basis of the calculated urban population figure here of 108,000, the total population in 1672 should rather be about 540,000. Perhaps the annual growth 1660-1672 was larger than 3,600.

As can be seen from Appendix Table 1, the average size of the households ('families') for the individual towns varies from 2.5 in Nykøbing Mors and 3.7 in Mariager to 6.1 in Roskilde and Fredericia and 6.6 in Hobro. The variations are considerable and this could call for a more detailed examination on the basis of church registers, tax lists etc. The variations, however, are no larger than those seen for instance between districts in Copenhagen in 1660.[14] For the towns as a whole it can be stated that a large group of 16 towns had households of an average size of 4.0-4.4 persons, 11 towns had averages of 4.5-4.9 persons and averages in 13 towns were 5.0-5.4 persons.

The size of the households ('families') varies only to a certain degree with the size of the towns. In the 12 towns with a population of fewer than 500 the average household size is 4.2, in the towns with population figures of 500-999 and the towns with the limits set at 2,000, 3,000 and 4,000 and more, the figures are 4.0 or 5.0.

The proportion of children under six years of age in the total urban population varies for the individual towns from Store Heddinge's 7.7 % and Thisted's 8.3 % to Fredericia's 21.2 % and Mariager's 21.4 %. Thus considerable differences are seen here too, and more detailed studies are needed to find out if this indicates different age pyramids in various towns. Perhaps some towns such as Fredericia had considerable immigration and growth, (these conditions have actually been examined on the basis of detailed population statistics, but for a later period).[15] In the towns as a whole, there is a large group of 17 towns with percentages for children under six years of age of 11.0-12.9 %, 14 towns have percentages of 13.0-14.9 % and 10 towns have percentages of 15.0-16.9 %.

Tax payers and structure of households

The city archives of Kolding have a unique list of the population of that town at the end of the 17th century.[16] The list is probably one of the best sources of material to analyse the population structure of a Danish town in the time before the first official census lists from 1787.[17] Fortunately the list also seems to give a representative picture of the population structure of a Danish town at that time. The list is undated but on the basis of the names of aldermen, recorder, vicars etc. it can be dated to the time around 1692. Thus it is about 20 years younger than the urban population list from 1672. Nevertheless it is relevant because the figures for households and inhabitants are close to the figures from 1672. With 257 households and 1,094 persons the figures in the 1672 list are only a little higher than those from around 1692: 244

households and 1,073 persons. The average size of the households is 4.3 and 4.4 respectively. Therefore it is of value that for every household, under the designation 'families', it gives figures for wives, children, lodgers, maids and labourers. Thus it is possible to see what lies behind a population figure like 1,073.

Of the total population of 1,073 people, 244 were heads of households and in addition taxpayers, 174 were wives, 397 children, 61 lodgers and 197 servants, namely 101 shop assistants and labourers and 96 maids. Most of the heads of households were married men, 13 were widowers, 45 widows (see Appendix Table 2).

Therefore, in a town like Kolding – population-wise the sixteenth largest town in Denmark around the year 1692 – for every 100 heads of households or taxpayers there were 70 wives, 161 children, 26 lodgers and 78 servants.

The average size of households was, as mentioned, 4.4. Households of four people dominated, followed by households of five and three people. Of the heads of households 54 or 22 % were women.

As a whole the children comprised 37 % of the population of the town. This is a figure similar to the figure for the proportion of people from 0 to 19 years of age in the Danish urban population in 1787.[18] The Kolding list says nothing about age limits for the definition of children, but it seems to be about 20 years, not 10-12 years as in the poll tax lists.

Households with only one child dominated, followed by households with 0 and 2 (cf. Appendix Table 3). Only 24 households had more than three children. For the households as a whole the average was 1.6 children. For the households that *had* children, the average was 2.1. This figure is somewhat lower than the figure of 2.7 known from Ribe in the first half of the 17th century, but corresponds with the one observed in several Copenhagen districts in 1660.[19]

Fewer than half of the households in Kolding had servants, and many had only one labourer, shop assistant or maid (cf. Appendix Table 4). Only a few widows and unmarried women had servants and of the male households only eight had more than three. For the households as a whole the average was 0.8, almost the same as the 0.7 known from Ribe in 1640.[20]

With the Kolding list we have a source from which we can gain an understanding of the relation between the figures for taxpayers and population. The number of heads of households corresponds to the number of taxpayers, and servants normally did not pay taxes. For each of the heads of households or taxpayers there were in this case 4.4 inhabitants. This, as we will see, is a little less than the average for the

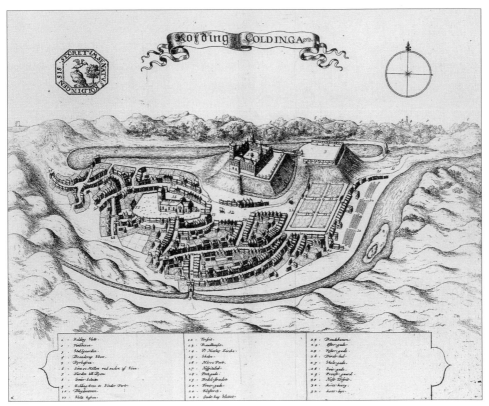

Fig. 3.

Kolding ca. 1670. Bird's eye view of the town, 1677.

towns in 1672. The explanation can perhaps be found in the economic situation in the town. Kolding had greatly declined in the years up to 1660. The population had decreased by 2 % in the years from 1672 to around 1692 and it has previously been observed that in periods of depression a decrease in the number of lodgers, for instance, could occur. In 1623 Ribe had 983 taxpayers and 22 % of these were lodgers. In 1640 when the number of taxpayers had fallen to 757, only 11 % of these were lodgers, the number had decreased from 217 to 86. In periods of depression there was no need for so many people in business life.[21]

The fall in the number of taxpayers

The figures in Table 2 are calculated on the basis of counting taxpayers on several tax lists.[22]

TABLE 2.

Taxpayers in nine towns before and after 1660 (ca. 1620-1682).

	Ca. 1620	Ca. 1640	Ca. 1660	Growth, %	Precise period	Ca. 1672	Ca. 1682	Growth, %	Precise period
Grenaa	158					147	111	-30	1612-1692
Horsens		375	356	-5	1632-1662				
Køge		474				210	228	-56	1640-1674
Randers		308	398	29	1640-1662/63	227	414	34	1640-1682
Ribe	917	749	421	-44	1640-1660	450	496	18	1660-1682
Varde		205	122	-40	1640-1666	148		21	1666-1671
Vejle	253					150		-41	1620-1671
Aalborg		549	467	-15	1643-1661	489		5	1661-1672
Aarhus	550	576				663	643	15	1636-1673

The precise years for the tax lists from the individual towns are the following: Grenaa 1612, 1674, 1692; Horsens 1632, 1662; Køge 1640, 1674, 1682; Randers 1640, 1662-63, 1674, 1682; Ribe 1620, 1640, 1660, 1672, 1682; Varde 1640, 1666, 1671; Vejle 1620, 1671; Aalborg 1643, 1661, 1672; Aarhus 1619, 1636, 1650, 1673, 1683. In 1671 Varde has two tax lists, here the number from the one list with the highest figure is chosen: in reality 192, but 44 of these are named as 'single persons', the other list has 126 taxpayers. Source: Tax lists, see Landsarkivet for Nørrejylland (The Provincial Archives of Northern Jutland), rådstuearkiver. Degn 1981a, vol. 2, p. 236. Bach, Degn and Strømstad 1993, p. 40. Engel 1999, p. 36.

A fall in the number of taxpayers in five of the towns can be seen in the period around 1620/1640-1660 from 5 to 44 %. Grenaa decreased from 1612 to 1692 by 30 %, and from 1640 to 1674 Køge had a fall of 56 %. Two towns had higher numbers of taxpayers: from 1640 to 1682 the number in Randers increased by 34 %, and from 1619 to 1673 numbers in Aarhus increased by 21 %. The average for the nine towns is a decrease of 23 %. This is in accordance with the 22 % decrease in the Danish population as a whole, which was calculated by Aksel Lassen in 1965 for the period 1645-1660.[23]

Table 2 presents figures for the time after 1660 showing progress for four towns of between 4 % and 21 %, with an average of 10.

In the period 1630-1672 Copenhagen presumably grew from around 25,000 to

41,000 inhabitants. From having had 25 % of the total urban population, Copenhagen had grown to having around 38 %. In a few decades the capital had become the completely dominant town. Its status is reflected in the King's understanding of the situation. Up to 1657 Frederik III always mentioned Copenhagen as *vor købstad København* ('our chartered town Copenhagen'). In 1658 this was changed to *vor residensstad København* ('our seat Copenhagen').[24] Copenhagen had become the capital of the monarchy.

The relation between the figures for the population of towns and their taxpayers around 1672 is illustrated with the figures for a number of chartered towns in Table 3. As can be seen, the figures vary greatly, from Kolding's 3.2 and 2.6 inhabitants per taxpayer to Randers' 8.9 and 7.9. But if Kolding is ignored, a certain relation is seen between the size of the town and the number of inhabitants per taxpayer. The large towns had more inhabitants per taxpayer than the smaller ones, which can also be seen from Appendix Table 1 as a whole (cf. above). In the large towns the business units, in accordance with the central place structure (cf. the map page 102), could be larger and have more personnel, shop servants and labourers, and the wealthier households could have more maids. These are the circumstances illustratively reflected in the average wealth of inhabitants in the different towns. In the years 1674-1676 for the towns with fewer than 500 inhabitants, with 500-1,000, with 1,000-2,000 and with 2,000-4,000 inhabitants, the average wealth was 126, 208, 262 and 369 *rigsdaler*, respectively.[25]

TABLE 3.

Urban population in 1672 and the number of taxpayers.

	Population 1672	Taxpayers around 1671/1674		Households ('families')	Inhabitants per taxpayer		Taxpayers per family
		With children under 6 years of age	Without children		With children	Without children	
Varde	567	475	148	128	3.8	3.2	1.2
Ringkøbing	623	559	130	64	4.8	4.3	2.0
Vejle	712	589	150	165	4.7	3.9	0.9

	Population 1672	Taxpayers around 1671/1674		Households ('families')	Inhabitants per taxpayer		Taxpayers per family
Kolding	1,094	884	339	257	3.2	2.6	1.3
Ribe	1,939	1,753	450	488	4.9	3.9	0.9
Randers	2,036	1,803	227	405	8.9	7.9	0.6
Viborg	2,704	2,458	475	662	5.7	5.2	0.7
Aalborg	4,181	3,719	489	820	8.6	7.6	0.6
Aarhus	4,474	3,094	663	684	6.7	4.7	1.0
Total	18,330	15,334	3,049	3,673	6.0	5.0	0.8

The years are: 1671 Varde, 1672 Ribe, Vejle and Aalborg, 1673 Kolding, Ringkøbing, Viborg and Aarhus, 1674 Randers.

Source: Appendix Table 1 and tax lists, see Landsarkivet for Nørrejylland, rådstuearkiver.

The fall in the number of new municipal licenses to trade

Municipal licenses to trade (*borgerskab*) were necessary in order to exercise self-employed occupations in commerce, shipping and trade in the towns. This included paying a sum of money to the town. The accounts covering this charge enable us in some cases to follow the development in the number of trade licenses taken out.

TABLE 4.

Persons taking out *borgerskab* (trade licenses) in some towns 1600-1680.

	Ribe	Aarhus	Assens	Køge
1600-09	204	163		
1610-19	236	220	95	
1620-29	161	258	45	239
1630-39	124	187	86	247
1640-49	90	184		215
1650-59	55	202		

	Ribe	Aarhus	Assens	Køge
1660-69	152	210		
1670-79	113	170		

For Køge and for Assens one and three years respectively are missing in the 1620s and to compensate the figures have been raised 1/10 and 3/10.

Source: Degn 1981a, vol. 1, p. 47. Fredericia 1889-90, pp. 214-16. Fussing 1957, pp. 75, 71 f. D 22 Ribe rådstuearkiv, 241. Borgerskabsprotokol 1585-1809.

Long, and almost complete, accounts of money paid for municipal trade licenses exist from a few chartered towns during the period. As can be seen from Table 4 the first decades of the 17th century were prosperous in Ribe and Aarhus. Then came a fall in the number of municipal trade licenses taken out up to 1660, and even after two decades, the two towns had not reached the former level.

Deserted houses in the towns

The decline in the population due to consequences of the wars 1657-1660 and several plagues during the 1650s, in particular in 1659, had the result of course that many houses in the towns were abandoned, without inhabitants. In addition, many houses were derelict, perhaps burnt down during the occupation by enemy troops and indeed by the Danish allies too.

The so-called house valuations (*hustakster*), prepared in 1661-1662 as the basis for planned taxation of houses, indicate this very clearly. The tax was to replace the collection of the old revenues from Crown lands. Most of these lands had been lost because of the wars and the subsequent sale to meet the debt of the Crown. This was the development by which Denmark changed from being a Crown land state to a tax state. The house valuations are still extant from several chartered towns in the Jutland dioceses Viborg, Aarhus and Ribe. In fixed routes through the streets, with the street names indicated, they name the individual houses, their owners, tenants and the valuation price. Here too the physical condition of the houses is noted, and the results of the wars are clearly seen. In Aarhus, for example in one street, there is a row of 12 small houses 'burnt down by the enemy' and completely abandoned.

The conditions in some towns can be seen from Table 5. In the eight chartered towns 25 % of the houses on average were deserted, although with large variations from 9 % in Varde to 45 % in Kolding. These towns must indeed have had an eerie

FIG. 4.

Deserted gårde, *houses and small houses in Aarhus 1683. Each* • *marks a deserted house, in all nearly 60. Two streets in particular and the area around one of the churches were greatly affected.*

atmosphere. And yet many years elapsed before the catastrophes had been overcome. Even in the successors to the house valuations – the site valuations (the *grundtak-ster*) of 1682, numerous abandoned *gårde* and houses can be seen. Of the 700 houses in Ribe, 29 are registered as unoccupied, 11 as abandoned, six as building sites and a further 58 as gardens and deserted sites, the last mentioned on sites that formerly had occupied houses, i.e. a total of 104 out of 700.

TABLE 5.

Houses and deserted houses in some Jutland towns 1661-1662.

	Number of houses	Of these, deserted	
		In numbers	%
Varde	108	10	9
Skanderborg	67	9	13
Randers	493	92	19
Ribe	695	132	19
Aarhus	749	188	25
Hobro	81	23	28
Mariager	109	34	31
Kolding	372	169	45
Total	2,674	657	25

Source: *Rigsarkivet (The Danish National Archives), Kommissionsakter vedr. taksation til matriklen af købstæder i Viborg, Aarhus og Ribe stifter, 1661-1662. [Hustakster]. Rentekammeret 311.71.*

The decrease in trade and shipping

No accounts showing the extent of trade in the 17th century exist. On the basis of local studies in the accounts for duty, toll, annual fairs etc. it is possible, however, to get an impression of the trend in many localities.[26]

For the very important exports of oxen, then Denmark's most important export article, there was a continuous decrease through the 17th century. The total annual exports of oxen from the Kingdom (including Scania) and the Duchy of Schleswig, fell from 55,000-60,000 oxen in the years 1600-1620 to around 35,000 in 1620-1630 and 20,000-30,000 in the years after 1630. Moreover, from the middle of the century even more of the exports were taken over by Netherlanders. This may very well be one of the explanations for the dramatic decrease, mentioned below, in the highest assessments in the tax lists from Ribe. The oxen exports had been a very lucrative business for the merchants.[27]

In the 17th century harbours were rather simple: small rivers with a wharf or quays or a construction of quays on the shore. In spite of this maintenance was costly, with deepening and dredging or replacement of timber, and building foundations as a protection against storm and ice drift etc. Many towns complained to the King about the damage to or destruction of the harbour because of storms. In several cases towns got permission to levy harbour dues and toll on ships and on commodities to maintain the harbours. This was the case for towns like Næstved, Horsens, Kolding, Aarhus and Ribe. Because of this there are still extant harbour accounts from Aarhus and Ribe that can throw light on shipping to and from these harbours.[28]

A study of the Danish merchant fleet for the year 1639, before the devastating wars, has shown that the Kingdom of Denmark at that time had a merchant fleet of 700 ships, of which 570 were registered in the chartered towns, with a total tonnage at around 18,000 *læster* (lasts) of 1.8 tons each.[29] In 1656 the tonnage had fallen to 14,500 *læster*, in 1670 the merchant fleet of 772 ships had a tonnage of 7,521 *læster*, this time partly explained by the loss of the Scanian provinces. Thus we see an enormous decline in the Danish merchant fleet and so the sea transport capacity was greatly reduced. In this sphere the earning power of the chartered towns shrank dramatically.[30]

Yet the decline was not the same for all the chartered towns. In 1639, 38 % of the merchant fleet capacity was registered in Copenhagen; in 1676 the figure was 49 %.[31]

On the basis of the accounts from the levying of the Sound Toll at Elsinore, European shipping between Western Europe and the Baltic provinces can be followed in detail. The reliability of the accounts has been discussed in the light of the possibilities for smuggling. But they are presumably correct concerning the number of ships. With Denmark's position in relation to the Sound the accounts reflect only a part of the Danish shipping. But with regard to the trend in the figures they are presumably indicative of conditions as the figures follow the trend for the merchant fleet.

As can be seen from Table 6, Danish shipping between Western Europe and the Baltic was increasing when the wars occurred in the 1640s and 1650s. Then the number of ships passing the Sound fell dramatically to one-third. The ships had been lost in the wars. Hardest hit were the chartered towns in the provinces. When a new increase began in the 1670s, Copenhagen had two-thirds of the total Danish shipping. The Jutland shipping through the Sound in the 1670s was about two-thirds of that in the 1630s.

TABLE 6.

Danish ships passing through the Sound 1620-1679, in %.

	1620-29	1630-39	1640-49	1650-59	1660-69	1670-79
Copenhagen	72	58	52	78	64	72
The rest of Zealand and Møn	11	14	16	12	15	9
Lolland and Falster	3	3	1	2	2	2
Bornholm	0	-	-	-	0	-
Funen and Langeland	2	2	1	-	1	1
Jutland	12	23	30	8	19	16
Total	100	100	100	100	100	100
Passages	1,361	1,741	2,550	926	993	1,268

Source: Nina Bang 1906-1933.

The increase in the taxation

In combination with the taxation imposed by the enemy, the looting and the dev-astation, the taxation imposed by the Danish King was crucial in the economic de-velopment of the towns. The King needed huge sums for building fortresses, fitting out the fleet, the recruitment of soldiers and the purchase of war equipment. The level of taxation does not appear directly from the letters concerning the taxation. These impose the above mentioned town tax and other taxation, including money for the maintenance of soldiers and boatmen (*bøsseskytterpenge*, *bådsmandsholdpenge*, *bådsmandsudskrivningspenge* or *borgelejepenge*), introduced in 1611, but they say nothing about what was actually paid.[32]

An examination of the real taxation for a chartered town has been made for Ribe and the amounts are seen on Table 7.

TABLE 7.

The taxation in Ribe 1620-1660.

	Assessed amount in rigsdaler	Of this			Number of taxes	Multiple of a single tax	Yield per multiple*
		Town tax	Boatmen and gunner tax	Levied by the enemy			
1600s	2,761	832			12	36	77
1610s	11,370	832	5,032		15	130	87
1620s	15,177	666	4,000	3,285	29	261	58
1630s	15,137	499	5,302		30	334	45
1640s	23,785	333	3,324	9,935	26	644	37
1650s	53,090	166	3,489	29,750	51	1,473	36
Total	121,320	3,328	21,147	42,970	163	3,041	40

* The figures in this column are found by division of the assessed amount in rigsdaler by the multiple, the figure with which the skilling figure for each of the taxpayers had to be multiplied in order to get the levied tax amount.

Source: Degn 1981a, vol. 2, p. 233, where the figures are specified for the types of taxes.

The figures illustrate what happened in detail. The previously mentioned old annual town tax played an unimportant role.[33] In reality other taxes were more important, but perhaps the chartered towns got their town tax reduced because as time went on they were so pressed and every single *rigsdaler* was vital.

And many *rigsdaler* were needed for paying the taxes. Taxes were increased four-fold as early as the second decade of the 17th century with the Kalmar War 1611-13, if one takes a starting point in the first decade of the century, a decade that much resembled the two preceding decades. Then followed a five-fold increase for the 1620s and 1630s, then a nine-fold increase, and finally, in the 1650s, nearly a twenty-fold increase. The war policy of Christian IV and armament expenses played a role, with the introduction of the above-mentioned boatmen and soldier taxes. But a still larger role was played by the enemy tax collections in the 1640s and especially the 1650s. A further burden was the billeting and unauthorised looting of the enemy troops as well as of the troops who came to the rescue of the Danes during the wars against

Sweden 1657-60, namely the Brandenburg, Imperial and Polish troops of Frederik III, who in accordance with treaties had been sent by the allies.

The number of taxes levied indicates the growth, too. At first one or two annual taxes were levied, and later three, and then in the 1650s the population experienced a spate of taxes, with five annual taxes. A comparison between the multiple and the yield shows the consequence of the tax pressure. The multiple had to be raised not only because the tax pressure was increased but also because assessments fell due to a decrease in income and fortune. As can be seen from Table 7, the yield fell gradually from decade to decade. The tax base was diminished, the total of the assessment of taxes decreased, the population was impoverished and the multiple had to be increased, to raise tax pressure.

This is really obvious when the level of the total taxation in the period, 121,320 *rigsdaler* is compared with the total valuation of Ribe's 695 *gårde* and houses in 1661. This valuation gave a total amount of 42,732 *rigsdaler*. In the six decades capital amounting to three times the total valuation in 1661 was taken from Ribe society. In the 1650s alone, the town had to pay an amount in taxes that was about 25 % larger than the total valuation at the end of the decade.

A demonstration of the serious consequences of the growing – and finally very oppressive – tax pressure is the fact that not only was the large underclass in Ribe impoverished, but also the merchants, ship masters and tradesmen who were so important for the business life of the town. Examinations of the tax pressure on the different occupational groups show that in the years before 1660 it was increasingly necessary to exploit the well-to-do people in the population, as no more could be taken from the others.[34] Yet the taxation of those with high assessments, as previously mentioned, had been gradually reduced over a long period. In the tax lists from the 16th century assessments of inhabitants at up to 480 *skilling* can be seen, in 1620 the highest assessments were 176, in 1629 they were 128, and in 1640, 88 *skilling*. Part of the explanation is found in the recession for the large merchants in the town, among other things a result of the decline in the export of oxen. But presumably the well-to-do with the high assessments could not afford the rising number of taxations.

Another demonstration of the serious consequences of the growing tax pressure can be seen in the fact that unpaid taxes were on the increase. In the 1630s towns began to fall behind with payment of taxes. They complained to the King about impoverishment and lack of means for necessary repairs and some were granted a deferment. Many Jutland towns managed for a time because in May 1646 the Jutland chartered towns were granted exemption from all ordinary and extraordinary taxes for three years because of damage and expenses in the war.[35] In the 1650s the situation was again calamitous and at the end of the decade tax debt had become an important element in many probate cases.[36]

Here it should not be forgotten that the growth in the levying of taxes on peasants in some ways corresponded to the levying of taxes on the chartered towns. It is more difficult to calculate the taxation on the countryside and presumably no accounts corresponding to those from the towns exist. At any rate there are no accounts of the taxes levied by the occupation troops in the countryside. A hint is given in the indications in the tax letters, as they can be converted to single taxes on tenants. For the seven decades from the 1590s to the 1650s, multiples of 2, 5.5, 13, 18.5, 16, 28.5, and 9.5 respectively can be calculated. The last figure could apparently indicate a reduction of the tax burden, but this was only because the King could not levy taxes during the occupation. And the reduction was more than balanced by the billeting and contributions extorted by the enemy.[37] Hence, there was a marked increase in the taxation in the countryside, and this was also important for the chartered towns as the merchants and tradesmen had many of their customers in the surrounding trade area. The problem also affected the otherwise tax-free landowners and is reflected in the complaints to the King in 1648 by the nobility – on behalf of the peasants – concerning the increasing taxes. The nobility claimed that because of the hard and incessant taxation, the farmers had become impoverished. Never before, they said, had it been the practice to levy tax in this way – as now was the case – even in good peace times. The taxes spoiled the productive capacity of the farmers in relation to their noble masters.[38]

The spoliation of the countryside through taxation and occupation by foreign troops was also of great importance for the towns. The 20 % of the population living in the towns had to subsist on the 80 % living in the countryside. They had to get food and raw materials for their own consumption and exports and sell imported articles and the products of the artisans to the countryside.

The importance of this can be seen by looking at the role of the peasants as customers for the merchants and tradesmen of the town, reflected in merchants' accounts and especially probate cases. For the prominent Ribe merchant Hans Friis (1587-1650), the peasant customers comprised nearly 30 % of his clientele in the 1630s and 1640s. Yet their purchases were no more than a tenth of the total business. In this case, however, this is explained by the fact that with the selection of commodities in his business, the merchant especially appealed to the noble customers and the upper class of citizens and clergy. For ten other Ribe merchants in the 1650s, the importance of the peasant customers was much more conspicuous. Only three of these had noble customers, only six had clerical customers, but all of them had townsmen and peasant customers. For several of them peasant customers were predominant and as a whole the peasants comprised two-fifths of the customers according to the probate cases after these merchants, and their debts amounted to nearly half of the total sum outstanding.[39]

Movements in the economy of the towns

The recession for the towns, visible in the size of the population, new citizens, business, shipping etc., is perhaps for some towns also reflected in the size of the town taxes, annual taxes which since the 16th century had been imposed with different amounts for the different towns, surely an indication of the economic capacity of the different towns. This is despite the fact that the amounts were not large compared with the other taxes. As can be seen from Appendix Table 5, these town taxes in 1576 varied from Copenhagen's 10,000 *daler* to Sakskøbing's 50 *daler*. But over time the figures varied quite a lot, presumably because of applications from towns affected by large fires, floods, exceptional tax pressures and devastation under occupation by the enemy etc.

Here the figures for the towns have been studied for the years 1576, 1621 and 1655, cf. Appendix Table 5. The years represent one year in peacetime at the end of the 16th century, one year before Christian IV's participation in the Thirty Years' War, and one of the last years before the wars in the 1650s, as town taxes were not levied after 1656. As the figures for the individual town varied with the total amount levied the figures for the years 1621 and 1655 have been calculated in proportion to the figures for 1576 and the two totals multiplied by 3.67 and 1.88 respectively, so that the figures are directly comparable.

It appears that for nine of the 54 chartered towns there were no remarkable changes in the period, while 16 had their town tax raised, 10 had it reduced, and 10 had first an increase and then a fall, and nine the reverse.

Of the figures for taxpayers studied here (see Table 2) only the figures for Ribe and Aarhus are from the period 1621-1656. Ribe's town taxes were almost unchanged but the number of taxpayers fell 44 % from 1620 to 1660. In contrast, Aarhus had slightly increasing town taxes corresponding to an increase of 22 % in the number of taxpayers from 1619 to 1650.

Generally there was a small displacement of the tax burden from Zealand and Møn to Lolland, Falster, Funen and Jutland, cf. Table 8.

The many changes over time and the increase or reduction of taxes can presumably be explained through studies of conditions in the individual chartered town. The raising of taxation in Elsinore may be connected with the increase in the shipping through the Sound. Holbæk's increased taxation could perhaps be explained by the activity of merchants as grain exporters. Køge's dramatic fall in taxation corresponds to a drastic fall in the population figure from the 1630s to the 1650s.[40] The halving of Copenhagen's tax is more difficult to explain as the population in the town rose dramatically but the reduction could perhaps reflect the favouring of the town by the King.

TABLE 8.

The distribution of the town taxes in the provinces 1576, 1621 and 1656 in %.

Province	Tax 1576	Tax 1621	Tax 1656
Zealand and Møn	43	35	34
Lolland and Falster	4	8	7
Funen	15	17	17
Jutland	38	40	42
In total 37,100 daler			

The table is a recapitulation of Appendix Table 5.

The growing crisis of the towns 1620-1680

Many features show us in considerable detail that most of the 17th century was a difficult time for the Danish chartered towns. Following some decades with peace and prosperity after the 1570s, the trend began to be reversed with the Kalmar War 1611-1613. From the 1620s, taxation, wars and occupation by enemies laid great pressure on the economy of the towns and opportunities for a positive development were lost. The effects of the recession were obvious in many ways: in the number of taxpayers, the number of people taking out trade licenses, the number of merchant ships, deserted houses, recession for business and shipping, and a neglect of maintenance of the harbours. In the years up to 1660 the urban population fell by around 23 %, corresponding to the fall in the Danish population as a whole. Several decades would elapse before Denmark had overcome the consequences of the wars and the corresponding taxation in the period.

Archival sources

RIGSARKIVET (THE DANISH NATIONAL ARCHIVES)
Rentekammeret (The Exchequer)

311.71 Kommissionsakter vedr. taksation til matriklen af købstæder i Viborg, Århus og Ribe stifter, 1661-62. [Hustakster].

14.4 Diverse til kontoreftertrctning og oplysning 1660-1848, V. Diverse befolkningsstatistik. Ao 1672 Befantes efterfølgende Familier og folch udi Kiøbstederne.

LANDSARKIVET FOR NØRREJYLLAND
(THE PROVINCIAL ARCHIVES OF NORTHERN JUTLAND)

D 8. Grenå rådstuearkiv, 65. Diverse kæmnerregnskaber, skattelister o.a. 1528-38, 1566-1692.

D 13. Horsens rådstuearkiv, 66. Dokumenter vedr. statsskatteoppebørselen 1627-1790.

D 14. Kolding rådstuearkiv, 14. Skattemandtaller 1673-99. 97. Skatmesterregnskaber med bilag og koncepter 1591-1699.

D 21. Randers rådstuearkiv, 14. Rodetakseringer 1631-56. 15. Kontributionsskatteregnskaber 1657-70. 36. Skattemandtal 1644-1749.

D 22. Ribe rådstuearkiv, 29. Skattebog 1622-37. 30. Skattebog 1638-55. 31. Skattebog 1660-78. 32. Skattebog 1657-59.

D 23. Ringkøbing, 2. Skattemandtaller og -takseringer 1593-1691.

D 31. Varde rådstuearkiv, 80. Varde bys bog 1639-1710.

D 32. Vejle rådstuearkiv, 89. Ekstraskatteregnskaber 1670-1775. 348. Skatteligninger 1602-95.

D 33. Viborg rådstuearkiv, 377. Viborg bys takst på næring og brug 1673.

D 1. Aalborg rådstuearkiv, 34. Skillingstakster 1644-46, 1650-79.

D 2. Aarhus rådstuearkiv, 114. Mandtal og regnskab over skatter 1612-1743. 117. Statsskatteregnskaber 1670-76.

LANDSARKIVET FOR SJÆLLAND (THE PROVINCIAL ARCHIVES OF ZEALAND)
Køge rådstuearkiv. Kæmnerregnskaber 1640, 1681-82.

BIBLIOGRAPHY

Bach, Marie, Ole Degn & Poul Strømstad 1993. *Køge 1500-1950*. (Scandinavian Atlas of Historic Towns, 7). Odense: Odense University Press.

Bang, Nina (ed.) 1906-1933. *Tabeller over Skibsfart og Varetransport gennem Øresund 1497-1660*. Vol. 1-2. Copenhagen.

Degn, Ole 1973. 'Perspektiver i et købmandsregnskabsmateriale fra Ribe fra første halvdel af 1600årene'. In: *Beretning. Det nordiske Historikermøde i København 1971*. Copenhagen, pp. 113-29.

Degn, Ole 1981a. *Rig og fattig i Ribe. Økonomiske og sociale forhold i Ribe-samfundet 1560-1660*. Vol. 1.2. Aarhus: Aarhus Universitetsforlag.

Degn, Ole 1981b. 'Oplandets betydning for byens sociale forhold'. In: Rolf Fladby and Harald Winge (eds.), *By og bygd. Stad og omland. Nordisk lokalhistorie*. (Seminarrapport nr. 3). Oslo: Norsk Lokalhistorisk Institut, pp. 36-45.

Degn, Ole 1983. *Ribe 1500-1950*. (Scandinavian Atlas of Historic Towns, 3). Odense: Odense University Press.

Degn, Ole 1991a. 'Small towns in Denmark in the sixteenth and seventeenth centuries'. In: Antoni Maczak & Christopher Smout (eds.), *Gründung und Bedeutung kleinerer Städte im nördlichen Europa der frühen Neuzeit*. (Wolfenbütteler Forschungen, 47.) Wiesbaden, pp. 151-69.

Degn, Ole 1991b. *Alle skrives i mandtal. Folketællinger og deres brug*. (Arkivernes informationsserie). Copenhagen: Gad.

Degn, Ole 2002. 'Danske, norske og svenske byhistorier og byudvikling og urbanisering.' *Heimen*. Vol. 39, pp. 7-17.

Degn, Ole & Erik Gøbel 1997. *Skuder og kompagnier. Dansk søfarts historie, 2, 1588-1720*. Copenhagen: Gyldendal.

Engel, Rolf 1999. *Randers 1500-1950*. (Scandinavian Atlas of Historic Towns, 10). Odense: Odense University Press.

Falbe-Hansen, V. & W. Scharling 1885. *Danmarks Statistik*. Copenhagen.

Fridericia, J.A. 1889-90. 'Statistiske notitser fra Aarhus raadstuearkiv'. *Historisk Tidsskrift*, 6th series, 2, pp. 214-16.

Fussing, Hans H. 1957. *Bybefolkningen 1600-1660. Erhvervsfordeling. Ambulans. Indtjeningsevne*. Aarhus: Aarhus Universitetsforlag.

Kancelliets Brevbøger vedrørende Danmarks indre forhold, 1621-1623-1660. Copenhagen: Rigsarkivet 1922-2005.

Lassen, Aksel 1965a. *Fald og fremgang. Træk af befolkningsudviklingen i Danmark 1645-1960*. Aarhus: Aarhus Universitetsforlag.

Lassen, Aksel 1965b. 'The population of Denmark in 1660.' *The Scandinavian Economic History Review*, 13, 1, pp. 1-30.

Munch, P. 1900. *Købstadstyrelsen i Danmark fra Kristian IV's tid til Enevældens ophør (1619-1745)*. Vol. 1-2. Copenhagen: Det nordiske Forlag. (Republished 1977. Copenhagen: Selskabet for Udgivelse af Kilder til dansk Historie).

Olsen, Albert 1932. *Bybefolkningen på merkantilismens tid*. (Merkantilistiske studier, 1). (Republished 1975. Copenhagen: Selskabet for Udgivelse af Kilder til dansk Historie).

Pedersen, Henrik 1928. *De danske landbrug fremstillet på grundlag af forarbejderne til Christian V.s matrikel 1688*. (Republished 1975. Copenhagen: Landbohistorisk Selskab).

Petersen, Erling Ladewig 1980. *Fra standssamfund til rangssamfund 1500-1700. Dansk social historie*. Vol. 3. Copenhagen: Gyldendal.

Rubin, Marcus 1881-82. 'Bidrag til Københavns befolkningsstatistik i hundredåret 1630-1730'. *Historisk Tidsskrift*, 5th series, 3.

Secher, V. A. 1889-1918. *Corpus constitutionum Daniæ. Forordninger, Recesser og andre kongelige Breve, Danmarks Lovgivning vedkommende*. Vol. 2-6, 1576-1660. Copenhagen: G.E.C. Gad.

Tuxen, Poul 1987. *Stege 1500-1950*. (Scandinavian Atlas of Historic Towns, 5). Odense: Odense: Odense University Press.

Appendices

Appendix Table 1.

The urban population in 1672: households ('families'), persons and average.

Chartered town	Families	Persons	Children below 5 years	The town total	Family average	Children in %
Zealand						
Copenhagen				41,000		
Elsinore	833	3,532	501	4,033	4.8	12.4
Hillerød	202	808	150	958	4.7	15.7
Holbæk	150	769	110	879	5.9	12.5
Kalundborg	187	895	163	1,058	5.7	15.4
Korsør	180	708	118	826	4.6	14.3
Køge	293	1,414	229	1,643	5.6	14.0
Nykøbing	114	399	64	463	4.1	13.8
Næstved	429	1,584	269	1,853	4.3	14.5

Chartered town	Families	Persons	Children below 5 years	The town total	Family average	Children in %
Præstø	101	363	72	435	4.3	16.6
Ringsted	134	600	100	700	5.2	14.3
Roskilde	352	1,936	260	196	6.2	11.8
Skælskør	117	544	73	617	5.3	11.8
Slagelse	362	1,628	204	1,832	5.1	11.1
Slangerup	90	450	63	513	5.7	12.3
Sorø	92	473	55	528	5.7	10.4
Store Heddinge	75	334	28	362	4.8	7.7
Vordingborg	147	629	107	736	5.0	14.5
Møn						
Stege	122	575	81	656	5.4	12.3
Lolland- Falster						
Maribo	11	379	65	444	4.0	11.0
Nakskov	318	1,649	271	1,920	6.0	14.1
Nykøbing	198	765	96	861	4.3	11.1
Nysted	152	599	92	691	4.5	13.3
Sakskøbing	62	242	30	272	4.4	11.0
Stubbekøbing	112	439	72	511	4.6	14.1
Funen						
Assens	227	922	162	1,084	4.8	14.9
Bogense	90	370	68	438	4.9	15.5
Fåborg	146	708	133	841	5.8	15.8
Kerteminde	119	539	103	642	5.4	16.0
Middelfart	139	631	125	756	5.4	16.5
Nyborg	191	1,007	153	1,160	6.1	13.2
Odense	779	3,331	477	3,808	4.9	12.5
Svendborg	186	861	148	1,009	5.4	14.7
Rudkøbing	104	400	78	478	4.6	16.3
Jutland						
Ebeltoft	189	665	152	817	4.3	18.6

Chartered town	Families	Persons	Children below 5 years	The town total	Family average	Children in %
Fredericia	322	1,253	338	1,591	6.2	21.2
Grenaa	118	388	65	453	3.8	14.3
Hjørring	189	644	138	782	4.1	17.6
Hobro	52	311	32	343	6.6	9.3
Holstebro	94	430	70	500	5.3	14.0
Horsens	311	1,288	228	1,516	4.9	15.0
Kolding	257	884	210	1,094	4.3	19.2
Lemvig	106	410	40	450	4.2	8.9
Mariager	99	291	79	370	3.7	21.4
Nykøbing	138	301	42	343	2.5	12.2
Randers	405	1,803	233	2,036	5.0	11.4
Ribe	488	1,753	186	1,939	4.0	9.6
Ringkøbing	64	559	64	623	3.8	10.3
Skagen	193	810	194	1,004	5.2	19.3
Skive	92	461	68	529	5.8	12.9
Sæby	158	592	78	670	4.2	11.6
Thisted	233	917	83	1,000	4.3	8.3
Varde	128	475	92	567	4.4	16.2
Vejle	165	589	123	712	4.3	17.3
Viborg	662	2,458	246	2,704	4.1	9.1
Aalborg	820	3,719	462	4,181	5.1	11.0
Aarhus	684	3,094	380	3,474	5.1	11.2
Total	12,881	54,578	8,323	62,901	4.9	13.2

Missing are Copenhagen (here added), the chartered towns on Bornholm and Rødby and Skanderborg, cf. note 10.

Source: Rigsarkivet, Rentekammeret 14.4 Diverse til kontorefterretning og oplysning 1660-1848, V. Diverse befolkningsstatistik. Ao 1672 Befantes efterfølgende Familier og folch udi Kiøbstederne. Rubin 1881-82, p. 527.

Kolding's inhabitants around 1692: The marital status of the heads of households and the size of the households.

Size	Head of household						Total persons
	Married men	Widowers	Widows	Unmarried women	Unmarried men	Total house-holds	
1		1	2	5	2	11	11
2	16	3	14	2	1	36	71
3	20	3	16	2	0	41	123
4	49	4	5	0	0	58	232
5	36	0	6	0	0	42	210
6	20	1	2	0	0	23	138
7	9	1	0	0	0	10	70
8	11	0	0	0	0	11	88
9	6	0	0	0	0	6	54
10	4	0	0	0	0	4	40
11	2	0	0	0	0	2	22
14	1	0	0	0	0	1	14
Total	174	13	45	9	3	244	1,073

The status of the heads of households is seen here on the basis of the household structure. We have either a man with a wife and possibly children = a married man. A man without a wife, but with children = a widower. A woman with children = a widow. A woman without children = an unmarried woman. And a man without a woman and children = an unmarried man.

Source: Landsarkivet for Nørrejylland D 14. Kolding rådstuearkiv, Mandtal over borgerskabet og samtlige indbyggere og deres huses familie, 97. Skatmesterregnskaber med bilag 1591-1699.

Appendix Table 3.

Kolding's inhabitants around 1692: Heads of households and the number of children.

	Head of household						Children total
Number of children	Married man	Widower	Widow	Single woman	Unmarried man	Total households	
0	35	1	5	9	3	53	0
1	50	7	24	0	0	81	81
2	47	2	9	0	0	58	116
3	23	2	3	0	0	28	84
4	6	1	3	0	0	10	40
5	8	0	1	0	0	9	45
6	4	0	0	0	0	4	24
7	1	0	0	0	0	1	7
Children total	174	13	45	9	3	244	397

On the status of the heads of households, cf. Appendix Table 2, the note.

Source: Landsarkivet for Nørrejylland, D 14. Kolding rådstuearkiv, Mandtal over borgerskabet og samtlige indbyggere og deres huses familie, 97. Skatmesterregnskaber med bilag 1591-1699.

Appendix Table 4.

Kolding's inhabitants around 1692: Heads of households and number of servants.

Servants (svende, karle *and* piger)	Head of household						Servants total
	Married man	Widower	Widow	Single woman	Unmarried man	Total households	
0	85	8	36	7	2	138	0
1	42	3	5	2	0	52	52
2	25	1	4	0	1	31	62
3	14	1	0	0	0	15	45
4	6	0	0	0	0	6	24

Servants (svende, karle and piger)	Head of household						Servants total
5	0	0	0	0	0	0	6
6	1	0	0	0	0	1	68
7	0	0	0	0	0	0	0
8	1	0	0	0	0	1	8
Households total	174	13	45	9	3	244	197

On the status of the heads of households, cf. Appendix Table 2, the note.

Source: Landsarkivet for Nørrejylland, D 14. Kolding rådstuearkiv, Mandtal over borgerskabet og samtlige indbyggere og deres huses familie, 97. Skatmesterregnskaber med bilag 1591-1699.

APPENDIX TABLE 5.

The taxes of the chartered towns 1576 (daler) and 1621 and 1655 (proportionate in rigsdaler).

Chartered town	Tax 1576	Proportionate 1621	Proportionate 1655
Zealand			
Elsinore	800	1,835	1,505
Holbæk	150	433	1,035
Kalundborg	400	440	752
Korsør	300	110	188
Copenhagen	10,000	6,312	5,643
Køge	700	1,541	752
Nykøbing	150	110	113
Næstved	600	624	752
Præstø	200	73	113
Ringsted	100	128	113
Roskilde	800	294	376
Skælskør	500	184	470
Slagelse	400	385	376

Chartered town	Tax 1576	Proportionate 1621	Proportionate 1655
Slangerup	200	367	282
Store Heddinge	150	118	113
Vordingborg	150	92	188
Møn			
Stege	600	184	188
Lolland-Falster			
Maribo	200	330	282
Nakskov	800	1,468	1,129
Nykøbing	200	459	470
Nysted	100	147	150
Sakskøbing	50	92	113
Stubbekøbing	200	275	282
Funen			
Assens	600	624	666
Bogense	100	367	376
Fåborg	300	239	256
Kerteminde	500	477	508
Middelfart	300	404	429
Nyborg	400	991	1.057
Odense	2,500	2,019	2,152
Svendborg	600	991	681
Rudkøbing	200	92	188
Jutland			
Ebeltoft	150	147	188
Grenaa	200	147	41
Hjørring	100	147	158
Hobro	100	73	79
Holstebro	200	367	102

Chartered town	Tax 1576	Proportionate 1621	Proportionate 1655
Horsens	1,200	1,101	1,174
Kolding	600	1,101	1,136
Lemvig	300	367	406
Mariager	100	275	293
Nykøbing	400	73	79
Randers	1,200	1,285	1,445
Ribe	2,000	1,835	1,956
Ringkøbing	300	367	418
Skagen	350	37	38
Skive	100	147	120
Sæby	250	275	256
Thisted	400	37	451
Varde	300	551	587
Vejle	500	734	715
Viborg	800	734	1,038
Aalborg	2,500	3,670	3,010
Aarhus	1,800	1,468	1,697

The figures for 1621 and 1655 are here calculated proportionately because the total tax in 1576 was 37,100 daler and in 1621 and 1655 at 10,110 and 19,716 daler respectively, and therefore the figures are multiplied with 3.67 and 1.88 respectively.

The chartered towns on Bornholm are missing, and also Hillerød, Sorø, Rødby and Fredericia, mentioned in the urban population list 1672.

Source: Secher 1889-1918, vol. 2-6, tables at the end of every volume.

NOTES

1   For useful discussions in connection with the elaboration of the article I would like to thank the editors.

2   Degn 1977, pp. 9-11. Here it is ignored that in connection with the foundation of Kristianopel, Avskær, Lykå(by) and Elleholm were abolished, in the foundation of Ny-Varberg, Gamleby

and Nyby, in the foundation of Kristianstad, Vä and Åhus, and that for the benefit of Malmø, Trelleborg was abolished as a chartered town.

3   Cf. Degn 1981a, vol. 1, pp. 416-24.

4   Population figures are missing for the chartered towns on Bornholm and for Rødby and Skanderborg, cf. Appendix Table 1.

5   Villages, single farms and manors are listed in Pedersen 1928.

6   On the town system, see Degn 1991a.

7   Pedersen 1928. On this basis calculations of farms and houses in the parishes lying within a radius of 20 km were made for the individual chartered towns, fully or with at least half of the area.

8   Degn 2002, p. 13.

9   See the list of archival sources: Landsarkivet for Nørrejylland (The Provincial Archives of Northern Jutland), rådstuearkiver.

10   Falbe-Hansen & Scharling 1885, pp. 566-69, and Lassen 1965, pp. 323-25 have only the total population figure.

11   Falbe-Hansen & Scharling 1885, pp. 564-65. Lassen 1965, p. 29. Gunnar Olsen 1943, p. 105, argues that the figures are not completely correct, as a rule too small, but this is not likely as the urban population percentage would otherwise be questionably high, cf. the following.

12   Lassen 1965a, p. 34.

13   Namely the figure for the towns in the 1672 list, 62,903 + Copenhagen's 41,000 + the calculated figures for the chartered towns on Bornholm (Rønne, Neksø, Aakirkeby, Svaneke and Hasle), Rødby and Skanderborg. The calculations for these last towns are based on the population figures in 1769 with the deduction of growth corresponding with the total growth for the provincial towns 1672-1769: 11.8 %. With these calculations we get the figures 2,730 (Bornholm), 581 (Rødby) and 506 (Skanderborg).

14   Petersen 1980, p. 107.

15   See for instance Degn 1981b, p. 39.

16   Landsarkivet for Nørrejylland (The Provincial Archives of Northern Jutland), D 14, Kolding rådstuearkiv, 97. Skatmesterregnskaber med bilag 1591-1699.

17   Cf. too a few lists from 1769 from Elsinore, Odense, Vejle and Horsens and the lists from the eight chartered towns in the diocese of Ribe 1748 (Landsarkivet for Nørrejylland (The Provincial Archives of Northern Jutland), B9 Ribe stiftamts arkiv, 1027 Indberetninger om stiftets købstæder 1714-1749) and the chartered towns of the diocese of Zealand 1753, Degn 1991b, pp. 16 and 14. The 1787 census is the first registration with lists of inhabitants from nearly all the Kingdom; only one parish is missing!

18   For the age groups 0-9 and 10-19 the figures were 21.7 % and 15.5 % respectively, calculated on the basis of Lassen 1965, pp. 370-72.

19   Degn 1981a, vol. 1, p. 260. Petersen 1980, pp. 106-07.

20   Degn 1981a, vol. 1, p. 189.

21 Degn 1981a, vol. 1, p. 256. In Kolding around 1692 only 5.7 % of the inhabitants were lodgers.

22 On the tax lists, see Landsarkivet for Nørrejylland (The Provincial Archives of Northern Jutland), rådstuearkiver. Presumably it will be possible to increase the material with tax lists from the chartered towns Elsinore, Holbæk, Kalundborg, Nakskov, Odense and Kerteminde.

23 Lassen 1965a, p. 11. Aksel Lassen 1965b.

24 Danske Kancelli, copy books 1657 and 1658, cf. the edition *Kancelliets Brevbøger 1657* and *1658*, 2002, 2004.

25 Degn 1991a, pp. 156, 159-60.

26 Cf. Degn 1981a, vol. 1, pp. 444-45, vol. 2, pp. 242-50.

27 Degn 1981a, vol. 1, pp. 118, 123.

28 Degn & Gøbel 1997, pp. 55-56. For instance *Kancelliets Brevbøger 1621-23*, p. 33, *1624-26*, p. 708, *1627-29*, p. 77, *1630-32*, p. 681, *1635-36*, p. 103, *1637-39*, pp. 624, 761, 953, 975.

29 Degn & Gøbel 1997, p. 48.

30 Degn & Gøbel 1997, p. 48.

31 Degn & Gøbel 1997, pp. 48, 52.

32 Degn 1981a, vol. 1, p. 425.

33 It is a little confusing that V.A. Secher in his edition of *Forordninger, recesser og andre kongelige breve, Danmarks lovgivning vedkommende*, 1558-1660, 1-6, 1887-1907, very carefully in a large appendix table lists every town tax for every chartered town.

34 Degn 1981a, vol. 2, p. 236.

35 Degn 1981a, vol. 1, pp. 429-31.

36 Degn 1981a, vol. 1, pp. 429-31 vol. 2, p. 241.

37 Degn 1973, p. 126. Degn 1981a, vol. 1, p. 426.

38 Degn 1981a, vol. 1, p. 427.

39 Degn 1981a, vol. 1, p. 140, vol. 2, pp. 87, 145.

40 Bach, Degn & Strømstad 1993, p. 31.

Michael Bregnsbo

Copenhagen – The capital of an empire

When the first official Danish census was taken in 1769, Copenhagen, the capital, was by far the largest city in Denmark and had 70,514 inhabitants. The second largest city in Denmark was then Odense with only 5,464 inhabitants.[1] Furthermore, when it came to the size and number of brick and stone houses, no other city in Denmark could even come close to Copenhagen. As well as being disproportionate to the rest of Denmark with regard to size, Copenhagen was geographically situated almost as far to the east as possible, Sweden being on the other side of the relatively narrow Øresund.

Even today, Copenhagen is still disproportionate to the rest of the country: the number of inhabitants being 501,285 in relation to 5,383,507 in Denmark as a whole, i.e. every tenth inhabitant in Denmark lives in Copenhagen. The disproportion is even more glaring if the metropolitan area or Greater Copenhagen with 1,085,813 inhabitants is included, which means that every fifth inhabitant in Denmark lives within this area. In comparison, the second largest Danish city, Aarhus, has only 291,258 inhabitants.[2] The same disproportion is seen in the size and administrative structure of the city government and city administration. Furthermore, Denmark has a strongly centralised political and social structure which means that the government, the state administration and most of the political, financial, economic, social and cultural institutions are located in Copenhagen.

It is true that capital cities often tend to be the largest cities of a country. Still, the size of Copenhagen, both today and formerly, seems extraordinarily disproportionate in relation to the rest of the country, compared with other Danish cities and with the size of the country as a whole. The question is why Copenhagen was, and still is, so oversized in relation to the rest of Denmark. What is the historical background for this?

FIG. 1.

van Wijks map of Copenhagen, 1611.

Research survey

In answering this question, some 19th century historians have highlighted the disastrous wars against Sweden from 1657 to 1660, when the whole country was occupied by enemy forces – except for the capital Copenhagen, which bravely and resolutely held out and repelled an enemy storm in February 1659. The citizens were afterwards rewarded with various privileges. These historians also pointed out the favouritism shown to the capital and its inhabitants, which accompanied the introduction of royal Absolutism in 1660 (these events will be elaborated on later in this essay). Due to a fundamentally liberal attitude these historians were strongly critical of Absolutism and tended to consider the favourable treatment of Copenhagen as politically and morally unsound and economically dubious, because it made the Absolutist rule and its activities and lavish expenditure more important for the growth of the city than the Copenhageners' trade privileges.[3] But the long-term consequences of the events of 1657-1660 have been scarcely discussed. Generally, the question of the favourable position of Copenhagen has caused little direct discussion among Danish historians, most of whom have seen it more or less as the natural course. Still, the theme *has* been discussed a couple of times from a more province-centred and provincially conscious point of view.[4] In his study of the province of Jutland in Danish history between 1814 and 1864, the historian Steen Bo Frandsen has advocated that a regional dimension be included in Danish history. This was a transitional period between Absolutism and the adoption of a free constitution, but also a period of Danish-German antagonism within the Duchies of Schleswig and Holstein which were under the Danish Crown. These conflicts culminated in the disastrous Danish defeat in the war against Prussia and Austria in 1864 when the Duchies had to be ceded. Frandsen concludes:

It can be argued that Copenhagen especially profited from the outcome of the war, because the defeat enabled the capital to extend its domination over the country forcing it into an inferior position. Having been a monarchy consisting of several provinces, Denmark became a nation-state, where there was only the capital and the province. Centralisation was at the top of the agenda after 1864. Regional solutions were no longer discussed with respect to representation or some kind of regionalisation. It was inevitable that regional differences found their way into the political sphere – for example, through the farmers' political movement. But in the small nation-state of Denmark, a regional opposition was never organised on a parliamentary level.

Frandsen does not deny the importance of the events of February 1659 for the dominant position of Copenhagen but emphasises that regional alternatives were indeed possible in the period from after 1814 until the fatal war of 1864.[5]

Yet, as the statistics from the 1769 census mentioned earlier show, the disproportionately dominant position of Copenhagen in relation to the rest of the country was indeed a fact before the period studied by Frandsen even if he is right in concluding that this tendency was reinforced after 1864. The emphasis by other historians on the events of 1657-1660 as decisive cannot be gainsaid. But still, do these events in themselves really explain exhaustively and satisfactorily the disproportion of Copenhagen in relation to the rest of Denmark? At least it would be useful to know exactly how these events (and maybe others as well) had an effect on the special position of Copenhagen which has continued until the present day.

The Danish empire

There has been a tendency in Danish historiography to project the present-day minor power called Denmark back to the past, but this has caused erroneous perceptions of events and decisions in Danish history, as formerly the Danish state consisted of more territories than it does today. The Danish state, however, has not always been a minor power. Quite the opposite: it was actually a leading and dominant power in Northern Europe. To a large extent this was due to the fact that the German Empire had a weak and decentralised political structure at that time, while the Danish state was larger and stronger than most of the German principalities. It is not that the territories which once belonged to the Danish state (among others, the Kingdom of Sweden, the Kingdom of Norway and the Duchies of Schleswig and Holstein) were part of the Kingdom of Denmark, but they were under the Danish crown in the sense that the King of Denmark was at the same time the ruling monarch (king or duke) of these territories. The Kingdom of Denmark was thus part of a larger state.

How should this state be characterised and conceptualised? One suggestion has been as a conglomerate state, patrimonial and decentralised, later developing into a unitary state, bureaucratised and centralised.[6] Another suggestion has been as a composite state.[7] But what should the characterisation of such a state be, if it is to cover all periods and developments? The 'Danish monarchy' (which is on a higher level than the 'Kingdom of Denmark', and not to be confused with it) could be a possibility. Certainly, the Danish state has always been a monarchy but this notion does not really capture the compositeness of the state. A recent study of Danish history, which endeavoured to write the history of the whole of this composite state and not just that of present-day Denmark projected back to earlier times, suggests using the term 'Danish empire' to describe the composite structure of the Danish state. The word 'empire' is defined as an extensive territory which is ruled by a single governing authority (in this case, the King of Denmark). This notion highlights the fact that while one power rules a whole territory, the various territories of the empire might consist of different cultures, languages, social, administrative, judicial and political structures and systems. Thus, the empire is larger than the nation called Denmark.[8]

From the Middle Ages until today

An empire is an entity characterised by diversity, antagonisms and/or fruitful cooperation. And this is exactly what the Danish empire has been like through history: in 1380 the Kingdom of Norway came to the Danish Crown by inheritance, and belonging to Norway were the old North Atlantic dependencies of Greenland, Iceland and the Faroe Islands. In 1397 the Kingdom of Sweden (which included present-day Finland) also joined the empire, as part of the so-called Kalmar Union between the three Nordic Kingdoms. In 1460 the King of Denmark was appointed Duke of Schleswig – this duchy had originally been part of the Kingdom of Denmark but had broken away during the Middle Ages – and Count of Holstein (from 1474 Duke of Holstein). Holstein was part of the German empire and thus as Duke of Holstein, the King of Denmark was a German prince. Sweden finally broke away from the Danish empire in 1523 but the union between the Kingdom of Denmark, the Kingdom of

Norway (including its North Atlantic dependencies) and the Duchies of Schleswig and Holstein still remained. The Danish empire was still the stronger power compared with Sweden, and was furthermore a major North European and Baltic power of international significance.

However, the 17th century marked the decline and weakening of the Danish empire, and Sweden now became the superior Nordic state. The Danish empire lost various wars and had to cede land. After the disastrous wars against Sweden in 1657-1658 and 1658-1660, the Danish empire had to cede some provinces in Norway as well as the Danish provinces of Scania, Halland and Blekinge on the other side of Øresund. The cession of these provinces meant that the Danish Kingdom lost a third of its territory, making its geopolitical position rather delicate and exposed. Copenhagen was situated in the front line against Sweden and several attempts to re-conquer the ceded provinces all failed. Instead the empire endeavoured to integrate the Duchies of Schleswig and Holstein where the ducal authority had previously been partitioned and was being executed jointly by several princes at a time (one of these being the King of Denmark). Some of these princes were, however, hostile towards the King of Denmark and were supported by Denmark's enemy. Because of this, the duchies constituted a serious security problem. The introduction of royal Absolutism in 1660 can thus be seen as an attempt to strengthen the rest of the state after the catastrophic loss of territory.

In addition, in order to utilise the opportunities within international trade, small overseas colonies or trade stations were procured, in India around 1620, and on the African Gold Coast (in present-day Ghana) during the second half of the 17th century. In the Caribbean three small islands St. Thomas, St. John, and St. Croix (the present-day US Virgin Islands) were acquired between 1672 and 1733. The Danish empire managed to stay neutral during the major European wars of the middle and second half of the 18th century so that its trade and shipping could prosper. However, the empire became involved on the side of the French in the Napoleonic Wars, and afterwards had to cede Norway to Sweden. The old Norwegian dependencies (Greenland, Iceland and the Faroe Islands) remained however in the Danish empire.

The 19th century, until 1864, witnessed the abolition of Absolutism and the adoption of a free constitution for the Kingdom of Denmark in 1849, but also national tensions and conflicts between Denmark and German separatists in the Duchies of Schleswig and Holstein. This led to an armed conflict from 1848-1850, which should be seen as a civil war within the empire, but with international involvement. According to international agreements after the war the members of the Danish empire had to stay together in the same state. This, however, proved unworkable and ended in the war of 1864 against Prussia and Austria, and the subsequent cession of the Duchies of Schleswig and Holstein. In 1920, the northern part of Schleswig was returned to the Danish empire after a referendum. The overseas colonies were abolished: Those in India were sold to Britain in 1845, the colony in Africa in 1850. The three West Indian islands were sold to the US in 1917. The Faroe Islands were represented in the Danish parliament after 1849, whereas Iceland at the request of the Icelanders themselves was not. Iceland got her own constitution in 1874 and became a kingdom in its own right in a personal union with the Kingdom of Denmark in 1918. In 1944 Iceland seceded from Denmark and gained full independence. The Faroe Islands got home rule in 1948, Greenland's status within the empire was changed in 1953 when it became an equal part of Denmark instead of a colony. In 1979, Greenland, too, got home rule.[9]

This brief summary by no means does justice to the history of the Danish empire. The picture should be much more detailed, among other things there are areas that have been part of the empire for a longer or shorter period but which are not mentioned here at all. The aim, however, has not been to tell the story of the Danish empire, but to emphasise that the Kingdom of Denmark has indeed been part of a larger empire for most of the time. Consequently, Copenhagen has been the capital not only of the Kingdom of Denmark, but of the much larger Danish empire. Thus, in order to find out why present-day Copenhagen is disproportionately oversized in relation to the rest of Denmark it could be worth examining how its status as capital of the whole Danish empire affected Copenhagen.

The capital of an empire

For Copenhagen, becoming a capital was a process that occurred gradually.[10] Originally it was not built as a capital and was not even founded by the king, but by the bishop of Roskilde Diocese in 1167. The King of Denmark did not take over Copenhagen until around 1415 and during the 15th century it gradually began to fit the role of a capital. In 1479 the first university of the Danish Kingdom was established here. During the reign of Christian III (1534-1559) the navy was expanded and its headquarters were located in Copenhagen.[11] These arrangements of course contributed to the growth of the city in size and number of inhabitants relative to the rest of Denmark. However, it is difficult to determine to what extent these should be seen as Danish or imperial measures.

Copenhagen's position as the capital of an empire clearly found expression in the development known as the military revolution, and in Danish historiography often as the transition from domain state to tax, military or power state.[12] To put it briefly, this concerned the fact that military technology had made the organisation of defence, on the basis of a noble cavalry, militarily obsolete, with infantry becoming the important thing. The consequences of this were, among other things, a standing infantry army (also in times of peace) and a permanent and growing taxation to finance this army. This again meant an expansion of public administration.[13] This development which in the Danish connection coincides more or less with the reign of Christian IV (1588-1648) had a strong impact on Copenhagen and its growth, because many of the new military and administrative functions were concentrated there. The growing military pressure and the wars which the Danish empire faced during the 17th century promoted this development. The naval installations in Copenhagen (*Holmen*) were further expanded as sovereignty of not only the Danish waters, but the Norwegian waters as well, was being challenged and had to be maintained, thus emphasising that the navy was not only for the Kingdom of Denmark but for the whole empire. The growth of a permanent infantry army was shown by huge brick buildings like *Tøjhuset* (the Royal Armoury), *Proviantgården* (the Royal Provision Depot), and *Kongens Bryghus* (the Royal Brewery). Furthermore, vast navy headquarters were built. No other town within the Danish Kingdom or within the Danish empire could even come close to matching the splendour and size of these buildings or military installations.

But this military and administrative expansion also left its mark on Copenhagen as an imperial capital in other ways. In order to increase wealth in society in general, to enable the state to prosper financially, the government sought to implement an active policy for promoting commerce, shipping and industry, a policy often characterised as mercantilism. Overseas trading companies were organised and provided with a government-backed monopoly and various tax, tariff and military privileges and support. The first trading company was *Ostindisk Kompagni* (Danish East India Company) founded in 1616. Three years later trade with Iceland was given to a monopoly, a Copenhagen-based trading company of which the partners were all Copenhagen merchants. Monopoly trading companies of a similar kind were established to handle trade and shipping in other parts of the world (Africa, the West Indies) as well as in other parts of the Danish empire (Greenland, Finnmark in Northern Norway). Not all of these companies had a long life, but new ones were founded to replace them. The Danish colonies in India, Africa and the West Indies were originally run not by the Danish state but by what were formally private firms and were not taken over by the government until the mid 18th century. The reason for establishing trading monopolies was the necessity to collaborate, if any trade connections at all with these distant areas were to have a chance to succeed. The formally private status of these chartered companies was supposed to encourage private investors. Furthermore, it could also give the Danish government the possibility to dissociate itself in the event of conflicts between representatives of the chartered – but formally private – company and subjects of other European colonial powers. Around the middle of the 18th century, trade connections had been consolidated to such an extent that monopolies could be abolished and replaced by free competition. Free competition would be impossible if the trade colonies were in fact owned and administered by a private company alone, as the other traders and companies would then have to rely on harbour and other facilities belonging to their competitor. Thus the government took them over.

A common feature of these trading companies was that they were usually based in Copenhagen. There were certainly a few exceptions. An African company was founded in 1659 in the city of Glückstadt in Holstein and a company in charge of the trade to Finnmarken was founded in the Norwegian city of Bergen in 1702. Furthermore, around 1720 endeavours to re-establish connections with Greenland (these had actually been severed since the late Middle Ages even though the Danish empire had never given up its claim of sovereignty over this island) were initiated in Bergen in Norway and a company for this purpose was founded there and got royal approval in 1723. In these endeavours missionary and commercial considerations went hand in hand. However, this Bergen-based company had to give up in 1726, as the missionary and commercial connections to Greenland were taken over by the state and moved from Bergen to Copenhagen. Thus, even though it was originally a Norwegian dependency, Greenland was administratively and legally transferred to the Kingdom of Denmark. Or to be more precise: it was transferred to the capital of the Danish empire rather than to the capital of the Kingdom of Denmark.[14]

It is characteristic that the trading companies based in cities other than Copenhagen were few and did not last long, after which their trade functions were moved to Copenhagen. Moreover, the cities in question were typically situated outside the

Kingdom of Denmark: Glückstadt in the Duchy of Holstein and Bergen in the Kingdom of Norway. Certainly, none of these areas had any city that was anywhere near the size of Copenhagen, but still, they had cities that were significantly larger than any city within the Kingdom of Denmark apart from Copenhagen.[15] Besides trading companies, the government in a mercantilist spirit sought to encourage, support and subsidise industrial production in order to increase wealth and self-sufficiency. Most of the factories resulting from that policy were located in Copenhagen and thus were another factor contributing to the huge growth of the capital.

These trading companies had striking effects on Copenhagen. Impressive administrative centres and warehouses were built. As the companies were Copenhagen-based, all shipping and trade went through Copenhagen necessitating extended warehouse and shipyard capacity and creating a significantly wealthy and trendsetting merchant class as well as jobs for many people of humbler rank. Thus the number of inhabitants in Copenhagen increased. This trend can be seen relatively early: an estimate of the size of the merchant navy of the Kingdom of Denmark and the Duchy of Schleswig around 1639 shows that 28 % of it was based in Copenhagen.[16] Exact statistical figures for later periods are difficult to obtain, but considering the expansion that took place during the following more than 150 years, it must be expected that Copenhagen's share grew enormously. Thus, it is known that in total size the merchant navy of the provinces of the Danish Kingdom around 1750 almost equalled that in Copenhagen, but already some twenty years later the Copenhagen fleet was 20 % larger than the provincial one.[17] Figures from the Duchy of Schleswig are not known from these years, but a list from 1782/83 shows that the capital then owned 57 % of the total merchant fleet in the Kingdom of Denmark and Schleswig, the Duchy of Schleswig had 28 %, and the provincial part of the Kingdom only 15 %.[18]

From the middle of the 18th century and onwards, the chartered trading companies gradually lost their monopolies and closed down. Yet, this development did not have negative consequences for Copenhagen. Quite the contrary, the liberalisation of trade and shipping once again favoured Copenhagen since the business, know-how, wealth, manpower, and financial institutions, as well as the storage, harbour, and shipping facilities necessary for private business were already there and existed almost nowhere else in the empire. Indeed, the second half of the 18th century was an age in which the Danish empire managed to stay neutral and keep itself out of the many major European wars so that commerce and shipping could prosper under the neutral Danish flag, thus making Copenhagen a major European trade centre from which large amounts of goods were re-exported. This was another factor reinforcing the growth and importance of Copenhagen as the capital of an empire at the expense of the rest of the Kingdom of Denmark.

Royal Absolutism

As previously mentioned, royal Absolutism had been introduced in Denmark in 1660. This was after the disastrous wars against Sweden 1657-1658 and 1658-1660 which had deprived the Kingdom of Denmark of one-third of its territories and caused the pillage and ruin of the remainder. A *stændermøde* (assembly of the Estates) took place in Copenhagen after the wars in the autumn of 1660. Its purpose was to levy taxes to help the disastrous financial condition of the Danish government. However, strong disagreements about the distribution of the financial burdens led to bitter strife between the nobility and the lower orders (burghers and clergy). The lower orders got in touch with the royal court and the result was the change in Denmark's constitutional status from an elective monarchy to a hereditary monarchy, a decision which the nobility was more or less forced to accept. This introduction of hereditary monarchy necessitated further political, administrative and political adjustments. The result was that the Estates left it to the king to draft a proposal for such measures. The lower orders had probably hoped – and maybe even expected – to be given a say in political matters, perhaps a status similar to the one the nobility had enjoyed before 1660. In January 1661, King Frederik III announced *Enevoldsarvere-geringsakten* (The Act of Hereditary and Sovereign Monarchy) which meant the introduction of royal Absolutism. This was hardly what the Estates had expected, but by then the assembly of Estates had long been over, so the representative of the Estates could not meet and protest about the royal proposal but had to comply. Danish Absolutism was further consolidated in 1665 when *Kongeloven* (*Lex Regia*) (the Royal Law) was drafted – this was something as unique and self-contradictory as an Absolutist constitution.

During the second war against Sweden 1658-1660 most of the territories of the Kingdom of Denmark had been occupied by Swedish troops, only Copenhagen had defended itself resolutely and held out until other powers intervened in support of Denmark. For this, Copenhageners were shortly afterwards rewarded with significant and lucrative trade privileges in comparison with other cities of the Kingdom of Denmark. Furthermore, the city was given its own special municipal constitution.[19]

Prospects of participation in government affairs, e.g. levying of taxes, had originally also been promised to the Copenhageners, but after the introduction of royal Absolutism 1660-1661 this was out of the question, being considered incompatible with the Absolutist system of government. The introduction of Absolutism however meant that Copenhagen became the permanent residence of the royal family and the royal court, and that central administration was further expanded. In addition, an ambitious naval expansion scheme was introduced, meaning a further growth of the navy whose base was still in Copenhagen.[20] Thus, the capital grew, not only with regard to the number of courtiers, civil servants, army officers, soldiers, naval officers and seamen, but also with regard to the shipbuilding industry and to providers of goods and services. Although these tendencies had begun long before 1660, the events of that year certainly reinforced them. The building programme of the early years of Danish Absolutism did not include a new and impressive residential royal palace but rather a very large citadel (*Kastellet*) in Copenhagen. In a comparative European perspective, the Danish monarchy after 1660 was indeed strongly prepared militarily[21] and it should once again be noted that this huge army and navy was not for the defence of the Kingdom of Denmark alone, but for defence of the whole empire.

As Copenhagen had become the city of permanent royal residence many noblemen thought it desirable to have a residential palace to enable them to be present at the royal court as well as to entertain and live in a manner befitting their rank. During the 1750s and 1760s a new district was added to Copenhagen, *Frederiksstaden* (Frederik's City, named after King Frederik V). This consisted of noble palaces as well as large houses for merchants who were prospering from the long-distance trade for which Copenhagen was the hub. This prosperous development lasted until the Danish empire involuntarily became involved in the Napoleonic Wars on the French side which led to the bombing of Copenhagen and the subsequent loss of the navy to Britain in 1807 and the cession of Norway to Sweden in 1814. The loss of Norway meant, among other things, that the population of the empire was significantly reduced, making the size of Copenhagen in relation to the rest of the empire even more markedly disproportionate.

The age of democratisation and military defeat

The trend to place all central political and administrative institutions in Copenhagen was for a short period broken when *rådgivende stænderforsamlinger* (advisory as-

FIG. 2.

Børsen, built 1619-1623.

semblies of Estates) were established in the 1830s. These were elected even though the number of enfranchised members was modest; the assemblies had the right to be consulted about and to discuss new legislative initiatives from the government. They could also introduce legislative bills themselves, but the government was not obliged to follow their advice and resolutions. In his capacity as Duke of Holstein, which was a member of the German Federation established in 1815, the King of Denmark was obliged to introduce an assembly of Estates for that duchy, but the King had long refused to do so fearing for his absolute power. Around 1830, however, due to pressure from the German Federation and fear of revolution – as had just been seen in France in 1830, no further delay was possible. Since it would be politically difficult to allow such an assembly in one part of the Danish empire and at the same time maintain unrestricted Absolutism in the others, assemblies of the Estates were extended to the whole empire. Thus, an assembly for the Danish islands, one for the province of Jutland, one for the Duchy of Schleswig and one for the Duchy of Holstein were established in principle in 1831 and in practice from 1834 onwards. In order to avoid causing too much political turmoil, the assemblies were held in economically less important towns away from the politically conscious and leading economic centres. Thus, the assembly for the Danish islands was not held in Copenhagen, but in the city of Roskilde about 30 kilometres west of Copenhagen. The assembly for Jutland was held in the small town of Viborg instead of in the towns of Aarhus or Aalborg, which were the largest and leading commercial cities of that province. The assembly for the Duchy of Schleswig got its seat in the city of Schleswig and not in Flensburg, which was the largest and economically most important town in this Duchy. And the assembly for Holstein was not held in the leading administrative centre and university town of Kiel in that Duchy, but in the sleepier town of Itzehoe. The assemblies within the Kingdom of Denmark were abolished after the fall of Danish Absolutism in 1848. Those in the Duchies, however, continued to exist after 1848 and their powers were extended.

But this decentralisation was the exception. When Absolutism was abolished in 1848 and a free constitution for the Danish Kingdom was passed in the following year, *Rigsdagen* (the Parliament) was located as a matter of course in Copenhagen. During the 1850s several futile attempts to create a constitution encompassing the whole Danish empire and not just the Kingdom of Denmark were made. *Rigsrådet* (i.e. a parliament comprising the Kingdom of Denmark and the Duchies of Schleswig, Holstein and Lauenburg) was located in Copenhagen but never had the chance to operate as was intended because of the intransigent antagonisms between the Danish and the German nationalities within the empire.

The defeat in the war of 1864 and the subsequent cession of the Duchies of Schleswig and Holstein meant that Denmark became a Danish nation-state – even though the empire still included the territories of Iceland, the Faroe Islands, Greenland and the West Indian islands, large in area but small in population. The Kingdom of Denmark was then to a large extent identical with the Danish state or the Danish empire if one prefers. This development reinforced even further the dominant position of Copenhagen in relation to the rest of the country. The historian Steen Bo Frandsen, mentioned previously, puts it like this:

The construction of a national economy placed Northern Jutland [i.e. the province of Jutland apart from Schleswig, MB] in the role of supplier of raw materials and of people for the expansion of Copenhagen. Denmark was organised completely on the terms of the capital city, and Copenhagen became even more, if possible, synonymous with the Danish state than be-

FIG. 3.

Copenhagen 1764.

fore (...) Everything of importance was placed in Copenhagen. Industrialisation strengthened the dominant position of the city (...).[22]

This development continued and was even hastened in the following century. The 20th century saw the development of a welfare state in Denmark which meant a huge expansion of the public sector both locally and nationally, including central administration which still had its seat in Copenhagen. The same applies to the rising number of semi-public institutions and organisations (e.g. trade unions and commercial organisations) as well as large companies who located their head offices in the capital city as the traditional political, financial, economic, cultural and administrative centre of Denmark.

Concluding remarks and perspectives

The question has been the historical background for present-day Copenhagen being so oversized (as has long been the case) in relation to the rest of Denmark. Historians have traditionally seen the reason as being either the privileges granted to Copenhageners in gratitude for their bravery and resolution during the Swedish siege 1658-1659, or the introduction of Absolutism in 1660 which led to the new regime expanding and concentrating nearly all political, administrative, financial, economic, cultural and military institutions in Copenhagen. Sometimes they may have seen the reason as being a combination of both events. The disastrous military defeat in 1864 after which Denmark became a small power has also been seen as a reason for Copenhagen's dominant position. Certainly, there is much to be said for all these expla-nations, they are not wrong, but they alone cannot be an exhaustive explanation. In this essay it has been argued that the dominant position Copenhagen still has today is due to the fact that the city used to be the capital, not of the present-day small state called Denmark, but of the much larger and more important Danish empire. Military, administrative, naval, cultural and commercial institutions used to be con-centrated there. In themselves these necessitated crew and manpower and all this led to an increased demand for goods and services, which again meant growth. Thus, a self-perpetuating process was started. This development took place before 1658-1660 (but was indeed later reinforced by those events). The 'military revolution' and the transition from 'domain state to tax state' have been considered important factors. Certainly, the empire shrank disastrously in 1658, fatally in 1814 and almost com-pletely in 1864. But still, in that period, the endeavours to centralise politically, ad-ministratively, culturally, militarily and commercially had indeed borne fruit. Thus, despite the fact that the empire was shrinking Copenhagen could still continue to grow disproportionately in relation to the rest of the country.

Many reminiscences of Copenhagen's former position as the capital of an em-pire can still be seen. The statistical, political and administrative reminiscences have all been mentioned earlier. So here, the focus will be on visible, physical localities in Copenhagen which reflect the former status as imperial capital. One of the many old churches in the centre of Copenhagen, the St. Petri Church, is, like most churches in Denmark, Lutheran – but this one is for a German-speaking congregation. And so it has always been, reflecting the fact that one-fifth of the inhabitants of Copenhagen used to be German-speaking, because the city was the capital of an empire in which a large proportion of the population (and not only in the Duchies of Holstein and Schleswig) had German as their native language. Beside the Christiansborg Castle, which is the seat of *Folketinget* (the Danish parliament), there is a beautiful renais-sance building from the age of King Christian IV called *Børsen* (the Exchange) built in 1619-1623 as a place for the interchange of goods imported by trading companies from various parts of the Danish empire as well as other parts of the world. Nearby is the *Proviantgården* (The Royal Provision Depot) which today houses part of the Danish National Archives and offices for *Folketinget*. Then there is the *Tøjhus* (Royal Armoury) which is today the Danish army museum. Both these buildings bear evi-dence of the transition from domain state to military-, tax-, or power state as a con-sequence of the military revolution that took place during the reign of King Christian

Fig. 4.

Copenhagen today. In the centre of the picture, The Parliament and The National Library.

IV. Their impressive size still reminds us of the fact that they functioned as central warehouses for the armed forces of the entire Danish empire, and not only the armed forces of the Kingdom of Denmark. The address of the Danish Ministry of Foreign Affairs is at *Asiatisk Plads* (Asiatic Square), the place where the cargoes of the company ships from Danish trade stations and colonies used to be discharged. The present-day Royal Cast Collection is in a building called *Vestindisk Pakhus* (West Indian Warehouse). Correspondingly, a popular, former working-class area near the harbour of Copenhagen is called *Islands Brygge* (the Icelandic Wharf). The Danish royal residence, the Amalienborg Palace, consists of a square with four identical palaces situated in *Frederikstaden* (Frederick's City). The middle of this square is ornamented by an equestrian statue of King Frederik V (king 1746-1766). The foundation stone was laid in 1760 to mark the 100th anniversary of the introduction of royal Absolutism. And the statue was donated by shareholders of *Asiatisk Kompagni* (the Danish Asia Company) to praise and thank the King for his wise rule of peace and prosperity which benefited colonial trade. Contrary to popular belief, the Amalienborg residence was not built as a royal residence from the start but as palaces for four different aristocrats to live in when they had court or government service in Copenhagen. It was not until after the Palace of Christiansborg burnt down in 1794 that Amalienborg became a royal residence.

Some might think the term 'the Danish empire' and the characterisation of Copenhagen as 'a capital of a former empire' rather misleading, e.g. in comparison to London and her status as the capital of a former worldwide empire. Indeed, the Danish empire was generally not based on conquest. The overseas possessions in Asia, Africa and the Caribbean, though prosperous for a period, were small in area and did not function as colonies for emigration and settlement to any large degree. During the period from 1870 till 1914, which in world historiography is known as 'The Age of Imperialism', the Danish empire had already begun to dismantle its overseas colonies and had no territorial aspirations whatsoever in other parts of the world. The core of the Danish empire was the Baltic area, Northern Europe and the North Atlantic, not overseas territories. For that reason, an obvious parallel between Copenhagen and the Danish empire should not be London and the worldwide British empire, but Vienna and the Central and Eastern European Habsburg (and formerly even German) empire. Both Copenhagen and Vienna are capitals demographically oversized in relation to the small states for which they are capitals but that is due to the fact that both used to be capitals of greater empires. Both Copenhagen and Vienna are situated disproportionately to the east in relation to the geography of their present-day states, indeed both can be considered border towns. Copenhagen is near the border to Sweden; Vienna is near Hungary, the Czech Republic, and Slovakia. But this geographical status is relatively new. The areas on the other side of Øresund were Danish provinces until 1658, while Hungary and Slovakia – together with many other areas – were part of the Austro-Hungarian Monarchy until 1918. Thus, present-day capitals Copenhagen and Vienna can be likened to a coat that is several sizes too big.

BIBLIOGRAPHY

Barfod, Jørgen H. 1995. *Christian 3.s flåde*. (Marinehistoriske Skrifter, 25). Copenhagen: Gyldendal.

Barfod, Jørgen H. 1997. *Niels Juels flåde*. (Marinehistoriske Skrifter, 27). Copenhagen: Marinehistorisk Selskab.

Bech, Sv. Cedergreen (ed.) 1980-1983. *Københavns historie*. Vol. 1-6. Copenhagen: Gyldendal.

Bregnsbo, Michael & Kurt Villads Jensen 2004. *Det danske imperium. Storhed og fald*. Copenhagen: Aschehoug.

Bruun, Carl 1890. *Kjøbenhavn. En illustreret Skildring af dets Historie, Mindesmærker og Institutioner*. Vol. 2. Copenhagen.

Degn, Ole & Erik Gøbel 1997. *Skuder og kompagnier (1588-1720). Dansk Søfarts Historie*. Vol. 2. Copenhagen: Gyldendal.

Elliot, J.H. 1992: 'A Europe of Composite Monarchies'. *Past and Present*, 137, pp. 48-71.

Feldbæk, Ole 1986. 'The Danish trading companies of the Seventeenth and Eighteenth centuries', *Scandinavian Economic History Review*, 34, pp. 204-18.

Feldbæk, Ole, 1997. *Storhandelens tid (1720-1814). Dansk Søfarts Historie*. Vol. 3. Copenhagen: Gyldendal.

Frandsen, Steen Bo 1996. *Opdagelsen af Jylland. Den regionale dimension i Danmarkshistorien 1814-64*. Aarhus: Aarhus Universitetsforlag.

Gustafsson, Harald 1994. 'Conglomerates or Unitary States? Integration Processes in Early Modern Denmark-Norway and Sweden'. In: T. Fröschl (ed.), *Föderationsmodelle und Unionsstrukturen. Über Staatenverbindungen in der frühen Neuzeit vom 15. zum 18. Jahrhundert*. Wien-München: Verlag für Geschichte und Politik, pp. 45-62.

Holm, Edvard 1886. *Danmark-Norges indre Historie under Enevælden fra 1660 til 1720*. Vol. 2. Copenhagen: Gad.

Jespersen, Knud J.V. 2004. *A History of Denmark*. Basingstoke, Hampshire: Palgrave Macmillan.

Kjersgaard, Erik 1987. 'Den gale ende af kikkerten'. In: *Politiken*, 21 February 1987.

Lind, Gunner 1987. 'Military and Absolutism: The Army Officers of Denmark-Norway as a Social Group and Political Factor, 1660-1848'. *Scandinavian Journal of History*, 12, pp. 221-43.

Mommsen, Ingwer Ernst 1996. 'Statistik des schleswig-holsteinischen Schiffsbestandes 1745-1865'. *Rundbrief des Arbeitskreises für Wirtschafts- und Sozialgeschichte Schleswig-Holsteins*. Vol. 66-67, no pages.

Petersen, E. Ladewig 1975. 'From Domain State to Tax State. Synthesis and Interpretation'. *Scandinavian Economic History Review*, 23, pp. 116-48.

Statistisch-Tabellarische Übersicht der Volks-Menge in den Königlichen-Dänischen Staaten. Beylage zu dem zweyten Theile der Materialien zur Dänischen Statistik 1787. Flensburg/Leipzig.

Statistisk Årbog 2004. Copenhagen: Statistics Denmark.

Statistiske Meddelelser 1911. Series IV. Vol. 37.1. Copenhagen: Statistics Department.

NOTES

1 These figures are published in *Statistiske Meddelelser* 1911.

2 The statistical figures are from 2003. *Statistisk Årbog* 2004, tables 38 and 42.

3 Bruun 1890, vol. 2, pp. 145-172. Holm 1886, vol. 2, pp. 394-411.

4 Kjersgaard 1987.

5 Frandsen 1996, pp. 582 ff.

6 Gustafsson 1994.

7 Elliot 1992.

8 Bregnsbo & Jensen 2004. The most recent general survey of the history of Denmark in the English language is: Jespersen 2004.

9 Bregnsbo & Jensen 2004. Jespersen 2004.

10 This theme about Copenhagen as a capital of the Danish empire which also includes part of Danish history is so huge that it will be impossible to make references to all relevant literature. Generally, references are made to the works already mentioned: Jespersen 2004 and Bregnsbo & Jensen 2004. And furthermore: Bech 1980-1983. Only if these works do not contain enough information about some of the topics mentioned will references to further literature be made.

11 Barfod 1995.

12 In the domain state the King's household and administration were financed by the incomes of the landed estates 'earmarked' for the crown, the defence based on noble cavalry, an army only raised in time of war and taxes were usually only imposed in times of war. In the tax, military or power-state the King's household and administration had expanded and had to be financed by taxation, the defence organisation consisted of a hired standing infantry army, the army was also kept in peacetime and taxation became a permanent phenomenon in times of war as well as in peacetime.

13 Petersen 1975.

14 Feldbæk 1986. Bregnsbo & Jensen 2004.

15 The numbers of inhabitants of the cities and towns within the Danish monarchy according to the census of 1769 are all published in: *Statistisch-Tabellarische Übersicht der Volks-Menge in den Königlichen-Dänischen Staaten. Beylage zu dem zweyten Theile der Materialien zur Dänischen Statistik* 1787.

16 Degn & Gøbel 1997, p. 48. Aarhus had the second largest part of the Danish merchant navy: 7 %!

17 Feldbæk 1997, pp. 14-16, 27.

18 Mommsen 1996, vol. 66, pp. 37-51, vol. 67, pp. 23-47.

19 The events of 1659 and 1660 are sometimes still used in Danish political discussions today, especially about the relations between the capital and the provinces. In 1987, the historian Erik Kjersgaard, then chief curator of the urban open-air museum *Den Gamle By* (The Old Town) in Aarhus publicly criticised – what he saw as – the pampered and self-pitying Copenhagen-centred attitude and pointed out how cultural institutions and public transport in

Copenhagen then received relatively higher proportions of government money than similar institutions in the provinces. According to Kjersgaard, Copenhagen and its inhabitants were 'married to the state' and did not care much about the cultural institutions of the city whereas the inhabitants in the rest of the country showed responsibility, commitment and support to their own institutions. The reason for this was according to Kjersgaard the privileges granted to the Copenhageners for their bravery during the siege 1658-1659 and with the introduction of Absolutism in 1660. Even though Absolutism had long since been abolished, the special position that Copenhagen enjoyed had, according to Kjersgaard, continued. Kjersgaard 1987.

20   Barfod 1997, pp. 9-40.

21   Lind 1987, pp. 222 f.

22   Frandsen 1996, p. 566. The translation into English is mine, MB.

Lars N. Henningsen

The towns of the Duchy of Schleswig, ca. 1700-1850
– A regional variant of Danish market town history

Introduction

The geographic borders of the Danish monarchy in the 18th century were not the same as in the present Kingdom of Denmark. Today, the part of the country called Sønderjylland or North Schleswig borders on Germany. In the west, the border is south of the town of Tønder, and in the east it is north of the town of Flensburg. This border was drawn through the old Duchy of Schleswig after a plebiscite in 1920.

Up until 1864, the territory of the Danish king went as far as the river Elbe. The Kingdom of Denmark had its southern border along the river Kongeåen. The border was south of the towns of Kolding and Ribe. South of this were the two Duchies of Schleswig and Holstein. Furthest to the south, between the Eider and the Elbe, was Holstein, and north of this was Schleswig or Sønderjylland. Both Duchies were ruled by the Danish king, but politically they were set apart from the Kingdom, and Holstein was even part of the German-Roman Empire (which was dissolved in 1806) and after that of The German League. Legislation and administration in the two Duchies were in many ways different from that of the Kingdom. Central administration and legislation were located in Copenhagen, but locally in the Duchies there were intermediate authorities between the towns and the central administration. Most important were the *statholder* (royal governor) and *Overretten* (the provincial government and the high court of justice), both based in the town of Schleswig. The *statholder* was the king's local deputy. He supervised the officials, the administration of justice, and especially the market towns. Between 1713 and 1834, *Overretten* was the supreme legal institution in the Duchy of Schleswig. As an intermediate administrative authority between the central authority in Copenhagen and the local authorities, *Overretten* dealt with matters concerning the judicial system, the church,

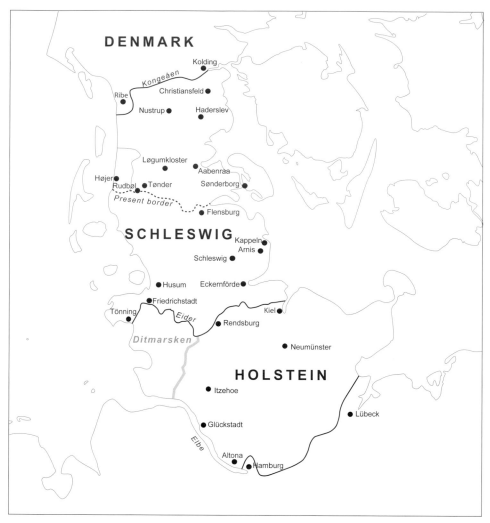

Fig. 1.

Map of Schleswig and Holstein showing the most important towns.

schools, poor relief, and public order. Kongeåen was a customs border. Products originating from the Duchies, however, were subject to a lower customs duty when brought into the Kingdom than products coming from further away.[1]

In a number of areas, town life in the Duchies differed from that of the Kingdom. The market towns were not supervised by the *amtmand* (the chief administrative officer of the county, prefect), but answered directly to the *statholder* and the central authorities in Copenhagen. The excise duty (consumption tax) called *konsumtion* did not apply south of Kongeåen. A limited degree of local administration was allowed to exist longer in the towns south of Kongeåen than in the Kingdom. The demands of central administration for supervision, control and ironing out of local differences were less manifest than in the Kingdom, but were still increasing in the 18th century.[2] Furthermore, in Schleswig there was a group of townships, the small market towns called *flækker,* which did not exist in the Kingdom. They were something in between regular villages and regular market towns. The *flækker* had been granted limited town rights. They were entitled to function as centres of trade and crafts and to arrange fairs. In contrast to the market towns, they were subject to the local *amtmand*. They did not constitute independent jurisdictions, and they had no magistrate as their local administrator.

In the following, we will limit the perspective to one of the two Duchies, namely Schleswig. For almost two centuries, up until 1713/21, Schleswig was divided between the Danish King and the Duke in Gottorp Castle in the town of Schleswig. This resulted in differences between the King's towns and those of the Duke's concerning legislation and trade connections. However, in 1721 the whole Duchy was united under the King. From then on, all the towns to a certain degree depended on the capital, Copenhagen, the administrative and economic centre of the monarchy. The geography of the Duchy of Schleswig permitted the emergence of a number of thriving towns with good opportunities for expansion in shipping and trade. Nearly every town was a port. Some were clustered to the west on the coast of the North Sea, and some to the east on the coast of the Baltic. Each was characterised by its geographical position.

The towns in west Schleswig were surrounded by fertile marshland with a considerable surplus of grain and especially cattle. The land was also suitable for the fattening of cattle and horses imported from the Kingdom. The towns were ideally positioned for trade connections to the south and west, to Hamburg and the Netherlands. Agricultural products from the town hinterlands and cattle and horses from Denmark were in demand on this market to the south which had great purchasing power. The only problem lay in the navigational conditions and harbour facilities of the towns. Large ships could not enter the ports. But even so, the west coast towns managed to have considerable transit trade with goods from the south and west to the middle of Schleswig and its east coast.

The towns of the east coast had better transport conditions. Only Haderslev in the north and the town of Schleswig in the south did not have adequate harbours. All the others, Eckernförde, Flensburg, Sønderborg, and Aabenraa, were situated with good natural harbours on bays or firths which went a good distance into the land. They were ideal bases for sailing on the Baltic with its good access to important raw materials that were wanted in Western and Southern Europe. Around and behind the towns was fertile moraine country with many farms and manors – with considerable cattle breeding, dairy farming, and grain production. The farmers of the surrounding area supplied goods to be exported by the town merchants and bought goods imported to the towns from the outside areas. The natural connections of the east coast towns were to the east and north.

The middle of Schleswig was characterised by poor land in comparison with the extremely rich marshlands to the west and the fertile agricultural areas to the east. No real towns arose here. The middle of the area was the natural hinterland of the coast towns, as a supplier of agricultural goods and articles of domestic industry as well as a buyer of goods from the towns.[3]

All in all, Schleswig, thanks to its location, had a good starting point for town development. Schleswig acquired a very dominant position in the Danish town landscape. Gauged by the number of inhabitants, the towns of Schleswig were among the largest Danish market towns.

TABLE 1.

Number of inhabitants of the Kingdom of Denmark and the Duchies of Schleswig and Holstein 1769 and 1801/03.[4]

	1769	1801/03
The Kingdom of Denmark	815,000	926,000
Schleswig	243,605	276,000
Holstein	279,000	326,000

TABLE 2.

Largest towns of the Kingdom of Denmark and the Duchies of Schleswig and Holstein 1801/03.

Copenhagen	Denmark	100,975
Altona	Holstein	23,085
Flensburg	Schleswig	10,666

LARS N. HENNINGSEN

Schleswig	*Schleswig*	*7,823*
Rendsburg	*Holstein*	*7,573*
Kiel	*Holstein*	*7,075*
Odense	*Denmark*	*5,782*
Aalborg	*Denmark*	*5,579*
Elsinore	*Denmark*	*5,282*
Glückstadt	*Holstein*	*5,178*
Randers	*Denmark*	*4,562*
Aarhus	*Denmark*	*4,102*
Husum	*Schleswig*	*3,658*
Haderslev	*Schleswig*	*3,635*
Fredericia	*Denmark*	*3,474*
Preetz	*Holstein*	*3,060*
Eckernförde	*Schleswig*	*2,921*
Aabenraa	*Schleswig*	*2,834*
Sønderborg	*Schleswig*	*2,761*
Tønder	*Schleswig*	*2,579*

Market towns between shipping and land trade

The ports of the east coast prospered in the 18th century. Among other things, they thrived on import of goods from the Baltic area – building timber, iron, lime, tar, flax, grain etc., and they supplied the surrounding area with these goods all the way to the west coast which lacked trees of its own.

Flensburg, 'the quite large, rich, and beautiful trade town', had the best hinterland. 'The people from the country would rather travel the long way to Flensburg than to other Schleswig towns to sell and buy what they need', it was said in 1799. Most of Northern Schleswig and great parts of South Schleswig, even Ditmarsken in Western Holstein, were both customer and supplier to Flensburg, and the merchants of Flensburg were wholesalers for their colleagues in North Schleswig. Flensburg's large trading firms supplied flax, salt, lime, iron, timber, groceries, and wine to the extensive surrounding area. Traders from Flensburg were often in the majority at the markets in the neighbouring towns to the north. Not unreasonably, the neighbouring towns complained incessantly about the overwhelming competition from Flensburg. Almost half of the total imports to the Duchy of Schleswig in 1765 were via Flensburg – consisting of 80 % of the imports from France, 75 % from Courland, Livonia and Russia, and about 60 % of the Swedish goods.[5]

On the west coast, the towns' sea trade was declining in the 18th century. Harbours that were beginning to fill up with sand were a problem in Husum, Friedrichstadt and Tönning. In Tønder, the building of dikes had long since blocked direct connection to the sea, and the goods had to be shipped instead from the small market town of Højer and the hamlet of Rudbøl. However this did not stop Tønder and Husum from having large-scale trade with Hamburg, Altona and the Netherlands both by land and sea. The imported groceries and especially tobacco were sent on even further, to the east coast. The export trade with grain, butter and cheese and with oxen and horses from the Duchy of Schleswig and Jutland provided a good income in the three biggest towns on the west coast. More than half the total exports from Schleswig went via Tönning, Husum, and Friedrichstadt, especially to Hamburg, Altona and the Netherlands. But things went a little slower in Friedrichstadt. This town had not existed, like the others, since the Middle Ages. It had been founded in 1621 by Duke Friedrich III of Gottorp, and had been populated by religious refugees summoned from the Netherlands. Given religious freedom and trade economic privileges, they were meant to establish widespread trade with France, Algeria, Spain, Portugal, and Persia. The town never achieved this sort of super-regional importance, and it never succeeded in gaining a greater surrounding area in competition with the neighbouring towns.

The towns' turnover would have been impossible without shipping, and the towns of Schleswig were well-developed when it came to matters of the sea. In 1699, the relatively small Duchy had a tonnage about half the size of that of the Kingdom. After Copenhagen, Altona in Holstein, and a number of Norwegian towns, the three towns Aabenraa, Flensburg, and Sønderborg, were easily the leading ports of the entire Danish monarchy.

LARS N. HENNINGSEN

TABLE 3.

Shipping tonnage in the Kingdom of Denmark and the Duchies of Schleswig and Holstein 1782/83 –
1800/06.[6] Shown in kommercelæster.[7]

	1782/83	1800/06
Copenhagen	28,770	25,791
The rest of the Kingdom[8]	8,133	12,325
Holstein	16,313	18,630
- of this Altona	14,209	12,456
Schleswig	14,000	27,707
- of this Flensburg	7,047	15,456
- Sønderborg	1,784	2,497
- Aabenraa	2,148	2,106

Aabenraa, Sønderborg, Flensburg, and Eckernförde together accounted for three-quarters of Schleswig's tonnage. A steady flow of smaller ships sailed from these towns to the Kingdom of Denmark and back. Especially Copenhagen's insatiable need for goods demanded many a shipload of grain, pork, firewood, bricks or textiles from the cottage industries of the Duchy of Schleswig. The towns' largest ships sailed on the Baltic, to Norway or to England, and got the basic materials for the domestic trade. Especially the ships from Aabenraa for a long period specialised in a triangular trade between Sweden, Norway, and England – until the Swedish protective legislation following 1724 transferred the export of lumber to Swedish ships. Many ships from the main town of Flensburg sailed all the way to France and brought home wine, plums, sugar or salt to be sold at home or in the Baltic region.

Transport of goods belonging to domestic ship owners and merchants, however, is not enough to explain the volume of shipping from Schleswig and Holstein in comparison with the Kingdom. The largest ports were also centres of carrying trade. In the years 1726-30, Copenhagen had a monopoly on the import of salt, tobacco, wine and foreign spirits. From 1742, all imports which did not come directly from the country of origin and on board Danish ships were highly taxed. That was a serious obstacle to trade between Schleswig's towns and Denmark. Flensburg in particular felt the blow, but other towns too complained continuously about 'the banning of

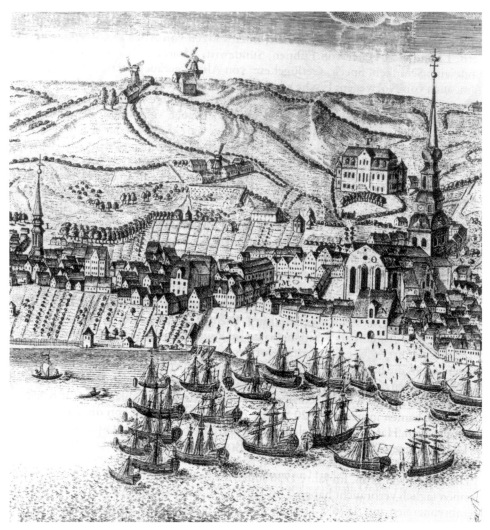

FIG. 2.

The central part of the harbour in Schleswig's largest town, Flensburg, in 1800. Drawing by G.G. End-
ner. The picture illustrates central elements of town economy at that time. The ships are tightly packed
in the harbour – above the quay lies the main street with large merchant houses and warehouses. This
is the background for the leading role of Flensburg and the Schleswig towns among the market towns
in Denmark: in part the shipping trade in Denmark and most of Europe and the Danish West Indies,
and in part merchant trade across the whole of Schleswig and large parts of Denmark – with contacts
in Europe – created a flourishing town life with work for constantly more people. There was a wider
horizon in the Schleswig towns than in most of the towns in the Kingdom.

trade with Denmark'. That meant that the sea trade of Schleswig's towns could not be based on the sale of their own or imported goods in the Kingdom. Instead, the ships began to engage in carrying trade for foreign or Danish customers. This was done so successfully that in the 18th century the Duchies were home to a sea trade hitherto unknown in the provincial towns of the Kingdom.

As early as the 1720s, ships from Schleswig were frequently used by ship owners in Copenhagen for carrying trade in the North Atlantic and between Sweden, the Netherlands, France, and the capital. In 1745, Copenhagen received 36 of its 128 shiploads from Norway on ships registered in Aabenraa and Sønderborg, and in the same year, 120 loads arrived from abroad on ships from Schleswig. Danish provincial ships accounted for only 36 loads. From Flensburg, the ships engaged in carrying trade between the Baltic and Western Europe – in combination with the transportation of goods at the owners' own expense. That gave progress – even in the otherwise quiet years of 1720-1740. In Eckernförde, the tonnage rose from 277 *kommercelæster* in 1720 to 597 in 1740, and a similar growth was experienced in Aabenraa. Here in particular, the growth was noticeable. In 1721, the population of Aabenraa was about 1,250, and the tonnage a little under 1,200 *kommercelæster*. Up until about 1750, the population increased to a little over 3,000 inhabitants and tonnage to about 4,300 *kommercelæster* – overtaking the hitherto most important town of Flensburg. The background for this was extensive trade with Sweden, Iceland, and England.[9]

But that was only the beginning. As late as the 1730s, the fear of falling into the hands of privateers from North Africa kept most ships away from Southern Europe. This improved when treaties from 1746 with the Muslim countries in North Africa and Turkey protected Danish ships when sailing on the southern seas. This newly found security was taken advantage of during the European wars in the years 1740-48. The freight rates increased for sailing with Baltic goods to France, Portugal and the Mediterranean and back to Northern Europe with groceries and salt. That meant that more people wanted to try their luck on the long routes. And that in turn caused a rise in shipbuilding in Flensburg, along the firth of Flensburg, in Eckernförde, and in the shipyards of other towns. The ships from the Dutchies and Denmark were employed on the route from the Baltic to the Mediterranean by merchants from the Baltic towns, Hamburg, the Netherlands, England, France and Southern Europe. The tonnage in the Duchies grew. In 1736, in the whole of Schleswig, there were about 250 ships over 5 *kommercelæster*. In 1745, the number was 384, a large increase.

The next period of prosperity was during the wars from 1755/56 to 1763. For a short time, ships under neutral, Danish flags could work almost without competition in freight trade to Southern Europe and into the Mediterranean. Investors who were willing to run a risk, merchants, high-ranking officials, and finally also a few prosperous farmers, invested in large ships which were employed on the lucrative routes. Flensburg's tonnage grew from 2,428 *kommercelæster* in 1754 to 4,058 *kommercelæster* in 1765. 'Freight money is a steady and nice income', said the successful ship owner Friedrich Wilhelm Otte in Eckernförde. In those years, he created Denmark's largest privately owned shipping company with about 25 ships of approximately 1,200 *kommercelæster*. That was more than the combined total of all the ships in Odense and Aarhus. He had been quick to take advantage of the opportunities that lay in the Mediterranean routes.[10]

But progress was greatly influenced by market trends. In 1763, the last year of the war, a vicar from Nustrup, Johan Arndt Dyssel, on a journey through Aabenraa noticed 'very good trade at more than a hundred ships, among which many are very large, sailing to Norway, England, France, Spain, and into the Mediterranean. Especially the uncertain times lately have given them good trade, since the Danish flag has stayed clear and secure'. In the following year, a very different tone was used in another report, 'After the war, sea trade looks bleak again. The warring nations as well as the others need no foreign ships now. Most want to do their trade themselves. Most of the summer of this year, 1764, 10 of the largest ships, accounting for a capital of 60,000 *mark* or more, have stayed at home thus making no profit, and a large proportion of those that have been at sea have lost more than they have earned'.[11] Dependency on international trade conditions rather than on domestic turnover of goods is characteristic of the Duchies' sea trade. European trade of this kind was a rare exception in the provincial towns of the Kingdom in this period. That was a special feature of town life in Schleswig.

Trade and sea trade divided the towns of Schleswig into two groups: To the east there were sea ports that were dependent on international trade and shipping conditions and therefore characterised by sharp rises and falls in income. To the west were towns with inferior port facilities which did not have the advantages of shipping. Here the towns had to concentrate partly on export of agricultural products from the surrounding area, cattle and horses brought in from the Kingdom, and partly on imports from the Netherlands and Northern Germany for their local markets. This too brought prosperity, but it did not allow for the dynamic development to be seen in the east. That is why there are many reports of stagnation in the towns on the west coast.

The merchants – the towns' upper class

It is clear that there were merchants of stature in many towns of Schleswig in the 18th century. Economically and socially, they took the lead. This is confirmed by the capital and trade tax of 2 % that was introduced in 1743.[12] This clearly documents that the merchants were of great importance in the towns of Schleswig.

The greatest wealth was in Flensburg. The merchants here accounted for 14 % of the tax payers. But they owned 77 % of the wealth. The equivalent percentage of wealth was 86 % in Tønder – the dealers in cattle, grain, and lace were rich. In the trading town of Haderslev, with the large and wealthy surrounding area, the merchants, being 7 % of the population, owned more than 55 % of the wealth. In Aabenraa and Sønderborg there were many sailors and fewer traders, accounting for 10 and 5 % of the population. But here too the trade capital was also considerable – 44 % in Aabenraa and 28 % in Sønderborg.

Versatility was the trademark of the great merchants. Merchant Jacob Schwennesen in Aabenraa was typical for the period between 1730 and 1770. From the people of the surrounding area, he bought meat and butter, cheese, bricks,[13] firewood and thousands of yards of homemade linen. The goods were usually shipped to Norway, Copenhagen or perhaps provincial ports of the Kingdom. Schwennesen leased the right to supply beer and spirits to the surrounding area, and he sold imported goods from the Baltic region all the way to the west coast.[14] The assortment of his colleague in Haderslev, Peter Raben, was the same until 1774 and the merchant also acted as a bank for his customers. At the time of his death, Raben had amassed more than 400 debenture loans, lent to citizens and farmers in the surrounding districts – amounting to a total of 32,000 rdl.[15]

Both merchants also made investments in ship's shares. All the merchants in the thriving ports of Schleswig did this. This was done on the basis of partnerships in order to share the risk, and the good trade conditions in 1740-48 and 1756-63 made it possible to increase one's commitment quickly. Only in Eckernförde were there shipping companies in the modern sense, owned by one or a few owners. In Aabenraa, merchant shipmasters often entered into ever-changing partnerships. In Sønderborg a very large group of people were underwriters of the ships, also country people. In the largest port, Flensburg, the many ships were financed by various merchant partnerships. Extremely wealthy business firms could easily own shares in 20 ships. The trade with many different kinds of goods, sea trade on one's own account, and carrying trade were interwoven. A very large part of the population

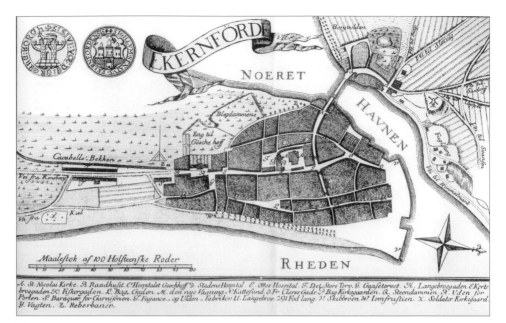

Beneath the figure, text inside the image reads:

Maaleſiok af 100 Holſteenſke Roder

RHEDEN

A. St. Nicolai Kirke. B. Raadhuſet. C.Hoſpitalet Goschhoff D. Stadens Hospital. E. Ottes Hospital. F. Det Store Torv. G. Gaaſetorvet. H. Langebroegaden E.Kort broegaden K. Fiſkergaden. L. Bag. Gaden. M. den nye Vaaning. N. Kattefund. O Fr Clares Gade. P. Bag Kirkegaarden. Q. Steendammen. R. Uden for Porten. S. Baraquer for Gurniſonen. T. Fayance - og Ulden - Fabriken. U. Langebroe 291 Fod lang. V. Skibbroen W. Iomfruſtien. X. Soldater Kirkegaard. Y. Vagten. Z. Reberbaner.

FIG. 3.

The ground-plan of the market town Eckernförde in 1768. On the plan the most important elements in the trade of the town can be seen. To the right, the deep, safe harbour, the prerequisite for the town's trade and shipping. Here too lay the shipyards and ropewalks (Z). Beside the church in the middle of the picture (A) the town's most important man, merchant, ship owner and factory owner, Friedrich Wilhelm Otte, had his large complex of buildings with residence, offices and warehouses. To the left in the picture, at the main road towards Rendsburg-Kiel, is Otte's two large factory buildings (T), at the top the textile factory and at the bottom the faience factory.

of the ports of the east coast depended on sea trade, as sailors, traders, craftsmen and investors.[16]

Basic goods such as flax, salt, lumber and iron were of great importance. The textile trade was also important. Woollen garments and homespun were produced on the west coast, in the middle of the area, woollen hats and socks were made, and almost everywhere flax or tow cloth. Some of these were traded, often through merchants who provided the raw materials and sold the goods. Some were exported to the Kingdom. But there was also a significant demand for foreign textiles. Almost all of these came from the south. A few merchants attended the fairs in Braunschweig or Leipzig or imported goods directly from Silesia, Westphalia, Brabant or other textile centres. Much of it came from merchants and traders in Hamburg, Altona and

Lübeck. In Flensburg, Husum and other towns, they had their warehouses, and they visited the annual fairs of Flensburg where merchants from most parts of Schleswig did business. Several large Flensburg business firms specialised in trade with textiles, directly or as wholesalers for merchants in the neighbouring towns to the north.[17] They depended greatly on deliveries and credit from the wholesalers of Altona and Hamburg.

Craftsmen and markets

The traffic at sea was important. But the craftsmen still constituted the largest proportion of the towns' citizens. In Husum it was calculated that they accounted for 51 % of the population in 1769, and the situation was similar in other towns. Tailors, shoemakers and bakers usually accounted for the major part.[18]

The guild rules regulated the crafts in detail. In the small towns, many of the craftsmen were not organised in guilds, or they were members of guilds in the larger towns. The hatters in Aabenraa were members of the guild in Itzehoe in Holstein about 200 kilometres away. Some guilds were closed, i.e. they only allowed a certain number of *amtsmestre* ('office-holding masters') who of course tried by all means to hold on to their privileges and prevent the admission of the *frimestre* ('free masters') from outside the closed guild. This rigid structure often caused friction between the craftsmen on the one hand, and on the other hand the state, the town or the traders who wanted a more liberal and flexible adjustment of supply and demand. Trade in Flensburg, for example, created a great demand for wooden barrels, and the demand changed with the fluctuations in business. But the coopers' guild was a closed guild, and the seven *amtsmestre* and their assistants could not always meet the demand when there was a rise in business. When trade was booming, the merchants would often complain about the lack of barrels, but the guild masters were reluctant to give a share of the work to new people. Only under especially good circumstances, as for example around 1780, was the number of *amtsmestre* increased.[19] A liberalisation of the guild system as such did not occur until the beginning of the following century.

The craftsmen in the towns were also struggling against the craftsmen in the country. In 1711, several decrees in both Duchies forbade trade and the hiring of craftsmen within a radius of 3 Danish miles (of 7.5 km) from a market town except for wheelwrights, blacksmiths, tailors and shoemakers. In the marshlands to the west where

FIG. 4A-B.

Schleswig had an extensive production of textiles. Weavers in the market towns and in the country districts made large amounts of linen. Some of the production was financed by the town merchants. Large quantities were sold at the fairs or exported directly to Denmark, often by sea. The picture shows two linen samples which a citizen in Aabenraa sent to the administration in 1765 with an offer to supply large quantities of linen to the armed forces.

the roads were often flooded and the connection between towns and countryside was especially problematic, the limit was two Danish miles. Authorised country craftsmen were only allowed to work in their own parish and were not allowed to attend the annual fairs. Unauthorised craftsmen and traders had to settle in a town.[20]

Locally, these ordinances were followed by special rules. In Haderslev the 'forbidden districts' were meticulously described in 1744. Within three Danish miles of

the town, no peasant was allowed to trade farming products, and the major share of the products had to be acquired in the towns. Outside this border, the rights to deliver foodstuffs and small commodities and beer and spirits to inns and parties were leased out, usually to town merchants. They leased the inns in the areas surrounding the town and thus had the right to sell foodstuffs and small commodities, wine and spirits in the district. Brewing and spirit distillation were the most important trade of many citizens, and by leasing inns and small shops in the countryside, the citizens tried to secure trade with the surrounding area.[21] But the legal provisions were usually ignored. In numerous complaints, the towns tried to stop wandering hawkers, illegal brewing, distilling, trade and craftsmanship in the country.

The craftsmen worked for the local consumers – but not only these. Many craftsmen also worked for an unknown foreign market. In Flensburg the button makers received orders for thousands of buttons for military uniforms, and weavers and people doing handicrafts also supplied the military with many items, often through the textile merchants of the town. In the 1750s, the weavers of Haderslev were able to send shiploads of tens of thousands of *alen*[22] of linen and drill to Copenhagen. The craftsmen or their wives attended fairs in Jutland and on the islands of Denmark[23] – in this way, the economy of each town depended on the world around it, whether near or far.

The fairs were important in the turnover of goods. Each town had two to three fairs annually which attracted traders from near and far. Many traders came to Northern Schleswig from Jutland and Funen, but further to the south, traders from the south were in the majority, especially from Hamburg and Altona or sometimes Lübeck and Bremen. Travelling Jewish traders and representatives for merchants in the large towns to the south were able to satisfy all demands for exotic merchandise.

Daily trade with consumer goods and foodstuffs was done at the weekly market days or at the towns' wharves and piers. Here, free trade was not allowed. Each town had its own methods to secure the goods at a reasonable price for the ordinary consumer and to protect the town against traders from the outside and large-scale trade. Market agendas determined the amount of turnover in order to fulfil the needs of the individual consumer. The bakers and ordinary citizens were allowed to buy foodstuffs for their own needs first, and after a certain hour, the merchants were allowed to buy larger quantities for trade. The grain that arrived at the harbour could not be sold until the municipal authorities had set a price, and traders were not allowed to buy until the ordinary households had had a chance to buy it. Any trade outside of the market was forbidden. The idea was clear, 'If the strongest people were allowed to buy everything by offering higher prices, the poor and weak people would never be able to buy anything', as it was said in Flensburg in 1783.[24]

Bread was a basic food for everyone, and in years with a scarcity of grain, it was often impossible for ordinary people to pay for it. Therefore, the bakers were subject to strict supervision. The municipal corporation of each town decreed how much a loaf of bread was to weigh, depending on the price of grain.

Protoindustry

Industry needs funding, and therefore merchants were part of many of the first 'industries'. Mills were the oldest industries. The copper mill near Flensburg stemmed from around 1612 under King Christian IV, and since 1632 it had been owned by merchants in Flensburg. From 1687 the mill benefited from the banning of the export of old copper and brass from Schleswig and the import of new copper and brassware. Employment at the mill in the 18th century was around 20 people on average.

In 1735 *Kommercekollegiet*[25] was founded in Copenhagen, and all other local authorities at that time were asked to send reports about manufactories and factories and suggest ways to help them prosper.[26] Most of them had nothing to answer. In Haderslev, there was a report about a Silesian who produced coarse cloth; in Aabenraa a discharged cavalryman who produced canvas was mentioned. In Flensburg there was a starch and powder factory and a paper mill. In Friedrichstadt there was an oil mill, and fabric was produced from wool and silk. But they were all small operations, craftsmanship rather than industry.

Not until the 1750s was there more of interest to mention. At that time, the concept of 'industry' was discussed, and free capital was invested in the hopes of making a profit. Faience was the latest new item, a fashionable commodity with prestige. In 1755 a duke, a baron and some citizens started a faience factory in the town of Schleswig in cooperation with the Otte family, wealthy ship owners and merchants from Eckernförde. The first sugar refineries were established in Schleswig in the following years, in Flensburg, Husum and Friedrichstadt, after establishment of these outside of Copenhagen was allowed.

Most important were the many attempts to start textile businesses. In the town of Schleswig nobility and citizens founded a subsidised factory in 1755 producing lace thread, and in the following year production of luxury linen was attempted. In Eckernförde, the Otte family was especially successful. In 1761/62 a large woollen manufactory was built, where different sorts of woollen fabrics, caps and socks were produced on 32 looms.

The accounts of the early 'manufactories' and 'factories' in the sources are quite long. But the words are misleading. These were not industries in the modern sense. In Eckernförde the wealthy merchants could pay for the construction of large central production premises for 30 weavers and about 80 textile workers as well as 80 employees in the faience manufactory. Such large premises, however, were the exception. In most cases, the work was done de-centrally in the 'putting out system' almost like a cottage industry. The yarn was spun by hundreds of home spinners and the weavers often worked individually or a few together as independent artisans, sometimes with the 'putter-out-cum-merchant' as the link between them. Large centralised enterprises did not come until the end of the century.[27]

The industrial experiments often had a social dimension. In 1762, the Otte merchant family in Eckernförde suggested that all the poor who got poor relief should spin yarn for the family firms – or lose their relief. Such ideas were welcome in government circles and, on the instructions of the central administration, many towns had to start establishing spinning mills to be manned by the poor.[28] The results must be said to have been less than impressive – but the experiment of using poor people in the textile industry was repeated time and again later in the century. Spinning and weaving was done in the prisons in Glückstadt, Neumünster, Rendsburg and Flensburg, and caps, homespun, horse blankets or fine cloth from these places made up a considerable proportion of the textile trader's compulsory trade in domestic goods.

There were many experiments – and many failures, because capital and the market were limited. Sale of the expensive textiles and faience from the businesses in Schleswig and Eckernförde was difficult, even though the state tried to help by banning imports and reducing duties. That type of artificial business disappeared when the supply of capital from the merchant-manufacturer or the state failed to materialise. Only the more everyday goods could be sold. The lace-thread factories in Schleswig town, Tønder and the *flække* Løgumkloster also had some sales to the many lacemakers in Tønder and Haderslev counties. Tobacco was twisted in most towns. The sugar refinery in Flensburg too and the hundreds of distilleries also had large turnovers in the Duchies and in Norway. But otherwise, manufacture and the so-called factories were on a weak footing throughout the 18th century. Not 'industry', but shipping and trade were the capital-creating businesses in the towns.

Municipal government

Municipal government differed considerably from town to town. In each town, a small group of so-called *deputerede borgere* (delegated citizens) formed a type of local authority representation for the citizens. The number varied: 12 in Aabenraa and Schleswig, 16 in Haderslev, Sønderborg and Tønder, 24 in Flensburg. They participated in tax assessment and endorsed the town accounts, and they held, in turn, the function of town treasurer or accountant for the poor relief fund. People from the same circle filled the other honorary offices in the town, for example as church warden or hospital superintendent. The 4-6 aldermen with one or more mayors constituted the *magistrat*, the municipal corporation proper. They made up the *rådstueret* (the town court), and like the mayors held office for life.

Well-to-do craftsmen could get a place in the ranks of the *deputerede borgere*, but merchants were in the majority and the merchants had almost a monopoly on the places in the municipal corporation. Close family ties linked the aldermen and the delegated citizens – not just within each town, but also between the towns. In many places the post of mayor was held by the wealthiest merchant until well into the 18th century, and this was an advantage because all the posts in the municipal corporation were in principle honorary posts, only rewarded with perquisites or considerable tax reductions. These posts could be a burden for busy businessmen, and time after time, wealthy merchants tried to buy freedom from this civic duty.

The municipal corporation had democratic elements. For example, all the house-owners in Haderslev on several occasions elected the mayor by direct, written vote. However, the aristocratic features were more characteristic. The aldermen originally co-opted members from the ranks of the delegated citizens and perhaps elected the mayor, possibly in accordance with a proposal from the delegated. The aldermen also elected new delegated citizens in accordance with proposals from the other delegated citizens or they co-opted members.[29]

However self-government was limited. At the end of the 17th century, the broad body of citizens in nearly all the towns objected to being governed by the council aristocrats and their administration of the tax and accounts system, and the state intervened.[30] This resulted in a strengthening of the broad body of citizens represented by the delegated citizens in relation to the municipal corporation, and in particular a gradual increase in the standardising influence of the state at the expense of local self-government. Election of aldermen or mayor had to have the King's approval. Time after time there was conflict between a town and the state about the election of aldermen or mayor, and royal appointments became increasingly common in the 18th century. The towns' independent choice of public authorities was on the way to becoming a right of proposal – the approval and confirmation rested with the central administration, and not infrequently, the state pressed its candidate through against local wishes. One of the consequences was that university educated people gradually took over the mayoral post from the self-taught merchants. The citizens had to accept an increase in salary expenses, but municipal administration was still extremely small.

The typical wage bill for a moderately large market town at the beginning of the 18th century seldom included more than just the town clerk, priests, cantor, organist, poor relief beadle, police officer, watchmen and executioners.

Control from above was of many different kinds and growing: in the 1720s, the individual *amtmand* supervised the towns in his capacity as *bypræsident* (town president*)*, until *statholderen* (the governor) took over the job from 1731. In 1736, all the Schleswig town privileges were called in for revision. After 1741 the towns had to get the *statholder*'s permission to raise new loans. From 1756 the town accounts had to be sent in to the governor, from 1772 to *Rentekammeret* (the Exchequer) in Copenhagen.[31] The tendency is clear – although there is no question of a systematic standardisation or disregard of the local leadership, as was the case in the Kingdom. The governor in Gottorp Castle did not supervise the towns as closely as the *stiftamtmænd* (the county governors) north of Kongeåen. The towns of the Duchies continued with a multiplicity of rules until long into the following century.[32]

The development pattern of the individual towns 1700-1806

In the first sections, it has been emphasised that the large Schleswig towns were part of a close network with their surroundings through trade and shipping. More than many towns in the Kingdom, their economy was based on shipping and trade by sea. Because of this, they were extremely dependent on international market trends. In time, this dependence resulted in changes that can be seen in the population, shipping tonnage and the differing importance of the towns as local trading centres within Schleswig. The fluctuation was particularly evident in the ports on the east coast – the other towns were more stable.

The position of dominant regional centre and most important trading and shipping town was held by Flensburg in the time before and all through the 18th century and into the 19th century. Nevertheless, considerable shifts can be noted with regard to the order of precedence between the towns. In connection with the wars in Europe 1688-97 and in the years 1701-1709, the towns generally benefited from the neutrality of the Danish King and the Gottorp Duke. This meant a growth in shipping trade in the Schleswig towns. Skippers and ship owners from non-neutral areas moved to the neutral towns in order to continue their shipping trade from there. In the years from 1709 to 1713 the neutrality applied only to the Gottorp areas – this greatly benefited the towns of Aabenraa and Eckernförde.[33]

The shipping trade expanded after the peace agreement in 1721 and until the 1750s. While Flensburg stagnated, the other east-coast towns grew in these years.

They put ships at the disposal of merchants and companies in Copenhagen and their ships sailed to Sweden, especially Gotland and Kalmar. Aabenraa advanced by leaps and bounds during these years. The town had considerable immigration, the population grew from an estimated 1,250 in 1721 to about 3,000 in 1753, the fleet grew from 779 *kommercelæster* in 1705 to 1,109 *kommercelæster* in 1710. From 1729 to 1748, it was almost trebled (from 1,643 *kommercelæster* to 4,332 *kommercelæster*), and shipbuilding expanded. For a short period, Aabenraa was a larger shipping port than Flensburg. This was not so much due to trade through the town as to participation in voyages to Gotland/Sweden and England and carrying trade for companies and merchants in Copenhagen on voyages to Iceland, Finnmark and Northern Europe. Something similar occurred in Eckernförde. The tonnage doubled from 1720 to 1740. Sønderborg, too, enjoyed progress. Among the Schleswig towns, it held first place in the voyages to Copenhagen and Norway.[34]

Sweden endeavoured to encourage the country's own shipping with legislation from 1724, 1726 and 1744. Foreign ships were forbidden to import goods to Sweden other than those from their home lands or colonies, and export was reserved for Swedish ships. After this, the Schleswig ships had to find other routes. Nevertheless, the North Schleswig ports continued to grow and up to a point also Eckernförde in the following years, helped in particular by the war years 1740-48 and 1756-63. They all took part in the large European carrying trade. In the years 1747-71, a total of 949 sea passes were issued to ships from the three Schleswig towns, Flensburg, Aabenraa and Eckernförde, for voyages to the Mediterranean – all the provincial cities in the Kingdom of Denmark together had only 100 passes issued and Copenhagen 398.[35]

TABLE 4.

Passes issued to Danish ships sailing to the Mediterranean 1747-1807.[36]

	1747-1771	1778-1792	1793-1807
Copenhagen	398	699	1,192
Kingdom market towns	100	149	333
Flensburg	415	658	1,107
Aabenraa	296	288	268
Eckernförde	238	-	-
Sønderborg	-	94	120

The pattern changed at the end of the 1760s. From abroad came the effect of the European wars, the American War of Independence 1778-1783 and the revolutionary wars from 1792 until 1807. The wars resulted in increased freight rates and new opportunities for international shipping and trade. At home, the consequences of the agricultural reforms, price increases and a slight rise in the population could be felt. The trend can be seen in the population of the towns and the shipping tonnage. They show that growth was very unequally distributed. Flensburg distanced itself more and more from the other towns, both as a Northern European shipping town and as a trading centre in relation to the hinterland in the rest of the Duchy of Schleswig.

The towns on the west coast had only moderate growth. Only Tönning developed considerably. This was connected with the fact that after the 1784 opening of the new waterway, the Eider Canal, from Holtenau at Kiel over Rendsburg to Tönning, the town got an important position on this direct international waterway between the Baltic Sea and the North Sea. All ships had to call at Tönning to pay customs duty and a large warehouse was built in the town. Later the town enjoyed a short-lived feverish growth from 1803. The English blockade of the Elbe 1803-05 meant that for a short time Tönning became the most important port of call for ships to Hamburg and Altona, it became the intermediate port for goods to these two large towns. In 1803, the population was 1,923, in 1807 approximately 5,760. In the following years the town benefited from the illicit trade bypassing the continental blockade.[37]

Husum was handicapped by its bad navigational conditions and the few large ships from the town sailed from Altona. However, a considerable number of small vessels provided for the sea-borne connection to Altona, Hamburg and Holland. This and the very substantial trade in cattle and horses gave the basis for an increase in population from 1769 to 1803. Prosperity also characterised Tønder, the most northerly market town on the west coast of Schleswig. All sea-borne contact to the west went over the neighbouring loading places of Højer and Rudbøl. But the purchase of cattle in Schleswig and the Kingdom for fattening and resale still gave good profits. The many lace traders too, who financed the production and export of the expensive lace from the large hinterland around the town, brought considerable incomes, though without increasing the population of the town.

On the east coast, from the 1770s up until Denmark's entry into the wars on Napoleon's side in 1807, there was a clearer differentiation between the towns. Flensburg outstripped all the others.

Haderslev was handicapped by its bad harbour. The farmers of the hinterland preferred to go to Aabenraa and Flensburg. Strong competition came from the town Christiansfeld, founded in 1771 by a Herrnhuter community just north of the town. Christiansfeld had got full rights for trade and crafts and the town's skilled craftsmen and traders gave the old market town considerable competition. As a commercial town, Haderslev lost ground. However, there was some prosperity on the basis of the ordinary progress of the time, sales to the extensive hinterland and the many travellers through the town, the many civil servants in the town and a large military garrison. It was not until after 1830 when the sailing channel was deepened that use of the harbour in Haderslev increased.[38]

Aabenraa stagnated after 1763. Trade to Sweden and England was made difficult by the navigation legislation in the two countries. It is true that the Aabenraa skippers utilised the extraordinary war trading conditions in 1778-83 and 1792-1806, and Aabenraa ships sailed on the long routes from the Baltic to the Mediterranean. But the fleet was never again as large as in the 1750s, employment for sailors fell from about 450 in the 1740s to about 300 at the end of the century. The fleet stagnated at between 2,000 and 2,300 *kommercelæster* and the population was also unchanged (1769: 2,701, 1803: 2,834). The town's share of the shipping to the Mediterranean from the Duchies fell from 17 % during the period 1747-71 to 9 % in 1793-1807.[39]

In Sønderborg there was perhaps a little greater dynamism. The starting point was the good harbour, and its excellent situation in relation to trade and shipping to the Kingdom and the Baltic. Many small vessels provided for the sale of agricultural goods and bricks from and to an extensive hinterland. The ships from the town also took part in the large foreign trade. In 1778-1807 Sønderborg accounted for 4-5 % of the Mediterranean voyages from the Duchies. But here too, competition from Flensburg was strong.[40]

To the south-east, Eckernförde lost ground as a shipping town from the end of the 1760s. The surrounding area was limited and from 1784 the construction of the Eider Canal meant that the transit function of the town in relation to Rendsburg disappeared. The estates in the surrounding area preferred to sell their goods and get their supplies in Rendsburg and Kiel. The shipping tonnage in the town decreased, businesses were crafts and the production of beer, malt and spirits. Only the establishment of a state military nursing institution, *Christianspflegehaus*, with a population of about 400 people, gave some growth.

The government town of Schleswig did better and had solid growth almost at the level of Flensburg, from a population of 5,629 in 1769 to 7,823 in 1803 and a little over 11,000 in 1835-45. This was due neither to shipping nor trade in relation to the surrounding area, but chiefly to the status of the town as the administration and government town. The number of ships calling at the harbour increased it is true when the harbour facilities were improved between 1762 and 1783, but Schleswig still could not make its mark as a shipping town.[41]

Flensburg in the centre

From 1778 to 1806 growth was increasingly concentrated in Flensburg. The town on the fjord with its good situation in the middle of Schleswig became the dominant shipping and trading centre, surpassing all the other towns. In 1769 the population was registered as 6,842, in 1803 stated to be 10,666. In 1799 a population of perhaps 15,000 was mentioned, if the suburbs, hundreds of day labourers from the surrounding country and military personnel were included.

The rapid progress in these years is shown by an extract of details: In 1795 permission to build in the suburb of Neustadt was given and it was incorporated in the town. A total of 200 stills produced spirits for sale in the hinterland, Denmark and Norway and 4,000 horned cattle were fattened on the residue. Flensburg was the only town in Schleswig which in the understanding of the time could be called an 'industrial town'. The most important industries were five sugar refineries, 40 tobacco factories, two starch works, two soap factories and with them candle factories, several dye-works, tanneries, paper mills, shipyards, ropewalks and canvas factories. The markets in the town drew customers from most of Schleswig, and traders from Flensburg were much in evidence in the markets in the neighbouring towns. The tonnage boomed. From 126 ships of 3,986 *kommercelæster* in 1777, there were 302 ships of 15,456 *kommercelæster* in 1806. In the period 1747-71, Flensburg's share of shipping to the Mediterranean from the Duchies was 24 %, in the years 1793-1807, this increased to 36 %.[42]

The development patterns of the towns after the Napoleonic wars

The war years of 1807-14 left a clear mark. The towns without a lot of shipping were not particularly affected, but the shipping towns had to undergo a radical re-organisation. During the war, the total tonnage in Schleswig was reduced from 27,707 *kommercelæster* in 1806 to 13,547 in 1815. After the war, competition on the long

LARS N. HENNINGSEN

sailing routes increased and the important Mediterranean routes dwindled to almost nothing. The shipping towns almost had to start afresh and the town network looked different. The result was that Flensburg indeed continued to be the largest town in Schleswig, but the absolute dominance of the town in shipping and trade and as middleman for the rest of Schleswig was weakened. On the other hand, other towns became more assertive. Flensburg began to meet competition that had been unknown at the end of the 18th century. For the towns that had had extensive connections with Copenhagen, the weakening of the capital meant a recession. Instead, Hamburg-Altona was strengthened as middlemen for the towns in Schleswig and in a few years Kiel became as large as Flensburg.

Town growth was thus more evenly distributed than in the earlier years. This was also because from the 1830s agriculture experienced new growth after the agricultural crisis of the post-war years. This gradually had an effect on the towns. The greatest growth was in Haderslev. The town had no ships to speak of so it did not suffer losses from captures in the war years. The basic business in the town – trade and crafts – could continue unchanged after the war. In 1830 the harbour was repaired and this gave an opening for a shipyard, the construction of iron foundries and other industrial-type activities. Sales to the large surrounding area really began to grow. The population rose from 3,635 in 1803 to 6,156 in 1840. The town experienced the greatest percentage growth of all the towns in Schleswig.[43]

The governing centre of the area, Schleswig town, also grew, from a population of 7,823 in 1803 to 11,551 in 1845. This was due to increased sales and increased demand as a result of new government offices, newly built hospitals and the garrison.[44] Growth in the small harbour towns could also be seen. They benefited from the agricultural progress and the rising prosperity. This was the case for Kappeln and Arnæs, among others, on the east coast.

The greatest reorganisations were needed in the large shipping and trading towns. The fleets in all the east-coast towns that had been committed to long European voyages, which were very dependent on market conditions, were reduced to under the half. Important shipping areas – the Mediterranean and Norway – were dropped after the war and new goals had to be found. The Aabenraa shipping circles began to collaborate with ship owners in Hamburg on large ships that sailed in the carrying trade for outsiders, chiefly to South and Central America and later to China and India. In just a few years, the setback as a result of the war years was succeeded by new impressive progress. As early as 1824 the fleet had grown to pre-war size, in

1848, it was more than doubled to 4,776 *kommercelæster*. In the 1850s Aabenraa took first place among the shipping towns in Schleswig – ahead of Flensburg. The population rose from 2,834 in 1803 to 4,086 in 1845. This was an expansion just as remarkable as in the period 1721-1750.[45]

With this, it has already been said that Flensburg did not regain its old dominance from the flourishing pre-war period. The fleet of ships decreased to less than half. The town committed itself to a marked extent to shipping and trade with the Danish West Indies. For a short time, Flensburg here had an initial advantage over Copenhagen and towns in the Kingdom – but from the 1830s Flensburg lost ground in relation both to these towns and their much stronger colleagues in Hamburg. Inexorably Flensburg lost terrain as a shipping town and an almost international trading town. To an increasing extent, goods came directly from Hamburg, and Kiel in Holstein became a serious competitor. Other towns disengaged themselves from Flensburg as middleman. In the 1850s Flensburg's time as the main trading centre in Schleswig was beginning to be over. Of greater importance for the town were instead the many state authorities and their officials, which were domiciled in the town after the war of 1848-50.[46]

The growth after 1830 in this way was broader than in the period when Flensburg had been the undisputed main town – the years around 1800. This phase lasted until 1864 when Schleswig was separated from Denmark and shortly afterwards became part of the Kingdom of Prussia. This again entailed the need for radical reorganisation in the towns. A new phase in their interdependent development history had begun.

BIBLIOGRAPHY

Andersen, Dan H. 2000. The Danish Flag in the Mediterranean. Shipping and Trade, 1747-1807. (Ph.D. dissertation). University of Copenhagen.

Becker-Christensen, Henrik 1988. *Protektionisme og reformer 1660-1814. Dansk toldhistorie.* Vol. II. Copenhagen: Toldhistorisk Selskab.

Beiträge zur historischen Statistik Schleswig-Holsteins 1967. Kiel: Statistisches Landesamt Schleswig-Holstein.

Dyssel, Johan Arndt 1924-25. 'Iagttagelser paa en Rejse gennem Nordslesvig i 1763'. *Sønderjydsk Maanedsskrift*, pp. 171-73.

Fangel, Henrik 1975. *Haderslev bys historie 1800-1945.* Haderslev: Historisk Samfund for Sønderjylland; Institut for Sønderjysk Lokalhistorie.

Feldbæk, Ole 1982. *Tiden 1730-1814. Gyldendals Danmarkshistorie.* Vol. 4. Copenhagen: Gyldendal.

Gregersen, H.V. 1961. 'Tiden 1660 til 1720'. In: Johan Hvidtfeldt & Peter Kr. Iversen (eds.), *Aabenraa Bys Historie indtil 1720.* (Skrifter, udgivne af Historisk Samfund for Sønderjylland, 25). Aabenraa: Historisk Samfund for Sønderjylland, pp. 185-239.

Gregersen, H.V. 1967. 'Fra Kielerfreden til Treårskrigen'. In: Johan Hvidtfeldt & Peter Kr. Iversen (eds.), *Aabenraa Bys Historie II 1721-1864.* (Skrifter, udgivne af Historisk Samfund for Sønderjylland, 25). Aabenraa: Historisk Samfund for Sønderjylland, pp. 130-83.

Greve, Klaus 1987. *Zentrale Orte im Herzogtum Schleswig 1860.* (Studien zur Wirtschafts- und Sozialgeschichte Schleswig-Holsteins, 12). Neumünster: Wachholtz Verlag.

Grove-Stephensen, F.S. 1985. Skibsfarten i Slesvig 1750 med særlig henblik på Åbenrå, Sønderborg, Flensborg og Egernførde. (Unpublished manuscript). Flensburg: Arkivet ved Dansk Centralbibliotek for Sydslesvig.

Haase, Nicolai 1925. *Das Aufkommen des gewerblichen Grossbetriebs in Schleswig-Holstein.* (Quellen und Forschungen zur Geschichte Schleswig-Holsteins, XI.) Kiel: Gesellschaft für Schleswig-Holsteinische Geschichte.

Henningsen, Lars N. 1977. 'Byboere, landboere og brændevin'. *Sønderjysk Månedsskrift,* pp. 13-22.

Henningsen, Lars N. 1978. *Fattigvæsenet i de sønderjyske købstæder 1736-1841.* (Skrifter, udgivne af Historisk Samfund for Sønderjylland, 47). Aabenraa: Historisk Samfund for Sønderjylland.

Henningsen, Lars N. 1984. 'Lebensmittelversorgung und Markverhältnisse in Flensburg im 18. Jahrhundert'. In: *Flensburg 700 Jahre Stadt – eine Festschrift.* (Schriften der Gesellschaft für Flensburger Stadtgeschichte, 36,1). Flensburg: Stadt Flensburg, pp. 207-29.

Henningsen, Lars N. 1985. *Provinsmatadorer fra 1700-årene. Reder-, købmands- og fabrikantfamilien Otte i Ekernførde i økonomi og politik 1700-1770.* Flensburg: Studieafdelingen ved Dansk Centralbibliotek for Sydslesvig.

Henningsen, Lars N. 1989. 'Et 'flittigt og oeconomisk folk''. Tilvirkning og salg af tekstiler fra Nordøstslesvig i 1700-årene'. *Sønderjyske Årbøger,* pp. 127-66.

Henningsen, Lars N. 1990a. 'Købmand Jacob Schwennesen i Aabenraa'. *Sønderjysk Månedsskrift,* 1990, pp. 35-41.

Henningsen, Lars N. 1990b. 'Penge og ånd. Flensborg-købmanden Hans Feddersens vej til brødremenigheden'. *Sønderjyske Årbøger,* pp. 57-72.

Henningsen, Lars N. 1990c. 'Bødkersvendene i Flensborg'. *Sønderjysk Månedsskrift,* pp. 243-50.

Henningsen, Lars N. 1991. 'Slesvigs og Holstens administration'. In: Erik Alstrup & Poul Erik Olsen (eds.), *Dansk kulturhistorisk Opslagsværk.* Aarhus: Dansk Historisk Fællesforening, pp. 808-12.

Henningsen, Lars N. 1992. 'Handelsbyen Haderslev i 1700-årene – set fra købmand Peter Rabens krambod'. *Sønderjyske Årbøger,* pp. 53-72.

Henningsen, Lars N. 1998. 'Die Zusammenführung Schleswigs unter dänischer Herrschaft – Idee oder Realität'. In: H. Becker-Christensen & U. Lange (eds.), *Geschichte Schleswigs vom frühen Mittelalter bis 1920,* pp. 61-79. Aabenraa: Institut for Grænseregionsforskning.

Hjelholt, Holger 1942. 'Tidsrummet c. 1660-1805'. In: Vilh. la Cour (ed.), *Sønderjyllands Historie fremstillet for det danske Folk.* Vol. III. Copenhagen: Reitzel, pp. 155-484.

Hjelholt, Holger 1943. 'Tønder under Kongestyre 1713-1864'. In: M. Mackeprang (ed.), *Tønder gennem Tiderne*. (Skrifter, udgivne af Historisk Samfund for Sønderjylland, 3). Tønder.

Hvidtfeldt, Johan 1960. 'Tidsrummet 1667-1807'. In: Holger Hjelholt (ed.), *Sønderborg bys historie*. Vol. 1. Sønderborg: Dy-Po Bogforlag, pp. 97-210.

Hähnsen, F. 1923. *Die Entwicklung des ländlichen Handwerks in Schleswig-Holstein*. (Quellen und Forschungen zur Geschichte Schleswig-Holsteins, IX). Kiel.

Ibs, Jürgen H. 2004. *Historischer Atlas Schleswig-Holstein vom Mittelalter bis 1867*. Neumünster: Wachholtz Verlag.

Momsen, Ingwer Ernst 1969. *Die Bevölkerung der Stadt Husum von 1769 bis 1860. Versuch einer historischen Sozialtopographie*. (Schriften des Geographischen Instituts der Universität Kiel, 31). Kiel: Geographisches Institut der Universität.

Momsen, Ingwer Ernst 1978. 'Die Berichte über die wirtschaftlichen Verhältnisse in den Städten und Ämtern der Herzogtümer Schleswig und Holstein … 1735'. *Rundbrief des Arbeitskreises für Wirtschafts- und Sozialgeschichte Schleswig-Holsteins*, 2, pp. 30-35.

Momsen, Ingwer Ernst 1996. 'Statistik des schleswig-holsteinischen Schiffsbestandes 1745-1865'. *Rundbrief des Arbeitskreises für Wirtschafts- und Sozialgeschichte Schleswig-Holsteins*, 66, pp. 37-51, 67, pp. 23-47.

Møller, Anders Monrad 1981. *Fra galeoth til galease. Studier i de kongerigske provinsers søfart i det 18. århundrede*. Esbjerg: Fiskeri- og Søfartsmuseet.

Niemann, August 1799. *Handbuch der schleswig-holsteinischen Landeskunde. Topographischer Teil. Erster Band. Herzogthum Schleswig*. Schleswig.

Nørr, Erik & Jesper Thomassen (eds.) 2004. *Slesvig, Preussen, Danmark. Kilder til sønderjydsk forvaltningshistorie*. (Kilder til dansk forvaltningshistorie, 4). Copenhagen: Selskabet til Udgivelse af Kilder til Dansk Historie.

Pingel, Fiete 2003. 'Von der Ruhe des Nordens bis zum Staatsbankrott (1713-1813)'. In: *Geschichte Husums von den Anfängen bis zur Gegenwart*. (Schriften der Gesellschaft für Husumer Stadtgeschichte, 3). Husum.

Schröder, Johannes von 1837. *Topographie des Herzogthums Schleswig*. Schleswig.

Schütt, Hans-Friedrich 1966. 'Flensburg in der Zeit des Gesamtstaates'. In: *Flensburg Geschichte einer Grenzstadt*. (Schriften der Gesellschaft für Flensburger Stadtgeschichte, 17). Flensburg: Gesellschaft für Flensburger Stadtgeschichte, pp. 169-235.

Schütt, Hans-Friedrich 1971a. 'Apenrade'. In: Hans Friedrich Schütt (ed.), *Schiffahrt und Häfen von Tondern bis Brunsbüttel, von Hadersleben bis Schleswig*. Flensburg: August Westphalen, pp. 171-87.

Schütt, Hans-Friedrich 1971b. 'Flensburg, Segelschiffszeit'. In: Hans Friedrich Schütt (ed.), *Schiffahrt und Häfen von Tondern bis Brunsbüttel, von Hadersleben bis Schleswig*. Flensburg: August Westphalen, pp. 89-114.

Staeglich, Helmut 1989. 'Schleswig-Holsteinischer Kanal und Elbblockade'. In: *Tönning im Wandel der Zeiten*. Husum: Stadt Tönning.

Vaagt, Gerd 1966a. 'Kriegsjahre und liberale Strömungen'. In: *Flensburg Geschichte einer Grenzstadt*.

(Schriften der Gesellschaft für Flensburger Stadtgeschichte, 17). Flensburg: Gesellschaft für Flensburger Stadtgeschichte, pp. 235-300.

Vaagt, Gerd 1966b. 'Die Jahre der nationalen Auseinandersetzung'. In: *Flensburg Geschichte einer Grenzstadt*. (Schriften der Gesellschaft für Flensburger Stadtgeschichte, 17). Flensburg: Gesellschaft für Flensburger Stadtgeschichte, pp. 301-46.

Worsøe, Hans H. 1967. 'Tiden 1721-1814'. In: Johan Hvidtfeldt & Peter Kr. Iversen (eds.), *Aabenraa Bys Historie II 1721-1864*. (Skrifter, udgivne af Historisk Samfund for Sønderjylland, 25). Aabenraa: Historisk Samfund for Sønderjylland, pp. 5-130.

NOTES

1   Becker-Christensen 1988, pp. 219-50, 424-56, 500, 523.

2   Henningsen 1991, pp. 808-12.

3   Greve 1987. Ibs 2004.

4   Feldbæk 1982, p. 125. Beiträge 1967, pp. 9, 13-15. Haderslev: Fangel 1975, p. 18.

5   Niemann 1799, pp. 562-607. Hjelholt 1942, pp. 357-58, 447-50.

6   Momsen 1996. For the rest of the Kingdom, however, see Møller 1981, p. 29 and appendix 3 (also available on http://www.byhistorie.dk).

7   The number of *kommercelæster* expresses a ship's cargo capacity. This figure was reckoned on the basis of measurements of length, breadth and depth at more detailed places on the hull. In 1830 more detailed measurement principles were introduced and at the same time it was determined that a *kommercelæst* was 150 cubic feet, i.e. about 4.6 m³. In the years up to and including 1824 all Danish ships (for tax reasons) were given a figure that was 1/6 under the real figure. To get the correct number, the figures above should be multiplied by 1.2.

8   The figures for the rest of the Kingdom are from 1780 and 1800, respectively.

9   Worsøe 1967, pp. 73, 85, 87, 92, 94.

10 Henningsen 1985.

11 Dyssel 1924-25, p. 173. Worsøe 1967, p. 95 (Fabricius 1764).

12 Landsarkivet for Sønderjylland (The Provincial Archives for Southern Jutland), Tønder by-arkiv 278: Skatteregistre over formue- og næringsskatten 1744. Rigsarkivet (The National Archives in Copenhagen), Tyske Rentekammer G 97: Sønderborg og Aabenraa, G 98: Haderslev. Stadtarchiv Flensburg XII Hs 2077: Flensburg. Landesarchiv Schleswig-Holstein, Abt. 167 AR 1746 Flensburg 93, 94.

13 Around Sønderborg and Aabenraa there were many tile works from which large quantities of bricks were exported – e.g. to Copenhagen, even all the way to the Danish West Indies.

14 Henningsen 1990a.

15 Henningsen 1992.

16 Schütt 1966. Grove-Stephensen 1985.

17 Henningsen 1989. Henningsen 1990b.

18 Pingel 2003, p. 105. Momsen 1969.

19 Henningsen 1990c.

20 Hähnsen 1923.

21 Henningsen 1977.

22 1 alen is 62.8 cm.

23 Henningsen 1989.

24 Henningsen 1984.

25 A central authority working especially with trade and industry.

26 Momsen 1978. Hjelholt 1942, pp. 334, 347.

27 Haase, 1925. Henningsen 1985, pp. 171-234.

28 Henningsen 1978, pp. 98-105.

29 Henningsen 1991, p. 812.

30 Hvidtfeldt 1960, pp. 102-04, 109-27.

31 Henningsen 1998, pp. 64-66.

32 For a general introduction, see Nørr & Thomassen 2004.

33 Gregersen 1961, pp. 226-30. Henningsen 1985, pp. 25-39.

34 Gregersen 1961, pp. 226-30. Worsøe 1967, pp. 91-97. Henningsen 1985, p. 44. Hvidtfeldt 1960, pp. 135-38, 143, 147-48, 162-63, 169.

35 Andersen 2000, pp. 98-99.

36 Andersen 2000, pp. 99, 221.

37 Staeglich 1989, pp. 48-57. Hjelholt 1942, p. 457.

38 Fangel 1975, pp. 15-146.

39 Worsøe 1967, pp. 87-97. Andersen 2000, pp. 99, 221.

40 Hvidtfeldt 1960, p. 169. Andersen 2000, p. 221.

41 Niemann 1799, pp. 681-720.

42 Niemann 1799, pp. 562-607. Andersen 2000, pp. 99, 221.

43 Fangel 1975.

44 Schröder 1837 II, pp. 228-42.

45 Gregersen 1967, pp. 139-44. Schütt 1971a, pp. 171-88.

46 Vaagt 1966a, pp. 242-47, 285-92. 1966b, pp. 334-41. Schütt 1971b, pp. 105-07.

Karsten Skjold Petersen

The garrison town during Absolutism, 1660-1849

On the introduction of Absolutism in 1660, Denmark got a standing army. Until then, the normal practice had been that regiments were disbanded when the contract between the state and the regiment commander expired. The enlisted regiments with whom there were contracts during the wars with Sweden 1657-1660 were not disbanded when the last of the wars ended and the Danish King arrogated absolute power to himself. The new standing army comprised predominantly enlisted soldiers. It is true that a few conscripted regiments had existed since 1614, but the soldiers in these were not called up for continuous service.

In 1701 King Frederik IV's *landmilits* (militia) was formed with conscripted young peasants as a supplement to the enlisted soldiers. Both this militia, which existed until 1730, and King Christian VI's *landmilits* which was formed in 1733, consisted of independent regiments, which assembled only once a year for 3-4 weeks. Apart from this, the young peasants, called *landsoldater* (national soldiers), were at home in their conscription districts (typically the estate where they belonged) and drilled for only a few hours on Sundays for part of the year. However, there were always enlisted soldiers for continuous service, and among other things they manned the fortresses of the realm.

The enlisted and conscripted military units were combined in 1767. The enlisted army was a great economic burden on the state, so therefore in pace with the growing wish that the country's own sons should be responsible for the defence of the realm, the standing army – consisting largely of foreigners, especially Germans – began to be phased out. The crucial step to accomplish this was taken with the compulsory military service system of 1802 and the army ordinance of 1803, according to which Denmark should have an army based on compulsory military service. Enlisted soldiers, however, remained in the army for a few decades, although in constantly smaller numbers. Non-commissioned officers and musicians continued to be recruited throughout the period of Absolutism.

The conscription of soldiers for the army was exclusively laid on the peasantry until 1849, when more general compulsory military service was introduced. Until then, towns had been exempt from conscription of soldiers, but in return had to assign quarters to the army. The towns that were ordered to have a military camp were called garrison towns.

The garrison towns were the capital and a number of the market towns. Those towns with garrisons, as well as the size and type of garrison, were changed innumerable times during Absolutism. Sometimes the changes were based on military considerations, at other times they reflected local or regional political considerations. In the monographs of Danish market towns, there is rarely more than half a page devoted to the town's garrison, and some of the studies simply give the impression that the town never had a garrison. Depending on the relative sizes of the garrison and the town, the garrison could nevertheless be of very great significance.

The Danish army, which included both the Kingdom of Denmark and the Duchies of Schleswig and Holstein (until 1773 also Oldenburg and Delmenhorst), was very large in proportion to the size of the population. On paper, throughout the 18th century, it amounted to about 30,000 men out of a total population of about two million. The army furthermore absorbed about a third of total state expenditure. That is why Denmark is generally considered to be one of the most heavily armed states in Europe up until the wars in connection with the French revolution. However, it must be noted that the actual serving army in peace time was only about 7,500 men, as the other soldiers were either the *landsoldater* mentioned earlier, who were only called up for the training period, or were on leave for various reasons.

It is part of the picture that the Danish King was also King of Norway where there was a mainly conscripted army of about 30,000 men.

This article will review the practical aspects of the relationship between garrison and town in the Kingdom of Denmark:[1] how billeting was administered, what duties the towns had, the importance of the garrison for the local economy and the local labour market, what significance the change from an enlisted to a conscripted army had, etc.

KARSTEN SKJOLD PETERSEN

Garrison towns

Copenhagen was not just the capital, but after 1658 it was also the border town to the east. It was also incontrovertibly the largest garrison town – and as the main stronghold of the Kingdom it had for long periods half-a-dozen infantry regiments, the two Royal Life Guards and about half of the artillery. The other pivotal point in the disposition of the Danish army was the Duchies of Schleswig and Holstein at the southern boundary of the monarchy, where Rendsburg was the main stronghold. For long periods, the garrison there consisted of three infantry regiments and some artillery companies.[2] Among the small Danish fortresses during the period of Absolutism were Fredericia, Korsør, Nyborg, Kronborg and Glückstadt. However the army was so large that there was not enough room in the fortresses, and it was continuously dispersed in at least 15-20 % of the market towns in the Kingdom. And during part of the 18th century, the cavalry regiments alone were spread over a third of these towns. This dispersal was primarily determined by the need for feed for the horses. In addition, the fact that the cavalry was more mobile than other parts of the army and could be assembled much more quickly gave fewer misgivings about spreading the squadrons of the single regiments.

Tables 1 and 2 contain surveys of the large garrison towns in Denmark and the Duchies respectively at the time of the first censuses.[3] The surveys show the size of the population and the size of the garrison.[4]

TABLE 1.

Large garrison towns in Denmark 1787 and 1801, inhabitants and garrison.

Garrison town	Garrison units in 1787 and/or 1801[5]	1787			1801		
		Total population	Of these, the garrison	Pct.	Total population	Of these, the garrison	Pct.
Copenhagen (Kastellet included)	Livgarden til Fods (The Royal Life Guards Infantry) Livgarden til Hest (The Royal Life Guards Cavalry) 6 infantry regiments 2 battalions of marines Ingeniørkorpset (The Engineer Corps) 7 artillery companies	90,032	8,444	9.4	100,975	9,347	9.3
Odense	Fynske Regiment (lette) Dragoner (The Funen Dragoon Regiment)	5,363	655	12.2	5,782	665	11.5
Aalborg	Aalborgske/3. Jyske Infanteriregiment (The Aalborg/3. Jutland Infantry Regiment)	4,866	653	13.4	5,579	678	12.2
Elsinore	Sjællandske Jægerkorps (The Zealand Chasseur Corps) Kronborgske Bataillon (The Kronborg Battalion)	4,829	799	16.5	5,282	379	7.2
Aarhus	Aarhusiske/1. Jyske Infanteriregiment (The Aarhus/1. Jutland Infantry Regiment)	4,052	653	16.1	4,102	678	16.5
Randers	Jyske Regiment (lette) Dragoner (The Jutland Dragoon Regiment)	3,645	655	18.0	4,562	665	14.6
Fredericia	Jyske/Fynske Infanteriregiment (The Jutland-Funen Infantry Regiment)	3,066	653	21.3	3,474	739	21.3
Viborg	Viborgske Infanteriregiment (The Viborg Infantry Regiment)	2,572	653	25.3	2,379	0	0

TABLE 2.

Large garrison towns in Schleswig-Holstein 1803, inhabitants and garrison.

Garrison town	Garrison units i 1803	Total population	Of these the garrison	Pct.
Rendsburg	Oldenborgske Infanteriregiment Holstenske Infanteriregiment 2. Jyske Infanteriregiment (The Oldenborg, Holstein and 2. Jutland Infantry Regiments) 2 companies of Artillerikorpset	7,573	3,081	40.7
Schleswig	Slesvigske Infanteriregiment (The Schleswig Infantry Regiment) 2 squadrons of Livregiment Ryttere (Life Regiment Cavalry)	7,823	1,171	15.0
Glückstadt	Dronningens Livregiment (The Queen's Life Regiment) 1 company of Artillerikorpset	5,178	1,051	20.3
Eckernförde	Slesvigske Jægerkorps (The Schleswig Chasseur Corps)	2,921	423	14.5
Kiel	1. Slesvig-holstenske Batallion let Infanteri (The Schleswig-Holstein Light Infantry Batallion)	7,075	379	5.4

The figures for the size of the garrisons have been calculated on the basis of the army plans and include officers, *understab*,[6] non-commissioned officers, and privates from all arms, i.e. cavalry, artillery and infantry. With regard to the privates, the figures include enlisted soldiers and *nationalrekrutter*,[7] both those on duty and those on leave of absence, but not *landsoldater*. Officers' servants as well as the wives and children of the military are not included. The real size of the garrison and its effect were therefore even greater than is apparent from the above figures.

For most of the towns, a careful scrutiny of the census figures will however reduce the size of the garrison, primarily because the *nationalrekrutter* were granted leave to go home to their conscription districts for most of the year. In addition, each regiment always had a few vacant numbers.[8]

In relation to the size of the population, Rendsburg had easily the largest garrison. After this came Viborg with 25.3 % in 1787. Viborg, though, was not quite as greatly burdened as the number suggests. For several periods, individual companies were transferred to other towns.

FIG. 1.

King Frederik V inspects some cavalry regiments during the annual exercise 1749. Each garrison town had to provide a drill ground.

During the spring training period, the *landsoldater* were called up, and the town garrisons then grew quite considerably. The garrison towns could rarely cope with this extra burden, and consequently many of the *landsoldater* were in tent camps or were billeted in the surrounding villages.

Billeting regulations

The market towns which were assigned a garrison had first of all to provide billets for the privates, non-commissioned officers and officers, as well as for their horses if they had them. In addition they had to provide a number of facilities (guardhouse, sickroom, a drilling ground, magazines etc.). The duties of the garrison towns were stipulated in the so-called 'billeting regulations'. Regulations for the Danish market towns are known from 1764, 1775, 1788 and 1816.[9]

According to the billeting regulations, a billeting commission should be set up in all garrison towns, where most questions concerning the town's obligations should be dealt with. The commission comprised the municipal corporation, one officer and two of the town's *eligerede borgere* (trusted citizens). The sole garrison representative was thus in the minority in relation to the representatives of the town, but, on the other hand, all cases should in principle be decided unanimously. If the commission could not agree about a case, it was to be handed over to negotiation between the county governor and the garrison commander in question. If the case was deadlocked, the chancelleries were the final court of appeal. The garrison then complained to *Generalitets- og Kommissariatskollegiet* (The War Chancellery), while the town went to *Danske Kancelli* (Danish Chancellery).

The commission typically met a couple of times a year to arrange a number of practical details. Most space in the minutes of the meetings is normally devoted to discussions about forage stores and the annual agreements about light and firewood for the guardhouse and sickroom.

The commission could assign expenses, and the money was taken from the billeting funds, which the *kæmner*[10] often administered. However there were local differences in the way the funds were administered. The economic aspects of the relationship between the town and the garrison will be discussed later.

Work in the commission can be regarded as one long tug-of-war between the garrison and the town. The garrison made continuous demands for the provision of billets and facilities, and equipment for these. The town's representatives scrutinised the billeting regulations each time to see if the demand was warranted. They were very careful about granting the garrison anything. On the administrative level, the disagreements were thus about the size and quality of the town's services to the garrison.

Billeting

Billets could either be procured from the citizens (private billets) or be in special buildings built for the purpose (barracking).

Until well into the 19th century, the majority of the Danish army were in private billets. The billeting regulations fixed the amount of billet money for the military, both officers and privates. The amount for privates, for example, was 1 *skilling* per day in the regulations from 1764, 1775 and 1788. The billeting commission calculated the total billeting amount on the basis of a muster roll, which the commander of the unit was obliged to hand over. The commission subsequently charged the town's citizens this amount as a billeting tax. The amount each citizen had to pay was determined in a special tax assessment.

All the money collected as billeting tax was repaid to the citizens who had billeting in kind. Private billeting was in a way voluntary. In principle people could just pay the tax. If they wanted the money back, they could choose to have soldiers as lodgers.

When the billeting tax was collected, the commission issued the requisite number of so-called bills of quartering (i.e. billets), one for each soldier, and a list of the citizens who were obliged to billet. If a town was a garrison town for several companies, efforts were made as far as possible to divide the town into company districts, so that the single companies lived reasonably clustered. There was a non-commissioned officer with each company, the *fourer* (the quartermaster sergeant) whose job, among other things, was to find billets in his district. As it was not considered refined to have soldiers billeted, the *fourer* was usually turned away by the servants in the houses of the fashionable citizens. He therefore had to have his men billeted with citizens who were less genteel. At each place, an arrangement was made with the billeting host about the lodging of a given number of people. The host received a corresponding number of tickets which he later cashed at the town hall. The *fourer's* round of the area, however, was seldom necessary in practice. When the billeting tax was paid, most of the people said whether they wanted billeting in kind at all – and in that case, how many soldiers they could take. In the billeting, accompanying wives were counted as privates, while non-commissioned officers were counted double, whether or not they were married. Until the end of the 18th century, about one-third of the enlisted soldiers were married.

Some few citizens simply made their living from billeting. In this way private barracks came into existence, which sometimes could be very large. At the 1801 census, it can be seen for example that a citizen in Copenhagen ran private barracks for a whole infantry regiment. However, it could also happen that there were not enough people who voluntarily took in soldiers for the fixed billeting money, and then billets had to be rented at a higher price. The citizens who had refused to billet in natura had to pay this extra expense.

The organisation of billeting in Copenhagen was rather different from that in the provinces. Here the system with billeting tickets was abolished in 1764. Instead the town paid a lump sum as billeting tax to *Generalitets- og Kommissariatskollegiet*. This central authority handed over the money to the regiments who then rented billets for cash.

Not all town dwellers had to contribute to billets. For instance all church people were exempted by a special privilege. This was also the case for the nobility, school heads, royal officials and members of the municipal corporation. The burden had to be borne by the remaining citizens, that is, the people who owned houses or land or were subject to the tax on business and trade. The wage earners of the town, whether they were artisan journeymen and apprentices, servants, or workmen etc., did not have to contribute to the garrison.

According to the billeting regulations, the billet host was obliged to provide a bed with straw mattress, a table, a bench and a chair. The bed was to be furnished with a feather duvet cover and a pillow. In addition, the soldier got a pair of sheets and a tow towel. The sheets and towel were to be exchanged for clean ones every month while the straw in the mattress was to be replaced every second month.

To have a horse billeted, first of all stabling had to be fitted out with a rack, a manger and stalls and in addition a hand light had to be acquired. Every month the host subsequently had to provide ¼ *skålpund* (about 496 gr.) candles and various tools such as one wooden bucket, one wooden shovel and two brooms annually.

The soldiers were not entitled to warmed bedrooms. On the other hand, according to the billeting regulations, they should 'enjoy fire and light in common with the host and be content with that'. If the host did not want the soldiers swarming over his living room, he had to allot them a room with a fireplace and give a specified amount, 8 *skilling* a month per person in the summer six months and double that amount in the winter, with which the soldiers could themselves buy candles and fuel. The regulations did not set any limits to how often or how long the soldiers were allowed to stay in the host's warm, lighted room. However it should be so 'that the host has the use of his room and must not suffer any harm or hindrance to his trade activities'. This weak wording was obviously often the cause of disagreements.

Since the billeting money was fixed as an absolute amount and therefore subject to constant depreciation in pace with inflation, the army could not compete in prices with other people looking for lodgings. The result was that the soldiers were assigned the most miserable quarters: back buildings, dark, dank basements and leaking attics which were stiflingly hot in summer and icy cold in winter. It is true that the billeting regulations laid down that married men should as far as possible be billeted in the so-called *boder* (small houses) and that they must not be assigned attics or damp, dark basements. The single soldiers on the other hand had to be satisfied with the apartments they were allotted by the host as long as they just had watertight roofs, windows and doors. A former regiment commander described the quarters of his people like this:

Most soldiers live in attics that are exposed to storm and rain; several are assigned lodgings in basement dens where there is no daylight, and yet they have to dress their hair and powder themselves and do their military toilette; that is why they also go when they can to public-houses, where it is warm, to get drunk on spirits and forget their sufferings.[11]

The soldiers were most usually billeted two by two, and the beds arranged accordingly. Not only did the soldiers have to share beds, they also had to share bedclothes. The advantage for the billet host was fewer expenses, and for the soldiers that they could share body heat in the cold winter nights.

According to the billeting regulations, the officers had the right to quarters of different sizes depending on their rank, and the regulations are thereby excellent sources to shed light on the military rank system. A colonel had the right to one room and two small rooms, a lieutenant-colonel or major two small rooms, and a captain just one small room. Each of these officers in addition had the right to a box bed. Moreover, in each small room, there should be a stove with a firebox and tongs as well as a table and three chairs. If the host had curtains in his rooms, the officer also had the right to curtains in his rooms. The commander who acted as garrison commander also had the right to a kitchen, dining room and basement. The officers themselves had to supply light, fuel and bedclothes, and they were also responsible for cleaning.

All officers in the Danish army were allowed a batman, colonels indeed two. In the quarters of the superior officers, there had therefore to be one, respectively two, small rooms for these servants. These small rooms had to have a stove, firebox and tongs, a table and three chairs and a candlestick.

With regard to the horses, a colonel was to have stabling for four-six horses, lieutenant colonels and majors, two-three horses, captains, two horses. Finally these officers were to be assigned a place to keep firewood. The stipulation about stabling applied not just to cavalry officers, but to all army officers.

The *subalterne* officers (captains, first- and second-lieutenants) and those of equivalent rank among the regiment's *understab* each had the right to one small room with stove, firebox and tongs, a table and three chairs. On the other hand they did not have the right to a bedstead. Finally they were to be offered stabling for one horse. The *subalterne* officers' batmen did not have the right to their own small room. There should just be space for them in their master's small room, whether or not their master had both wife and children.

The officers of the period had a very well-developed awareness of rank. If they could possibly afford it, they rented suitable quarters themselves. In this way, they were not obliged to accept the billet the town assigned them. Instead they could choose to take billeting money, contribute a little themselves, and independently rent a dwelling.

Barracks

Billeting in state barracks was the exception. In Copenhagen, there was *Kastellet* (the Citadel) whose six detached blocks were completed in 1664. Most of Rendsburg's garrison were quartered in 21 barracks that were built 1691-99. *Kastellet* and Rendsburg had their garrisons quartered in barracks because they were built as regular fortresses without the citizens of a normal town where the garrison would otherwise have been billeted. Besides, *Kastellet* was special in that it was an independent fortress with its own headquarters which functioned independently of the fortress of Copenhagen.

The next regular barracks building after *Kastellet* and Rendsburg was Sølvgade Barracks in Copenhagen which was built 1765-71. The municipal corporation got the idea of letting Copenhagen's garrison be billeted in barracks in 1763.[12] They had calculated what it would cost if the town itself built and ran barracks for the levied billeting tax. The arrangement would make a profit already after seven years. In 1764 the military central administration took over the project which meant that Copenhagen with its billeting tax paid a fixed annual amount to the state, which in return undertook to build and run barracks for the garrison. Until then, the soldiers were still to be billeted among the citizens for the rate existing up until then.

Initially barracks were to be built for the two regiments that were highest in order of precedence. Construction lasted many years because of increases in the price and personal differences among the army commanders. The actual building work was done by the garrison's own enlisted soldiers.

In 1771, each of the two regiments could move into its own wing of Sølvgade Barracks. The barracks was so spacious that there was also room for the soldiers who had leave, wives and children, non-commissioned officers, the *understab* and the majority of the officers. Additionally some *landsoldater* could be billeted there during the annual training time. In the year Sølvgade Barracks was put into service, an enthusiastic debater wrote about the new quarters:

Never have soldiers lived better than in barracks (. . .) in the barracks for one thing, the soldier does not need to lie in a leaky attic or in a water-logged basement, and put his health at risk, there he does not need to drink a skilling's worth when he sometimes wants to warm himself a bit. (. . .) In the barracks there is no self-seeking host who tempts the soldier to spend more than his wages with an offer, yes sometimes forcing credit on them.[13]

The quarters in the new, smart, bright rooms were in many respects a considerable improvement. The disadvantage for the privates was that they were now under the constant supervision of the officers. In spite of this, the pleasure seems to have been great among the troops. However the pleasure did not last long. In 1775 the regiments were ordered to leave the barracks on 29 September, and again be billeted with the citizens. According to the order the reason for this was, among other things, to return to the citizens the earnings that they had lost when the barracks were built.

After this, the Copenhagen barracks project was in the doldrums until Crown Prince Frederik assumed power in 1784, at which time it was brought to life again. In October 1785, the military could again take over Sølvgade Barracks and the next stage in the barracks project was a barracks for *Den Kgl. Livgarde til Fods* (The Royal Life Guard), which was put into service in April 1786. Two years later, a South American general visited Copenhagen. He moved at ease at the court and during his stay he visited The Royal Life Guard's new barracks:

We were shown around by a private, very polite and very sensible. He showed us the dormitories, very nice and with good beds in which two men slept in each. Only married soldiers had a whole bed at their disposal, in which they in turn slept with their wives, without any curtain or other separation; everyone slept in the same room and the beds stood quite close to each other. We asked him if this did not encourage impropriety, to which he carelessly remarked that everyone minded their own business. I also saw some very beautiful 12-year-old girls from the same families, all with the confidence of innocence about them. One could only admire the great moral purity that is found among these people. Of everything that is to be found in Copenhagen, this surprised me the most![14]

It was not until about 1803 that the last military units in the capital were successfully accommodated in barracks. At that time, 40 years had passed since the beginning of the barracks project. With the exception of Rendsburg, the garrisons in the provinces were still billeted on the citizens. This continued well into the 19th century, and right up to the beginning of the 20th century in some few towns.

For the soldiers, the barracks meant better and more uniform quarters, where they escaped the constant bickering with the billet host. Physically they were moved away from the more socially disadvantaged environments and came under the officers' almost constant supervision.

Facilities

According to the billeting regulations, the garrison towns were to make a number of facilities available for the military units. These facilities included one or more guardhouses (*Corps de Gardes*) complete with gaol, a hospital/sickroom, an exercise ground, depots for the regiment's vehicles, an armoury and a military stores depot to keep the equipment of the *landsoldater* outside the training time. Finally, in connection with each of the company commanders' quarters, a military stores depot was to be fitted out for his enlisted force. If the garrison was a cavalry regiment, the town also had to provide a workshop for the farrier, a cutting box for chaff, and stores for forage and bedding.

The town was to provide the hospital with beds, light and firewood. The number of beds and the amount of light and firewood was not fixed in the regulations, but was to be negotiated with the billeting commission.[15] The beds, as in the private billets, were to be two-man beds. The town was to supply bedclothes and towels. All other expenses for the running of the hospital were to be paid by the regiment. As with the hospital, the town was to supply light and firewood to the guardhouse during the six winter months.

It quickly became the practice that the towns made the rural inhabitants pay for the firewood. In many places, the guards at the gates of the town were thus detailed to collect a piece of firewood from every load that passed into the town (the so-called guard or customs firewood). This collection was done in connection with payment of the tax on the consumer goods brought into the town. Correspondingly, four-five pieces of peat were taken from each load of peat. The collection of firewood and peat for the use of the military apparently caused some controversy between the peasants and the gate guards, and so the billeting regulations of 1775 laid down that the towns could collect this tax all right, but they must not let the military be in charge of the collection. In 1781, Elsinore had also been given leave to collect guard fire-

FIG. 2.

The changing of the guard on Kongens Nytorv in Copenhagen 1753. This ceremony took place on the central square of every garrison town each forenoon. The guards drilled for about four hours before they dispersed across the town to change with the guards from the previous sentry duty. Unfortunately the print has been partly damaged by moisture.

wood from the firewood that was imported by sea. Here the skipper either had to hand over two pieces from each cord or pay 3 *skilling* in cash. The arrangement had always existed in Copenhagen, and in 1782 it was extended to the other provincial garrisons in the Kingdom.

Guard duty

Among the many duties of the soldier, guard duty was absolutely the most time-consuming. All garrison towns, and particularly fortification towns, had a wealth of guard buildings. As a starting point, there was a main guard building, and in the large garrison towns there were also guardhouses at the town gates.

Privates were posted as sentries at all the guardhouses. This was primarily done at the town gates and at the quarters of the regiment commander (colour guard), but also at other important places such as the regiment's armoury and ammunition store. In Copenhagen sentries were also posted at the residences of a number of important people such as generals and diplomatic representatives, and at important buildings such as The Royal Mint, the Supreme Court, powder magazines and barracks.

The sentries normally stood alone, on rare occasions, in pairs. A watch lasted 24 hours, but the individual soldier stood sentry for only two hours at a time, in cold winters just one hour. To protect himself from the elements he was provided with a sentinel's cape and guard gloves, and if the weather became really bad, he could go into his sentry box. When he was not on sentry duty, he had to stay in the guard room.

One of the fixed duties of the guard was to announce the beginning and end of the day for the garrison soldiers. Each watch had its own section of the town through which a non-commissioned officer, a couple of privates and a drummer trudged, while the drumhead was beaten for reveille and tattoo. The reveille was sounded and beaten every morning a little before sunrise. The tattoo was sounded between 8 p. m. and 10 p. m. depending on the season. After the tattoo, the troops were meant to be in their quarters. To enforce the curfew, patrols were sent from each guardhouse through the town streets several times during the night. If a soldier was caught out of his billet, he was immediately arrested and dragged back to the guard room. The guardhouses in this way were also used as military gaols. The prisoners stayed there until their case had been before the special military court, *krigsretten*, and a sentence, if there was one, had been carried out.

To ensure that the guards of the town did not sleep or in other ways neglect their work, the commanding officer had special patrols, *ronder,* sent out 3-4 times during the day and night. Each *ronde* consisted of an officer or a non-commissioned officer and a handful of privates. They all began their round at the main guardhouse, after which every guardhouse and every sentry was checked. If a sentry had to be arrested because he was sleeping or was drunk, the *ronde* left one of its own men on sentry duty and brought the prisoner to the nearest guard. The *ronde* again ended at the main guardhouse, where a report was made.

In addition to the ordinary guard duties, the gate guards had to check the passports of all those coming into and leaving the town, and assist the customs and *konsumtion* officers, who controlled all the imports of goods into the town. The authorities found it difficult to stamp out smuggling of goods. To prevent fraud in the customs and *konsumtion,* the prospect of potentially large rewards were held out to

Fig. 3.

The main Corps de Garde in Copenhagen on Kongens Nytorv. Sentinels from each guardhouse were posted in the neighbourhood. Drawing by C.W. Eckersberg 1807.

the military guards in 1781. If they succeeded in confiscating goods that were being smuggled, they got the value of them (with the deduction of the costs of the case). The lucky sentry, however, had to share his reward with the guard commander and the other guards according to a special scale.

Each morning the guards for the coming day assembled at the changing of the guard in the central square in the town. After this, these soldiers drilled for up to four hours. Around 11 o'clock they were lined up nicely while the guard commanders were given the day's password. This word was a watchword that had to be exchanged every time two guards met each other during the activities of the day. After being given the password, the single commands dispersed to music, to relieve the guards of the previous day around the town.

All considered, military music played a prominent part in the Absolutist garrison towns. This was true not just for the regiment where most events were accompanied by music, but also for the civilians who had to listen to fifes and drums every day.

The garrison's other duties

After guard duty, practice and drill were the most important duties of the serving soldier. Recently enlisted recruits were usually drilled for a few weeks under a drill sergeant until they had learned the basic skills. During the rest of their period of service, training was limited to the annual training period of three-four weeks in the spring, and the drill at the guard parades.

In the regiments, there was a difference between the *permitterede* and *kommanderede* soldiers and the garrison force. The *permitterede* (soldiers on leave of absence) and their significance for the garrison towns will be dealt with later. The *kommanderede* soldiers were people the regiment had supplied for other duties – often by order of *Generalitets- og Kommissariatskollegiet* or other central authorities. Some of these duties concerned the regiment itself; they could be recruitment of new soldiers, transport of recruits from the place of recruitment to regiment headquarters and the training of *landsoldaterne* in their native districts. Among duties for other authorities can be mentioned *soldateske* (marine soldiery) and public works.[16] *Soldateske* involved service as marine infantry on navy ships. On board, the most important function for the *soldateske* was to man the guns.

The state used soldiers for public works to implement a number of projects cheaply. The soldiers' wages for instance were considerably lower than those of civilian workers. In spite of critical voices in the officer corps, the state considered it completely natural to take advantage of the huge manpower potential of the large army. For the same reason, the officers in charge of recruitment of new soldiers were instructed to take on people who were skilled in a trade as far as possible. The public works could consist of jobs such as barracks building, improvement of fortifications, the prevention of sand drift, maintenance and building of roads, bridges, canals, harbours and castles. The soldiers were also frequently drafted to assist the gardeners in the royal gardens and parks.

The army's most important duty was of course to defend the state against external enemies. But it also served as a means to uphold peace and order inside the state. For instance the army had standing orders to take action against all riots and disturbances. Police preparedness was often inadequate in the period and local authorities could ask for assistance from the military at any time. However the army was also duty bound to restore order without being asked. This duty is specified for example in *reskript* (an ordinance) of 16 November 1781:

Should a gathering of a mob occur, a non-commissioned or commissioned officer must immediately summon his guard to arms, and if such a gathering should be caused only by curiosity or other unimportant reasons, he must keep the crowd so far from *Corps de Garden* that he can stand with the guard unobstructed (. . .); but should the mob for instance conspire for suspicious reasons and make a move to commit some impertinence or other, the guard on duty shall try to prevent such in time and report it to the town commander and procure his orders, after which the necessary arrangements should be made to disperse the crowd.

The army was put into action several times in connection with civil disturbances. When the inhabitants of the island of Bornholm in 1770 created a disturbance over the levying of an extra tax, a corps of 1,000 men was assembled. After this the disturbance came to nothing and the force was not embarked. The tax on distilled spirits provoked disturbances in 1776 and the army was then put into action in Hinge near Randers in East Jutland and in Nysted on Lolland. In 1781, there was a mutiny on the Wadden Sea island of Föhr, where the inhabitants resisted conscription to the navy. During the great carpenter strike in Copenhagen in 1794, it was also the army that was set in against the strikers.[17] Besides these large actions, the army took care of a number of minor police functions. Public executions were often the occasion of disturbances, and a military command was therefore always present to ensure that everything proceeded in an orderly fashion. If a fight or the like started near a guard, he had a duty to separate the fighting parties and if necessary to make arrests. And if people who had been summoned to court proved to be unwilling to appear, it was the military that had to fetch them etc.

Every Sunday and Holy Day, the soldiers had to assemble before the headquarters of the regiment commander for Church Parade. Here the so-called *krigsartikler*,[18] some of the rules of obedience and other provisions considered relevant were read. After this, the men marched in formation to the church where there was a service. Church parade was compulsory for everyone who was not on duty. The same was true for actual church attendance. The various Christian communities represented among the enlisted soldiers were allowed to attend their own churches. For Lutherans, efforts were made to have regular sermons in both Danish and German.

In Copenhagen there were two separate churches for the army, *Garnisonskirken* for the Copenhagen garrison, and *Kastelskirken* for the Citadel garrison. Each had both a Danish and German congregation. The Reformed Christians and Catholics attended churches of their own religion. In the provinces, the arrangement was that priests

KARSTEN SKJOLD PETERSEN

from these two religions travelled between the garrisons from time to time and held services. In Rendsburg and Fredericia, there were also special garrison churches, but otherwise, the garrisons had to be satisfied with the ordinary parish churches.

The garrison and the local labour market

In the 18th century, about half of the enlisted soldiers had leave of absence without pay for most of the year, normally the 11 months outside the annual training time. These soldiers on leave were called *frifolk* or free men. As already mentioned, the term *permitterede* was also used. If a *permitteret* soldier stayed in the garrison town during his leave, he was, like those in service, subject to the curfew between tattoo and reveille.

Among the enlisted soldiers, there were many who had learned a trade or something similar, and these people were given preference when the commander selected those who were to be free men. In 1769, the commanders were forbidden to disband their men to unemployment. The regiment had to ensure that there was work for their *frifolk*. If a free man suddenly became unemployed, the regiment had a corresponding duty to take him back, i.e. give him work, wages and lodgings.

Many enlisted soldiers found work as tradesmen, as workers in factories and shipyards, as workmen or as labourers. In the provincial garrisons, there could also be the possibility of farm work on neighbouring estates and farms or on the agricultural holdings of the town.

In principle, the *permitterede* could take work anywhere. If the local area could not support its free men, the regiment commander thus had the possibility of issuing a passport so that they could look for work further away. It is true that it was meant to be possible to assemble the men of the regiment at short notice. But in practice this was not so simple. The rule was that no one should be disbanded further away than about half a Danish mile from the garrison without a passport, and the regiment in any case should know the address and employer of the free man.

The soldiers who had served their apprenticeship in a trade were glad to be employed as journeymen by the local masters. This was not always popular with the civilian journeymen who forced through the rule that the soldier journeymen should be laid off first if employment fell.

Compared with soldiers' pay, wages for journeymen were high. However, part of the picture was that there was extensive unemployment in the building trade during the winter. For carpenters in Copenhagen, this seasonal unemployment was seldom less than three months, very often more. In addition to this, the soldier journeymen as *frifolk* had to get themselves lodgings. Finally, all those on leave of absence who had permanent work had to pay certain taxes. Their wives and children, though, were exempt.

The rules about how the free men were allowed to support themselves were laid down in the ordinance of 10 March 1725. With various additions and restrictions, this was valid for the remainder of the period. The free men could freely take work with the master artisans and other citizens of the town. On the other hand, nearly all self-employed work was forbidden. For instance they could not take out a trade licence in the towns or become masters.[19] However, they could do work for other military people. In such self-employed activity, their wives and children could help, but they were forbidden to employ anyone. In spite of the restrictions, the permission easily gave rise to dissatisfaction among master artisans who felt their businesses and privileges were encroached upon.

The ordinance forbade nearly all forms of trading for the soldiers. They could not run any sort of shop, including public houses or canteens, nor could they carry freight by boat. On the other hand, their wives were allowed to peddle fish, oysters, fruit and vegetables. They were allowed to fish and cultivate the crops mentioned as well. However this needed a plot of land. They could also buy up crops from the farmers in the area surrounding the garrison town and bring them to market. When bringing them into the market town, they had to pay *konsumtion* like everyone else. Finally soldiers were forbidden to shave civilians or cut their hair, or distil spirits, brew beer or bake. They could not even brew or bake for their own use.

As mentioned, the free men were granted leave for 11 months annually. The rules about the number of *frifolk* and the duration of leave were really intended as a guide. They were minimum demands if the regiment budgets were to be met. As long as the service duties of the regiment were not neglected, it could therefore keep more *frifolk*. The only real limit was that the regiment had to keep so many men on duty that the individual soldier was not on sentry duty more often than every third day.

The relationship between the garrison and the local labour market had the greatest potential for conflict. Relations to the individual parties in the labour market differed greatly however. The relationship to the master artisans of the garrison town for example was two-sided. The masters were undoubtedly glad for the extra manpower the soldiers could offer. Many had high qualifications and could impart knowledge about new techniques and the like. At the same time they acted as scabs, as they always had their military income to fall back on. On the other hand, the masters could be extremely dissatisfied when the soldiers encroached on their business.

Among the hucksters, bakers, butchers and publicans of the garrison towns there was generally a positive attitude to the enlisted soldiers. The more soldiers in the garrison, the larger the turnover. But here too there could be conflict about the right to run a business, for example when the soldiers ran an illicit bar.

The relationship to the civilian journeymen was probably mainly bad. Of course there could be personal friendships, and collaboration in individual work places could be very good, but generally, the journeymen seem to have had great animosity towards their military colleagues. Professional solidarity could be very strong, and the soldiers often got the cold shoulder. The journeymen tried to put pressure on the masters not to take on soldiers – and when this occurred, it could happen that they refused to work with them. The authorities turned a blind eye to this behaviour for a long time, but in 1800 it was put on record that the journeymen who refused to work with *frifolk* from the army were to be punished with four days imprisonment on bread and water. If the offence was repeated, the punishment was doubled.[20]

If there was plenty of work, the soldiers were accepted, but if there was unemployment, the relationship became critical. It is known that the Copenhagen carpenter journeymen succeeded in forcing through the arrangement that soldier journeymen could not be employed as long as journeymen who were members of a guild were unemployed. The consequence of this was that the soldiers were the first to be sacked if the order book was empty.

Contact and conflict

Contact between the enlisted soldiers and the town inhabitants was on both a formal and an informal level. When the enlisted soldiers were on duty and acted as people in authority, for example as gate guards, the formal contact prevailed. They acted then as royal officials – and as such regularly earned the displeasure of the citizenry. The authorities, for instance, found it necessary at intervals to impress on the inhabitants that they should show the sentries respect and not insult them.

When the enlisted soldiers were on leave or just had time off, they behaved as private persons – and the contact with the inhabitants of the town could therefore

FIG. 4

The Royal castle in Copenhagen 1698. Like other important buildings it had its own Corps de Garde. In front of the guardhouse are two punishment devices: the pole and the wooden horse. All military punishments were carried out in public.

be characterised as informal. This was primarily the case when the soldiers were working, but also in more social types of contact. The contact between the town inhabitants and garrison could also be positive. The garrison naturally took part in the town festivities which could be in connection with the King's and Crown Prince's birthdays, but the occasion could also be the entry of the regiment into the town or the dedication of new colours. Finally, there were naturally the local market days.

The differences in station set reasonably clear limits to acceptable social behaviour: who could associate with whom. For the officers it meant that they mixed socially with the town citizens. But even here, there were class differences. The regiment commander could indeed mix with the town bailiff, town councillors, the bishop, the estate owners, or the largest merchants, but not an ordinary master carpenter. However, the social codex became a little less strict during the period. In particular, the French Revolution in 1789 brought a considerable upheaval in its train. A second lieutenant quoted in his memoirs a letter that he wrote in 1793 to his sweetheart at home in Germany:

You cannot imagine the effect the French Revolution has already had on our customs here in the Northern countries. Today, Koch, the manufacturer, invited me to go and play billiards with him and then have an evening meal with him. Later in the evening *Gnav*[21] was played; the players were a distiller, a sexton, a major, a captain, a lieutenant, an ensign, the town musician, a merchant, the Reformed Evangelical schoolmaster and the manufacturer; we all sat at one table without difference in rank or station. It could not have happened a year ago.[22]

However, there was no room for privates or non-commissioned officers at the table. Socially, privates as a rule ranked under the trained artisan journeymen, though this could depend on their personal background, appearance and ambitions.

The presence of the many young unmarried men from the garrison naturally caused a stir. The young ladies of the town were doubtless grateful for the large choice of males. The garrison on the other hand was hardly popular among the young men of the town in this regard, and the girls' parents were also probably worried about their daughters' virtue. Indeed this fear was not without ground.

From olden times, a soldier was exempt from punishment the first time he had sex outside marriage. The second time the soldier offended, he was to be punished with arrest on bread and water for four weeks, and be exhorted by the priest to live a Christian and seemly life. The third time, he was to be removed to the nearest fortification and work at the King's pleasure. How long such an indeterminate sentence was, was thereby dependent on how puritanical the sitting King was.

Financial advantages and disadvantages for the town

The towns often complained about the expense connected with having a military camp. In the historical accounts about the garrison towns, the histories of market towns, the relationship between the garrison and town is usually dealt with very briefly. The camp is often described as a great burden, especially a financial burden. Detailed studies of the financial relationship are almost non-existent.[23]

If the financial aspect of the case is considered alone, having a garrison, however, was not such a great burden. The contemporary complaints, which those who wrote later uncritically accepted, were probably just part of the political posturing that always goes on when public expenses have to be paid. It is true that the town had great expenses in connection with the garrison, but it also had earnings.

Going through the expenses and earnings, one should distinguish between the communal items and the individual ones. The communal items were those that concerned the town, while the individual ones were those that concerned the individual citizens.

As already mentioned, the town had to make a number of facilities available, such as a drill ground, guardhouse or houses, military stores depot and sickroom. Once the facilities had been procured, the running expenses however were relatively small. One of the big running costs, firewood for the guards and sickroom, for instance, was passed on to the rural people.

The main expense for the citizens was the billeting tax. The citizens who chose to accept billeting in natura had expenses for the establishment of rooms with furniture as described in the section on billeting.

The town's income consisted primarily of the billeting tax it levied on its own citizens. Next it included at times the so-called auxiliary tax from other market towns, and finally the town had income from the guard firewood. The auxiliary tax was a system of adjustment between towns that had garrisons and towns that did not have them. The system was administered by the state.

In contrast to the town, the citizens had a wide range of incomes as a result of the presence of the garrison. Primarily this comprised the billeting money which was paid to those who had billeting in natura. Then some citizens had income from the sale, construction and maintenance of the garrison facilities. Furnishing the buildings that the town had to put at the garrison's disposal was indeed an expense for the billeting funds, but the contracts for their construction and maintenance were always given to the local master artisans. In the fortification towns, responsibility for the maintenance of the defences lay with the central military administration. Soldiers did the work as a rule as public work, but sometimes local artisans here too had an opportunity to make money from the military. Finally the citizens had the profit from the garrison's daily consumption of goods and services. With the cavalry garrisons, the greatest expense for the army was the rent of grazing land for the horses as well as the purchase of winter feed and bedding for them. In addition the garrison at times bought all the soldiers' bread from local bakers. Some of the soldiers' wages were in this way paid in kind. The farrier, the armourer, the saddle maker, and the barber-surgeon apparently bought most of what they needed locally. These were things like coal, iron, tools, leather, medicaments etc. In addition, the town shoemakers normally supplied the garrison footwear. All these incomes for the citizens were due to purchases by the garrison. To this must be added what the individual soldier bought for his own wages. The whole garrison, from the commander to the privates, got wages from the state. All, or nearly all, this money was spent in the local community.

The size of this financial injection can be calculated on the basis of the budgets according to which the army units had to order their affairs.[24] They contained wage expenses, outlay for the care of the horses, and various other expenses for nursing, writing requisites etc.

The garrison of an infantry regiment with about 1,100 officers, non-commissioned officers and privates implied for example that, according to the army plan of 1774, an annual sum of about 30,022 *rigsdaler* was put into circulation (see Table 3). This amount included wages and expenses for writing requisites, the hospital and an offering for the priest.[25] Expenses for equipment, recruitment and wages for the *land-soldater* on the other hand are not included, since only an insignificant part of this money was spent in the garrison town. The *landsoldater*'s wages were mainly spent in the rural parishes where they lived for most of the year. The wages that were saved on free men *are* set off. As another example it can be shown how much money a squadron of hussars put into circulation (Table 4).

TABLE 3.

Budget for an infantry regiment in the Duchies of Schleswig and Holstein, 1774-1803.

Year	Rigsdaler
1774	30,022
1777	29,796
1785	33,188
1789	33,023
1803	35,828

TABLE 4.

Budget for a hussar *squadron, 1778-1842.*[26]

Year	Rigsdaler	*Total number of persons in the squadron*
1778	5,103	65
1785	7,205	162

Year	Rigsdaler	*Total number of persons in the squadron*
1799	9,013	-
1803	9,220	188
1816	10,698	163
1840	10,250	123

On this basis, it can be summarised that it was financially advantageous to have a military camp, and the longer the garrison stayed in the town the better the return on the investment in the established facilities, stabling and billets.

The garrison was still an expense for the town treasury, but in contrast to the citizens the town did not get a share of the garrison's daily consumption. Among the people of the town, not everyone profited from the garrison. The military presence was most lucrative for the canteen man, shoemakers, bakers, farmers, brewers and distillers. These last three businesses were often run by the same persons. Briefly it can be said that everyone who dealt in food and drink had direct earnings from the garrison.

Summary

The garrisons had an appreciable effect on the garrison towns. As a rule, they constituted quite a good proportion of the total population, and their daily duties made them very visible and audible. Guard duty with its *ronder* and changing of the guard was a daily spectacle. This was also true of the musicians who marked the beginning and end of each day. There were also the drills, marches, public punishments, church parades, funerals and nightly patrols – all together they helped to make the garrison conspicuous.

Because of all this official activity, the garrison was extremely noticeable. The effect however was even greater and more direct. This was because of two circumstances: the majority of the soldiers were privately billeted with the citizens, and about half of the garrison were on leave as *frifolk* who earned their living in various civilian jobs. In this way they were an active element in the life of the towns.

Even though the enlisted soldiers were active in town life, as a group they were never regarded as fully integrated. They were and remained an alien element. It is true that their billeting with the people and their links to the local labour market showed integration, but in contrast, there were a number of things that resulted in separation. The military with its own jurisdiction and its own criminal code maintained a distance to civilian society. In the large garrison towns, the garrison was isolated with regard to attendance at church and school. Socially, the enlisted soldiers belonged to the lower class in the towns. Their wages were low, and the billeting system with the fixed billeting money put them in the most inferior housing. The poor living conditions in turn meant that the soldiers had a lenient attitude to property rights. The fact that the soldiers were people of authority was yet another thing that distanced them from the civilian population of the garrison towns. It can be easily imagined that a soldier who felt disdained and humiliated had great pleasure in inconveniencing people in his official capacity.

The local labour market often had difficulty absorbing the sudden surplus which the encampment of a large military unit entailed. Conflicts resulted. Soldiers who could not get work – or who wanted to earn more – worked as self-employed. This dabbling meanwhile threatened the master artisans' businesses and immediately provoked protests. The presence of the soldiers was also a threat to wage earners, even if this was for different reasons. The soldiers simply meant a general risk of a reduction in wages and deterioration of working conditions. In this way, the conduct of the soldiers on the labour market affected the two opposing forces in the labour market.

If one regards the relationship to the town as a social unit, the soldiers in the garrison by all accounts were never fully integrated. In relation to the total economy of the town, the garrison however represented a stimulus, both as consumers and as manpower. It can therefore be summarised that naturally not everyone was happy to have the enlisted soldiers garrisoned. The people who had the greatest advantage of the military camp were the tradesmen and the master artisans, those who had least were the workers.

There were great differences in the enlisted garrisons in the first three-quarters of the period and the conscripted garrisons at the end of the period, that is, after the Napoleonic wars. A general characteristic was that the enlisted garrisons were considerably larger, seen in relation to the civilian population. This was partly due to the general increase in the civilian population from about 1790, and partly because of the introduction of drill schools[27] at the end of the 18th century. Moreover, the enlisted garrison was characterised by the fact that many soldiers had wives and children. Another big difference was that where the enlisted soldiers were granted leave as *frifolk* in the town, the conscripted *frifolk* were sent to their native districts in the country. Because of this, the conscripts never had the connection to the town that the enlisted soldiers had, for better or worse. To recap, it can thus be stated that the effect of the garrison on the town and its daily life, economically as well as socially, was considerably greater in the time before 1814 than in the period after.

BIBLIOGRAPHY

Abrahamson, W.H.F. 1771. *Tanker om Krigsstanden og dens Forbedring*. Copenhagen.

Bjerg, Hans Chr. (ed.) 1983. 'En revolutionær turist. General Mirandas besøg i København 1788'. *Historiske Meddelelser om København*, pp. 139-71.

Danske militære enheders garnisonering. The Danish National Archives' unpublished survey.

Falkenskjold, Seneca Otto von 1847. *Gamle Erindringer*. Copenhagen.

Købke, J.P. 1892. *Indkvarterings- og Kaserneringsforhold i Kjøbenhavn fra Byens Belejring i 1659 indtil nu*. Copenhagen.

Petersen, Karsten Skjold 2001. 'Landsoldater og nationalrekrutter. To typer udskrevne 1767-1802'. *Personalhistorisk Tidsskrift*, 2, pp. 235-41.

Petersen, Karsten Skjold 2002. *Geworbne krigskarle. Hvervede soldater i den danske hær 1774-1803*. (Tøjhusmuseets Skrifter, 15). Copenhagen: Museum Tusculanum.

Petersen, Karsten Skjold 2003: *Husarer i Roskilde. En garnison og dens by 1777-1842*. (Tøjhusmuseets Skrifter, 16). Roskilde: Roskilde Museum.

Petersen, Karsten Skjold 2005: 'Garnisonsbyen under enevælden'. In: Søren Bitsch Christensen (ed.), *Den klassiske købstad*. (Danske Bystudier, 2). Aarhus: Aarhus Universitetsforlag, pp. 347-82.

Rosenstand Goiske, P. (ed.) various years. *Rescripter, Resolutioner og Collegialbreve den danske Krigsmagt til Lands angaaende*. Copenhagen.

Wagner, Ludvig 1880. *Et Soldaterliv i forrige Aarhundrede*. Copenhagen: Konrad Jørgensen.

NOTES

1   This article is based on the research in Petersen 2002 and Petersen 2003. An earlier version was published in Danish in Petersen 2005. For bibliographical information about laws and ordinances see Petersen 2005, note 1, p. 378.

2   A regiment consisted of 10-12 companies and included a total of about 1,100 officers, non-commissioned officers and privates. A company thus was about 100 men.

3   The very first census in Denmark in 1769 did not count military personnel.

4   A complete record of the garrison towns in the country can be seen in The Danish National Archives' unpublished survey: Danske militære enheders garnisonering.

5   The names of the enlisted regiments did not have any local connection. *Oldenborgske Infanteriregiment* was thus just a name and the regiment had no connection with the province of Oldenburg. The only exception to this rule was that four regiments (*Aarhusiske, Aalborgske, Riberske og Viborgske*) were actually named after the town where they would be garrisoned in the 1785 army plan. However the names were already changed again in the 1789 army plan.

6   In every regiment *understaben* included the following people: the quartermaster (who was in charge of the billeting and catering service), a drum major, five barber-surgeons, six oboists (the oboe was the most important melodic instrument in the military orchestras of the time), a judge advocate, a *gevaldiger* and a *stokkeknægt* (who both had the job of carrying out the physical punishment sentenced at the regiment's internal court), and an armourer.

7   National recruits were conscripted soldiers with duties like those of the enlisted. With regard to the difference between national recruits and landsoldater, see Petersen 2001.

8   Each soldier in the regiment had a number. The number could not be changed and thus could be either occupied or vacant. In principle, the commanding officer was obliged to keep all numbers occupied, unless there were special arrangements with the army command.

9   Billeting regulations for the Danish market towns were stipulated in *forordninger* (ordinances) of 21 April 1764, 8 May 1775, 4 August 1788 and 15 November 1816. Similar stipulations were issued for the Duchies on 7 June 1775 and 31 October 1788. Finally a mention should be made of the billeting regulations of 1806 for units on the march. From the earlier period, among others a billeting regulation for the cavalry is known from 23 June 1740.

10 *Kæmneren* was in charge of the market town's municipal funds. The task was a civic duty and normally a new *kæmner* was appointed each year. If a town's billeting accounts have been preserved, they are usually as documents in *kæmnerens* accounts, which are part of *rådstuearkiverne* (the municipal archives).

11 Falkenskjold 1847, p. 306. Falkenskjold was commander of *Danske Livregiment* from 13 February 1771 to 22 January 1772.

12 Købke 1892, pp. 507 f.

13 Abrahamson 1771, pp. 29 f.

14 Bjerg 1983, p. 163.

15 The billeting regulation of 21 April 1764 stipulated in paragraph 17 that one sickroom with three beds should be fitted out per company. Irrespective of the number of patients, the town should pay 48 *skilling* every month for light and firewood in the summer half of the year and 1 *rigsdaler* in the winter half. Such details are not found in later regulations.

16 In Danish called *kronarbejde*.

17 The episode was considered very serious, as the Absolutist fear of social unrest was very strong after the French Revolution.

18 *Krigsartiklerne* contained rules about the mutual relations between the troops and the officers, about the punishment for crimes committed and about the forms for enforcement of discipline.

19 The 1725 ordinance, it is true, allowed soldiers to 'work with their own hands', that is to act as master artisans without being members of a guild. However, this privilege was taken from them with *Verfügung* of 10 December 1736 and 7 January 1737, respectively. See also: *forordning* of 20 April 1739; *reskript* of 10 August 1742; *forordning* of 21 May 1745; *reskript* of 23 October 1767 (see note 1). *Generalitets- og Kommissariatskollegiet*s letter of 28 April 1792, in: Rosenstand Goiske.

20 *Forordning* of 21 March 1800.

21 *Gnav* was the most popular game of carentury.

22 Wagner 1880, p. 94.

23 An exception, though, is Petersen 2003.

24 The so-called *gageringsplaner*.

25 For religious ceremonies, the priest was paid a small cash fee.

26 The figures 1816 and 1840 are in *rigsbankdaler*, a currency introduced in 1813.

27 The rise of drill schools meant that, by and large, new soldiers did not stay in their fixed garrison town in the first months of their service.

Community and 'zünftig' culture in Danish craft guilds

The Danish term *lav* is equivalent to the English term guild. Basically *lav* means community, and the phenomenon of craft guilds refers to trade organisations within the field of crafts in the Danish cities and towns.

In order to draw a distinction between the original craft guilds and modern-day organisations within the crafts, some of which still calling themselves guilds, it is important to emphasize that membership of the historical guilds was compulsory and that it comprised all master craftsmen, journeymen and apprentices within each trade.[1]

Four phases

The period of guilds in Denmark begins in the early Middle Ages and ends with the Freedom of Trade Act of 1857 which came into force in 1862. For clarity, the period can be divided into four phases.

The first phase stretches from the early Middle Ages to the end of the 15th century. Here we meet the earliest craft guilds, which evolved in the newly founded market towns. It is evident that the craft guilds were inspired by those in the German towns, just as it is clear that the craft guilds were influenced by the religious guilds. However, special mention should be made of the fact that the most essential factor in establishing the guilds was the simple necessity of organising in communities.

The second phase stretches from the end of the 15th century to the guild reform in 1681/82. This period is the heyday of the guilds and a period from which there is excellent source material that enables us to analyse the function and character of the guilds in detail.

The third phase, from the reform in 1681/82 to the abolition of the guilds with the coming into force of the Freedom of Trade Act in 1862, is characterised by governmental measures against the guilds and a gradual economic liberalisation, which by degrees eliminated the basis of the guilds' existence.

From 1862 and from the 1870s in particular, new organisations were established in the form of trade unions and employers' associations.

Theme and outline

This outline will focus on the period from the end of the 15th century to the abolition of the guilds in 1862, and the focal point will be the guild community and the special guild culture, the so-called *zünft* that characterised the craft guilds.

The phenomenon of craftsmen organising themselves in guilds was widespread across most of Europe and there was a close network between the guilds. Here the focus will be on the Danish towns of which Copenhagen was by far the largest, while the provincial towns with a population of typically 1,000 to 5,000 were fairly small seen from a present-day perspective. I will especially concentrate on the development outside Copenhagen.

The aim is to give an overall description of the different aspects of the functions of the craft guilds: their social activities, organisation, education, administration of the so-called moral economy and the *zünftig* customs, which were maintained solely by virtue of the strong international network to which the guilds belonged.

Finally, I will analyse the driving forces underlying the struggle between the growing power of central government and the traditionally self-governing guild communities, and which eventually led to the abolition of the guilds in the 19th century.

Sources that bring us closer to the grass-roots level of history

When I was exploring sources for subjects for my dissertation, I had the opportunity to research the history of crafts. I was deeply fascinated by the extensive and largely unused source material kept in the guild archives.

One thing is what the laws and rules of the guilds tell us about what the conditions *ought to be*, but they perhaps do not tell so much about what they *actually were*. Something else is that the records in the guild archives show quite another reality, as they include detailed information on rules and inventory, meetings and internal wrangles, apprentice contracts and letter copies, income and expenditure, all events, great and small, that took place in the course of time. Often an almost inaccessible and enormous amount of source material, but on the other hand an amazing source, which from as early as the late 16th century and particularly from the 17th century gives us a unique insight into the mentality and behavioural pattern of craftsmen of that time, and thus brings us closer to the grass-roots level of history.

Furthermore, good survey material is available in the form of reports submitted by the guilds and market towns to the governmental guild commissions from 1800 and 1853.[2]

Research

Danish research into the history of craft guilds is very limited, and for many years it has been an easy task to keep apace with developments in this field. If one is familiar with Camillus Nyrop's numerous source-based monographs from the decades around 1900, one is practically up-to-date. And having read Helge Søgaard's doctoral thesis from 1940 on the craft guilds in Aarhus during Absolutism, one has a thorough, qualified and indispensable account of the development in a single market town.[3]

Other, partial, studies have appeared, such as Albert Olsen's major article on the state and the guilds; however, this is mainly based on laws and regulations, which, as already mentioned, say what the conditions ought to be, rather than what they actually were. In the beginning of the 1980s, a work series on the cultural history of the crafts was published, which in this connection does not contribute new material, as the account is characterised by a modernist approach according to which the craftsmen are regarded as individuals and not as members of guild communities.[4]

The major works in in the history of Danish crafts are still Nyrop's monographs and Søgaard's doctoral thesis.

In contrast to Denmark, a range of important works has been published in Germany and Sweden during the last twenty years, of which I would like to single out two Swedish doctoral theses: namely, Lars Edgren's major book from 1987 on handicrafts and craftsmen in Malmö 1750-1847, and Lars Magnusson's thesis from 1988 on investors and smiths in Eskilstuna 1800-1850. Both works are based on thorough studies of the original source material, they offer a good comprehensive view of international research within the field, and theoretically and methodologically they are inspired by cultural history, which provides a fruitful combination of historical solidity and theoretical vigour.[5]

FIG. 1.

Craft guilds in Denmark in the 17th and 18th centuries. Town craftsmen were organised in guilds to safeguard common interests during the Middle Ages, but a reliable overview of the extent of the guild system is first possible from the 17th and 18th centuries. As the map shows, there was quite a hierarchy of guild towns: from the large trendsetting towns down to the small towns with only one or very few guilds. Many small market towns, however, especially in North and West Jutland, were completely without guilds. If a craftsman from these towns wanted to assert himself, he had to request admission to one of the organisations for his trade outside his home town.

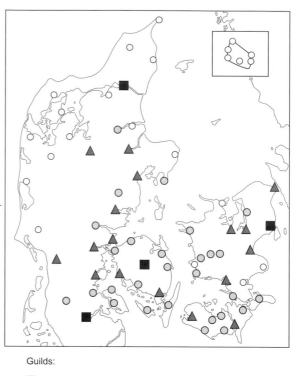

Guilds:

- ■ 15-
- ▲ 5-15
- ◯ 1-5
- ○ None

Distribution and hierarchy

It was during the 1400s that the craft guilds really became visible in the medieval townscape, and by the 1600s it is possible to form a comprehensive view of the guilds in the Danish market towns.

Here, the principle of hierarchy prevailed, where the major German guild towns are at the top of the system followed by Copenhagen and then Aalborg, Odense and Flensburg, all of which had more than 15 guilds.

One step further down the hierarchy we find guild towns of some calibre, such as Viborg, Randers, Aarhus, Horsens, Kolding, Ribe, Svendborg, Holbæk, Roskilde, Køge, Elsinore, Næstved, Nykøbing Falster and Nakskov – all well-established market towns according to Danish standards, each having between 5 to 15 guilds.

Yet another step down in this hierarchy were a large number of smaller market towns with only a few guilds, which were often subordinate guilds to those in the larger market towns.

And at the very bottom of the hierarchy were the small market towns that did not have any guilds at all. However, a few ambitious craftsmen from these small towns applied for membership of the guilds located in the more important market towns. Thus, a number of craftsmen from the market towns around the inlet Limfjorden were organised in the guilds in the nearby towns of Viborg and Aalborg.

The craft guilds

A craft guild consists of three groups: master craftsmen, journeymen and apprentices, and membership was compulsory. Guilds as associations solely for master craftsmen belong to the period after 1862. Despite differences between the various groups, they were all connected to the trade and were thus members of the guild community. The different terms master craftsman or master, journeyman and apprentice merely represented phases in the normal lifecycle of the craftsman from apprentice over journeyman to master, and during this period it was the rule rather than the exception that any apprentice in the fullness of time could set up for himself as master and citizen in the market town.

The guilds had many different functions. They were responsible for teaching the trade, supervising the training of the apprentices and the making of the masterpieces. The guilds had their own courts. They set prices for work and materials, allocated journeymen and apprentices to the masters, prevented competition between masters in the same trade, and on the whole had extensive powers to prevent certain masters from growing big at the expense of others. The guilds also provided financial assistance in the form of sickness benefit and burial expenses to the masters as well as to their journeymen, apprentices and the entire household. And finally, the guilds were the forum for a whole set of complicated rituals, the so-called *zünft*, all with the purpose of showing that the members of a certain guild were people of quality and rank. It was maintained by the strong international network, the *zünft*, which in fact is the German word for guild.

Government and the guilds

During the Middle Ages, the craft guilds were granted a monopoly to practise their trade. In return, the guilds had an implicit duty to ensure that the trade involved an appropriate number of qualified craftsmen working at a fair price.

If this balance was disturbed, for instance when the masters in one particular craft tried to exclude new masters, and this occurred now and then, it could happen that the King would intervene.

King Christian IV did this when he abolished all craft guilds in Denmark in 1613. But the fact that already in 1621 he had to accept the fact that the craftsmen organised themselves in guilds says much about the real balance of power, and although, on paper, his decrees on guilds ensured considerably more control over the craftsmen than before, the guild archives show that after a short period of time everything continued as usual.[6]

Absolutism and mercantilism

In the 17th century mercantilism and Absolutism were two closely connected lines of development. Both mercantilism and Absolutism were results of the competition between states during this period, combined with the emerging commodity economy and military technological development. The aim was to create a strong government that could intervene in the development of society by imposing regulatory measures with a view to achieving the highest level of self-sufficiency and national independence. The existence of a large and prosperous population was essential for tax reasons, military reasons, as well as for labour reasons. But what was required was, of course, a population that worked, that created and was productive, and did not waste a non-productive life in idleness.

Guild reforms of Absolutism

On a wide range of issues these governmental views collided with the craft guilds' community and *zünftig* culture. During early Absolutism, several reform attempts were made, and with the guild reform that resulted in two major decrees in 1681-1682, government tried in earnest to take measures against the guild culture. The reform abolished the old rules and issued new statutes that were dictated from above.

Furthermore, the reform intervened notably in three areas:

FIG. 2.

The baker's shop sign with King Frederik IV's monogram and crown. The sign comes from Aarhus.
This and the other illustrations of objects can be seen at Den Gamle By Open Air Museum.

Firstly, it intervened in the guilds' autonomy – and this meant that all meetings and social gatherings that were not expressly authorised by the local authorities were banned and it was also required that a representative of the town attended every meeting.

Secondly, measures were taken to foil the efforts of the guilds to minimize internal competition – this was done by demanding that the town authorities became involved in the approval of master pieces which previously had normally been approved by the guilds alone, and it was expressly forbidden to demand money, feasts and barrels of beer from the new masters. Furthermore, the guilds' rules that each

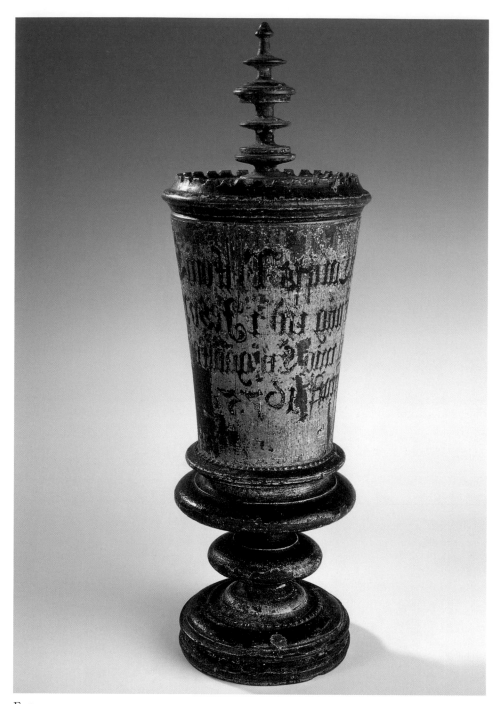

FIG. 3.

The cup was used as a drinking vessel when the new journeymen were admitted to the guild. This is the Aarhus joiner journeymen's cup in wood from 1675.

master was allowed to have a maximum of two to three journeymen were abolished. Instead there would be no limit to the number of journeymen. And the masters were forbidden to make agreements about fixed prices for their work.

And thirdly, strong measures were taken against the *zünftig* customs of the guilds and those of the journeymen in particular. Basically, all the laws and rules specific to journeymen were revoked. The requirement that the journeymen had to prove legitimacy were banned, the journeymen's social gatherings were banned, and finally their Saint Mondays and their many different traditional festivities were banned.

Just after the guild reform had been implemented, government began to permit craftsmen to set up for themselves as independent craftsmen without being members of a guild. Such craftsmen were called free masters. Throughout the 1700s, admission to become a free master was extended several times, but as admissions of this kind were primarily aimed at giving people in straitened circumstances the opportunity to support themselves by becoming independent, this incentive was no genuine threat to the guilds.

The various rules of the reform were followed up several times during the 18th century, and the reform work of Absolutism culminated in the major reform of the Copenhagen guilds in 1800. The reform banned – once again – all guild prejudices, rules or customs including Saint Mondays and letters of legitimacy. It introduced a free contractual relationship between masters and journeymen and extended admission to become free masters in such a way that this could, for the first time, be to the detriment of the guild masters.

However, this reform, and especially the opportunity to become free masters, was weakened in the years that followed, during which the economic revival of the late 18th century was followed by depression.

By 1832 the application of the reform was also extended to the provincial towns, however, in a version that was so weak that it can hardly be characterised as a radical guild reform.

Copenhagen and the provincial towns

When speaking of the period of Absolutism, it is important to distinguish between the development in Copenhagen and the development in the provincial towns.
In Copenhagen the governmental power of the state was close at hand, while there was a long distance to Royal Copenhagen for bailiffs and mayors from the provin-

cial towns scattered all over the country, where living in harmony with fellow townsmen was regarded as much more appropriate than conforming to the letter of the distant law.

While the provincial towns generally experienced economic stagnation until the beginning of the 19th century, Copenhagen, on the other hand, enjoyed economic expansion and growth in the 18th century. Here, factories were established, new town districts were built, and the basis for an extraordinary development within the crafts in Copenhagen was created. Especially within the large building trades, major master craftsmen emerged with many journeymen and considerable capital power. The traditional generational cycle where a craftsman started off as an apprentice in order to become a journeyman and then a master was broken. This again resulted in a clash of interest between masters and journeymen, which in the provincial towns was a phenomenon that occurred much later.[7]

Own court and police authority

It is widely believed that local courts were the lowest legal authority in Denmark during Absolutism. However, on closer examination it appears that below the surface of the perfect power structure of Absolutism was a whole network of local organisations which at a grass-roots level attended to a range of important administrative and legal tasks; tasks which at a later date would typically belong to public authorities. The villages had their village community and the market towns had their craft guilds.

The master of the guild was the chairman and a special sign showed where he lived. Usually the meetings of the guild took place there in the master's house. The sign on the lodging house showed where the travelling journeymen could find lodging when they arrived in a town.

In the guild the central element of the meeting was the casket. The casket or chest was where the guild kept its rules, records, seals, moneybox and other articles of value. The master of the guild 'threw open' the casket by knocking on the lid with a stick, and the casket was opened. From then on everything was taken seriously. The casket symbolised the dignity of the guild, and 'for open casket' simply meant: The court is now in session!

The master of the guild would typically assemble with his assessors once a week to settle cases between the members of the guild, irrespective of whether the case con-

FIG. 4.

The guild casket was the unifying focal point for the craft guilds in the market towns. This is where the guild's regulations, records and other valuables were kept and important issues were decided 'in the presence of the open casket', as it was put. This is the casket of the Aarhus bakers' guild from the 18th century.

cerned masters, journeymen or apprentices. And despite the many governmental prohibitions and interventions in the guilds' autonomy, it seems that most of the guilds, unconcerned, continued to settle petty cases between the members, also in the 1700s and 1800s. They just watched their steps more carefully. Typical cases could be incidents where the journeyman of one master had been lured to work for another, or where a master had purchased a large consignment of raw material without sharing it with his fellow masters in the guild. Or they could be fights or wrangles between the journeymen or between a master and his journeyman, or cases where a master or journeyman had failed to attend a funeral although he was next in turn and had been summoned.

Besides acting as court of justice, the guilds also acted as a kind of police authority. That is, the officials of the guild were the executive power, which ensured that the guild court decisions were effected. The means of enforcement were first and foremost the right to seize someone's goods or, in extreme cases, exclusion from the guild. The rules of 1738 of the Aarhus smith guild thus stipulate that if any guild brother 'has been fined for any offence, and does not pay before the next guild meeting, then the master of the guild, with the assistance of the guild messenger and two other guild brothers, shall be free to seize his goods for the amount owing'. Then if the debtor does not redeem the pledge, the master of the guild has the right to have the pledge valued within 12 weeks and subsequently sell it at auction.[8]

In practice the guilds did not seem to be a strict police authority due to the fact that the overriding consideration for the community often meant that meticulous justice was replaced by an amicable settlement acceptable to everyone.

When the governmental reform commission in 1800 asked about conditions in the market towns, most towns and guilds wisely evaded the question concerning the future existence of the guild courts. The guilds were aware that enforcement of their own laws was illegal, so on this point, they had better stay silent and the local members of the commission, who naturally knew what was going on, for the sake of a quiet life and future cooperation, saw no reason to report such knowledge to the central administration.

However, in the towns of Fredericia and Assens they revealed themselves, and in Assens the guilds informed the commission that

(…) disputes between one master craftsman and another or between master craftsmen and journeymen shall be settled in the guild by a majority decision (…), and disputes between one journeyman and another shall also be settled at the journeymen's meeting in the presence of two master craftsmen. If the disputes cannot be settled, settlement must be reached in the above-mentioned manner by the master craftsmen.[9]

This gives us a rare opportunity to look into the real world of the guilds. And there is little doubt that events of this type happened in the same way in other towns.

Education and protection of the trade

Masters, journeymen and apprentices had a common interest in protecting the trade and the people who performed it, and the guild was the forum for the professional training in the trade and the guarantor that the quality was up to standard.

It was not the individual master who made a contract with a new apprentice. It was a matter for the guild, and the apprenticeship contract was often copied into the guild's record. If the guild did not already know the new apprentice, he would be required to furnish proof that he was born in lawful wedlock of honest parents of an unblemished reputation.

As far back as 1620, the King had tried to put a stop to the craft guilds' demands for letters of legitimacy. But law was one thing, reality another, and up until the mid 1700s there are occasional written testimonies that the guilds wanted to be certain that no bastards were taken on.

It was also in the guild that the journeymen, after having gone through various rituals, received their certificate of completed apprenticeship, the proof that they had gone through a *zünftig* education in conformity with international guild customs, and were now entitled to travel all over Europe. It was in the guild that the masterpiece of the young master craftsman was approved, an event which also included entertainment and festivities. In addition he was supposed to give a proper party and donate a fairly large sum of money in connection with his admission into the guild.

This very feature was a constant source of conflict with the state, as the guilds tended to increase the costs from time to time, in order to limit the number of masters in the trade, and naturally the authorities could not accept this. It was against this background that the guild reform of 1681/82 intervened in an attempt to keep a tight rein on the irregularities. However, numerous notes in the guilds' archives show that the system continued to be strong and powerful.

The guild protected the trade by acting – almost as a kind of police authority – against the so-called tricksters, that is, people who plied the craft without being master craftsmen and members of the guild. What usually happened was that the guild sent three masters to confiscate the tools of the person in question – and very probably he also got a good thrashing.

With the increasing number of free masters, it became legal for people to ply their craft outside the guild, and throughout the 1700s there were numerous conflicts between guilds and authorities concerning the rights of these free masters.

Preventing competition between guild members

Equality was a key word, and one of the guild's most important objectives was to ensure that everybody within the community had more or less equal conditions, so that no one would rise too high or sink too low. The English social historian E.P. Thompson has applied the term 'moral economy' to this system.[10] The term refers to the basically medieval attitude that economic enterprise was an integral part of human behaviour, and thus subject to the commitments of moral laws. This attitude persisted in wider circles despite the policy of government by which growth and competition were increasingly given pride of place.

In the craft guilds joint attempts were made to regulate the economy in such a way that all within the trade could maintain the dignity of their position. Tendencies that some might grow big at the expense of others were strictly restrained. For that reason all competition was forbidden and prices and wages were the same for everybody and fixed in accordance with the so-called *justum pretium* principle, which meant that not only were they to be trade-economically reasonable, they were also to be fair. Although the reform of 1681/82 stipulated that master craftsmen were not allowed to make price agreements, there is plenty of documentation that the policy of fixed prices remained the norm as long as until the first half of the 19th century.[11]

All journeymen within each craft earned the same wages, and it was forbidden to leave one master in order to work for another in the same town. Similarly, the masters were not allowed to poach each other's journeymen, and if these rules were broken the guild court imposed suitable fines.

When a strange journeyman arrived in town after having travelled abroad, he was an asset in whom all masters were interested. But in order to avoid any competition between the masters on gaining the right to employ the journeyman in question, most guilds had an arrangement that ensured that all masters, from time to time, were given the opportunity to have such a widely travelled journeyman in their employment. In brief the arrangement meant that once a strange journeyman had arrived in the town he reported to the guild master or to the journeymen's lodging house and then his services were offered to the guild's masters in turn. The principle of this arrangement was, as a report from Aalborg puts it in 1800, that 'a master craftsman of less fortune could thereby often be given assistance to employ a journeyman', so that it 'in the small places where there is often a shortage of journeymen could be of assistance to a poor, yet able and good man'.[12]

With the reform in 1800, coming into effect in the provincial towns in 1832, this system was abolished, and the reason why the abolition in fact seemed to be successful is not that the authorities were capable of forcing it through, but that the increasingly independent journeymen of the Enlightenment period would no longer put up with the system.

Saint Mondays and other drinking days

The guilds also regarded it as important to define themselves downwards in society. Even if the craftsmen were not men of property, they could present themselves as honest people with a special *zünftig* culture. In the mid 18th century, it was still common for stone masons to wear wigs, and for travelling journeymen to wear three-cornered hats and rapiers – the guilds had their own special customs and traditions. And the craftsmen had a lot of self-respect: they would not tolerate accusations of being rogues, rascals, or even worse – thieves or illegitimate. The craftsmen were people of quality and rank and the trade was regarded as 'das ehrsahme Handwerck', to use the German term.

In his manifesto for the newly reorganised *Kommercekollegium*[13] from 1735, the far-seeing government official, Otto Thott, complained about journeymen who much too often took a 'Saint Monday off, which is often followed by a sleeping Tuesday and a sick Wednesday'.[14] Otto Thott belonged to the circle of officials who had a real ambition to take measures against what among reformist officials was regarded as laziness. Not only because this culture belonged to an earlier time, but primarily because it was a hindrance to the efforts to implement economic development in order to provide increased wealth for the country.

Information on Saint Mondays is generally very limited. Saint Mondays were banned by the reform of 1681/82, and therefore no one talked much about this custom. But it is certain that in former times it was a custom among the craftsmen to take a day off now and then, and research shows that quite often a considerable number of working days were spent drinking and on practising *zünftige* customs. The occasion could be the celebration of Shrovetide, but it could just as well be the celebration of an apprentice who had been admitted as a journeyman, or simply a meeting at the journeymen's inn – although it was forbidden, officially.

Scattered notes in the guilds' archives provide an occasional glimpse underneath the official surface. And in the report from the town of Sakskøbing to the guild commission of 1800 it is said in direct terms that the journeymen work no more than necessary to provide themselves with clothing – 'and spend the rest of their earnings at the inn'. 'Not seldom it happens that they idle away as much as four days a week without going to work'. Examples of similar occurrences are indicated in a range of other reports from the large amount of existing material from the guild commission of 1800.[15] English, German as well as Swedish research shows that in these countries the Saint Monday lived on despite bans and interventions.[16]

Furthermore, a long range of customs, games and festivities were connected with work. These traditions were all aimed at illustrating that the craft and its practitioners were something special, and at the same time they were aimed at providing a few minutes' rest and a drink. The Swedish historian Lars Magnusson describes the working hours as being 'porous', in contrast to the concentrated working hours of modern times.[17]

Well-known are probably the initiation customs when a journeyman was to be admitted. But the so-called pranks where the new apprentice was sent for all kinds of crazy things are also characteristic, and there are many amusing examples. Thus, the painters sent the apprentice to get upwards-paint while the shoemakers used tartan-sewing thread, and the baker sent the boys to get dough gloves or a basket of steam.[18]

It is characteristic that work was not regarded as an existential necessity as it is today, shortly after the turn of the millennium. People worked as much as they had to and no more. The remaining time was spent enjoying life and having a good time.

Minimal effect

The guilds in the capital as well as in provincial towns had their heyday until around 1800. And although from 1681 on, the Absolute monarchy intervened several times to control the activities of the guilds, important traits of their culture lived on as a cultural undercurrent – practically unaffected by the political and economic ideals of that time. One could point out three aspects of explanation:

Firstly, the relationship between the authorities and the guilds was probably more ambivalent than is revealed by the fundamental proclamations of the reform in 1681/82. The guilds administered a long range of duties that no one else would attend to, and it was obvious to everyone that they actually did this quite well. The restless journeymen were under control, new craftsmen were trained and the guilds

THOMAS BLOCH RAVN

FIG. 5.

The lodging house sign for the Aarhus ropemaker journeymen's guild. The sign hung outside the Journeyman's Inn and was removed when a new master was elected as innkeeper for the journeymen, and accordingly had to provide for the inn. This removal of the sign was celebrated with great festivity.

provided substantial social welfare, a duty that the authorities could not take over straight away. At the same time, as a present-day observer, it is not difficult to imagine that mayors, bailiffs and aldermen in the market towns might be more loyal to their fellow townsmen than to a distant government in Copenhagen.

Secondly, in the relatively static town communities there was no economic incentive for the craftsmen to break with the guild community. Only in Copenhagen was development taking place that made it attractive for the individual to try to break with the traditional systems in favour of the new and unknown.

Thirdly, the significance of the craftsmen's international organisation, the *zünft*, should not be disregarded. It worked with various means to maintain the old system and here the journeymen in particular played an important part. The Danish playwright and satirist Ludvig Holberg (1684-1754) has given an excellent description of this in one of his epistles in which he points out that the journeymen

(…) are the only persons in society that cannot be forced. They have no permanent dwelling and without the slightest trouble or the least loss can move from one place to another. When they threaten to desert one should believe that they are in earnest, and their masters must then be tactful unless they wish to see their work and trade lie idle. For wherever a journeyman goes he will be in his native land, and when he comes to a foreign land in the evening, he will be in service again the very next morning. Thus, the journeymen are the only ones who can travel abroad without cost, and with empty hands can wander about the world as long as they have enough pennies to pay with in a couple of lodging houses on their way.[19]

Modern times

In the years around 1800 a new phase of development began, which over a few decades resulted in fundamental changes in the conditions of the guild craftsmen.

Firstly, the administration and police authority became increasingly efficient, and – for the first time – a close connection between the political proclamations and practical policy actually began to appear. The fear that revolutionary journeymen would enter the country plays a part here, and the authorities' control of the travelling journeymen was intensified considerably. Thus, the craftsmen's international network was greatly impeded.

Secondly, the economic decline in the first decades of the 19th century meant that for the first time in many years, the demand for qualified craftsmen decreased, and unemployment became common and sometimes prevalent. The travelling journeymen who used to carry themselves like gentlemen in three-cornered hats with rapiers in their belts now turned into increasingly shabby labourers who had to struggle to earn their daily bread.

Thirdly, as a result of the agricultural reforms in the late 18th century, division of labour in the countryside increased, and especially from the 1820s and the 1830s the number of craftsmen working in the countryside grew explosively – with or without a license. Consequently, the craftsmen of the market towns who until then had had the agrarian hinterland more or less to themselves had to face competition from the craftsmen in the countryside.

Fourthly, and finally, as the towns began to experience economic growth in the

Fig. 6.

In the 18ᵗʰ century, a silver cup became a status symbol for the journeymen's guilds. It was the custom that a new journeyman donated a sign to the guild in connection with his admission. This is the cup of the Aarhus joiner journeymen from 1824.

1840s, it became more and more relevant for the guilds' masters to consider if it would be profitable to reorganise into an individualistic and competitive way of working.

To make a long and complicated explanation brief, an effective control system had been created and at the same time a range of economic incentives formed the basis for fundamental changes in the organisation of the crafts. Things started to move fast, and with the abolition of the guilds by the Freedom of Trade Act taking effect from 1862, it could be said that legislation had been adapted to a development that had more or less already occurred.

Rupture or continuity?

On the other hand, one cannot disregard the fact that development in Denmark was characterised more by continuity than rupture.

It was not rapid industrialisation that formed the basis of the Freedom of Trade Act.

The manufacturers of mercantilism and the factories of the early 19th century did not fundamentally affect or threaten crafts, and the craftsman-like organising of the manufacturing sector continued to exist until the 1890s, in some sectors perhaps until after the Second World War.

It is also characteristic that the first organisation of workers and employers took place within the trades that had previously had strong guild organisations, and for many years these skilled craftsmen had the decisive influence in both the workers' and the employers' organisations.

On a voluntary basis the tests to prove ability to practise the trade that had been abolished by the Freedom of Trade Act were reintroduced. A special legal system with arbitration and labour law was introduced, which in the beginning did not differ much from the systems that existed within the craft guilds. And within many trades, spirits were kept up in the social field by awarding grants and the establishment of foundations, many of which still exist.

The American labour market researcher, Walter Galenson, who spent some years in Denmark after the Second World War, pointed out that the guilds in Denmark lived on in the modern-day labour market organisations to an extent that cannot be seen in other European countries.

What is interesting here is that Galenson identified a particular traditional dislike of economic individualism and free competition and he ascertained that the competitive spirit in Denmark had never been as radical as in his own country USA, or for that matter in any other country that he knew of. He gave plenty of examples of how various competition-restricting arrangements from the period of guilds were imperceptibly embedded in the new organisations and in the set of rules that regulated interaction between these organisations.[20]

While some traits of the guild communities thus lived on in the new organisations, the power of the *zünft* was without doubt broken. Of course there were still some who adhered to the various kinds of initiation rituals for journeymen, of course there were still craftsmen who went travelling, and of course there was a Saint Monday, not unusual within the building trade until as recently as the 1970s. But the special customs of the *zünft* – and especially the international network that they were based on – were definitively gone.

BIBLIOGRAPHY

Dybdahl, Vagn et al. (eds.) 1982-84. *Håndværkets Kulturhistorie*. Vol. 1-4. Copenhagen: Håndværksrådet.

Edgren, Lars 1987. *Lärling, gesäll, mästare. Hantverk och hantverkare i Malmö 1750-1847*. Lund: Dialogos.

Galenson, Walter 1955. *Arbejder og Arbejdsgiver i Danmark*. Copenhagen: Det danske Forlag.

Griessinger, Andreas 1981. *Das symbolische Kapital der Ehre. Streikbewegungen und kollektives Bewusstsein deutscher Handwerksgesellen im 18. Jahrhundets*. Frankfurt a.M.: Ullstein TB-Verlag.

Henningsen, Henning 1960. *Behøvling og hønsning. Indvielses- og optagelsesskikke i håndværkerlav*. Copenhagen: Håndværksrådets Forlag.

Holberg, Ludvig 1750. *Epistler Befattende Adskillige historiske, politiske, metaphysiske, moralske, philosophiske, Item Skiemtsomme Materier*. Tomus III. Copenhagen.

Hübertz, J.R. 1846. *Aktstykker vedkommende Staden og Stiftet Aarhus*. Vol. II. Copenhagen.

Magnusson, Lars 1988. *Den Bråkiga Kulturen. Forläggare och Smideshantverkare i Eskilstuna 1800-1850*. Stockholm: Författarförlaget.

Nyrop, C. 1887. *Kjøbenhavns Tømmerlav: Industrihistoriske Meddelelser*. Copenhagen: C.A. Reitzel.

Nyrop, C. 1893. *Træk af dansk Lavsordning. Lavenes Ophævelse i det Sekstende og Syttende Aarhundrede*. Copenhagen.

Nyrop, C. 1903. *Haandværksskik i Danmark. Nogle Aktstykker samt nogle Oplysninger om Handwärksgebrauch und Gewohnheit*. Copenhagen: Det Nordiske Forlag.

Nyrop, C. 1907. *Kjøbenhavns Murer- og Stenhuggerlav: Historiske Meddelelser*. Copenhagen: Kjøbenhavns Murer- og Stenhuggerlav.

Nyrop, C. 1909a. *Kjøbenhavns Skomagerlav 1509-1909*. Copenhagen: Nielsen & Lydiches Bogtrykkeri.

Nyrop, C. 1909b. *Den danske Enevoldsmagt og Lavene. En lavshistorisk Undersøgelse.* Copenhagen.

Olsen, Albert 1927-28. 'Staten og lavene'. *Historiske Meddelelser om København.* 2nd series, vol. III, pp. 81-136.

Ravn, Thomas Bloch 1980. Fra tømmermænd til lønarbejdere og kapitalister. Private print.

Ravn, Thomas Bloch 1982. 'Fra svendelav til fagforening. Brud eller kontinuitet?' *Arbejderhistorie,* 18, pp. 3-16.

Ravn, Thomas Bloch 1983. 'Arbejdet mellem nødvendighed og dyd'. *Den Jyske Historiker,* 26, pp. 4-20.

Ravn, Thomas Bloch 1984. 'Håndværks- og fabriksvirksomhed i Christiansfeld'. In: A. Pontoppidan Thyssen (ed.), *Herrnhutersamfundet i Christiansfeld.* Vol. 1. Aabenraa: Historisk Samfund for Sønderjylland, pp. 143-274.

Ravn, Thomas Bloch 1985. 'Snapsting og markedshåndværk: Omkring en Christiansfeld-skomagers besøg i Viborg 1779'. *Fra Viborg Amt,* 50, pp. 41-68.

Ravn, Thomas Bloch 1986. 'Oprør, spadseregange og lønstrejker i København før 1870'. In: Flemming Mikkelsen (ed.), *Protest og oprør. Kollektive aktioner i Danmark 1700-1985.* Aarhus, pp. 47-85.

Ravn, Thomas Bloch 1988a. 'For åben lade'. *Skalk,* 6, pp. 18-27.

Ravn, Thomas Bloch 1988b. 'Fortiden i nutiden – mental inerti og moralsk økonomi i Danmark fra middelalderen til i dag'. In: Vagn Wåhlin (ed.), *Historien i kulturhistorien.* Aarhus: Aarhus Universitetsforlag, pp. 235-55.

Ravn, Thomas Bloch 1988c. *Håndværk og købstadsliv: Omkring skomager Hammershøjs beretning om Viborg i forrige århundrede.* Viborg: Historisk Samfund for Viborg Amt.

Ravn, Thomas Bloch 1997. 'Byens mennesker. Befolkningsforhold og mentalitet'. In: Ib Gejl (ed.), *Århus. Byens Historie 1720-1870.* Aarhus: Århus Byhistoriske Udvalg, pp. 81-109.

Søgaard, Helge 1940. *Håndværkerlavene i Århus under Enevælden – en socialhistorisk studie.* Copenhagen: Munksgaard.

Thompson, E.P. 1971. 'The Moral Economy of the English Crowd in the Eighteenth Century'. *Past and Present,* 50, pp. 76-136.

Thott, Otto 1735. 'Uforgribelige Tanker om Kommerciens Tilstand og Opkomst'. Published in: Kristof Glamann & Erik Oxenbøll 1983, *Studier i dansk merkantilisme,* pp. 139 ff. Copenhagen: Akademisk Forlag.

NOTES

1   This article is based on my previous publications: Ravn 1980. Ravn 1982. Ravn 1983. Ravn 1984. Ravn 1985. Ravn 1986. Ravn 1988a. Ravn 1988b. Ravn 1988c. Ravn 1997.

2   The guild archives are primarily kept in *landsarkiverne* (The Provincial Archives of Zealand, Funen, Southern and Northern Jutland). The records from the guild commissions are in Rigsarkivet (The Danish National Archives).

3   Nyrop 1887. Nyrop 1893. Nyrop 1903. Nyrop 1907. Nyrop 1909a. Nyrop 1909b. Søgaard 1940.

4   Olsen 1927-28. Dybdahl 1982-84.

5   Edgren 1987. Magnusson 1988.

6   Nyrop 1887, p. 45. Olsen 1927-28, p. 91.

7   Here, I will concentrate on the market towns and as far as the capital is concerned, I refer to my previous research published in Ravn 1982 and Ravn 1986.

8   Hübertz 1846, p. 294.

9   Rigsarkivet, Danske Kancelli, 5. Departement: K7 A-B, Bilag til Ordre af 8 August 1800 om Kommission ang. Lavene i Danmark. (Assens and Fredericia)

10 Thompson 1971.

11 See note 1.

12 Rigsarkivet, Danske Kancelli, 5. Departement: K7 A-B, Bilag til Ordre af 8 August 1800 om Kommission ang. Lavene i Danmark. (Assens and Fredericia).

13 A section of the central administration dealing with commerce and industry.

14 Thott 1735, p. 139.

15 Rigsarkivet, Danske Kancelli, 5. Departement K7 A-B, Bilag til Ordre af 8 August 1800 om Kommission ang. Lavene i Danmark. (Assens and Fredericia)

16 Thompson 1971. Edgren 1987, p. 241. Griessinger 1981. Reulecke 1976.

17 Magnusson 1988, pp. 265 ff.

18 Henningsen 1960.

19 Holberg 1750.

20 Galenson 1955, pp. 36, 117 f., 143-49, 389.

Anders Monrad Møller

The seaports of the Kingdom and their shipping trade, 1660-1850

The market towns in the Kingdom of Denmark have always been viewed in relation to the capital, Copenhagen – the polarity between province and capital indeed still exists. The position of the metropolis during Absolutism was strengthened from the end of the 17th century and throughout the 18th century. The small market towns in the Kingdom quickly construed this as being something that was happening at their expense. Around the country, a golden past at the beginning of the 17th century was remembered, when every market town with respect for itself had export trade and shipping, resulting in great wealth. Testimony to this could be seen in many places in the form of solid, old, half-timbered houses dating from the good times, like the many sepulchral tablets in the town churches showing well-fed merchants and their wives and children. In contrast, in the 18th century, the provinces had to be onlookers at the remarkable progress of Copenhagen with the build-up of large-scale commerce with ships in overseas trade and on the Mediterranean, and they felt, despondently, that others were denied a share in this expansion. Very quickly the idea was established that Copenhagen was deliberately being favoured to the detriment of the provincial towns. As will be argued in the following, there is reason to add some nuances to this black-and-white formulation.

Division of labour between the capital and the provinces

To a certain degree it is true that the capital was favoured. The way the central administration saw the situation was revealed in a report written in 1709-10 by Thomas Jørgensen Hørning,[1] the secretary of *Kommercekollegiet*.[2] He emphasised that only the capital city had sufficient capital to handle overseas trade, including connections to the colonies, which the Danish King also had the pleasure of having in his realm. However, apart from the North-Atlantic possessions of Iceland and the Faroe Is-

FIG. 1.

The most important localities in the article.

lands,[3] these comprised only a small locality in India – Tranquebar on the Coromandel coast – and some forts on the Gold Coast (Guinea) in Africa. Of greater importance were the Danish West-Indian islands, St. Thomas, and St. Jan, and from 1733 also St. Croix, which *Vestindisk Kompagni* (the Danish West India Company) had advantageously bought from France. In addition, a regular sailing to China was started in 1730, and two years later, *Asiatisk Kompagni* (the Danish Asia Company) was formed, replacing the ailing *Ostindisk Kompagni* (The Danish East Asia Company). Overseas shipping was thus organised by trading companies domiciled in the capital city, and the establishment and running of such companies was completely beyond the scope of the provincial towns – only some scattered futile attempts were made. One had to be satisfied with possibly procuring shares in *Asiatisk Kompagni*, but on the other hand, that was one of the best investments of the time.

This localisation of the trading companies was entirely as it should be, according to Thomas Jørgensen Hørning, because power was concentrated in the capital city. But he also had some perceptive views about the role of the market towns. He was glad for the geographical circumstances of the long Danish coasts, which meant that most of the market towns were situated on the coast, and goods to supply the capital city could be easily shipped. Hørning's views on the relationship between the capital and the provinces are crystalised in the sentence about Copenhagen being like a mother for the others. In reality, he saw the relationship as a division of labour.

But Hørning also enthusiastically established another basic fact, namely that while the Kingdom of Denmark had a surplus of grain, the opposite was the case in the Danish King's other Kingdom, Norway. In this way the two Kingdoms supplemented each other, as Norway in turn had fish, timber and iron, which among other things could be exchanged for the Danish grain; from Hørning's point of view, an exceedingly satisfactory situation.

Again a division of labour; and this division of labour depicted in such positive words by Thomas Jørgensen Hørning would prove to be maintained throughout the 18th century. The leading role of the capital was to a certain degree also determined legislatively. The ordinance concerning the so-called 'four *species*' (type of commodity) is famous, which for a few years after 1726 gave Copenhagen the exclusive right to import salt, tobacco, wine and cognac to the Kingdom.[4] In later liberal-oriented history writing, this was regarded as a dreadful mercantilist attempt at centralisation by favouring the capital. However the fact is that it was actually the codification of an existing situation; in 1726, there were no Danish provincial towns with ships that imported salt from Portugal.

In 1735, there was a similar codification concerning trade between Denmark and Norway.[5] This was in the form of a Danish monopoly on supplying Southern Norway with grain, which corresponded with a Norwegian monopoly (introduced in 1733) on supplying iron to Denmark. Again it should be noted that, fundamentally, this was legislation that just set a framework for existing economic relations.

But the development did not pass without expressions of dissatisfaction from the provinces. This was clearly expressed in 1735 when *Kommercekollegiet* carried out an inquiry in all the market towns in the land, where they were to answer a great number of questions, among them about their business life.[6] Here it transpired that in many places people felt that the situation was wretched, and as previously mentioned there was a recollection of a golden past when the economy had been so much better. Many of the answers were in a very pitiable tone with complaints and a plea for financial help and support from the state. But to a certain extent this was the style of the time. And who has ever boasted of wealth if asked by official authorities, who, it could possibly be thought, would remember it the next time tax was to be collected. So it would be better to emphasise the negative aspects.

Although people in the provincial towns felt they were locked into a subordinate role to some extent, this role was not however without importance; Copenhagen and Norway had to be supplied.

18th century provincial ships in shuttle service

This meant that during the whole sailing season, from March/April until the end of the year, provincial ships sailed from their home ports to the capital with firewood, grain, bacon, fruit and other provisions, which were either sold as full cargoes or sold in small lots on the quays in Copenhagen's large harbour. This was done from all the localities on the islands of Zealand, Lolland, Falster and Funen, and from the east coast of Jutland. This could be very regular, and the same skipper with the same vessel could sail from six and up to eight voyages a year in this constant shuttle. The hold had few or no goods on the voyage home, but often small quantities of groceries, salt and manufactured products.

An example from 1733 is Poul Nielsen from Svendborg with his small sloop of five *kommercelæster* (see note 14). On the fourth of the year's six voyages, he carried oats, apples, pears, bacon, eggs and earthenware, while the return cargo consisted only of 22 barrels of Spanish salt. On the last voyage to Copenhagen, he got inward clearance to the capital on 10 October. Subsequently he lay at anchor for weeks to sell his goods. Not everything got sold because he had 19 barrels of butter when he went through customs in Svendborg on 21 December. He clearly wanted to get home for Christmas.

This net of connections between the capital and the provinces was naturally not only important for the exchange of goods, but also for communication in a broader sense. At a time when the conditions of the roads left much to be desired, sea transport was in many cases far easier and cheaper for traveling from one place to another – especially if one had a lot of luggage or a whole load of furniture. It is just difficult to get an impression of its extent. The reason is that while the customs service painstakingly recorded every single consignment of goods, including the absolutely duty-free furniture, passengers were of no interest to the customs. So it is impossible to calculate the number of those who used the opportunity to travel by ship instead of over land. In many instances the traveller had of course to board a ship in any case, because the many Danish islands were linked by a net of ferry connections, the majority run by monopoly ferrymen, who thus worked under conditions different in principle from the other seamen.

There was naturally a certain degree of specialisation in the goods carried by provincial shipping to Copenhagen. From Frederikshavn (at that time called Fladstrand) in North Jutland, there were dried flat fish in large quantities. From the Limfjord area, a little to the south, there were salted herring which were sent via the main town of the area, Aalborg. Further south, there were harbours where beech firewood was the dominant cargo, while in the 18th century a tradition for fruit farming was developed on South Funen, which meant that in the late summer and autumn the vessels carried barrels of apples and pears.

A parallel to the relationship between Copenhagen and the east-facing provincial districts is found in the southern part of Jutland's west coast, where the traffic from the small shipping communities of Ho and Hjerting on the mainland and the islands of Fanø and Rømø was to the south. Some sailed to Altona and Hamburg on the Elbe and some to the Netherlands, where many Danish sailors also got work.[7] The outward-bound cargo from Jutland consisted of provisions such as grain, tallow, butter and other delicatessen goods (smoked or salted bacon) as well as a couple of specialities, black pottery and oysters. The return cargo was dominated by groceries, wine, cognac, and spices etc., typical luxury goods which were imported in very small quantities.

From the Danish provincial towns, the slightly larger ships mainly sailed similar shuttle voyages to Norway. Grain and bacon were the main cargo that went north, while the return load was most often timber. This timber trade has left lasting traces in Denmark, because while the Danish woods included beech trees that gave good firewood, building timber was more difficult to find – oak wood was expensive and was to be mainly reserved for ship building. So there is therefore a very good chance that the pinewood beams and boards to be found in the surviving 18th century Danish houses in the towns and countryside are of Norwegian origin, even though a less significant amount of timber cargo did come with small vessels from the Swedish Kattegat coast.

An example of a seaman who sailed with goods to Norway is Jens Nielsen from Horsens with the sloop *Den dobbelte Krage* (The two crows). He set out for Norway in March 1733 with malt, rye, oats, peas, smoked bacon, butter and two barrels (of 38.64 litres) of distilled spirits. At the beginning of June he had returned from Drammen with about 200 boards of various lengths and 200 battens.

With regard to the Norwegian trade too, there was a certain specialisation. While the skippers from Aalborg and other Jutland towns most often sailed to places in the southernmost Norway, very close connections developed between the town of Odense on Funen and the largest Norwegian town of the time, Bergen. This was not just a matter of exchanging Norwegian fish for Danish grain; there are also several examples of larger ships in a jointly owned shipping company with shares divided among owners, skippers and merchants both in Odense and Bergen.

There were very few Danish seaports that did not have a direct connection to Norwegian harbours with their own ships. These few towns, for example Bogense on Funen, were called on by other Danish ships (from the Kingdom or from the Duchies of Schleswig and Holstein), which collected cargo to be sailed north.

From the Jutland west coast there was an exchange of goods with Norway corresponding to that described for the districts east of Skagen at the northern tip of Jutland. Otherwise Skagen was a dividing line of crucial significance. Quite simply, there was no direct shipping connection between places on the west coast of Jutland and other places in the Kingdom, including Copenhagen.

Most of the provincial ports on Zealand, Lolland, Falster and Møn also conducted shipping to the south. Each year, one or more vessels from each of these ports sailed to Lübeck, and the skipper had wide-ranging order forms submitted by the town's shopkeepers and merchants. In Lübeck, a rather varied assortment of goods was loaded. For example, a Skælskør skipper with a galliot of nine *kommercelæster* brought home the following merchandise in November 1733 for three of the town merchants: salt, alum, glass, paper, hooks and eyes, dolls, sugar, vitriol, prunes, raisins, currants, ginger, cloves, cardamom, nutmeg, cinnamon, saffron, rice, cloth, flax, hops and wine – the idea was clearly to stock up for the Christmas trade. There were only small quantities of each category, so now and then the large vessels had to supplement with bricks as ballast.

In the ports of entry, a watchful eye was kept on the Lübeck voyages because the vessels had heavily excised goods, and the customs officials were told to be vigilant because there was a great temptation to smuggle. The Copenhagen wholesalers were also vigilant. Because where did all these goods come from? They were not produced in Lübeck of course, nor were they imported directly from foreign countries. The bulk of them were transit goods that came from Hamburg and thereby from the largest competitor to the capital city. All authorities agreed that it was advisable that the provinces got their imported goods via the capital, but this meant that the Copenhagen importers not only had to compete on the selection and price, they also had to compete on credit facilities. This was evidently a problem. In any case, in many inventories of the estates of skippers and merchants during the 18th century there are considerable debts to people in Lübeck. To a great extent the provincial merchants in East Denmark can be regarded as retailers who traded on credit from the wholesalers in the old hanseatic city. An example is Jacob Detmer in Nakskov who, in 1740, left a stock of small goods valued at upwards of 1,300 *rigsdaler*, but against this were debit items to five different merchants in Lübeck in the amount of more than 1,100 *rigsdaler*.

But shipping to Lübeck declined both in the number of voyages and the total amount of goods, the reason being that during the 18th century the imported merchandise via Copenhagen to the provinces had become larger and more differentiated. So in a number of fields the capital supplied the goods that had previously come direct from the south: for example things like groceries and various manufactured goods – from porcelain to cloth. However, it was still necessary to go to Lübeck to get *nürnbergerkram* (various small hardware products) and many other specialities.

Expeditions to the towns further east along the coast of the Baltic were rare, even though the volume increased during the century. In addition to a frequent ferry to Rostock, there was a small export of grain to the port, but this trade was mainly with ships from Schleswig and Holstein. A small number of provincial ships brought rye, flax and hemp from Danzig, Königsberg, Memel and Riga, while late in the 18th century they began to take part in the transport of firewood from Pomerania to Copenhagen. The Danish beech forests were actually not sizable enough to meet the growing demand.

Canal construction

A special initiative was the construction of the Eider Canal in the years from 1777 to 1784, which connected the Baltic with the North Sea.[8] An old dream of establishing a sea route across the Duchy of Schleswig was thereby realised. The canal went from the Kiel Fjord and was excavated over a stretch of just less than 34 km to the Eider, which was navigable 10 km east of Rendsburg, after which ships could continue without any great problem to the mouth of the river west of Tönning. The canal system included six large locks and was made to take ships with a draught of up to three metres, so it was a proper ship canal, not just for barge navigation. The Eider Canal was the largest of its kind at the time and was rightly admired as a great feat of engineering. On the other hand, the expectations of flourishing transit traffic were not fulfilled in practice; the canal was primarily of local significance.

Another system important to shipping from the end of the 18th century should also be mentioned, namely the 1.8 km long canal from Odense Fjord to an excavated harbour a few hundred metres north of the town. The work began in 1796, but completion took time, so it was not finally finished until 1806. For Odense, Denmark's largest provincial town, this canal was very clearly of benefit for maritime trade but the Exchequer had nevertheless to write off a large loss. It had been optimistically expected that operational income could cover payment of interest and capital, but this was far from the case.

Skippers in market towns and in rural districts

It was their own skippers from the provinces who were responsible for the two most important fields of activity, the coastal service to Copenhagen and shipping to Norway and Lübeck. Copenhagen ships participated only to a very small extent. According to *Danske Lov*,[9] the skippers were to live in the market towns and be registered as citizens there. Many of them also did this, but not all. This caused conflict in some places because the local skippers refused, for various reasons, both to move to town and to register as citizens as demanded.

The Bergen sailors who sailed from Odense Fjord are a good example. Until the construction of the canal, it was impossible to sail right into the town with large ships. Odense River was not navigable, and in the winter the ships lay out in the fjord while the skippers lived in the villages of Stige and Hauge nearby. They wanted to be close to their ships to keep an eye on them and at the same time they could save the expense of registering as a citizen and in addition could avoid the other financial obligations incumbent on a market town citizen. Using a modern term, one might call it a form of tax shelter.

In Odense, the municipal authorities understandably protested by complaining to the central administration. The views of the municipal authorities were upheld in principle, but in spite of several attempts, nothing was done to force the skippers to move to the town. Ironically, a contributory fact was that the skippers had leased farms and houses that belonged to the Crown, and the local royal official did not have the slightest wish to see his tenants move away, which would mean less income for his coffers.

Similarly, there was a concentration of skippers who settled in Rørvig at the approach to Isefjord and Roskilde Fjord on Zealand.[10] It is true there were a total of four market towns on the fjords, Holbæk, Roskilde, Frederikssund and Nykøbing, but only very few ships belonged to these towns due, among other things, to the atrocious sailing conditions in the shallow fjords. Since 1680 the whole area had been under one customs official living in the village of Rørvig just inside the entrance to the fjords where there was excellent safe anchorage, and it was also here that in the second half of the 18th century a settlement with a flock of skippers in farms and houses was established with a total of 10 vessels. In contrast, the skippers in the market towns disappeared almost completely.

The Rørvig skippers sailed mainly to Copenhagen. From the large hinterland along the coasts of the fjords, grain and firewood were loaded, while the return load was far more varied and could for example consist of tobacco, linen, paper, oil, caraway, coffee, iron, whale oil, flax, hops, soap, salt, dried cod, rice, sugar, rock candy, glass, bottles and groceries.

The skippers from Odense Fjord and Rørvig were not the only skippers in rural districts. Actually, there seemed to be a tendency that relatively more skippers settled outside the market towns in the course of the 18th century. This could be individually along the coast, but it occurred particularly because of the emergence of proper town communities without market town status. This was the case for Dragør in the Kingdom and Marstal on Ærø, which at that time, though, was under the authority of the Duchy of Schleswig.

The hard-working Dragør residents

Dragør is situated on the island of Amager close to Copenhagen and here a constantly growing band of skippers[11] specialised in sailing cords of wood and grain to the capital on both public and private accounts. They collected the wood in the Danish provinces and in Holstein, Mecklenburg and Pomerania. It is true that Amager was the larder of the capital, but all the agricultural products went over land with horse and cart, so there was no surplus production to be exported from the home port. That is why the skippers from Dragør almost exclusively took cargoes for others.

While skippers from the provincial market towns were bound to a great extent by their rigid sailing patterns – to and from Copenhagen or shuttle trips to Norway – the Dragør skippers could organise sailing plans much more flexibly. They bought relatively large, but inexpensive, second-hand galleasses in Pomerania and underbid other skippers on tenders for the transport of firewood for the Copenhagen bakers' ovens and brewing and distilling coppers, and, in addition, the ordinary consumption of beech firewood for heating. Firewood was not generally considered a very attractive load by other skippers, but rather something to be tolerated for want of something better. But the Dragør skippers made a virtue of necessity and latched on to the firewood trade during the 18th century. While their ships were bigger than the usual provincial ships, the manning of the ships did not increase proportionately with the size. In this way they gained a further competitive advantage.

The skipper community on Amager grew in pace with the purchase of more, and bigger, ships. As late as 1740, it is said there were 36 vessels, but in 1769, the number had increased to 92, while the average size increased from 12 to 18.5 *kommercelæster*. And thanks to the flexible sailing pattern, more voyages could be made per year than was usually the norm for provincial skippers.

The success in Dragør was not unnoticed. The authorities regarded the development favourably, and the local customs official could proudly report on the busy and hard-working skippers who with the greatest exertion endeavoured to exploit their ships – they were almost regarded by their contemporaries as an ideal of initiative and frugality worthy of imitation. The skippers in Copenhagen were less enthusiastic. In the venerable Copenhagen skipper guild, they maintained strongly that according to their guild ordinances they had the sole and exclusive right to cargoes from the capital and demanded the assistance of the authorities to stop these 'criminals'.[12] One argument, in itself legitimate and well-known, was also that a skipper registered as a citizen in a town had an obligation to pay tax, etc., something people from outside could largely avoid. But the Copenhagen skippers did not succeed, and their complaints ceased in the last decades of the 18th century when the skippers from the capital had more than enough employment in the growing overseas trade. In this regard, provincial skippers and men had to a great extent to be used to crew the Copenhagen ships as the city could not man its large merchant fleet itself.[13]

The provincial fleet in the 18th century

The number of provincial skippers increased in the 18th century, and even though the provincial fleet could not show such immense growth as in the capital in that century, the tonnage was doubled. Close to one-and-a-half times as many ships came on the scene and the average size was a nearly one-and-a-half time as big, as can be seen from Table 1.

To a certain degree the growth was derivative, as can be seen. The progress in the capital city and the growing need for supplies pulled, as it were, the provincial shipping with it. In traditional histories, this aspect has not been particularly noticed. The capital and the provinces have been regarded as two completely separate sectors, but considered correctly, they were financially interdependent. And it was thought that the provinces lay in a 'sleeping beauty' idyll, but that is not true either. There was definitely growth in the country areas which can also be read from the bare figures for the total provincial fleet.

TABLE 1.

Vessels in the provincial towns in the Kingdom of Denmark.

	Number	Kommercelæster[14]
1707	656	6,130
1731	721	6,075
1733	723	5,906
1750	725	7,298
1760	722	7,816
1770	719	8,716

	Number	Kommercelæster[14]
1780	671	8,133
1790	884	11,281
1800	910	12,325
1807	935	13,315
1813	986	11,643
1818	1,223	13,900
1824	1,091	11,226

Source: Anders Monrad Møller 1981 and 1988.

The type of ships in the fleet was not constant either. Some older types became rarer, such as the three-masted *krejerter* and *skibe* and the two-masted *skuder* and *bysser. Skib* (ship) and *skude* (craft) are really type designations and not general names for large and small vessels respectively. By far the most common type throughout the century however was the one-masted sloop, which constituted 40 % of the total cargo carrying capacity. Over the years, they were built increasingly large, from an average of 5.7 *kommercelæster* in 1733 to 10.9 in 1798. The most common types among the slightly larger vessels were the so-called one-and-a-half masted ships, such as the round-sterned galiot and its successor the square-sterned galeas. This latter type constituted just over 30 % of the total provincial tonnage in 1798.

The harbours in the 18th century

One of Copenhagen's great advantages was the excellent natural harbour, which into the bargain was located extremely conveniently for north-south voyages in the Øresund. In the provinces too, a few harbours of this type could be seen in the 18th century, for example in Svendborg on Funen. Svendborg lies on a slope that continues relatively steeply out into the water and has always made it easy to erect quays at a suitable depth while numerous ships could lie safely anchored further out in the bay, sheltered from west, north and east, and towards the south even sheltered by a small island (Tåsinge).

But in many cases, the market town lay at the bottom of a fjord on the mouth of a river, for example the East Jutland towns of Vejle, Horsens and Randers. And this automatically gave problems with sanding up. There are innumerable com-

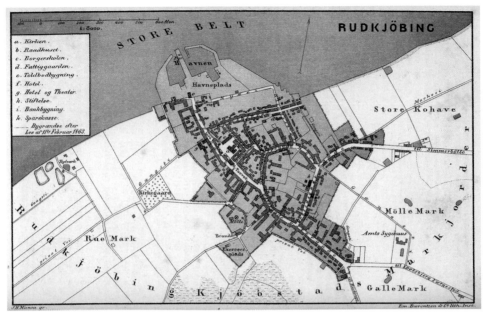

FIG. 2.

The map of Rudkøbing harbour is a clear illustration of a typical harbour extension. The broad middle pier is really a descendant of the original quay built in prolongation of Brogade. Later, the southern arm of the mole was built first, and then the northern one to make space for the growing fleet of small and large vessels.

plaints about streams that became muddied and sanded up; the technical facilities for dredging were limited, and in any case, it was extremely expensive work. Part of the trouble was self-inflicted as skippers who arrived with ships with a ballast of sand or stones often sneakily got rid of the ballast in the wrong places.

The problem was not reduced by the fact that the vessels gradually increased in size. Therefore, in many places, sailing lighters had to be used to sail cargoes out to the ships that lay anchored some way from land. And even where the ships could sail right into the coast, something like a quay was a rarity. Most often there was just a primitive *bro* (pier) where only a small number of ships could come alongside at a time. In many old market towns there is a *brogade* (Pier Street) leading down to the harbour where the town pier was situated at one time.

In other places it was even worse, as there were no harbour facilities at all. This was the case on the north coast of Lolland at the loading place of Bandholm where the water was extremely shallow. Grain was loaded by first being driven with a horse and cart a little way out in the water, from where it was reloaded onto a lighter that

FIG. 3A-B-C.

Around 1780 naval officer Georg Albrecht Koefoed compiled his maritime encyclopaedia, which has only recently been published. He used a French source for his information and copied shamelessly – as was typical at that time – from its plates. The Frenchman, for good reasons, was not familiar however with the local Danish types of vessels. So Koefoed had to draw them himself, and did this on his 'plates', among them fig. 131, a sloop, fig. 115, a krejert, *and fig. 129, a ketch. The last two were given a fine Danish flag at the stern, strangely enough not quite correct in its proportions.*

sailed the grain out to the waiting ship that had anchored several hundred metres out because of the lack of depth. This was an awkward procedure, particularly in the winter period, and it was not without risk for both men and animals.

Conditions for shipping in the 18th century can seem very primitive and time-consuming. But precisely the factor of time did not play the same role as in later periods. The running costs for sailing vessels were relatively low and actually the period spent in lay-days for provincial shipping was much longer than the sailing times. One has to envisage weeks spent loading and unloading and only a few days sailing. This explains the small number of annual voyages, 6-8 for a vessel plying between the provinces and the capital and 3-4 for a vessel in the Norway trade. Only the efficient Dragør skippers managed a higher number of voyages.

At the end of the century, there was a growing interest in improved harbour facilities. From 1797 the government consultant in this area was the very energetic naval officer, Poul Løvenørn. He travelled all over the country, surveyed and drew up proposals for improvements. From 1798, harbour commissioners were introduced in the individual seaports, so that administration of harbours was separated from the ordinary local administration. The harbour commissioners corresponded with central administration through the supervising *amtmand* (the chief administrative officer of the county), so both the technical expertise and the administrative apparatus were on hand, but no great results were achieved before the Napoleonic wars interrupted the modernisation work in progress.

The Napoleonic wars

Not only was the large-scale trading in Copenhagen hit hard during the Napoleonic wars, but the provincial fleet was also greatly affected. For political reasons, great emphasis was placed on supplying Norway, and this meant that provincial vessels were requisitioned for the risky transports, and many were captured and confiscated by the English, while quite a number of Danish seamen were imprisoned. The regular coasting trade was also threatened, because it could be hazardous to sail over Great Belt, which was patrolled by English warships. It was sometimes necessary to resort to sailing by night, something that was not otherwise common.

But as a replacement for the losses, new ships were continuously being built, so that after the peace settlement in 1814, there was, on the whole, just as large a tonnage outside Copenhagen as before the war.

FIG. 4.

'Fredsøen' was a small sloop built in 1817 at Vindeby on Tåsinge. Characteristics are the open bulwark stanchions and the flat stern with the four small windows giving light to the skipper's cabin. As usual in ship portraits, the vessel is shown from two different angles, so different spreads of canvas could be demonstrated.

The thing that frequently comes to mind in connection with the Napoleonic wars is the War of Privateering, the legalised piracy.[15] In these war years, Danish ship owners could get a letter-of-marque from the Danish government, which meant that they had the right to capture enemy merchant vessels and neutral vessels carrying contraband. The legality of capture, however, always had to be adjudged by a special court. If this found that it was a lawful prize, the skipper could be entitled to a considerable reward. The vast majority of privateers were equipped in Copenhagen, but the provinces were also involved and there were vessels primarily from Aalborg, Randers, Elsinore and Rønne. These were mainly boats that could succeed in taking a good prize, especially in calm weather.

One of the lucky ones was Captain Corfix Nielsen with the boat *Juliane Marie* of Elsinore. The vessel was small, only 1.5 *kommercelæst*, but the crew on the other

FIG. 5.

The ketch 'Providentia' of Svendborg was built there in 1818 and had a very high rigging, which was usual for this type of ship in the first half of the 19ᵗʰ century. In the 'small' version to the right, it can actually be seen 'unrigged', as the topmast has been taken down, which was quite usual if there was a threat of rough weather.

hand was large, 17 men. It was armed with two small cannons. In the spring of 1810, Corfix Nielsen captured the pink, *Graf Carl Lieven* and some time in the summer the kuff, *Wilhelmus Kayser*. Both vessels with their cargoes were adjudged good prizes and sold at auction. Nielsen must have become a prosperous man, but not everyone succeeded nearly as well. Many obtained a letter-of-marque and put out to sea without ever seeing as much as the shadow a prize.

The general assessment of the results of the whole privateering period is that financially it had minimal importance. Probably the English were hampered, a number of their warships being tied up controlling Danish waters. Although they were merely pinpricks, the psychological effect, on the other hand, was obvious. Even though Denmark had been forced to cede the whole of the Danish navy to England, one *could* nevertheless do something, and afterwards there were stories about the brave privateer captains who so daringly pulled the whiskers off the British lion. All things considered, this guerrilla war at sea – being a parallel to the gunboat war – was what the Danes were restricted to after the loss of the navy in 1807.

The lean post-war years

The peace and the cession of Norway to Sweden in 1814 meant that the Danish merchants and seamen could no longer count on having the Norwegian market for themselves, even though they retained a good market share. But the Danish grain surplus had in any case to be sold at world market prices in competition with the Baltic countries, among others.[16] Here, though, Denmark had an advantage on account of its geographical situation closer to the most important markets in Western Europe. The Danish coastal waters are ice-free earlier than the Baltic Sea, so they could normally move out earlier at the start of the year.

Much adaptation was necessary to gain a foothold for grain sale in the Netherlands and Great Britain. For example it was necessary to arrange to buy the grain in the autumn and store it in warehouses over the winter so it could be sent off in the spring at the most favourable time, that is, when prices were highest. The time factor played a completely different role than previously and the need for capital was growing.

As late as the 1820s, times were lean and the provinces were feeling their way, greatly hampered by falling world market prices. It was not until the second half of the 1830s that the situation finally changed and selling prices began to increase.

In Copenhagen, on the other hand, the large-scale trading of earlier times was still remembered and vain efforts were made to resume it. Insistence on the notion that 'great' shipping was what the merchant fleet of the capital should be engaged in clearly blocked any new thinking. Just after the peace agreement in 1814, it was thought in Copenhagen that things could continue as before the war, for instance the West Indies trade, with ships that were hastily procured at a high price. But when the West Indies trade almost collapsed after a few years, a real recession began for Copenhagen shipping. At the beginning of the 1820s, several of the large, well-reputed, commercial firms from the flourishing trading years at the end of the 18th century went bankrupt.

In the provincial towns, they were not bound in the same way by a great past, but started from their usual modest level. In the Danish market towns, the merchants still bought grain in the surrounding area and tried to sell it at the greatest possible profit. A trade convention entered into with Great Britain in 1824 and changes in the English Corn Laws in 1828 helped to pave the way for the Danish grain ships, enabling them to gain pivotal access to English, Scottish and Irish harbours. And from the 1830s, the provincial towns made definite progress, while, economically, Copenhagen continued to stagnate. The balance was definitely about to tip in favour of the provinces. While the merchant fleet increased considerably in these towns in the period until the middle of the century, the numbers stagnated in the capital: whereas in 1833 there were 300 ships registered giving a total of 16,118 *kommercelæster,* in 1850 there were just 274 giving 14,846.5 *kommercelæster.*

Table 2.

Vessels in the provincial towns in the Kingdom of Denmark.

Five year average	Number	Kommercelæster*
1833-1837	1,339	16,702
1838-1842	1,339	19,574
1843-1847	1,513	24,310
1848-1852	1,763	31,195

Source: Anders Monrad Møller 1988.

* See note 14.

The type of vessels in the fleet changed too. It is true that the sloop was much the most common type of small ship with a share of about 1/3 of the total tonnage of the Danish merchant fleet outside Copenhagen. And the sloops were built larger, up to 50 *kommerclæster.* But with this, an upper limit was clearly reached, because the mainsail became increasingly unmanageable with increasing size. It was then easier to go over to a schooner rig with the same or even a larger sail area divided between two almost equally tall masts. As late as 1820, there were only just over 20 schooners in the provincial fleet, but thirty years later, the number had increased more than tenfold, and the two-masted schooner had become the standard ship among the medium and very large ships.

Harbour expansion

In other ways too, developments meant changed conditions. As already mentioned, it was necessary to build warehouses, so the merchant could export on time. At the same time there must also have been a growing interest in better loading and unloading conditions, i.e. better harbour facilities. Parallel with the increase in grain

FIG. 6.

'Mathilde' of Nyborg belonged to Hans Kruse, one of the leading ship owners in the provinces in the first half of the 19ᵗʰ century. The designation at the time was just 'schooner', even though the rigging could vary quite a lot – here the version with many square sails on the foremast.

exports, a start was made on extending existing harbours or establishing proper new facilities. Technologically, there was no question of any new departure. Many still remembered Poul Løvenørn and his proposals. It was well known what could be done if it could be afforded, and the means gradually became available. While the enterprising merchants, who wanted to have harbour construction started probably did not have any technical expertise themselves, the state had expert consultants, as Løvenørn had successors who were made available according to need, and without charge, around the country. Collaboration between the state consultants and the harbour commissioners who administered the harbours in the individual towns seems to have gone surprisingly smoothly.

It could be that the already existing facilities were extended. A start could be a pier that lay quite unprotected from the pounding of the waves. Here a curved jetty could safeguard the pier and also form a basin where ships could moor safely.

In addition, the extension could be with quays, dredging could be done, better approaches could be made, a slip established to haul up vessels, etc. All this cost money but could be covered by rising harbour income. It was a good circle where progress in one field determined corresponding progress in another. And the state was willing to give loans on favourable terms.

A good example was Rudkøbing on the island of Langeland where a pier, 125 metres long, lay at Brogade. (See fig. 2, p. 249). In 1799 Løvenørn had prepared a completely finished plan, but the project had never been realised, clearly for financial reasons. But from 1815 onwards, a good annual increase in harbour income was noted, and at the beginning of the 1820s construction of a protective mole was started south of the quay in a close collaboration between the local harbour commission and the state harbour consultant, who reported the local initiative in laudatory terms – to a certain extent voluntary labour was used. The mole was finished in 1826 and subsequently there was a basin where ships could be moored safely, which was a great advantage because of the strong current along the coast.

But that was not all. Soon the facility was considered too small and in 1847 the construction of another mole north of the quay began. The north mole was completed in 1850 and after that there was enough space. To this very day, the whole facility is still in Rudkøbing, with the quay, the two moles and basins preserved more or less intact.

In some places there was more than just an extension, namely a completely new facility, which was the case at Bandholm where a pier, 320 metres long, was completed in 1837. Six years later an extension with a harbour basin was built and a steam-driven dredger had been borrowed from the Danish navy so that a dredged channel ensured that ships could put into the harbour. Subsequently cargoes could be loaded directly from horse and cart, eliminating the difficult and cost-increasing transport with lighters. As in most cases, the initiative was local – here an extremely enterprising landowner – but the goodwill of the state was clear and the harbour consultant was on the spot.

At Bogense, there was also a new facility, but here is an example of something that was anything but a success. Løvenørn had been in Bogense in 1799 and had suggested digging a canal from the coast to the town – obviously inspired by what was happening at the time in the neighbouring town of Odense. At the time, though, nothing was done about it, but the idea surfaced again in 1802 and 1807, and in 1820 the harbour consultant of the day proposed constructing an embankment or pier no

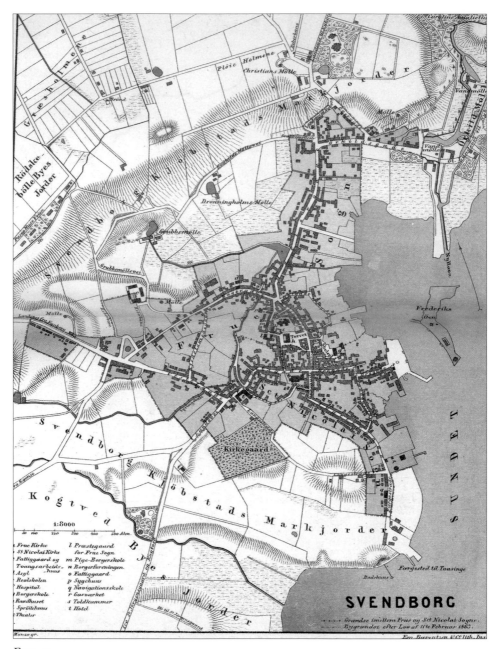

FIG. 7.

Svendborg has always been known for its excellent natural harbour. The town is situated as it were in
a hollow, the sides of which descend steeply downwards into the water. That is why it has been easy to
build a quay. In addition, the natural build-up of sand as well as any superfluous ballast thrown over-
board from ships diminished the depth of water, making it possible to merely build on the outside.

less than 380 metres from the coast and beside it excavating a seven-foot-deep basin. In addition, dredging should be done at this pier. Unfortunately the total cost would amount to a sum of 45,000 *rigsbankdaler*. And there were strong doubts about whether the harbour income would cover interest, payment, maintenance and running costs. In Bogense they therefore went back to the old idea of a canal and excavation then began. By 1828 they had a channel that could be used for boats. However, it transpired that the channel became full of seaweed very easily, which meant that stone embankments had to be built on either side of it. But in Bogense they were determined to have a proper harbour for ships, and in 1841 they got the kind assistance of King Christian VIII who had fond memories of the town from the time when he as heir apparent was governor of Funen. The Absolute monarch cut through difficulties and granted a loan, despite objections from civil servants in central administration. The canal was deepened and the protective embankments were broadened – there were also seawalls but two instead of one. However, there was so much debt that the town had a financial millstone around its neck for many years afterwards.

Many other harbour constructions could be seen in the Danish seaports in the first half of the 19th century, with the result that the waterfronts of many towns had completely changed character by the middle of the 19th century. The harbour was the pride of the town and the goal of the daily promenade. Here people met each others and exchanged news, and here they could delight in the profitable activity that was going on, and as time passed, they could also see a steamship call at a number of places. Steamships did not yet require major harbour facilities at that time, but just a jetty where general cargo and passengers could disembark.

With grain and coal

But the steamships needed something else, namely coal. And coal and coke were also needed for the growing number of steam engines and for the iron foundries being established in the provincial towns from the 1830s. The coal was brought from England and Scotland, countries to which a large proportion of the exported grain was already being delivered. Therefore coal gradually became the obvious return cargo in the Great Britain trade. As late as the 1820s, coal was seldom carried in Danish ships, but from the 1840s, it was becoming the rule when vessels returned home from a voyage to Western Europe. This was an ideal situation for the provincial shipping. Shipping with an assured cargo both ways had much greater freight income, and coal in the hold on the return voyage was certainly better than just ballast. This trade of grain exchanged for coal would also be the backbone of the foreign trade of the provincial towns during the time after 1850.

In this regard an example is *Caroline Margrethe* from Stege on the island of Møn, east of Zealand, a sloop of 17.5 *kommercelæst,* captained by Hans Nicolai Sørensen and partly owned by the town's most prominent merchant business, C. Hage & Søn.[17] It was for this shipowner that *Caroline Margrethe,* on its third voyage to England at the end of July 1844, loaded 560 barrels of barley and 10 barrels of peas. The ship weighed anchor on 30 July and sailed up through the Great Belt, where, much to his annoyance, the skipper was delayed in Slipshavn where *strømtold*[18] had to be paid. Under continued difficulties, *Caroline Margrethe* could at last put into dock in Hull on 17 August. Here there was also a delay, but at last the vessel was unloaded and could be shifted to the other side of the dock to load coal. On 26 August, it left Hull. When it passed the island of Samsø in Danish waters, it was hailed by a revenue cutter and an officer came on board to search – because contraband goods could also be concealed under the coal. On 4 September, the ship anchored at Samsø where the skipper, who had bought the coal on his own account, tried in vain to sell it. Then the voyage went to Aarhus where he succeeded in selling the cargo to a distiller. The fourth voyage set out from Samsø with a cargo of barley for Leith, after which the sloop called at Dysart to get the obligatory coal that ended in Næstved. From there the fifth voyage, with another cargo of barley, went to Leith. Christmas Eve was celebrated in the coaling port of Alloa, while New Year's Eve was celebrated on *Caroline Margrethe* as it sailed in a stiff breeze on the North Sea on its return voyage. There was one more voyage before Hans Nicolai Sørensen could lay up his ship for the winter.

Summing up, developments in the Danish seaports in the 18th century can be said to have been determined by the sure sale of grain in Norway and supplies to Copenhagen. There was a certain progress, although at a moderate pace and to a great extent derived from the strong growth in Copenhagen. In the first half of the 19th century, there were, it is true, some financially lean years with low world market prices after the Napoleonic wars, but the seaport merchants gained a foothold in the Western European markets, in particular in Great Britain. But when prices improved, things gained speed. People in the provinces could then manage on their own and be completely independent of the capital. Around 1850 a rapid process of change began with the increasing exchange of Danish grain for British coal. And this development continued for a further few decades after the middle of the century.

BIBLIOGRAPHY

Hassø, Arthur G. 1934. *Københavns Skipperlav 1634-1934*. Copenhagen: Hagerup.

Larsen, Kay 1972. *Danmarks Kapervæsen 1807-1814*. 2nd edition. Copenhagen: Rosenkilde og Bagger.

Meier, Peter Uffe 1981. *Omkring de fire species. Dansk merkantilistisk stabel- og navigationspolitik i 1720'erne*. Copenhagen: Akademisk Forlag.

Møller, Anders Monrad 1981. *Fra galeoth til galease. Studier i de kongerigske provinsers søfart i det 18. århundrede*. Esbjerg: Fiskeri- og Søfartsmuseet.*

Møller, Anders Monrad 1983. *Frederik den Fjerdes Kommercekollegium og Kongelige Danske Rigers inderlig Styrke og Magt*. Copenhagen: Akademisk Forlag.

Møller, Anders Monrad 1988. *Jagt og skonnert. Studier i den danske provinssøfart i tiden fra 1814 til 1864*, Copenhagen: Falcon.*

Møller, Anders Monrad 1992. 'Måneden drejer – om søfolk til den københavnske handelsflåde 1777-87'. In: *ODERINT, DUM METUANT. Festskrift i anledning af Ole Ventegodts 60-års fødselsdag*. Copenhagen.

Møller, Anders Monrad 1998. *Med korn og kul. Dansk søfarts historie 4, 1814-1870*. Copenhagen: Gyldendal.

Møller, Anders Monrad 2001. 'En fuldkommen sikker Ankerplads. Historien om Rørvig Toldsted og søfarten fra Isefjorden 1680 til 1903'. In: Bo Bræstrup and Kurt Sørensen (ed.), *Mellem Kattegat og Isefjord. Rørvigs natur og kulturhistorie*. Rørvig: Rørvig Naturfredningsforening.

Olsen, Albert 1936. *Danmark-Norge i det 18. Aarhundrede*. Copenhagen: Gyldendal.

Rasch, Aage 1978. *Ejderkanalen*. Aabenraa: Historisk Samfund for Sønderjylland

*The appendices of these books with data of the merchant fleets of all towns in the period from 1720 to 1832 are available on www.byhistorie.dk/provinsens_soefart/

NOTES

1 Thomas Jørgensen Hørning's paper, see Møller 1983.

2 *Kommercekollegiet* was a section of the central administration and dealt with commerce and industry.

3 Greenland was first colonised later in the 18th century.

4 Meier 1981.

5 Olsen 1936.

6 Here, and in general in the following, see Møller 1981.

7 Whole shiploads of sailors were sailed annually to Amsterdam, Middelburg, Delft, Rotterdam, Enkhuizen and Hoorn. Around 1700, there were at least 6,500 Danish sailors employed in the merchant navy of the Netherlands, much to the concern of the Admiralty, who thus saw innumerable potential seamen evade conscription.

8 Rasch 1978.

9   'Statute of the Danes', the codified statute-book dating back to 1683 (issued by King Christian V).

10   Møller 2001, pp. 189-207.

11   In Danish these skippers are called *selvejerskippere* (freehold skippers). This refers to the fact that they belonged to the farming class, but were not tenants, they owned their own houses and ships.

12   Hassø 1934, pp. 78, 98.

13   Møller 1992, pp. 21-26.

14   The number of *kommercelæster* is an expression for the cargo carrying capacity of a ship. This number was calculated on the basis of measuring the length, breadth, and depth of different places on the hull. In 1830, more detailed measuring principles were introduced, and at the same time it was decided that a *kommercelæst* was 150 cubic feet, i.e. about 4.6 cubic metres. For the years up until 1824, all Danish ships (for tax reasons) were given a capacity figure that lay 1/6 under the real figure. To come to the correct figure, one must therefore multiply the numbers by 1.2.

15   Larsen 1972.

16   Here and in the following, see Møller 1988.

17   Møller 1998, pp. 43-46.

18   *Strømtolden* (dues) were levied on vessels that passed through Great Belt and Little Belt from the 15th century until 1857. They were a counterpart to the Sound Dues on Øresund.

Market town agriculture

Introduction

A Danish market town 200-300 years ago looked very different from a Danish pro-vincial town at present. The narrow streets seethed with animals. Horses drawing wagons and coaches, cattle in large herds on their way to or from pastures outside the town, pigs in yards and in back buildings, stray hens and half-wild cats were all part and parcel of the townscape. So with regard to animals, there was no real dif-ference between living in a market town or a village. And outside the town lay the undeveloped land where cultivated areas alternated between pasture, meadows, bogs, thickets, watering places and manure heaps. Market town agriculture was part of the everyday life of the inhabitants and could not be ignored.

The town ground, the fields, the common and the gardens

In the Absolutist period, the town ground – the built-up part of the market town area – was usually surrounded by a hoarding. Here the inhabitants lived in houses and the citizens carried on their trades. The built-up part of the market town was surrounded by the *markjorder*. The term is difficult to translate from Danish as it is, literally, 'the field lands', but the term covers not only farmland, it also includes the common, meadows etc. In other words *markjorder* means the town's total land area outside the town ground. The *markjorder* were used for farming and animal hus-bandry, and there were only a very few buildings there, such as a powder magazine, a mill or a house for the night soil men, buildings unwanted within the hoarding. As a rule, the *markjorder* covered a much larger area than the town ground. In 1837, the *markjorder* in the market towns of the Kingdom covered a total area of 94,996 *tønder land* (ca. 52,402 hectares).[1] This figure had been largely unchanged since the 17th century. The three market towns with most land in 1837 were the Jutland towns of Viborg with 9,669 *tønder land* (ca. 5,333 hectares), Skagen with 8,803 *tønder land* (ca. 4,856 hectares) and Varde with 7,100 *tønder land* (ca. 3,916 hectares). On the other hand, the land in these towns was of a very poor quality. The three market towns with least land were Sandvig on Bornholm with 151 *tønder land* (ca. 83 hectares) and the two Zealand towns, Præstø with 103 *tønder land* (ca. 57 hectares) and Sorø with only 8 *tønder land*.[2] However, the inhabitants of Sorø had grazing rights on the land that belonged to the town's academy for young noblemen.[3]

In the Middle Ages, the open fields of the Danish towns were used exclusively for communal grazing for the inhabitants' livestock. Only the so-called *toftejorder* or corn gardens which lay alongside or close to the town ground were cultivated at that time. This changed in the 16th century when in many places *markjorder* were divided into individual plots that were allocated to each of the houses in the town. This *udskiftning* (division) was done with a view to tillage and thereby better utilisation of the land.[4] In several towns, part of the *markjord* was uncultivated until well into the 19th century, and at least part of the common in most market towns was not ploughed and was used for grazing.

Definition of market town agriculture

To fit the definition of market town agriculture, at least three conditions must be fulfilled. First, farming had to be done on land that was in some way the property of the market town or its inhabitants, with the result that the land was under the jurisdiction of the market town. The circumstances of ownership could be complicated and cause many disputes both between the inhabitants in the town and between the town itself and the surrounding rural districts, but the crucial fact was that the market town land belonged to the town and that the inhabitants of the town were the people who made decisions about its use.

Second, the land had to be exempt from tax. Thus, in contrast to farmers in the country, the market towns did not pay *hartkorn* taxes to the state.[5] There were, though, a very few exceptions to this rule, but at the time this could give rise to deliberations about whether the towns in question could be regarded as real market towns at all.

Third, the farming had to be done on the basis of a property in the town. In the middle of the 19th century, the agricultural land of many towns began to become concentrated into large lots. These were bought by farmers who built dwellings and farm buildings on their newly acquired land. This development accelerated in the following decades while the inhabitants of the market towns concentrated to an ever increasing extent on urban occupations proper: commerce, trades and industry. At the beginning of the First World War, in many towns there were so few courtyard houses with outbuildings on the town ground that still farmed the *markjorder* that, strictly speaking, it no longer gave any meaning to talk about market town agriculture in these towns.

The field structures of Aarhus, Randers and Skanderborg

In the following sections, agriculture in three different East Jutland market towns in the 18th-19th century will be discussed. Judging from the research (although there is little) into the agricultural structure of the Danish towns, a description of agriculture in these three towns together gives in many ways quite a good impression of conditions in the towns of the Kingdom before industrialisation. However, it should be noted that some towns differed markedly from the rest on account of the particular nature of the land etc.

Aarhus and Randers were large market towns for the time, as they both had just over 4,000 inhabitants at the census in 1801. Skanderborg, which at the time had just fewer than 500 inhabitants, must be considered a very small market town. Aarhus got market town privileges in 1441 and in the 18th-19th century was an enterprising commercial centre with a reasonably good harbour that was enlarged in 1805 with a new jetty. Randers got its market town privileges in 1302 and, like Aarhus, was doing well in business in the 18th-19th century. The harbour facilities in the town were not good because the Gudenå river flowing into the sea at the town tends to silt up. On the other hand, the town had the advantage of a large hinterland. Skanderborg came into existence around a royal castle in the 16th century and got market town privileges in 1583. However the castle lost its importance at the end of the 17th century and after this trade in the town declined. According to two reports from 1735 and 1806 respectively, there were only 4-5 small shopkeepers in the town. In 1735 agriculture and fishing were described as the main occupations, while several sources from the 19th century stated that agriculture, distilling and handicrafts were the dominant occupations.[6] The town suffered greatly from its location far inland, which meant high prices for goods from the outside that had to be transported on difficult roads. And

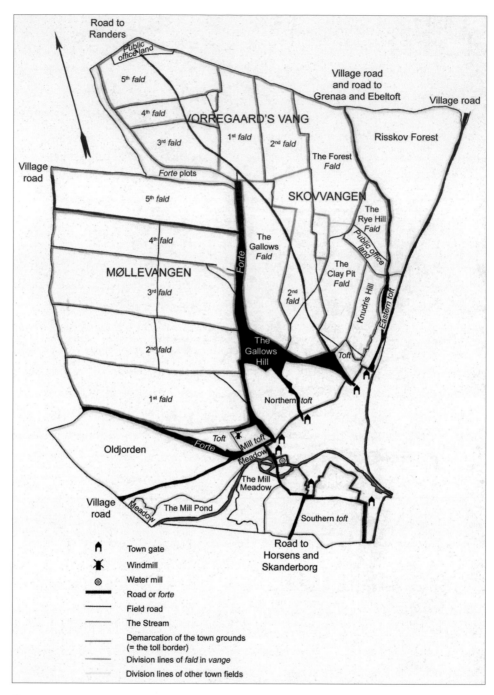

Road to
Randers

Public
office land

5th fald

4th fald

3rd fald

VORREGAARD'S VANG

1st fald   2nd fald

Village road
and road to
Grenaa and Ebeltoft

Village road

Risskov Forest

The Forest
Fald

Forte plots

Village
road

5th fald

SKOVVANGEN

The
Rye Hill
Fald

Public office land

4th fald

MØLLEVANGEN

3rd fald

The
Gallows
Fald

Forte

The
Clay Pit
Fald

Knudris Hill

Eastern toft

2nd fald

2nd
fald

The
Gallows
Hill

Toft

1st fald

Northern toft

Oldjorden

Toft

Forte

Mill toft

Meadow

The Mill
Meadow

Village
road

Meadow

The Mill Pond

Southern toft

Road to
Horsens and
Skanderborg

♠   Town gate
✹   Windmill
⊗   Water mill
━━   Road or forte
──   Field road
──   The Stream
──   Demarcation of the town grounds
     (= the toll border)
──   Division lines of fald in vange
──   Division lines of other town fields

FIG. 1

The town fields of Aarhus around 1801-1802.

An illustration of the town grounds (the bygrund*) and the town fields showing the cultivation and the new road system after the* udskiftning *in 1801-1802.*

the farmers of the district preferred to drive to the nearest shipping towns of Aarhus and Horsens, where they could get a better price for their agricultural products.

As in the other Danish market towns, the *markjorder* in Aarhus, Randers and Skanderborg can be divided up into a number of large or small, physically separate, land areas. And, as in many other places, a large part of these areas were designated as *vang* (field). In Aarhus, for instance, they spoke of three *vange*: Møllevangen, Skovvangen and Vorregårdsvang. In addition there were different smaller plots of land and meadows, the wood, Risskov, and lanes, roads and the *forter*. These last-mentioned were very broad grass paths which in addition to serving as roads were used for grazing, primarily for the livestock of visitors to the town.[7] In all, Aarhus had 1,586 *tønder land* (ca. 875 hectares) fields and meadows in 1837 (besides Risskov).[8] It is not clear when the town got most of this area, but according to tradition, Queen Margrethe I at the end of the 14th century fixed the borders of the town area and thereby ensured among other things the ownership of Risskov.[9] In the oldest known privileges for the market town from 1441 the borders of the *markjorder* are established 'as they thus have been from time immemorial', and in addition the privileges ensured that the citizens had access to fields, wood, pasture and fishing.[10] The privileges were confirmed by Royal Charter from 1490. In 1542 the privileges meanwhile were extended, as King Christian III gave the inhabitants permission to use Vorregårds Mark too, and in 1561 the municipal corporation and citizens also got the ownership of this *vang* – on payment of an annual fee to the cathedral chapter.[11] There were no later extensions of Aarhus' *markjorde*.

In Randers, there were six *vange* north and west of the town, five *vange* in a belt a little further north – and finally, most northerly, Voldum Mark and a number of smaller plots of land. In addition there were various roads and *forter* as well as large meadow areas beside the Gudenå river. In all, the *markjorder* in 1837 covered 2,340 *tønder land* (ca. 1,291 hectares).[12] According to a legal document from 1616, all the land with the exception of Voldum Mark belonged to the town as early as 1477, and most of it had long done so at that time. In 1554 King Christian III gave Voldum Mark to the municipal corporation and the citizens by copyhold in perpetuity on payment of a fee.[13]

Skanderborg's land consisted of 3 *vange*, some *toftejorder* and roads, some meadow and bog areas as well as the woods Hestehaven and Dyrehaven. In 1837 the *markjorder* consisted of 440 *tønder land* (ca. 243 hectares) fields, meadows and bog and, in addition, the wooded area.[14] Apart from some few privately owned *toftejorde*, which

FIG. 2

The town fields of Randers 1803.

The map is dominated by vange. *Most of the unspecified areas to the north were public land and to the south near the river Gudenåen ('the Stream') the land was predominantly meadows.*

were already owned by the town inhabitants, the town got all the *markjorder* in 1767 when they were acquired at auction. Before that time the inhabitants had some of the same land by copyhold from the king. The *markjorder* remained subject to taxation after the town had taken them over.[15]

Udskiftning and tillage

During the years 1559-1580, the land in Møllevangen, Skovvangen and Vorregårdsvang in Aarhus was divided among the properties in the town with a view to cultivation. With this *udskiftning* each of 272 properties in the town got a certain amount of land, called a *gårdsavl*. One hundred years later, the three *vange* were fully cultivated.[16] Later other parts of the *markjorder* were brought under cultivation, among them the plot called Oldjorden, which was originally a *forte* road to the village of Ry.[17] In 1751 and 1757 this area was surveyed, divided into plots and part of it was designated as glebe land – i.e. land that belonged to particular official posts in the town, not exclusively clergy, and in practice was part of the payment of the official in question. The rest of Oldjorden was leased for cultivation and payment was made to the town treasury.[18] At the end of the 18th century, practically all of Aarhus *markjorder* were cultivated.

The Randers *markjorder* went through a similar process. Four *vange* were divided into strips called *agre* which were allotted to various properties in the town.[19] Large properties got a whole *ager* in each *vang*, smaller properties a half. In one *vang*, 101 small plots were for the most part allotted to cottages. Voldum Mark, which was old monastery land, had been cultivated for a long time when it was incorporated into Randers *markjorder* in 1554. The rest of the land which was called 'The Old Pasture Land' was left uncultivated until the second half of the 18th century, when it was brought under cultivation, plot after plot. At the end of the 18th century, the town's *markjorder* were by and large cultivated.

In Skanderborg, the situation was completely different. The town citizens as already mentioned had to lease land for tillage and pasture until 1767. Since the land did not belong to the town, it could not be divided into plots as was done in Aarhus and Randers. When the citizens acquired the plots in 1767, they were completely cultivated apart from meadows and peat bogs.

Ownership

Originally only the small plots of land, the *toftejorder*, immediately outside the town ground, were privately owned. The rest of the land belonged to the market towns. But crucial changes occurred in this ownership situation in connection with *udskiftning* in the 16th century and afterwards.

In Aarhus, the *gårdsavl* were regarded as private property right from the beginning and were traded independently of the town property to which they were at-

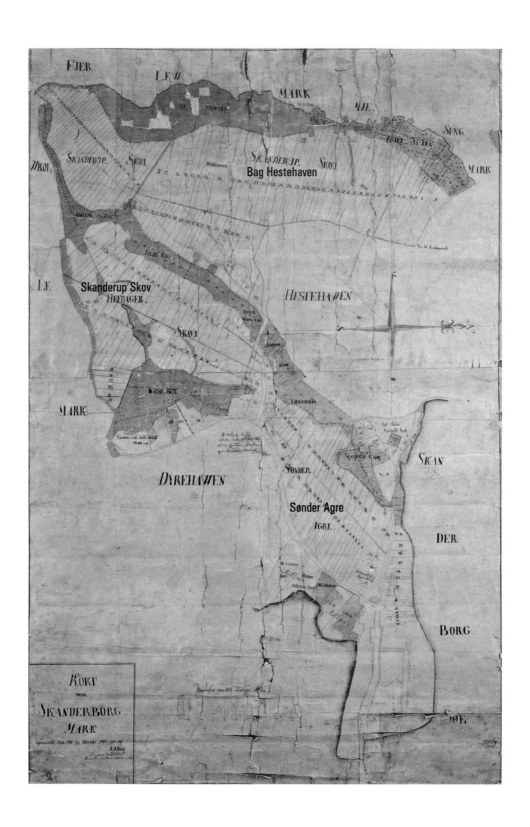

FIG. 3.

The town fields of Skanderborg 1791-1792.

The map was drawn to illustrate how property was to be divided after the udskiftning *of the town fields in 1792-1793. The land surveyor carefully sketched the scattered strips of each farm holder or landholder. The land was still cultivated individually except for the common grazing, which lasted until 1827. The three-field system remained. The fields were Bag Hestehaven ('Behind the Horse Garden Plot'), Skanderup Skov ('Skanderup Forest'), and Sønder Agre ('The Southern Land').*

tached. The town's *gårdsavl* gradually became concentrated in the hands of much fewer owners, and many of these did not live in the town. In 1727, non-residents – usually farmers from the neighbouring villages – thus owned or leased about half of all *gårdsavl*.[20] It was a good business deal for the town citizens to sell or lease to people from outside the town, but the central authorities were displeased about farmers evading taxes and duties by cultivating the tax-exempt town land, and the practice was therefore checked by an ordinance of 14 August 1741. The ordinance, which was valid for all Danish market towns, established that town land could only be cultivated by the town inhabitants, and that tax should be paid on the town land that had already been handed over to non-residents.[21] On the other hand, it appears from an ordinance of 26 March 1756 that the authorities did not have any objections to the sale or lease of the plots in Aarhus to men from the town.[22]

The *udskiftning* in Aarhus meant that around 1800 only very little actual common land was left, namely the grazing areas Forten and The Gallows Hill. A reckoning from the beginning of the 19th century indeed shows that 1,202 (76 %) of the 1,586 *tønder land markjorder* were then in private hands.[23] Much of the remaining 384 *tønder land* in the course of time had changed status from common land to town treasury land; this meant that the municipal corporation could do as they wished with the land in question, and in practice the land was leased for a number of years to give an income to the town treasury. In addition, as already mentioned, Aarhus had some glebe land. As in many other towns, the mayors, the aldermen, the bailiff and the town clerk each had some land at their disposal, and the same was the case (in any case from 1751 and afterwards) for the county governor of Aarhus who lived in the town.[24] Finally, Aarhus had some land owned by institutions; for instance in 1801 the cathedral was the third largest plot owner with a total of 17 *gårdsavl*, while the hospital had three.[25]

Developments in Randers were in many ways similar to the situation in Aarhus, but striking differences can also be seen. In Randers too, the *agre* (the strips) were the object of brisk trade independent of the properties to which they had originally been allocated. In 1694 several *agre* were even sold at public auction.[26] And in the field regulations of the town from 1772, it appears that farmers from the surrounding villages also owned land in the *markjorde* of the town.[27] That the *agre* were considered to be the private property of the *avlsbrugere* (the farmers) can be seen for instance from the fact that four of the town *vange* were always called 'the private fields'. In 1805 these fields comprised 1,057 *tønder land* (ca. 583 hectares), while the *markjorder* that belonged to the town comprised 1,265 *tønder land* (ca. 698 hectares).[28] In Randers the private land was therefore only 46 % of the *markjorder*, that is, considerably less than in Aarhus. This difference was mainly due to the fact that the largest *vang*, Voldum Mark, remained in the possession of the town treasury after the town had bought this *vang* from the King in 1740. Long before 1740, Voldum Mark had been divided into strips which had been leased for cultivation and grazing, and this leasing practice continued after ownership had passed to the town.

In Randers, the four private *vange* lay in between the common land of the town. This was undoubtedly due to the particular configuration of the ground: efforts were made to avoid the hilliest ground when the private *vange* were established. The common land was called the Pasture Land, because it had originally been used exclusively for grazing. However, much of the common land was brought under cultivation in the 18th century, but it was decided to allow the land to remain as public property as, like Voldum Mark, it was leased for the benefit of the town treasury. Finally Randers had its glebe land, as in 1606, the members of the municipal corporation as well as the bailiff and town clerk were each allotted land, and three clergymen had shares in Voldum Mark.[29]

In Skanderborg, the 438 *tønder land* (ca. 242 hectares), including wooded areas, which the town acquired in 1767, were divided among all the town's property owners in 1792-1793.[30] This was the same sort of *udskiftning* that had been done in Aarhus and Randers 200 years previously, but this was a most unusual action at the end of the 18th century. The argument for such an *udskiftning* was usually that this would lead to cultivation of the land to the advantage of the town, but Skanderborg's *markjorde* at that time had been cultivated for several hundred years. Besides, at the end of the 18th century, people had become aware that it was not a good idea that common land be transferred to private ownership, which into the bargain was known from experience to be concentrated in the hands of just a few owners. When this was done, the town was deprived of a public amenity value that would be to the benefit of posterity. Nevertheless, the land in Skanderborg, after having belonged to the town as common land for 25 years, passed to private property – though with the proviso that it must never be sold separately from the plots.[31] After the *udskiftning* all *markjord* in Skanderborg was in private hands.

Common grazing and communal farming

The market town land was utilised by the inhabitants in several different forms of co-operation, and clear rules for the use of the *markjord* were therefore necessary. These rules were written in bylaws, which are also known from the Danish villages. According to these regulations for Aarhus (1760)[32] and Randers (1772),[33] a field committee to be responsible for observance of the rules should be appointed in both towns.

The oldest form for co-operation on the town fields was the common grazing. The field regulations give rules for the number of animals that could be grazed on the land. In both Aarhus and Randers, large properties could graze six horses or cows. In Aarhus medium-sized properties and so-called 'houses with a gateway' (i.e. larger houses) could have two cows on grass. In Randers medium-sized properties could graze three-four horses or cows, small properties and houses two horses or cows. The inhabitants of small houses or cottages in both towns had grazing rights for one cow. These figures reflect the typical number of horses and cows in the different property categories. A grazing assessment was prepared in the individual towns each year. In this, the grazing was divided among those with grazing rights and in return these people paid grazing money to the town. Since grazing was a limited resource, there were strict rules about what animals could graze on the common pasture of the towns. In general it can be said that, with the exception of geese, the animals that were excluded were those that could find feeding other places, or those that could cause great damage to the fields (the geese were normally put on grass in their own meadow or the like). Thus in both Aarhus and Randers, it was forbidden to put goats, pigs, bullocks, stallions and geese on pasture – and the same applied to sheep in Aarhus.[34] In contrast, sheep were allowed on pasture in Randers because the cattle in this town could not utilise the grazing resources completely.[35] Both towns also gave the people coming to town (among them farmers with business in town and fair keepers) a chance to graze their animals in certain parts of the *markjorder* – in Randers for instance this was in a hilly area west of the town. In both

Aarhus and Randers – as well as in other towns with pasture – there was a differentiation between summer pasture and aftergrass. Summer grazing was on the fields that lay fallow a certain year, while aftergrass was on the cultivated fields after harvest. Finally, specific plots of land could be assigned to constant grazing. In Aarhus this was the case for instance for the *forter*.

After the *udskiftning* in the 16th century, there was also communal farming among the plot owners in Aarhus with regard to the utilisation of the *gårdsavl*. This co-operation was a direct result of the division of land. The *vange* were divided into smaller units, *fald* (approximately a furlong), whose form was dictated by the configuration of the ground (see fig. 4). Møllevangen was divided into five *fald*, Skovvangen into six and Vorregårdsvang into five. To get the fairest possible division of good and poor land – with regard to both quality and distance from the town – a *gårdsavl* of land was apportioned with five-six strips in Møllevangen and five-six in Skovvangen and Vorregårdsvang, located in different *fald*. So if a man owned just six *gårdsavl*, he had 30-36 shares merely in that part of the town fields that was cultivated a particular year.[36] Møllevang and Skov- and Vorregårdsvang were cultivated alternately. Incidentally, such a two-field rotation was also practised in many East Jutland rural parishes.[37] The complicated field structure in Aarhus resembled the situation in countless Danish villages before the land reforms at the end of the 18th century, and indeed, town bylaws also contain – like the villages – a detailed set of rules for how the fields should be cultivated so that the risk of conflict between individual farmers was reduced as much as possible.[38] The field committee had to make decisions about when ploughing, sowing and harvesting should be done, when gates should be repaired, when fences should be erected and when harvested fields should be opened for pasture. And to prevent theft of the grain, it was decided that people, horses and carts must not be on the fields between 10 p. m. and 3 a. m.[39] In addition, men were employed to dig ditches and throw up dikes and other practical jobs, and there were guardians who supervised that the times for sowing, harvesting etc. were observed. The communal farming in Aarhus occupied by and large the same field area as the communal grazing.

At the *udskiftning* in Randers in the 16th and 17th century, every house with a courtyard got a strip in each of the private *vange*, but just as had happened in Aarhus, the strips quickly became concentrated into the hands of a few owners. Even though the farmers had their land spread in many different places in the *vange*, the land was not cultivated in common. On the contrary, each used his own land at will for cultivation or pasture.[40] This could have various unfortunate consequences –

for example that the winter seed sown in some of the *agre* could be damaged when the herder drove the town's livestock to aftergrass in the private *vange*.[41] In contrast to the private *vange*, the town common was cultivated jointly after it had been brought under cultivation and leased in the 18th century. Randers' bylaws had rules for this communal farming, and among other things there was a strict prohibition against town people getting help for cultivation from the farmers of the surrounding area.[42] Here too people, horses and carts were forbidden to be on the field at night.[43]

After the acquisition of Skanderborg's *markjorde* in 1767, the land that the inhabitants of the market town previously had held by long-term copyhold continued to be cultivated jointly in a three-field system.[44] At the *udskiftning* in 1792-1793, the large properties each got one strip in each of the three *vange* in addition to three meadow and peat plots. The small properties got one cultivated plot and one peat plot.[45] But even though each property thus got some plots scattered around the town fields, there was no joint tillage after the *udskiftning*.[46] The joint pasturage however continued on the land until 1827 when it was abolished after a citizens' meeting in the town hall.[47]

Farming and animal husbandry

When the population figures from the censuses at the beginning of the 19th century are compared with information in the land register of 1844 (which is based on surveys done in the 1820s and 1830s), it is obvious that the towns as a whole had much less land at their disposal per inhabitant than the villages.[48] So even though some market town farms were the same size as the average farm in the villages, the total importance of farming as a source of income was considerably less for the towns than for the rural parishes. This confirms – not surprisingly – that farming was the primary occupation in the country while commerce and trades were the primary occupations in the market towns.

Farming in market towns was primarily organised to meet the inhabitants' own needs. This can be illustrated for example by a quotation from J.P. Trap's memoirs about his childhood in a merchant's house in Randers. Trap, who was born in 1810, relates how they baked rye bread, brewed beer, boiled soap, and made candles themselves, and continues: 'milch cows were kept and pigs reared. Poultry and pigeons were part of the stock of the farm, most often one had *agre* and meadows on the

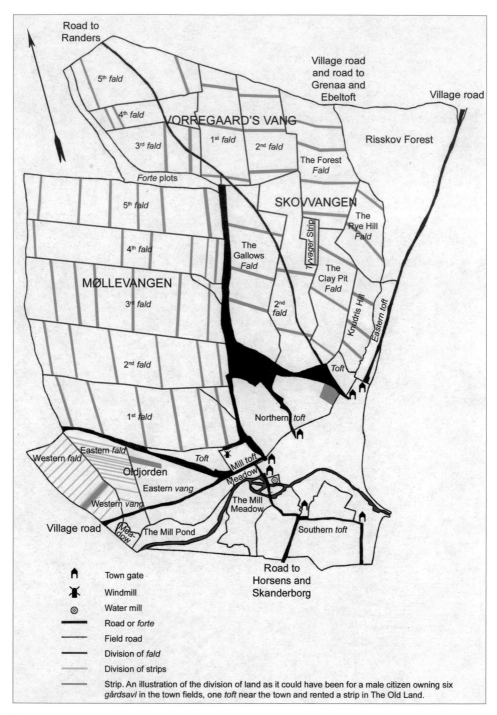

Road to
Randers

5th fald

4th fald

3rd fald

1st fald

2nd fald

VORREGAARD'S VANG

Village road
and road to
Grenaa and
Ebeltoft

Village road

Risskov Forest

The Forest
Fald

Forte plots

5th fald

4th fald

MØLLEVANGEN

3rd fald

2nd fald

1st fald

SKOVVANGEN

The
Rye Hill
Fald

The
Gallows
Fald

Tvager Strip

The
Clay Pit
Fald

2nd
fald

Knudris Hill

Eastern toft

Toft

Northern toft

Eastern fald

Western fald

Oldjorden

Eastern vang

Western vang

Toft

Mill toft

Meadow

The Mill
Meadow

Southern toft

Village road

Mea-dow

The Mill Pond

Road to
Horsens and
Skanderborg

♙ Town gate

✳ Windmill

⊗ Water mill

▬▬ Road or *forte*

── Field road

▬▬ Division of *fald*

│ │ Division of strips

▬▬ Strip. An illustration of the division of land as it could have been for a male citizen owning six *gårdsavl* in the town fields, one *toft* near the town and rented a strip in The Old Land.

FIG. 4.

The town fields of Aarhus around 1800. Division of land in regard to cultivation
A fald *is: approx. a furlong.*

town land which were cultivated with the help of the two or four horses that were kept for transport in the business'.[49] He also relates that the town had a 'distinctive summer smell' (…) from the many cows which each morning and at midday were driven out to the field to graze on the common and again, midday and evening, came home to be milked. 'The cowherd (…) was driven out to graze, and called home for milking by sounding a large cow's horn'.[50]

The town fields were primarily used to grow grain. It is true that an ordinance of 14 August 1741 enjoined that a quarter of the cultivated land in the market towns should be sown with hemp, flax or tobacco, but evidently this was not worthwhile as it was not much observed.[51] In addition, hay was saved on all large and small areas that were unsuitable for tillage. In 1806 the yield from Aarhus' town fields was stated to be 18 loads of winter wheat, 16 loads of rye, 802 loads of barley, 420 loads of oats, 10 loads of peas and 185 loads of hay.[52] In Randers in the previous year the harvest was 1,526 loads of grain and 953 loads of hay,[53] while the total grain and hay harvest in Skanderborg in 1806 was stated to be 200 loads.[54]

Comparable figures for farming and animal husbandry in the Danish market towns are first available after the *Statistisk Tabelværk* began publication in 1835. The first figures for market town agriculture in the Kingdom are from 1837. Table 1 shows the figures for seed and yield in proportion to the seed sown in the three market towns.

TABLE 1.

Seed used in Aarhus, Randers and Skanderborg 1837.[55]

Crop	Aarhus	Randers	Skanderborg
Barrels of wheat seed	27.5	82	-
Yield	6.5	7	
Barrels of rye seed	115	138	122
Yield	6.5	6	5
Barrels of barley seed	368	251	104
Yield	6.5	6	5
Barrels of oats seed	883	974	174
Yield	6.5	5	6
Barrels of buckwheat seed	-	-	9
Yield			5
Barrels of peas seed	-	-	-
Yield			

Crop	Aarhus	Randers	Skanderborg
Barrels of potatoes*	99	80	54
Yield	10.5	8	9
Grass seed or clover seed, yield	1,632	1,600	408
Winter rape, tønder land	8	2	3
Flaxseed, tønder land	-	4	-
Tobacco, pounds	-	3,504	-

Outside the gardens

As can be seen from the figures, oats (which were mainly used as horse feed) were by far the most important type of grain in all three market towns. Barley (which among other things was used for beer brewing and distilling spirits) was the next most important grain apart from in Skanderborg, where a little more rye was grown. Oats were also predominant in most of the other Jutland market towns, whereas barley was the most widespread type of grain in the rest of Denmark. Compared with the other types of grain, the production of wheat was very small in Aarhus, Randers and Skanderborg, indeed in the last mentioned town, no wheat at all was grown. In that way too, the East Jutland pattern corresponded well with the situation in other parts of the country; for example even well into the 19th century, wheat was grown to a large extent only on the islands of Lolland and Falster and other parts of East Denmark with heavy clay soil. The table shows that peas were not grown on the town fields of the three market towns in 1837; other written sources however contain numerous examples of growing peas both on the town fields and in the gardens. It can also be seen that potatoes were grown in all the towns and the same was the case for grass and clover which were important feeding components for the livestock. Finally it is worth mentioning that the farmers in Randers lived up to the requirements in the ordinance from 1741 to grow flax and tobacco. As well as the crops on the town fields, the inhabitants of the market towns grew potatoes, cabbage and other vegetables in their gardens on the town ground and the vast majority of towns were self-sufficient in vegetables. However this was not the case in Randers, because the town ground was so densely built-up that there was almost no room for gardens.

Table 1 shows that all three market towns had yields of 5-7 for grain and 8-10.5 for potatoes. These were high figures for that time, but the East Jutland market town land was also the most fertile in Jutland.[56] Perhaps there is also a connection between this fertility and the fact that the land of the three towns was cultivated so early compared with many other market towns. On the basis of the figures for sowing and yield, the total harvest of grain and potatoes from the *markjorder* can be calculated. The results are shown in Table 2:

TABLE 2.

Harvest yield in Aarhus, Randers and Skanderborg 1837.

Crop	Aarhus	Randers	Skanderborg
Barrels of grain	9,058	7,778	2,174
per inhabitant	2.2	1.7	4.5
Barrels of potatoes	1,040	640	486
per inhabitant	0.3	0.14	1.0

A total of 85,417 barrels of potatoes were harvested on Danish market town land in 1837, which gives an average of 1,275 barrels for each of the 67 market towns in the Kingdom. As mentioned the figures do not include the potatoes grown in the gardens in the town, which differed greatly from town to town. In spite of this uncertainty, there seems to be little doubt that Skanderborg was the town which was the most self-sufficient in this crop of the three towns studied.[57]

With regard to the grain harvest, in 1837 a total of 220,851 barrels were harvested on the market town land in the Kingdom, which gives an average of 3,296 barrels of grain per market town. As can be seen, production in the East Jutland towns varied from 1.7 barrels per inhabitant in Randers to 4.5 barrels in Skanderborg. For comparison it can be mentioned that the yield in all the Danish rural parishes together was 11 barrels per inhabitant.[58] The figures clearly show a much greater degree of self-sufficiency in Skanderborg than in Aarhus and Randers – especially when one takes into consideration that the towns produced only for their own use and not for export. In other words, the inhabitants of Skanderborg based a greater part of their economy on the utilisation of the *markjorder* than the large market towns. However the figures also show that the crops from the town fields even in the large market towns were a not unimportant contribution to the food supply, even if most food had to be bought from the farmers.

Animal husbandry in Aarhus, Randers and Skanderborg 1837.

Animals	Aarhus	Randers	Skanderborg
Horses	688	636	79
Colts and foals (1838)	14	17	-
Cows	434	626	171
Bullocks and bulls	24	100	7
Young stock for rearing	-	10	3
Pigs and piglets	112	84	12
Sheep and lambs	11	98	23
Beehives (1838)	31	-	6

Animal husbandry was an important part of everyday life for the market town inhabitants of that time. All households kept animals to some extent. The number of animals in the Danish market towns in 1838 included 12,372 horses, 272 colts and foals, 18,094 cows, 1,494 bullocks and bulls, 1,161 young cattle, 8,392 pigs and piglets, 14,049 sheep and lambs and 1,086 bee hives.[59]

Horses and cows were the most important farm animals in the market towns. The horses were used both for transport and work in the fields. Randers and Aarhus had more horses than cows, because these towns – which are situated on large roads – were strictly obliged to provide for the further transport of people and goods. That is why they – like most other market towns – had a carters' guild with its horses. These horses were often grazed on a specific place in the town fields or on a meadow that had been assigned to the carters. Skanderborg had fewer horses than cows and on this point too was more like the villages than the large market towns. There was no great need for transport in Skanderborg anyway after the town castle had lost its significance.

The cows were indispensable to the town dwellers because it was impossible to transport milk over long distances, and it was therefore important for a town to be self-sufficient in milk products. Those who could not afford a cow themselves could have a share in one. Both in villages and market towns, there was also a town bull.

In the 16th and 17th century, Jutland had quite a considerable production of bullocks for export, and as late as the 19th century there were a number of bullocks in certain towns. This was the case for instance in Randers, but definitely not in Aarhus and Skanderborg. Probably many of the bullocks mentioned in the lists from 1837 belonged to the numerous spirits distillers who in this way made good use of the residue from spirits production.

Two groups of users

One can distinguish between two groups of users of the town fields: those with rights to pasture and the *avlsbrugere* (the farmers). The first group probably, in practice, always included all the people who wanted to graze their horses and cows on the fields. But in connection with *udskiftning* there were often vigorous discussions about whether the grazing rights included only the people who owned property in the town.[60] The group of *avlsbrugere* included the people and institutions that, in addition to grazing rights, had the right to cultivate a large or small part of the town fields (and in some cases also had ownership of this land). A local enquiry in connection with a redistribution of the land in Aarhus in 1801 gives a good insight into the composition of the circle of *avlsbrugere* in that town. At that time, there were 58 *avlsbrugere* in Aarhus, where the population of the town in the same year was calculated at 4,104 inhabitants.[61] Six of the *avlsbrugere* were church positions, church institutions or public foundations, while the other 52 were private people, 10 of them women. The biggest taxpayers of the town owned most *gårdsavl*.[62] There were three people of rank, two clergymen, 15 merchants or skippers, nine master craftsmen and an apothecary among the male farmers. In addition there were seven with unknown occupations and five people who were just designated as what can be translated as peasants, and who must therefore be assumed – as the only people – to have had farming as their main occupation.[63] The man who was the largest plot owner was the merchant Hans Raae, who had 24 *gårdsavl*. He was an important figure in Aarhus and later sat as a member of the advisory town council from 1804 to 1834. The next largest plot owner was master tailor Peder Villadsen with 18 *gårdsavl*. Then came the Cathedral with 17, apothecary Reddelin with 14 and merchant Peder Herskind with 13. Herskind, like Villadsen, was a member of the advisory town council in 1801. The sixth largest plot owner was the Deanery of the Cathedral with 12 *gårdsavl*. Together the 24 largest *avlsbrugere* owned 205 *gårdsavl*, corresponding to 75 % of the town fields.

To illustrate the circle of farmers in Skanderborg, there is a so-called cart list, that is, a list of transport obligations, from 1835. The list shows that there were 44 *avls-brugere* out of a population of 831 inhabitants.[64] Forty of them were men and they were categorised as follows: the county governor, two people of rank, one clergyman, two military people, eight merchants, four master craftsmen, one apothecary, one innkeeper, one district surgeon, one master builder, four managing clerks – and finally 14 uncategorised, who in theory could all have been full-time farmers.

The economic significance of the *markjorder* for the market town

The *markjorder* not only had great economic significance for the farmers and the actual users of the land. They could also be a great asset to the towns where a large part of the land was leased for the benefit of the town treasury. As mentioned, this was the case in Randers and an examination of the town budget from 1830 gives a clear impression of the importance of the farming in the economy of the town. The budget operated with expenses of 12,000 *rigsbankdaler* for the town treasury.[65] Of this, the largest post was billeting soldiers at 6,000, followed by 2,236 for wages. Among the other expenses we find 500 for administration of the town fields. On the income side the assessed taxes were estimated at 4,000 *rigsbankdaler*, while other taxes and the money in hand and various minor incomes amounted to 4,230. The other income for the town treasury – 4,100 *rigsbankdaler* – was income from the town land, divided between 3,500 for rent of the fields and 600 in pasture money. This last, as already mentioned, was paid by those with rights to pasture and was fixed each year at the grazing assessment. It was usual that this sum was fixed so that it covered expenses for the administration of the town fields, items such as wages to herders and supervisors, and this, then, was also the case in Randers where the expenses for administration of the town fields had been estimated at 500 *rigsbankdaler*.

The size of a town's income from leasing agricultural resources was determined by a large number of more or less random factors. In general, however, it can be said that towns with a large area of land, other things being equal, had more land that could be leased for cultivation. Another general characteristic concerns the time of cultivation. The land that was cultivated at an early stage was mainly divided among the town properties – i.e. it changed into private land no longer at the disposal of the town. The land that was not brought under cultivation until after the middle of the

18th century, on the other hand, was normally leased. It therefore either retained its status as common, as was the case in Randers, or it passed to town ownership, as was the case in Aarhus. In both cases the income normally went to the town treasury. But only in the cases where the land remained a common could the inhabitants decide how the rent income should be spent; in the other cases only the leadership of the town decided how the money was spent. However, generally, the common that was leased for cultivation changed status quickly and became the property of the town.

As a summary of the analysis of farming in Randers, Skanderborg and Aarhus, it can be said that farming on the fields of the market town had most economic importance for the small in-land market town, whereas the supply of milk – and with that pasturage – was important for all market towns irrespective of size. On the whole there is no doubt that farming had great importance for the daily life of the inhabitants in a great number of Danish market towns. Finally the study gives grounds to conclude that at least some towns with considerable amounts of land had a large income from leasing the land.

Enclosure and the dissolution of market town agriculture

Since 1800, agriculture in market towns was marked to a great degree by *udskiftning* and divison[66] – two concepts that are sometimes confused. *Udskiftning* as mentioned was a familiar phenomenon in the towns, but at the end of the 18th century – as part of the Danish agricultural reforms – *udskiftning* were also implemented in countless villages. This process, which involved the dissolution of the open-field system and relocation of many farms from a village to the open fields, inspired a new wave of *udskiftning* in the towns – as will be discussed later. Division of the towns' land holdings – that is division of a land area into plots which were then sold with full ownership and right of use to the buyers – was first of real importance in the second half of the 19th century. In these divisions the former *vange* were generally changed into residential areas.

In the years around 1800, many towns wanted to enclose their uncultivated common in order to divide the plots among the property owners of the town for the purpose of cultivating the land and gaining more revenue. An example of this is the *udskiftning* of the 400 *tønder land* common in the Zealand market town of Skælskør in 1797. Here the 70 landowners each got a share that corresponded to the land tax assessment; this meant that the larger a ground they had in the town, the larger the share of the common they got. But since the quality of the land on the common was very varied, it was also decided to award each landowner plots of both good and bad land – as had been the practice in *udskiftning* in earlier times. However in Skælskør, there were on average only three plots per owner.[67] In *Danske Kancelli* (The Danish Chancellery) which at that time had to consider all the requests for changes in market town land, they quickly became reluctant to give permission for this kind of enclosure. The reason was regard for posterity, because the right of disposal of the land was lost when it passed into private ownership. Thus Randers and Elsinore were refused when these towns requested permission for *udskiftning* among the town properties of cultivated and uncultivated common land in 1802 and 1798 respectively.

In 1811 an ordinance was promulgated which ordered that an annual fee be paid to the town treasury for trade in land plots that now belonged to individual property owners.[68] The ordinance also stated very precisely what the purchaser should pay per *tønder land*. At the same time permission was again given for *udskiftning* of common land among the town properties; the people who might acquire new land with such *udskiftning,* however, should pay an annual fee to the town treasury – and do so right from the very moment of the *udskiftning*. The reason for this payment arrangement was that the property owners did not have any right to the land and the town should therefore be indemnified. This was done by converting its ownership into the receipt of a fixed fee. On the basis of this reasoning *udskiftning* of cultivated and uncultivated common land was implemented among other places in Ringsted (1813), Stege (1815), Vejle (1824), Sæby (1838), and Hobro (1842).[69]

In the 18th and 19th centuries, enclosure of market town fields with the subsequent distribution of land among the town properties was normally done in a single process. This also included total dissolution of all kinds of farming communality. On the other hand, market town fields that were subjected to early enclosure – such as Aarhus town fields that were divided among the town properties in the 16th century – were most often subject to *udskiftning* more than once before all the land was included and all forms of farming communality dissolved. Some market town fields were never enclosed and divided among the town properties. They were used jointly and then at some time divided into plots and leased or sold. In other places, such as Randers, there was a considerable amount of private fields which had been divided among the town properties at an early stage, but which did not form part of a farming communality. In Randers the different owners' *agre* lay in between each other in the fields. As far as is known, there are no other examples of such a field system *without* at the same time joint cultivation among the users. The opposite situation – that fields had been subjected to *udskiftning* but were still jointly cultivated – on the other hand was quite usual. This was the case for example in Aarhus after the *udskiftning* in 1801-02.

Most market towns had both common land and private land, which were jointly cultivated in various complex forms. Generally it can be said that most forms of farming communality were in the towns that had undergone an early *udskiftning* and it was therefore often very difficult to implement enclosure in these towns in particular. This was the case for instance in Aarhus where the town fields went through the final *udskiftning* in 1840-1841; in this process all the land of each of the plot owners was gathered into one place, and at the same time all forms of joint cultivation were abolished. At this time almost 80 % of all market town land in the Kingdom of Denmark had been subject to *udskiftning* to some extent or another.[70]

The dissolution of the open-field system did not just result in improved farming, but in a complete change of cultivation and the cultural landscape. Lands now had to be fenced. Each owner decided himself what crops were to be cultivated on his land, and which fields should be under pasture. There was no longer one or more very large cultivated *vange* and a corresponding one laid out for grazing. People could no longer walk freely in the half of the town fields, that were lying fallow and used for grazing, but had to stay on the paths. The *forter* had disappeared – on the other hand there were parks and footpaths.

The dissolution of joint cultivation and the distribution of the town fields was the end of an era when agriculture went hand in hand with commerce and trades as a natural part of citizens' life.

BIBLIOGRAPHY

Begtrup, G. 1808. *Beskrivelse over Agerdyrkningens Tilstand i Danmark, Nørrejylland*. Vol. I-II. Copenhagen A. & S. Soldins Forlag.

Beretning og Betænkning fra den i Anledning af et Forslag til en friere Afbenyttelse af Aarhuus Kjøbstads Fællesjorder nedsatte Committee 1838. Copenhagen.

Bergsøe, A.F. 1847. *Den danske Stats Statistik*. Copenhagen.

Bjerge, P. & T. Søegaard 1908-1910. *Danske Vider og Vedtægter*. Vol. 2. Copenhagen: Lehmann & Stage.

Brasen, J.A. 1845. 'Historisk Fremstilling af Skielskiørs Bymark, dens forskiellige Skikkelser og Udskiftninger'. *Historisk Tidsskrift*, pp. 563-92.

Clausen, J. (ed.) 1939-40. *Aarhus gennem Tiderne*. Vol. 1-2. Aarhus: Nyt Nordisk Forlag.

Fogtman, Laurids 1786-1918. *Kongelige Rescripter, Resolutioner og Collegialbreve for Danmark og Norge, udtogsviis udgivne i chronologisk Orden (1660-1870)*. Copenhagen: Gyldendal.

Frandsen, Karl-Erik 1983. *Vang og tægt. Studier over dyrkningssystemer og agrarstrukturer i Danmarks landsbyer 1682-83*. Esbjerg: Bygd.

Hald, J.C. 1827. *Bidrag til Kundskab om de danske Provindsers nærværende Tilstand. Randers Amt*. Copenhagen: Schultz.

Hertz, Michael 1989. 'Avlsbrugere og avling på købstadsjorder'. *Bol og By*, pp. 72-92.

Hofman, H. de 1756. *Samlinger af Fundationer og Gave-Breve vedkommende Aarhuus Stift*. Vol. II. Copenhagen.

Hofman, H. de 1758. *Samlinger af publique og private Stiftelser, Fundationer og Gavebreve, som forefindes udi Danmark og Norge*. Vol. III. Copenhagen.

Holtet, C. 1933. *Blade af Skanderborg Bys Historie*. Skanderborg.

Madsen, H. 1983. *Skanderborg*. Skanderborg: Centraltrykkeriet i Skanderborg.

Mørup, E. 1880/1893. *Samling af collegiale og ministerielle Circulairer og Skrivelser m.m. vedr. Landinspecteurernes Virksomhed 1782-1879 og 1880-92*. Copenhagen: Landinspecteurforeningens Forlag.

Neckelmann, L.C. 1988. *Kortfattet Udsigt over Randers Kjøbstad i Aaret 1830*. Randers.

Schou, Jacob Henric 1795-1849. *Chronologisk Register over de kongelige Forordninger og aabne Breve, samt andre trykte Anordninger, som fra Aar 1670 af ere udkomne*. Copenhagen.

Schythe, J.C. 1843. *Bidrag til Kundskab om de danske Provindsers nærværende Tilstand. Skanderborg Amt*. Copenhagen: Qvist.

Stadfeldt, S.A. 1804. Chorographisk og oeconomisk Beskrivelse over Randers Kiøbsted i Nørre Jylland. Copenhagen.

Statistisk Tabelværk, 1837, 2nd *hæfte*., 1842, 5th *hæfte*, 1842, 6th *hæfte*, new series, 1852, vol. 4-5.

Thane, L. 1908. *Skanderborgs Historie*. Skanderborg.

Trap, J.P. 1859. *Statistisk-topographisk Beskrivelse af Kongeriget Danmark*. Copenhagen: Gad.

Trap, J.P. 1870. *Fra fire Kongers Tid*. Vol. I. Copenhagen.

Wedel, L.M. 1806. *L.M. Wedels indenlandske Rejse*. Vol. 2. Copenhagen.

http://www.folketimidten.dk.

http://www.dengamleby.dk/cgi-files/landbruget/landbruget.asp.

NOTES

1   1 *tønde land* is 0.5516 hectares.

2   *Statistisk Tabelværk,* 5th *hæfte*, 1842, contains the oldest comparable figures for all the market towns in the Kingdom of Denmark. The figures from this source are reproduced on the web site http://www.dengamleby.dk/cgi-files/landbruget/landbruget.asp.

3   However this right was abolished by a royal decree of 15 April 1842, which confirmed an agreement between the town and the academy whereby the town acquired some land as com-

pensation for the grazing rights. The legal provisions are taken from Fogtman 1786-1918 and Schou 1795-1849.

4   In a Danish context, *udskiftning* simply means a change of land distribution among the land users and does not necessarily imply changes of property, farming community or the location of the farms. However, *udskiftning* was often followed by dissolution of the open-fields system and a division of the plots, typically fenced, among the property owners of the town. In these cases, we could use the English term, enclosure. However, in many of the examples in this article, this was not the case and consequently the Danish term *udskiftning* is used.

5   *Hartkorn* taxes were chargeable on the individual farm on the basis of the *hartkorn* number. This number was an expression of the productivity of the land, as it took into consideration both the area and quality. Not just arable land, but also meadow and wooded areas were assessed for *hartkorn*. The different taxation treatment of country and town land was discontinued by a law of 20 June 1850; after this all users of agricultural land etc. had to pay *hartkorn* tax.

6   Rigsarkivet (The Danish National Archives in Copenhagen), Kommercekollegiet, pk. 29: Relationer over de danske Stifters Tilstand…1735, Skanderborg. Begtrup 1808, vol. I, p. 578. Schythe 1843, p. 503.

7   *Beretning og Betænkning*, 1838, p. 27.

8   *Statistisk Tabelværk*, 5th *hæfte*, 1842. According to *Statistisk Tabelværk*, new series, vol. 5, 1852, 123 *tønder land* should be added to this.

9   *Beretning og Betænkning*, 1838, p. 3.

10 Hofman 1756, pp. 27-30.

11 Hofman 1758, pp. 189-92.

12 *Statistisk Tabelværk*, 5th *hæfte*, 1842. *Statistisk Tabelværk*, new series, vol. 5, 1852, gives the area as 2,381 *tønder land*.

13 Stadfeldt 1804, pp. 401-403.

14 *Statistisk Tabelværk* 5 th *hæfte*, 1842. *Statistisk Tabelværk*, new series, vol. 5, 1852 gives the area as 488 *tønder land*.

15 Begtrup 1808, vol. I, p. 579.

16 Clausen 1939, vol. I, p. 254.

17 *Beretning og Betænkning*, 1838, p. 39.

18 *Beretning og Betænkning*, 1838, p. 20 and Clausen 1939, vol. II, pp. 10 f.

19 These were Østervang in 1551, Vestervang in 1582, Næstnyvang in 1606 and Udervang in 1637.

20 Clausen 1939, vol. I, p. 334.

21 *Forordning* 14 August 1741 (reproduced in Schou 1795-1849).

22 *Reskript* 26 March 1756 (reproduced in Fogtman 1786-1918).

23 Begtrup 1808, vol. I, p. 555.

24 *Beretning og Betænkning,* 1838, pp. 20 ff. With regard to land that belonged to secular posts, the rule was that the land reverted to the town if a post was abolished.

25 Erhvervsarkivet (The Danish National Business Archives), Århus Købstads Arkiv, Aarhus. E14 Åstedsforretning 1801, pp. 64-65, 82-83, 93-94. Kort- og Matrikelstyrelsens arkiv, Copenhagen (Archives of The National Survey and Cadastre in Copenhagen). K-63 Møllevangen. Kort- og Matrikelstyrelsens arkiv, Copenhagen. K-63 Worregård og Skovvangen, K-63 Møllevangen.

26 Stadfeldt 1804, pp. 365 f.

27 Bjerge & Søegaard 1908-1910, vol. II, p. 203.

28 Begtrup 1808, vol. II, p. 137.

29 Stadfeldt 1804, pp. 369-73.

30 Begtrup 1808, vol. I, p. 579.

31 Op.cit.

32 Bjerge & Søegaard 1908-1910, vol. II, pp. 272 ff.

33 Op.cit. pp. 192 ff.

34 Pigs were often kept in the back buildings of the houses, where hens were also kept.

35 Since sheep could manage with poorer quality grass than cattle, it was usual in the Danish towns to relegate the sheep to the marginal areas of the town, among other places, moors, bogs and dunes. Some of the largest numbers of sheep were also to be found in towns with land of very poor quality; for instance Skagen which was surrounded by sand on all sides had over 1,000 sheep in 1837.

36 Erhvervsarkivet, Århus Købstads Arkiv, Aarhus. E14 Åstedsforretning 1801, pp. 37 f.

37 In other parts of the country, other forms of rotation were more widespread. For instance the three-field system was completely dominant in the eastern part of Denmark. In a typical three-field system, the single *vang* was sown one year with barley, the next year with rye, and lay fallow the third year. About Danish tillage forms, see Frandsen 1983.

38 Bjerge & Søegaard 1908-1910, vol. II, pp. 272 ff.

39 Op.cit. p. 286.

40 Begtrup 1808, vol. II, p. 139.

41 Op.cit. p. 137.

42 Bjerge & Søegaard 1908-1910, vol. II, p. 197.

43 Op.cit. p. 203.

44 Thane 1908, p. 18.

45 Begtrup 1808, vol. I, p. 579.

46 Thane 1908, pp. 75 f.

47 Holtet 1933, p. 167.

48 *Statistisk Tabelværk*, new series, vol. 4, 1852. Trap: *Danmark* II and http://www.folketimidten. dk.

49 Trap 1870, p. 8.

50 Op.cit. p. 6.

51 *Forordning* 14 August 1741 (reproduced in Schou 1795-1849) and Bergsøe 1847, vol. 2, p. 112. The cultivation of these cash crops is discussed in Hertz 1989, pp. 72-92.

52 Begtrup 1808, vol. I, p. 555, 580. Begtrup 1808, vol. II, p. 139.

53 Begtrup 1808, vol. II, p. 139.

54 Begtrup 1808, vol. I, p. 580.

55 *Statistik Tabelværk*, 5th *hæfte*, 1842. The figures from this work can now be seen on http://www.dengamleby.dk/cgi-files/landbruget/landbruget.asp.

56 Hald 1827, p. 89.

57 *Statistisk Tabelværk*, 5th *hæfte* 1842, and http://www.dengamleby.dk/cgi-files/landbruget/land-bruget.asp. These sources contain comparable figures for all the Danish market towns.

58 *Statistisk Tabelværk*, 2nd *hæfte*, 1837.

59 *Statistisk Tabelværk*, 5th *hæfte*, 1842, and http://www.dengamleby.dk/cgi-files/landbruget/land-bruget.asp.

60 See for example *Beretning og Betænkning* 1838, where the question is a recurrent theme.

61 Erhvervsarkivet, Århus Købstads Arkiv, Aarhus. E14 Åstedsforretning 1801, pp. 64 f., 82 f., 93 f. and Kort- og Matrikelstyrelsens arkiv, Copenhagen. K-63 Møllevangen. K-63 Worregård and Skovvangen.

62 Clausen 1939, vol. I, p. 334.

63 Lokalhistorisk Samling, Aarhus. Borgerskabsprotokol 1674-1862.

64 Madsen 1983, p. 93.

65 In addition, 14,200 *rigsbankdaler* to run the poor relief, the school system and the church. Cf. Neckelmann 1988, pp. 40-45.

66 In Danish: *Udstykning*.

67 Brasen 1845, pp. 585 ff. Cf. Reskript of 3 October 1794 (reproduced in Fogtman 1786-1918).

68 *Forordning* 18 October 1811 (reproduced in Schou 1795-1849).

69 *Kancellipromemoria* 5 January 1813 (Ringsted), *reskript* 30 May 1815 (Stege), *reskript* 28 May 1824 (Vejle), *reskript* 30 May 1838 (Sæby) and *reskript* 15 July 1842 (Hobro). All these texts are described in Fogtman 1786-1918.

70 *Statistisk Tabelværk*, 5th *hæfte*, 1842.

Henrik Harnow

The early contours of a Danish industrial city –
Danish towns between the pre-industrial and the
industrial period, ca. 1800-1850

Introduction

Looking at the total number of Danish industrial workers halfway through the 19th century one can tell that Denmark had yet to experience industrialisation on a wide scale. In Copenhagen, the capital, the estimated number of industrial workers was 8,500 out of a population of 130,000 in 1847.[1] In 1855, Odense, Aarhus and Aalborg – the second, third and fourth largest towns in the Danish Kingdom – had 651, 472 and 390 industrial workers respectively according to the censuses of that year.[2] Even fewer industrial workers were found in the medium-sized Danish towns and the smallest towns were largely unaffected by industrialisation during most of the 19th century.

Strictly speaking it is not possible to identify a single industrial city[3] in Denmark by 1850 – unless the factory village of Frederiksværk in Northern Zealand is counted as such. This is not to say that industrialisation had not yet set its mark on a number of towns – indeed it had – or that there were no factory villages. Copenhagen was by far the most industrialised city by 1850, when industrial enterprises and dwellings for industrial workers were beginning to spread beyond the city gates. The old capital was bursting at the seams and sending its industrial lava over the surrounding countryside, but it was still a far cry from what had happened in Birmingham, Liverpool or Manchester.

This article deals with early industrial development and especially its effect on towns in the Kingdom of Denmark. In spite of the opening lines this is still a worthwhile effort. Industrialisation was not a sudden change but a process that took place over several decades, finally reaching its zenith with the mature industrial city in the late 19th and early 20th centuries. Development was not spread evenly, and most small towns were still relatively untouched by industrialisation around 1900. Nevertheless there was a general feeling of dramatic physical change, of the old world giving place to something new. It is characteristic that in 1918 the first buildings preservation act came into force. Apart from listing a large number of rural estates, several old provincial town houses were listed in the years that followed. They were all threatened by destruction created by the forces of industrialisation.

Our cities of today are the result of this all-consuming process and still basically reflect the changes brought about by industrialisation. The transformation from the pre-industrial city to the industrial city was not only a change in town morphology but at the same time a break up of social structures, status and the perception of the city.

To provide an overall frame for the understanding of the general nature of Danish cities in the early and mid 19th century the article briefly presents the concepts of the pre-industrial city in contrast to the industrial city. The article endeavours to relate Danish research in industrialisation and in the history of Danish towns to these concepts at a meta level. In this article the term 'industry' normally refers to the prevailing Danish definition of industry as production units with six employees or more, but a pragmatic approach is applied where useful, acknowledging the problematic nature of the definition – not least in a transitional period such as the early and mid 19th century.

Characteristics of the pre-industrial and the industrial city

It is paradoxical that the city preceding the industrial city has come to be known as the 'pre-industrial city', a city defined not by what it was but by what it was going to become.[4] Though a number of reservations must be made, in very general terms, the pre-industrial city was characterised by a pre-eminence of the central area over the periphery, especially in the distribution of social classes, the existence of finer, spatial differences according to ethnic, occupational and family ties etc. and low functional differentiation outside the very centre of the city.[5]

The city centre was the domain of the social elite. The buildings of power, the church, the town hall and the houses of the privileged were located in the centre.

FIG. 1.

Bird's-eye view of Copenhagen seen from Østerbro ca. 1863-1864. The capital was on the verge of burst-
ing its old boundaries but it was still not an industrial city. In the following decades industry with its ac-
companying physical and social change spread across the city and the areas outside the old city centre.

The pre-industrial city was characterised by a gradual decline of status from the centre towards the city limits, where the poorest houses and the outcasts of society were located.

The social structure of the pre-industrial city was one of very subtle divisions. The family structure often consisted of large households, for instance master artisans provided dwellings for their employees within their home, and prosperous families often had a number of servants living in the same household. With regard to segregation at household level, the front street had a higher status than the back street, reflected in the social status of the inhabitants. Though there was a contrast between centre and periphery it would be incorrect to see the city centre as the preserve of the rich. The pre-industrial city had a relatively small spatial differentiation between rich and poor – the latter often living just around the corner from the main street.

This, of course, is a sweeping generalisation where nuances and specific conditions tend to be overlooked. Most Danish towns of the 18th and early 19th centuries show recognisable traits of this general structure, as we will see later, but in general they were also considerably smaller than the cities that constituted the empirical background for the theory.

The industrial city, on the other hand, is not a clear-cut concept either, but generalising on the same level one can mention a number of characteristics caused by industrialisation and population growth.

The theories of the industrial city boast a long tradition. The American sociologist E.W. Burgess' concentric circle-theory from 1925 is often mentioned as the starting point.[6] Burgess pointed out some universal development traits that characterise the industrial city. First of all, in the industrial city the suburbs have social pre-eminence over the city centre as an important contrast to the pre-industrial city. Burgess described the industrial city as a structure of circular zones growing as additions to the old city centres. In brief, the theory of concentric zones describes the industrial city ideally as a central business district surrounded by a transitional zone with older housing in gradual decline. This inner part of the city is then surrounded by industry and by zones of housing. Dwellings for the rich are located in suburbs due to historical, natural and other factors. The rich and powerful have, so to speak, left the city centre to live in quieter surroundings. The process of change from a pre-industrial to an industrial city was slow and gradual and often with several historical 'layers' represented at the same time.

It is no doubt correct that the zonal structure of the industrial city as described by Burgess is the best known theory because 'its popularity was (...) sustained by the appealing simplicity with which it could be depicted diagrammatically', but also because it was the first explicit generalisation of the structure of 'the industrial city'.[7]

Today it is generally accepted that a number of other factors must be taken into consideration as well as specific historic and natural conditions, but it is fair to acknowledge that Burgess pointed out elements that can be found in the physical reality of most western cities that grew under the influence of industrialisation. When the Danish municipal engineer R.V. Rygner in 1926 contributed to a one-volume history of Odense on Funen, the third largest city in Denmark at the time, he had never heard of Burgess and his theory of concentric circles, but Rygner's description of the development of the city during the past more than fifty years nevertheless was in the form of a circular movement around the old town centre, showing an underlying sense of a new city structure.[8]

A special aspect of the industrial city is the factory village, which strictly speaking was neither an industrial nor a pre-industrial city. Factory villages were dramatic results of early industrialisation. Internationally there are a number of well-known examples such as Robert Owen's model village New Lanark in Scotland, Saltaire at Bradford and Krupp's factory village at Essen. Factory villages owed their existence to one factory or a certain branch and were typically built where a supply of labour, certain natural conditions or waterpower were available. They were totally new villages with no older city structure as their precursor.

Danish research on the industrial city

The history of Danish industrialisation in general is relatively well researched. Classic works include Axel Nielsen (ed.), *Industriens historie i Danmark* (A history of Danish industry) from 1944 in four volumes, followed by Richard Willerslev's *Studier i dansk industrihistorie* (Studies in Danish industrial history) in 1952. Of specific interest to foreign readers is Svend Aage Hansen's *Early industrialisation in Denmark* from 1970.

Svend Aage Hansen's *Økonomisk vækst i Danmark* (Economic growth in Denmark) from 1978 presents an overview of the general economic development. The latest works in this genre are Ole Feldbæk's *Danmarks økonomiske historie 1500-1840* (The economic history of Denmark 1500-1840), 1993, and Ole Hyldtoft's *Danmarks økonomiske historie 1840-1910* (The economic history of Denmark 1840-1910), 1999. Recently the research project, Danish industry after 1870, has been published in seven volumes.[9]

Hyldtoft's research into Danish industrialisation and economic growth has resulted in a number of publications spanning from *Københavns industrialisering* (The industrialisation of Copenhagen), 1983, to his latest book on the history of the technological development of Denmark. Though the subjects covered have been wide ranging, Hyldtoft has consistently worked over the years on developing and refining a synthesis of the general Danish process of industrialisation. He has described Danish industrialisation as proceeding in alternating phases. Hyldtoft's view is that a development with growth 'in depth' with the introduction of new technology and new branches in the 1840s and 1850s was followed by periods with differing weight upon growth in depth and periods of diffusion and general growth.

This research is relevant to the subject of this article but treats town development only indirectly. It is fair to say that Danish research on the transitional period from the pre-industrial to the industrial city has been limited. Only a small number of publications have set out to achieve an understanding of the changes in the physical structure of Danish cities and the social stratification brought about by industrialisation.

Though a number of other publications have followed since its publication, the introduction to the subject given by Ole Degn in *Urbanisering og industrialisering* (Urbanisation and industrialisation) in 1978 is still a cornerstone and an internationally oriented presentation of the subject.

A number of local town histories have been published over the last two decades, most of them well researched and using new empirical material, but rarely with the aim of analysing structural changes or involving more complex theories of the morphology of cities under the influence of industrialisation. The history of town growth during the early industrial period must still basically be pieced together from the relatively large number of town histories and several publications on different subjects related to the development of Danish cities and Danish industrialisation.

A few works stand out as pioneering efforts in this field. Peter Dragsbo's *Mennesker og huse i Aabenraa* (People and houses in Aabenraa) from 1978 was an early effort to analyse the structural development of areas in Aabenraa in Southern Jutland in the period from 1850 to 1920.[10] Dragsbo combined studies of the town plan, building structure and building types with empirical studies of social stratification enabling him to present well-researched conclusions on the process of transformation from a pre-industrial to an industrial city. Hans Chr. Johansen, Per Boje and Anders Monrad Møller's *Fabrik og Bolig* (Factory and Dwelling) from 1983 was another pioneering work making use of databases in analysing the development of Odense. Inspired by works on English industrialisation and the different theories of town growth, the study presents analyses and conclusions very relevant to the subject of this article.

Following the founding of the Danish Centre for Urban History in 2001 a number of different research projects originating within the centre have contributed to and revitalised this area of research, e.g. the structural approach by Jens Toftgaard Jensen and Jeppe Norskov in *Købstadens metamorfose. Byudvikling og byplanlægning i Århus 1800-1920* (The metamorphosis of the market town) published in 2005. The bottom line is still, however, that a standard work on the general history of the Danish cities of the period does not exist.

FIG. 2.

A view from the cathedral tower of Odense towards the new street, Albanigade, in 1861. In the background to the right is the new courthouse and prison, while the church-like complex to the left is the Albani Brewery from 1859. The area behind the brewery developed into an industrial area with factories south of the river and areas with workers' housing. Along the river to the right, with a view to the cathedral and the old centre of town, pretentious villas for the new entrepreneurs were erected in the following years. The area was designated as a national industrial monument in 2007, chosen to represent the characteristic traits of the early industrial city in Denmark.

Industrialisation – the first impact on Danish towns

The early attempts to start up industrialisation in Denmark differ greatly from the spontaneous industrial revolution in Britain. From the 1730s and until the 1830s the Danish state played an active and direct role in the attempts to further industrialisation according to the English role model. This was done by encouraging and supporting new initiatives, for instance with loans and grants and by directly establishing new workshops and proto-factories (the Danish term for these pre-industrial production units was a *manufaktur*). The state's initiatives involved industrial espionage and the transfer of technology, mainly from Britain, in the form of technicians and engineers and to some extent machinery and other technology.[11]

The attempts to initiate an early industrialisation were all in all not successful. Danish society was not sufficiently developed to allow a broader industrialisation to take off. The many activities nevertheless left their mark and were visible. One result was a more widespread woollen industry using new technology in the Danish provinces in the first decades of the 19th century. The active role of the state declined around 1830.

From the 1830s there were the first visible signs that the development of the modern industrialisation of Denmark was gradually gaining momentum. The population of the Kingdom of Denmark grew from ca. 925,000 in 1800 to 1.3 million in 1850. From the late 1820s the economy began to grow following years of crisis including war with England (1807-1814), state bankruptcy (1813), the loss of Norway (1814) and a stagnant economy from about 1814 until 1825.

It is outside the context of this article to discuss the dating of an industrial breakthrough in Denmark, but it remains a fact that the development from the 1830s was connected to the longer and continuous process that by the late 19th century had transformed Denmark into a country, where agriculture was still dominant in volume, but industry had become the dynamic and driving force in the changes in society and city development.

From the 1730s a long period of mercantilist policy began, which lasted throughout the century. The policy of the 1730s had been to further industrial growth in and around the capital, but this changed to a policy aimed at establishing workshops, proto-factories and industries in the provincial towns too.[12] During the period there were large-scale state initiatives, namely the digging of Europe's largest ship canal, the Eider Canal in 1777-1784, connecting The North Sea with the Baltic Sea, and the construction of the somewhat smaller Odense Canal in 1796-1806. In 1764 the French engineer Jean Marmillod was put in charge of a large-scale project to improve the main highway system.[13]

A number of attempts were made in the 18th century to establish large-scale industrial enterprises in Copenhagen and its surroundings, all backed by the state. Industrial buildings were not totally new. The large *Gjethus* (a building for casting metal, from the German *giesen*) with a central location at Kongens Nytorv in Copenhagen had been built as early as 1661 for casting bronze cannon. A large sugar refinery was built at Christianshavn in Copenhagen in the first part of the 18th century using raw materials from the Danish West Indies. A shotgun factory complex was built at Hellebæk in Northern Zealand in the 1760s, and large textile workshops, e.g. the royal silk factory from 1753 and the royal wool manufactory from 1760, were erected, but the most remarkable enterprise was the Manchester Factory built at the Sortedams Lake in Copenhagen in 1779.[14] It is arguably the first real introduction of the English factory system to Denmark, modelled after early Arkwright factories, the early purpose-built and compact multi-storeyed factory buildings with an integrated central power source (normally a water wheel, but in the early factories a horse gin was commonly used as the source of power).[15] The Manchester Factory was powered by a horse gin and equipped with modern machinery made on the basis of industrial espionage in England. The factory had no success. Production lasted only into the 1780s and was never commercially profitable. It is too far reaching to treat the large naval complex at Holmen in Copenhagen in any detail, but it must be stressed that Holmen during the period remained the centre of technological competence in Denmark and it was the first place to erect a steam engine in 1790.[16]

It is characteristic that when the provincial towns reported on the state of industry in 1735, nearly all replied that no or very few *manufakturer* or factories existed.[17] From the middle of the 18th century a number of provincial towns experienced attempts to establish *manufakturer* outside the prevalent guild system. Some were on a small scale, but larger projects too saw the light of day. These *manufakturer* were often housed in complexes that seemed large for their time but as building types they remained traditional and they hardly qualify as factories, though there was a kind of industrial production in the sense that a large number of people were employed under supervision in the same buildings.

The grandest project in the Danish provinces in the 18th century was the attempt to move a complete woollen mill from Wiesbaden in Germany to Odense in 1756.[18] This state-financed project under the leadership of the textile manufacturer Anton Hübner involved moving about 400 people by ship to Odense through Odense Fjord. Not only did this huge project involve quite large buildings, the immediate effect on the town was also considerable. The population of the old town behind the tollgates was suddenly increased by 10 %, and accommodation as well as the religious element – the workers were a mixture of Lutherans, members of the Reformed Church and Catholics – caused problems. The factory complex was located close to the centre of town and consisted of four two-storey wings, in all 1,000 m² for spinning, weaving and other processes. However, in 1757 an attempt was made to move the factory from the town to a rural location. The number of workers had diminished and production was never successful. Some workers stayed in Odense but a larger number left and wandered through the provinces creating a problem of begging on their way. What effect did Hübner's manufacture have on the city of Odense? Quite a large sum of money was directly and indirectly spent on buildings, in taverns etc. and the social consequences were immediately felt. But when the factory complex was sold at auction in 1761 there had been no industrial spin-off from this adventure, which had instead proved that it was problematic to move a large number of foreigners to a small town.

Manufakturer were also established on private local initiatives.[19] In Odense a sugar refinery was established in 1751 using sugar cane from the Danish West Indies, and though never prosperous it functioned until 1789. Only 10-15 people worked at the refinery, and the overall effect on the town was limited. In Aarhus attempts to establish new industries in the 18th century were of a more limited nature: a couple of textile *manufakturer*, of which only one survived, and the most successful, a soap-making *manufaktur*, which was established in 1772 by two local merchants. Production was small, and neither it nor the number of workers reached an industrial scale.

In Aalborg a woollen mill began production in 1736 in a factory in the southern part of town close to the river, which was used to drive a fulling-mill and for dyeing. The factory made use of people receiving poor relief, and consequently the wages of the approximately 50 workers were very low. Other attempts were made to put the poor to work in early *manufakturer*, but this pragmatic solution to the combined problem of poverty and unemployment never resulted in sustained industrial growth.

Aalborg likewise experienced the establishment of a fully state-financed *manufaktur*. A silk *manufaktur* began production in 1753 with around 60 workers and employed the large number of 133 in 1761, but problems with overproduction in Copenhagen and with personnel etc. made it a limited success. It closed in 1763. Parallel to Odense, a sugar refinery was also established in 1752, producing sugar until 1822. All in all there were six sugar refineries in the provinces in the late 18th century: two in Elsinore, one each in Roskilde, Odense, Randers and Aalborg. Other branches that were relatively successful were soap making and the tobacco industry. The overall picture of industrialisation in the towns outside Copenhagen shows a limited number of rather short-lived enterprises until the 1830s.

Industry takes off

One of the crucial problems during the early attempts to kick-start Danish industrialisation was that the projects were isolated in the sense that they had no connections with the surrounding community and lacked technical expertise when the foreign technicians left. An important precondition for more widespread industry was the development of a Danish iron and metal industry located in all areas of the country. Earlier enterprises existed but Heinrich Meldahl's foundry, casting iron from a cupola furnace, from 1811 is generally considered the first modern iron foundry in Denmark. Meldahl had trained in Norway, which had previously supplied Denmark with cast iron. The twin Kingdoms of Denmark and Norway came to an end with Norway's secession in 1814.

Copenhagen was the centre of the early development of the iron industry and early machine shops, although the factory village Frederiksværk in Northern Zealand had a considerable production too (see below). Starting with Thomas Potter in 1769, a number of early enterprises were established before foundries and machine shops began spreading in the provinces. Shortly before 1850 the largest firms in iron and metals were still to be found in Copenhagen, with Baumgarten and Burmeister as the most notable example, growing from 30 workers in 1847 to more than 211 workers in 1855.[20]

Industrial competence spread from Meldahl and a few other early firms in Copenhagen to other parts of the country during the 1830s and 1840s. In Odense, Meldahl's former foreman of model making, M.P. Allerup, established the town's first iron foundry in 1836, and quite characteristically the competence spread from Allerup to other new firms in Odense and finally to other parts of Funen.[21]

An overview of the foundation of early Danish iron foundries clearly shows why industrialisation gained a firm hold at this time. Not only the largest cities but also the next level of provincial towns and their surrounding regions could sustain local foundries and mechanical works. These were established all over the country during the next two decades, for instance in Hjørring in Northern Jutland in 1831 and 1843, Horsens in Eastern Jutland in 1843, Ribe in Southern Jutland in 1848, Nyborg on Funen in 1841 and Køge on Zealand in 1842.[22]

The important effect of this relatively even distribution in the regions was the establishment of regional or local competence and the opportunity to deliver products and also spare parts to the local area. The mechanisation of Danish agriculture has a strikingly parallel chronology, and the use of new ploughs and other mechanical equipment on a wider scale from the 1830s is closely connected with the spread of iron foundries and machine shops, which often produced a wide variety of products for both agriculture and the local urban economy.

In the 1830s and 1840s the traditional branch of textiles was still quite dominant as an industrial branch, in Copenhagen employing 41 % of the total workforce in industry by 1839.[23] Before modern industrialisation set in with a more diverse industrial palette, textiles were the most important industry if assessed by the number of workers employed. Not only the capital but also the country in general was dominated by a widespread textile industry, almost resembling handicraft and on a generally low technological level. The rural population was to a great extent self-sufficient, spinning and weaving their own cloth. On a number of estates attempts were made to establish a putting-out industry or proto-industry, but the products had no chance in a market that was overwhelmingly self-sufficient.

Following the above-mentioned attempts at large-scale industrialisation in Copenhagen in the late 18th century a number of textile mills using the first Danish-made textile machinery and waterpower were established relatively successfully, notably Modeweg at Brede (close to Copenhagen), Bruun's at Fredericia (Jutland) and Grejs Mill at Vejle (Jutland). In contrast to England these Danish textile mills were without exception woollen mills. In the cities small industrial establishments using handicraft technology were in function in the 1830s and 1840s weaving English-spun cotton yarn.[24]

The industrial workforce, its localisation and the use of steam power

The total number of industrial workers in the first part of the 19th century is difficult to estimate with any great certainty. The sources are mainly the annual factory records *(fabrikslister)*, which are, at the same time, a rich and unique material and incomplete.[25] With some reservations it is possible to give a rough picture of the location of and employment in *manufakturer* and factories as well as other establishments with six workers or more.

The number of industrial workers in the provinces rose from around 600 in 1820 to about 3,000 in 1850.[26] That must be seen in perspective with the growth in the number of industrial workers in Copenhagen from about 5,900 in 1830 to about

8,500 in 1848.[27] A more realistic estimate of the total number of the industrial work-force in 1855 is about 20,000 out a population of about 1.5 million.[28]

Around 1850 about 70 % of all industrial workers were in Copenhagen, while a further approximately 12 % were employed in the three largest cities Odense, Aal-borg and Aarhus together. The localisation of workers in rural districts and towns shows that industrialisation even in the provinces was not a markedly rural phenom-enon. In counties where there were large cities, by far the largest proportion of in-dustry was located within the cities.[29]

Around 1850 industry was more unequally divided between countryside and city, and more products were made in mass-production factories for commercial sale to consumers than in the 1820s. The rise in the industrial workforce does not represent an average growth in company size, which stagnated at a level of approximately 20 workers through the 1830s and 1840s, while growth was because of a greater number of firms. The location of firms was not influenced by major improvements in infra-structure before 1850. The railroad from Copenhagen to Roskilde opened in 1847, and the large railway projects linking the country were not carried out before the 1850s and 1860s.

The use of power by industry can be described more precisely.[30] Much rural in-dustry was based on waterpower throughout the period, and before 1850 only a few industries in the cities had installed small steam engines.

The first Danish-built steam engine was made in Frederiksværk in 1828 by the mechanic Martin von Würden and afterwards used to run a copper rolling mill.[31] By 1839 there were 15 steam engines with a total horsepower of 183 in Copenhagen. Ole Hyldtoft specifically notes that 126 hp – more than two thirds – were located at five large enterprises and that these figures therefore might give the wrong impres-sion of the general level of mechanisation.[32] Steam power was still a rarity in indus-try, though certain branches such as the paper industry, where plants were located in the countryside, had relatively large steam engines.

In the larger provincial cities the first few steam engines appeared in the 1830s and especially the 1840s and 1850s. The first steam engine in Odense was set up in 1839 and used in a centrally placed textile mill housed in old monastery buildings, a complex very unlike the modern factories of the day. In Aarhus the first steam engine was put to work in 1838 and in Aalborg in 1841. A characteristic trait of the 1840s was the use of small steam engines, typically of 4-5 hp, in the distilleries.[33] Mecha-nisation was under way, but in Aalborg, for instance, the historian Henning Bender characterises the 1870s as a breakthrough in the use of prime movers in the form of steam engines.

Early industrialisation and its influence on the city

It is relevant to raise the question of where, in this process of transformation from pre-industrial to industrial city, the capital Copenhagen and the provincial cities were to be found. Were they pre-industrial or industrial cities, and to what extent?

For Copenhagen this discussion has been explicitly treated for the period from 1840 to 1910.[34] In 1840 Copenhagen was still basically a pre-industrial city showing all the typical signs of such. Its structure reflected its background as a fortified city with a huddling together of social groups and workplaces in the inner city. A two-kilometre wide strip of land outside the city walls, where there were almost no permanent buildings because of defensive considerations, encircled the capital.

The historian Ole Hyldtoft concludes that workplaces and dwellings in Copenhagen in the 1840s were intertwined, situated as they were in the mainly low houses, rarely more than three storeys high. A fine web of social segregation was to be found even at house-level: the first and second floors typically housed middle-class families, while workers were to be found in the basement or in the upper storey and in back-houses. A total of 90 % of the capital's population lived inside the city walls in 1840. High-status streets surrounded the city centre with the royal residences. A gradually lower status and lower land prices were found towards the periphery.

The capital of the 1830s was dominated by pre-industrial occupations like military, civil servants and artisans, who made up a total of 55 % of the working population. A third of the working population was employed in handicraft alone. A concentration of certain branches could also be seen, i.e. coopers at Christianshavn close to the harbour.

Tendencies to a break up of this traditional structure can be observed, e.g. in a gradual change in the household tradition of artisans. Married artisans with their own households were already common by 1840. At that time industry employed only 10 % of the population, and the small number of 14 industrial establishments used steam power. By far the largest part of industry was localised within the city walls by 1840, and the traditional type of industry still prevailed: textiles made up 40 % of all industry.

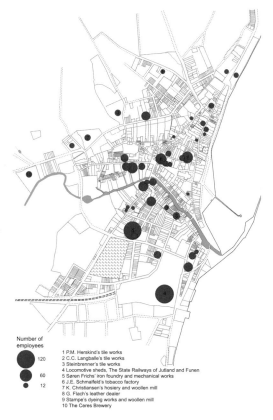

Number of
employees

● 120

● 60

● 12

1 P.M. Herskind's tile works
2 C.C. Langballe's tile works
3 Steinbrenner's tile works
4 Locomotive sheds, The State Railways of Jutland and Funen
5 Søren Frichs' iron foundry and mechanical works
6 J.E. Schmalfeld's tobacco factory
7 K. Christiansen's hosiery and woollen mill
8 G. Flach's leather dealer
9 Stampe's dyeing works and woollen mill
10 The Ceres Brewery

FIG. 3.

*Graphic presentation of industrial firms in Aarhus 1870. Quite a large proportion of all industry was
still located within the old parts of the city.*

Space does not allow a detailed look at the nature of the provincial towns of the
1830s and 1840s, but they can be characterised without exception as pre-industrial –
and only a very few of them broke the traditional structure until the 1870s or even
later.

For Aarhus a new detailed study confirms the pre-industrial structure of the city
in 1801 and 1845. It also indicates a visible development around the middle of the
century, which by 1880 showed typical signs of an industrial structure: the enlarge-
ment of the city area beyond the old toll gates, a change in occupational structure in
favour of industrial branches, the creation of new areas of high social status outside
the old city etc.[35] A situation parallel to that of the capital is worth noting. The localisation of industry in Aarhus was as a rule within the old city in 1845, and while

this pattern had undergone dramatic changes by 1870 with larger industries placed circularly around the old city, quite a large proportion of industry was still based in the old city centre (see fig. 3).

In 1983 Hans Chr. Johansen presented a physical map on the basis of the 1787-census of a number of variables giving a clear picture of a pre-industrial pattern in the city of Odense, a picture that was undergoing change by 1850, but still basically kept the structure of a pre-industrial city.[36] Well-known industrial cities of the early 20th century such as Horsens and Vejle in Jutland were small cities of only approximately 5,000 and 3,000 inhabitants by 1850, and though industrial establishments existed, industry was not the driving force in the transformation of the physical landscape of these towns before the 1870s.[37] Peter Dragsbo's study of Aabenraa in Southern Jutland clearly shows a general development much later than the 1850s with respect to overall structural changes, but still indicates an early tendency to a kind of zonal structure in the periphery of town. Small 'suburbs' for poor people and early workers developed on the periphery of the inner city, a development known from other market towns too.[38]

With a population growing at the rate of 2 % per year in the 1850s and 1860s greater pressure was put on the buildings in the inner city of Copenhagen. By 1850 the situation was so critical that doctors publicly warned against further overcrowding, and the first workers' housing on a philanthropic basis were erected. Most renowned were *Lægeforeningens boliger* (the Doctors' Union's dwellings) built in 1854 in the quarter of Østerbro, consisting of eight blocks with 31 small apartments in each. A large area was allocated for building by 1852, and the early *brokvarterer* ('bridge neighbourhoods')[39] began to grow. Both with respect to size and quality, the buildings from the early period around 1850 were of a higher quality than the buildings in the classic workers' housing zones, which grew from the 1870s. The early apartments often had 2-3 rooms with a kitchen and became the homes of better off workers.[40]

The first modern villas in Copenhagen were built in the 1850s and 1860s in the new suburbs, especially in Frederiksberg. The young engineer-to-be, Frits Casse, and his family were interested and quite inspired by the new way of life:

We were greatly surprised one morning in Spring when walking to school we saw workers cutting down a hedge and building a temporary timber bridge (…) It was the poet Carit Etlar, who had bought a large area and was now busy building a magnificent villa, which he had

HENRIK HARNOW

drawn himself (…) My mother talked a lot about what a pleasure it would be if my father could follow Carit Etlar's example so that we could exchange our small apartment in Brede-gade for a magnificent new home on Frederiksberg Allé.[41]

Casse's family actually built a new villa as early as 1851 designed by the well-known Danish architect J.D. Herholdt. The structure of the industrial city was beginning to take shape, and the middle class magazine *Illustreret Tidende* (Illustrated News) noticed the new villas in the street Rosenvænget in 1863:

A whole colony of elegant buildings rises between the trees (…) The inhabitants do not dis-turb each other, as the buildings are far apart (…) one feels that here it will be impossible to build amusements or pubs (…) here one cannot build tenement houses for large numbers of families, the privilege of Nørrebro …[one of the 'bridge neighbourhoods'].[42]

After the 1850s Copenhagen experienced a marked fall in pre-industrial occupations within the old city, and industry, formerly dominated by textiles, diversified into a wider spectrum. A number of new factories were built outside the former gates, but still a large proportion of all industrial workers were employed within the old city centre.

When the first Danish shed factory[43] – Salmonsen's Cotton Mill – was built in 1847 the owners 'chose to build the factory in a more spacious location'. This did not mean that they bought a plot of land outside the city, but instead an area at Nyhavn, quite close to the old high status centre of Copenhagen. In this area they built a large weaving shed with power looms, steam-driven ventilation and a four-storey factory for spinning, as well as a dyeing works. A steam engine of 20 hp powered the factory.[44]

This pattern, with several years 'latency' in industries leaving the older parts of the city, can also be seen in the larger provincial cities – still only cities of 5,000-10,000 inhabitants or less. New factories were built and new building materials such as cast iron were taken into use, e.g. in Ribe in 1850 in Giørtz' Cotton Mill. The first villas were built and from the 1860s also early workers' housing, but the general pattern of the industrial city could not be seen in the provinces before the 1870s. At that time traits of the pre-industrial structure were still visible with quite a high concen-tration of industry in the old city centres and with high status dwellings along the main streets and the market places.

To sum up, in 1850 no Danish city could rightly be characterised as fully transformed from pre-industrial to industrial, but new areas in Copenhagen in particular had an unmistakably industrial character. The Carlsberg Brewery moved from the old city to an area close to the new railway to Roskilde in 1847. Carlsberg is symbolic of the new development: it had begun in traditional surroundings in the city centre but then a completely different brewery – a factory – took form in the village of Valby, three to four kilometres from the old city centre in the open fields.

The larger provincial cities did not show many visible signs of a process of transformation around 1850. The factories were few and with a few exceptions rather traditional and located in the old city centre. Among the exceptions were the new iron works and machine shops. They were built as the first in a line of industrial enterprises, which followed in greater numbers in the years to come. Housing patterns in the provincial cities were still in the 1850s and 1860s basically pre-industrial in their form, with the wealthy households located centrally and the outskirts of town occupied by people of the lowest social status. A few modern villas had been built, but they were exceptions, and it was commonplace for the owner of a factory to live on the premises.

Factory villages

Different types of pre-industrial enterprises existed at a relatively early stage in Denmark, some located in the countryside because of the need for waterpower. Corn mills, rolling and hammer mills etc. would typically have one or a few dwellings around them in the 17th and 18th centuries, but factory villages in the classical form and of more than negligible size were rare in Denmark.[45]

As mentioned, Danish industrialisation on a wider scale occurred mainly in already existing cities, and Denmark had only a limited amount of heavy industry that depended on specifically located raw materials and needed the concentration of a large workforce around the production plant. Danish industry grew from the 1840s and only on a wider scale from the 1870s. Therefore Danish industrialisation did not depend on waterpower as the primary motive power unlike the early English textile factories that had to be built in remote places in the countryside. Danish factories were only built in larger numbers when steam power was a well-tried technology and coal could be supplied by rail or sea.

However, certain industries depending on waterpower or other locational factors of a non-urban character did create small villages before 1850. Tile works, glass works, some textile and paper mills needed a population of workers living nearby, but these settlements were in only a few cases large enough to be considered factory villages. Two examples are worth mentioning, and with 100 years between them, they both represent a combination of state initiative and active private entrepreneurship characteristic of the early industrialisation of Denmark. The first and most important Danish factory village was Frederiks Werck (today Frederiksværk) in Northern Zealand, named after King Frederik V (1723-1766), while the paper-industry town of Silkeborg began its protracted growth process a century later.

A village for armament production – Frederiksværk

In Northern Zealand sand drift had hindered the outflow of water from Denmark's largest lake, Arresø, in the 17th century and caused the severe flooding of peasants' fields and houses in the early 18th century.[46] This was the background for a royal charter that in the years 1717-1719 resulted in the digging of a canal from Arresø to Roskilde Fjord, a stretch of only a couple of kilometres. The canal allowed the water from Arresø to flow to the sea – and at the same time created one of the best sources of waterpower in Denmark.

The first use of the new source of power was for a grinding mill to polish semi-precious agate, the use of which was a fashion phenomenon amongst the royalty and nobility of Europe. This initiative involved German artisans and lasted from 1728 to 1746, but was not followed by a more permanent settlement of any scale.

In 1751 the French engineer Etienne Peyrembert was summoned by the state to establish a cannon forge, i.e. he was to construct cannon from wrought iron and not from cast iron or bronze. Waterpower was necessary to drive the hammers in the forge and other mechanical equipment such as the boring mill. The basic idea was that Peyrembert's cannons would be lighter than the conventional cast ones, but he was not successful and had to leave Denmark in 1755 – one of several unsuccessful attempts at technology transfer.

The cannon works had a side effect. It was during Peyrembert's leadership that the first permanent settlements were made in the area that shortly afterwards became the most rigidly planned and largest Danish factory village ever. The place was chosen solely for its waterpower and until then had been an unused sandy stretch of land between the fjord and Arresø.

When Peyrembert left, a number of buildings had been erected, in particular

FIG. 4.

A view of Frederiksværk in 1773 with symmetrical grid, the large Gjethus to the left, workers' and artisans' dwellings and the gunpowder works to the right.

Peyrembert's former production plant and several workers' and artisans' dwellings. Shortly after Peyrembert had left, a young man of Norwegian origin, who is now considered the founding father of Frederiksværk, Johan Friedrich Classen (1725-1792), and his companion, the wealthy Copenhagen merchant Just Fabritius, took over. Fabritius withdrew from the project as early as 1761, and it was Classen who undertook the impressive construction of a factory village with a detailed plan for the layout of streets, the digging of ditches, the construction of fences, the planting of trees and bushes and the building of a large number of houses in the years from 1756 and for several decades after. The economic incentive was to establish a works for casting cannon in bronze and later on grenades, cannon balls etc. in cast iron. It is highly probable that the first production of cast iron in Denmark took place at Frederiksværk in 1769 with the unlikely use of reverberatory furnaces normally used for casting bronze. In addition Classen and Fabritius were contracted to construct a gun powder mill and had to dig another stretch of canal to feed the water wheels.

Frederiksværk is simply the most remarkable example of a factory village in Denmark. It became a small society in itself and was the centre of Danish armament production until the early 19th century, the production of gunpowder continuing through most of the 20th century. In 1777 it had grown to a considerable size numbering 504 male and 416 female inhabitants.

The economic prospects of Frederiksværk depended heavily upon orders for the Danish army and navy as well as considerable orders when Denmark, like other countries, paid the so-called 'Algerian presents', bribes in the form of cannons and gun powder to allow Danish ships to pass Algiers on voyages to destinations in the Mediterranean without being attacked by pirates.

In the summer of 1756 the two men took over Peyrembert's former works. During the following twenty years the plan for the street grid was realised and a large number of buildings were erected. The ownership of Frederiksværk changed several times. Originally the works had been a present from the state – with certain obligations – and from 1761 Classen was the sole owner. In 1767 he sold the complex to the state but remained in charge, now with the title of major general, and shortly after he bought it back again.

While Peyrembert was there, the early Frederiksværk covered around 120 acres. This was not enough for Classen who was successful in enlarging the area several times. Finally he could establish two estates, Arresødal in 1769 and Grønnæssegaard in 1776. The estates had the jurisdiction over the villages and the peasants in the area, and all peasants were obliged to work at the cannon works or powder-mill or do service for the works transporting goods, gunpowder etc.

Under Classen's leadership a baroque-like symmetrical grid was laid out with parallel and diagonal streets and park-like areas. In the centre of town a large park with diagonal paths and surrounded by trees was laid out and the factory village was surrounded by rampart-like fences and ditches. A large number of hazel and hawthorn trees were planted on the bastions as well as other trees, streets and open spaces were lined with trees, and the planting numbered several thousands trees. Classen's Frederiksværk, the ambitious symmetrical plan, the well-built houses and the tree planting were evidently not created with only practical purposes in mind. Aesthetic elements were obviously important in the construction of Classen's ideal factory village.

Classen began the construction of a new main factory, a building with stone walls and tiled roof, in 1761. The building – *Gjethuset* – was vast by the standards in Denmark in the 18th century and is generally considered to be the work of the Danish royal architect Laurids de Thurah. In the relatively small and low-rise factory village the stately *Gjethus* with its smoking chimneys towered over the whole area and was visible as soon as visitors came to the village.

Classen was generally successful in creating a prosperous village, but not all his ideas were implemented. His idea was to attract competent artisans to live in the factory village and take up various small industries and handicrafts. In this he was not fully successful, but about 15 houses, all of the same type – timber-framed and tiled twin houses of 1½ storeys, were built to accommodate artisans and their families. Three of these buildings are still standing in Strandgade, one of them a listed building. Strandgade is one of the oldest streets and part of the original plan as the street that formed the southern limit to the large park-like area.

Apart from the large stonewalled and tiled *Gjethus*, Classen also built a number of other production buildings of which only a few are still standing. The large saltpetre store and the charcoal ovens building are both from the 18th century and built from heavy natural stone.[47]

In 1850 Frederiksværk gained formal status as a trading station with its own town council and jurisdiction. The local administration from then on was similar to that of the market towns. Frederiksværk formally became a market town in 1907.

A paper town out of nowhere – Silkeborg

Paper production had a long tradition in Denmark where a number of paper mills located near adequate water resources produced hand-made paper made from collected old cloth. The years around 1800 saw a dramatic change in technology in the form of the paper making machine producing rolls of continuous paper, soon after to be made from wooden pulp, which in principle could be produced endlessly.[48]

The first mechanical production of paper in a steam-powered factory took place in 1829 at Strandmøllen located where the river Mølleåen meets Øresund north of Copenhagen.

The energetic entrepreneur J.C. Drewsen installed an English-made Donkin paper machine and began producing paper – still based on old cloth as raw material.

The Drewsen-dynasty stayed in the paper industry, and in 1844 J.C. Drewsen's sons, Christian and Michael, took over after their father. A deserted area in Mid-Jutland gave the Drewsen family a golden opportunity to establish a large, modern paper factory a few years later, thereby creating the foundation for the new planned city of Silkeborg.

The area is a length of landscape with lakes and valleys through which the river Gudenåen runs, surrounded by large forests. Through the first part of the 19th century only a few small villages, a single farm and an estate in a rather derelict condition were the only buildings in the area.

During the 1830s plans for establishing a trading station on the spot and thereby starting economic development and settlement in the area were a subject for discussion at government level. For this purpose it would be useful, indeed almost a precondition, if not alone artisans chose to settle there, but also if a large enterprise chose this place for large-scale production. Following contacts and visits to the area in 1842 and 1843 the Drewsen family signed a contract obliging them to build a paper factory, while the state intended to lay out the trading village.

The history of how a company of 30 artisans and the entrepreneur Michael Drewsen travelled to Silkeborg and how the first paper machine was ferried on Gudenåen to the new factory is fascinating, but not the subject of this article.[49]

It has been pointed out that the paper factory and the trading village, which took shape from 1846, were in many ways separate 'societies', but the paper factory was a precondition for the growth of the city of Silkeborg in the years immediately after 1850, a development which transformed Silkeborg into a regional centre and one of Mid-Jutland's largest cities. The county of Silkeborg today numbers 55,000 inhabitants.

In 1844 the building of the foundations in the swampy area began, and with impressive speed the paper factory was ready for production. It used a large water wheel as its primary source of power from the very start and then, in addition, after the installation of a second paper machine, the first two water-driven turbines in Denmark were introduced. Competent workers were brought from the paper factory at Strandmøllen, and the large population growth of the area ensured the necessary workforce. On 1 January 1845 the first paper, which was still cloth-based, was made on the paper machine.

The relatively large number of people in the nearly empty area made certain initiatives from the factory owner necessary. The outbuildings of the old estate were soon converted into dwellings for workers and their families, and in addition four large houses were built to accommodate workers at Smedebakken.

During the following decades the factory was enlarged, another paper machine was installed, and the factory evolved into a large complex east of what became the centre of the new trading station. In 1845 Silkeborg had 149 inhabitants, who were nearly all connected with the paper factory. In 1850 the new village had a population of 462, a number that had risen to 1163 in 1855.[50]

As part of the state initiative a commission was appointed in 1843 to plan the form and function of the new trading station. The early Silkeborg was a strictly

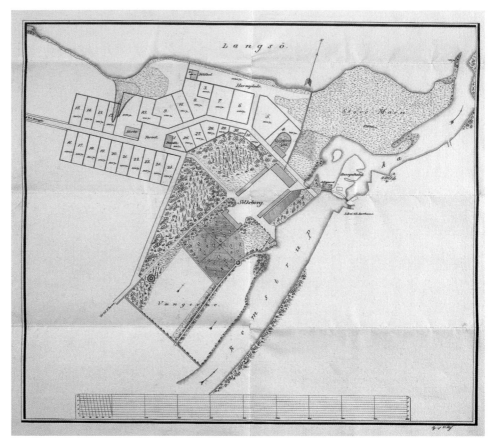

FIG. 5.

C.F. Schlegel's plan from 1845 was the first layout for the trading station of Silkeborg.

planned village – not according to an ideal plan like Frederiksværk on the basis of a symmetrical pattern with obvious weight upon aesthetics, but built according to a town plan that had to be adjusted to the course of Gudenåen. In 1843 Major C.F. Schlegel sketched out the plan that was realised but which soon proved to be much too small (see fig. 5). Silkeborg was a success, and the growth of what began as a factory village and a planned trading station surpassed all expectations.

Schlegel's small plan was east-west oriented with Gudenåen as the eastern border and Silkeborg Langsø (the lake) as the northern limit. Though a planned city, which was partly a factory village, Silkeborg's first plan shows a number of deliberate similarities with the medieval Danish towns. The ideas of the commission were realised in Schlegel's plan as a town with a central market place, a church and a town hall placed nearly symmetrically opposite each other across the market place, a church-yard and a small harbour. The similarities with the old market towns stopped here, for even though the town plan followed the organic shape of Gudenåen and Silke-borg Langsø, the most important road was Hovedlandevejen (the main road), which was straight as a ruler.

The new town was divided into 30 building sites. The few plots of land could not be sold to just whoever wanted to buy. The new town council was to be selective, and artisans could establish themselves only after having applied for a trade license. This meant that the town council could select competent artisans who had a satis-factory economy.

The rapid growth had the effect that as early as in 1851 the town had to be en-larged to three times its original size with a grid of straight streets, which today make up the central part of Silkeborg: Vestergade, Søndergade, Nygade and Tværgade with the rounded Østergade as an exception.

Other factory villages and industrial settlements

A number of small villages have been left out of this account, but strictly speaking a mill with a few dwellings hardly qualifies as a real factory village. Frederiksværk and Silkeborg have been chosen as examples of large plans that were realised and which have sustained development until the present. An example of a Danish factory vil-lage engaged in the textile industry is the well-preserved and grade-A listed complex in Brede on Mølleåen, now owned by the Danish National Museum, which plans to open a large new industrial museum in the future.

Brede is a large complex consisting of an old main building like that of a small estate, a huge factory complex gradually enlarged well into the 20th century and a large number of workers' dwellings dating from different periods. A school, a kinder-garten and a lunch house etc. are also preserved, but several of these buildings were erected after the 1850s and during the late 19th and early 20th centuries. Brede was a textile village of considerable size and grew from around 200 workers in the early 19th century to around 900 in the early 1930s.[51] Hellebæk, too, north of Copenha-gen, with its hammer mill, gun factory and textile mill, had a factory village charac-ter, and this could even be said of some paper mills, glass works and tile works es-tablished in the decades after 1850.

Large Danish factory villages were exceptions to the general pattern of Danish industrialisation. Frederiksværk and Silkeborg are different examples of factory villages, planned villages, which left lasting traces and continued to grow. Both cities still possess easily recognisable traits from their early history. To a great extent Frederiksværk was realised during the 18th century as the vision of one man, under the strict control of its owner, while Silkeborg only partly tells the story of a classical factory village – though the paper factory and the small community around it are an essential part of the town's early history and created the potential for fast growth.

The industrial city is a technical city

The terrible living conditions in early industrial cities, which grew at great speed and with basically no restrictions and highly unsatisfactory sanitary conditions, are well known. The public role in modernising cities in order to deal with the pressure of a growing population is an important part of the problems of the industrial city, and the technification of the city is also an indication of a certain level of industrialisation. The creation of an adequate and qualitatively better water supply, the first attempts at creating sewage systems and the lighting of the streets, organised removal of garbage and excrement are all part of this story.

It is too wide ranging to give a full overview of this subject but a few examples act as an indication of the level of city development around the middle of the 19th century.

The first plans for modern water works in Denmark originate in the 1840s, when the new English system of technology employing sand-filters, cast iron tubes and steam engines appeared. Though Copenhagen was the first city to plan a combined waterworks and gasworks, and a sewage system, the city of Odense actually was first when the first water dripped from the 700 taps in 1853. Soon after, a number of larger cities followed suit, many waterworks being planned and carried out in combination with gasworks providing street lightning and lightning of public buildings and factories. The early phase in the 1850s was dominated by the first Danish firm of consulting engineers, English & Hanssen, both with a background in England and in English technology. Soon after, Danish engineers from The Polytechnical Institution (today DTU, The Technical University of Denmark) in Copenhagen were able to compete with their practical colleagues with a background in workshop practice.[52]

Almost no sewers existed in Danish towns in 1850. In most small towns this was not a major issue through the rest of the 19th century, but in Copenhagen, where living standards were under pressure, the first unsatisfactory sewage system was built in 1855. It was a much reduced plan consisting of a few main sewers in the inner city leading mainly surface water to the harbour. A complete and fully modern system was not put into function for the next forty years.

One of the rare accounts of the technical state of the capital in the 1840s was given by the above-mentioned engineer Frits Casse, who untypically paid attention to these subjects, when as a boy and young man he experienced Copenhagen at a time of dramatic growth and technical change. Later he described the state of things in the 1840s:

The paving of the streets was generally in a very bad condition and a sewage-system was non-existent with the exception of a few underground pipes leading into the harbour. Everywhere gutters lined both sides of the streets and received all sewage from the back yards (...) Concerning the collecting of soil tubs, it was of an even more incredible standard. In each back-yard a large pit covered by planks was used to store excrement for one to two months until it was completely full, and these pits were hardly ever watertight, meaning that the surroundings were penetrated by these niceties (...) The lighting was extremely backward compared to today's standards [1890s].[53]

In Copenhagen graduates from the Polytechnical Institution held various technical positions as early as the 1840s. In 1857 the first position as municipal engineer was held by Ludvig August Colding, and in the following decades the largest Danish towns also employed municipal engineers. The industrial city was a technical city, which had to be planned and run by the new experts: educated engineers.

Summary

This article has outlined the overall characteristics of Danish industrialisation from the middle of the 18th century to the 1850s. The theories of the pre-industrial city and the industrial city have – on a broad-spectrum level – acted as a background for the general understanding of the development of Danish cities in this period. The article has pointed out new building types, changes in the locational patterns of industry and population, and given a number of examples. What was the state of Danish cities then, around 1850? Can the larger Danish cities be characterised as industrial cities or was industry still waiting to transform them?

In conclusion it can be said that no full-blown industrial cities existed in 1850, not even the capital of Copenhagen. Different levels of development towards the industrial city were obvious though, and not only in Copenhagen.

The capital was the most industrialised city of all. It had the largest new factories and the largest number of industrial workers, and from the late 1850s the first villa suburb and especially large new areas of workers' housing were manifesting themselves and putting pressure on the fast growing city. Copenhagen was far from a 'complete' industrial city by 1850, but from the 1850s certain areas could be characterised as industrial enclaves.

Secondly, a number of the next largest cities (Odense, Aalborg, Aarhus and a few others) were at the beginning of a transition to the industrial city. New industries, some located outside and around the old city, the first workers' housing and the first villas were a reality, but at the same time clearly visible patterns of the pre-industrial city still remained for several decades. The change from the main street as the place of the highest social status in town and the first priority for the location of wealthy households was often hesitant and could be found in the 1880s and 1890s, when the larger cities had all undergone deep structural changes and now covered much larger areas.

The medium-sized towns were not completely untouched by industry, but like the small towns they were far from industrial cities and through most of the 19th century they remained largely untouched by the forces of industrialisation.

BIBLIOGRAPHY

Becker-Christensen, Henrik et al. 1996. *Vejles industri 1732-1996. Vejles historie*. Vol. 3. Vejle: Vejle Kommune.

Bender, Henning 1987. *Aalborgs industrielle udvikling fra 1735 til 1940. Aalborgs historie*. Vol. 4. Aalborg: Aalborg Kommune.

Boje, Per 1976. *Det industrielle miljø 1840-1940. Kilder og litteratur*. Copenhagen: Akademisk Forlag.

Burgess, E.W. 1925. 'The Growth of the City'. In: R.E. Park et al., *The City*. Chicago: University of Chicago Press. Reprinted in M. Stewart (ed.) 1977. *The City: Problems of Planning*. Harmondsworth: Penguin.

Carter, Harold 1983. *An introduction to Urban Historical Geography*. London: Edward Arnold.

Casse, Frits 1913. *En gammel ingeniørs erindringer*. Copenhagen: G.E.C. Gads Forlag.

Chapman, Stanley D. 1972 (1987). *The Cotton Industry in the Industrial Revolution*. London: Mac-Millan.

Christensen, Carl 1926. *Frederiksværk*. Copenhagen: Gyldendalske Boghandel.

Christensen, Dan Ch. 1996. *Det Moderne Projekt*. Copenhagen: Gyldendal.

Degn, Ole 1978. *Urbanisering og industrialisering, En forskningsoversigt*. Copenhagen: Akademisk Forlag.

Doughty, Martin (ed.) 1986. *Building the industrial city*. (Themes in urban history). Leicester: Leicester University Press.

Dragsbo, Peter 1978. *Mennesker og huse i Aabenraa, Et etnologisk studie af kvarterudvikling i en nordslesvigsk købstad 1850-1920*. Esbjerg: Sydjysk Universitetsforlag.

Due, Jeppe Klok 2005. En undersøgelse af industriens udvikling og forankring i de kongerigske provinskøbstæder fra 1817-1847 med udgangspunkt i fabrikstabellernes opgivelser. (Unpublished thesis). University of Aarhus: The Danish Centre for Urban History.

Feldbæk, Ole 1990. *Den lange fred, Danmarks historie 1700-1800. Gyldendal og Politikens Danmarkshistorie*. Vol. 9. Copenhagen: Gyldendal & Politiken.

Feldbæk, Ole 1993. *Danmarks økonomiske historie 1500-1840*. Herning: Systime.

Gejl, Ib (ed.) 1997. *Århus, Byens historie 1720-1870*. Vol. 2. Aarhus: Århus Byhistoriske Udvalg.

Hansen, Jens Erik Frits 1977. *Københavns forstadsbebyggelse i 1850'erne*. Copenhagen: Akademisk Forlag.

Harnow, Henrik 1988. Tekstilfabrikker i Odense 1835-1935. (Unpublished MA thesis). Southern University: History Department.

Harnow, Henrik 1998. *Den danske ingeniørs historie 1850-1920*. Aarhus: Systime.

Harnow, Henrik 2000. 'Den fynske industris fader – M.P. Allerup og det danske industrimøde i Odense 1858'. *Fynske Minder* 2000, pp. 23-45.

Harnow, Henrik 2001. *Industribyen Odense, en nutidig fotografisk vandring i industrialismens Odense 1840-1945*. Odense: Odense Universitetsforlag/Odense Bys Museer.

Harnow, Henrik 2004. *Odense Havn og kanal gennem 200 år*. Odense: Odense Bys Museer.

Hellesen, Jette Kjærulff & Ole Tuxen (eds.) 1988. *Historisk Atlas Danmark*. Copenhagen: G.E.C. Gad.

Historiske huse i Frederiksværk 1986. Frederiksværk: Frederiksværkegnens Museum & Nationalmuseet.

Hyldtoft, Ole 1980. 'Arbejderboliger og bymiljøer'. In: Poul Strømstad (ed.), *Mennesket & maskinen*. Copenhagen: Nationalmuseet, pp. 72-97.

Hyldtoft, Ole 1984. *Københavns industrialisering 1840-1914*. Herning: Systime.

Hyldtoft, Ole 1987. 'Med vandkraft, dampmaskine og gasmotor – den danske industris kraftmaskiner 1840-1897'. *Erhvervshistorisk Årbog*, pp. 75-125.

Hyldtoft, Ole 1994. *Den lysende gas*. Aarhus: Systime.

Hyldtoft, Ole 1997. 'Von der Festung zur modernen Grosstadt: Kopenhagen 1840-1914'. In: Th. Riis & Jann M. Witt (eds.), *A Tale of Two Cities*. Odense: Odense Universitetsforlag, pp. 81-116.

Hyldtoft, Ole 1998. 'København. Fra fæstning til moderne storby'. *Fabrik og bolig*, pp. 3-25.

Hyldtoft, Ole 1999. *Danmarks økonomiske historie 1840-1910*. Herning: Systime.

Illustreret Tidende, 1863.

Jensen, Jens Toftgaard & Jeppe Norskov 2005. *Købstadens metamorfose, Byudvikling og byplanlægning i Århus 1800-1920*. (Skrifter om dansk byhistorie, 2). Aarhus: Aarhus Universitetsforlag.

Johansen, H. Chr., Per Boje & Anders Monrad Møller 1983. *Fabrik og bolig: Det industrielle miljø i Odense 1840-1940*. (Odense University studies in history and social sciences, 79). Odense: Odense Universitetsforlag.

Johansen, H. Chr. 1983. *Næring og bystyre, Odense 1700-1789*. *Odense Bys Historie*. Vol. 4. Odense: Odense Universitetsforlag.

Johansen, H. Chr. 1988. *Industriens vækst og vilkår 1870-1973*. *Dansk industri efter 1870*. Vol. 1. Odense: Odense Universitetsforlag.

Jørgensen, Steffen Elmer 2001. *Fra chaussé til motorvej. Det overordnede danske vejnets udvikling fra 1761*. Copenhagen: Dansk Vejhistorisk Selskab.

Kragh, Helge 1992. *I røg og damp, Dampmaskinens indførelse i Danmark 1760-1840*. Copenhagen: Teknisk Forlag.

Larsen, Keld Dalsgaard 2000. *Dansk Papirindustri 1829-1999*. Silkeborg: Silkeborg Museum.

Larsen, Keld Dalsgaard et. al. 1996. *Silkeborg 1846-1996, Historie – Natur – Kultur*. Silkeborg: Silkeborg Kommune.

Larsen, Keld Dalsgaard & Kurt Balle Larsen 1994. *Michael Drewsen*. Silkeborg: Midtjysk Forlag.

Melchiorsen, Mogens 1985. 'Silkeborg papirfabrik – en tidlig storindustri i ødemarken'. *Fabrik & bolig* 1985/1, pp. 3-19.

Mikkelsen, Jørgen 1994. 'Købmandens kontaktflade – en regionalundersøgelse'. *Erhvervshistorisk Årbog*, pp. 106-45.

Nielsen, Axel (ed.) 1943-44. *Industriens historie i Danmark*. Vol. I-III. Copenhagen: G.E.C. Gad.

Norn, Otto 1973. *En købstads industrialisering*. Horsens: Horsens Bogtrykkeri.

Nyrup, Camillus 1887. *J.F. Classen. Skaber af Frederiksværk og Stifter af Det classenske Fideikommis*. Copenhagen: G.E.C. Gad.

Pollard, Sidney 1964. 'The Factory Village in the Industrial Revolution'. *English Historical Review*, 79, 1964, pp. 513-31.

Rawert, O.J. 1850 (1992). *Kongeriget Danmarks industrielle Forhold*. Copenhagen: Fred. Høst.

Rygner, R.V. 1926. 'Byens vækst'. In: H.St. Holbech (ed.), *Odense Bys Historie*. Odense, pp. 597-645.

Sestoft, Jørgen 1979. *Arbejdets bygninger*. (Danmarks arkitektur, 3). Copenhagen: Gyldendal.

Silkeborg Kommuneatlas: Byer og bygninger 2000 2000. Copenhagen: Skov- og Naturstyrelsen.

Sjoberg, G. 1960. *The Preindustrial City. Past and Present*. New York: The Free Press.

Thestrup, Poul et al. 1986. *Mod bedre tider, Odense Bys Historie 1789-1868*. Vol. 5. Odense: Odense Universitetsforlag.

Trinder, Barrie 1982 (1997). *The making of the industrial landscape*. London: J M Dent.

Tønsberg, Jeppe 2004. *Brede Klædefabrik*. Aarhus: Erhvervsarkivet.

Whitehand, J.W.R. 1992. *The Making of the Urban Landscape*. Oxford: Blackwell.

Notes

1 Hyldtoft 1984, p. 48.

2 Johansen, Boje & Møller 1983, p. 36. See Johansen's remarks on the principles for the statistics based on the 1855 census; the numbers for Odense represent only branches with more than 10 employees all in all. See also Thestrup et al. 1986, pp. 145-76, Gejl (ed.) 1997, p. 199 and especially the chapter by Erik Korr Johansen, pp. 157 ff., and Bender 1987, pp. 239 ff. It is important at this early point to stress that these numbers are generally considered to be somewhat too low, and it is equally important to note that they must be multiplied by at least two to give an impression of the number of people who depended on industry.

3 Most Danish towns covered in this article were market towns of limited size before 1850. I purposely use the terms 'industrial city' and 'pre-industrial city' throughout the article as they are internationally well known concepts.

4 See Sjoberg 1960. The validity of Sjoberg's general theory was discussed by P. Wheatly 1963, 'What the greatness of a city is said to be. Reflections on Sjoberg's 'Preindustrial city', *Pacific Viewpoint*, 4, pp. 163-88. See also the presentation in Carter 1983, pp. 171-83.

5 Carter 1983, p. 171.

6 Burgess 1925.

7 Whitehand 1992, pp. 1 ff.

8 Rygner 1926.

9 Johansen 1988 was the first volume in the series. It gives an overview of the economic and industrial development of the period.

10 Aabenraa was Danish until 1864, but for most of the period covered by Dragsbo it was German. Since 1920 it has been Danish again.

11 See Nielsen 1944, III, 1, III, 2 and Feldbæk 1993.

12 Feldbæk 1990, pp. 159-64.

13 Harnow 2004, pp. 15-24, and Jørgensen 2001. Concerning canals see also Anders Monrad Møller's article in this volume.

14 Sestoft 1979, pp. 51 ff.

15 Chapman 1926, pp. 17-25.

16 Kragh 1992, pp. 35 ff.

17 In 1735 as part of the more active role of the Danish state in promoting trade in general, all sections of local administration were asked to return descriptions of the state of commerce and industry. These reports are called *Stiftsrelationerne* and date from 1735-1736. They are in Rigsarkivet (The Danish National Archives), Kommercekollegiet, Dansk-norske sekretariat: Relationer over de danske stifters tilstand ... (no. 28-30). They are also published by The Danish Centre for Urban History on www.byhistorie.dk.

18 Johansen 1983, pp. 106 ff.

19 See Johansen, Boje & Monrad Møller 1983. Bender 1987. Gejl 1997.

20 Hyldtoft 1984, pp. 85-86. Baumgarten and Burmeister later changed its name to Burmesiter & Wain, known as B&W. The company was established in 1843 and developed into the larg-

est Danish industrial enterprise employing 1,400 workers in the 1870s. Several times B&W were technical pioneers and held an international position in the production of diesel engines during the first decades of the 20th century. B&W built a large number of steel vessels but also produced more traditional mechanical products for industry.

21 Harnow 2000, p. 25.

22 Bertelsen 2005. Some caution must be taken in using this new registry. There are a number of anniversary publications most of which are listed in Johansen 1988.

23 Hyldtoft 1984, p. 70.

24 Becker-Christensen 1996, pp. 72-74 and Nielsen 1944, III, 2, pp. 48 ff.

25 The factory records cover the period from 1774-1855. They are in Rigsarkivet (The Danish National Archives), Kommercekollegiet, Industri- og fabriksfagets sekretariat, no. 1558-1586 (1801-1816), Generaltoldkammer- og Kommercekollegiet, Industri- og fabrikkontoret (1817-1847) and Statistisk Bureau (1848 ff.). For a more detailed presentation of factory records as a source for Danish industrial history see Boje 1976, pp. 29 ff. and Due 2005.

26 Due 2005, p. 10. Please note that these rough figures are based on the factory records. Due takes a number of reservations on pp. 6 f. and 9 f. It must also be emphasised here that the overall numbers are somewhat too small.

27 Hyldtoft 1984, pp. 46 ff.

28 The author would like to thank Ole Hyldtoft for his contribution to discussions on the growth rate and number of industrial workers in the 1840s and 1850s.

29 Hellesen & Tuxen 1988, p. 177 is based on the factory records but leaves out a number of branches and especially Holmen in Copenhagen, which creates a marked difference from the figures in Hyldtoft 1983.

30 Hyldtoft 1987.

31 The first steam engine in Denmark was *Ildmaskinen* (The Fire Machine) installed at Holmen in 1790 to power the hammers at the anchor mill. See the article by Fl. Steen Nielsen in Kragh 1992, pp. 35-53.

32 Hyldtoft 1984, pp. 96-115.

33 Johansen, Boje & Møller 1985, pp. 34 ff., Bender 1987, pp. 251 ff. and Gejl (ed.) 1997, pp. 198 ff.

34 Hyldtoft 1992.

35 Jensen & Norskov 2005, pp. 71 ff., 155 ff.

36 Johansen 1983, p. 200, Johansen, Boje & Monrad Møller 1983, pp. 26-35.

37 Norn 1973, Becker-Christensen et al 1996, pp. 121 ff., 171-73, 178 ff.

38 Dragsbo in his early study of Aabenraa even speaks explicitly of these areas as workers' areas and claims that they illustrate 'the concentric zonal structure of the early 19th century market town'. This kind of concentricity must be understood basically as a center-periphery contrast and not as a zonal structure parallel to the mature industrial city. Dragsbo 1978, pp. 68, 75 ff. Certain local natural conditions later pushed development in the direction of a radial rather than a concentric structure. The completely ideal picture of a pre-industrial city also

had exceptions. For instance it has been pointed out that the periphery of towns was not always an area exclusively for the poor. In a number of Danish towns large merchants were located at the periphery close to the main roads, thereby attracting customers, see Mikkelsen 1994.

39 So named because of the bridges that cross the lakes between the old city and the new areas.

40 Hansen 1977, especially pp. 70-78, 79-84 and Hyldtoft 1998, pp. 8 f..

41 Casse 1913, pp. 39 ff.

42 *Illustreret Tidende* 1863, p. 292.

43 'Sheds' after the roofing originating in sheep's sheds in England.

44 Rawert 1850, pp. 514-15.

45 An early pioneering work on factory villages is Pollard 1964. The major issue is the standard of living, but Pollard also discusses the nature of factory villages.

46 No modern history of Frederiksværk exists. Part of its industrial history has been covered by Christensen 1996, pp. 319 ff. See also Nyrop 1887, Christensen 1926 and *Historiske huse i Frederiksværk 1986*.

47 *Historiske huse i Frederiksværk 1986*, pp. 8 f., Christensen 1926 pp. 25 ff.

48 In Denmark the use of wooden pulp began in the 1860s. The first Danish wooden pulp mill was built by Th. Weber in Haderslev in 1862 soon followed by others.

49 Larsen et al. 1996. More specifically the production of paper is covered by Larsen 1994 and Larsen 2000. See also Melchiorsen 1985.

50 Larsen et al. 1996 and Melchiorsen 1985. In 1854-1855 Silkeborg acquired the status of trading post and thereby had an administration basically like the market towns. It was not until 1900 that Silkeborg formally became a market town.

51 Tønsberg 2004, p. 109. A bit late for the time frame of this article, but nevertheless another planned town must be mentioned. The harbour city of Esbjerg at the southern part of the western coast of Jutland mirrors in its whole structure its origin as a planned city. Esbjerg was established in connection with the huge project of constructing a harbour connected with main railway lines in 1868 with the aim of creating a central shipping port for exporting Danish agricultural products mainly to Britain. The oldest streets of Esbjerg are considerably wider than in the old medieval towns, they form straight lines and right angles. The main street is the one-kilometer-long Kongensgade. Esbjerg experienced massive growth and developed into Denmarks's fourth largest harbour and later on a regional centre. Esbjerg is today the fifth largest city in Denmark with more than 72,000 inhabitants.

52 Hyldtoft 1994 and Harnow 1998.

53 Casse 1913, pp. 18-21.

Peter Henningsen

Copenhagen poor relief and the problem of poverty, ca. 1500-1800

Poverty in the early modern city

Poverty, destitution and utmost misery were the lot of the great majority of people living in the big cities of early modern Europe. Most people accepted poverty as an unavoidable fact of life and some, like the Danish moral philosopher and theorist Johannes Boye, even thought it a necessary phenomenon in a well-ordered state. Thus poverty was not an evil as such. In 1798 Boye claimed that misery and poverty actually served the function of enhancing the mood of more prosperous people, who might otherwise be discontented with their lot: 'What bigger encouragement to patience [exists] than seeing the crowd that is even worse off'.[1] Thus, poverty functioned as a lightning conductor for the middle classes' potential dissatisfaction with their own material conditions of life and served to reassure them that they belonged to the fortunate few.

German historians have shown that the misery and squalor of the eighteenth century German cities was immense. In Berlin, 8-10 % of the inhabitants were beggars and indigents, while nearly one-third of the whole population received poor relief from the authorities. In Cologne, 25 % of the inhabitants were reckoned as beggars, and in Hamburg – which was about the same size as the Danish capital Copenhagen – it was calculated in 1811 that 50 % of its population were poor. But of course that number did not receive poor relief from the Hamburg city authorities.[2] German historians estimate that nearly 10 % of the entire German population in the eighteenth century was made up of beggars and vagrants and the country was flooded with wandering gangs of bandits. Particularly the smaller Catholic and clerical states and domains in the southwest were much favoured places for beggars and vagrants as these areas offered them shelter and protection.[3]

The German conditions were not unusual or exceptional in any way. More than half of the population in Italian, French, English and Spanish cities consisted of poor and indigents. A destitute urban population of between 50 and 70 % was actually quite common in the early modern period. Of course, not all of these people were beggars or living on charity. A very large number of the poor belonged to the group of working poor. These were people who made their way through life on very low incomes and accordingly were in constant danger of sinking into destitution, dependent as they were on the state of the market, trading conditions and grain prices. A single year with a bad harvest followed by high prices for bread would bring them on the verge of ruin or even make them cross the narrow line between survival and death.[4]

What rising grain prices meant for the poor, and for the poor law authorities who had to support them in times of shortages, can be seen in a report from *Fattigdirektionen* (the Copenhagen poor relief board) from 1807: If the price of grain went up by one *skilling* a pound, and a family consisting of a husband, wife and four children had to have one pound of bread per person per day, the additional expenditure for the household would amount to 14 *rigsdaler* and 46 *skilling* for a whole year. That was not a small amount for a poor family, 'and as the cost of accommodation, clothing, lighting, heating and the like rises in the same manner, then it can only be expected that poverty in a city like Copenhagen will increase'.[5]

Shortages and high prices were an economic catastrophe for the poor law authorities: When grain prices rose by one *skilling* per pound, the poor law authorities would have an additional expenditure of 30,000 *rigsdaler* per year for grain alone.[6]

Copenhagen and the poor in the eighteenth century

Copenhagen was the residence of the King, the court and all the major institutions in the country. It had a very large military garrison and a large number of small dwellings for seamen and the naval staff, all situated in the north-eastern part of the city. Compared with other European capitals, it was not a large city. According to the census of 1787, the city was inhabited by slightly more than 90,000 souls. At the time of the next census in 1801, the number had increased to a little more than 100,000; in 1834 it was 119,292; and in 1850, 129,695. The population continued to increase during the remainder of the century, especially after the abolition of the fortifications and ramparts in 1857.[7] And poverty and destitution increased at the same rate – or even more rapidly – as the population.

In 1783 Copenhagen was reported to have 4,000 tenement houses, 'which are densely inhabited, even the basements in most houses'. In addition to these ordinary dwellings there were 4,000 houses for the naval seamen in the district of Nyboder, and quarters for 800 soldiers from the military garrison in the citadel Frederikshavn – or Kastellet as it was commonly called. There were also four royal castles, 20 aristocratic palaces, a number of citizen houses 'resembling palaces', the official buildings and churches and, of course, the charitable institutions for the poor and sick – 23 in all. The largest institution was *Almindelig Hospital* (The General Hospital) established in 1769 with room for 6-700 people (or inmates). *Helligåndshospitalet* (The Hospital of the Holy Spirit), in daily speech called *Vartov* had about 400 dwellers – many of them belonging to the genteel poor; and *St. Hans Hospital* just outside the city walls had room for hundreds of insane and syphilitic people. The city also had a number of smaller public and private institutions for people of other religious confessions, three orphanages for boys and girls (*Opfostringshuset, Vaisenhuset* and *Lorchs Stiftelse for Unge Piger*), an institution for foundlings *(Hittebørnsstiftelsen)*, a birth clinic for the poor *(Fødselsstiftelsen)*, a hospital for the sick *(Frederiks Hospital)* and two hospitals for the soldiers and the naval seamen *(Christians Plejehus* and *Søkvæsthuset)*, and of course a prison for criminals and beggars *(Børnehuset)*.

With regard to poverty and indigence, Copenhagen did not differ from other major European cities. In the autumn of 1717 the chief constable of police estimated that only 20 % of the city's inhabitants had enough money to have a stock of food and firewood for the coming winter, while the remaining 80 % had to purchase their daily necessities where they could find them.[8]

Reliable accounts of the size of the population in eighteenth century Copenhagen do not exist before 1787, when the second census of the century was carried out. The first census from 1769 has many flaws, and lacks so many details about the inhabitants that it only can be used with caution. However, the censuses from 1787 and 1801 listed the occupations of the inhabitants. If we consider the people in the lowest income groups – soldiers, sailors, merchants' and manufacturers' labourers and apprentices, as well as the journeymen and apprentices of craftsmen; shipmasters, fishermen and seafarers; farmers, innkeepers, servants, day-labourers, pensioners and paupers – to be identical with the working poor and the paupers, as many as 72.4 % of the population in 1787, and 73.4 % in 1801 belonged to this group.[9]

All these people were at risk of sinking into misery if they became sick or widowed and in the case of children, orphaned. It was claimed in 1795 that indigence was in-

Fig. 1.

In the 1780s about 85,000 – 90,000 people lived in the old city inside the ramparts. We must suppose that there was terrible overcrowding in the city and sources confirm that the inhabitants had very little space in which to play. The city had no way of really being able to create specific well-to-do districts and specific poor districts. On the whole, rich and poor lived side-by-side until the ramparts were demolished in 1857. The drawing shows an interior from a typical Copenhagen lower-class home in the 19th century.

creasing in all levels of society, and that 'the number of poor is growing annually'.[10] It can be seen that a little more than 8,000 people – 1/12 of the city's population – were regarded as belonging to the deserving poor in 1799 and received poor relief from the authorities,[11] but the real number of poor was much higher. One of the directors of the board of the city's poor relief estimated in 1774 that more than 1/8 of the population 'cannot live without public support'.[12] And the number of poor was rising constantly: In the wake of the English bombardment of the city in 1807 during the Napoleonic wars, 7,000 people became homeless or were injured and 'deprived of everything they owned'.[13]

With the British historian Alexander Cowan, we can distinguish between four main types of poverty in early modern Europe. All of these could be found in early modern Copenhagen as well:

1. The structural poor. This group comprised the working poor, who were either so badly paid that they had to supplement their small income by begging, theft or both, or who just worked intermittently due to the nature of their job, for instance on construction sites and the like, which always closed down in winter. The group also comprised the old and sick who were not able to work at all, the orphans and foundlings who did not have any 'friends' to take care of them, and the widows, who were left with small children after the death of the breadwinners.

2. The cyclical or the crisis poor. At times of crises resulting from famine, war or plagues, the structural poor were joined by the crisis poor who were thrown into poverty as a result of the high price of food, especially of grain. The group also comprised those poor who had been victims of bad luck by being injured in an accident or who had suffered from fire etc.

3. The genteel or 'shamefaced' poor. These people suffered from a more relative deprivation than the other two groups. These were former well-to-do people – sometimes even nobles who had fallen on hard times – who had suffered material misfortune and losses, and as a result their social status had declined rapidly. This meant that they could no longer fulfil the obligations and social norms demanded of them by their social equals. A person of a certain social status was expected to have the economic means to support it. These people felt ashamed to turn to the poor relief board for fear of losing their 'social honour' and they preferred, if possible, to handle the situation on their own.[14] Of course, this was not always possible, and in Copenhagen there were a number of private, philanthropic institutions – *Budolphi Hospital* (The Budolphi Foundation for Genteel Poor), *Harboes Jomfrukloster* (Harboes Convent for Noble Maidens and Widows) and *Petersens Jomfrukloster* (Petersens Convent for Maidens) – all reserved for the shamefaced poor. The poor relief authorities also had special apartments reserved for the shamefaced poor. First and foremost *Abel Cathrines Boder* (Abel Cathrine's Dwellings) and *Helligåndshospitalet/Vartov*, which was something between a private and public institution supported by private donations.

4. The voluntary poor. These were people who had voluntarily chosen a life as vagrants and idlers (if such people ever existed in reality).

Although contemporaries often attempted to put the poor into certain categories, there was little recognition that most of the urban population lived in conditions of poverty with few, if any, resources to fall back on in times of crisis.[15] 'Sickness can weaken the working hands' as it was said in 1795, 'and make the esteemed family miserable'. And poverty was not always to blame on individual lack of industry. Some professions were dependent on fashion and were affected by passing vogues. When, for instance, a citizen had a profession in decline, like the wig makers and hairdressers in the 1790s, there was no way they could maintain their economic position in the usual way, and they would quickly fall into poverty.[16] Except in times of general crisis, the presence of the non-indigent poor did not impinge on the sensibilities of their more prosperous contemporaries with the same force as the sight of vagrants, homeless children, the old, the deformed and the disabled begging on the streets.

These groups were always in focus for the social empathy of the well-to-do people of the day, while the poverty of the working poor was somewhat more hidden. Moreover, this might explain why there was often a lack of accord between the proposed solutions to poverty problems and the underlying causes of poverty itself.[17] The government, the city authorities and the poor law authorities treated the symptoms of poverty while having no idea of its causes: the economic and social structures that made employers pay such low wages to their workforce meant that the workers could hardly earn a living from them, to say nothing of supporting a large family. The low wages were the result of the common mercantilist perception that the ordinary man was born lazy and had to be forced by circumstances to work.[18] Thus, high food prices and small earnings made the common man work harder, contributing more to the common well-being than would have been the case if the wages had been higher. National interest required that the workers remained relatively poor.

Another category of working people who were at risk of sinking into poverty were the servants. As long as they served, they were provided with food and housing, but if they became seriously ill, or suffered an injury and therefore did not have their employment renewed, they could immediately hear poverty knocking on their door. Servants and domestics were 10-15 % of the population in the early modern city, while the working poor, dependent on low incomes and intermittent work, were about 20 %. The old, the sick and the disabled, who made a living by begging, stealing or receiving alms, were between 5 and 10 %. When all the occupations assessed to low taxations in the tax registers are added to these groups, as many as 50-70 % of the households in the early modern city can be counted as poor.[19]

A well-made polity of beggars

The beggars were glaringly obvious in the streets of Copenhagen during the whole early modern period. Although begging had been totally banned in 1698 and the poor law authorities had hired a number of 'beggar chasers' – the so-called 'beggar kings' – to arrest beggars and put them in prison, it did not change the fact that poverty and destitution were overwhelming and the beggars too many. [20]

The beggars were everywhere, their favourite spots being the squares next to the town gates, the market squares, outside the churches and at the square in front of the customhouse – places with a lot of traffic and people passing by, where the begging pauper had a fair chance of receiving some alms.[21] Not even the royals and the Royal court were sheltered from the begging crowds. In 1731 a begging woman had made her way right into the royal castle of Christiansborg and begged before His Majesty himself. She was quickly arrested and put in prison.[22] In March 1785 the court staff found two beggar children in the royal stables, where they had spent the night – unfortunately one of them had passed away – and later they found a begging girl in the arcades of the castle.[23] In 1788 Princess Sophie Frederikke was the target of a ragged crowd of beggars, who had been waiting outside the German Church while she was attending service. It took great efforts of the vicar and his helper to keep the insistent beggars away from the Princess as she left the church.[24]

When the King and his court left Copenhagen for the royal palaces outside town during the summer, the roadsides swarmed with beggars. In 1705 *Danske Kancelli* (the Danish chancellery) had to warn the *amtmand* (the chief administrative officer of the county), Knud Juel, from the county of Copenhagen, to do something about the numerous beggars, 'who without any form of bashfulness perpetually overrun people by begging for alms'.[25] All beggars seemed to leave their hovels and dwellings, when the court was expected to pass by. In 1738, when the court was expected at the royal castle of Hirschholm in Northern Zealand, the local authorities had to visit the peasants of the area and warn them to keep all beggars away from the 'royals on their journey'. The most efficient measure to be taken in these instances was, wrote the local county administrator, to have the beggars whipped off the road by some grooms riding in front of the royal procession, as 'they did not respect threats and warnings'. Beside the tavern in the nearby village of Usserød, where the court usually stopped, such a great number of beggars were gathered that the court officials and other passing strangers did not dare to stop there for fear of 'intimidation and inconveniences'.[26]

In the suburbs of Vesterbro and Frederiksberg, just outside Copenhagen, where the royals had to pass on their way to the summer residence at Frederiksberg Castle, large tableaux of strategically placed beggars displaying their sorry state were always to be found. In 1786 it was told that the long avenue at Frederiksberg, which led to the castle, was filled with 'beggars, who are deformed and badly marked by diseases and wounds although a patrol is being kept in order to keep the avenue clean and tidy'.[27] The Vesterbro district in particular was famous for its many taverns, amusing hang-outs and the many beggars who gathered there, according to the writer Peter Andreas Heiberg. In his journal *Rigsdalerseddelens Hændelser* (The Happenings of a Rigsdaler-Note) from 1793, Heiberg claimed that the beggars after being given alms in downtown Copenhagen went out to Vesterbro to play games of chance in the taverns while laughing behind the backs of decent people.[28]

Nobody could walk in peace without being intimidated by beggars, it was claimed in 1791. Particularly a stroll in the Amalienborg district, where all the large palaces and houses of the wealthy citizens were situated, could be a tiring experience: 'For every fifty steps, he [the pedestrian] can certainly expect to be asked for alms, either by sturdy women with hired children in their arms or by scabbed boys or adolescent girls, who pinch the wretched infants they carry with them until they scream, to move people to compassion'.[29] But the beggars were not content with begging on the streets alone. They also went from door to door to ask for alms.

In 1738 the poor relief authorities of Copenhagen distinguished between two different types of beggars: the honourable beggars and the rough and coarse ones. These latter beggars begged only in the streets and had all the usual characteristics of a poor and miserable soul: the rags, the wounds, the deformities and the unmistakable smell of poverty. The honourable beggars were different. They were perhaps some of the shamefaced poor – poor folk of 'a decent station in life', as it was said in 1778.[30] The honourable beggars were well dressed and looked like polite people. They went from house to house, either on their own or with hired 'staff', and pretended to sell perfumed letters and supplications for help. It was beneath their personal feeling of dignity to beg in the streets or to apply for poor relief. Instead they tried to cope with their condition by 'selling' masked supplications for alms, and of course it was also often beneath their dignity to do it themselves. Thus, it was sometimes done 'by their children, and even by hired people'. According to the poor relief authorities, this type of begging was increasing during the 1730s: 'In Copenhagen, this way of begging is almost more common now than the rough one; therefore de-

FIG. 2

In the 18ᵗʰ century, it was quite usual that beggars appeared 'at the doors' as it was called, and begged from private homes. This situation is depicted on a print by Daniel Chodowiecki.

cent people, who are daily being overrun by these, become unwilling to give something to the [collection] book that is brought around quarterly'.[31]

These beggars naturally made it difficult for the 'beggar kings' to recognise them as such, as they bore none of the 'typical' signs of a beggar, i.e. the rags and the smell of poverty and dirt. The professional beggars were another problem; they knew how to circumvent rules directed against vagrancy and begging. Thus the bishop of Zealand, Christen Worm, reported in 1730 that the ferrymen who transported passengers between the provinces were also transporting beggars – which otherwise was strictly prohibited – as they could not always recognise them, complaining that some beggars were dressed as fine folk, while carrying their professional equipment – the rags – in bags that they brought along.[32] Fooling officials in this way is also known from other European countries: Thus the gatekeepers of Strasbourg were being tricked in the same manner in the winter of 1530-31, when they allowed many fairly well-dressed people – who later turned out to be beggars – into town.[33]

There are some indications that the extensive begging in the capital was being organised by professional gangs of beggars – beggar corporations as some contemporaries called them – who had split up the city between them in certain districts and who, by bribing the beggar kings, could operate unchallenged by any authority, as the police officers were not entitled to arrest beggars and regarded it as beneath their dignity to do so. Beggars who did not bribe the beggar kings or let these officials have some of their money, on the other hand, were mercilessly dragged to prison.[34] This was not pure imagination or mere exaggeration: In 1774 the beggar king Niels Jensen was dismissed as he had been 'treated' by some beggars and hence had confiscated their collected alms for himself, and in 1779 the beggar king Mathias Pedersen was dismissed for more or less the same reasons.[35]

Niels Ditlev Riegels, who at the time was a well-known writer and polemicist, claimed that the professional beggar corporations were a result of the beggars getting together in prison, where criminals and beggars mingled, and this resulted in even more criminal activities in the city following their release. In fact, the prison functioned as an 'academy' for future criminals, as the youngsters learned their skills from the older beggars, who taught them the skills of their profession:

There [they] tell each other about their acquired knowledge and experiences. They have united, put together a capital, distributed shares (big patterns are infectious) and now they go on begging forcefully. The company sends out factors to the public spaces and equips small ships for domestic trade. Thus, a blind man navigates Vingaard Street, where he trades blessings and the name of Jesus. Several burdened cargo barges (a pregnant wife with a couple of kids by her side, a woman who suckles her child in the freezing cold) in whose wake a number of ragged lads are sailing, beat up and down the canal, right into the castle Square, where they sell sobbing, crying and nakedness with good profit.[36]

Beggars flooded the streets of Copenhagen: the dismissed soldiers, the sick, the old and the disabled, the cripples and the homeless orphans. Actually whole groups of homeless siblings could be seen wandering around, seeking shelter in alleys and basement passages until a compassionate soul felt sorry for them and took care of them.[37]

In this respect Copenhagen was no different from other major European cities.

Defining the worthy poor, 1522-1660

As the problem of begging was no novelty in the era of Absolutism (1660-1848) and as the organisation of poor relief in Copenhagen dated back to the early 16th century, it is appropriate by way of introduction to give an account of Danish poor policy in the period preceding the 18th century. Begging had been an official problem since the beginning of the sixteenth century, when the King and his council had taken several measures to eliminate it. Fighting against begging was a common trend all over Western and Southern Europe where, since the late Middle Ages, the state governments and city authorities had done all in their power to cleanse the streets of the annoying idlers. Starting in Lyon and Ypres in the 1520s, the authorities had taken systematic measures to distinguish between worthy and unworthy poor, the former being allowed poor relief from the municipality and the latter being whipped out of town or set to forced labour.[38] This distinction also gained currency in Denmark with the 'ordinance on country and town' in 1522, where it was decided that the old, sick and disabled poor and the orphans were to be supplied with a sign that allowed them to go begging for alms in their home parishes. The sturdy beggars, on the other hand, should be put into prison or evicted from the towns.[39]

When the Catholic convents and hospitals vanished as a consequence of the Lutheran Reformation in 1536, the collective distributions of alms and the social work of the Catholic Church vanished as well. Instead, the city authorities replaced the Catholic hospitals with temporal institutions for the poor, and organised recurrent collections for the worthy poor in the churches. Another consequence of the Reformation was the effort of the authorities to abolish illegal begging on the streets, i.e. begging without an official sign. Begging could no longer be legitimised by religious perceptions of atonement and indulgence, the influence of good deeds on the afterlife etc. Instead it was regarded as an evil – sometimes a necessary evil – that had to be dealt with.[40] The many ordinances from the 16th and 17th centuries that tried to regulate or prohibit begging testify to these new ideas about the matter.

A circumstance that seems to have influenced the general view of beggars was the notion that their number was increasing steadily. During the 16th and 17th centuries more and more complaints were heard about the growing number of poor and thus also the growing number of beggars. By all accounts the complainers were probably right.[41] After a dramatic decline during the Black Death in the middle of the fourteenth century, the population had recovered by the 1520s, and indeed had increased and continued to do so, whereas the resources of society did not. The number of farms in the villages was fixed and in the towns, the guilds did not accept any new-comers. The consequence was an increasing pauperisation of the population.

Even if the Copenhagen authorities probably had the best of intentions about eliminating the extensive begging, they did not have the economic means to do so, and in addition the institutions did not have room for all the deserving poor. The worthy poor, who could not come into a hospital, were given permission instead to beg 'according to customary practice'.[42] This was meant to be a temporary solution, but – as time would show – it helped to maintain the perception of begging as a morally based and legitimate method of making a livelihood, even when Copenhagen set up its first proper system of poor relief in 1549. As the Copenhagen poor relief revenues came mainly from voluntary donations and various duties, this meant that the authorities were not in a position to offer enough support to all the worthy poor and so the poor still went on begging, even though they got alms from the poor relief funds. One of the main objectives of the poor relief system was to get adequate funds to support the poor. Thus, in 1549 a regular collection was introduced in the capital. A number of citizens were appointed to make weekly collections in the churches and to collect at the royal castle when the court was present.

The final goal was to put all the deserving poor into the hospitals, and according to this it was decided that no poor person, once hospitalised, could leave the hospital. If a poor person did so, he was banished from town. This regulation shows that it was the intention of the King and his chancellery, who were in charge of the Copenhagen poor relief system until 1781 (after which *Københavns Magistrat* – the municipal corporation of Copenhagen – took over), that all poor should be hospitalised. It also shows that the Danish authorities were abreast of the recent developments in countries such as England and France.[43] In order to control the deserving and undeserving poor, the overseers from the Copenhagen poor relief system had to keep a register, in which the names of all the worthy poor had to be written.[44]

However, the royal efforts do not seem to have borne fruit. Unworthy beggars still roamed the streets of Copenhagen and took the bread out of the mouths of the worthy poor. Repeated ordinances and regulations through the 16th and 17th centuries show that the authorities in reality were powerless against the problems of poverty and begging. Public begging in the streets was prohibited in 1576, even for those with a token. The King then stipulated that only begging at doors was allowed.[45] In 1599 it was ordered that the *lensmænd* (noble holders of fiefs, from the 1660s replaced by the *amtmænd*) of Zealand should round up sturdy beggars without tokens, and set them to forced labour on the rebuilding of the royal castle in Copenhagen, and in 1602 a similar order was issued to the *lensmænd* all over the country. In 1613 arrested beggars were to be sent to forced labour at Frederiksborg Castle in Northern Zealand.[46] In these ordinances, the idea of combining the struggle against illegal begging with forced labour of the sturdy beggars and vagrants for the benefit of the state was introduced in Denmark for the first time. With inspiration from England and the Netherlands, a prison – a house of correction – for beggars and homeless children called *Børnehuset* (The Children's House) was established in 1605. In order to make the inmates self-supporting, they were to learn a craft, and it was the wish of the King 'that begging, which in this Kingdom and particularly in our city Copenhagen more than anywhere else is rampant, can be abolished by reasonable means'.[47]

In the beginning, the authorities had great expectations for this new industry employing the poor as they expected to kill two birds with the one stone: on the one hand, it became possible to create new jobs for the unemployed rabble, thus eliminating the problem of begging, and on the other hand, a domestic manufacturing industry could get off the ground. Unfortunately for the authorities, this did not happen. Time after time, they had to realise that, in practice, the paupers represented a poorly skilled and unreliable work force, and the factories were constantly running at a loss. The initiative did not solve the problem with the beggars either. The house of correction could not employ, to say nothing of house, all the poor and wretched beggars in Copenhagen, and as long as beggars from the countryside continued to flow into the city, it seemed almost impossible to eliminate begging.

Furthermore, the efforts of *Københavns Magistrat* to round up beggars were not always as vigorous as the King could wish. At any rate, the various Kings often grumbled at the city council, *Fattigdirektionen* and the chief of police for not complying with the issued ordinances and orders. Actually, it is characteristic for the business of *Københavns Magistrat*, that it did not take any independent initiatives to eliminate the problem of begging. Instead the city council left it to the King and his chancellery and the various appointed commissions to deal with the poverty problems of the city, both before and during the years with Absolutism.

With an ordinance from 1631 the King made all forms of begging in Copenhagen illegal, and gave a large sum of money to the city's poor relief system. Moreover, he decreed that a number of overseers should go to the burghers and collect money for the poor four times every year.[48] But as early as 1643, the total prohibition against begging seems to have been repealed and tokens were reintroduced with the royal statute from that year. However, it is not clear whether the statute, when it speaks of 'all Denmark, in towns as well as in villages' also included the capital or if Copenhagen was excepted and was thus still subject to the total ban on begging from the 1631-ordinance.[49] In any case, in 1646 it was ordered that all beggars in the city should be taken into custody and brought to the 'Plague House', a hospital for the insane and people with venereal disease, where they had to be questioned about whether they were inhabitants of the city. Beggars who were not inhabitants were to be sent back to wherever they came from, while the others should be taken care of by the authorities.[50]

In 1650 a special regulation dealing with begging was issued for Copenhagen. In this it was stated explicitly that begging again was allowed for the chosen few – the poor who carried one of the officially issued tokens. However, it was specified that the authorities should seek to hospitalise as many poor as possible. Only the poor, for whom there was no room in the hospitals, had authorisation to beg in the streets. To make sure that nobody misappropriated their tokens, it was decided that all beggars should be rounded up quarterly, and their tokens investigated.[51]

Thus, the total ban on begging in Copenhagen was short-lived. It was not until 1698 that the ban was again revived, and this time for good.

Fighting the beggars, 1660-1771

No major changes to the poor relief system and begging were made in the period between 1660 and 1698. The year 1698 saw the introduction of an Act on Poor Relief, which for the first time since 1631 attempted to draw up a coherent plan for the city's whole system of provision for the poor. A number of stipulations in this Act were to be carried over to the great Act (ordinance) on Poor Relief from 1708, which in general historical usage is considered to be the first profound and 'real' regulation of poor relief in Copenhagen.[52]

In the Act from 1698 no real effort was made to identify the worthy and unworthy poor. It was left to the judgement of the overseers to decide who could claim relief. This was remedied in the following ordinance from 1708, an Act which was much more detailed than the 1698 Act and which was in force right up until 1799, when the Copenhagen poor relief system was radically altered in accordance with the principles of the Enlightenment. In the ordinance of 1708 it was made absolutely clear that begging in the streets and squares was strictly prohibited, and that it was illegal to accommodate beggars or to give them alms 'at the doors'. If the citizens wanted to give alms to a poor person, they were not to give to him or her personally, but were to put the money into the official poor boxes, which were to be brought around by the overseers to each individual citizen from that time on. In this way the authorities could make sure that the money went to the deserving poor and not into the pocket of some scoundrel or sturdy beggar faking sickness and destitution.

Moreover it was dictated that it was a public duty for 'honest and beautiful' (i.e. respectable and honourable) citizens to function in turn as *fattigforstandere* (superintendents of the poor). One of the duties of these men was to investigate how many poor people, beggars etc. were living in the various parts of town. Then they were to draw up a register and hand it over to the newly established *Fattigkommissionen på Konventhuset* (The Poor Commission at the Convent House), who in turn had to use the register during the examinations of arrested beggars and the poor who applied for poor relief. It was the thankless task of *Københavns Magistrat* to appoint these 'beautiful' citizens, who did whatever possible to avoid the burdensome assignment.

The poor who were detected in this way were admonished to present themselves to *Fattigkommissionen på Konventhuset* to be questioned about their circumstances. If they were recognised as deserving poor, they were subsequently provided with a parchment note documenting their worthiness. The note was to be shown to the commissioners at *Konventhuset* every time the poor person went to receive his weekly alms. The poor were also obliged to attend communion on a regular basis and to let the vicar endorse the parchment note in order to prove that they had frequently visited 'the house of God, and attended communion and catechising, if they intend to enjoy their awarded alms'.

The following categories of people were considered to be worthy and deserving poor:

1. Foundlings.

2. Old people, who because of age and sickness were incapable of working, and who had formerly been citizens in the city or had lived there for at least three years, including soldiers and naval seamen, their wives and children, who, with regard to alms, enjoyed the rights of citizens.

3. The sick and bedridden, unless they had brought the 'unhappiness' upon themselves by leading a dissolute life.

4. The sick and disabled.

5. The temporarily ill.

6. Poor people who were able to prove that they could not provide for their families with their work.

7. Minors (under the age of 14), fatherless children of citizens.

Beggars and vagrants, prostitutes and other women living an irregular and slovenly life should immediately be arrested and thrown into prison. Foreign beggars were not allowed to live in the city, but had to leave when they were detected. If they did not, they were thrown into prison as well. Beggars from other Danish provinces, on the other hand, were sent back to their place of birth.[53]

The novelty in this Act was the decision that the poor no longer had to apply for poor relief. Now relief was granted as a public right as long as the poor met the conditions in the Act. The poor and needy were sought out – at least in principle – by the appointed 'beautiful' citizens and led to *Fattigkommissionen på Konventhuset*, who would grant them poor relief. However, in the beginning this stipulation posed some problems for the authorities because the poor hid when the 'beautiful' ones made inquiries about them. They were afraid of being locked away in the hospital or being sent out of town, as had previously been the case. Accordingly, the director of *Fattigdirektionen* got the vicars to announce from the church pulpits that they had nothing to fear.[54]

As the poor person could not, as mentioned, receive relief without attending church frequently, there was thus an aspect of social and religious control in the Act. Despite the secularisation of poor relief by removing the link to the churches and the clergy and attaching it instead to the temporal *fattigkommission*, there was no dissension with religious dogmas and thinking, simply an administrative reorganisation from ecclesiastical alms to governmental relief. It was precisely the question of the poor attending communion regularly as a prerequisite for poor relief that was later to cause great administrative problems for the authorities, and the stipulation was a major source of trouble and suffering for the poor themselves: Johan Heinrich Bärens, one of the leading specialists in matters of poor relief, said in 1799:

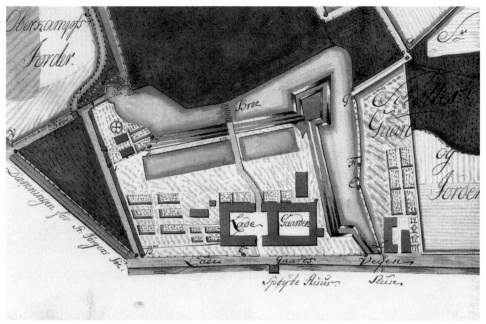

FIG. 3.

Ladegaarden *lay outside the city ramparts. Until 1768 it functioned as a military hospital, i.e. poor house and hospital for poor people from the armed forces. In 1768 a hospital for mentally ill and syphilitic patients was established here. After the hospital was moved in 1816, the building stood empty until 1822 when it was fitted out as a workhouse under the Copenhagen Poor Relief Authority. In 1833, a house of correction was added. The building functioned as a factory and workhouse until 1908.*

(...) it is made a duty for the relief commissions to provide for every poor person in their own parish, but in this respect the parishes have no fixed boundaries or territory. Every poor person is regarded as belonging to the parish where he last attended communion. Accordingly, the poor of the parish could be dispersed all over town and this is especially the case for certain congregations, for instance St. Petri [the German congregation in Copenhagen]. This necessarily makes the attendance and managing of the relief commissions so much more difficult and troublesome.[55]

It is important to note that *Fattigdirektionen* required nothing in return for the poor relief granted and that the poor did not have to work in order to receive public assistance. But they had to behave in an orderly manner, and abstain from 'indecency, gluttony, drunkenness, fights, quarrels, scolding and raging, frivolousness and looseness or any other vice and indecency'. However, this did not mean that the authorities did not want the poor to work at all, but according to the law it had to be done on a voluntary basis. As the poor could not be forced to work, the authorities sometimes tried to 'persuade' them with 'harsh' arguments instead. In the city's largest hospital, *Almindelig Hospital*, founded in 1769, it was common practice in the 1770s to heat only the workrooms and the dormitories for the very old and bedridden poor during the winter months, whereas the rooms for the somewhat more sturdy poor were only heated on Sundays. In this way the hospital management tried to 'drive the more fit inmates to the warm workrooms in the daytime, partly because these inmates should not waste their time in idleness, and partly in order to clean the dormitories in the daytime and open up the windows to improve the air'.[56]

Finally, it should be noted, that the ordinance of 1708 encompassed all inhabitants of the city of Copenhagen, including pensioned soldiers and seamen. However, these occupations were separated from the civil system of poor relief in 1734, when it was ordained that they should be transferred to newly established institutions for the relief and assistance of military and naval staff. The background for this separation were the many complaints from *Fattigkommissionen på Konventhuset* that the main bulk of arrested beggars comprised soldiers and seamen. In the period from 1733 to 1738, 450 civilian beggars were arrested, while the number of arrested beggars belonging to the army and navy was 734 and 617 respectively.[57]

It was preposterous, the poor commission claimed, that the citizens should provide for all these soldiers and seamen. That ought to be a task for the military and naval departments, not for the city of Copenhagen. The complaints were acknowledged and complied with, and thus the duty of providing for soldiers and seamen was transferred to special military and naval poor commissions: *Krigshospitalet på Ladegaarden* (The War Hospital at the Barn House) for the soldiers and *Kvæsthuset* (The House for Maimed) for the seamen.[58] But this, of course, did not diminish the number of beggars from the military departments. Søren Hempel, the inspector of *Almindelig Hospital*, claimed in 1769 that the military beggars had nothing to fear from the civil authorities as the military department flatly denied that anyone from their ranks was begging in the streets. Subsequently the military beggars, when captured, were released right away without further ado. This gave rise to the obvious problem that the military beggars did not fear any punishment at all: 'Some of the young females and pregnant women from other services even claim to belong to the military departments in order to be released immediately'.[59]

There is no indication that the ordinance of 1708 on poor relief and begging changed the face of street begging in any appreciable way. The city still abounded with beggars and, as if nothing had happened, people continued to hand out alms in the streets and at their own doors. *Fattigkommissionen på Konventhuset* was power-less and could do nothing to change this. Even the Queen and her court regularly handed out alms to the beggars who appeared at the court and so did a great num-ber of priests who frequently distributed alms at the church doors. And the ordi-nary citizens followed suit: 'Some particular inhabitants, such as bakers, innkeepers and others, also hand out to the poor at their doors on certain week days, and thus give occasion to the beggars to go visiting other good people in the neighbourhood'. When, for instance, the Duke of Braunschweig-Bevern, who was attached to the dip-lomatic corps in Copenhagen, complained to the chief of police in 1774 about the increasing number of beggars and urged him to do something about it, he received the answer that the police would use all means possible to do so, with the sarcastic addition that the job would be much easier to do if the Duke would abstain from handing out alms from his house, 'which attracts beggars to him'. Accordingly he was strongly advised to send the money to the poor board instead.[60]

The business of *Fattigkommissionen på Konventhuset* and the beggar kings was not made any easier by the fact that many citizens defended the beggars when they were arrested by the beggar kings. 'In general it is the inhabitants themselves that sus-tain the begging in this city, as they defend certain beggars, when the attendants come to grab them, and, they allow others to be grabbed, just as if it is at their dis-cretion to decide which beggars are to be arrested and which are not', as *Fattigkom-missionen* reported in 1738.[61] The inspector of *Almindelig Hospital* even reported how noble masters let their servants beat the beggar kings on occasions when they had arrested beggars at their houses and subsequently told the beggar kings to stay away 'as they would have the liberty to hand out to whoever they pleased'.[62]

Fattigkommissionen did not even have the means to protect their employed assis-tants – the beggar kings. They were frequently hunted down and beaten up by the mob, sometimes consisting of more than one hundred people at a time. This hap-pened in particular when the attendants had arrested a beggar, and afterwards dragged him or her to prison. On one known occasion in 1714, assistants and the commission even had to barricade themselves in *Konventhuset* as the mob went wild with rage.[63]

Obviously, the violent treatment of the beggar kings meant that a great number of them resigned from their positions to find a less hazardous occupation elsewhere.

This happened in 1789, when nine extra beggar kings had been hired. In the first few days they were harassed by the mob several times, and on one occasion they were attacked by more than 100 people even though they were protected by the military. The mob chased them all the way from the prison at Christianshavn to the front door of *Almindelig Hospital* about a mile (one Danish mile = 7.5 km) away. The new beggar kings were so frightened by this experience that they immediately resigned, as 'they would not serve in a business connected with so much danger' – and new employees were not easy to find anywhere.[64]

The brawls and fights between beggar kings and the mob were not just a curious 18th century phenomenon. When the practice of hiring beggar kings was abandoned in 1813, the job was instead given to the police, who, understandably, were somewhat reluctant to accept this assignment. The Copenhagen mob still had a fierce resentment towards officials catching beggars in the streets, as the chief of police and president of *Københavns Magistrat*, A.C. Kierulff, reported to *Danske Kancelli* in 1832:

For the opinion among the lower orders of Copenhagen on the arrest of beggars is such, that when a beggar on his apprehension makes resistance, the result is always that the general compassion for him calls for public action on behalf of the captive, who is released, while the police officers are frequently abused.[65]

Decentralisation and *Københavns Magistrat*, 1771-1799

In 1771 the system of Copenhagen poor relief was changed radically, as the centrally situated *Fattigkommissionen på Konventhuset* was abolished, and new decentralised poor commissions – eight at the time – were established in every parish of the city. From then on, it was up to the individual parish commissions to decide whether or not a poor person was worthy of relief. But what was worse, it was also up to the individual commission to keep the beggars off the streets of their parish. This would later prove to be a very unwise decision as the parish commissions did not have the finances or the practical means to do so and the result was a foregone conclusion: the number of beggars increased considerably during the following years.

The parish commissions referred to a central board – *Fattigdirektionen* – who had the main responsibility for the finances and for the working of all parish commissions. The reason for the change was the belief that the old commission at *Konventhuset* had been too costly and too ineffective because of its centralised position in one spot of the city. This would be improved by the decentralised commissions which, it was believed, would have a much better opportunity to know every single poor person in their parish and thus also a better overview of the situation on the street.[66] The commission at *Konventhuset* did not know if a poor person received relief from more than one place at a time, which was actually possible if the receiver was a little sly.

Another problem had been the lack of means to make the poor work in return for the relief granted. Work had by and large been a voluntary option for the poor. Although this was still the case after 1771, the parish commissions could urge the poor person to work and convince him that this was for his own good. The authorities also began to realise that it was not a good idea after all to gather all the poor for 'indoor' relief at the hospitals. It was not only a very expensive solution, but hospitalisation also had a tendency to split families from each other. From then on, the Copenhagen poor relief system relied on 'outdoor' relief to a much greater extent.[67]

Both before and after 1771 the weak spot was the economy of the poor relief system as it was not based on taxation, but on voluntary gifts, donations, regular collections by the citizens and in the churches, a fixed sum from the land register tax and, likewise, a fixed sum from the revenues from the lotteries.[68] However, in 1762 and 1764 the King decided that 9,000 *rigsdaler* should be paid to *Fattigdirektionen* annually. The money should be assessed from the land register of Copenhagen and be paid for the running of *Konventhuset*, *Børnehuset* (the prison for homeless children and beggars at Christianshavn) and *Fødselsstiftelsen* (the institution for newborn foundlings) at Frederiks Hospital, the city's first somatic hospital, founded in 1757. This was the first attempt to assess a poor tax on the inhabitants of Copenhagen. Not until 1815 – under the influence of another view about the distinction between what was public and what was private – did the central authorities venture to impose a more general poor tax on the city.[69]

An administrative change took place in 1781 as the management of the Copenhagen poor relief system was put in the hands of *Københavns Magistrat*. *Fattigdirektionen*, which had worked independently of the town council (the board had been managed directly under the auspices of *Danske Kancelli*), was therefore dissolved.[70] However, the legal basis was still the Ordinance on the Poor from 1708 and its successor from 1771 and this was also the case for the finances. This turned out to be fatal for the city government and its poor relief in the following years, as the deficit kept increasing in spite of the fact that Copenhagen was becoming wealthier as a result of flourishing trade during the 1780s and the 1790s. Already at the time of the takeover in 1781, the poor relief administration had an enormous deficit, and in 1782 *Københavns Magistrat* warned the King and *Danske Kancelli* that if nothing was done to change this, ruin was approaching.[71]

The decentralised parish commissions of 1771 made things even worse, as the local commissioners totally lacked an overview of the finances of the poor relief administration. The parish commissions were entrusted to grant poor relief, but they just sent the bill to *Københavns Magistrat* as they were not entrusted to deal with finances. *Københavns Magistrat*, on the other hand, had no control over the parish commissions and could not check if they granted too much relief to the poor. According to the Ordinance on the Poor of 1771, they just had to pay whatever the parish commissions required. Naturally, the costs shot up and *Københavns Magistrat* ate into the capital of their funds for the poor with terrifying speed.[72]

The situation was untenable, and in 1792 another ordinance on poor relief – ordering the poor to work in return for the relief granted – was issued. It was stipulated that every parish in Copenhagen should erect a workhouse. In fact, a number of parishes already had such workhouses, erected on a voluntary basis, but now they were made compulsory. From then on the obligation on the poor person to work if he wanted to receive poor relief, was indispensable. The ordinance further declared that the poor had to be guided towards diligence and industry, should be encouraged by rewards, and should 'compete to achieve rewards'.[73]

A new age was dawning.

The Enlightenment and the poor

In the late 1760s and early 1770s the idea emerged that it was useless to punish beggars and vagrants with prison sentences. It was also claimed that it was bad state policy to fob off the worthy poor with small alms on which they could not survive without begging. Instead the state should make greater efforts to rehabilitate the lazy and the dishonest, while the worthy poor should enjoy an increase in their alms. More important, however, was that the local authorities now became obliged, through re-education, to 'instil' in the poor the same view as that held by the patriotic elite, i.e. the bliss of hard work.

Believing with John Locke – and mediated by Danish intellectuals such as Ludvig Holberg, J.S. Sneedorff and Tyge Rothe – that man was a *tabula rasa*, and thus

PETER HENNINGSEN

FIG. 4.

To the left is Tugt- og Børnehuset *(prison) on Christianhavns Torv, built by Philip de Lange*
1739-1741. In the yard behind the imposing main building a rasp-house for the male prisoners was built
later. In 1790, Børnehuset *was closed as an institution as the name was changed to* Tugt- Rasp- og
Forbedringshuset. *The building burned down during a prisoner revolt in 1817.*

susceptible to change as he was entirely a product of learning from experience, the
pioneers of Danish welfare policies and poor relief introduced new ways of dealing
with the poor, particularly the undeserving vagrants and beggars.[74] The beggar was
now regarded as a victim of circumstance, and it was the task of the poor relief system not only to hand out alms, but also to transform the beggar from an idler into
a hard working, 'happy' man. But how was this to be done?

During the final third of the 18th century, the problems of poverty in Copenhagen became ever more pressing as immigration from the country steadily increased
and did not seem to end: 'In the end the capitals will look like besieged fortresses,
which, because of the size of their own population, will be forced to surrender', it
was said in a Copenhagen newspaper in 1808. The anonymous writer further pointed
out that the new liberal thoughts were what created misery and poverty and caused
the situation that 'every tenth or twelfth inhabitant of the capital is a pauper living
on assistance from the poor relief'.[75]

The traditional social and economic system favouring all kinds of monopolies and forced membership of guilds for artisans and trades people was rapidly vanishing. As a consequence, the old traditional forms of insurance and reciprocity, where masters through the guilds supported their journeymen in case of illness, were no longer as effective as they were meant to be. A great number of journeymen – no longer forced to serve a master for decades and also save money to make the costly master piece necessary to join the guild as a master (if indeed there was a vacancy as in many cases the number of masters was fixed) – now set up on their own as *frimestre* (free masters) or built their own homes, got married and had children, even though they were still working as journeymen. In many cases the result was that competition between the masters became fiercer than before, forcing down the profits, and a great number of masters and journeymen had to throw in the towel and turn to the poor relief administration. Thus the transition from a quasi-feudal order, based on reciprocity and obligations between the orders, to a liberal way of thinking and a liberal mode of production, where old ties of social bonds were gone, implied more poverty and destitution than ever before.[76]

The Enlightenment and the cameralist and patriotic perception of the common good gave rise to a strong interest in the education of the peasants and the rabble of the cities, on the one hand, and a renewed interest in proper care for the poor on the other. The cornerstone in the thinking of the cameralists was the notion of the people – particularly the riffraff – as utterly stupid and sluggish people who did not know what was for their own good.[77] However, time had made it abundantly clear for many that poverty and destitution were not solely the fault of the poor themselves. Instead, a great number of the poor were victims of the economic structures of both mercantilism and liberalism and the profound social changes that had taken place during the 18th century. Coercion and control no longer sufficed to keep the poor in check.

At the dawn of the 18th century, poor relief had been considered an act of mercy; at the end of the century it had instead become an essential instrument in society's political struggle against destitution and crime. Since the Reformation in 1536 the poor relief administered by the Copenhagen authorities had consisted of a mixture of the provision of charity and the implementation of punishments. The sturdy poor should be intimidated from becoming a burden on society and the propertied social groups should be protected from beggars, vagrants and criminals. Hitherto, the means to this end had consisted of attempts to imprison the paupers in houses of correction, prisons, hospitals and workhouses. At the end of the century nobody regarded this to be an adequate solution to the problems of poverty, nor as the aim of the poor relief administration.

Led by trend-setting creators of 'public opinion' – most of whom were government and municipal officials such as Johan Heinrich Bärens (1761-1813), Christian Elovius Mangor (1739-1801) and Ove Malling (1747-1829) – poor relief became the principal instrument in the planning of the future happiness of the people by directing new generations of poor towards a thrifty and industrious life. On the one hand, society had a Christian obligation to take care of the old, the sick and the weak, but on the other hand it also had an obligation to punish and re-educate lazy idlers. These people had to be forced to work, but – and this was important – the coercion had to look like help and not punishment. Through compulsion, idlers should become acquainted with the bliss of hard work, and if they were unable to find a job themselves, they should be offered work in the public workhouses.[78]

During the Enlightenment, work was regarded as a universal solution to all kinds of social problems. Work was not only useful for the state, it was also for the benefit of the individual. Only by putting everybody to work could poverty and indigence be avoided. The means to this noble purpose was a systematic programme of re-education and rehabilitation and this was to be tested on defenceless paupers who were in no position to make effective objections.

Among social historians, it is commonly claimed that the obligation of the Copenhagen poor to work was stipulated by law for the first time in 1792, but actually *Danske Kancelli* had stipulated back in 1779 that all sturdy paupers, who received support from the Copenhagen poor relief administration, had to be put to work at spinning unless they could earn just as much or even more by work in 'the tobacco plantations or other factories and the like'. The stipulation, which was included in an ordinance from 15 September 1779, thus anticipated the 1792 ordinance and has to be regarded as the law that in reality introduced the duty of the Copenhagen paupers to work.[79] Even the sick in *Almindelig Hospital* were put to work, as work was considered an effective medicine which could cure scurvy, scabies and idleness.[80] Also in 1779 it was suggested that spinning rooms for the poor should be established in all parts of Copenhagen and it should be compulsory for the paupers to attend work there, and even though the proponents of the idea did not succeed in their enterprise, it clearly shows that the idea of public workhouses for the poor was not new, as these houses were actually established in the late 1780s.[81]

However, it was not until the great Poor Reform of 1799, that the duty to work had its breakthrough. There was no longer any discussion about whether the pauper should work or not. It had become imperative.[82] Johan Heinrich Bärens, the most important observer of late 18th century poor relief administration, put the absolute obligation to work in this way:

Anybody who signs in for poor relief in the workhouse of his parish (….) must be put to some sort of work at the very moment he enters the house, whether he is poor or not, whether he comes there in the morning or in the afternoon, whether he stays only briefly or remains for several days (…) Anybody who receives assistance has to sign in every day for a certain time even if he cannot work at all. This is to make sure that this pauper does not receive assistance from elsewhere or walk around begging.[83]

Not surprisingly, it was Bärens who in the late 1790s thought up the idea of establishing a new house of correction, where the sturdy paupers and beggars were to be set to forced labour. If they were caught begging in the streets or if they would not work in return for their granted assistance, they were locked up for a certain time and put to work. In common with the English and American prison pioneers (e.g. John Howard and Jeremy Bentham) it was the belief that prisoners should not be allowed to talk to each other, so they were ordered to stay silent. In silence they were to contemplate their wretched lives, hopefully come to terms with God and themselves, and thus start a new life on their release. The prisoners in the correction house who could not stay silent were locked up in isolation in small cellars in the basement for a number of days or weeks according to the 'crime' they had committed: that is, how much disturbance they had created in the workrooms. It was also Bärens, who was the leading force behind the actual establishment of the correction house in Copenhagen in April 1800.[84]

The poor relief system in Hamburg – which had been reformed and reorganised in 1788 – inspired most, if not all, North European poor relief efforts in the following years. Hamburg had been divided into 60 small poor districts, which were allocated among five main districts each managing 12 poor districts. At the head of each main district were two *Armenvorsteher* (superintendents) responsible for six districts each. In each of the 60 small poor districts, three citizens were appointed as *Armenpfleger* (unpaid attendants). Their job was to take care of the paupers in their area and to consult the superintendent in cases of doubt. *Der Armenkollegium* (The Poor

Assembly) was in charge of the five main districts, and the assembly was composed of people from the city council and supervisors from hospitals, workhouses and various charitable institutions of the city. The supervisors of each poor district in Hamburg were obliged to visit the poor regularly to discover their state of poverty and decide if they should be sent to a hospital or a workhouse, or if they perhaps could manage with 'outdoor' relief in the form of economic help from the poor box. They also had to account for all the paupers in their districts and make sure that everyone received the necessary help. As it was essential that all sturdy paupers were put to work, if there were no jobs the poor relief authorities were obliged to create jobs in their workhouses. The allotted work usually comprised spinning, weaving and knitting, which the poor could do at home. A special school was established for the old and weak, thus making them also capable of spinning and weaving. And youth were not forgotten either. Therefore an industrial school was established, where the children of paupers could get used to an industrious life. The fundamental principle of the *Armenanstalt* consisted in a combination of poor relief, forced labour, education and rehabilitation.

Similar efforts to reform the system of poor relief had been initiated in other German cities: In the city of Bremen, assistance and the allotment of work had – just as in Hamburg – been introduced in 1779, and in Lübeck the *Armenanstalt*, established in 1773, was reorganised in 1801 according to the model of the *Armenanstalt* in Hamburg. In Braunschweig, the old *Armenanstalt* was also reorganised according to the Hamburg model in 1805.[85] A number of German cities had actually reorganised their poor relief during the 1770s and 1780s, but none as successfully as Hamburg.[86]

However, the Poor Reform in Hamburg in 1788 was not as innovative as has later been claimed. In fact it was modelled on a variety of different poor relief systems already in existence. But these different features were integrated in a special manner, which at the time seemed astonishingly effective. Thus the Hamburg *Armenanstalt* became a role model for a whole generation of poor relief reformers, and by the dawn of the nineteenth century it represented the zenith of what a 'rationally organised' poor relief system should encompass and what could be achieved if cities organised their own systems in the same way as the Hamburg poor relief system.

The great plan, 1799

The new and comprehensive 'plan for poor relief' that was introduced in Copenhagen in July 1799 was almost completely modelled on the Hamburg *Armenanstalt*. 'The arrangement in Hamburg, whose position, climate, size of population, manners and customs are so intimately in agreement with Copenhagen, has mainly been complied with' as Bärens related in 1799.[87] The overall intention of the 'plan', as it was commonly called, was once and for all to get rid of the beggars, to provide adequate but not too abundant support for the worthy poor and to make sure that no new generations of beggars and vagrants was hatched out among the poor. The plan was not only the most radical and thorough scheme for poor relief that Copenhagen had ever seen, it was also the most ambitious.

In all its outlines it bore the mark of the Enlightenment with its firm belief in future progress and its rational belief in the idea that systematic and scientific analysis could ensure a happy future for everyone by marking out the lines for the creation of a new human type: the industrious and patriotic worker.[88] While the Poor Ordinance of 1708 could be contained in 18 pages with 42 paragraphs, the 'plan' of 1799 consisted of no less than 78 pages with 215 paragraphs. Furthermore, the new organisation of poor relief was specialised in particular subject areas to a degree never seen before.

The notion of 'the improved poor' was most strongly expressed in the paragraphs on the schools for the poor and the upbringing of the poor children. Nothing was more evident than the belief that the neglected upbringing of the poor led to the future destitution of their children, as was said by *Fattigdirektionen* in a report to *Danske Kancelli*. Thus, it was one of the noblest tasks of *Fattigdirektionen* to make sure that all poor children received an adequate education according to their station in life. Even people who were not poor enough to be entitled to poor relief, but on the other hand could not afford to send their children to school, were allowed to send their children to the schools for the poor. Education was considered to be of such great importance that the state would not leave it to the parents to make sure that their children were properly educated.[89]

The purpose of schooling – attendance was compulsory – was to mould the neglected youngsters into 'enlightened, good and industrious men and citizens'. They should be prevented from falling into 'idleness and vices and become accustomed to good manners and morals, tidiness and cleanliness'. It was also important that they were guided to 'such knowledge' as was beneficial to man and 'by means

PETER HENNINGSEN

of which, they, in case of lack of work in the future, can earn their living or usefully engage themselves in vacant hours'. They were to acquire only the knowledge 'appropriate to the common man', which meant reading, writing, arithmetic, religion and morals. Moreover, they were meant to acquire 'general knowledge of nature and its arrangements and mode of operation, of civic organisations and duties, of the most important rules that would preserve their health, and of the polity and position of their fatherland and other countries'.

To this can be added that the children should be 'led to proper and harmonious singing, particularly chorals and decent folk songs'. The bodies of the poor were also on the agenda: In order to turn out strong workers and good soldiers and defenders of the fatherland, the children were to be exercised in gymnastics: 'The exercising of the body shall be of the kind that contributes to strength, pliability and agility which are necessary and useful to the working classes'.[90]

For the outcasts of society – the vagrants and the rude beggars – other and more stringent means were required: 'Beside a well scheduled poor relief, begging can by no means be tolerated. This evil, which debases humanity, disgraces the public, troubles their fellow citizens and weakens the desire of the wealthy to support public poor relief, thus has to be generally prohibited'.[91] No mercy should be shown towards beggars, who ought to be condemned to forced labour in a correction house specially made for this very purpose. This was because they had evaded honest work and instead wanted to make their living 'in an illegal way', as it was said in § 127 of the 'plan'. All paupers should work as much as they were able to in one of the public workhouses. Just like Hamburg, Copenhagen was divided into a number of main poor districts – a total of 12 – each headed by a superintendent, who was assisted by a number of subordinate and unpaid attendants. They had to make sure that the daily business of their districts was properly taken care of. In addition, a large number of specialised commissions were established – for education, for industry, for the provision of assistance etc. At the head of these was the so-called *Direktionskommission* (The Directions Commission, i.e. the board) to which all the individual commissions referred (this was changed in 1815, but that is a different story).

A new and revolutionary element of poor relief in the 'plan' was the stipulation that the directors, superintendents and supervisors were meant to work actively to prevent pauperism, instead of merely providing the paupers with poor relief. The Copenhagen poor relief administration should not only take care of people who were 'pushed down to destitution', but also of people, 'who accidentally got close to such

FIG. 5.

Copenhagen Municipal Authority had given the contract for sweeping the city streets to the Copenhagen Poor Relief Authority. The drawing shows paupers from Ladegaarden *(the workhouse) on their way into Copenhagen to do the daily sweeping. Drawing from the 19th century.*

a condition. To support the first is to relieve destitution, to engage the latter is to prevent it'.[92]

The most essential change was that poor relief was now distributed on the basis of a carefully prepared plan instead of perfunctory handouts to the benefit of nobody in the long run. A proper poor relief implied that no poor person was without the absolute necessities of life, and 'that no one by such want is debilitated or forced to beg'. Relief should be offered proactively and not withheld until requested by the pauper himself. What the outreaching operations implied for the unpaid district attendants can be seen from the recollections of the Copenhagen citizen Jens Friborg, who in his autobiography noted:

I still recollect the extreme cold, which still prevailed in the Easter days [1799] and meant that instead of attending church service, I had to run around among the poor to check their condition. I had to provide bed linen at the expense of the board [*Fattigdirektionen*] for those who did not have any; the same was the case with food etc. This winter was the most severe I have known. That year, as late as Whit Sunday, the snow was piled up in two huge heaps along Kongens Nytorv [a central square in Copenhagen] with only a passage in between. This was not a good omen for the new poor board, and the Crown Prince, our present King [Frederik VI], who pitied the poor suffering from the cold and, urged the board to spare no effort to relieve their misery.[93]

Thus the main purpose of the 'plan' was not only the relief of material needs, but also – and perhaps most important – the moral and patriotic rehabilitation of the poor individual. This was a natural consequence of the common perception of the ordinary pauper as a work-shy and lazy person who was somehow responsible for his or her own destitution. It was still uncommon to consider the poor as people struck by accidental unemployment or sickness. Even though a large number of the pioneers of poor reform were acquainted with the notion that unemployment and poverty were to a great extent the result of social inheritance and bad market conditions, they nevertheless often spoke as if this was not the case. This schism in the perception of who was worthy of help and who was not has lasted right down to our own time, when politicians still debate whether the unemployed should be forced to work or not, whether the dole is too high etc.

Poverty was still regarded as the moral problem of the individual pauper and accordingly public help had to be meagre in order to prevent the poor from relying on it so much that he or she did not bother to work. Thus poor relief had to be kept at an absolute minimum (§ 1 in the 'plan'). Furthermore it was crucial that the granted relief was followed by moral instruction and education. After all, the aim of the great poor relief project was moral reform of the poor. According to the reformers there was nothing wrong with society as such.[94]

However, a crucial weakness of both the Hamburg and the Copenhagen Poor Relief reforms of 1788 and 1799 was financing based on voluntary gifts, wills and donations. It was true that since 1708 the authorities had collected some revenues from fines, taxation of various amusements, a certain percentage of civil servants' salaries, lotteries, taxation on real estate (from 1764) and tax on marriages between persons of rank, but these were, after all, just a drop in the ocean. Not even the taxation on real estate in 1764 was sufficient. *Fattigdirektionen* constantly lacked enough money to fulfil the great ambitions of the plan and the golden promises of work and provision of assistance for everyone in need. The situation became even worse as Denmark was grudgingly dragged into the Napoleonic wars on the French side. This led to war with England and the fatal loss of the fleet in 1807 – the cornerstone of Danish prosperity – and the catastrophic bombardment of Copenhagen, which ruined large parts of the city and brought an otherwise prosperous and industrious era to an end. Of course, the great city fire of 1795 had not made the situation any better.

In 1813 the country went bankrupt and the following year saw the end of the Napoleonic wars. The subsequent peace treaty in Kiel in 1814 wrote the end of the union between Denmark and Norway. This was certainly not the most propitious moment for the completion of great plans concerning the poor.

Conclusion

The development of temporal poor relief in Denmark between 1500 and 1800 closely resembled the developments in other parts of Western Europe, thus showing that Denmark was in line with general European trends in the field. With some delay, the new ideas came to Denmark, most probably through Germany, as was definitely the case with the great reform of 1799, but also sometimes from the Netherlands, as seems to have been the case in the beginning of the 17th century when King Christian IV established *Børnehuset*, modelled on principles from the Amsterdam correction house. The same line of development can be seen in the 19th century, when industrialism and liberalism blossomed and made even greater numbers of poor people more miserable than ever before. In this matter, too, Denmark resembled the other West European countries.

The great plan of 1799 was in force for most of the 19th century, and thus the abolition of Absolutism in 1848 did not change the main features of Copenhagen poor relief. Not until the 1890s did the 1799-plan become obsolete. It was replaced by new stipulations that were inspired by other political visions of social welfare.

BIBLIOGRAPHY

Bärens, J.H. 1792. *Udkast til en Plan for Fattigvæsenets specielle Bestyrelse i Kiøbenhavn*. Copenhagen.

Bärens, J.H. 1799a. *Forestilling fra Direktionen for Kiøbenhavns Fattigvæsen om sammes bedre Indretning tilligemed den indsendte Plan hvorefter Direktionen skal overtage Bestyrelsen*. Copenhagen.

Bärens, J.H. 1799b. 'Kjøbenhavns Fattigvæsen'. *Kjøbenhavns Magazin for Skole-, Industrie- og Fattigvæsen*. Vol. 1. Copenhagen.

Bonderup, Gerda 2002. 'Health Care Provision and Poor Relief in Enlightenment and 19th Century Denmark'. In: Ole Peter Grell, Andrew Cunningham, Robert Jütte (eds.), *Health Care and Poor Relief in 18th and 19th Century Europe*. Aldershot: Ashgate, pp. 172-88.

Bruun, Carl 1890. *Kjøbenhavn. En illustreret Skildring af dets Historie, Mindesmærker og Institutioner*. Copenhagen.

Callisen, Henrich 1809. *Physisk Medizinske Betragtninger over Kiøbenhavn*. Copenhagen.

Christensen, C. 1976. *Hørsholms Historie fra 1305 til 1875*. Copenhagen: Nordlundes Bogtrykkeri.

Christensen, Villads (ed.) 1919-20. 'Daglige Begivenheder i København 1716-22. Indberetninger fra Politimester Ernst til Kongen'. *Historiske Meddelelser om København*. 1st series, vol. 7, pp. 325-83, 405-46.

Christensen, Villads 1912. *København i Kristian VIII's og Frederik VII's Tid 1840-1857*. Copenhagen.

Cowan, Alexander 1998. *Urban Europe 1500-1700*. London & New York: Arnold.

Dahlerup, Troels 1979. 'Den sociale forsorg og reformationen i Danmark'. *Historie. Jyske Samlinger*. New series XIII, 1-2, pp. 198-202.

Ehrencron-Müller, H. & L. 1950. 'Uddrag af Johan Philip Kneyln Rosenstand-Goiskes Efterretninger'. *Historiske Meddelelser om København*. 4th series, 2, pp. 169-244.

Elvius, Sofus & P. Fr. Rist (eds.) 1891. 'En kjøbenhavnsk Urtekræmmers Levnetsløb'. *Museum. Tidsskrift for Historie og Geografi*, pp. 90-98.

Endres, Rudolf 1976. 'Das Armenproblem im Zeitalter des Absolutismus'. In: Franklin Kopitzch (ed.), *Aufklärung und Bürgertum in Deutschland*. München: Nymphenburger Verlagshandlung.

Fairchilds, Cissie C. 1984. *Domestic Enemies. Servants & their masters in Old Regime France*. Baltimore: Johns Hopkins University Press.

Geremek, Bronislaw 1994. *Poverty. A History*. Oxford: Blackwell Publishers.

Hansen, Holger (ed.) 1916. *Kabinetsstyrelsen i Danmark 1768-1772. Aktstykker og Oplysninger*. Vol. 1. Copenhagen.

Hansen, Holger 1915-16. 'Fattigvæsenets Lotterier'. *Historiske Meddelelser om København*. 1st series, vol. 5, pp. 503-15.

Hansen, Peter Wessel 2004. 'Til nytte for det almindelige. Trinitatis Arbejdshus 1790-1841'. *Historiske Meddelelser om København*. Copenhagen, pp. 5-30.

Heiberg, Peter Andreas 1793. *Rigsdalerseddelens Hændelser*. Copenhagen.

Henningsen, Peter 2004. 'Det philadelphiske system. Københavns Fattigvæsen og tvangsarbejdshuset i Pustervig 1800-1807'. *Fortid og Nutid*. Vol. 2, pp. 3-28.

Jensen, Carsten Selch 2004: 'Byerne og de fattige – den internationale baggrund for den danske udvikling'. In: Søren Bitsch Christensen (ed.), *Middelalderbyen*. (Danske Bystudier, 1). Aarhus: Aarhus Universitetsforlag, pp. 295-324.

Jütte, Robert 1994: *Poverty and Deviance in Early Modern Europe*. Cambridge: Cambridge University Press.

Jørgensen, Harald 1982. 'Det offentlige fattigvæsen i Danmark 1708-1770'. In: Karl-Gustaf Andersson et al. (ed.), *Oppdaginga av fattigdomen. Sosial lovgiving i Norden på 1700-talet*. Oslo: Universitetsforlaget, pp. 31-107.

Kolderup-Rosenvinge, J.A. (ed.) 1824. *Samling af gamle danske Love*. Vol. 4. Copenhagen.

Kongelig approberet Plan for Fattigvæsenets bedre Indretning og Bestyrelse i Staden Kiøbenhavn og dens Forstæder, 2 July 1799 1799. Copenhagen.

Kopitzsch, Franklin (ed.) 1976. *Aufklärung, Absolutismus und Bürgertum in Deutschland*. München: Nümphenburger Verlagshandlung.

Leeuwen, Marco van 2002. 'Histories of Risk and Welfare in Europe during the 18th and 19th Centuries'. In: Ole Peter Grell, Andrew Cunningham, Robert Jütte (eds.), *Health Care and Poor Relief in 18th and 19th Century Europe*. Aldershot: Ashgate, pp. 32-68.

Lindemann, Mary 1990. *Patriots and Paupers. Hamburg 1730-1812*. New York: Oxford University Press.

Lis, Catharina & Hugo Soly 1979. *Poverty and capitalism in Pre-Industrial Europe*. Atlantic Highlands, New Jersey: Humanities Press.

Lund, Georg Henric 1795: *Om Fattigvæsenet og den offentlige Understøttelse*. Copenhagen.

Løgstrup, Birgit 1970. Fattigvæsenet i København omkring 1700 med særligt henblik på fattigforordningen af 24. september 1708. (Unpublished thesis). University of Copenhagen.

Malling, Ove 1840. 'Udtog af Kjøbenhavns Fattigvæsens Direktions Indberetning til Hans kongelige Højhed Kronprindsen angaaende det kjøbenhavnske Fattigvæsen, dateret 20de Nov. 1807'. In: Frederik Thaarup (ed.), *Penia eller Blade for Skole-, Industrie-, Medicinal- og Fattigvæsen,* 5. Copenhagen.

Malling, Ove & V.K. Hjort 1799/1801. *Efterretninger fra det kiøbenhavnske Fattigvæsen*, 7. Copenhagen.

Markussen, Ingrid 1995. *Til Skaberens Ære, Statens Tjeneste og vor egen Nytte*. Odense: Odense Universitetsforlag.

Nielsen, Oluf (ed.) 1884. *Københavns Diplomatarium. Samling af Dokumenter, Breve og andre Kilder til Oplysning om Københavns Forhold før 1728*. Copenhagen: Gad.

Nyeste Skilderie af Kjøbenhavn 1808, 41, 43. Copenhagen.

Olsen, Olaf 1978. *Christian IVs Tugt- og Børnehus*. Højbjerg: Wormianum.

Pontoppidan, Carl 1793. 'Tanker til høiere Eftertanke angaaende Alimentations- og Fattig-Væsenets Tilstand i Dannemark, især i Hovedstaden Kiøbenhavn, baade i ældre og nyere Tider'. *Magazin for almeennyttige Bidrag til Kundskab om Indretninger og Forfatninger i de kongelige danske Stater, II. Deel*. Copenhagen.

Porter, Roy 2000: *Enlightenment: Britain and the Creation of the Modern World*. London: Allen Lane.

Ribov, Marion 1971. Struenseetidens fattiglovgivning og dens resultater. (Unpublished thesis). University of Copenhagen.

Riegels, N.D. 1786. 'Tiggerie'. *Maanedsskriftet Kiøbenhavns Skilderie*, 1, pp. 8 f.

Rubin, Marcus 1879. *Oversigt over Kjøbenhavns Fattigvæsens Historie*. (Tabelværk til Kjøbenhavns Statistik, 4). Copenhagen.

Rørdam, H.F. (ed.) 1883. *Danske Kirkelove samt Udvalg af Bestemmelser vedr. Kirken, Skolen og de Fattiges Forsørgelse fra Reformationen indtil Christian V's Danske Lov, 1536-1683*. Copenhagen.

Sachsse, Christoph & Florian Tennstedt 1980. *Geschichte der Armenfürsorge in Deutschland vom Spätmittelalter bis zum 1. Weltkrieg*. Stuttgart: Kohlhammer.

Schulze, Winfried 1987. *Vom Gemeinnutz zum Eigennutz. Über den Normenwandel in der ständischen Gesellschaft der frühen Neuzeit*. München: Stiftung Historisches Kolleg.

Schwartz, Robert M. 1988. *Policing the Poor in Eighteenth Century France*. Chapel Hill: University of North Carolina Press London.

Secher, V.A. (ed.) 1891-94. *Corpus Constitutionæ Daniæ. Forordninger, Recesser og andre kongelige Breve Danmarks Lovgivning vedkommende, 1558-1660*. Copenhagen.

Sellin, Thorsten 1944. *Pioneering in Penology. The Amsterdam Houses of Correction in the Sixteenth and Seventeenth Centuries*. Philadelphia: University of Pennsylvania Press.

Statistiske Oplysninger om Staden Kjøbenhavn 1881. 2. hæfte, Copenhagen: Københavns Magistrat.

Thestrup, Poul 1971. *The Standard of Living in Copenhagen: some methods of measurement 1730-1800*. Copenhagen: University of Copenhagen.

Trier, Herman 1913-15. 'Fattigvæsensplanen af 1799'. *Historiske Meddelelser om København*. 1st series, vol. 4. Copenhagen, pp. 1-56.

Villadsen, Kaspar 2004. *Det sociale arbejdes genealogi. Om kampen for at gøre fattige og udstødte til frie mennesker*. Copenhagen: Hans Reitzel.

Voght, Kasper 1798. *Over Hamborgs Fattigvæsen – med nogle Anmærkninger om Fattigvæsenet i Almindelighed af Johannes Boye*. Copenhagen.

Woolf, Stuart 1986. *The Poor in Western Europe in the Eighteenth and Nineteenth Centuries*. London: Methuen.

NOTES

1   Voght 1798, p. 84.

2   Sachsse & Tennstedt 1980, pp. 101 f. Endres 1976, p. 223. Lindemann 1990, p. 53.

3   Sachsse & Tennstedt 1980. Jütte 1994, pp. 143-56.

4   Woolf 1986, p. 6.

5   Malling 1840, pp. 68 f.

6   Malling & Hjort 1801, p. 106.

7   Thestrup 1971, pp. 23, 136-43. Christensen 1912, pp. 497-526. *Statistiske Oplysninger* 1881, pp. 8 f.

8   Christensen 1919-20, pp. 348 f.

9   Thestrup 1971, pp. 23, 136-43.

10 Lund 1795, pp. 7 f.

11 Rubin 1879, p. 46.

12 Pontoppidan 1793, p. 231.

13 Callisen 1809, pp. 406 f., 413.

14 In a letter from *Trinitatis Sogns Plejekommission* (The relief commission of Trinitatis parish) from 1778, this social group is particularly mentioned and their characteristics explained. Rigsarkivet (The Danish National Archives), Danske Kancelli F74-d: 1778-79 Kommissionen ang. Fattigvæsenet i København.

15 Cowan 1998, pp. 152-55.

16 Lund 1795, pp. 7 f.

17 Cowan 1998, p. 153.

18 North European economists and civil servants expressed these views on numerous occasions during the 18th century, see e.g. Lis & Soly 1979, p. 117. Sachsse & Florian 1980, p. 97.

19 Woolf 1986, pp. 6, 13. Fairchilds 1984.

20 The Act of 18 October 1698 concerning poor relief in Copenhagen.

21 Bruun 1890, pp. 284 f.

22 Københavns Stadsarkiv (Copenhagen City Archives) MC 387: Københavns Magistrats Kollegiebreve 1731, Report of 28 December 1731 from Chief of Police Erik Torm to *Københavns Magistrat*.

23 Københavns Stadsarkiv, FV 132A: 1782-85 Dokumenter vedr. Almindelig Hospital, Abel Cathrines Stiftelse, Uldmagasinet og Friskolerne (I. Diverse vedr. betlere og fattigfogeder).

24 Københavns Stadsarkiv, FV 124A: Partikulære Dokumenter 1738-1789 (I. Sager vedr. tiggere 1738-89).

25 Rigsarkivet, Danske Kancelli D20-4: Sjællandske Tegnelser 1705-06, no. 237 & 239.

26 Christensen 1976, p. 169.

27 Ehrencron-Müller 1950, p. 178.

28 Heiberg 1793, p. 100.

29 'Betlernes Opbringelse' 1791, *Skilderie af vore Tider*, p. 45.

30 Pontoppidan 1793, p. 264.

31 Report from *Fattigkommissionen på Konventhuset*, 17 September 1738 to *Fattigdirektionen*, and the following report from the Poor Board, 2 May 1739 to *Danske Kancelli*. Rigsarkivet, Danske Kancelli D21-82: Koncepter og Indlæg til Sjællandske Tegnelser 1739, no. 601-610.

32 Rigsarkivet, Danske Kancelli D19-49: 1731 Koncepter og Indlæg til Sjællandske Registre, no. 330.

33 Cowan 1998, p. 169.

34 Heiberg 1793, pp. 57-63.

35 Pontoppidan 1793, p. 211. Københavns Stadsarkiv, FV no. 136a: 1779 Dokumenter vedk. Almindelig Hospital mv. Plejedirektionens Dokumenter (I. Sager vedr. betlere og fattigfogeder mv.), Report from Claus Meden, warden at *Almindelig Hospital* to *Københavns Magistrat*, 10 February 1779.

36 Riegels 1786, pp. 8 f.

37 In the archives of the Copenhagen poor law authorities can be found several documents on homeless children and groups of siblings wandering around town. København Stadsarkiv, FV 124-127 Partikulære Dokumenter 1709-1800.

38 Geremek 1994, p. 44. Cowan 1998, p. 157.

39 Kolderup-Rosenvinge 1824, Kong Christian 2.s. Ordinantz eller saakaldte verdslige lov: Om Fattige siuge Mendiske Gudtz Almösse tage.

40 Geremek 1994, pp. 120-41. Dahlerup 1979, pp. 198-202.

41 Jensen 2004, p. 296.

42 King Christians III's first Copenhagen Statute. Rørdam 1883, p. 7.

43 Cowan 1998, pp. 162 f. Schwartz 1988, pp. 14 ff.

44 Vedtægt om de Husarme. Nielsen 1884, p. 77.

45 Letter to *Københavns Magistrat*, that begging in the streets from now on is prohibited, 28 February 1576, Nielsen 1872, p. 462.

46 Letter to *lensmændene* of Zealand 1599, to *lensmændene* all over Denmark in 1602 and to *lensmændene* in Zealand 1613. Secher 1891-94, pp. 75, 143 and 403.

47 Sellin 1944, pp. 20-30, 87. Olsen 1978, p. 26.

48 Royal mandate to the clergy, the mayor and the council in Copenhagen, that they shall enter into an agreement on an ordinance concerning the relief of the poor in Copenhagen (1630). Nielsen 1874, p. 786. The poor ordinance of 10 April 1631.

49 Christian IV's recess from 27 February 1643. Secher 1903, vol. 5, p. 319.

50 Royal letter to *rigshovmesteren*, that the beggars should be transported to the Plague House to be questioned (1650). Nielsen 1882, vol. 5, pp. 293-94.

51 Ordinance on beggars. Royal letter to the mayor and council of Copenhagen. Nielsen 1882, vol. 5, pp. 337-38.

52 Act on the Copenhagen poor relief of 18 October 1698, and Act of 24 September 1708 'on relations with beggars, poor children, worthy paupers and vagrants in Copenhagen, thus also on alms for their provision.'

53 Act of 24 September 1708 'on relations with beggars …'

54 Løgstrup 1970, p. 70.

55 Bärens 1799b, vol. 1, pp. 66-89.

56 Københavns Stadsarkiv, FV 134: Dokumenter vedk. Almindelig Hospital, Abel Cathrines stiftelse, Uldmagasinet og Friskolerne (Vedr. Kommissionssagen mod inspektør Meden), The former steward of *Almindelig Hospital*, Sørens Hempel's letter to *Københavns Magistrat*, 30 June 1791.

57 Rigsarkivet, Danske Kancelli D21-82: Koncepter og Indlæg til Sjællandske Tegnelser 1739, no. 601-610.

58 Løgstrup 1970, p. 78. Ordinance concerning the military as well as the civil poor's provision in Copenhagen, 8 February 1734.

59 Københavns Stadsarkiv, FV 128B: 1708-1846 Fattigvæsenets Styrelse. Underdanigst Betænkning om Betleriet at hæmme, by Søren Hempel.

60 Pontoppidan 1793, pp. 206 f.

61 Rigsarkivet, Danske Kancelli D21-82: 1739 Koncepter og Indlæg til Sjællandske Tegnelser, no. 601-610.

62 Københavns Stadsarkiv, FV 128B: 1708-1846 Fattigvæsenets Styrelse. Underdanigst Betænkning om Betleriet at hæmme, by Søren Hempel.

63 Rigsarkivet, Danske Kancelli D21-18: Koncepter og Indlæg til Sjællandske Tegnelser 1714, no. 48, Report from *Fattigkommissionen på Konventhuset* to *Fattigdirektionen*.

64 Københavns Stadsarkiv, FV 133A: 1787-90 Dokumenter vedr. Almindelig Hospital, Abel Cathrines Stiftelse, Uldmagasinet og Friskolerne (I. Diverse sager vedr. betlere og fattigfogeder), Report from Inspector Claus Meden of *Almindelig Hospital* to *Københavns Magistrat*, 18 May 1789.

65 Københavns Stadsarkiv, FV 142A: Betænkning og Indstilling af 29.5.1832 til kgl. danske Kancelli om Ladegaardens Indretning fra 1 Okt. 1832. Fra Fattigvæsenets Direktion ved Overpræsident Kierulff, p. 28.

66 It should be noted, that the new arrangement and the new ordinance of 16 November 1771 did not make the Act of 24 September 1708 obsolete.

67 Hansen 1916, vol. 1, pp. 254-78. Ribov 1971 (available at The Royal Library, Copenhagen).

68 Hansen 1915-16, pp. 503-15.

69 Rescript to *Københavns Magistrat* 10 April 1762; Town hall placard concerning a tax, to be put on the land register in Copenhagen for the payment of the expenses of the poor relief, 13 August 1764; Bill concerning a poor tax in Copenhagen, 9 March 1814; Bill concerning the poor tax in Copenhagen, 20 October 1815.

70 Rescript to *Københavns Magistrat*, 4 April 1781 to say that it should take over the management of poor relief in Copenhagen.

71 Københavns Stadsarkiv, FV 128B: 1708-1846 Fattigvæsenets Styrelse, Magistratens Forestilling om Kjøbenhavns Fattigvæsen og underliggende Stiftelser af 21de Martii 1782, pp. 68, 79 f.

72 Bärens 1799b, vol. 1, pp. 66-89.

73 Hansen 2004, pp. 10 ff.

74 Porter 2000, p. 263.

75 *Nyeste Skilderie af Kjøbenhavn* 1808, no. 41, p. 645 and no. 43, p. 676.

76 See for example Schulze 1987. van Leeuwen 2002, pp. 40-42.

77 Markussen 1995, p. 58.

78 Endres 1976, p. 226.

79 Pontoppidan 1793, p. 293.

80 Op. cit. p. 275.

81 Op. cit. p. 278.

82 Trier 1913-15. Jørgensen 1982, pp. 31-107. Rescript 15 September 1779, 'that those who in Copenhagen receive poor and hospital money and are able to work should be spinning wool for *Guldhuset* [the Gold House, a manufacture in Copenhagen]'.

83 Bärens 1792, p. 9.

84 Henningsen 2004, pp. 3-28.

85 Sachsse & Tennstedt 1980, p. 126. Lindemann 1990, pp. 135-76.

86 E.g. Augsburg in 1782-83, Berlin in 1774, Hannover in 1785, Lübeck in 1784, Lüneburg in 1776, Mainz in 1786, Strasbourg in 1767 and Vienna in 1784. Lindemann 1990, p. 111.

87 Bärens 1799b, p. 85. The Danish historian Gerda Bonderup erroneously claims in a work from 2002 that this plan was drafted by a commission in 1787, as she confuses the 1798 commission with an earlier commission. Bonderup 2002.

88 To me it seems rather strange when Bonderup in the above-mentioned work claims that 'the humanitarian tendencies of the Enlightenment were not reflected in the public poor relief system'. Op. cit. p. 176.

89 Bärens 1799a, p. 63.

90 *Kongelig approberet Plan for Fattigvæsenets bedre Indretning og Bestyrelse i Staden Kiøbenhavn og dens Forstæder, 2 July 1799*, § § 61, 63, 65.

91 Bärens 1799a, p. 87.

92 Op. cit. p. 41.

93 Elvius & Rist 1891, pp. 29 f.

94 Villadsen 2004, p. 66.

Jørgen Mikkelsen

Poor relief in provincial towns in the Kingdom of Denmark and the Duchy of Schleswig, ca. 1700-1850

A comparison of the legislation and the economic, social and administrative conditions in the individual parts of the Absolutist monarchy reveals many similarities and differences. By mirroring the conditions in the individual areas in each other, one can often gain many interesting insights into inconsistencies as well as sources of inspiration and parallel development. In this article, I will mainly concentrate on provincial towns in the Danish Kingdom, but I will also involve the Duchy of Schleswig to illustrate this 'mirror effect'.

The study can be regarded as a combination of social and administration history. The main problem complex is how the local town authorities administered the social legislation of Absolutism in practice. Specifically, it is about how the economic basis for the poor relief system was procured, who received poor relief, how the relief was paid and what demands were made in this connection. In addition I will look at the attitudes of the authorities and social polemicists, and the changes that occurred in this sphere. A subject of special interest is the change in attitude that can be seen in the first decades of the 19th century in the trend to concentrate the poor in special institutions with strict discipline. The article however is not just a study of public poor relief. The extent and nature of private assistance will also be discussed, and in this connection, I will look at how the two forms of relief could supplement each other.

The article is based exclusively on literature and therefore inevitably reflects the central points in the research that has been done until now. A particular problem in this connection is that many aspects are examined in depth for only a single or a few towns, and in some cases it can be problematic to generalise on the basis of these examples. On balance, however, it must be admitted that urban poor relief has attracted much interest – in any case in comparison with many other subjects pertinent to Danish towns during Absolutism. For instance many substantial specific results about urban poor relief can be found in Harald Jørgensen's dissertation, *Studier over det offentlige Fattigvæsens historiske Udvikling i Danmark i det 19. Aarhundrede* (1940), which in spite of its relatively great age is still the most important reference work on poor relief in the Kingdom before 1900 – especially with regard to legislation and the ideas underlying the various laws. Another central work is Lars Henningsen's book *Fattigvæsenet i de sønderjyske købstæder 1736-1841* (1978), which contains meticulous comparative analyses of the administration of poor relief in the towns of Schleswig, and in addition gives a splendid insight into the changes in attitude to the poor that occurred during the period. Poor relief is also mentioned in most Danish town histories, but the extent of this treatment varies greatly. Likewise, there are a number of articles about the poor relief system in the local history annuals. Some of the best analyses of the subject are found in books and articles about the towns of Odense, Aarhus, Kalundborg and Elsinore, and this article therefore contains particularly many references to these accounts. With regard to private assistance, I have benefited from a new, unpublished dissertation by Tine Bro about the charitable institutions in provincial towns.[1]

Towards a public system of poor relief

The oldest traces of Poor Laws in Denmark are found in King Christian II's laws from 1521-1522, where for the first time in Denmark a distinction between deserving and undeserving poor can be observed.[2] The first category, consisting of sick and disabled people, was to be provided with a special badge to wear on their chests which showed that they had the right to beg. The undeserving poor – i.e. the beggars who had the use of their limbs – were to be chased away from where they lived unless they got work. The principles in these regulations were repeated and amplified in several later laws from the 16th and 17th centuries. For instance it became possible to set the undeserving poor to forced labour.[3] In the 1587 ordinance on begging, however, a way was opened to allow people who had been the victims of fire, shipwreck or other misfortune to be provided with a so-called 'begging letter' by the local authorities. This letter gave people permission to collect money for one year to get on their feet again. Several town histories mention examples of the use of such documents in the 17th century.[4]

In the Middle Ages, the Catholic church in Denmark was responsible for large-scale help for the poor, and it was very common to give alms, as this was considered to be a means to achieve salvation. Earlier, it was generally assumed that social services suffered a perceptible blow in connection with the Protestant Reformation in 1536, when the Crown took over all church property and estates, and Lutheran theologians rejected the notion that good deeds were important for salvation. In recent decades however, several scholars have argued that there was greater continuity between the conditions during Catholicism and Protestantism. Among other things, they have pointed out that the Danish Church Ordinance of 1539 (which laid down the administrative framework for the future Danish Church) as well as the large code of statutes, *Koldingske Reces,* from 1558, and Bishop Peder Palladius's journal of pastoral visitations from 1538-1543 all, directly or indirectly, contain clear admonitions about the individual's duty to help his neighbour.[5] In addition some of the former monasteries and convents were converted into foundations for the sick, the handicapped (especially the mentally ill, the blind, the deaf-and-dumb, and the disabled) and other people in distress. But even the Franciscan hospital in Odense, which according to its charter was to admit residents from the whole diocese of Funen, had only 60-70 places around 1570.[6]

During the 16th and 17th centuries, a number of social institutions were also established on the initiative of members of the nobility or town citizens. Tine Bro could trace a total of 32 charitable institutions established in the provincial towns of the Kingdom between 1500 and 1700, and in 1672 there were charitable institutions in all nine provincial centres, in nine of the 15 regional centres and in nine of the 40 local centres. As could be expected, the average size was greatest in the large towns; for instance charitable institutions in the provincial centres had room for a total of about 300 residents at the end of the 17th century, while the institutions in the regional and local centres could hold about 200 and about 70 people, respectively.[7] The total number of residents for all institutions was thus a little under 600, equivalent to the population of one of the smallest market towns of the time. When one further takes into consideration that a number of institutions also admitted people from the country, it is clear that these institutions were able to give shelter only to an extremely small section of the population of the towns. However it must be added that some town residents also benefited from the many endowed local charities. These were typically established by a prosperous person who set aside a sum of money for the poor in a town or a parish and decided that the annual interest should be allotted to a fixed number of people. Some grants were given for life, while in other cases they were one-off disbursements.[8]

FIG. 1.

Gråbrødre Kloster *(Franciscan monastery) in Viborg is one of the building complexes that was converted into a charitable institution for poor, old and disabled people shortly after the Reformation. According to the first charter from 1583, two-thirds of the residents were to come from the town, while the remaining places were reserved for people living in the diocese of Viborg. In 1739, some accommodation for mentally ill patients was also established in the buildings. Incidentally,* Gråbrødre Kloster *is still used as a charitable institution for seven elderly residents.*

The charitable institutions were self-governing institutions, but in accordance with their charters, they were often administered by local or regional officials. And in the cases where the charter did not limit the target group to people from specific families, occupations or the like, but included the destitute in general, a charitable institution in practice was often regarded as being part of the public poor relief system.

Until the beginning of the 18th century, however, the public poor relief system in most of the towns of the Kingdom seems to have been extremely limited. In many places it has presumably been just about emptying the town's poor boxes (in the churches and ale-houses etc.) a couple of times a year to disburse the money in them to some of the most destitute. In other places, though, the poor relief system also owned various buildings and land that could be rented out to town citizens and in this way produce some income.

In the years around 1630 meanwhile, steps were taken to organise the system much more efficiently in two of the largest provincial towns, Odense and Ribe, and the same was the case in Copenhagen.[9] These years were characterised by high prices, and there was social unrest in several towns, which was probably an important motive for the reorganisation of the poor relief system in the three towns. The decision was made in these towns to supplement the existing funds for public assistance with a regular collection from the citizens.

At a meeting in Ribe town hall in 1630, the citizens and officials as well as the *lensmand* (the noble holder of the fief) and the bishop agreed that in future a sum of money for poor relief would be collected four times a year from the citizens who put down their names as contributors. A disbursement would be made once a week and the money was to go to the people who were registered on a special list of the needy as well as the grammar school pupils. In the first year, 229 contributors were registered, among them merchants, tradesmen and officials. But the numbers quickly declined and during the war in 1643-1645 the voluntary contributions fell away completely. However the weekly disbursement of money was successfully continued with the help of other poor relief income, but the number of recipients was reduced. On the other hand, the ambition to eliminate begging had to be abandoned, and in 1647 the town corporation decided to make 200 new beggar badges.[10] While the arrangement in Ribe was thus based on voluntary contributions, the municipal authorities and the *lensmand* in Odense introduced a proper poor-rate – incidentally, after strong opposition from the town artisans. At the same time, begging was prohibited. The arrangement existed until 1659 when it broke down in connection with the Swedish occupation of the town and extortionate taxation.[11]

The organisation of the poor relief system in the towns of the Kingdom after 1708

On 24 September 1708 two major ordinances were issued regarding the organisation of the public assistance and a prohibition on begging in the Danish Kingdom. One ordinance concentrated on Copenhagen while the other was divided into two – very different – chapters concerning the towns and rural parishes.

The provisions for the towns had clear similarities with the arrangements that had been made in Odense and Ribe. For instance, it was decided that a book was to be prepared in all towns in which 'every subject' (in practice probably: every head of household) according to his financial situation was to register what he 'as a voluntary gift' would pay for the poor annually. In addition all clergymen and civilian officials were to pay a tax of 1 % of their income. The amounts were to be collected by a special authority, the poor inspectorate, consisting of a member of the corporation, a clergyman, and two citizens and they were also in charge of a weekly disbursement of alms. The people who did not pay what they had promised before the end of the year were to have their names read out from the pulpit; other sanctions were not mentioned. The ordinance is more verbose with regard to the shortcomings and failings of the poor. For instance it was clearly emphasised that alms should not be given to people who were capable of doing work or who were themselves to blame for their poverty on account of drunkenness or other vices. Likewise, the poor inspectorate was to take away assistance from people who were guilty of improper behaviour and who continued with this in spite of warnings from the inspectors. Finally the ordinance has a number of paragraphs about the education of poor children. For example, it appears that the inspectors should make sure that academically interested boys should go to grammar school while the others were to be apprenticed to a tradesman.

The vague wording of the ordinance about the collection of the poor relief money quickly proved to be a major problem in many towns. This was especially because the ordinance was issued at a time of profound crisis when many people – the better off people too – could have difficulty finding a financial surplus to help the poorest segment of the population. In the years from 1709 to 1720 when Denmark was involved in the Great Nordic War, the annual amount of voluntary subscriptions in Aarhus fell steadily from 712 *rigsdaler* to 326.[12] It was perhaps better in Assens, where as early as 1709 they resorted to a tax assessment of some citizens, because in the opinion of the municipal authorities these had not put down their names for a large enough sum as a voluntary gift.[13] It is not known if something similar was done in other towns at that time. In 1734 meanwhile, the legislation was tightened up. The town authorities were given express authority to assess 'unwilling residents' and at the same time they got the right to seize goods from residents who had repeatedly refused to pay the stipulated amount. Several local history accounts also write about the introduction of a poor-rate during the 1730s.[14] But several of them also relate that unpaid taxes of long standing were general, or that the local authorities could be very reluctant to undertake seizure of goods.[15]

In 1722, the rural dean in Aarhus wrote in his collection book that the citizens preferred to pay the needy directly rather than pay the poor-rate to the authorities.[16] The dislike of (or rather perhaps indifference to?) the public poor relief system did not abate with time, if anything it got worse. In any case, the town's voluntary subscriptions reached an absolute low point in 1755 when only 131 *rigsdaler* was collected, i.e. 40 % of the amount in 1720. The lists of contributors in the 1750s also show that even the *byfoged* (the town judge and chief of police) and several prominent business men were either in arrears or had failed to put their names down for a contribution, and plainly this cannot have been motivating for the ordinary citizens. It was not until 1769 that the town corporation introduced tax assessment of the 'unwilling residents', and even that happened only after a direct order from the *stiftamtmand* (the county governor) and the bishop, who had the overall supervision of the town's poor relief system. However, some citizens refused to pay as they maintained that no payment for the poor could be demanded from them against their will! And when the corporation apparently dared not take a strong line with the impudent citizens, the poor relief income remained just as low as ever. But in 1793 the income was more than quadrupled in one fell swoop, and the new level was successfully maintained for the next number of years. The good result in 1793 was achieved after great efforts from the town poor inspectors who went from house to house to put pressure on the individual heads of households. This time, though, the initiative also seems to have come from the *stiftamtmand* and the bishop who had both personally put their names down for quite a large sum for the poor.[17]

Odense too had great problems getting the citizens to make their contributions and often only about half of the assessed amount was received. After having to eat into the capital of the poor relief system for several years, in 1759 the poor inspectorate decided that in future they would not disburse a greater amount than came in. The number of permanent recipients who until then had been about 180-200

FIG. 2.

Beggars were a characteristic element in the life of Danish towns and villages in the early modern
period. Therefore it is only natural that a few beggars appear on some of the drawings found in the
topographical works from the 18th century. This is a part of a picture of the market town Hobro in
Eastern Jutland.

was reduced to about 125 (at the time the town had a population of over 5,000).[18] The retrenchment continued in the following decades in such a heavy-handed fashion that taxation could gradually be reduced to under the half. The total expenses of the poor relief system in 1790 amounted to only 30-50 % of the total in the 1750s. However this was not because the need for help was smaller – on the contrary. The rising prices for basic foodstuffs at the end of the 18th century in any case must have been a great problem for the least-favoured section of the town population. In the 1770s there were also vehement complaints that beggars from the town were pestering the rural parishes around Odense. An investigation was then made of the real need for poor relief in Odense. This showed that 236 people needed help and that they needed annual assistance totalling about 1,500 *rigsdaler* (at the time the poor relief disbursements were ca. 700 *rigsdaler*). The municipal authorities tried to solve the problem by urging the citizens to supplement the poor-rate with voluntary contributions, but without result. Some citizens refused directly by referring to the extent of the begging. In 1791, the poor inspectors once more drew attention to the problem and proposed that the town should procure the necessary amount by the introduction of property tax.[19] The proposal was presented to all the guilds in the town. They rejected it completely, but several of them now supported the idea of making a voluntary contribution in addition to the poor-rate. The *stiftamtmand* and the bishop accepted this solution, but put extraordinary pressure on the population – among other things by announcing that lists would be printed showing what each person had given. The result was overwhelming, as people put their names down for a total of 1,759 *rigsdaler*. But already in the following year the income again began to show a slowly declining trend.

In Kalundborg too, the poor inspectorate made a point of having a surplus in the accounts. In this medium-sized town with 1,300-1,400 inhabitants, a sum of 400-500 *rigsdaler* was disbursed annually from the 1730s to the 1780s and the number of alms recipients was about 70, in any case in the 1770s and 1780s. But when the voluntary gifts declined steadily in the last decades of the century, it was decided in the 1790s to make a drastic reduction in the permanent assistance – to just under 300 *rigsdaler* divided among about 50 poor people.[20] A few others though could possibly receive acute, temporary assistance – and this was also probably the case in most other towns.

These examples clearly show that conditions for the poor in the 18th century could vary greatly from town to town, and indeed from decade to decade too. A comparison of the three towns mentioned must take into account that Odense had four times as many inhabitants as Kalundborg, while Aarhus had three times as many. So undoubtedly they had many more actual poor people than Kalundborg. In light of this, the amount of assistance paid out to the poor in Kalundborg until the beginning of the 1790s is striking. In some of the years in the 1780s, the total disbursement of alms in Kalundborg was perhaps even larger than in Odense! The favourable situation for the people of Kalundborg is connected with the fact that the town poor relief system was quite well off. From olden times, it was in possession of large land areas that could be rented out. And through sensible investments of the frequent surplus on the annual accounts, quite a considerable interest income was gained in time. The income from rent and interest together made up 49 % of the total income of the poor relief system in the period 1720-1770, whereas voluntary gifts accounted for only 23 %.[21]

When conditions in the individual towns are compared, it should also be noted that there were great differences in the extent of the assistance that was given outside the actual public poor relief system. An example of a town, which in this connection was very well off, was Elsinore where conditions have been thoroughly studied by Nynne Helge. This town with just over 5,000 inhabitants developed a public poor relief system during the 1730s that functioned well, and between 1737 and 1803 its income increased steadily from 1,644 to 5,458 *rigsdaler*.[22] This was due to a relatively efficient collection of poor-rates, good income from interest and especially frequent endowments from private individuals and town guilds. The poor relief system could therefore afford to treble its disbursements between 1737 and 1797. The number of permanent recipients though was quite modest, 60-100, but in addition some assistance was probably given to people in acute need. Elsinore also had a large charitable institution, namely one of the monasteries that had been converted into a social institution after the Reformation in 1536.

Of greater significance however was the special poor relief fund linked to the The Sound Tolls administration. In connection with foreign ships passing the town and paying Sound Tolls to the Danish state, the ships also had to pay a fee to this local fund. Shipping passing the town increased up through the 18th century and especially at the end of the century, and the annual income of the poor relief fund therefore also increased – from 1,500-2,000 *rigsdaler* in the 1730s, 1740s and 1750s to nearly 7,000 *rigsdaler* in 1794.[23] These proceeds were divided among a large number of recipients; thus both the public poor relief system and the charitable institution got a fixed amount, and this was also the case for the German church, the hospital, the three schools for children of poor parents, the two midwives etc. Moreover, the customs house poor relief fund had a large disbursement once a year for people of limited means in Elsinore and other parts of North Zealand. Random checks show that at the end of the 18th century about 500 people a year benefited from this assistance – that is 5-8 times more people than those who got permanent help from the public poor relief system in the town.

18th century alms recipients

The ordinance from 1708 had no criteria for recipients of poor relief in the towns or how the poor inspectorates should prioritise the needy when it was impossible to meet all the needs. On the other hand the ordinance gave instructions about the categories of country people who could get alms. Here assistance should first and foremost be given to the 'blind, the bedridden and those who cannot earn anything at all', and then to 'young orphaned children' who were to be put into care. Finally those who 'on account of bad health, many young children or other legitimate reasons' could not earn enough to survive should be given 'some help'.

These guidelines seem to have been used in the towns in practice, and in Odense and Aarhus, the poor were simply divided into a number of classes according to their need.[24] Everywhere elderly women living alone seem to have been dominant among alms recipients, whereas very few married couples and men living alone are found in the 18th century lists of those entitled to assistance.[25] This is attributable to the fact that generally there were more women than men in the oldest age group, but there was also a great difference between the sexes with regard to their ability to support themselves when they were old and alone. Foster children are also mentioned in several town histories, and a story from Svendborg in 1733 indicates that children could be compulsorily removed from their families as early as that time. In any case, we hear about six poor children who got their food around the town because it was thought that the parents could not be trusted with money for their maintenance.[26]

This type of assistance – that a poor person was taken on by three to seven neighbours in turn – was quite common in the country in the 18th century and indeed far into the 19th century; such a person often had to eat dinner and supper at several different places during a week. Another possibility was that each of the poor people was instead allotted a quantity of barley and rye (and possibly malt, grain, peas or pork) from specified peasants; the poor then had to prepare the food themselves.[27]

In the towns, where money economy was more widespread, disbursement of money seems to have been the dominant form of assistance in the 18th century. However it should be noted that there are very few studies of this at present. One of the towns where we can follow the disbursement system over a long period is Viborg, where there is a poor relief journal from 1783 to 1810. In this town with ca. 2,500 inhabitants, the number of alms recipients for the vast majority of the years was 45-55, and normally new people could only be put on the list when someone died or moved away. However, it also happened that a woman was excluded because the poor inspectorate thought that the person in question was able to support herself. For that matter, exclusion could be just for the summer half-year, when it was easier to find casual work. In addition, the journal contains several examples of an alms recipient losing assistance for a short or long period because of bad behaviour, just in accordance with the spirit of the ordinance from 1708. Some cases were about drunkenness; in other cases the poor person had refused to share in sweeping the town squares or had not attended the funeral of another alms recipient.[28]

At the end of the 18th century the alms recipients in Viborg received 4-24 *skilling* a week, that is, 2-13 *rigsdaler* a year. This level corresponds quite well with figures from other towns. Hans Chr. Johansen for instance calculated that the poor in Odense in 1775 on average received ca. 6 *rigsdaler* a year, while the corresponding figure seems to have been ca. 7 *rigsdaler* in Kalundborg in the 1770s and 1780s and 7-9 *rigsdaler* in Aarhus in the years just after the reform of the collection system in 1793.[29] By way of comparison, Johansen notes that an unskilled worker at the end of the 18th century could probably earn ca. 50 *rigsdaler* a year. The comparison is weakened by the fact that many workers seem to have been unemployed for part of the year and that the typical worker had to maintain several people, while the typical recipients of poor relief only had to take care of themselves. But nevertheless the figures give a clear impression that it could indeed be very difficult for an alms recipient to manage for the money that came from the poor relief system alone. In a letter from 1791, the poor inspectorate in Odense also asserted that 4 *skilling* per day per person (i.e. ca. 15 *rigsdaler* a year) was the absolute minimum that could be given to the poor, if the person in question was to be kept from begging.[30]

As previously mentioned, Odense and the surrounding area seem to have been plagued by begging in these decades. In the neighbouring town of Svendborg, the practice of earlier years of giving begging badges to the deserving poor was contin-

FIG. 3.

When the number of recipients of public assistance in some Danish towns at the end of the 18th century
is compared with the population of the towns at that time, it can be seen that about 2-5 % of the inhabit-
ants got assistance from the authorities. The real number of people requiring help from others to survive
was much higher, and undoubtedly differed greatly from year to year, depending on the economic con-
ditions at the time. One of the few Danish researchers who has ventured to make an estimate of the total
number of poor people is Henrik Fangel. On the basis of extensive study of the archives, he estimated that
about 35 % of the population of Haderslev lived at subsistence level at the beginning of the 19th century
(Fangel 1975, p. 105). This is a drawing of one of the more curious characters among the poor inhabit-
ants of Haderslev ca. 1820.

ued in the 18th century when the money in the poor relief fund was inadequate.[31]
However it must also be presumed that many of the poor got the most essential of
their necessities through help from family and relations, including possibly other
guild members. In addition Hans Chr. Johansen has observed that when some of the
Odense poor died, their estates had considerable debts for staple goods with some of
the large shopkeepers in the town. Johansen believes that there must have been an
element of charity in this 'credit', as the shopkeepers probably knew that they had
little chance of getting their money.[32]

Even though it is not really alms, it should also be mentioned that it was seemingly quite common that in special crisis years with shortage of grain and high grain prices the public authorities purchased large amounts of grain in order either to make the grain available free of charge to the poor or sell it at a reduced price.[33] Such initiatives can very well have been motivated both by social considerations and the wish to avoid social unrest.

The Schleswig poor system of 1736

The ordinance of 1708 was valid only for the Danish Kingdom, but in several other parts of the monarchy similar initiatives were taken during the 18th century. In Norway this was in the form of diocesan decrees, first for Akershus and Bergen dioceses in 1741 and 1755 respectively, and later for Kristiansand and Trondheim dioceses in 1786 and 1790.[34] But some Norwegian towns did not get a proper public poor relief system until well into the 19th century.

The towns in the Duchy of Schleswig on the other hand got a common poor ordinance in 1736. This was two years after the tightening of the Poor Laws in the Kingdom of Denmark, and it is possible that the strong Pietistic currents of the time played an important role in both places. In any case, the Pietistic-oriented King Christian VI had very central significance for the establishment of the common system in Schleswig.[35] The ordinance of 1736 had many similarities with the 1708 ordinance in the Kingdom;[36] but the Schleswig ordinance laid down that the local authorities could assess the town inhabitants if the voluntary contributions proved to be inadequate (i.e. as had been possible in the Kingdom since 1734). Besides, the ordinance permitted towns that already had an independent poor relief system to continue with this, if they just complied with the spirit of the new legislation. This was the case in Friedrichstadt, Tönning, Haderslev and Flensburg.[37] In the other towns, the 1736 ordinance formed the basis for the future poor relief system. Lars Henningsen's comparative analysis of administrative practice in the various towns shows that there was great variation and that the central authorities more or less let the municipalities rule themselves – as was, incidentally, the case in many other spheres of the urban policy in the monarchy in the 18th century. Thus the extent to which the Schleswig towns used tax assessment differed greatly, but in most places a good amount was continually collected successfully, which was used for the weekly disbursement of money. The only real exception was Ærøskøbing, where – after an unsuccessful attempt to introduce voluntary contributions – they were content to let the poor collect alms from the other inhabitants every Saturday in the form of money, bread, beer and milk. It was not until the 1820s that this town got a proper public poor relief system.[38]

As in the towns in the Kingdom, the average disbursement of alms in the Duchy of Schleswig was too small for the poor to be able to live on it alone. It also seems to have been a general principle that the alms should never exceed the difference between what a person could earn and what was necessary to survive, as it was formulated in a book on poor relief from 1769.[39] And in Aabenraa, in any case, the expenses of the poor relief system were carefully matched to the level of income of the system, and therefore large reductions were sometimes made in the amount of the alms.[40]

In contrast to the towns in the Kingdom, several Schleswig towns were divided into two or three districts. Each of these got its own poor relief system, but there were often difficulties about cooperation between them. However the two districts in Haderslev decided to introduce a joint poor relief system in 1736 and this apparently worked well until 1759. At that time the town suffered a major fire, which meant that a great proportion of the taxpayers were exempted from paying tax. As a result a drastic reduction in the disbursement of alms had to be made, and it completely stopped in one of the districts for a time. It was not until 1834 that Haderslev again got a joint poor relief system for the two districts of the town.[41]

On the other hand, there are several examples that less serious crises could be managed in a way that benefited the poor. For instance this was the case during several periods with high prices and/or severe winters, when the town authorities in Tønder either bought up grain to reduce the price or made special collections for the poor.[42]

Work for the poor during mercantilism and the Enlightenment

In 1738 Roskilde town established a spinning mill with 20 spinning wheels and 10 reels. A spinning master from the Royal Spinning Mill in Copenhagen was employed as the daily leader, and it was her job to teach the female alms recipients of the town how to spin flax. But it was soon obvious that they could only manage to spin rough and uneven yarn that was difficult to sell. So when production proved to be completely uneconomic, the mill was closed down four years later.[43]

Similar undertakings were established in several other places in the Kingdom at the beginning and the middle of the 18th century. They were inspired by the mercantilistic idea that domestic production should increase in order to limit the need for imports, but it was also wished to make use of the labour of those who got public assistance. However, the operations made great losses and were therefore closed down after a few years.[44]

While efforts in the Kingdom to activate the poor probably all had local roots, the corporations in the Duchy of Schleswig in 1763 were presented with an initiative from above. They were issued with a decree – on which their opinions were sought – prescribing a proposal that, in future, alms could only be disbursed to completely incapacitated people as well as to the poor who could prove that they had worked in a factory or the like – and those who had worked most should get most alms![45] When the corporations voiced some misgivings about this, a new decree was issued in 1766 ordering the towns to arrange for work for the poor – for example by letting them spin flax or wool on behalf of the poor relief fund. Lars Henningsen's studies show that at least seven towns complied with the order – but, in the case of Haderslev, not until seven years after the decree had been issued. Four of the towns established spinning mills while the others let the poor work at home so that it was only necessary to buy and distribute raw materials, collect the finished products and pay wages for them. Some of the arrangements stopped after only a few years, while others lasted several decades. But there were losses everywhere because of production and marketing difficulties. The fact that spinning was generally hated among the workers and the payment was very poor was a great problem.[46]

In spite of the many fiascos, the spinning mill concept got a new impetus after 1780 when patriotic ideas found favour in both the Kingdom and the Duchy of Schleswig.[47] Even though the balance of trade was still in mind, more weight was put on the possibility of helping the poor to a better life by means of an 'offer of work'. This change in attitude should be seen in light of the new understanding that poverty could actually be created by society and that unemployment was not necessarily a person's own fault. The state therefore had an obligation to help all citizens to achieve a reliable means of support. Views of this kind can be seen in Montesqieu and afterwards in many texts from various parts of Europe, for instance in the French constitution of 1793.[48]

In Schleswig and Holstein we find these ideas in many texts from ca. 1780.[49] One of the most influential writers in the Duchies was Professor Aug. Chr. Heinrich Niemann, who wrote a sort of catechism for a better organisation of the poor relief system in 1792.[50] He argued for the necessity of investigating the individual needs of the poor, so that each individual could get the most appropriate help. He also attached great importance to preventive initiatives to avoid the complete impoverishment of the needy person. In Niemann's opinion, work was the most important form of poor relief, and he believed that alms should be disbursed only to the people who were completely helpless, because alms had the effect of making people passive. That is why Niemann was in favour of denying help to the able-bodied poor who did not want to work. On the other hand he hoped that the poor who accepted an 'offer of work' developed greater diligence and independence and in this way (again) became good citizens. He was also a strong supporter of work schools where children did not just learn theoretical skills, but also spent a lot of time on practical work that could instil in them a good work ethic.

Niemann was greatly inspired by the new poor relief system that Hamburg had implemented in 1788. In this, the town had been divided into five main districts, each consisting of 12 'poor districts' with an *Armenpfleger* (poor-guardian) in charge. This person had the job of keeping a close eye on the conditions of the poor, getting work for the unemployed and care for the sick. In addition he had to disburse the necessary alms and keep the leadership of the town continually informed about conditions. With his texts, Niemann inspired similar arrangements in various towns in Schleswig and Holstein, and in the course of a few decades, the *Armenpfleger*-institution had been introduced in nearly all the Schleswig towns.[51] It should be noted that this was done completely without intervention from higher authorities. As is clear from Peter Henningsen's article in this book, the Hamburg arrangement also inspired the 1799 Copenhagen plan for the poor. In contrast, the *Armenpfleger*-arrangement does not seem to have left any impression on the provincial towns in the Kingdom.

The Kingdom's poor relief regulations of 1803 in practice

In the Kingdom, it was probably mostly Copenhagen intellectuals who embraced the new ideas of the Enlightenment with regard to the nature of poverty, but a new tone could also be heard in the provinces. In a speech in 1788, the Odense Professor Ole Nicolai Bytzov declared that the unemployed too deserved respect, since 'the fault was not theirs'. He also suggested that Odense should introduce higher assistance, better education of poor children and the establishment of a workhouse where the unemployed could be given work. At the time, however, his words fell on deaf ears.[52]

By 1803 the Kingdom's towns and rural districts had meanwhile each been given a replacement for the old 1708 ordinance. The ideas of the Enlightenment had clearly coloured the two regulations – in spite of the fact that the texts must be regarded as a modernisation and clarification of the existing system rather than as a radical reform.

The new system for towns meant that the existing poor inspectorates were replaced by poor commissions, but these had almost the same composition as the inspectorates, as the posts in the commissions were to be filled by one or more parish clergymen, a member of the municipal corporation, the *byfoged* and two or more 'worthy' men. The bishop and the *stiftamtmand* (or another *amtmand*) continued to have the overall supervision of the poor relief system in a town. The regulations, however, gave much more specific guidelines for administration than hitherto. One of the central tasks was to prepare a complete public relief plan at the end of every year. This plan was to have a list of all the needy with information about their needs, condition and life until then. Those entitled to poor relief were divided into three classes, which accords quite well with the division in the 1708 ordinance in the chapter concerning poor relief in rural districts. However, it is remarkable that the second class now included not only orphaned children, but also children 'whose parents' intelligence, health or morals are such that the children's rearing and upbringing should not be entrusted to them'.[53] And with regard to the poor in the third class (the people 'who because of infirmity, many children, increasing age or other such reasons are unable to earn as much as is needed for their own or their children's bare necessities'), the poor relief system was ordered to get them suitable work at normal wages.[54]

The points about the financing of the poor relief system were also of great importance. Here taxation played a greater role than heretofore; for instance a property tax is mentioned as one of the possible sources of income. In addition it was emphasised that the assistance plan was to form the basis for the tax assessment of citizens; the starting point could no longer be the amount of cash in hand at the disbursement of alms. The interest in education of the ordinary people during the Enlightenment was also evident, because the poor regulations required that all children in public care went to school from the age of 6 or 7, and that they got the money for school material from the poor relief fund. In addition a poor commission was authorised to remove a child from its parents or foster parents if these did not ensure that the child went to school.

The most controversial points in the regulations however were those that dealt with *where* exactly the poor were entitled to assistance. Generally speaking this question was not touched upon in the 1708 ordinance, but a 1736 decree established that a person had the right to assistance in his/her current place of residence only after he/she had lived there for two years. That was changed in the new regulations, which meant that a town was obliged to give assistance not only to the needy who were born in the town, but also to the people 'who in the last three years, either continuously or at least for longer periods than in any other place, have had a fixed address there and have made their living legally[!]'. This wording, which is also found in the regulations for the rural districts, understandably gave rise to many interpretations – particularly by poor commissioners who with all their might tried to minimise their assistance obligations and did everything they could to pass the task over to other parishes where the poor person might have lived. The archives of the poor commissions and the counties from the first half of the 19th century contain numerous cases of this nature.[55] The legislators had to make clarifications and adjustments of the provisions several times. In 1817, for instance, it was emphasised that a poor person who was entitled to assistance was to get this in the town or rural parish where he or she had most recently had an unbroken stay of at least three years. In 1839 this time limit was increased to five years – undoubtedly in order to limit the constant inter-municipal conflicts about the obligation to give assistance.

One of the intentions of the 1803 poor ordinance was to make it possible for the local authorities to disburse more poor relief than before. Local history literature also gives a very clear impression that this was the case. In Odense, the disbursement amounts were more than trebled all at once, and in Kalundborg, almost a trebling occurred between 1803 and 1805.[56] And even in Aarhus where the weekly amount disbursed had been increased by more than 50 % between 1795 and 1803, a further increase of 64 % was made between 1803 and 1805. At the same time, both the number of recipients as well as the average amount of alms increased; the latter increased from ca. 7½ to over 11 *rigsdaler* a year.[57] In Kalundborg and Elsinore too there was a substantial increase in the average assistance to the permanent alms recipients; in Elsinore, the amount even went up to 26 *rigsdaler* (calculated for the years 1804-08 together).[58] Poul Thestrup's meticulous study of conditions in Odense shows however that condition certainly did not continue to be so rosy. The war years 1807-14 were characterised by drastic price increases and even though the weekly portions were increased, they could not keep pace with the prices at all, so in 1813, the real value of the disbursed money assistance in the town was only about 10 % of the assistance in 1804. On the other hand, the years after the peace settlement in 1814 were characterised by a sharp fall in prices, so in 1824 the real value of the money assistance was again almost up to the 1804 level.[59] Just as in the 18th century, conditions for the poor could undergo very great changes in the course of a short time.

The 1803 regulations are pervaded with the view that as far as possible poor relief should be given in kind instead of in monetary form. *Amtmand* P.C. Stemann, who was one of the main architects of the 1803 ordinance, argued that payment in kind was particularly called for in towns, partly because of the high prices for the necessities of life and partly because the town poor could all too easily be tempted to spend money on 'coffee, spirits and such luxury items'.[60] There are a number of specific studies of the method of assistance in the towns of the Kingdom in the 19th century, but they show a very varied pattern. Some places continued to give monetary assistance almost exclusively, while other towns had made assistance in kind the absolute dominant form of assistance within a few years. This was the case in Slagelse, where the poor commission at the beginning of the 19th century was led by one of the most enthusiastic people in the Danish poor relief system at that time, the Rev. Hans Bastholm.[61] It is also conceivable that the galloping inflation during the 1807-14 war got more towns to make greater efforts to have assistance in kind because it was hoped that in this way an increase in begging could be avoided. In any case the poor commission in Odense in 1812 began to supplement the disbursement of money with a supply of rye bread and peat (and in certain periods, pork, peas, potatoes and butter too).[62]

Assistance in kind could however also have forms other than the simple supply of basic goods. For instance in Kalundborg in 1805 a Madam Petersen was employed to prepare a daily midday meal for 28 poor people, who in return had a certain amount deducted from their assistance. But the arrangement was discontinued after a couple of years.[63] In other places, such as Roskilde and Køge, a large number of the poor were allocated food in the houses of town citizens in turn. In Roskilde this arrangement also included the people who were housed in the town poorhouse around 1820.[64] And according to a statement from the governor of Funen in 1816, nearly every house owner in Svendborg had some poor people to feed on certain weekdays.[65]

During the 1820s, meanwhile, the pendulum seems to have swung back again. Even in towns such as Slagelse and Ringsted, where assistance in kind had been in the forefront up to then, more emphasis was beginning to be placed on monetary help. As Harald Jørgensen points out, there could be great logistical problems in dealing with widespread assistance in kind in a town where the population and the number of the poor were clearly growing.[66] But perhaps another factor could be the fact that the prices of grain and other foodstuffs were again beginning to rise at the end of the 1820s, so from the point of view of the local authorities, it could be more expedient to disburse poor relief in money. In any case, monetary assistance became the completely dominant form of assistance in the towns during the 19th century.[67]

In his analysis of the poor relief system in Kalundborg up to 1840, Tyge Krogh has pointed out another striking shift in poor assistance, namely that the clientele receiving alms changed far more quickly than previously. The number of people on permanent help fell from 61 in 1804 to 55 in 1838, but in the same period, the number of people on temporary assistance grew from 4 to 139, and their share of the direct assistance correspondingly increased from 6-7 % to ca. 50 %![68] This was due mostly to the fact that families with illness and unemployment had their expenses paid for medicine, rent and firewood, and also received money to buy some clothes, such as a pair of wooden shoes or a coat. In addition each year a small amount was given to some travelling journeymen who were moving on after having worked in Kalundborg for a while.

A study by Nynne Helge also shows an increase in the temporary assistance in Elsinore from as early as the 1780s, but the extent of that does not yet seem to have been studied in other towns.[69] But it would certainly not be surprising if it can be shown that other towns too experienced great growth in this regard. Should this prove to be the case it could reflect the fact that unemployment was then considered a legitimate cause of poverty. In addition the 1803 regulations and a supplementary statutory provision from 1810 obliged a town to pay temporary assistance to a poor inhabitant who came from another place – until the money was refunded from the previous parish or town.[70] Finally, Krogh observes that a changed occupational structure could perhaps underlie the growth in the number of people on temporary assistance in Kalundborg. For instance the town noted a large increase in the number of wage earners, because it became more common for journeymen and merchants' employees to set up their own homes instead of continuing to live with their employers.[71] And just a small misfortune could cause great poverty for these workers.

There is no systematic study of developments in childcare in the poor relief system. So it is impossible to say whether the direct authority to remove a child compulsorily from problematic parents had any rapid or strong effect on the social services in the towns. But the local history literature has some examples of poor commissions using this provision, especially in the case of children of unmarried mothers.[72] Some of the orphaned children and those compulsorily removed were placed in an institution (cf. discussed in more detail below), but – as in the 18th century – it was more common to house them with foster parents in the town in question or in a neighbouring rural parish, where fostering payments were often lower.[73] The poor commissions often endeavoured to place the children as cheaply as possible, because the fostering payment could easily amount to a significant share of the total budget of the poor relief system. In many cases, foster children were simply put out to public tender.[74]

The delegation of the care meant that the foster parents had to pay for board and lodging, and look after the upbringing of the child. In return they could benefit from the child's work. That is why the fostering payment was highest for young children who were not able to work. A study of the occupations of foster parents in Randers in the 1830s shows that most were artisans, but there were also teachers, sailors, shopkeepers and widows among them.[75] In the country too most foster parents seem to have come from the less well-off milieu. It could be imagined that the fostering payment was often a welcome financial supplement for these hosts, and that some of them can have been tempted to exploit the children's labour. In any case, the literature has several examples of a poor commission being compelled to move a foster child, because it was being treated badly by its host.[76] Normally the commission allowed a foster child to stay in a home as long as all the parties involved were satisfied with the arrangement, but some places had an annual tendering process for all children who were placed by the authorities. This gave the possibility that even children who were well placed in a foster relationship could be forced to move for purely financial reasons.[77] The supervisory role of the poor relief system stopped at the age at which children were confirmed, usually 14. But it was probably common that the poor commission also made efforts to get the foster children apprenticed or into service as this was the best insurance that they would not again be a burden on the authorities. In any case we know about such an employment service in Kolding, Vejle and Viborg.[78]

Limitations in the rights of the poor and the establishment of institutions

In his evaluation of the significance of the 1803 regulations for Kalundborg, Tyge Krogh notes that the reform 'on the face of it' seems to have been of great benefit to the town poor, because their economic situation was improved. But then he adds: 'The cost to the poor, however, was their freedom to administer their own lives and probably, in the long term, also a loss of social standing'. Kalundborg's poor suffered the first restrictions as early as 1807 when the poor commission decided to establish a special journal to register the possessions of the poor when they began to get permanent assistance. This enabled the commission to call the individual to account if he or she sold, for example, some clothes to get money for alcohol and afterwards asked the commission for new clothes.[79] In the following year, *Danske Kancelli* (the Danish Chancellery) sent a letter to all the relevant authorities in Denmark in which a demand for such a registration was made, as well as for an official record of the possessions of the poor person.[80]

The difficult years during the Napoleonic wars and especially after 1814 resulted in several local requests for a tightening of the Poor Laws in the Kingdom. For instance several wanted to limit the freedom of movement of the alms recipients, and their possibility of marriage. In 1817 complaints about the heavy expenses of public assistance reached such a volume that *Danske Kancelli* requested recommendations from all the *amtmænd* about which means could be used to reduce these expenses. In addition, the *amtmænd* should determine to what extent the rising number of poor people was due to the young getting married without having any reasonable prospect of supporting themselves. The inquiry was answered not just by the *amtmænd*, but also by a large number of clergymen and other local officials, and nearly all the respondents found it necessary to set certain limits for contracting marriage.[81] However these requests were first transformed into legislation with the marriage ordinance of 1824. That contained a provision that two people could not marry each other if just one of them, as an adult, had received assistance from the public poor relief system, and if that assistance had not been repaid. However a dispensation from this rule could be given, but only by the poor commission in the town or the parish where the man was entitled to assistance. In the following decades this provision gave rise to numerous discussions in the poor commissions, and the chancellery was not infrequently involved in cases where a local authority went right to the limit in an effort to avoid paying poor relief.[82] In 1857 the legislation was moderated some-

FIG. 4.

Basket making was one of the jobs that inmates in poor houses were set to do. The photograph, from the poorhouse in the rural parish of Kværkeby in Mid-Zealand, was taken at the end of the 19th century. But the picture could just as well have been taken in a town poorhouse.

what, as from then on a municipal council could only deny marriage if the man had received poor relief within the previous five years and had not yet repaid the assistance.

The questionnaire in 1817 also showed a clear acceptance of the idea of establishing work institutions for the poor. However, there was no question of new ideas at that time. Between 1787 and 1800, for instance, seven workhouses were established in Copenhagen, each of them covering a parish. Between 1800 and 1807 the capital city had in addition a house of correction for the poor who either would not work for their poor relief or who continued to beg; here the individual inmates were kept in isolation in the hope of getting them to reflect on their life and in this way be re-socialised to a better life.[83] In his 1802 proposal for re-organising the Danish poor relief system, P.C. Stemann also advocated the establishment of a house of correction for beggars in every county.[84] Stemann's wishes in this area were first realised however in the second half of the 19th century. But many of his ideas about the treatment of the poor may have been an important source of inspiration for Hans Bastholm, when in 1806 he took the initiative to establish a new poor institution in Slagelse.[85] The institution, which had room for a total of 56 inmates,[86] clearly differed from the poorhouses in provincial towns until that time, as the individual inmates there were left to themselves and in principle only had housing in common. In the institution in Slagelse, on the other hand, the leadership kept a close eye on all the inmates who were kept working in the wool-spinning mill attached to the institution. The inmates were also given a hot midday meal, ca. ½ kg bread and ca. 1 litre beer daily. Furthermore the leadership decided to have separate dormitories for men and women and tried to separate the inoffensive inmates from those who were more problematic.[87]

In 1812 Bastholm published a full account of his institution, and in 1817 this was followed by comprehensive 'theoretical and practical directions for the efficient management of the poor relief system in Denmark'. In this Bastholm advocated collecting all the poor from a town or district into one place where they could be under proper supervision. Bastholm's texts seem to have had a wide circulation and to have inspired a large number of institutional establishments. And in the middle of the 19th century most of the towns in the Kingdom had either a combined poor- and workhouse (in Danish: *fattiggård*), or at least a large poorhouse. After 1860 there was also a tremendous growth in the number of combined poor- and workhouses in rural areas, and around 1885, there was a total of 350-375 of these in the rural parishes.[88]

A characteristic feature of the new institutions was that they had detailed regulations which were similar from place to place and which set a very restrictive framework for the life of the inmates. In this way, the inmates were to be taught to be good citizens who could do steady work outside the walls of the institution.[89] The strict discipline was the most important reason that, as time passed, poor commissions readily placed neglected children in a combined poor- and workhouse. As Dean G. Koch wrote in 1836: 'The children become (...) healthier and better behaved, do not witness their parents' former disorder (...) do not become accustomed to wandering idleness (...) are kept steadily in school'.[90] The discipline included very strict day rhythms, and the inmates could not leave the institution without permission, which was normally given only on Sundays.[91] Most combined poor- and workhouses also separated the sexes at night. The regulations prescribed that the inmates were given

FIG. 5.

In the 19th century, it was commonplace that inmates in poorhouses and houses of correction worked outside the walls of the institutions, for example cleaning the streets of the town. This picture shows a line of inmates from the Copenhagen institution Ladegaarden *on their way to their daily work equipped with brooms and shovels. In Copenhagen they were bluntly called the 'ragged army' from* Ladegaarden.

good, nourishing food, but there was a prohibition on spirits and in many places on coffee and tobacco too. However it seems to have been quite common that the poor used the weekly day out to get drunk or to smuggle in forbidden goods. These and other offences could be punished with exclusion from a meal, temporary forfeiture of permission to go out, a short stay in a 'dark cell' or various forms of corporal punishment. It was the custom in some places that the punishment was administered in the presence of everybody.[92]

The inmates were obliged to 'perform the work that suited their strength and was assigned to them and to obey their superiors and behave properly', as written in regulations from 1845.[93] In practice the work was most frequently various forms of textile work such as the manufacture of cloth, rugs and horse blankets.

A new study shows that quite a considerable part of the total production of these goods in the Kingdom in 1827, 1837 and 1847 was manufactured in work institutions, but in each of these three years, the institutions had between them 400-500 workers and many of the places also had skilled masters and journeymen.[94] And in contrast to previously, a financial surplus was successfully achieved, in any case in some places. The institution in Slagelse had a loss in only four of the years between 1825 and 1853, and there was even quite a considerable surplus in some of the years.[95] It was apparently also common that an institution offered its labour out in the town, for example for street cleaning. But there are also tales in several places about renting out people as day labourers for private citizens; the leaders of an institution could use this to reward the most worthy of the inmates. And in Ribe in any case, it was also possible to rent out the inmates as permanent servants.[96]

When the combined poor- and workhouse in Aarhus was ready for occupation in 1820, all the recipients of poor relief until then were presented with an ultimatum by the poor commission: either they moved into the institution or else they waived their right to all assistance. Some of them chose the latter. Hans Sejerholt observes too that nearly all monetary assistance from the town poor relief system stopped after 1820 (because the inmates in the institution got assistance only in kind), but 15 years later, large sums were again paid to the poor who lived in the town.[97]

It is not known to what extent the Aarhus 'either-or' model was used in other towns. But local history literature has several testimonies that the combined poor- and workhouses had a deterrent effect. For instance Bodil Vestergaard gives an account of a woman in Randers who at the beginning of the 1830s asked the poor commission for an increase in her poor relief, but when the commission offered to admit her to the combined poor- and workhouse, 'she vehemently refused and went away angrily', as is recorded in the commission minutes.[98] And Sv. Aage Bay mentions a long report from 1830 in which Mayor Ræder in Horsens noted with pleasure that the number of adults receiving poor relief had been greatly reduced since the establishment of the work institution seven years previously. Ræder was in no doubt about the necessity for such an institution, because as he wrote:

As you are aware, the poor person in general is depraved and lazy, because had he been respectable and hard-working and otherwise had healthy limbs, he would not have become destitute. In particular, the beggar does not know any greater evil than having to work. If this has to be done under supervision and unwillingly as far as it goes, the evil in his opinion goes beyond all limits, and therefore no matter how well the work institution takes care of him, he will be most reluctant to be admitted to the same. If the police then do their job and pursue every beggar and tramp with inflexible rigour, these people become involved in double danger, and to avoid this they have no other choice than to begin to work themselves![99]

These are undeniably points of view that have much greater similarities with the widespread attitudes at the beginning of the 18th century than those which were asserted in the ideas of the Enlightenment...

However, not all poor commissions seized the new institution idea with such great enthusiasm. Some towns refrained completely from building combined poor- and workhouses because they feared great expense, especially in the building phase. Other commissions weighed up the economic and moral arguments against each other for a long time. This was the case in Ribe where, for instance, the critics expressed grave doubts about putting children and adults – who could not be blamed for their misery – together with all kinds of 'evil people'. This ended with the establishment of a combined poor- and workhouse in the town in 1845. As in Aarhus 25 years earlier, it was only in very special cases that a recipient of poor relief was allowed to live outside the institution. But here too, this uncompromising attitude had to be abandoned after some years.[100]

The Schleswig poor relief system in the first half of the 19th century

Schleswig did not get a new poor law in 1803. But the towns in the Duchy experienced increasing social problems because of inflation during the Napoleonic wars and stagnation after 1814. And it was definitely not improved by the fact that in the first decades of the 19th century the towns experienced a growth in population caused by immigrating farm workers and others. After 1814 the increasing pressure on the public poor relief funds breathed new life into the discussion about social services, writes Lars Henningsen. He divides the critics of the existing social legislation and the practice of public assistance into two groups, and in this connection he draws parallels with the contemporary discussion in England, which led to the implementation of the Poor Law Amendment Act of 1834.[101] One group of debaters believed that the right of the poor to assistance had simply laid the groundwork for the rising poverty. For instance they claimed that the poor-rate had resulted in widespread apathy and begging, and that many threw themselves into hasty marriages in the belief that the public authorities would help if they were reduced to distress. These critics argued therefore for the total abolition of public poor relief (including the obligation of the public authorities to provide work for the unemployed) and they thought that all charity should be handed over to private initiative. Some even went as far as to say that it was an encroachment on the inviolability of private property to burden citizens with poor-rates!

The other group of critics insisted that the public authorities had an obligation to help the poor and that the poor had a right to claim assistance. But they found it necessary to introduce strict rules so that only a negligible sum was paid. Several spoke warmly about helping people to help themselves, among other things by the establishment of savings banks and the allotment of free gardens to the poor.[102] But work institutions also became more prominent in the discussion, especially because of the deterrent effect. As Lars Henningsen emphasises, some of these views were a further development of ideas from the Enlightenment, while others marked a clear break with these. A shift of focus also occurred: poverty was increasingly regarded as something self-inflicted, and the most important goal at the time was to keep the public expenses in check. It can also be observed that Niemann in his 1792 catechism directly rejected collective assistance in special institutions, because according to Niemann the aim should be to bring the poor back to ordinary active life, not to segregate them as a group for themselves.[103]

A study of developments in the towns of the Duchy shows that in several places the treatment of the poor became markedly more severe between ca. 1820 and 1835.[104] This is seen most clearly in Sønderborg where drastic reductions in assistance were implemented to reduce the poor-rate – just as had been done in some of the towns in the Kingdom in the 18th century. It was openly acknowledged that it would be necessary to supplement public relief with private charity, and indeed there were several private initiatives. In 1833 the town also established a house of correction for men where, under strict supervision, the inmates were put to grate dyewood for the town merchants.[105] Such rasp-houses otherwise normally belonged in prisons.

In 1835, modelled on the Prussian example, four-socalled *rådgivende stænderforsamlinger* (advisory assemblies of Estates) were introduced, each comprising a region – the islands in the Kingdom, Jutland, Schleswig and Holstein, respectively. The assemblies met every second year and consisted of elected representatives of the estate owners, the peasants, and the town house owners, respectively, and they had the task of advising about laws and proposing legislation.

The printed debates from the *stænderforsamlinger* therefore give a good insight into which social and political questions occupied a section of the population with a somewhat broader composition.[106] Expenditure on the public poor relief system was a subject that was regularly discussed in the assemblies in both the Kingdom and

Duchies. The sharpest points of view emerged in the Schleswig assembly. Here in 1836 a committee was set up who were to formulate a proposal for the King about a revision of the Schleswig poor laws. The committee prepared a report, which was well supported in the assembly. It is true that it acknowledged the obligations of the public authorities, but there were strong arguments for the establishment of more work institutions with strict discipline and for limitations in the right of the poor to marry. And when an able-bodied person asked the poor relief system for help, the person in question, in Lars Henningsen's words, should be regarded as 'a ward who handed over to his guardians the right to enjoin his person, possessions, time, energy and way of life'.[107]

The report formed the basis for three laws that saw the light of day in the years 1839-41. One determined that a person who had received and not repaid poor relief after he had reached 18 years of age could only contract marriage after having got permission from the local authority where he had his home. While this provision had a parallel in the legislation in the Kingdom, this was definitely not the case with the second law. This contained an obligation for children and other relatives of a person who requested poor relief; a local authority could order these relatives to help the person in distress, if this was financially possible. Finally the poor ordinance of 1841 gave rules for public poor relief common to all the towns in Schleswig, and with this the 1736 ordinance was finally replaced. The new law codified a number of administrative innovations from the previous years and made them generally valid, but it also added several new elements. Some of the most important features were:

- The *Armenpfleger* arrangement became obligatory for all towns
- Great weight should be placed on giving poor relief in kind (this form of poor relief had also gained ground in Schleswig since ca. 1820)
- An obligation to repay was introduced, also for temporary assistance
- There were penalties if paupers disobeyed the administrators. At worst, such a person could be condemned to prison on bread and water for 30 days.

Finally it was emphasised that in general the fact that a person could not find work was not an adequate criterion for obtaining poor relief. With this, the 1841 poor law meant a definite break with the Enlightenment tradition.

Private charity and other help without limitation of civil rights

Rising pressure on the public poor relief system seems to have led to a growth in private charity in both the Kingdom and Schleswig during the 19th century. This subject however has not yet been thoroughly studied in the case of the Duchy, but we know that in the decades after 1814 various local associations were established which endeavoured to find more work for the poor. Similarly, many examples are known of extraordinary relief measures during severe winters and in other critical situations. For instance there could be special collections and lotteries for the benefit of the poor as well as the establishment of private feeding institutions.[108] Similar emergency measures are known from several of the towns in the Kingdom,[109] and in some of these, it also became popular in time to have charity concerts for the benefit of the poor.[110] There are indications that the towns in the Kingdom experienced a general growth of charitable societies in the middle of the 19th century, and if that is the case, it must be taken as a sign that it had become popular among the towns' middle class to show social engagement and social responsibility. One of the reasons is possibly that it could help to consolidate one's social position in town society to give to charity. As Tine Bro has formulated it, one can simply say that charity became a 'public occasion'.[111]

Thanks to Tine Bro's analysis of the history of the charitable institutions, we now also have a good overview of this segment of the social services in the 19th century. She has reckoned the number of charitable institutions in the towns of the Kingdom to be 63 in 1800, 106 in 1850 and 212 in 1900, and her calculations show that the total number of inmates increased from fewer than 1,000 in 1800 to ca. 2,000 in 1850 and ca. 3,000 in 1900.[112] This is certainly not a striking increase when seen against the background of the total growth in town population during the 19th century. But it is interesting to look at the development in the different types of institution. Nearly all towns got at least 1-2 charitable institutions. In the small towns these were typically an old people's home for widows and other elderly and infirm people. Such broadly defined institutions were naturally also found in larger towns, but here there were also charitable institutions aimed at a narrower target group, for example widows and unmarried daughters from the family of the founder of the institution. In addition, from the middle of the 1830s, there was strong growth in the number of orphanages and day nurseries, although some of these offered only a place for the children to stay while the poor parents were at work. Tine Bro sees this

FIG. 6.

In 1767 merchant Peter Eilschou built a number of houses in Odense which, after the death of the married couples who had lived in them, were to be used as a charitable institution for three poor widows and three poor spinsters, who should all be of merchant or clerical rank and also have a good reputation and live respectable lives. De Eilschouske Boliger *(the Eilschou Almshouses) functioned as a charitable foundation from 1799 to 1920, and during these years the inhabitants not only enjoyed free lodgings but also received a pension. They were neither subjected to specific rules of conduct nor assigned tasks. The charitable foundation is a typical example of private institutions for the genteel poor during the period. In 2005, the buildings were re-erected in the open-air museum,* Den Gamle By, *and are furnished in a way that corresponds with the original furnishing.*

development as an expression of the fact that children were increasingly being considered as individuals with special needs, but also notes the desire to exert a moral influence on the children so they would be able to develop into good citizens.[113]

Other new types of institution were the so-called homes for retired artisans. However, they first gained ground in the second half of the 19th century and this is connected with the abolition of the craft guilds in 1862 and the social obligations these had had.[114] Many of the old guilds established associations, which considered that one of their most important tasks was to collect money to build inexpensive or free housing for members of the association. But these charitable institutions, which were established by means of members' contributions and gifts and directly aimed at helping people from specific occupations, can also be regarded as a reaction to the increasing stigmatisation of the poor. The charitable institutions in fact gave the possibility of assistance that was not linked to the loss or limitation of civil rights.[115] A similar motive could perhaps have been the underlying reason for the establishment of many other charitable institutions in the 19th century – especially the institutions directed at people who had been well off but who had been the victims of illness or misfortune. Tine Bro therefore concludes that the charitable institutions in towns during the 19th century developed from being a supplement to the public poor relief system to being more of an alternative option.[116]

Several other scholars write about a general change in attitude to social services in the time around 1850. They believe that yet again it had become common to differentiate between deserving and undeserving poor and that many people gradually became aware of the absurdity of making hard-working people into second-class citizens just because illness or age forced them to get poor relief.[117] The first cautious steps on the part of the authorities were four laws and circulars from 1848, 1853, 1855 and 1856, which all opened the way for giving financial help from the public authorities without this being associated with limitations of civil rights. Three of these laws concerned temporary assistance in special circumstances. The last one was a law about the establishment of so-called free poor relief funds in the single local authority areas. The idea was that people could sign up for voluntary contributions to help the poor as had been done in the 18th century, and that the amount paid in should be disbursed to the most destitute. Studies from a number of towns however all give the same impression that the free poor relief funds never played a role of any significance because the voluntary contributions were too small.[118]

It was not until around 1890 that there was a decisive break with the 19th century stigmatising treatment of the poor. The laws about old age pension and the public poor relief system, which were both promulgated in 1891, meant that needy people over the age of 60 who had not received poor relief in the previous 10 years, as well as various groups of physically and mentally handicapped people, could from then on get assistance from the public authorities without limitation of their civil rights.[119] At the same time the local authorities were obliged to waive repayment of a person's poor relief when the person in question had not received any form of assistance for five years.[120] The 1892 law on health insurance societies was also important; it really gave an impetus to the idea of self-insurance. The law gave extensive state aid to the approved health insurance societies that admitted only people of limited means as members. These members then had the possibility of medical treatment completely or partly free, subsidised medicine and a maintenance allowance during illness for up to 13 weeks a year.[121]

The 1910s and 1920s too were characterised by many socio-political initiatives (for example on unemployment assistance and temporary assistance in crisis years), and these initiatives made it more acceptable to receive assistance from the public authorities. The many laws were codified, combined and further developed in the comprehensive social reform of 1933. This law complex formed the basis for Danish social policy for several decades and still plays a considerable role in the perception of the Danish system of welfare, and its general principle is that every form of social assistance is a right and that all citizens who fulfil certain requirements have the right to a certain payment from the public purse.

Conclusion and perspective

When the poor relief system and conditions for the poor in the different parts of the Absolutist monarchy are compared, the natural starting point is legislation. Here the lack of simultaneity is quite striking. In particular it is surprising that all the towns in Schleswig did not have the same legislation until 1841, i.e. 133 years after the towns in the Kingdom. With regard to content, however, there is generally good agreement between the legislation in the two parts of the monarchy, even though several provisions were valid in only one of the areas. This is the case for example with the 1766 decree, that the Schleswig towns should provide work for the poor, and with many of the provisions that were the result of the energetic work of the Schleswig *stænderforsamling* on the question of the poor.

On the administrative level, the *Armenpfleger* arrangement is clearly the greatest difference between the Kingdom and the Duchy of Schleswig. Whereas in the Kingdom, this was apparently realised only in Copenhagen, it gained a foothold in many Schleswig towns in the first decades of the 19th century, and in 1841 it became obligatory in all towns in the Duchy. Many other local variations in the administration of the poor relief system can also be pointed out – especially *within* the Schleswig area – but it is perhaps more important to mention a feature that administration in the provincial towns in the Kingdom and the towns in the Duchy had in common. In both areas and throughout the whole period poor relief was a matter for the local authorities, and the responsibility was generally given to a special administrative body with representatives from the municipal corporation, the clergy and the citizens.[122] It is true that the body was under the supervision of higher authorities, but in the 18th century this control was very limited – even though the article has several examples that an active effort from the regional inspectorate could make a considerable difference. Be that as it may, the social administration could be implemented in many different ways – especially because the 18th century legislation put so much emphasis on voluntary efforts and, on the whole, contained few restraints. Some towns established poor relief systems that functioned quite well, while others let things slide.

For the vast majority of the towns whose administration have been described, it must be said however that during the 18th century they created a public poor relief system that worked reasonably well, with annual collections of contributions from the citizens and regular disbursements to the people who were registered as paupers. Here the towns differ from the numerous rural parishes in both the Kingdom and the Duchy where there does not seem to have been any essential difference between the state of things in the 18th century and in the previous centuries. But conditions for the poor in a given town could undergo great changes from decade to decade, depending on how the poor inspectors did their job. These differences had probably diminished in the 19th century, when local authorities came under stricter control from above. Still the legislation and the central authorities could not change the fact that there were great differences between how much property (in the form of land, buildings and capital) the individual poor relief systems had at their disposal – and how much interest income could be distributed to the town paupers. Likewise, there were great differences in the extent and nature of private and semi-official social services.

With regard to the trend in the views of the authorities on poverty, a clear common feature can be observed for the towns in the Kingdom and in the Duchy. During most of the 18th century, the overriding purpose was to overcome the problem of begging. The most important means used in this struggle were regular disbursements (normally in the form of money) to the most disadvantaged. But it seems that the authorities were seldom particularly interested in what the poor spent the money on and how they managed. However, a number of spinning mills etc. were established, but they had a purely financial objective. Under the influence of the ideas of the Enlightenment, greater weight was laid on the obligations of society to the poor at the end of the 18th century. First and foremost the idea then was to provide work for the unemployed to give them the chance to become re-socialised. The new poor-law legislation for the Kingdom introduced in 1803 was marked in several ways by these ideas. For instance, it laid the ground for considerably better financing than had been the case before, but the stage was also set for stronger intervention from the authorities, e.g. with the provisions concerning the compulsory removal of children from problem parents.

The idea of bringing up the poor to become good citizens and the wish to practise stricter control took a sharp turn in a more repressive direction under the effect of the crisis after the Napoleonic wars, which meant rising pressure on public funds. Locally, in both the Kingdom and in Schleswig, there was a desire to make greater demands on the poor and to limit their rights, and some of these wishes were complied with politically. Both parts of the monarchy also experienced a great increase in the number of combined poor- and workhouses from about 1820. It is true that the poor received what, at the time, was quite reasonable board and lodging in these houses, but their everyday life was regulated in a way similar to conditions in prisons, and there was much greater exploitation of their work than had been seen before. One of the most important aims of the institutions was to deter the poor from looking for assistance from public funds and this worked in many cases. Several examples are also known of the poor commission in a town giving the poor an ultimatum: either to let themselves be put into the institution, or otherwise forego assistance from public funds.

While the repressive tendencies in poor relief in the 19th century are very well documented, more studies are needed to see if temporary assistance to a wider circle of the population gained ground at the expense of permanent alms for a relatively small and closed group of people. If such a general development can be shown, it could be interesting to study to what extent this can be attributed to changes in the social structure, among them a weakening of guild organisations and other networks that had traditionally carried out considerable poor relief functions.[123]

The history of Danish social services is not just about breaks, but also about continuity. For instance the fundamental differentiation between deserving and undeserving poor can be found right from the late Middle Ages until the present. In the first ca. 200 years, the deserving poor, i.e. the sick, the handicapped and old people who were unable to do any work, had the exclusive right to beg. Legislation at the beginning of the 18th century meant that this group of people had, from then on, to live on what the public authorities could collect for them – as well as what they could get from family and friends etc. The ideas of the Enlightenment also brought the unemployed in from the cold – though only on condition that they would take the work they were assigned. But in the crisis years after 1814, the pendulum began to swing the other way, and indeed there was a tendency whereby all recipients of public assistance began to be considered as undeserving poor – in any case, they were stigmatised. The growth of various types of charitable institutions and other private initiatives during the course of the 19th century can be seen as a reaction against this, as they offered help to the poor without depriving them of their civil rights. In the period ca. 1850-1930, in addition, there was a gradual reduction in the stigmatising assistance by means of legislation. And during the 20th century, Denmark – like a number of other countries – developed a so-called 'universal' welfare system, which gives all citizens the right to a wide range of tax paid social benefits.

Epilogue

One might expect this to be the end of the story. However, the old distinction between deserving and undeserving poor is perhaps in the process of being revitalised. As part of a discussion at present about the future of the Danish welfare society, many politicians and economists have advocated limiting the access of the most affluent section of the population to some social benefits. But some social scientists have warned against such initiatives, as they believe they can weaken popular support for the welfare state,[124] their argument being: in a 'universal' welfare system, the distinction between 'recipient' and 'donor' is wiped out, because everybody comes to both give and receive in the course of their lives. It is therefore felt to be morally acceptable to receive help from public funds. In contrast, in a so-called 'goal-oriented' system, where an effort is made to limit recipients to certain sections of the population, there will often be a tendency to stigmatise certain types of recipients.[125] Typically these are recipients of cash assistance, who are accused of laziness and lack of will power. On the other hand, here too there is wide acceptance of the view that old people, the sick and the handicapped deserve to get help from the public authorities. The parallel to the Danish discussion in the 19th century is quite striking!

BIBLIOGRAPHY

Andersen, Knud Holch 1987. 'Bondelægen. En lokalhistorisk synsvinkel på praktiserende lægevirksomhed og sygdomsbehandling ca. 1900-1935'. In: Finn H. Lauridsen (ed.), *Festskrift til Vagn Dybdahl*. Aarhus: Aarhus Universitetsforlag, pp. 7-29.

Bay, Sv. Aage 1982. *Horsens historie indtil 1837*. Horsens: Horsens Kommune.

Blomberg, Aage Fasmer 1980. *De magre år. Odense 1660-1700*. Odense: Odense Kommune. (A volume of: Tage Kaarsted (ed.), *Odense bys historie*. Vol. I-X, 1978-88).

Blomberg, Aage Fasmer 1955-56. *Faaborg By's Historie*. Vol. I-II. Faaborg: Faaborg Byhistoriske Arkiv.

Bro, Tine 2005a. Stiftelsesvæsenet i de danske købstæder 1700-1900 – et studie i relationen mellem stiftelser, fattiglovgivning, social forsorg og privat velgørenhed. (Unpublished thesis, The Danish Centre for Urban History, Aarhus University).

Bro, Tine 2005b. 'Stiftelser i de danske købstæder – fattigvæsenets ven eller fjende'. *Den Gamle By 2005*, pp. 32-41.

Bro-Jørgensen, J.O. 1959. *Svendborg købstads historie*. Vol. 1. Svendborg: Svendborg Kommune.

Brønfeld, Poul et.al. (eds.) 1998. *Vejles Historie*. Vol. 2 *(Moderne tider – 1786-1970)*. Vejle: Vejle Kommune.

Bundsgaard, Inge & Peter Korsgaard 1991. 'Fra fattigforsorg til socialpolitik. Kommunal socialforsorg fra 1800-tallet til i dag'. In: Per Boje et.al. (eds.), *Folkestyre i by og på land. Danske kommuner gennem 150 år*. Herning: Poul Kristensens Forlag, pp. 161-204.

Christensen, John Stampe 1985 – see Nyberg, Tore & Thomas Riis 1985.

Degn, Ole 1981. *Rig og fattig i Ribe. Økonomiske og sociale forhold i Ribe-samfundet 1560-1660*. Vol. 1-2. Aarhus: Universitetsforlaget i Aarhus.

Due, Jeppe Klok 2005. En undersøgelse af industriens udvikling og forankring i de kongerigske provinskøbstæder fra 1817 til 1847 med udgangspunkt i fabrikstabellernes opgivelse. (Unpublished thesis, The Danish Centre for Urban History, Aarhus University).

Dyrvik, Ståle 1982. 'Avgjerdsprosessen og aktørane bak det offentlege fattigstele i Norge 1720-1760'. In: Ståle Dyrvik (ed.), *Oppdaginga av fattigdomen. Sosial lovgiving i Norden på 1700-talet*. Oslo, Bergen, Stavanger & Tromsø: Universitetsforlaget, pp. 109-84.

Fangel, Henrik 1975. *Haderslev bys historie 1800-1945*. Vol. I. Haderslev: Haderslev Bank.

Filipsen, Vibeke 1990. 'De fri fattigkassers relationer til det kommunale fattigvæsen 1856-1907'. In: Jan Kanstrup & Steen Ousager (eds.), *Kommunal opgaveløsning 1842-1970*. Odense: Odense Universitetsforlag, pp. 147-62.

Hansen, Bente Dahl 1984. *Betler eller almisselem. Studier i offentlig fattigforsorg i Sjællands stifts landsogne 1708-1802*. Copenhagen: Landbohistorisk Selskab.

Hansen, Peter Wessel 2006. 'Fra frihed til tvang: Fattigvæsenet i Trinitatis sogn 1771-1841'. In: Inger Wiene et.al. (eds.), *Runde Kirke, Taarn og Sogn. Trinitatis gennem 350 år*. Copenhagen: Nyt Nordisk Forlag, pp. 124-45.

Haugner, C.C. 1938. *Maribo Historie*. Vol. 2. Published by the author.

Haugner, C.C. 1935. *Nakskov Købstads Historie*. Vol. 2. Copenhagen: Nyt Nordisk Forlag.

Helge, Nynne 1987. 'Offentlig og privat forsorg i Helsingør 1737-1808'. *Helsingør Kommunes Museer 1986*, pp. 5-72.

Henningsen, Lars N. 1978. *Fattigvæsenet i de sønderjyske købstæder 1736-1841*. Aabenraa: Historisk Samfund for Sønderjylland.

Henningsen, Peter 2004. 'Det philadelphiske system. Københavns Fattigvæsen og tvangsarbejdshuset i Pustervig 1800-1807'. *Fortid og Nutid 2004*, pp. 3-28.

Holmgaard, Jens 1983. 'Fattigvæsenet i Viborg stift i 1730erne'. *Fra Viborg Amt 1983*, pp. 48-71.

Jensen, Carsten Selch 2004. 'Byerne og de fattige – den internationale baggrund for den danske udvikling'. In: Søren Bitsch Christensen (ed.), *Middelalderbyen*. (Danske Bystudier, 1). Aarhus: Dansk Center for Byhistorie & Aarhus Universitetsforlag, pp. 295-323.

Johansen, Hans Chr. 1983. *Næring og bystyre. Odense 1700-1789*. Odense: Odense Kommune. (A volume of: Tage Kaarsted (ed.), *Odense bys historie*. Vol. I-X, 1978-88).

Jørgensen, Harald 1940. *Studier over det offentlige Fattigvæsens historiske Udvikling i Danmark i det 19. Aarhundrede*. Copenhagen: Institut for Historie og Samfundsøkonomi. (Repr. 1979).

Kinch, J. 1884. *Ribe Bys Historie og Beskrivelse, 2den Del. Fra Reformationen indtil Enevoldsmagtens Indførelse (1536-1660)*. Copenhagen: G.E.C. Gad.

Krogh, Tyge 1987. *Staten og de besiddelsesløse på landet 1500-1800*. Odense: Odense Universitetsforlag.

Krogh, Tyge 1985 – see Nyberg, Tore & Thomas Riis 1985.

Ladewig Petersen, E. et.al. (eds.), *De fede år. Odense 1559-1660*. Odense: Odense Kommune. (A volume of: Tage Kaarsted (ed.), *Odense bys historie*. Vol. I-X, 1978-88).

Larsen, Christian Albrekt 2006. 'Fattiggård. Målretning af velfærd skaber polarisering'. *Politiken* 23 May 2006.

Maaløe, Lauritz 1936. *Assens gennem 700 Aar*. Odense: Historisk Samfund for Odense og Assens Amter.

Mikkelsen, Jørgen 1999. 'Befolkning og erhverv 1726-1850'. In: Henning Ringgaard Lauridsen et.al. (eds.), *Viborgs historie*. Vol. 2 *(1726-1940)*. Viborg: Viborg Kommune, pp. 63-128.

Mikkelsen, Keld 2005. 'Københavns Fattigvæsen 1770-1840'. In: Peter Henningsen (ed.), *Patrioter og fattigfolk. Fattigvæsenet i København ca. 1500-1850*. (Historiske Meddelelser om København, 2005). Copenhagen: Københavns Stadsarkiv & Københavns Kommune, pp. 57-140.

Nielsen, M.H. 1932-35. 'Fattiggaarde i Ribe Amt og By'. *Fra Ribe Amt 1932-35*, pp. 406-73.

Nyberg, Tore & Thomas Riis (eds.) 1985. *Kalundborg historie*. Vol. 1 *(Tiden indtil 1830)*. Kalundborg: Kalundborg Kommune.

Pedersen, Laurits 1929. *Helsingør i Sundtoldstiden 1426-1857*. Vol. II. Copenhagen: Nyt Nordisk Forlag.

Rasmussen, Anna 1996. *Forsørget og forfulgt. Om offentlig forsorg på landet i første halvdel af 1800-tallet*. Viborg: Udgiverselskabet ved Landsarkivet for Nørrejylland.

Sejerholt, Hans 1940. 'Omsorgen for de Fattige'. In: Jens Clausen et.al. (eds.), *Aarhus gennem Tiderne*. Vol. II. Copenhagen: Nyt Nordisk Forlag, pp. 346-97.

Thestrup, Poul et.al. 1986. *Mod bedre tider. Odense 1789-1868*. Odense: Odense Kommune. (A volume of: Tage Kaarsted (ed.), *Odense bys historie*. Vol. I-X, 1978-88).

Tønnesen, Eva 2005. 'Fattigforsorg i Roskilde'. *Historisk Årbog for Roskilde Amt 2005*, pp. 59-94.

Vedel-Larsen, Birgitte 2005. 'Kampen mod de uværdige fattige. Arbejdshuse og tvangsarbejdsanstalter i København'. In: Peter Henningsen (ed.), *Patrioter og fattigfolk. Fattigvæsenet i København ca. 1500-1850*. (Historiske Meddelelser om København, 2005). Copenhagen: Københavns Stadsarkiv & Københavns Kommune, pp. 141-62.

Vestergaard, Bodil 1999. 'Træk af Fattigvæsenets historie i Randers ca. 1830-1834'. *Historisk Aarbog fra Randers Amt 1999*, pp. 31-45.

Wøllekær, Johnny 1993. *Fattiggårdene på Fyn*. Odense: Landbohistorisk Selskab.

NOTES

1   Bro 2005a. Some of the results in the dissertation are published in Bro 2005b.

2   Such a distinction is seen in many other places in Europe from the end of the 14th century, cf. Selch Jensen 2004, pp. 305 ff.

3   Krogh 1987, pp. 52-55.

4   Ladewig Petersen 1984, pp. 399 ff., Pedersen 1929, II, p. 263 (where forged begging letters are also mentioned), and Bro-Jørgensen 1959, I, p. 402.

5   The discussion is presented in Selch Jensen 2004, p. 314. There are also several examples from Odense at the end of the 16th and beginning of the 17th century that gifts were donated to the poor as an act of penance (for example to relieve the giver's guilty conscience about a murder). See Ladewig Petersen 1984, p. 397.

6   Ladewig Petersen 1984, p. 403.

7   Bro 2005a, pp. 38, 47 and 48. In the study Tine Bro used the urban hierarchy constructed by Ole Degn and which is reproduced on page 102 in this book. The reckoning is based on three large works from 1755-1904 which give information about the establishment, charter, founders, recipients and economy for every single charitable institution.

8   The charitable institution and grant were often linked, which meant that people admitted to the institution also received a certain amount for maintenance.

9   Cf. Peter Henningsen's article in this book.

10 Degn 1981, I, p. 366, and Kinch 1884, II, pp. 780-89.

11 Ladewig Petersen 1984, pp. 406-11, and Blomberg 1980, p. 274. The two writers seem to disagree about whether the poor-rate arrangement in Odense was re-established after the war.

12 Sejerholt 1940, pp. 356 and 358. Similarly, Jens Holmgaard believes that the widespread crop failure in 1709 was mainly responsible for the fact that there was no public system of poor relief at all in many rural parishes in the years after 1708. The great agricultural crisis in the 1730s created further problems for the poor relief system, cf. Holmgaard 1983, pp. 55 ff. Bente Dahl Hansen's study of the public assistance in rural areas in the 18th century also has several

specific examples that acute crises such as epidemics of cattle plague could cause the break-down of the poor relief system in a parish, cf. Hansen 1984, pp. 60 ff.

13 Maaløe 1936, p. 251.

14 Haugner 1935, II, p. 267, Haugner 1938, II, p. 58, Helge 1986, pp. 5 ff., and Johansen 1983, p. 252.

15 Haugner 1938, II, p. 59, Helge 1986, p. 6, and Johansen 1983, p. 253.

16 Sejerholt 1940, pp. 359 ff. A similar point of view is found in a statement from Aarhus 1771 (cf. Sejerholt 1940, p. 372) and a declaration from *byfogeden* in Svendborg ca. 1790 (cf. Bro-Jørgensen 1959, I, p. 406). And in his description of the poor relief system in Fåborg, Aage Fasmer Blomberg refers to a declaration from 1792 where the clergyman and *byfogeden* inform *stiftamtmanden* that Fåborg did not have any form of public collection or disbursement to the poor. But 'when one or another had need of help, there had always been some who had given them money or food when asked', and that was why the town streets were allegedly completely free of begging. Cf. Blomberg 1955, I, p. 186.

17 The former de facto prime-minister Ove Høegh-Guldberg was *stiftamtmand* in the county of Aarhus at the time. There is general agreement that he carried out this task very efficiently and competently.

18 Johansen 1983, pp. 252 ff. However, information about the number of poor relief recipients is available for only a few years after 1759.

19 Thestrup 1986, pp. 110 ff.

20 Christensen 1985, p. 228, and Krogh 1985, pp. 317 f.

21 Christensen 1985, p. 226. The money that was put into the poor boxes made up 12 % of the total income and was thus the third highest item of income.

22 Helge 1986, pp. 6 ff.

23 Helge 1986, pp. 28 ff.

24 Sejerholt 1940, p. 352, and Johansen 1983, p. 254.

25 See for instance Johansen 1983, p. 258, and Helge 1986, p. 19.

26 Bro-Jørgensen 1959, I, p. 403.

27 A meticulous analysis of poor relief in rural areas in the 18th century can be found in Hansen 1984, pp. 50 ff.

28 Mikkelsen 1999, pp. 104 f.

29 Johansen 1983, p. 255, Krogh 1985, p. 318, and Sejerholt 1940, p. 375.

30 Thestrup 1986, p. 111. However this information was mentioned as an argument for a collection reform in Odense, and perhaps it is somewhat coloured by these circumstances.

31 Bro-Jørgensen 1959, I, p. 403.

32 Johansen 1983, p. 271.

33 See for example Bay 1982, p. 181, Maaløe, 1936, p. 251, and Helge 1986, p. 48.

34 Dyrvik 1982, p. 111.

35 Henningsen 1978, pp. 33 f.

36   Direct inspiration from the Kingdom ordinance is seen incidentally in the Schleswig town of Tønder, where a poor relief system was established on the initiative of a prosperous merchant after the very severe winter of 1708/09. However, the weekly collection of voluntary contributions stopped after just two years. Flensburg introduced a similar system in 1721. Cf. Henningsen 1978, pp. 28 and 30.

37   Friedrichstadt's system is particularly noteworthy. It went back to 1633 and was thus the oldest in the Duchy. Here each of the three congregations was responsible for its own poor. Cf. Henningsen 1978, pp. 59 f.

38   Henningsen 1978, p. 46. Ærøskøbing was apparently the only town in the Duchy where alms payments were made in kind.

39   Henningsen 1978, p. 76.

40   Henningsen 1978, p. 90.

41   Henningsen 1978, pp. 60-68, especially p. 66.

42   Henningsen 1978, p. 86.

43   Tønnesen 2005, pp. 66 f.

44   See for instance Helge 1986, p. 16 (about the spinning establishment in Elsinore 1738-46), and Sejerholt 1940, pp. 364-68 (about the factory in Aarhus 1758-63 which gave the town poor relief system a total loss of 1,839 *rigsdaler*).

45   Henningsen 1978, p. 98. The decree was issued by *statholderen* (the governor) who supervised the towns, but it was done on the order of J.H.E. Bernstorff, who had the main responsibility for industrial policy in the monarchy from 1753 to 1767.

46   Henningsen 1978, pp. 104 f. People's attitude to spinning can have been affected by the fact that convicts were set to the same type of work.

47   The factory in Ribe established in 1789 had an unusually long life, as it was not closed down until 1835. Cf. Nielsen 1932-35, pp. 421 f. See the mention of spinning schools in Juliane Engelhardt's article in this book.

48   In Henningsen 1978, p. 115, this constitutional resolution is reproduced in this way: "Society should ensure the existence of unfortunate citizens either by getting them work or giving those who cannot work the means of subsistence.'

49   Cf. Henningsen 1978, pp. 117 ff. Lars Henningsen also believes that the new attitudes had particularly fertile breeding grounds in the region because rising grain prices and several severe winters in the 1780s and 90s caused great social problems.

50   Henningsen 1978, pp. 118-21.

51   Henningsen 1978, p. 168.

52   Johansen 1983, p. 257. With regard to the contributions of the Copenhagen intellectuals, see Peter Henningsen's article.

53   This extension is in keeping with the new perception that it was important to identify the causes of poverty in order to improve conditions for the poor if possible.

54   On the other hand, the regulations said nothing about work institutions.

55 An excellent presentation of the potential for conflict in such cases is given in Rasmussen 1996. See too Sejerholt 1940, pp. 381-82, and Mikkelsen 1999, pp. 109 f.

56 Thestrup 1986, pp. 115-17, and Krogh 1985, p. 318.

57 Sejerholt 1940, p. 375.

58 Krogh 1985, p. 318, and Helge 1986, p. 12.

59 Thestrup 1986, pp. 120 f.

60 Cf. Jørgensen 1940, p. 337.

61 Jørgensen 1940, pp. 337 ff. Incidentally, Copenhagen made strong efforts to give assistance in kind in the first decades of the 19th century, cf. Mikkelsen 2005, pp. 115 ff.

62 Thestrup 1986, pp. 120-21. See also Bro-Jørgensen 1959, I, pp. 407 f. about emergency help in 1812-13.

63 Krogh 1985, p. 320.

64 Jørgensen 1940, p. 354, and Tønnesen 2005, pp. 67 f.

65 Bro-Jørgensen, 1959, I, p. 408.

66 Jørgensen 1940, pp. 340 and 350.

67 Jørgensen 1940, p. 382.

68 Krogh 1985, p. 321. Krogh also notes that the portion of the town population who received some sort of assistance from the public funds grew from 5½ % in 1804 to 10 % in 1838.

69 Helge 1986, p. 22.

70 Cf. Jørgensen 1940, p. 45.

71 Krogh 1985, p. 321.

72 See for instance Vestergaard 1999, pp. 39 f.

73 Jørgensen 1940, pp. 374 ff. However, Bodil Vestergaard also gives examples of a poor commission giving assistance to a mother so she could bring up the child herself, cf. Vestergaard 1999, p. 35.

74 Incidentally, adults on public assistance could also be put out to tender. These were people who were so weak that they could not have their own household or live alone. For instance some poor commissions tried to place insane people in private care, which could of course cause great problems for the hosts. An example of this is described in Vestergaard 1999, p. 42.

75 Vestergaard 1999, p. 35.

76 See for example Nielsen 1932-35, p. 457.

77 Jørgensen 1940, pp. 255 ff. However it is not clear if Harald Jørgensen also has examples of such annual total tendering processes from towns.

78 Jørgensen 1940, p. 379, Brønfeld et al. 1998, p. 76, and Mikkelsen 1999, p. 108.

79 Krogh 1985, p. 320. The decision of the poor commission was brought about because a couple of the paupers had done exactly that sort of thing.

80 Jørgensen 1940, p. 87.

81 Jørgensen 1940, pp. 43 and 49 f. The answer from the mayor of Horsens is printed in Bay 1982, p. 282.

82 Jørgensen 1940, p. 56. As part of her study of the poor relief system in Randers in the 1830s, Bodil Vestergaard has studied a few marriage cases. The number is too small to draw any real conclusions, but it seems as if the poor commission was more inclined to agree to a marriage when the woman was rather old, and there was therefore less likelihood of a large number of children. Vestergaard 1999, pp. 37-39.

83 The organisation of the house of correction was greatly inspired by new American ideas about prison organisation (the Philadelphia system). The short history of the institution (it burned down during the English bombardment of Copenhagen in 1807) is described in Henningsen 2004, pp. 3-28. On the Copenhagen poor institutions around 1800 see Vedel-Larsen 2005 and Hansen 2006.

84 Jørgensen 1940, p. 33.

85 The following section is based on Jørgensen 1940, pp. 337-39, and Nielsen 1932-35, pp. 408 f. As *amtmand* for the county of Sorø, Stemann had a supervisory function for the institution in Slagelse that was in this county.

86 Most poorhouses at that time had fewer than 10 inmates.

87 Another early example of a work institution in the provinces is the one established in Odense in 1804 as a school for poor children and housing for the homeless, the sick and others. Everyone who got assistance from the public authorities was obliged to work here – in so far as age and vigour allowed – unless the poor commission gave permission to work somewhere else. Cf. Thestrup 1986, p. 125.

88 Jørgensen 1940, p. 38, and Wøllekær 1993, p. 10. The impulse for the establishment of combined poor- and workhouses in rural areas came from Schleswig, where a number of parish institutions of that type were established from the 1830s.

89 See for instance Jørgensen 1940, pp. 289-94, and Sejerholt 1940, pp. 387-90. There are clear parallels between the treatment meted out to inmates in combined poor- and workhouses and that imposed on the inmates in Danish prisons from ca. 1840, and there were the same basic underlying attitudes.

90 Nielsen 1932-35, pp. 455 f. The remark pertained incidentally to a combined poor- and workhouse in the countryside.

91 In Sejerholt 1940, p. 389 f., there is an account of the joint Sunday excursion for the children in the institution in Aarhus. The children who had family in Aarhus however had permission to visit them instead of following the flock!

92 Tønnesen 2005, p. 72.

93 Cf. Nielsen 1932-35, p. 439.

94 Due 2005, pp. 14 f.

95 Jørgensen 1940, pp. 341 f.

96 Nielsen 1932-35, p. 451, Tønnesen 2005, p. 72, Bay 1982, p. 283, and Jørgensen 1940, p. 373.

97 Sejerholt 1940, pp. 386 and 390 f.

98 Vestergaard 1999, p. 39.

99   Bay 1982, pp. 283-84. See too Blomberg 1956, II, p. 233.

100   Nielsen 1932-35, pp. 425-31 and 440 f.

101   Henningsen 1978, pp. 150-56.

102   The idea of allotting free gardens to the poor was taken up by the central authorities in Copenhagen, in that two circulars from the end of the 1820s encouraged the municipal authorities in the Kingdom to lay out such gardens. This is also known to have happened in Aarhus and Ribe. Cf. Engberg 2005, I, p. 34, Sejerholt 1940, p. 392, and Jørgensen 1940, p. 371.

103   Henningsen 1978, pp. 119 and 156.

104   In the case of Aabenraa, however, Lars Henningsen notices a change in the attitudes of the officials already in 1811. See Henningsen 1978, p. 136.

105   Henningsen 1978, pp. 161-64.

106   Even though only 3 % of the population were eligible to sit in the assemblies, these institutions had great significance for the awakening political life in the last years of Absolutism. See Michael Bregnsbo's article in this book.

107   Henningsen 1978, p. 180.

108   Henningsen 1978, pp. 171-74.

109   Feeding institutions are known from Aarhus (Sejerholt 1940, p. 391) and Ribe (Nielsen 1932-35, p. 525).

110   Cf. Brønfeld et al. 1998, pp. 82-83, and Blomberg 1956, II, p. 231.

111   Bro 2005a, pp. 60 and 82.

112   Bro 2005a, pp. 38 and 46.

113   Bro 2005a, pp. 42, 44 f. and 58 ff.

114   Cf. Thomas Bloch Ravn's article in this book.

115   In time these were not just limitations on the right to marry but also disenfranchisement and non-eligibility for parliament and municipal councils and certain limitations in inheritance and indemnity rights.

116   Bro 2005a, p. 90.

117   See in particular Jørgensen 1940, pp. 97 ff., and Thestrup 1986, p. 131.

118   Jørgensen 1940, pp. 103-11, Thestrup 1986, p. 132, and Filipsen 1990, pp. 147-62.

119   Bro 2005a, pp. 27 and 30.

120   Bundsgaard & Korsgaard 1991, p. 178.

121   Andersen 1987, pp. 15-17. The law meant an increased uptake of members in the health insurance societies, and in 1915, about half the population over the age of 15 were members of such a society.

122   Lars Henningsen observes, however, that the citizens had only a little influence on the administration of the 18th century poor relief system in the Duchy; their influence gradually increased after 1814. Henningsen 1978, pp. 210 and 213.

123   In his article about developments in the Copenhagen poor relief system 1770-1840, Keld Mikkelsen, for instance, lays crucial weight on the dissolution of the old patriarchal and socially binding relationships in town and country. Cf. Mikkelsen 2005, pp. 58 ff.

124 Cf. Larsen 2006.

125 The classic example of a country with a 'goal-oriented' system is USA, where public welfare systems are reserved for people who are not covered by private insurance.

Christian Larsen

Urban schools, 1537-1850

Introduction

During the period 1537-1848 there were two types of school in the Danish market towns: *latinskoler* (Latin schools, i.e. grammar schools) providing a preparatory education for university with a view to a career in the public sector thereafter, and *danske skoler* (Danish schools, i.e. national schools) providing an elementary education.[1] This article is concerned with these two types of school. The starting point is the period after the Reformation in 1536, as the foundations of the school system of the Absolutist period after 1660 were laid in the 16th century. The school system in Copenhagen and the Duchies of Schleswig and Holstein, where there were special local conditions will be outside the scope of this study.[2] We will however consider the conditions in Norway until 1814 (when Sweden assumed control), Iceland and the Faroe Islands.

The national school system was under the control of *Danske Kancelli* (The Danish Chancellery)[3] until 1848. Local inspections were the responsibility of the bishop as the highest authority in each individual see, the local administration, however, was the responsibility of the deans and parish priests. This was also the case for the grammar schools until 1805, when along with Copenhagen University they came under the control of *Direktionen for Universitetet og de lærde Skoler* (The Department for University and Grammar School Affairs). From 1848 all educational institutions became the province of *Kultusministeriet* (The Ministry for Ecclesiastical and Educational Affairs).

There is a wealth of archival information concerning grammar schools for the 16th – 19th centuries, in contrast to the relative archival poverty for national schools in the early part of this period. This is the result of a low document survival rate and the fact that there was less legislation for national schools than for grammar schools, even though the larger proportion of those being educated in market towns attended a national school. Grammar schools have received greater attention from educational historians in the form of comprehensive studies and monographs concerning individual schools. The literature concerning national schools in the period 1550-1850 is meagre and the standard works are antiquated. Most research has concentrated on the period 1870-1930.[4]

Schools in the 17th and 18th centuries

Grammar schools, 1537-1784

In 1536 King Christian III reformed the Church in Denmark and Norway, deposed the Catholic bishops and confiscated the episcopal lands. Thereafter the Lutheran national church was introduced. These changes were enshrined in the Church Ordinance of 1537-1539.[5] In this ordinance we find the regulations concerning grammar schools which were to be closely connected to the Danish Church until 1805. The ordinance stated that at a grammar school 'children are to be reared and have their minds prepared for evangelism', the school should also be the lynchpin ensuring that the child grew up to be a Christian, God-fearing person. Children should be taught about the glory of God and to 'uphold and preserve a good, civil life and the established regime'. Grammar schools should also however provide candidates for the civil service. The primary function of a grammar school education, until well into the 1800s, was to equip pupils to take a theological civil service qualification at university.

It was decided that a grammar school was to be established in every market town, with teachers competent to educate pupils. However, the schools were not established as quickly as they might have been, as the ordinance did not specify who exactly was to be responsible for their foundation. Despite this, every market town established its own grammar school in the 1500s. By 1600 there were 56 grammar schools in Denmark, 11 in Norway, one on the Faroe Islands and two in Iceland (70 in all). By 1660 this total had increased by 10, partly because the larger towns of Odense, Roskilde and Oslo (at that time called Christiania) had by then *gymnasier* (preparatory colleges). There was a concentration of schools on Zealand, Lolland, Falster and Funen, while Jutland, with fewer market towns, consequently had fewer schools. (See fig. 4, p. 425).

The inventory and educational scope of the schools were dependent on the economic resources available in their market town. Expenditure included teachers' salaries, musical instruments, necessities for reading and writing and clothes for the poorer students. The Church was responsible for the upkeep of the building; lighting was only used for festivals and holy days. The schools' finances were ensured by the redistribution of church land and tithes in 1536, the guarantee of free food for pupils at royal castles and the granting of the office of parish clerk to the teachers as an additional source of income. In many market towns, citizens were obliged to contribute financially to teachers' salaries.

The pupils, or 'disciples' as they were then known, were also ensured a variety of incomes, the most important being their right to beg. This right was upheld until 1805. Another was the right to sing for the burghers or the gentry. 'Disciples' were also given the right to hold the office of parish clerk in a local church. Finally, many schools had a series of trusts to finance food or clothing for its pupils and in some cases 'boarding school' systems were in place providing board and lodging for the poorer pupils. At Ribe Cathedral School in 1591, 191 of the 250 pupils received some form of support. Parents were therefore not required to contribute to their children's education as the school was able to provide for their basic needs, which could be augmented by the supplementary incomes available to the students themselves.

Grammar schools were for the sons of Protestant parents. Jewish boys were first permitted to attend in 1798 and Catholics after 1849. Girls were finally given the opportunity to attend in 1903.

According to the Church Ordinance, grammar schools were to be divided into several classes (from first to fifth form). Where there were three teachers at a school, four forms were provided; where only two teachers were available, the number of forms was limited to three. Small towns had minor schools (1-3 teachers), whereas major schools could be found in the cathedral cities, i.e. Copenhagen and Roskilde on Zealand, Odense on Funen, Haderslev, Ribe, Aarhus, Viborg and Aalborg in Jutland, Bergen, Hamar/Kristiansand, Oslo/Christiania, Stavanger and Trondheim in Norway. In these schools there could be as many as nine teachers.

The pupils in the first to fourth forms were taught Latin, scripture, choral singing, deduction, and in the lower forms, reading, writing and arithmetic. It is not quite clear what was taught in the fifth form, but the pupils received grounding in Greek. At the centre of the curriculum for all school years was Latin, comprising grammar, translation, conversation and essays. For those in the fourth form, it was decided that, 'so that they should speak nought but Latin, they shall daily read some verses by Virgil, just as they shall diligently practice diction and each week shall write an essay or verse'. For the men behind the Church Ordinance there was no doubt that the success of a child's studies was, 'intimately entwined with the fear of God (...) Therefore every Saturday should be set aside so that on that day pupils may especially hear about what pertains to religion'.

The school reforms of 1604, 1632 and 1656 increased the number of classes to eight and accordingly broadened the curriculum ensuring more room for scientific and practical subjects and Danish. However there were no real innovations to the original Church Ordinance and in *Danske Lov* and *Norske Lov* (the legal compilations for Denmark-Norway of 1683 and 1687) the older law was merely codified.

The entrance examination for university (*examen artium*) was not held at the individual schools but at Copenhagen University, which until 1811 was the only university in the Danish and Norwegian Kingdoms. In the Duchies, there was the University of Kiel, founded in 1665. It was not until 1845/1850 that the entrance examination was held at the individual schools.

The only innovation in this period was the introduction of *gymnasier* (preparatory colleges), which as an extension to the grammar schools were to function as a prelude to university. Preparatory colleges were established in Lund in Scania (part of Denmark until 1658) and Odense in 1619, Roskilde 1622, Ribe, Viborg, Aarhus and Oslo 1636 but with little success. Already by 1640 the preparatory colleges in Ribe, Viborg and Aarhus were closed. The schools in Roskilde and Lund continued for several decades before they too were forced to close. Only in Odense did the preparatory college survive for a longer period. Preparatory colleges represent only a short-lived aberration without any lasting significance.[6]

The philologist Kristian Jensen has investigated the age and social and demographic backgrounds of grammar school disciples for the period 1539-1660 which, within reason, may be seen as indicative of the rest of the 1600s. In the minor schools the pupils were mainly from the local area. In the major schools such as that in Roskilde the picture was very different. Here there were 365 boarders in the period 1637-1660, and as most of the students received stipends, the 365 boys were undoubtedly the great majority of all the pupils in the school in these years. Of these, there are details of the geographical origins of 225 pupils: Zealand 111, Jutland 48, Norway 26, Scania 22, Schleswig seven, Gotland six and Funen five. Despite Zealand's dominance in the figures, other regions are well represented. 94 pupils came from villages, 71 from market towns and the origin of 60 is unknown. The preponderance of country children is presumably explicable by the fact that many were the sons of clergymen. From the towns, the higher social groups (tradesmen, civil servants etc.) as well as the 'middle class' (craftsmen) were well represented, while the children of the lower classes were poorly represented amongst the pupils.[7]

The government was aware that some of the minor grammar schools in small market towns were surplus to requirements. Those with small numbers of pupils could be replaced by national schools where pupils were educated in scripture, arithmetic, reading, writing, book-keeping and, at coastal ports, navigation. This awareness was founded on a report by the bishops to *Danske Kancelli* in 1681. In 1682 the King set up a commission to find out which of 'the ineffective grammar schools in small market towns' could be closed down and which could continue. However, apart from the conversion of Stege Grammar School into a navigation school the commission's work was without result.

The problem of a plethora of minor schools continued. In the beginning of the 18th century there were 59 grammar schools in the Danish Kingdom, 11 in Norway, one on the Faroe Islands and two on Iceland – a total of 73 in the monarchy (excluding the Duchies). The historian Carl E. Jørgensen has investigated conditions in grammar schools in the early 18th century. Not one school could actually boast the full complement of eight classes called for in the reform of 1656. Copenhagen Grammar School had seven classes while the cathedral schools had only six and the majority of grammar schools in smaller towns only one or two. In the large or medium-sized towns, the aim of a grammar school education was to prepare the pupil for university – this was not the case in the small provincial towns. Here the teaching was at a lower level, the pupils only learning a little Latin but receiving a grounding in Danish, scripture, singing and, perhaps, writing. Individual students in the small towns studied further at a major grammar school before going to university.

A glance at all grammar schools in the early 18th century reveals a relatively homogeneous intake: children of the local church employees – the priest, the chaplain, the verger and the headmaster – made up the major portion of the pupils. The next largest group consisted of children of burghers while the number of children from the countryside was not very large. As in the previous century the primary goal for a grammar school education was a theological university education. Of 300 graduates from Viborg Cathedral School between 1700 and 1739, 250 became priests, parish clerks or teachers.[8]

Fig. 1.

In the 1739 reform, many of the small grammar schools were converted into 'script schools', as was the case in Kerteminde. The old grammar school was demolished in 1740 and a new building was erected in the churchyard. This building was taken down and re-erected in Den Gamle By *in Aarhus in 1934. The tables and benches in the school are from the 19th century, but it may be presumed that the grammar and 'script' schools of the 18th century were furnished in the same way.*

After a request from the headmaster of Ribe Cathedral School, Christian Falster, King Christian VI set up a school commission in 1733 with the head of *Danske Kancelli*, the bishop of Zealand, *gehejmeprokurøren*,[9] a historian and the Royal Chaplain as members. In 1732, *Danske Kancelli* had collected suggestions to improve the grammar school system as well as information pertaining to the individual schools. The bishop suggested converting many of the minor schools into national schools and redirecting their resources to the remaining grammar schools. In this way the remaining schools would benefit economically and teaching salaries would increase. This suggestion was met with opposition within the commission but Christian VI was convinced by the bishop's arguments and the commission thereafter began to consider concrete reductions.

In 1739 the final bill was enacted reducing the number of grammar schools from 72 to 26, a reduction of 40 schools in Denmark and six in Norway. The ex-grammar schools now became national schools. As compensation for the reductions in the number of grammar schools, the government raised the salaries of 18 headmasters, five deputies and three teachers, two further deputy posts were created and one teaching post. Finally, the remaining grammar schools received increased stipends from charitable trusts formerly belonging to the ex-grammar schools. In the small market towns, bereft of a grammar school, educational opportunities became limited. Parents had to decide whether their children should continue their education at a major grammar school, leave school or continue at the national school. The commission received protest letters from citizens in Sakskøbing on the island of Lolland, Stavanger in Norway, Lemvig in Jutland and Næstved and Holbæk on Zealand. In Holbæk the locals offered to run the school from the town budget and to ensure that only the most suitable students were enrolled.

In the preamble to the Grammar School Act it was asserted that an improved grammar school would enable its students to gain more from their university careers, which would in turn be of benefit to the university. Consequently, the university would supply better candidates for 'God's church, Our service and that of the fatherland'. In the detailed act, there was an attempt to include all aspects of the grammar school system: teachers' salaries, school budgets, curricula, teaching materials, holidays and examinations etc. Many of the act's paragraphs were codifications of previous laws. The curricular stipulations concerning religious education, Greek, Latin and Hebrew show that the schools were still regarded as a basis for a theological university education:

All schools should be the foundries of the Holy Ghost, all the teachers in the schools should with all the diligence and the skills endowed them by God strive to engender, not merely learning, but especially a true fear of God in the hearts of the disciples.

F$_{IG}$. 2.

Skælskør Grammar School was a typical example of grammar schools in the small market towns. The school house was a very small brick-building with two window bays facing Algade and one window bay on to the churchyard. The building was erected in the first half of the 16th century and had originally been the church tithe barn for grain. When the school was closed down, the house was sold in 1740 to one of the town merchants.

On a purely pedagogical level, the act contained progressive points concerning educational methods and the introduction of subjects such as history and geography. The importance of Danish as a mother tongue was emphasised, with much of the teaching now being conducted in Danish and the introduction of Danish textbooks. There was also emphasis on reverence for the Danish language. Hereafter the curriculum was partly linguistic and partly humanist with history and geography added to scripture, arithmetic, geometry and philosophy.[10]

CHRISTIAN LARSEN

In 1756 the government sharpened the terms of the act of 1739, asserting (amongst other things) that poor parents should not seek to use the grammar schools as a form of support for their children. By the early 1770s it was felt that the Grammar School Act of 1739 was outdated, springing, as it did, from the pietistic scholastic ideals of the period. *Gehejmekabinetssekretær* (the Privy Secretary) and de-facto government leader Ove Høegh-Guldberg set up a school reform commission. It was asserted in the commission that the schools were 'derelict' and that the students enrolling in the university were most unsatisfactory. Høegh-Guldberg became chairman of the commission and six months later the King signed the final bill, consisting of no less than 93 paragraphs.

The Grammar School Act of 1775 was marked by its conservatism, following the bent of the Government. It did however have some reforming characteristics in areas such as the teaching of Danish. The King hoped that the schools would in time mould 'young people with righteous instruction and thorough erudition into wise servants of Ourself and the country'. The teachers were to imprint the 'knowledge of faith' as they always had, but now they were also to espouse 'the duties, amongst which are that love and sacrifice they owe to King and fatherland'. Religious education and the classics remained dominant in the curriculum. Danish received a more independent position, Danish textbooks were to be used and Danish was to be developed orally and stylistically. The increased importance of Danish was part of the government's national-patriotic strategy, a reaction to J.F. Struensee's regime of 1770-1772.[11] The languages taught were Latin, Danish, Greek and Hebrew. Hebrew was optional for those not wishing to take a theological degree later. The other subjects on offer were scripture, history, geography and astronomy. The teaching of mathematics, physics and philosophy was taken over by the university. Though the reform shows progress, it was not a break with the traditions of 1537-1539.[12]

National schools, 1537-1789

The term *dansk skole* embodied the idea that Latin was not taught in the school, the term however was a 'catch all', covering a large variety of educational options, including Danish, German and private schools. The Church Ordinance stated simply:

The so-called 'Script-schools' for boys and girls, which are unsuited for teaching Latin, must be paid for by private subscription. The teachers of these schools shall however be vigilant that true fear of God is instilled in these children along with their education.

After this, there was no actual regulation throughout the 16th and 17th centuries. A standard law for *danske skoler* was first introduced in 1814. *Danske Lov* of 1683 repeated the terms of the previous ordinance that the local authorities in a market town should provide means for a school and that local authorities and parish priests should be its inspectors. All those teaching in private education were to have had a university education or be approved by the bishop or at least by the parish priest.

In the Poor Act of 1708, it was asserted that no one was to teach before being examined in scripture, writing, and arithmetic by the priest in the presence of the municipal corporation. Each town was to be allocated a number of students (as potential teachers) relative to the town's population. Only teachers approved by the municipal corporation had the right to teach. These rules were also enforced for women in handicraft education. School teachers were exempt from ordinary municipal taxes. Children in the care of the relief system were to have free access to education. The act did not have any great effect as no financial provision was made for salaries or schoolhouses and the following years were affected by the Great Nordic War of 1709-1720. However, some schools were established.

In the larger towns there had been a national school system since the Reformation, but in smaller ones, schools began to appear in the 1600s. Compared with the grammar schools, national schools were far more heterogeneous in nature as there were no central guidelines. There were, however, certain general trends. Typically, a national school was either established by a private individual who, upon receiving citizenship from the municipal corporation, was entitled to give lessons – or by an endowment from a nobleman, priest or citizen. The latter were referred to as endowed schools and were notable in the 17th and 18th centuries. In some towns there were German schools with the emphasis on teaching German. Notable examples were found in Ribe, Fredericia, Aarhus, Aalborg, Randers and Horsens in Jutland, Odense on Funen, and Slagelse and Elsinore on Zealand. In Fredericia and Elsinore, lessons were in German because the children came from German-speaking homes. Elsinore had a German schoolmaster as early as 1578 where at that time there was already a Danish schoolmaster. Education in Danish and German schools appears to have been of the same type and content.

In a few towns, such as Elsinore and Ribe, there were two types of schools: national schools teaching reading (and the catechism) and those teaching writing and arithmetic. In other towns there were elementary schools for girls and small boys where matrons gave elementary lessons in reading and the catechism. Finally there

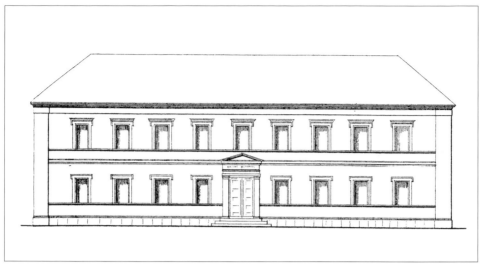

FIG. 3.

Kolding Grammar School was established shortly after the Reformation. The school was one of the small grammar schools with two teachers and four classes. In 1809 the Latin school was changed into a grammar school, but was still a small school with 5-6 pupils finishing each year. In 1845 the school got a new building, but it was closed down only 11 years later. (Drawing from the prospectus for the inauguration of the school's new building 23 October 1845.)

were sewing and crocheting schools, which taught girls handicrafts. Alongside these schools, there was private education, many (especially the more wealthy) of the burghers of the towns employed private tutors to educate their children at home.

In many towns, the municipal corporation supported the national schools. This assistance could take various forms, e.g. paying the school's costs, the corporation could give the teacher a monopoly to run the school, or there could be provision for stipends and bursaries to fund the education of poor children. In many churches, there were collections for schools. It was also possible, to a certain extent, for a school to be exempted from paying taxes and rates. Often, it was difficult enough to fund the local grammar school – so in many small towns, the grammar school also functioned as a national school giving an elementary education.

The teacher was responsible for his own survival as he was not paid by the town. His income came from parental or magisterial school fees that were paid in cash or kind. Many teachers had a second profession, such as verger or undertaker. He could also supplement his income by writing applications or doing accounts for his neighbours.

No teacher training colleges (in Danish: *seminarier*) existed before 1791. And in fact, most teachers in the 17th and 18th centuries had a background as merchant, artisan or soldier. There are a few examples of grammar school students who had not yet finished their studies becoming teachers. The schoolmistresses, mainly in the larger towns, were employed in needlework and elementary schools to teach girls and small boys. In towns such as Elsinore and Odense schoolmistresses were only allowed to teach boys under six and girls.[13]

As part of the policies of pietistic Christian VI, the Confirmation Act of 1736 introduced compulsory church confirmation for all children with attendant religious instruction as a preparation. The act's second paragraph states that no child:

(…) should be entered for confirmation, who has not received the necessary religious instruction at school, or where there is no public school, learned to know God from the parish clerk or another suitable person before they come before the priest to be catechised, examined and confirmed.[14]

The act's insistence on school-based education demanded an educational system that could deliver such instruction. This led to the first school law for the rural districts of Denmark and Norway in 1739, which was met with widespread resistance amongst the population and was accordingly revised in 1740. This resistance could have been the reason that no bill concerning market towns was promulgated. However, it could be that the government felt that the reform of the grammar schools in 1739 had been sufficient. The grammar schools that had been closed were converted into *kristendomsskoler* ('script-schools') which, as a rule, took over the grammar school buildings and retained the old headmaster as teacher. These schools were to teach scripture, reading, writing and arithmetic. Their establishment caused problems for previously established national schools which were faced with a new competitor in the 'script' school and in several instances were forced to close.

Our knowledge of conditions in the national schools of the mid-18th century is patchy due to a lack of source material. However a picture of conditions can be created from several disparate sources. Bishop Peder Hersleb in the Zealand diocese noted in his journal of pastoral visitations in the 1740s that education in the market towns was of a mediocre standard with some differences from one locality to another. The directions given to the teacher at Svaneke on Bornholm in 1751 show the standard of a school in an average Danish market town. Children should learn to read clearly and fluently from Danish books, know their letters, be able to recite Luther's catechism and have begun to learn the instructions from the authorised religious primer before they learned writing and aritmetic.

Information on the schools was collected in 1784 as a basis for a contemplated reform of the Danish school system in the provincial towns. According to these reports, there was one school in half the towns in the country and in the other half, two. In towns with two schools, one was generally run by the parish clerk primarily for poor children, while the other was run by a teacher for paying pupils, though this could vary with the locality. Scripture and reading were the core subjects and in some areas writing and arithmetic supplemented this. A look at the teachers' background shows that around a third were students and several had a degree in divinity. The rest had been merchants, hatters, farmers, non-commissioned officers, bailiffs, sailors, private tutors etc. Compared with earlier in the century, there had been improvements but there had been no decisive breakthrough in public education. Reform was still required to prevent unsatisfactory school attendance, which impeded an effective public education system.[15]

Schools in the 19th century

The coup of 1784, when the Danish Crown Prince (later King Frederik VI) toppled Ove Høegh-Guldberg's regime, was the catalyst for sweeping reforms, which also came to include public education. In 1788, Copenhagen University was given a new charter, in 1791 the first Danish teacher training colleges were established, in 1805-1806 there was a reform of the grammar schools, and in 1814 the national schools came under new legislation.

Grammar schools, 1784-1850

Despite a number of reforms to the grammar schools, the last one in 1775, they were subjected to a great deal of criticism in the 1780s as it was felt that the reforms had not produced the necessary improvement and that a more fundamental reform was required. At this time there were 27 grammar schools (19 in Denmark, six in Norway, one in Iceland – and one on the Faroe Islands, which was closed in 1794). A commission for the grammar schools was appointed in 1785, but only really began its deliberations when the Crown Prince's brother-in-law, Duke Frederik Christian of Augustenborg, was appointed its head in 1790.

The head of the commission and several of its members were influenced by the philosophy of philanthropism, with its vision of creating – by education – a rational, enlightened and contented population. They were, however, also inspired by the German pedagogical movement, neo-humanism. According to neohumanistic principles, the classical languages were not a tool subject, but instead the basis for the students' culture, an intellectual, moral and aesthetic background which could be used in the study of other subjects. Thus, spiritual education could be achieved through the study of classical authors. Duke Frederik Christian opened the debate in 1795 with the publication of the pedagogical programme 'Ideas concerning our grammar schools' organisation' in the prominent periodical *Minerva* and the distribution of this article to the headmasters all over the two Kingdoms. Frederik Christian's 'Ideas' programme was to be influential for the task ahead. According to the Duke, grammar schools should partly impart the skills necessary for further education and partly equip the student with those skills thought essential for a refined and cultured person.

As a result of the Duke's article and replies from the headmasters, an experimental reform was started at three schools in Denmark and Norway, and a training college for grammar school teachers (*Seminarium Pedagogicum*) was established at Copenhagen University (1799-1810). A modified version of the reform was introduced in the remainder of the grammar schools in 1805. The reform called for the abolition of pupils' choir duties in church and the clerk tasks held by teachers. The choir duties, it was felt, had led to 'frequent neglect of scholastic efforts'. At the same time Norwegian grammar schools gained the right to hold matriculation examinations for the university (otherwise reserved for the university itself), this was the government's reply to strong demands for a Norwegian university.[16]

The final bill was passed in 1809 and became the foundation for grammar schools until 1903 when modern preparatory colleges were introduced into Denmark. The act had a statement of intent in which it was said that the schools should give their pupils 'an appropriate improvement of skills, talents and abilities in order to be able to continue their studies at university'. Grammar schools were no longer merely a preparation for theological studies but for all university studies, thus breaking with the tradition of the Lutheran Church Schools of 1537-1539.

One of the innovations in the reform was the science and scholarship based cur-

1660

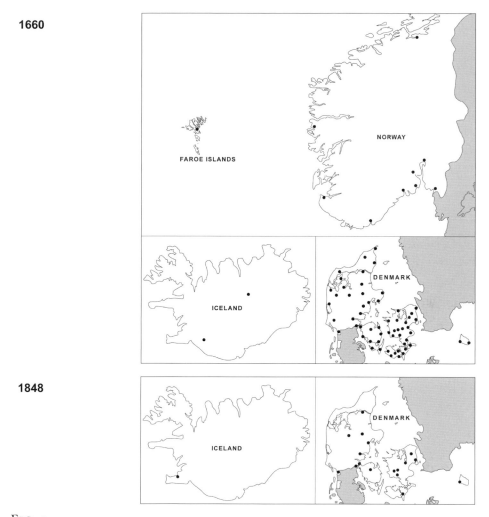

1848

Fig. 4.

Grammar Schools 1660 and 1848. In 1660 Denmark (with Iceland and the Faroes) had 64 grammar schools. 200 years later, the number was reduced to 18 schools.

riculum plan. The scientific nature of education was accentuated and every subject now had its own master. Curricular planning was expressed in the development of lesson plans, syllabus and curricular criteria, which were to be approved by the central administration, thus effectively creating a national curriculum.

The act introduced two forms of grammar school: 21 *fuldstændige skoler* ('finishing schools') with direct access to the university, and four *middelskoler* (middle schools) with the four lower forms and no direct access to the university. The finishing schools taught Danish, Latin, Greek, Hebrew, French, German, religion, ethics, geography, history, arithmetic, geometry and calligraphy. The middle schools taught the same subjects, except for Hebrew which was never taught, and French and German which were only taught where it was possible. In both schools there was also the possiblity of teaching natural sciences, anthropology, English, drawing, singing and gymnastics, if there were sufficient teachers. The schools were under *Direktionen for Universitetet og de lærde Skoler* (The Department for University and Grammar School Affairs) which supervised teachers, teaching and pupils.[17]

Denmark's involvement in the Napoleonic wars, the state bankruptcy in 1813 and the economic hardships that followed, meant that the promises of the reform could not be realised and nothing happened concerning educational reform until the 1830s. After the loss of Norway, there were 17 grammar schools in Denmark and two in Iceland in 1820, which declined to 13 (and the two Icelandic schools) by 1850 after the government closed a number of schools. Many schools had a small number of students, with only 1-3 graduating each year. The government wanted to increase the number of graduates by closing schools and using the surplus funds to finance the remaining schools, thereby raising standards. Therefore, between 1839 and 1846, four towns lost their grammar schools.

In the 1830s the grammar schools were subject to criticism, as it was felt that the natural sciences were not adequately represented in the curriculum. The new urban middle classes in particular were vociferous in advocating the inclusion of modern subjects (such as English, German, French and the natural sciences) as a preparation for a career in trade or production. There was a demand for more schools equipped to teach these subjects (*realskoler*). As in the 1790s there was an experiment with educational methods at three schools between 1845 and 1850. This provided the basis for the Grammar School Act of 1850, which strengthened the place of science and Danish in the curriculum while retaining the central role of classics and religion. It was the government's intention to satisfy both scientists and humanists with this reform. The other innovation of the reform was to transfer the entrance examination for the university to the schools themselves.[18]

National schools, 1789-1848

In 1789 the government set up *Den Store Skolekommission* (The Commission for the Better Organisation of National Schools), which existed until 1814. The commission initially addressed the condition of village schools as part of the government's agrarian reforms. It was only in 1806 that the commission finally looked at the condition of education in the market towns. The citizens of these towns had been much more active however in the process of reforming municipal education at a local level. In the vanguard was Slagelse where in 1799 there was a reform of the school system. A so-called literary and practical school (*læse- og arbejdsskole*) was founded which, in the words of the founders and in line with the ideals of the Enlightenment, was designed to encourage thought, sharpen understanding, enrich the language, ennoble the heart and promote refinement in the pupils. Girls were to learn spinning, stocking knitting and crocheting, while the boys learned to make boxes, pipe racks, pencils and the like. Teaching geography, history, natural sciences, German, drawing, writing and arithmetic was the responsibility of the parish priest. Several market towns followed this lead and in more and more towns, commissions for the modernisation of schools were set up.

The reports about private schools show that in 1802 there were 73 private schools in Denmark and Norway, of which the majority were in Copenhagen. There were 28 boys' schools, 31 girls' schools and 14 co-educational schools with a total of 2,224 pupils, 201 schoolmasters and 53 schoolmistresses.

In 1806 the governmental commission began to frame a new school act for the market towns, and Professor Friedrich Münter was sent on a fact-finding tour to German schools. However, due to the Napoleonic wars, the report was first finished in 1810. The aim was to create uniformity in the national school system and the commission therefore made the village school system the benchmark for the changes necessary in the towns. The bill was given royal consent in 1813 and became law in 1814.

Municipal schools were, according to the act's statement of intent, to form children into 'good and righteous people' in the spirit of the Protestant Lutheran doctrine, but 'also to give them the skills and abilities necessary to be productive citizens of the state'. In all market towns there were one or more national schools teaching 'the skills necessary for ordinary folk' and these were aimed at the children of the lower classes. The curriculum consisted of religion, writing, reading, arithmetic and singing. Where a trained teacher was available, there was also to be gymnastics for an hour each day. Children went to school at the age of 6-7 and finished at the time of their confirmation at 13-14. In conjunction with the municipal schools there could be technical schools, where crafts and practical skills were taught.

According to the act, in larger market towns, *realskoler* (secondary schools) could be established for children aged 14-17 years who did not need an academic education, but needed specialised technical and commercial skills. These schools attracted the sons of the better-off families and provided a curriculum including Danish, religion, calligraphy, arithmetic (including accounting and book-keeping), practical mathematics (for use by artisans), natural sciences, history, geography (including the study of international trade), German, French, English (occasionally) and, if required, draughtsmanship, singing and gymnastics. In ports, there could be lessons in navigation and swimming.

Teachers were paid out of the school fund. The income came partly from gifts, fines and church income, and partly from municipal tax. The school fund and local education system were under the control of the *skolekommission* (the town's school board) consisting of the parish priest(s), the municipal corporation or bailiff and two or three members selected by the *skoledirektion* (the county school board consisting of the *amtmand* and the dean) for a two-year term. With the Municipal Act of 1837, the town school boards were retained but were now elected by the town council and at least one member was to be a councillor. The school boards of the provincial towns and villages were under the authority of the the county school board who were to approve the decisions of the boards. *Danske Kancelli* was the ultimate authority, approving the curriculum, and overseeing the development of education in the towns, the number of schools, the size of school districts, teachers' salaries and teachers.[19]

The national school acts of 1814 for town and county remained in force until well into the 20th century, even though there were some changes in 1841, 1856, 1868, 1871 and 1899. The introduction of the 1814 acts was impeded by the financial crisis caused by the state bankruptcy of 1813. Despite the plan for two types of school there were for a considerable time only municipal schools with the same curriculum as that in the countryside. The planned system of *realskoler* remained only on paper, lacking the money, the teachers and the interest of the local population to come to fruition. There were instead *realklasser* (secondary school classes) at the national schools that taught history, geography, biology and physics – and, in some towns, mathematics, drawing or German. In some special cases, navigation and bookkeeping were taught. In other places, there were *realklasser* held at the local grammar school or in privately funded schools, and reports from 1836 show that such classes existed in several towns. In some places teachers offered lessons after school hours in languages and technical subjects for a fee. In 50 market towns there were one or more private schools. In 1836 there were 98 publicly managed schools with 15,253 pupils and 211 private schools with 3,389 pupils. By 1850, 16,100 pupils out of 22,500 children of school age went to a publicly managed school.

In conjunction with general progress, particularly in urban business, there was an increased demand for the education of children who needed more than an elementary education while not needing an academic education. In the years after 1830, there was a great debate about the establishment of *realskoler* teaching subjects useful for future merchants, industrialists and seamen. There was a demand for such an education promised by the act of 1814 but never delivered. In 1838, *Danske Kancelli* called for the establishment of fee-paying schools for boys. Many were founded in the following decade thus finally satisfying the need for *realskoler*. This development was aided by the government closure of eight grammar schools and their replacement with municipal *realskoler*. The era of the technical schools came after 1850 however.[20]

Conclusion

In the 16th and 17th centuries education was an urban phenomenon. From the 1730s compulsory education became nation-wide and towns lost their monopoly on educational opportunity, especially after the reforms of 1814. However, there were no advanced schools established in the countryside at this time and urban children retained the advantage they had over their country cousins. In market towns, there was a range of educational opportunities designed for different target groups, viz. grammar schools for those who wished to advance to further study and national schools for those who wanted a basic education. From the early 19th century there were also *realskoler* intended for those who required more than an elementary education but who did not need classical grammar school education. It could be difficult for the towns to establish and maintain these institutions if there were too few pupils – a particular problem for the grammar schools. For the elementary schools the greatest problem was truancy which first began to be dealt with in the late 19th century.

SCHOOL ACTS

Grammar School Act 1739/1963. *Forordning angaaende hvor mange latinske Skoler i Danmark og Norge skal vedblive, samt hvorledes med Ungdommens Information, Ingeniorum prøve, den aarlige Examen og*

Stipendiers distribution, med viidere efterdags skal forholdes. Friderichsberg 17 Aprilis Anno 1739. (Skolehistoriske aktstykker i facsimiletrykk, 13). Oslo: Norsk pedagogisk studiesamlings Venner.

Grammar School Act 1756/1963. *Forordning angaaende fattige Børns Antagelse i de publique Latinske skoler og Forsendelse til Academiet, Ingeniorum prøve og Stipendiorum Uddeeling, med viidere. Fredensborg Slot 23de Julii Anno 1756.* (Skolehistoriske aktstykker i facsimiletrykk, 14). Oslo: Norsk pedagogisk studiesamlings Venner.

Grammar School Act 1775/1963. *Forordning angaaende Skoele-Væsenets Forbedring ved de publique Latinske Skoeler, og hvad den studerende Ungdom, de saavel fra publique som privat Information kommer til Academiet, skal giøre Reede for. Christiansborg Slot 11te Maji 1775.* (Skolehistoriske aktstykker i facsimiletrykk, 15). Oslo: Norsk pedagogisk studiesamlings Venner.

Grammar School Act 1809/1963. *Forordning angaaende de lærde Skoler i Danmark og Norge. Kbh. 7de Nov. 1809.* (Skolehistoriske aktstykker i facsimiletrykk, 17). Oslo: Norsk pedagogisk studiesamlings Venner.

Municipal Education Act 1814/1981. *Anordning for Almue-Skolevæsenet i Kjøbstæderne i Danmark, Kjøbenhavn undtagen. Frederiksberg Slot den 29 Juli 1814.* Faksimileudgave. Vejle: Kroghs Skolehåndbog.

BIBLIOGRAPHY

Appel, Charlotte 2001. *Læsning og bogmarked i 1600-tallets Danmark.* (Danish Humanist Texts, 23). Copenhagen: Museum Tusculanum.

Collegial-Tidende for Danmark og Norge 1802. Copenhagen: Johan Frederik Schultz.

Hahn Kristensen, Curt 1962. *Seminarium Pædagogicum. Det pædagogiske Seminarium ved Københavns Universitet 1800-1811.* (Kirkehistoriske Studier, II, 15). Copenhagen: G.E.C. Gad.

Haue, Harry 2003. *Almendannelse som ledestjerne. En undersøgelse af almendannelsens funktion i dansk gymnasieundervisning 1775-2000.* (University of Southern Denmark, Studies in History and Social Sciences, 259). Odense: Syddansk Universitetsforlag.

Japsen, G. 1968. *Det dansksprogede skolevæsen i Sønderjylland indtil 1814.* (Skrifter udgivet af Historisk Samfund for Sønderjylland, 40). Tønder: Th. Laursen.

Jensen, Kristian 1982. *Latinskolens dannelse. Latinundervisningens indhold og formål fra reformationen til enevælden.* (Antikken i Danmark, 3). Copenhagen: Museum Tusculanum.

Jørgensen, Carl E. 2001. 'Latinskolereduktionen 1740'. *Uddannelseshistorie* 2001, pp. 70-142.

Kong Fridrich den Fierdes Allernaadigste Forordninger og Aabne Breve fra Aar 1708 til 1709. Copenhagen 1709, pp. 37-56.

Kong Christian den Siettes allernaadigste Forordninger og aabne Breve fra Aar 1735 til 1736. Copenhagen 1736, pp. 14-29.

Kong Christian den Syvendes allernaadigste Forordninger og aabne Breve for Aar 1805. Copenhagen: Schultz 1806, pp. 100-06.

Kopitzsch, Franklin (ed.) 1981. *Erziehungs- und Bildungsgeschichte Schleswig-Holsteins von der Aufklärung bis zum Kaiserreich. Theorie, Fallstudien, Quellenkunde, Bibliographie.* (Studien zur Wirtschafts- und Sozialgeschichte Schleswig-Holsteins, 2). Neumünster: Wachholtz.

Kornerup, Bjørn 1947-1952. *Ribe Katedralskoles Historie. Studier over 800 Aars dansk Skolehistorie.* Copenhagen: Gyldendal.

Kyrre, Hans & H.P. Langkilde 1926. *Byens Skole. Københavns kommunale Skoles Historie.* Copenhagen: Gyldendal.

Lange, Paul G. 1995. 'Et latinskoleforsøg for 200 år siden'. *Uddannelseshistorie* 1995, pp. 67-94.

Larsen, Christian (ed.) 2003. *Hoveriet og arbejdet skal gøres, kroppen skal bruges – sjælen kan have, hvem der vil. Biskop Peder Herslebs visitatsindberetninger 1739-1745.* Copenhagen: Selskabet for Udgivelse af Kilder til Dansk Historie.

Larsen, Christian (ed.) 2005. *Dansk Uddannelseshistorisk Bibliografi 1948-2004.* (University of Southern Denmark, Studies in History and Social Sciences, 299). Odense: Syddansk Universitetsforlag.

Larsen, Joakim 1881. *Bidrag til Kjøbenhavns offentlige Skolevæsens Historie.* Copenhagen: Schubothe.

Larsen, Joakim 1984a/1916. *Bidrag til Den danske skoles historie 1536-1784.* (Unge Pædagogers serie, B 37). Copenhagen: Unge Pædagoger.

Larsen, Joakim 1984b/1893. *Bidrag til Den danske skoles historie 1784-1818.* (Unge Pædagogers serie, B 38). Copenhagen: Unge Pædagoger.

Larsen, Joakim 1984c/1899. *Bidrag til Den danske folkeskoles historie 1818-1898.* (Unge Pædagogers serie, B 39). Copenhagen: Unge Pædagoger.

Lausten, Martin Schwarz (ed.) 1989. *Kirkeordinansen 1537/39. Det danske Udkast til Kirkeordinansen (1537), Ordinatio Ecclesiastica Regnorum Daniæ et Norvwegiæ et Ducatuum Schleswicensis Holsatiæ etc. (1537), Den danske Kirkeordinans 1539.* Copenhagen: Akademisk Forlag.

Nørr, Erik 2000a. 'Almue- og borgerskolevæsenet i det 19. århundrede'. In: Leon Jespersen, E. Ladewig Petersen, Ditlev Tamm (eds.), *Dansk Forvaltningshistorie I. Fra middelalderen til 1901. Stat, Forvaltning og Samfund.* Copenhagen: Jurist- og Økonomforbundet, pp. 757-86.

Nørr, Erik 2000b. 'Den lærde skole i det 19. århundrede'. In: Leon Jespersen, E. Ladewig Petersen, Ditlev Tamm (eds.), *Dansk Forvaltningshistorie I. Fra middelalderen til 1901. Stat, Forvaltning og Samfund.* Copenhagen: Jurist- og Økonomforbundet, pp. 787-806.

Rørdam, Holger Fr. (ed.) 1883-1889. *Danske Kirkelove samt Udvalg af andre Bestemmelser vedrørende Kirken, Skolen og de Fattiges Forsørgelse fra Reformationen indtil Christian V's Danske Lov. 1536-1683.* Copenhagen: Selskabet for Danmarks Kirkehistorie.

Notes

1   Translated by archivist, cand.mag. Robert Sunderland. The author wishes to thank archivist, dr.phil. Erik Nørr and professor, dr.pæd. Vagn Skovgaard-Petersen (†) for comments to the article.

2   For Copenhagen see Larsen 1881. On conditions in the Duchies see Japsen 1968 and Kopitzsch 1981.

3   *Danske Kancelli* was the ultimate authority for the courts, the clergy and the education system. The Chancellery also functioned as a cabinet office.

4   For a summary of research on education in Denmark see Larsen 2005.

5   Lausten 1989.

6   Larsen 1984a/1916, Appel 2001. Vol. 1, pp. 223-30 og Jensen 1982, pp. 22 f., 51-61, 110-27, 159-74, 186-90.

7   Jensen 1982, pp. 24-47.

8   Rørdam 1883-1889 III, p. 529, III, p. 541, Larsen 1984a/1916, pp. 117 f., Jørgensen 2001, pp. 71-86, 92-96.

9   *Generalprokurøren* was reponsible for the implementation of the government's decrees and the supervision of the civil service.

10 Jørgensen 2001, pp. 96-121, Kornerup 1947-1952 II, pp. 207-09. Grammar Schoool Act 1739/1963. (*Forordning angaaende hvor mange latinske Skoler i Danmark og Norge skal vedblive,* 1739).

11 The German physician J.F. Struensee, as chief minister in the government of insane King Christian VII, 1770-72, had been deposed by a coup in January 1772 and subsequently executed. Hereafter, executive power resided with the Dowager Queen Juliane Marie and Ove Høgh-Guldberg.

12 Kornerup 1947-1952 II, pp. 269-73, Grammar School Act 1756/1963. (*Forordning angaaende fattige Børns Antagelse i de publique Latinske skoler og Forsendelse til Academiet, Ingeniorum prøve og Stipendiorum Uddeeling, med viidere,* 1756).

13 Act to make provisions about begging in towns and rural districts ('Poor Act') 24 September 1708, in: *Kong Fridrich den Fierdes Allernaadigste Forordninger og Aabne Breve fra Aar 1708 til 1709* 1709, pp. 37-56. Appel 2001, vol. 1, pp. 230-46, Larsen 1984a/1916, pp. 107-26.

14 The Confirmation Act 13 January 1736 (*Forordning angaaende den tilvoxende Ungdoms Confirmation og Bekræftelse udi deres Daabes Naade,* 1736).

15 Larsen 2003, et passim. Jørgensen 2001, pp. 123-28, Larsen 1984a/1916, pp. 325-50.

16 Attempted reforms at Copenhagen Grammar School is described by Lange 1995. The teacher training college is covered by Hahn Kristensen 1962. Act to make provisions for changes in the 1775 Grammar School Act 22 March 1805 in: *Kong Christian den Syvendes allernaadigste Forordninger og aabne Breve for Aar 1805* 1806, pp. 100-06.

17 Grammar School Act 1809/1963. (*Forordning angaaende de lærde Skoler i Danmark og Norge. Kbh. 7de Nov. 1809*). Haue 2003. Nørr 2000b.

18 Haue 2003. Nørr 2000b.

19 Larsen 1984b/1893, pp. 253-79. Collegial-Tidende 1802, p. 523. Municipal Education Act 1814/1981. (*Anordning for Almue-Skolevæsenet i Kjøbstæderne i Danmark, Kjøbenhavn undtagen. Frederiksberg Slot den 29 Juli 1814*).

20 Larsen 1984c/1899, pp. 63-69, 99-109. Nørr 2000a.

Jens Henrik Koudal

Stadsmusikanter and urban culture in the Danish empire during the Absolute monarchy

Music is an individual human expression and at the same time a many-facetted social phenomenon. In the article, I will show how music during Absolutism was integrated in urban culture in the form of the *stadsmusikant* institution. A *stadsmusikant* was a town musician employed by the town council.[1] First, it will be shown how urban music culture was just one among several music cultures in Denmark in the period 1660-1848. Then, the structure and history of the *stadsmusikant* system will be examined. Third, the discussion that took place in the 18th century will be briefly touched on, and finally, the focus will be on some international aspects of the Danish *stadsmusikant* system.

A music culture can be defined as the totality of a group of people's musical repertoire, musical instruments, music theory and aesthetics plus the organisation and behaviour associated with music. In the Danish state in the period covered here, there were three essentially different music cultures emanating from the court, the village and the market town. To illustrate the distinctiveness of the market town music, I will initially characterise the three music cultures on the basis of the purpose and structure of each of them.

Court and village

The royal court brought cultural elements to Denmark from all over Europe. The Kings wanted the best and most modern music of the time and engaged eminent musicians and composers from many countries.[2] The key word for the music life of the court is: ceremonial. The power of the Absolute monarch was displayed in the daily ceremonial and ritualised court functions, of which the most important were the entrances, anointings, weddings and funerals. This display should not only impress and demonstrate that there was a bottomless chasm between the King and everyone else. It should also, symbolically, represent society's underlying religious and political values. The European courts competed in dignified displays, in which music was one of the indispensable elements. For daily use, the monarch had the Royal Trumpeter Corps, the trumpeters of the Royal Life Guards, the royal orchestra and the wind bands of the two military units *Livgarden til fods* (The Royal Life Guards Infantry) and the Grenadier Corps. In addition, the Absolute Kings wanted to have a ceremonial opera as known from, among other places, the court in Versailles, but this was only partly carried out.

The repertoire of the court music was international in principle, and used a broad spectrum of the professionally produced instruments of art music. For the conductor, it was important to be broadly familiar with European trends and be able to renew and readjust. Contemporary music was played and the conductors were obliged to compose new pieces continuously on a high artistic level.

Things were completely different with the second music culture: village music, which concerned 80 % of the population. In the typical village, work and socialising, fun and gravity were woven together. Song and music blossomed most exuberantly at the annual festivals and people's red-letter days, but were also linked to everyday work and social contact. Music did not exist as a professional occupation, at most as a sideline. At the annual festivals and red-letter days, people did mutual favours for one another, and dance music could be played by relatives, neighbours or travelling musicians without cash payment being needed. Peasants wanted instrumental music primarily at weddings and christening parties. At the beginning of our period, that is the decades after 1660, village music was characterised by a number of old, traditional instruments: old drone instruments like hurdy-gurdys and bagpipes, fiddles like *gige* and *fedel*, shawms, and drums including *rumlepotte* (a kind of friction drum), animal horns and other instruments with a practical-ritual function. Many of these instruments were made by the musician himself. Moreover, it was characteristic for this music culture that people danced not infrequently to song. All in all, a traditional music culture was handed down by ear, without professional musicians, without formalised training or payment for music. The repertoire was traditional. People danced the Polish dance,[3] played singing games and sang secular ballads, lyrical love songs and religious songs. This changed in the 18th century, especially because of the *stadsmusikant* system, which we will see below.

JENS HENRIK KOUDAL

The *stadsmusikant* institution

The third music culture, the burghers' music life in the market towns, was marked by contacts with Germany, Holland and the large trading towns in the Baltic Sea area, that is, Protestant Northern Europe. In the churches, the music was led by a cantor who had at his disposal a choir of school boys, the organist and on special occasions, the *stadsmusikant*. Secular music life in the market towns had the privileged *stadsmusikant* as its central figure, and therefore we will look more closely at this.

A *stadsmusikant* was in the Danish state one of the town's *embeds-* and *bestillings-mænd* (civil servants and officials) and was appointed by the *magistrat* (the town council) with duties and profession privileges. Thus he was not an independent tradesman. In exchange for his duties to the town council and the burghers, he had the right to play music as a profession in a certain area.

The European roots of town music go back to the medieval era, and *stadsmusikanter* were known in most of Europe.[4] There were *stadsmusikanter* from Dublin to Vyborg (in present-day Russia), from Lille to Krakow, and from Barcelona to Zagreb. To the north, the office of *stadsmusikant* was established as far north as Trondheim. The earliest *stadsmusikanter* we know about were appointed in Northern Italy at the beginning of the 13th century. The *stadsmusikant* system became most widespread however between 1500 and 1800 and it is not until after the year 1500 that we know about the phenomenon in Denmark. The earliest known *stadsmusikant* in the Danish Kingdom was appointed in Aarhus in the year 1500. Jes Lassen, the name of the musician, swore his allegiance to the town and at the same time had to promise not to take an engagement elsewhere without the mayor's permission.

In the period prior to the setting up of the Absolute monarchy in 1660, there were probably a score of towns in Denmark, Norway, Schleswig and Holstein which appointed *stadsmusikanter* to take part in the church music, to support the functions of the municipal authorities, for *tårnblæsning* (i.e. use of wind instruments in church and town hall towers), and especially to lend lustre to the burghers' weddings and other festivities. In general, one displayed one's prosperity and one's place in the society of rank by engaging musicians, and in the bridal procession, the music was a ringing proclamation that a marriage had taken place.[5] The idea was from the countries to the south, where the town music in Hamburg, Lübeck, Bremen and Danzig was admired far and wide.

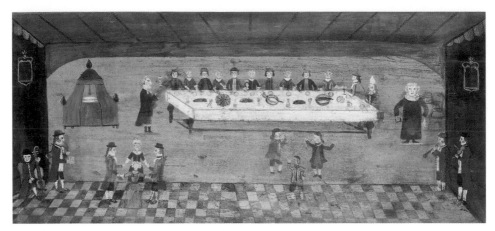

FIG. 1.

A peasant wedding in Northern Zealand ca. 1790. This is dinner with the vicar (to the right) and parish clerk (to the left), dance and marriage bed. Presumably they are stadsmusikanter who are playing the violin, oboe or clarinet, French horn and cello. Painted panel from the Grimstrup room.

It is fascinating to follow how the European *stadsmusikant* idea came to Denmark from the south – and became reshaped in a special Danish version. Such a transformation process took place in the period of the Absolute monarchy after 1660. In 1670, Denmark and Norway got a centrally controlled *stadsmusikant* system. The Absolute monarch arrogated to himself by an ordinance of 3 August 1670 the right to approve all local *stadsmusikant* appointments, and the musician in question was at the same time ordered to make trumpeters available for the navy. That is, the appointments of *stadsmusikanter* by the municipal authorities were valid only after they had obtained royal confirmation. As a type of payment for the new duties to the King, the *stadsmusikant* got a royal license which supplemented the right to play in the town with the right to play in rural areas. The *stadsmusikant* – with assistants and apprentices – simply had the monopoly on all paid music for burghers and peasants! It is not known if similar ordinances were promulgated for Schleswig and Holstein at the same time, but in practice, a similar system developed in the Duchies. The Kingdom of Denmark during the Absolutist period was divided into just under 30 *stadsmusikant* districts, where each appointment typically covered one to two *amter* (counties) (see fig. 2). Norway was divided into 10 districts and Schleswig-Holstein into approximately 20 districts. In the 18th century the number of *stadsmusikant* posts in the Danish state stabilised around 60, thereafter the number decreased until the system disintegrated after the middle of the 19th century.

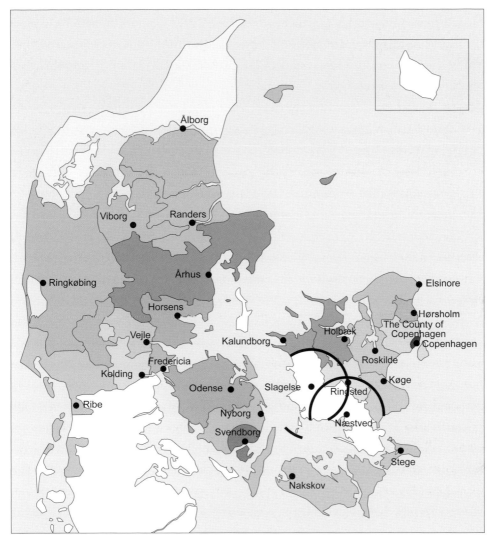

FIG. 2.

Stadsmusikant *districts in the Kingdom of Denmark (except the Duchy of Sleswig) 1730. The economic basis for many of the Danish offices was the peasantry (i.e. the tenant farmers) who in many cases contributed half the income of the* stadsmusikant.

This Absolutist music system – which in Europe is known in a similar form only in Mecklenburg[6] – was unchanged for 150 years, until the government at the beginning of the 19th century felt obliged to introduce deregulated music as a profession in the rural districts. A royal decree of 25 April 1800 laid down two important elements. First, the organist and *stadsmusikant* post in a market town should be combined when the *stadsmusikanter* then in office retired. Second, the monopoly of playing music in the rural districts should be revoked when these posts were combined. The free liberal constitution (1849) and the Trade Act (1857) completely abolished the privileged *stadsmusikant*.[7]

The characteristic aspect of the music culture in market towns was that professional musicians were involved in a number of very varied traditional situations: playing wind instruments from church and town hall towers, four-part church music for church festivals, music for banquets in the town hall, music for burghers' traditional customs (popinjay shooting, moving guild signs etc.)[8] and for private parties and dance music in town and country.

The *stadsmusikanter* were an internationally oriented group of musicians, German was the common language, and the music was more or less the same all over Northern Europe. The *stadsmusikant's* activity was somewhere between handicraft and art. There were no demands that he should be an innovative composer, but great demands on his flexibility and versatility. A master should ideally (1) own and maintain a large collection of musical instruments, of which he played four-five instruments himself, (2) he should work as a music teacher in the training of assistants and apprentices as well as for the burghers' children, (3) he should act as conductor of the ensemble both by arranging the music for the available instruments and by practical leadership, and (4) he should at short notice be able to supply the requisitionists with the music they wanted.

The *stadsmusikant's* work was clearly integrated into Absolutist society. Firstly, the musician's privileges concerned only the middle classes and lower social groups. The *stadsmusikant* could not assert his claim towards a person of rank – but they used him anyway. Particularly in the 17th century the musician all over Europe had the role of spotlighting the social hierarchy, in that it was specified in sumptuary decrees which social groups were allowed to use which music. In the Danish state, sumptuary decrees with detailed stipulations about music are known only from Schleswig-Holstein, which at this time had a special position. In the 18th century, however, there were traditions all over the Danish state concerning which instruments and ensembles were suitable for which occasions.

The relationship between culture and rank changed over time. Around 1660, it was fashionable to be able to celebrate a wedding in style, but around 1720 the situation had changed completely. In the play *Barselsstuen* (1723) (Childbirth room), the poet Ludvig Holberg thus let the servant Troels defend his master from the lower social class with the following words:

FIG. 3.

Distinguished wedding procession in Bremen 1646. In front are four stadsmusikanter, *one cornet player and three trombone players. Similar processions took place in towns on Zealand and in Scania during the 17ᵗʰ century.*

Just look at weddings! If you go to a tailor's or shoemaker's wedding, you're received with trumpets and French horns, placed at a table as long as from Candlemas to Easter (…) full of expensive dishes. If you go to people of the second class, who are higher, you get only tea, coffee and compliments; and to people of the first class, sometimes you get nothing except hearing the marriage ceremony and a pinch of snuff (…).[9]

The quotation cannot be taken as proof that a Copenhagen tailor or shoemaker had trumpets and French horns at his wedding – just as an indication that it could happen. But Holberg's satire reflects the phenomenon that, in Copenhagen of the 1720s, it was the ordinary burgher class who were most eager to use wedding music as a status symbol. The higher classes at the time often preferred to have a 'quiet wedding' without music. Incidentally, we know that *stadsmusikanter* in several Schleswig-Holstein and a few Danish-Norwegian towns succeeded in having a fixed fee introduced to be paid to the *stadsmusikant* for weddings without music.

It is characteristic that the *stadsmusikant* system in the Danish state gave rise to a cultural encounter between town and country. In the period around 1660-1800, the *stadsmusikanter* had, as mentioned, a monopoly of all paid music in the country. The *stadsmusikant* system also had a marked influence on village instrumental music. At a

FIG. 4.

Guild procession in Copenhagen in the first half of the 19th century. In front are two stadsmusikanter *(presumably journeymen).*

time between 1660 and 1720, the violin became the peasant musicians' main instrument at the expense of traditional, homemade string instruments. In the same period the peasants' old drone instruments disappeared[10] – either completely (like the bagpipe) or in any case as dance instruments. The drum as a dance instrument was discontinued around the middle of the 18th century. By the year 1800, the preferred instruments of the peasant musicians were the same as the *stadsmusikant's*: violin, clarinet, flute and cello.

One can regard the spread of music privileges in the country as a cultural clash between the professional *stadsmusikant* music and the peasants' traditional music. The monopoly *stadsmusikanter* appeared in the second half of the 17th century as a new element, as opposed to a peasant culture where music, as mentioned, was a tradition without professional carriers. The musicians from outside came with what the peasants regarded as new norms, new instruments and new music. Among the new norms, was the demand for payment for the music, which in this way became, so to say, a commodity.

Contemporary criticism of music life

The special aspect of the Danish music circumstances was something that was noticed abroad, for example, the country-wide *stadsmusikant* system was positively stressed in the 1780s in a book by the Swabian music writer C.F.D. Schubart.[11]

The state of music life, however, also aroused criticism, especially after the 1740s. My point in calling attention to examples of this criticism of music life is to show that there were varied views of the role of the *stadsmusikant* in society, according to the music culture to which one belonged.

King Christian VI's Court conductor, J.A. Scheibe, who was dismissed from the court in 1748 and settled thereafter in Sønderborg to run a music school, thus wrote in 1757 in a letter to the composer Telemann in Hamburg:

All Schleswig-Holstein is swarming with *stadsmusikanter*, musician assistants as well as organists and organist assistants; all in their own opinion are composers. God help us, they are nothing but utter bunglers who are surprised when you would teach them rules. They shout and rage when you would show them their weaknesses. (...) That is the way it is with music in the Duchies, and honestly, it is no better in Copenhagen. Young Danes begin to compose and there is no one who can teach them some rules – or even know one.[12]

With these bitter words from a dethroned Court conductor, Scheibe pointed out the ideals of court music and art music: a craftsman-like refined music, which expressed certain aesthetics, which the *stadsmusikanter* obviously did not live up to. Scheibe himself stood for what he called 'a sensible imitation of nature' in the form of a sensitive and simple – though refined – music.

Another form of criticism came from the organist in Kastellet (the Citadel) in Copenhagen, Carl August Thielo, in the book *Tanker og Regler fra Grunden af om Musiken* (Basic thoughts and rules about music) which was published in Copenhagen in 1746. The book was one of the first Danish-language music-teaching books, and it was intended for a broad middle-class public. After showing in the second chapter of the book that music is indispensable in churches, in the royal palaces, in the military, for students and in the middle class, the writer used the third chapter to illustrate the contempt with which music is met in some places. In church, music should be entirely at the service of the word, Thielo thought, but unfortunately that was not always the case. Outside church, music was misused by those who believed that music existed just to cheer the mind:

One finds indeed even more people who know nothing except that the best characteristic of music is dance music, and in their ears, English, Dutch, sailors- and Polish or Swiss pieces are the most beautiful. O stupidity! If these people had knowledge of the difficult study and the hidden power of music, they would think much differently.[13]

Thielo thus thought that music suffered great contempt through drunkenness in connection with parties, 'one says that wine tastes better when musicians play a rondeau[14] on their wind instruments'.[15] Thielo's criticism was based on a religious/moral point of view, while Schiebe's was artistic-aesthetic.

A third form of criticism appeared in the book by *stadsmusikant* Lorents Nicolaj Berg in Christiansand, *Den første Prøve for Begyndere udi Instrumentalkunsten* from 1782. Berg was annoyed firstly because the social symbolism of musical instruments was no longer respected and gave an example concerning the trumpet:

(...) it has happened for this royal instrument as for many other magnificent things that should only exist for the most distinguished people's adornment etc. The trumpet is misused in several places for humble people who want to be modern. In Denmark and Holstein, the peasants dance minuets for 4 *skilling* [a small amount] to the sound of the trumpet on their wooden shoes (...).[16]

Another recurrent line in Berg's textbook was a humorous, but pitiless, criticism of *fuskere* (dabblers), especially the village fiddlers. He did not think much of playing by ear, learning notes was necessary. He bluntly compared the unlettered performer with an animal:

Many go in for playing the violin by ear, which is called playing wildly; because all that they learn they have to get by listening to others, and, just as one whistles for the bird, that is how he learns the melody (...). Those who thus play wild or who do not know what they are doing are like the parrot who would teach the starling to speak.[17]

Stadsmusikant Berg in addition gave examples of how the playing method and ideal sound were different for the professional musician and the *birfedler*.[18] The professional musicians for example held the violin bow in a certain way described in detail. Some *fuskere* by contrast,

(...) hold it (the bow) like a bread knife, and scrape the bow on the poor strings with a stiff arm in such a way that the violin, even if it is only second-rate, is forced to screech and grunt, like butchering time in Jutland. One can often hear wise stories about how someone who plays wildly or *birfedler* (...) has taken the melody from 4 or 5 musicians. That is why some people would prefer to dance to *fuskere* [dabblers] (...).[19]

Berg thus attached great importance to defending his professional honour and thereby also the *stadsmusikanter*'s privileged position. According to him, one could use the wrong music, for example trumpets for peasants, and one could play music in a wrong way. He did not accept that 'common people' could have their own music culture without professional performers.

However, court cases show that the peasants too could be sharp critics of the *stadsmusikant*'s music. At a wedding party in the village of Hundstrup on South Funen in 1732, those present thought, according to the court records, that the *stadsmusikant*'s dance music sounded 'like when you twist the ear of a pig'.[20]

Parallel with the discussion about the legitimacy of the monopolies of guilds and market towns in the second half of the 18th century, the timeliness of the music monopolies was also discussed. This was particularly when the subject was dealt with in the central and regional administration, when a new *stadsmusikant* applied for royal confirmation of his monopoly. In 1789, for the first time, an energetic, liberal-minded *amtmand* (the chief administrative officer of the county) succeeded in preventing a *stadsmusikant* from getting a monopoly of performing music in the traditional rural district of the office.[21]

Stadsmusikant system in an international perspective

In Denmark – as everywhere in the area around the Baltic Sea – the *stadsmusikanter* had basically the same duties: to play for the corporation on official occasions, to play at burghers' private parties and for urban society's traditional customs, and to assist in church music in cooperation with the organist and grammar school. The blowing of wind instruments from the towers in many places was a custom in itself, a sonorous expression of the town's identity. The citizens loved to hear hymn melodies played by trumpets and trombones from the church tower when they promenaded after church service. In some places in the Baltic Sea area, the office was characterised by duties such as serving as tower watchman; in Denmark however the watchman and musician function were always separate. The obligation to keep assistants and teach apprentices was implicit in the period treated here. In Denmark-Norway, there was additionally the special obligation to procure *skibstrompetere*, that is, trumpeters for the Royal Navy.

In Denmark and the whole Baltic Sea area, it was also the case that the *stadsmusikant*'s most important right was the actual monopoly. It is true that the council in the large Hanseatic towns paid a good fixed salary, but the incidental earnings were of great importance everywhere. The *stadsmusikanter* in Denmark-Norway seldom got a fixed salary from the town officials. It was therefore crucial how far the monopoly of playing stretched. Normally the monopoly was valid for the middle class and lower social groups. In the large prosperous towns – such as many of the old Hanseatic towns – there was a formalised division of the town population into social groups, which were reflected in the so-called wedding or sumptuary ordinances. It was precisely in these places that there was a hierarchy of musicians – some appointed by the council (in German called among other names *Ratsmusikanten*) and some organised in guilds – who had a monopoly on playing for specified social groups. Nothing similar is found in Denmark. The Absolute Danish King's rank ordinances, however, defined who, as a social upper class, was superior and above the *stadsmusikant*'s monopoly.

There were two different ways to supplement earning opportunities by extending the monopoly: either by incorporating the rural districts around the town in question or by combining the offices of organist and *stadsmusikant*. In the two instances, it was thus the peasants and the church, respectively, who guaranteed the *stadsmusikant* function.

What were the social consequences of the Danish system? The *stadsmusikant* mas-

FIG. 5.

The housey-housey (lottery) draw in front of the Copenhagen city hall 1773. Above the draw is a group of stadsmusikanter *with their instruments.*

ters were normally in charge of the training of the professional assistants. Neither other professional musician groups nor *fuskere* could really come into the picture. The Crown succeeded only to a certain extent in using the posts as comfortable positions for retiring military musicians and royal orchestral musicians, because this met vigorous local opposition. Locally, a *stadsmusikant* post was normally taken over by one who had been a musician's assistant, because the assistants as a rule were more broadly qualified than military musicians and organists. The selection of *stadsmusikant,* however, was not just dependent on professional considerations. It was also decisive to establish functional families so that the local community did not have any problems, for example, with having to provide for *stadsmusikant* widows with small children. In several towns, the same family had the post of *stadsmusikant* for three to four generations.

While it was not uncommon in the first two-thirds of the 17th century for towns to have several musicians appointed as *stadsmusikanter* at the same time and on an equal footing, the organisation of one master with assistants and apprentices became the norm in the final third of the 17th century. Studies of households show that *stadsmusikant* principals in the Kingdom of Denmark in the 18th century often had only one permanent assistant and a single apprentice. A larger number of assistants and apprentices can be found in the towns: Copenhagen, Elsinore, Roskilde, Næstved, Odense, Nyborg, Aalborg, Randers and Aarhus. The Copenhagen *stadsmusikant* post was the largest in the Scandinavian countries, as the *stadsmusikant* in the Danish capital in the 18th century typically had 6-7 assistants and 3-6 apprentices.

The *stadsmusikant*'s work as music teacher is illustrated among other things by the preserved articles of apprenticeship and certificates of completed apprenticeship, by probate registrations of books and notes etc., and by two Danish-language music text books published by *stadsmusikanter*. It can be concluded that the Danish *stadsmusikanter* in the question of training (the apprenticeship system) on the whole behaved in accordance with 'the articles of the Saxe musicians' – which were some guild-like rules drawn up in 1653 by 107 Saxe musicians.[22] These laid down the following headings: An apprentice must be legitimate and conviction-free. The boy must be taught on many instruments, both wind instruments and percussion, but disreputable instruments such as the bagpipes, animal horn, hurdy-gurdy and triangle are unacceptable. The duration of apprenticeship must be at least five years. Both the articles of apprenticeship and the certificate of completed apprenticeship must be in written form. After the end of apprenticeship, the assistant must travel for three years before he can become a master. The wages for an assistant can be agreed according to the custom of the place, but the amount agreed upon must be written down. A master (or an assistant who wants to become a master) must submit to a test in playing the pieces determined for the test in the presence of two other masters and a competent assistant, before he is appointed and before he is admitted to the musicians' guild. A master must have a maximum of three apprentices and should preferably have at least one assistant. Finally the Saxe articles have a number of rules about good behaviour. For example, apprentices and assistants have to be obedient to their master, behave properly, not play music with *fuskere*, and apprentices who run away must not be employed by other guild brothers.

The requirement in the articles for training in percussion has not been generally followed in Denmark (there was no need for it), and there are Danish examples of a master having more than three apprentices. In addition, the requirement of three years' travel before an assistant could become a master was not always complied with in Denmark. But apart from these, the Saxe articles seem to have been followed by and large. This was done not because they were the law in the country, but because the profession in general was influenced by German practice.

Incidentally, it appears that in the Baltic Sea area, there was a common tradition for the drafting of the certificates of completed apprenticeship.[23]

Through the professional assistant training, the Danish *stadsmusikanter* were part of a fellowship across national boundaries. The lack of guilds did not prevent the Danish *stadsmusikanter* from keeping in contact with colleagues in the Baltic Sea area, who – it seems in the 17th century especially – were very mobile.[24] Travelling assistants were common in the whole period, and they were responsible for the replacements of people that occurred between the individual posts; a position as *stadsmusikant* master in Denmark being a top position. Denmark was influenced by contacts abroad via Hamburg, Lübeck and Rostock, while it was seldom that musicians immigrated from the eastern part of the Baltic Sea area. The immigration was typically from the south; Germans, but virtually never other nationalities, settled down and became *stadsmusikanter*. The predominant movement from south to north, however, was modified on many levels by the interaction between the centre and periphery within the Denmark-Norway boundaries (for instance between Copenhagen and all of Denmark-Norway, between Odense and all of Funen, between Aarhus and all of Jutland).

There were two partly opposing tendencies built into the system: on the one hand, there was an endeavour to have continuity, as vacant positions were prefer-

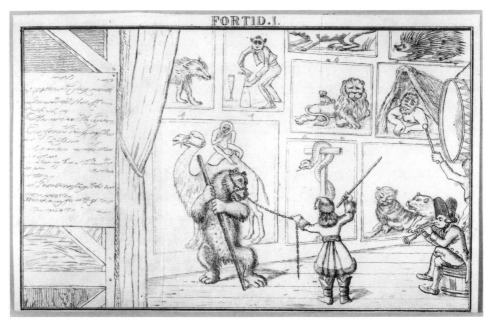

FIG. 6A.

Musical scenes from the past ('Fortid') and the present ('Nutid') as seen by a satirical cartoonist 1833.
In fig 6a is a man with a dancing bear, while the stadsmusikant *of the town is playing the shawm*
(oboe) and his son is playing the bass drum.

ably filled with sons, sons-in-law, widows of the deceased or their new husbands, and
trusted assistants. On the other hand, the system was open in principle and by taking part in the functions mentioned, many from outside were taken into the country's *stadsmusikant* positions. Immigrating German musicians left their mark on the
stadsmusikant system especially in the period until the beginning of the 18th century;
after this their descendants worked side by side with Danish musicians. Many *stadsmusikanter* in Denmark were bilingual (Danish and German), and they had a relatively high proficiency in reading and writing. In addition they could read music.
These qualities promoted contacts with colleagues in the area around the Baltic Sea
and the rest of Germany.

Due to the lack of guilds, the *stadsmusikanter* had informal networks, which were
often structured as familial relations or borne by contacts stemming from their apprenticeship and assistant time. The network disseminated news and professional cooperation – for instance lending money, notes and musical instruments – and trac-
ing assistants and apprentices who had run away. There are also examples that they
played together or in other ways performed together across the positions.

FIG. 6B.

Fig. 6b shows a Sunday evening song entertainment at a town theatre. A small orchestra is playing, presumably consisting of stadsmusikanter *and perhaps other musicians.*

In the Baltic Sea area, social status often seems to fall from the cantor over the organist to the *stadsmusikant*, but in Denmark there does not seem to have been any crucial social difference between organist and *stadsmusikant*. Nevertheless, the social position of the *stadsmusikant* in Denmark must be characterised as relatively low, on a par with ordinary master artisans. The earning potential varied greatly, though, between the largest and the smallest towns. It is characteristic that many *stadsmusikanter* had a sideline, because it was only in the fewest towns in Denmark-Norway that it was possible to live well from being a *stadsmusikant*. (But in this they are not different from so many other burgher tradesmen in the Danish-Norwegian market towns of the time). The high social status enjoyed by *stadsmusikanter* in some Schleswig-Holstein towns, corresponding to *die Ratsmusikanten* in large towns in Germany, is not found in Denmark. The Danish *stadsmusikanter*'s lack of fixed wages and their relatively low social position is supported by two circumstances: the market towns were small and the period when the position culminated, approximately 1660-1800, fell at a time of general economic depression for the market towns (in contrast to the capital, Copenhagen).

The Danish *stadsmusikanter*'s self-perception contained two main elements: they were honourable (in Danish: *ærlige*) musicians and had royal privileges. It was important to be an honourable musician, because it was only by that means that the *stadsmusikant* got his societal recognition and thereby the possibility of achieving a living wage. To honesty belonged the fact that one had 'learned the art' and thereby belonged to an occupational group which, in principle, was international. In the 17th century, there seems to be traces of a clash between, on the one hand, the immigrating German assistants' strict expectations of honesty, and, on the other hand, the local Danish practice, which was milder. There are strong indications that German assistants – and Danish assistants when travelling – transferred general practice from the North German *zünft* system to Denmark in the 17th century. The awareness of being the King's musician was, in contrast, specific for *stadsmusikanter* in the Danish state. Loyalty to the Crown, family feeling and the Evangelical-Lutheran religion, together with professional pride, were important guidelines in everyday life.

With their work in the market towns and as a result of their good contacts, both upwards to the court and military circles and downward to the peasants, the *stadsmusikanter* were mediators of musical currents. They brought foreign music to Denmark and the music of the nobility and middleclass – especially dance music – to the peasants. Within the boundaries of the Danish state, the *stadsmusikant* system meant that musicians, musical instruments and repertoire circulated among those holding the positions and this created a certain uniformity in musical life. New musical instruments for instance quickly became widespread everywhere. With the consistent spread of the *stadsmusikant* system after 1660, a broader stratum of townsmen and peasants had contact with a music that increasingly became European.

Both the increasing private music-playing of musical amateurs in the 18th and 19th centuries and the appearance of a public concert system in the first half of the 19th century changed the basic circumstances of musical life in a decisive way all over Northern Europe. The old *stadsmusikant* system was the loser because the *stadsmusikanter* could neither uphold the monopoly nor live up to the ever increasing technical demands of art music, which needed musicians who were specialised in one instrument. Pathetically, in 1847 the Copenhagen *stadsmusikant* G.G. Füssel brought an action against the pleasure garden Tivoli's musical director, the composer H.C. Lumbye. The musical director was accused of having violated the monopoly of the *stadsmusikant* with his public concerts in Tivoli. The Copenhagen court though did not think that Copenhagen's privileged *stadsmusikant* could extend his monopoly to cover the public music in Tivoli, and *stadsmusikant* Füssel lost the case. All this development had two important consequences. In the first half of the 19th century a new type of light music appeared, produced for an anonymous market. And new ideas about musical art with Beethoven's music made a great impact on the elite, who were no longer defined by class and rank. There were romantic ideas about the artist as a 'genius' and music as an art that opens up for awareness of an extrasensory, idea-less world.

The Danish system, which consistently linked town and country with the help of privileges from the sovereign, was the exception in Europe. Outside the Danish state (and the affiliated manor of Oldenburg in Northern Germany),[25] however, something similar is known from limited parts of the Electorate of Hannover, the Duchy of Westphalia and the Electorate of Saxony.[26] In the last three cases, however, it was the *stadsmusikant* who leased the rural district from the sovereign, and the purpose of the arrangement was to procure income for the sovereign. In Denmark-Norway, on the other hand, the right to play in the country was never bought by the musician, but belonged to the position, because it was a necessary precondition for its maintenance. In addition, towns in Germany can be found where the *stadsmusikant* had the right to play in a circular area around the town, corresponding to the protection area (shelter belt) for the trade and crafts of the town in question.[27] However, this concerns enclaves in a larger context and not, as in Denmark, a centrally controlled parcelling out of a whole country. Up to now, the only known parallel to the Danish system is found, as mentioned, in Mecklenburg (i.e., the then Duchies of Mecklenburg-Schwerin and Mecklenburg-Güstrow), whose ruler in the 18th century had an almost Absolutist status.[28] Here the Duke in the period 1650-1700 forced through an alteration of the *stadsmusikant* system, from locally appointed *stadsmusikanter* whose right to play was limited to the towns, to *stadsmusikanter* who were awarded privileges from the central authority, with the right to play in a town and the rural district belonging to it. The new organisation was part of a power struggle between the Duke and the cities, but was also due to the fact that the state of the *stadsmusikant* posts after the Thirty Years War was extremely poor. There is a striking parallel, both structurally and chronologically, between the developments in Denmark and Mecklenburg.

If one looks around the Baltic Sea, one can see in the 17th and 18th century three ways, different in principle, of organising the *stadsmusikant* system:[29]

• First, there was the centralised *stadsmusikant* system where the sovereign had decisive influence. Here town and country in an Absolutist state were linked together through privileges from the sovereign. As a rule these privileges were given to individual masters, as was the case in the Danish state and in Mecklenburg. It could also be that the sovereign confirmed appointments that were limited to the area of the town, as found in Braunschweig after 1671.

- The second was the locally based, secular, *stadsmusikant* system. In the one main form, the town council appointed a corps of musicians on the same footing (*Ratsmusikanten*); and in addition there was perhaps a musician's guild. The towns used the council musicians for ceremonies as could be seen in Hamburg, Lübeck, Danzig, Königsberg, and other old Hanseatic towns. In the other main form, the council appointed a single privileged master. This was the case in many smaller towns in Scania, Northern Germany and along the south coast of the Baltic Sea.
- The third system was the locally based, church-dominated *stadsmusikant* system. Here the organist had the monopoly of playing music and if there were assistants they were subordinate to him. This form of organisation is known from that part of Sweden north of the old Danish provinces and Finland.

In spite of some differences in the organisation of the *stadsmusikant* system, there was nevertheless a common character with regard to the *stadsmusikant*'s rights and duties in the Baltic Sea area. The similarity can only be explained structurally: the towns of the area had the same type of institutions with the same need for music. Underlying phenomena such as the common Evangelical-Lutheran religion, the influence of the guild system and the extensive commercial relations also played a part.

The *stadsmusikant* system was a distinctive and important cultural factor in the Danish Kingdom especially in the 17th and 18th century. The interaction between the interests of the Absolute royal power and the market towns gave the institution a special profile. The international aspects of the system led to an international cultural exchange. With the liberation of the peasants, commercialisation and the dissolution of the old monopoly society, which occurred in a continual process from the middle of the 18th to the middle of the 19th century, the rug was pulled from under the *stadsmusikant* group with its particular trade profile.

BIBLIOGRAPHY

Andersson, Greger 1994. 'Der Ostseeraum als Musiklandschaft. Musiker – Musikinstitutionen – Repertoires im 17. und 18. Jahrhundert'. In: Klaus Wolfgang Niemöller & Helmut Loos (eds.),

Die Musik der Deutschen im Osten und ihre Wechselwirkung mit den Nachbarn. (Deutsche Musik im Osten, 6). Bonn: Gudrun Schröder Verlag, pp. 73-85. Short edition published in: Irma Vierimaa (ed.), *Balticum – a Coherent Musical Landscape in 16th and 18th Centuries.* (Studia Musicologica Universitatis Helsingiensis, 6). Helsinki 1994, pp. 9-17.

Andersson, Greger (ed.) 1997. *Musik i Norden.* (Kungl. Musikaliska akademiens skriftserie, 85; Föreningen Nordens årsbog 1998). Stockholm: Kungl. Musikaliska akademien. German translation: *Musikgeschichte Nordeuropas.* Stuttgart and Weimar: Metzler Verlag 2001.

Berg, Lorents Nicolaj 1782. *Den første Prøve for Begyndere udi Instrumentalkunsten.* Christiansand: A. Swane.

Braun, Werner 1981. *Die Musik des 17. Jahrhunderts.* (Neues Handbuch der Musikwissenschaft, 4). Wiesbaden: Akademische Verlagsgesellschaft Athenaion.

Charles-Dominique, Luc 1994. *Les Ménétriers Francais sous l'Ancien Régime.* Paris: Klincksieck.

Gehler, Ralph 1995. 'Kunstpfeifer, Pfuscher und Bierfiedler. Der Kampf der Musikanten des 17. und 18. Jahrhunderts auf den Dörfern Mecklenburgs'. In: *Stier und Greif. Blätter zur Kultur- und Landesgeschichte in Mecklenburg-Vorpommern. Sonderheft '1000 Jahre Mecklenburg'.* Schwerin, pp. 88-92.

Gehler, Ralph 1996. Dorf- und Stadtmusikanten im ländlichen Raum Mecklenburgs zwischen 1650 und 1700. (Unpublished MA-thesis). Berlin: Humboldt-Universität.

Gehler, Ralph 1997. 'Dorf- und Stadtmusikanten im ländlichen Raum Mecklenburgs zwischen 1650 und 1700'. In: Doris Stockmann and Jens Henrik Koudal (eds.), *Historical Studies on Folk and Traditional Music.* Copenhagen: Museum Tusculanum Press, pp. 47-58.

Greve, Werner 1998. 'Stadtpfeifer'. In: Ludwig Finscher (ed.), *Die Musik in Geschichte und Gegenwart, Sachteil.* Vol. 8, 2nd ed. Kassel et al./Stuttgart et al.: Bärenreiter and Metzler, column 1719-32.

Grosse, Hans and Hans Rudolf Jung (eds.) 1972. *Georg Philipp Telemann. Briefwechsel.* Leipzig: VEB Deutscher Verlag für Musik.

Jansen, F.J. Billeskov (ed.) 1984. *Samtlige komedier i tre bind af Ludvig Holberg.* Vol. 1. Copenhagen: GAD.

Koudal, Jens Henrik 1993. 'Musikermobilitet i Østersøområdet i 1600- og 1700-tallet'. *Dansk Årbog for Musikforskning,* 21, pp. 9-32. Short English version: 'Mobility of Musicians in the Baltic in the 17th and 18th Century'. In: Ekkehard Ochs, Nico Schüler, Lutz Winkler (eds.), *Musica Baltica. Interregionale musikkulturelle Beziehungen im Ostseeraum.* (Deutsche Musik im Osten, 8). Sankt Augustin: Academia Verlag 1996, pp. 137-47.

Koudal, Jens Henrik 2000a. *For borgere og bønder. Stadsmusikantvæsenet i Danmark ca. 1660-1800.* Copenhagen: Museum Tusculanum Press.

Koudal, Jens Henrik 2000b. *For Townsman and Peasant. The Stadsmusikant Institution in Denmark c. 1660-1800: English Summary.* (Studier, 21). Copenhagen: The Danish Folklore Archives.

Krickeberg, Dieter 1971. 'Zur sozialen Stellung des deutschen Spielmanns im 17. und 18. Jahrhunderts, besonders im Nordwesten'. In: Walter Salmen (ed.), *Der Sozialstatus des Berufsmusikers vom 17. bis 19. Jahrhundert.* Kassel-Basel-Tours-London: Bärenreiter Verlag, pp. 33-35. English translation: 'On the Social Status of the Spielmann ('Folk Musician') in 17th and 18th Century Germany, Particularly in the Northwest'. In: Walter Salmen (ed.), *The Social Status of the Professional Musician from the Middle Ages to the 19th Century*. New York: Pendragon Press 1983.

Linnemann, Georg 1956. *Musikgeschichte der Stadt Oldenburg*. Oldenburg: Gerhard Stalling Verlag.

Moser, Hans Joachim 1910. *Die Musikergenossenschaften im deutschen Mittelalter*. Rostock: Carl Hinstorffs Buchdruckerei.

Müller, Harald 1985. *Ulrich Johann Voigt 1669-1732. Stadtmusikus zu Celle und Lüneburg*. Celle: Der Stadt Celle.

Salmen, Walter 1963-1967. *Geschichte der Musik in Westpfalen*. Vol. 1-2. Kassel-Basel-London-Paris-New York: Bärenreiter Verlag.

Schiørring, Nils 1977-1978. *Musikkens Historie i Danmark*. Vol. 1-3. Copenhagen: Politikens Forlag.

Schubart, Christian Friedrich Daniel 1806. *Ideen zu einer Ästethik der Tonkunst*. Wien: Mörschner und Jasper.

Schwab, Heinrich W. 1978. 'Krise und Auflösung des Stadtmusikantentums'. In: Uwe Haensel (ed.), *Beiträge zur Musikgeschichte Nordeuropas. Kurt Gudewill zum 65. Geburtstag*. Wolffenbüttel and Zürich: Möseler Verlag, pp. 271-82.

Schwab, Heinrich W. 1982. *Die Anfänge des weltlichen Berufsmusikertums in der mittelalterlichen Stadt. Studie zu einer Berufs- und Sozialgeschichte des Stadtmusikantentums*. (Kieler Schriften zur Musikwissenschaft, 24). Kassel-Basel-London: Bärenreiter Verlag.

Schwab, Heinrich W. 1993. 'Der Ostseeraum. Beobachtungen aus seiner Musikgeschichte und Anregungen zu einem musikhistoriographischen Konzept'. In: Nils Grinde, Idar Karevold, Even Ruud (eds.), *Nordisk musikkforskerkongress, Oslo 24.-27. juni 1992, Innlegg og referater*. (Skriftserie fra Institutt for musikk og teater, 1993:2). Oslo: Universitetet i Oslo, pp. 11-33.

Techrich, Hermann 1932. *Sächsische Stadtpfeifer. Zur Geschichte der Stadtmusikwesens im ehemaligen Königreich Sachsen*. Dresden: Buchdruckerei Otto Franke.

Thielo, Carl August 1746. *Tanker og Regler fra Grunden af om Musiken*. Copenhagen: J.C. Groth.

Wolschke, Martin 1981. *Von der Stadtpfeiferei zu Lehrlingskapelle und Sinfonieorchester. Wandlungen im 19. Jahrhundert*. Regensburg: Gustav Bosse Verlag.

NOTES

1   The article is based on many years' studies of the Danish *stadsmusikant* system published in Koudal 2000a. This thesis contains an English summary which is also printed separately as Koudal 2000b. If not otherwise mentioned, the statements in the article are documented in the thesis.

2   In general see Schiørring 1977-78 and Andersson 1997.

3   A pair dance that spread from Poland to Scandinavia about 1600 and in some places has lived on in folk tradition until today.

4   Greve 1998. Schwab 1982.

5   It should be noted that the registration of marriages and other religious ceremonies in the church register did not begin until 1645.

6   The *stadsmusikant* system in Absolutist France had certain resemblances to the Danish system, but also clear differences, see Charles-Dominique 1994.

7   The general decline of the *stadsmusikant* system in Europe is discussed in Schwab 1978.

8   When a guild changed its *oldermand* (president), the members in procession – often with professional music at the head – moved the guild's sign from the former residence to the new *oldermand's* residence. This was marked afterwards by a celebration, to which the *stadsmusikant* likewise often played the music.

9   Act 1, scene 1, quoted from Billeskov Jansen's edition of Holberg's *Samtlige Komedier i tre bind*, 1984, vol. 1, p. 388. In Holberg's *Den Pantsatte Bonde-Dreng*, too, Act 3, Scene 2, the trumpeting at a shoemaker's wedding is mentioned 'when the guests arrive'.

10   Instruments with one or more holding notes over which the melody is played, e.g. the hurdy-gurdy and bagpipe.

11   Schubart 1806, pp. 242-44.

12   Grosse and Jung (eds.) 1972, p. 333. (Letter from Scheibe to Telemann dated Sønderborg 8 February 1757. The original letter is in German).

13   Thielo 1746, p. 9.

14   A musical form where a fixed refrain alternates with continually new interludes (Italian: rondo).

15   Thielo 1746, p. 9.

16   Berg 1782, p. 65.

17   Berg 1782, pp. 7 f.

18   One who plays in beer houses or plays for beer, often used in general about inferior musicians and travelling fiddlers.

19   Berg 1782, pp. 20 f.

20   Koudal 2000a, pp. 437-38, where similar court cases are also discussed.

21   Koudal 2000a, chapter 6 (pp. 197-207).

22   The articles are printed and commented on in Wolschke 1981, pp. 33-36 and 240-45.

23   Such a (German-language) certificate of completed apprenticeship, issued in Aalborg in the year 1700, is reproduced in Koudal 2000a, p. 629 and commented on in the same pp. 231-36.

24   Koudal 1993.

25   Linnemann 1956, pp. 158-61, 163.

26   Krickeberg 1971, pp. 33-35. Salmen 1963-1967, 1, p. 83, and 2, p. 189. Wolschke 1981, pp. 45 f., 55 f. Techrich 1932, pp. 21 f..

27   Müller 1985, p. 39 (five miles around Stade). Braun 1981, p. 25 ('Wer die Kirchenmusik ausführt, hat im Umkreis dieser Kirche die Aufwartungsberechtigung'). Moser 1910, p. 120 (town pipers in Strassburg in the 16th century had the right to play in a four-mile circle around the town).

28   Gehler 1995. Gehler 1996. Gehler 1997.

29   See – besides Koudal 2000a – also Schwab 1993 and Andersson 1994.

Juliane Engelhardt

Enlightenment in the provinces — The patriotic societies in the towns and country of the Danish state

Numerous salons, coffee houses, learned academies and societies, freemason lodges, Jacobin clubs, reading societies and patriotic societies were established in the Danish state in the 18th century, and this article deals with one particular group: the patriotic societies.[1] The geographic area of the study covers the core countries of the Danish state: Denmark, Norway, and the two Duchies Schleswig and Holstein. Here 59 patriotic societies were established from 1762 to 1814. The survey of the societies – a list of which is printed at the end of this article – shows that they were scattered all over the empire. In every city and almost every provincial town the bourgeoisie gathered in local societies in order to promote the common welfare and progress of the fatherland. The members did not consider love of the fatherland an innate feeling, but as an activity, an ambition to do practical work for the common good. Thus, the main purpose of the societies was to initiate agricultural reforms and education among the population at large.

Why are the patriotic societies interesting? They are interesting because they reflected very central sociological and ideological currents in the late era of the Enlightenment. In addition, the patriotic societies illuminate to what extent the central thoughts of the Enlightenment reached the urban communities and provinces in the Danish state. Finally, the work of the societies contributes to our information about how the reforms were carried out on a local level, and how the lower orders responded to the societies' attempts to modernise society.

The establishment of the patriotic societies

Det kongelige danske Landhusholdningsselskab (The Royal Danish Society of Agriculture) was founded in 1769 and was the first patriotic society in the Danish state.[2] It

FIG. 1.

*Map of the distribution
of societies in Denmark.*

● Economic Society
✕ Society for Relief and Philanthropy
△ Society for Education and Enlightenment

was also the only society which worked in Denmark, Norway and the overseas dependencies.[3] The society was founded as a private enterprise, but several of the 12 founders had close contacts with the political inner circle around the King. Thus the society was accorded the honorary 'royal' title shortly after it was founded, the King and the Crown Prince became patrons of the society, and its committee was continuously named in *Hof og Statskalenderen* (The Court and State Calendar), an official publication of the Absolute monarchy, in which all public professions and institutions were named. So, *Det kongelige danske Landhusholdningsselskab* was, in fact, a semi-state institution.

The first regional patriotic societies were established in Norway. Here nine societies were established in the years 1773-1782, while there were none in the rest of the state. One explanation for why the society movement was manifest earlier in Norway was that this country had a relatively high degree of urbanisation; the majority of the Norwegian population was concentrated in and close to the cities and some of these were markedly larger than the cities in Denmark.[4] Additionally, Great Britain was the country's primary trading partner, and the Norwegians were influenced by the British industrial movement at an early stage.

As well as long-term factors promoting the establishment of the societies in Norway, specific motives played their part. Firstly, the harvest failed in the years 1771-1774, and parts of the country suffered from famine. Secondly, until 1788 Denmark retained exclusive right to sell corn to the southern parts of Norway. Thus, the idea of establishing societies gained a footing because Norwegians had an interest in improving the productivity of agriculture. The Danish corn monopoly and the acute harvest crisis led to an increasing realisation that it was necessary to increase productivity within Norway and not to rely on imports.

In Denmark, Schleswig and Holstein the patriotic societies were established in two waves. The first regional patriotic society in Denmark, *Det patriotiske Selskab i Næstved* (The Patriotic Society of Næstved), was started in 1780, but the movement did not break through until 1784 onwards. One important reason why the first wave of activity occurred was that Crown Prince Frederik (the later King Frederik VI) took over government that year from his father, the schizophrenic Christian VII. The Crown Prince relaxed restrictions on the press, and a critical public opinion, engaged in affairs and conditions within the state, began to flourish. The relaxations also encouraged association life, and between 1784 and 1799, 16 patriotic societies were established in Denmark and four in Schleswig and Holstein. The press restrictions were reinforced in 1799, and both public opinion and the many associations lost momentum. The next wave of activity occurred during the war, which started with the British attack on Copenhagen in 1807, whereupon Denmark supported Napoleon and the blockade of England. During the war, which lasted until 1814, 25 new patriotic societies were established in the state. However, the new societies were of a quite different character from the older ones. The members of the first wave of societies expressed much criticism of the power structure and stated demands for reforms in many areas of society. The societies established in the second wave, on the other hand, were intensely loyal to the system. The political climate had changed markedly and the demands for reforms were toned down and replaced by calls for a spirit of self-sacrifice and solidarity among the inhabitants. Patriotism was not the same in peace and war.

External influences

I have explained in the previous sections, the rise of the patriotic societies in a domestic context. However, the movement should also be considered in a larger perspective, since the societies stemmed from a development taking place at the same time in the rest of Northern Europe.[5] In Great Britain clubs and associations had existed since the end of the 16th century, but from the 1780s and until the turn of the century, a remarkably greater number were established, and many of these were patriotic societies.[6] The same development could be seen south of Denmark; between 1757 and 1800, 63 patriotic societies were established in Germany and Switzerland, encouraged by the war years 1756-1763 and the famines of the 1770s, which emphasised the need for improvements in agriculture.[7]

Thus the patriotic societies came into being at about the same time all over Northern Europe. The question is therefore whether there was a formalised collaboration between the societies and whether they can be characterised as an actual association movement. The founders of the patriotic societies in the Danish state were clearly inspired by the foreign societies. Especially, *Det kongelige danske Landhusholdningsselskab* had many similarities with *The Royal Society for the Encouragement of Arts, Manufactures, and Commerce*, founded in London in 1754, in terms of both goals and organisational structure. Several of the founders of the Danish society were also members of the British sister society.[8] In the same way *Die Hamburgische Gesellschaft zur Beförderung der Künste und nützliche Gewerbe*, founded in 1765, was a model for *Die schleswig-holsteinische patriotische Gesellschaft*, which was established in Kiel in 1786. There was no formal cooperation between the societies, but the founders of the societies in the Danish state clearly imported foreign thoughts and ideals and applied them to domestic conditions. They emphasised that they regarded their societies as part of a larger European movement, and made no attempt to hide the fact that they borrowed extensively from the foreign societies as they drew up their rules and regulations.

The patriotic societies within the Danish monarchy had almost identical rules and regulations. But there was no formal cooperation between the societies, they were all self-organising and established on local initiative. At no time was there an attempt to establish a central organ in Denmark, which could take over the functions of the local societies, not even by *Det kongelige danske Landhusholdningsselskab*, in spite of the fact that it both worked and had members all over the monarchy. In Norway, on the other hand, *Selskabet for Norges Vel* (The Society for the Well Being of Norway) incorporated the previously established regional societies when it was founded in 1809, and it aimed at a firmer and more centralised organisational structure. This society also established a number of parish societies, which all referred directly to the central society, in order to attain its goals on a local and regional level. In 1813 there were 66 parish societies scattered all over Norway.

Association life in the Danish state developed later than in Great Britain. There were several reasons for this; The Glorious Revolution and the abolition of the licensing laws in 1695 encouraged the culture of the free associations among the Britons. In the Danish state the right to speak and assemble freely was not secured until the constitution of 1849. Prior to this there was, briefly, freedom of the press from 1770 to 1773, starting when the radical enlightener J.F. Struensee, assumed power.[9] From 1784 to 1799 there was a fairly liberal interpretation of the restrictions on the press and the right to assemble. But the Absolute monarchy still kept the publications under close control, assemblies had to be reported to the local police chief superintendent beforehand, and the government had spies present during the meetings of the associations. Thus the rules had a disciplining and self-censoring effect among the debaters, and they also dampened the intensity of association life.

Another aspect was the relatively low degree of urbanisation in Denmark. In 1801 the population in the Danish Kingdom was one million people. 80 % still lived in the country, 10 % in Copenhagen and another 10 % in the 67 market towns. These were quite small; the biggest were Odense, Aalborg and Elsinore, which each had 5-6,000 inhabitants (see more in 'Introduction'). The low degree of urbanisation is of importance to association life, because an association needs a certain population density so that it can be established and recruit members.

The goals and means of the patriotic societies

What did the patriotic societies in Northern Europe have in common and how did they differ from other types of associations in the 18th century?

While the salons and early societies were highbrow cultural debating societies for arts and literature, the patriotic societies were much more practical. The members attached great importance to the fact that the patriotic disposition was expressed in concrete actions and practical work. Thus the patriotic societies had many outward-looking activities; they disseminated technological knowledge among peasants and craftsmen, they reorganised the health care and poor relief in several towns, and they established peasant libraries and secondary schools for the middle class. Several of the societies also compiled topographical descriptions and demographic statistics, which they published in periodicals. In addition, all the societies distributed prizes to peasants and villagers. The prizes were regarded as an effective means to overcome the laziness of the lower classes, which the members considered to be one of the main impediments to the implementation of reforms.

When the members demanded reforms in farming, industry and in the social area, it was emphasised that they acted out of love for their country, that they had established or joined a patriotic society to express their commitment to the common welfare, and that they felt obliged to help their fellow citizens and the state. This is why the societies were described as patriotic.

During the meetings of the societies the members made speeches and discussed the political and social conditions in the state. The patriotic societies in the Danish state published the speeches in pamphlets and magazines in order to keep their members and the public informed about what was discussed during the meetings. Today these publications are an important source of information about the members' attitudes to the state, Absolutism, reforms, general education, and enlightenment. The publication of the debates was one of the ways by which the patriotic societies distanced themselves from the esoteric and secretive freemason lodges. In addition, several of the patriotic societies in the Danish state had close relations with the royal family, and this was also in contrast to the lodges, which did not want interference from the state.

Like the learned societies that were established earlier in the century, the patriotic societies wished to present science and technological innovations for broad circles of the population. But whereas members of the learned societies were university professors and intellectuals, the core members of the patriotic societies were from the middle classes in the provinces who had an all-round education. The geographical spread of the patriotic societies also shows that the ideas of the Enlightenment had reached a larger audience than earlier in the century. The foundation of the patriotic societies represents a clear shift in the opinion of who should be enlightened. The members clearly dissociated themselves from the general belief held in the first half of the 18th century: that enlightenment was a matter for the learned and the educated sections of the population. They not only wished to enlighten themselves, they also explicitly stated that the object of their societies was to spread the rays of the 'Enlightenment's Sun' to every citizen in every backwater of the empire. They believed that every single inhabitant, peasant or landed proprietor, fisherman or aristocrat, was important in terms of bringing prosperity and welfare to the state, and they established the societies in order to spread the joys of civilisation among all sections of the population.

It is characteristic of the patriotic societies, that their point of departure was practical conditions and local circumstances. But the members announced that they had also long-term goals in mind. In their perception, human progress should begin in what was immediately accessible, and they hoped that their initiatives would spread like ripples in the water. In the same way they wanted to mobilise the entire population, so that every citizen was aware of his or her obligation towards the community and acted in a way that was for the benefit of the fatherland. The patriotic societies looked to the future and believed that in the course of one or two generations the inhabitants of the state would be able to harvest the fruits of the seeds the societies had planted. In the same tone the members claimed that their work was not in their own interest and that they did not benefit from it themselves. They strongly believed that they were preparing the way for the progress, welfare and happiness of the entire population.

Admission criteria and members

Who joined the patriotic societies? Did they attract certain groups or social segments in the population? Several of the societies published member lists with their members' names and professions. These lists will be used to investigate both the size of the societies and what occupational and social groups formed the basis of recruitment.

Both the majority of the societies and the largest in terms of members were in the largest cities in the Danish state: Copenhagen, Bergen, Christiania,[10] Kiel and Altona. In Copenhagen there were several societies with 300-400 members, and some even had more than 1,000. One example is *Det søsterlige Velgørenhedsselskab* (The Sisterly Charity Society), which had 1,233 members in 1813. The society is different from the other societies in that it accepted only women as members. Women were not formally excluded from the other societies, but these had none or only a few female members.

FIG. 2.

The house to the left is that of amtmand *Johan Rudolph Bielke in Næstved. This is where Næstved's Patriotic Society was founded on 20 July 1780, and the house was also used for society meetings. Bielke himself was president of the society and Næstved town recorder, Ewald Wulff, was the secretary. The drawing is from 1863.*

Altona in Holstein was the seat of another large society, *Die Schleswig-holsteinische Patriotische Gesellschaft*, which had 357 members in 1816. *Selskabet for Norges Vel* had 2,652 members in 1813. They lived all over the country, mostly in Trondheim and Kristiania.[11] In comparison, *Det kongelige danske Landhusholdningsselskab* never had more than 359 members, despite the fact that this society was very active all over the monarchy. One of the reasons was probably that the society subscription was rather high; ten *rigsdaler* per year when it was founded in 1769, whereas the subscription in the other societies was only 1-2 *rigsdaler* per year.[12]

In the provinces the societies were somewhat smaller and typically had 50-100 members. One example is *Det patriotiske Præmie-Selskab i Kalundborg* (The Patriotic Prize Society in Kalundborg), which had 45 members in 1792, its first year. The number rose to 92 in 1796 and to 118 in 1799, and then it quickly declined. *Det patriotiske Selskab i Næstved* had 70 members in 1789 and 88 in 1789, about the same as *Selskabet for Efterslægten paa Bornholm* (The Society for Posterity in Bornholm), which had 79 members in 1808.

The majority of the members belonged to the social group that can be termed the bourgeoisie. However, it was far from being an economically and occupationally homogeneous group; the members were recruited among both the haute bourgeoisie of Copenhagen and the middle class in the provinces, and among both the business bourgeoisie and the well educated *(Bildungsbürgerschaft)*. But in the patriotic societies the members acted in unity and believed they shared bourgeois attitudes and values.

Thus the patriotic societies reflected a development in which the term bourgeoisie changed from being a formal class designation, defining the craftsmen and traders in the cities and market towns who had a trade licence. In the patriotic societies, the term bourgeoisie was used as a social distinction, in which education, morals and good manners were informal indicators.[13] This semantic change shows that new kinds of communities had begun to develop. This new bourgeoisie was not a social or professional community, but a group of people who shared a lifestyle and values.

It was true for all the societies that either the first or the most conspicuous article in the respective set of rules proclaimed that the society in question was an open association, of which anybody could become member, regardless of rank and social status. But in reality admission was not open. The records of the societies show that nobody was accepted into a society unless the person in question had been proposed by another member beforehand. Due to this practice almost all applicants were accepted and the societies had a socially exclusive character. In just one case is an applicant known to have been turned down. This was Levin Ballin, who was refused admission to *Det patriotiske Præmie-Selskab i Kalundborg*. The society gave as the reason for the refusal the fact that Ballin was Jewish and therefore a stranger, from whom the city did not profit in any way. In contrast to a large number of the other members, Levin actually lived in Kalundborg, so he was not a stranger in the sense that the members did not know him. The denial of admission was based solely on Ballin's faith and ethnicity, and this was done as something completely natural. The reference to the fact that he was Jewish was stated as a reason that could stand by itself. However, in all fairness, it should be said that it was only in this society that there were expressions of hostility toward Jews. The other societies admitted Jewish members, and there was even a society founded with the purpose of integrating the Jewish population in trade and industry; *Præmieselskabet til at anføre den jødiske Ung-*

dom til Kunstner og Haandværk (The Prize Society to Lead Jewish Youth into Arts and Crafts).

In all the societies the most important admission criterion was the applicant's moral reputation. The societies attached the utmost importance to the cultured and decent behaviour of the members, and made it clear that members who lived immorally and offensively would be excluded. Thus the admission criteria were based on a code different from the traditional estate society; they gave higher priority to the behaviour and moral character of the individual than his rank. Through their admission procedures the societies maintained the personal demands made on the potential member; only by virtuous conduct and by considering the common good could the citizen make himself worthy of admission and thereby the designation 'patriot'. This reflects the fact that the bourgeoisie wanted new ground rules for what should give prestige in the society. They emphasised inner virtue instead of outer appearance. In their opinion it was the integrity and sense of duty of each individual, his commitment and will to do good, which should be rewarded.

In many cases there were a relatively high number of members who were not resident in either the hometown or the nearest environs of the society of which they were members. In some societies the non-resident members even constituted a majority. This is especially remarkable in the case of the small provincial societies because their object was to carry out reforms in the town or the environs in which they were founded. One example is *Det patriotiske Præmie-Selskab i Kalundborg*. Even though the town is situated 100 km west of Copenhagen, 25 % of the members were resident in the capital in 1799 and 31 % in distant provinces. Only a minority of 44 % of the members lived in Kalundborg or environs. Another example is *Det patriotiske Selskab i Næstved*, 90 km southwest of Copenhagen. Here 55 % of the members lived in the capital, 14 % in other parts of Denmark and 3 % in Schleswig or Holstein. Only 16 % of the members lived in Næstved or environs.[14]

What incentives did the non-resident members have to join the societies? Some of them may originally have had an affiliation with the towns concerned, but nostalgia was hardly a motivating factor in itself. In addition, they were unable to participate in the meetings or the activities of the society in question, so they had little opportunity to gain influence. In my opinion the high quota of non-resident members reflects the fact that communities had begun to emerge, which was characteristic of modern societies. This calls for an explanation:

Several sociologists, among others Anthony Giddens and Ernst Manheim, characterise pre-modern societies as being based in locally bounded areas. The social connections between people were primarily family and kinship, and secondarily the communities of the village or the parish where they lived and where they often had been born. It was characteristic for these types of communities that they had a high degree of physical nearness; people lived close to each other and saw each other more or less every day.[15] Modern societies differentiate themselves from traditional societies by having means of communication that makes interaction across physical distance (space) and immediate closeness (time) much easier. A part of a person's social relations are lifted out of the local context, and communities based on closeness in time and space are no longer the only communities. Social relations in modern societies can work even between people who live apart from each other. Traditional communities are thereby replaced by other forms of integration, and modernity is characterised by the rise of communities across time and space. This implies that modern human beings are able to show solidarity and feel connected with people they do not know personally and have never met.[16]

This theory can be applied to the patriotic societies. Obviously, these were organised locally and attached to geographically bounded areas, which is also reflected in their names. But as mentioned, the societies had a high quota of non-resident members, and these presumably knew only a few, if any, of the other members personally. They used means of communication other than the face-to-face relation. However, the members strongly believed that they were connected by their shared opinions, and that they had norms and values in common. Thus the patriotic societies were to a certain extent abstract communities, or – in Benedict Anderson's famous statement – imagined communities.[17] The societies made contacts across the traditional structures of society and created new kinds of communities. They are thereby symptomatic of a new culture of integration, which was made possible by the increasing circulation of the printed media, and which reflected underlying social and structural transformations in society. It is therefore an essential aspect of the patriotic societies that they recruited members from a very wide area. They represented a break with the traditional forms of society and fellowship, and reflected a way of establishing communities that is characteristic of modernity.

Meetings and organisational structures

Seen from the outside the societies were socially exclusive, but internally the societies had an educational function in creating democracy among the members. Once a person was admitted to a society he was formally placed on an equal footing with the other members. The societies attached great importance to the member's right to participate in decision making through debates and ballots. Every member had a right to express his views and to vote, and ballots were based on the principle of one man, one vote. Furthermore the rules of the societies emphasised that the administration should be open and transparent; every member had access to the accounts, protocols and minutes of the society. In most of the societies the presidency was divided between several members, typically from three to nine persons, and there were also several assistant directors and a board. Thus the societies aimed at having as flat a governance structure as possible. The rules of the societies also stressed that the presidency was solely an administrative assignment, that a strong leader was not welcome, and that it was important to maintain the society as a decentralised organisation.

This democratic way of organising the societies is also reflected in their lists of members. All the members were listed in alphabetic order, and this meant that the Secretaries of State were listed co-ordinately with brewers and black smiths. This was a break with the hierarchic conventions of the estate society, and a way in which the patriotic societies sent a clear signal to the public. In the rules and way of organising the societies they exposed a form of order in which civic virtue and deeds for the fatherland were set above birth, rank and title. Nor did the societies follow the style of address which prevailed at the time; all the members were addressed as patriots. The hierarchy of ranks that existed outside the societies was thereby suspended inside the societies. Thus the societies had a homogenising and equalising function among the members.

In the societies' publications the members clearly demonstrated a distance to the aristocracy, whose lifestyle they represented as superficial and unrestrained, a world of dance, concerts and carnivals, and characterised by a lack of commitment to the problems of society. The patriotic bourgeoisie contrasted the decadence of the aristocracy with their own puritan lifestyle, good manners, decency and restraint. In contrast to the traditional aristocratic view of work as déclassé, the bourgeoisie had a strong work ethic, although they did not do manual labour. And whereas the aristocracy, according to the patriots, lived secluded lives in their palaces and estates, they themselves were actively committed to the welfare of the fatherland. In this way the patriotic societies created a bourgeois identity among the members, and the societies functioned as forums in which the middle class developed its self-image in opposition to the aristocracy.

However, several members of the societies were nobles. During the meetings of the societies they could listen to the sharp attacks on the hierarchical society, which they represented. This raises the question of whether the bourgeois members believed that nobles could become good patriots. They could, in so far as they accepted the patriotic values and acted in line with the bourgeois norms. The bourgeoisie did not mind personal nobility either. The bourgeoisie's attack was first and foremost directed at inherited nobility, because it supported a society in which some people were assigned good positions and prestige, even though they had not worked for it.

Enlightenment among common people; spinning schools and poor houses

Even though common people were not invited to participate in the patriotic societies, they had a very central position, since they were the target group for the outward going activities of the societies. This chapter is about the societies' attempt to propagate agricultural and industrial reforms among this section of the population.

The patriotic societies aimed at improving every profession and doing this in every detail. One example is *Randers Amts Husholdningsselskab* (The Society of Agriculture in Randers County), which offered prizes for cattle breeding, pig breeding, bee-keeping, gardening, potato growing, tree planting, and the cultivation of flax and hemp; as well as for using peat coal, for making shoes, clothes brushes, woollen clothes and coffins of straw. No subject was considered too big or too small to attract the attention of the society. In the same spirit the societies published magazines, from which the readers could learn how to economise on light and fuel, make soap from fish, bake bread from bone meal, schnapps from sugar, how to avoid rot in shoe soles and dry-rot in building timber – just to mention some examples. Because of the grain shortage in Norway the Norwegian societies concentrated on propagating information about various grain substitutes, such as moss, rose hips, bone meal and lichen.

The societies were engaged in practical matters and did not subscribe to any particular economic theory. Their work was based on a belief that it was possible to gen-

FIG. 3.

Sct. Peders Kirkeplads in Næstved. Furthest to the left is Næstved Spinning School, which was established in 1782 and was in existence until 1804. After the spinning school had been closed, the building was used for a time as the garrison hospital. Painting by Just Michael Hansen, 1833.

erate economic growth by a decrease in consumption and by creating a spirit of enterprise among the peasants. They often drew attention to the peasants' laziness and aversion to change, which they considered to be *the* major hindrance to the implementation of reforms. The prizes offered by the societies were considered as a pedagogical means to stimulate the peasants to be innovative, and give them an incentive to be industrious and thrifty. It is thus interesting that what mattered most when the members decided whether a person should be awarded a prize was if the person in question was hardworking and had a decent lifestyle *in general*, whereas the product he or she had made mattered less.

How did common people respond to prizes offered by the societies? There were far from enough applicants for all the prizes offered, and far from all the applicants were considered worthy of reward by the societies. Instead the societies attempted to kick start progress in another way. One example is *Det patriotiske Præmie-Selskab i Kalundborg*, which bought a boat in 1794 and hired a fisherman, Peder Johnsen. The town is situated on the west coast of Zealand, and the fisherman had to sail people to the inlet west of the town. Here they were able to catch more fish than by fishing from the shore, which was common at that time. Peder Johnsen was obliged to write down carefully how many fish he caught and sold, and hand over the money to the society. After this, the society paid him two-thirds of the earnings from selling the fish. The society also paid part of his rent.

However, things did not go as planned. Apparently Johnsen did not get any fishermen from the town to sail with him, and in the first year the society's expenses for materials and wages were four times higher than the income. In the following two years, expenses were twice and three times the income, respectively. The members of the society had a growing feeling that Johnsen sold the catch and reaped the whole profit himself. This suspicion was deepened when the fisherman informed the society that since he had not caught any fish in 1800 they should not bother to pay him any wages for that year. In 1803 the society gave up the whole idea and sold the boat.

The patriotic societies had many experiences like this; they tried to initiate reforms of different kinds, but often unsuccessfully. The efforts of the societies did not gain a hearing among common people and the patriots often expressed their frustration that the peasants did not know what was for their own good.

Another and very widespread means of implementing reforms were spinning schools. A keen spokesman of spinning schools in Denmark was the wealthy merchant Niels Ryberg (1725-1804). He bought an estate in Køng, situated in South Zealand between Næstved and Vordingborg, in 1778 and established a spinning school in a village nearby. He then founded *Det patriotiske Selskab i Næstved* in order to develop a regional textile industry. During the 1780s the society established 13 spinning schools in market towns and villages in Mid- and South Zealand. Most of the schools had 10-20 spinners attending. Some were poor elderly women, but the spinning schools preferred children from four to thirteen years of age. As was said by the chairman of the society, the physician Christian Mangor: 'the younger the better'.[18] The members preferred children as labour, for one thing because they spun a finer thread, for another the children were considered to be a long-term investment; if the children learned to be industrious at a young age, it would benefit both themselves and the state when they grew up.

Thus a very central purpose of the schools was to give the children an industri-

Fig. 4.

In 1794 a spinning institution was established in Kalundborg in the double building to the right in the picture. The institution was established on the initiative of The Patriotic Prize Society in Kalundborg. The picture of the square in Adelgade in Kalundborg was taken in 1871.

ous upbringing. Hardworking and well-behaved children were rewarded with prizes, in order to teach them that it paid. Another method was songs; the children should sing while they spun. These were devotional spinning songs, in which the texts in an amused tone told about the joy of working and that it was healthy to be occupied, just as they expressed surprise that there were people who did not want to spin. All the songs were written in the first-person, to make it easier for the spinners to identify themselves with what they sang.

The societies made plans to set up reading schools in connection with the spinning schools, so that the children could get elementary teaching for half of the day and work the other half. However the plans were never implemented. Thus the children's working day started at five o'clock in the morning and ended at eight o'clock in the evening, with a two-hour lunch break in the middle of the day.

The spinning schools started by *Det patriotiske Selskab i Næstved* never really got well established. One of the reasons was the shortage of flax, and even though the society made a great effort to encourage the peasants to grow flax, it was still necessary to import it from abroad. The greatest hindrance to the success of the spinning schools was the aversion of the local population to working there. All the head teachers complained that the children's attendance was too unstable, and that the parents disliked sending them to the schools; some days only 2-4 children showed up, and they worked for only a couple of hours. The spinning schools eventually closed and in 1808 the society gave up the whole idea.

Spinning schools were not only established in Zealand; according to a statement from the central administration there were 38 spinning schools in market towns and villages all over Denmark in 1788. Some 1,582 spinners were attached to these institutions. However this statement does not give the complete number, the actual number of spinning schools was much higher. A comprehensive investigation into how many there were has not yet been made.

Seen in a wider perspective, the spinning school movement was widespread all over Europe in the decades around 1800, and the Danish schools had several sources of inspiration. One source was the pietistic working schools for poor children founded by Hermann Francke in Halle. Another was the spinning schools in Göttingen, in which the priest Ludwig Gerhard Wagemann was a leading figure.[19] During the years 1789-1803 he published the magazine *Göttingisches Magazin für Industrie und Armenpflege*. A third source of inspiration was the *British Society for Promoting Christian Knowledge*, which combined elementary teaching, practical work and Christian upbringing by establishing several thousand reading and spinning schools in Great Britain. Here the spinning schools were established in two waves; the first from ca. 1723, but they had all closed by 1744. The second wave were established from the 1780s and lasted a couple of decades.[20]

The founders and supporters of the spinning schools in Northern Europe shared a number of reasons for establishing the schools, and their arguments can be summarised as follows:

Firstly the textile industry was taken into consideration. It needed a work force that had relevant technical skills and practical experience. Secondly the national economy was considered. In most countries the public debate was very focused on the balance of trade and payments. In Denmark a crucial point in the economic discussions was the balance of payments deficit on yarn and textiles. It was often argued that the spinning schools would expand domestic production and also reduce the import of textiles. A third argument for the spinning schools was that they would make the poor self-supporting. Instead of poor relief they should be offered work at the spinning schools and thereby earn their own money. If they did not want to work there they would lose the right to poor relief. This argument was based on the opinion that poor relief kept the poor in poverty, whereas the spinning schools gave the mental and technical qualifications so that the poor could get active employment. A fourth, and frequently stated, argument was that the spinning schools had a preventive aspect. When children attended the schools, they learned to work at a young age, and thus they would not be a burden on the state later in life.

Finally it was the general belief that the spinning schools improved the morals of the spinners and taught them good manners. Thus pastor Steinhöfel in Göttingen maintained that boys often became thieves and girls became whores, but that this was prevented by the spinning schools. Here they would learn to speak decently and have useful conversations. Slander, lies, smutty songs, and indecent, filthy and blasphemous speech were not allowed at the spinning schools. Steinhöfel argued that the school's continuous upbringing would awaken the conscience of the spinners and soften their hearts. Furthermore the spinners learned to be thrifty and keep things tidy; to make sure that everything was in the right place and that everything was done in time. Finally the schools would improve the children's hygiene, because they were not allowed to attend the schools in dirty clothes or with slovenly loose hair.[21]

To sum up, the spinning schools were considered both as a solution to acute economic and social problems, and as part of a long-term preventative strategy. The educational aspects of the schools were also stated as the reason why children were put in the spinning schools at the age of four, even though they probably were not able to do real work at this age. The promoters believed that when the children were this young, it would be easier to influence their attitude to work and thus instil a new work ethic in the future generation. They considered the spinning schools to be a social investment, and expected the future returns to be industrious citizens.

The promoters of the spinning schools had great expectations from them, and Steinhöfel enthusiastically praised them as a splendid means to achieve enlightenment quickly.[22] However the spinning schools were not received with the same enthusiasm by the common people. Everywhere in Denmark the same picture as in Zealand emerged; the spinning schools were not viable because the workforce was too unstable. This was partly because the ideas of the middle class met with no response among the peasants, and partly because they ran into the same practical problems that had also hampered the reading schools, i.e. that the distance between the chil-

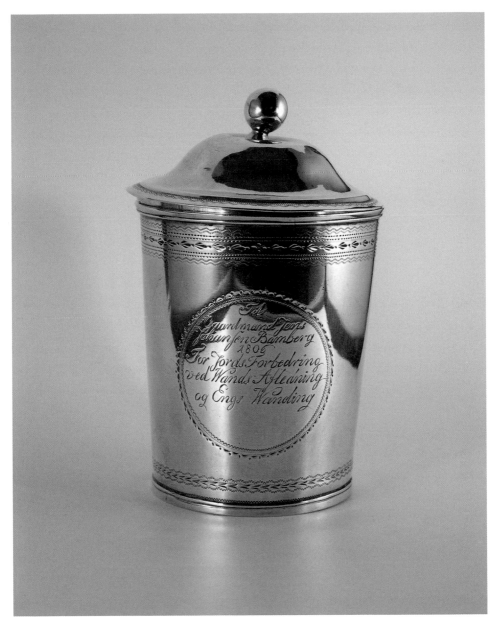

FIG. 5.

The patriotic societies were eager to reform society and members often complained about the common
people being averse to change. That is why they gave prizes to those who were diligent, and who used
new technology and new agricultural practices. The Agricultural Society gave the most lavish prizes.
The reward could be gold or silver medals, or, as here, a silver cup with the engraved words: 'From the
Royal Agricultural Society' and 'To Farmer Jens Johansen Bamberg 1806 for the improvement of the
land by draining and watering meadows.' Height: 10.1 cm.

dren's homes and the schools was often too great, and the parents needed the children's labour. According to *Die Schleswig-Holsteinische Patriotische Gesellschaft*, the idea of relieving poverty through spinning schools was abandoned by 1817.[23] The picture is the same in Germany and Great Britain. Here most spinning schools ceased around 1800, although some survived until the 1820s.

From an overall point of view the disciplining aspects were very prominent in the reforms the patriotic societies wanted to implement. The members considered progress and a sound economy as a question of communicating a culture, according to which hard work and an industrious spirit were inherently valuable. The reformers not only attempted to regulate the behaviour of common people, they also aimed at internalising this work ethic, so that each individual felt an inner urge to be industrious, and act in a way that was characterised by discipline and self-restraint. In this way the societies were a condensation of the civilising process, as described by Norbert Elias, and they accord with Max Weber's explanation that capitalism is just as much a cultural and psychological concept as it is an accumulation of money.[24] Most of the projects the societies initiated were short lived and did not live up to the expectations of the members. Both the middle class and the peasants lacked understanding for each other's way of reasoning. In my judgement, however, the societies had a profound cultural influence in a longer time span, first and foremost because they highlighted the idea that change was a positive thing, i.e. it was good to do things in a different way from the usual one, and that habits and traditions in themselves were not an argument for thinking and acting in a certain way. It is in this way that the societies had an important influence on the process of modernisation.

Reading schools and book clubs

Several of the patriotic societies in Copenhagen, among others *Det kongelige danske Landhusholdningsselskab* and *Selskabet for Efterslægten*, published useful and devotional literature, which they distributed among the peasants. The societies in the provinces established libraries and book clubs for common people in towns and in the country. Here the members read to the locals and they subsequently had 'useful conversations' about it, i.e. the members explained and interpreted the text.

Which kind of literature did the libraries contain? It was primarily useful literature, which presented practical knowledge especially about farming, and devotional publications, which admonished the lower orders to be obedient and inoffensive. A popular way of propagating these ideas was parables, in which the lower orders were described as prejudiced, tradition-bound, contrary and superstitious, but learned to be industrious, self-motivated and sympathetic toward change from progressive enlighteners.

Why did the societies find it important to enlighten common people? Their motives were both utilitarian and humanist. The utilitarian idea was that the socially lower classes were increasingly considered to be an unexploited economic resource. It was recognised that if the general level of education in the population increased, it would promote economic growth in the state as a whole. The members also believed that public mass education prevented riots and social disturbances. They argued that if the peasants learned about the laws and why they were made, they would become more inclined to comply with them. Thus the patriots reasoned that enlightened citizens would be both more hardworking and more law-abiding.

The humanist motive stemmed from social indignation. The members thought it below the dignity of a human being not to be able to read books and acquire knowledge. They considered education to be a human right and believed that it developed a person's social empathy, whereas ignorance led to brutality and cynicism.

However, at the meetings in the societies the members also discussed how much enlightenment common people could tolerate. They were clearly frightened that they would lose control of the development if the reforms were carried through too fast, and that the reforms would end in lawlessness and subversion. The fear of revolution was constantly present in the debates of the societies, and this moderated the expectations as to when, how and at what speed the social reforms should be carried out. The members continually stressed the necessity of maintaining order, just as they closely followed any suspicion of revolt among the population.

For the same reason the peasant literature distributed by the societies emphasised that the lower orders should stay within the occupation and social framework to which each was born. The patriots clearly dissociated themselves from transverse mobility with regard to occupation and social group in the case of the lower orders. They often claimed that the purpose of enlightening common people was to preserve, and not undermine, the social borders. Peasants who broke the social patterns were not pointed out as role models, but as the result of lack of enlightenment. The patriots' goals were that all the inhabitants of the state should be equal before the law, but social equality was not their ambition. Although the members wanted common people to be hard working, they only intended them to prosper *within* their social group, i.e. as villagers, not *outside* their social group. They did not mind circulation inside each branch of profession, for example that a copyholder should become a freeholder, but he should not become anything other than a peasant.[25] Apparently the members did not see anything paradoxical or contradictory in having different goals and ideals for the lower orders from themselves – the bourgeoisie – who sought social and political recognition through the patriotic societies.

Some of the societies established *realskoler* (secondary schools) for the members' own children. The schools were meant to meet the educational needs of the growing mercantile class, and taught subjects that were more relevant to commercial life than those taught in the grammar schools. The students learned the modern commercial languages, English and Dutch, and they learned economics, accounting and bookkeeping. In contrast to the grammar schools, which attached most importance to the classical subjects and prepared the student for a university education, it was expected that the students in the secondary schools should end their education after their final exams and start a career in business.

The schools were for boys only and to match this *Det søsterlige Velgørenhedsselskab* founded a school for girls in 1790. Here the girls had classes for 38 hours a week, of these 22 were reserved for teaching embroidery, knitting, spinning and sewing. During the remaining classes the pupils learned basic academic subjects such as reading, writing and mathematics.

Thus there was a big difference between what was considered to be an academic minimum and what norms the pupils should learn. It depended both on the social status of the pupils and whether they were boys or girls. The peasants learned first and foremost to be obedient and industrious. Boys from the middle class were taught subjects that prepared them for a career in trade and business, while the girls were guided to become good wives and good mothers.

The functions of the patriotic societies

This article has described how the patriotic societies were organised and some of the occupational and educational reforms they initiated. The large number of patriotic societies and their high level of activity show that the bourgeois middle class played a central role in carrying through reforms in the towns and provinces of the Danish state. Furthermore the societies worked as channels to communicate the values and social understanding of the bourgeoisie to wider circles of the population both peasants and the nobility.

To round off this essay it is important to answer two questions.

Firstly, what was the relationship between the patriotic societies and the Absolute monarchy? Several of the Secretaries of the State and high officials in the government were members of the societies, and the societies received considerable economic support from members of the royal family. As an example *Det patriotiske Selskab i Næstved* received 7,915 *rigsdaler* from the royal family in the period 1788-1805. But what interest did the monarchy have in cooperating with the patriotic societies?

The government at that time had the implementation of agricultural, social and educational reforms as a high political priority. Earlier in the century the government had made an attempt to carry through reforms of the poor relief and of public education, but they failed because of the local inhabitants' aversion to the projects and their wish to maintain well-established rights. The attempts had clearly shown that the state was not powerful enough to carry through reforms at the local level. The administrative infrastructure and the local organs had been too weak to force the plans through, and the state beat a hasty retreat. Seen in the light of these failures the government had an interest in cooperating with highly motivated people who had an insight into local conditions and problems, and could and would do the job. A large part of the members were resident in the rural provinces and small towns, and it was easier for them to establish contact with the local population than it was for the chancellery and administrative organs. From a governmental perspective the societies functioned as tools to implement reforms in those parts of the empire where the state organs were weakly represented. Thus the societies filled out an administrative vacuum.

Secondly, it is also a relevant question to ask what function the patriotic societies had for the bourgeoisie.

The societies were communities with bourgeois norms and values, and thus created a feeling of identity among the members. Furthermore the societies gave the bourgeoisie a platform from which they could actively participate in society. The members assigned themselves a social responsibility by stressing their solicitude for the welfare of the inhabitants and for the economic growth of the state, and they positioned themselves as players on the political scene – as patriots – by emphasising their duty and willingness to work for the fatherland. To be patriotic gave the bourgeoisie a position, through which they got a status and a function in the state.

Thus the establishment of the patriotic societies must be seen in connection with the appearance of the bourgeoisie as a social and economic influential section of the population, and its need to have comparable political influence. Furthermore, as explained earlier in this article, the debates and organisational structure of the societies reflected the bourgeoisie's need to confront the political culture of the time, which was based on privileges of birth and estate hierarchies. The members did not directly demand formal political power and representation, but they participated in establishing the bourgeoisie as an informal power by creating semantic concepts of opposition; they accentuated inner virtue as opposed to outer status, and their own ethical duties as opposed to the aesthetic pleasures of the nobility. It was a rhetorical device by which they appeared as morally superior and the nobility as decadent. Furthermore, the patriotic societies argued that the central issue in politics was *values*, not traditions.

The societies functioned as forums, in which the bourgeoisie could practice debating in a parliamentary way and in this way prepare themselves for actual political participation. The patriots did not write down that they wanted a free constitution: that would be politically too dangerous. But they were clearly very sure of themselves and wrote and worked in complete certainty that they were the men of tomorrow. They described themselves as 'Friends of Truth' and praised the societies as forums for free debates, as opposed to the flattery and dissimulation that they maintained characterised the court around the Absolute monarchy. The patriots were in no doubt that their cause was the winner of the future, and they saw themselves as a minority in the population, who represented truth and justice.

Survey of the patriotic societies in the Danish state 1769-2005

This is a list of all the patriotic societies that were founded in Norway, Denmark, Schleswig and Holstein between 1762 and 1814. They are grouped as economic societies, societies for relief and philanthropy and societies for education and enlightenment. The classification is based on the principal activity of each society, but should not be taken too narrowly since most of the societies were active in several areas.

In each group the societies are listed in chronological order according to the year they were founded. In those cases where there is uncertainty about when a society was founded or shut down, I have simply noted the first or the last time there are references to them. In several cases a society was not formally shut down, it just faded away. Some of the societies survived the age of Enlightenment, but they were depoliticised in the course of the 19th century, and their ideological character vanished. Today they exist as agricultural councils, which are occupied with – literally – down-to-earth themes and questions.

Danish societies are marked with *
Norwegian societies are marked with **
Societies in Schleswig or Holstein are marked with ***

Economic Societies

***   Die Königlich-Dänische Acker-Academie. Founded in Schleswig and existed 1762-1786.

*   The Royal Danish Society of Agriculture. Founded in Copenhagen on the 29th of January 1769 (the birthday of King Christian 7th). The society still exists.

*   The Economic Society in Nysted. Founded in 1771.

**   The Useful Society for Bergenhus. Founded in 1773 and still exists.

**   The Practical Society of Agriculture in Synnmøre. Founded in 1773 and dissolved in 1779. Re-established in 1805.

**   The Practical Society of Agriculture in Romsdal. Founded in 1776.

**   The Society of Agriculture in Stavanger County. Founded in 1776, the activities of the society stopped circa 1785.

**   The Society of Agriculture of Inderøyen. Founded in 1776 and dissolved circa 1782.

**   The Economic Society of Encouragement in Bratsberg County. Founded in 1777.

**   The Patriotic Society of Akerhus. Founded in 1778, its activities stopped in 1790. The society was re-established in 1808 and incorporated in The Royal Society for the Welfare of Norway in 1810.

*   The Patriotic Society in Næstved. Founded in 1780 and dissolved in 1809.

**   The Economic Society in Christiansand. Founded in 1782 and dissolved in 1790.

**   The Patriotic Society in Aamot. Founded in 1782.

***   Die schleswig-holsteinische patriotische Gesellschaft. Founded in Kiel in 1786 and re-established in Altona in 1812. Dissolved in 1858.

*   The Patriotic-Practical Society for the Promotion of Industry and Trade. Founded in Copenhagen in 1788.

**   The Corresponding Topographical Society in Norway. Founded in Kristiania (Oslo) in 1791, but faded away around the turn of the century. It was re-established in 1807 and incorporated in The Royal Society for the Welfare of Norway in 1809.

*   The Patriotic Prize Society in Kalundborg. Founded in 1792 and dissolved in 1819.

*   The Economic Welfare Society. Founded in Copenhagen in 1796.

*   The Danish Fishing Society. Founded in Copenhagen, existed in 1801.

* The Danish and Norwegian Patriotic Society. Founded in 1803 (?).
** The Patriotic Society in Kristiania. Existed in 1807.
** The Society for the Welfare of Aker Parish. Existed 1808-1811.
** The Society for the Welfare of Asker Parish. Founded in 1808 and existed until at least 1810.
* The Society for Domestic Arts and Crafts. Founded in Copenhagen in 1808.
** The Royal Society for the Welfare of Norway. Founded in 1809 and still exists.
* The Society for the Promotion of Enlightenment and Industry in Lolland-Falster County. Founded in 1809.
* The Society for Industry and Domestic Crafts in Holsteinborg County. Founded in 1809.
* The Parish Society in Kristiania. Established in 1810.
* The Society of Agriculture in Randers County. Founded in 1810 and still exists.
* The Patriotic Society in Funen Diocese. Founded in 1810 and still exists.
* The Economic Society of Aalborg County and Diocese. Founded in 1810.
* The Economic Society of Aarhus County. Existed in 1810.
* The Economic Welfare Society in Viborg. Existed in 1810.
* The Society for the Promotion of Welfare of Peasants in Øster Flakkebjerg District. Founded in 1811.
* The District Society for Useful Occupations in Randlev. Founded in 1810.
* The Economic Society in Holbæk County. Founded in 1812.
** The Agricultural and Industrious Society in Berg Parish. Founded in 1812.
* The Economic Society in Møn. Founded in 1813.

Societies for Relief and Philanthropy

*** Verein freiwilliger Armenfreunde. Founded in Plön in 1785.
* The United Relief Society. Founded in Copenhagen in 1788. In 1900 the name was changed to The Citizen Friend. The Society still exists.
* The Prize and Relief Society for faithful Servants in Copenhagen. Founded in 1786 and existed until at least 1812.
* The Sisterly Charity Society. Founded in Copenhagen in 1790.
*** Die Gesellschaft freiwilliger Armenfreunde zu Kiel. Founded in 1792. Similar societies were founded in Elberfeld, Halle, Heide (1801) and Ratzeburg (1808/1809).
* The Society that Supports Unmarried Women whose Circumstances do not Correspond with their Upbringing. Founded in Copenhagen in 1792 and existed until at least 1917.
*** Die Unterstützungsgesellschaft in Altona. Founded in 1799.
*** Sich freywillig vereinigenden Armenfreunde. Founded in Husum i Schleswig in 1805.
* The Philanthropic Society. Founded in Skive in 1808.
** The Relief Society in Røken Parish. Founded in 1811.

Societies for Education and Enlightenment

* The Reading Society in Lolland. Founded in 1782.
* The Society for Civic Virtue. Founded in Copenhagen in 1785 and dissolved circa 1791.
* The Society for Posterity. Founded in Copenhagen in 1786.
* The Nordic Topographical Society. Founded in Copenhagen in 1792.
* The Society for the Improvement of Craftsmen. Existed in Copenhagen in 1792 and until at least 1806.
* The Prize Society to Lead the Jewish Youth into Arts and Crafts. Founded in Copenhagen in 1793 and existed until at least 1837.
* The Anthropological Society. Founded in Skive in 1795 and was dissolved in 1806.
* The Society for Rescuing Drowning People. Founded in Copenhagen in 1796.
** The Society for the Dissemination of Enlightenment and Good Manners. Existed in Christiansand in 1799.
* The Society to popularise the Art of Swimming. Founded in Copenhagen circa 1804.
* The Society for Posterity in Bornholm. Founded in 1805 and still exists.

BIBLIOGRAPHY

Anderson, Benedict 1991. *Imagined Communities: Reflections on the Origins and Spread of Nationalism.* 2nd edn. London: Verso.

Bosse, Heinrich 1996. 'Patriotismus und Öffentlichkeit'. In: Ulrich Hermann (ed.), *Volk – Nation – Vaterland.* Hamburg.

Bödeker, Hans Erich 1999. 'Medien der patriotischen Gesellschaften'. In: Ernst Fischer, Wilhelm Haefs, York-Gothart Mix (eds.), *Von Almanach bis Zeitung. Ein Handbuch der Medien in Deutschland 1700-1800.* München.

Christensen, Dan Ch. 1996. *Det moderne projekt. Teknik og kultur i Danmark-Norge 1750-(1814)-1850.* Copenhagen: Gyldendal.

Clark, Peter 2001. *British Clubs and Societies 1580-1800. The Origins of an Associational World.* Oxford Studies in Social History. Clarendon Press.

Dann, Otto 1981. *Lesegesellschaften und bürgerliche Emanzipation. Ein europäischer Vergleich.* München.

Dülmen, Richard van 1986. *Die Gesellschaft der Aufklärer. Zur bürgerlichen Emanzipation und aufklärerischen Kultur in Deutschland.* Frankfurt a.M.

Elias, Norbert 1997. *Über den Prozess der Zivilisation. Soziogenetische und psychogenetische Untersuchungen.* Suhrkamp.

Engelhardt, Juliane 2004. De patriotiske selskaber i den danske helstat 1769-1814. Borgerskab, foreningssociologi og statstænkning. (Unpublished Ph.d. dissertation). Copenhagen: Copenhagen University.

Essen, Manfred von 1992. *Johann Daniel Lawätz und die Armenkolonie Friedrichsgabe.* Quellen und

Forschungen zur Geschichte Schleswig-Holsteins, 97. Neumünster: Karl Wachholtz Verlag.

Feldbæk, Ole 1988. 'Denmark'. In: Otto Dann & John Diwiddy (eds.), *Nationalism in the Age of the French Revolution*. London: Hambledon.

Feldbæk, Ole 1998. *Nærhed og Adskillelse 1720-1814. Danmark-Norge 1380-1814*. Vol. 4. Oslo: Universitetsforlaget.

Fuchs, Peter 1991. 'Vaterland, Patriotismus und Moral. Zur Semantik gesellschaftlicher Einheit'. *Zeitschrift für Soziologie*, vol. 2, pp. 89-103. Stuttgart.

Giddens, Anthony 2002. *Modernitetens konsekvenser*. Copenhagen: Hans Reitzels Forlag.

Habermas, Jürgen 1990. *Strukturwandel der Öffentlichkeit. Untersuchungen zu einer Kategorie der bürgerlichen Gesellschaft*. Frankfurt.

Hardtwig, Wolfgang 1990. 'Verein'. In: Otto Brunner, Werner Conze and Reinhart Koselleck, *Geschichtliche Grundbegriffe. Historisches Lexikon zur politisch-sozialen Sprache in Deutschland*. Vol. 6, pp. 789-829. Stuttgart.

Hasund, S. 1941. *Det Kgl. Selskab for Norges Vel 1809-1909*. Gjøvik.

Henningsen, Lars N. 1978. *Fattigvæsenet i de sønderjyske købstæder 1736-1841*. Aabenraa.

Hubrig, Hans 1957. *Die patriotischen Gesellschaften des 18. Jahrhunderts*. Berlin.

Im Hof, Ulrich 1982. *Das gesellige Jahrhundert. Gesellschaft und Gesellschaften im Zeitalter der Aufklärung*. München: C.H. Beck.

Jensen, Johan Fjord et al. 2000. *Patriotismens tid 1746 – 1807. Dansk litteraturhistorie*. Vol. 4. Copenhagen: Gyldendal.

Jones, M.G. 1938. *The Charity School Movement. A Study of Eigthteenth Century Puritanism in Action*. Cambridge.

Jørgensen, J.O. Bro 1973. *Industriens Historie i Danmark*. Vol. II, 1730-1820. Copenhagen.

Kopitzsch, Franklin 1996. 'Schleswig-Holstein im Gesamtstaat 1721-1830. Absolutismus, Aufklärung und Reform'. In: Ulrik Lange (ed.), *Geschichte Schleswig-Holsteins. Von den Anfängen bis zur Gegenwart*, pp. 281 – 332. Neumünster.

Koselleck, Reinhart 1959/1973. *Kritik und Krise. Eine Studie zur Pathogenese der bürgerlichen Welt*. Freiburg/Suhrkamp.

Lowood, Henry E. 1991. *Patriotism, Profit, and the Promotion of Science in the German Enlightenment. The Economic and the Scientific Societies 1760-1815*. New York & London.

Mangor, C.E. 1782. *Efterretning om Nestveds Patriotiske Selskab*. Copenhagen.

Manheim, Ernst 1979. *Aufklärung und öffentliche Meinung. Studien zur Soziologie der Öffentlichkeit im 18. Jahrhundert*. Frommann-Holzboog Verlag.

Markussen, Ingrid 1995. *Til Skaberens Ære, Statens Tjeneste og Vor egen Nytte. Pietistiske og kameralistiske idéer bag fremvæksten af en offentlig skole i landdistrikterne i 1700-tallet*. Odense: Odense Universitetsforlag.

Melton, James Van Horn 1988. *Absolutism and the eighteenth-century origins of compulsory schooling in Prussia and Austria*. Cambridge University Press.

Munck, Thomas 2000. *The Enligtenment. A Comparative Social History 1721 – 1794*. London & New York.

Scott, James C. 1990. *Domination and the Arts of Resistance. Hidden Transcripts.* Yale University Press.

Tenbruck, Friedrich H. 1989. *Die kulturellen Grundlagen der Gesellschaft. Der Fall der Moderne.* Westdeutscher Verlag.

Vierhaus, Rudolf (eds.) 1980. *Deutsche patriotische und gemeinnützige Gesellschaften.* (Wolfenbütteler Forschungen, 8). München.

Weber, Max 1920. *Die protestantische Ethik und der Geist des Kapitalismus.* Thübingen.

Wood, Henry Trueman 1913. *A History of the Royal Society of Arts.* London.

NOTES

1   Today the words patriotism and nationalism are often used as synonyms. However, patriotism must be distinguished from nationalism when it comes to the study of the 18th century. Patriotism implied another conception of the relationship between citizen and state than the national ideology of the 19th and 20th century. The members of the patriotic societies did not ascribe importance to the mother tongue, history or cultural peculiarity of the population and they did not see any conflict between cultural diversity and a feeling of unity among the population within the state. A person was considered a good patriot when he or she sat their own interests aside and worked for the welfare and progress of the fatherland.

2   There was an earlier society, *Die Königlich-Dänische Acker-Academie*, which was founded in Schleswig in 1762, but it never really got established and slowly dissolved.

3   Norway and Denmark entered into a union in 1397 and had a joint sovereign until the peace agreement in Kiel in 1814, where Frederik VI was forced to surrender Norway to the King of Sweden. Not until 1905 did Norway gain independence as a sovereign state. Norway brought the overseas dependencies: Iceland, the Faroe Islands and Greenland, into the Danish-Norwegian shared realm, and they remained under the Danish crown after the resignation of Norway.

4   Feldbæk 1998, p. 66.

5   Bödeker 1999. Clark 2001. Hubrig 1957. Vierhaus 1980.

6   Clark 2001, pp. 8, 95, 128, 132, 195.

7   Dülmen 1986, pp. 152-55.

8   The Society for the Encouragement of Arts, Manufactures, and Commerce Archive: Minutes of the Society, vol. 1, 1754 1757; Plans, Premiums and Members List 1754-1756; Rules and Orders of the Society, Established at London, for the Encouragement of Arts, Manufactures, and Commerce. London 1758; List of Members 1764.

9   As mentioned King Christian VII was schizophrenic. Struensee, who was the King's personal doctor, increasingly undertook political power, and was the actual ruler of the state 1770-1772. Struensee implemented several enlightened reforms of the administration and the state, which were considered to be radical at the time. This, and the fact that he had intimate

relations, and a daughter, with the Queen, led to a 'Palace Revolution', in which he was de-throned and sentenced to dead.

10 The city was originally named Oslo, but after a fire in 1624 the Danish King, Christian IV, had it rebuild and named it after himself. It was not until 1925 that the city was named Oslo again after a referendum.

11 Hasund 1941, p. 5. L.S. Platou: *Fortegnelse over de Norske Sogne-Selskaber, der have vedtaget at staae i Forbindelse med det Kongl. Selskab for Norges Vel.* (List of the Norwegian Parish Societies, which have decided on establishing relations with the Royal Society for the Welfare of Norway). *Budstikken* nr. 3, 1812, pp. 143-50.

12 In comparison, the price of one *tønde* (barrel) barley was 1 ¼ – 2 ⅓ *rigsdaler* in 1769.

13 Habermas 1990, chapter 3, § 9.

14 The remaining 12 % had not stated their address.

15 Manheim 1979, pp. 20-22. Giddens 2002, pp. 89-98. Tenbruck 1989, pp. 215-26.

16 Giddens 2002, pp. 22-26, 72-75.

17 Anderson 1991.

18 Mangor 1782, p. 65.

19 Melton 1988.

20 Jones 1938.

21 Nachricht des Herrn Pastor Steinhöfel zu Wake bei Göttingen, über die in Wake eingerich-tete Arbeitsschule vom 30ten November 1786. *Göttingisches Magazin für Industrie und Armen-pflege*, vol. 1, 1789, p. 57.

22 '[...] *dies herrliche Mittel zur schnellen Aufklärung'*. Nachricht des Herrn Pastor Steinhöfel zu Wake bei Göttingen, über die in Wake eingerichtete Arbeitsschule vom 30ten November 1786. *Göttingisches Magazin für Industrie und Armenpflege*. Vol. 1, 1789, p. 62.

23 Letter from J.L. Gazert to the central administration, dated 27 May 1817. Schleswig-Hol-steinisches Landesarchiv Abt. 422.3, no. 1.

24 Elias 1997. Weber 1920.

25 Markussen 1995, pp. 87, 100, 128-130, 178-179 and 184.

Danish vocabulary

Proper nouns of ships, theatre plays etc. are not included.

Accise: a duty

Admiralitets- og Generalkommissariatskollegiet: the central administration for the navy

Agre: strips of fields

Alen: measure of length (1 *alen* is 62.8 cm)

Almindelig Hospital: the General Hospital, Copenhagen

Amt, amter: app. county and counties (in 1793, e.g. there were 24 of these in the Kingdom of Denmark)

Amtmand: chief administrative officer of a county

Amtsforvalter: administrator of Crown lands

Amtsmestre: 'office-holding masters' (Schleswig-Holstein)

Armenpfleger: poor-guardian, a German term

Asiatisk Kompagni: the Danish Asia Company

Asiatisk Plads: the Asiatic Square, Copenhagen

Avlsbrugerne: the farmers

Birfedler: One who plays in beer houses or plays for beer, often used in general about inferior musicians and travelling fiddlers

Boder: small houses

Borgelejepenge: a tax, 'money for maintenance of soldiers and boatmen'

Borgerrepræsentanter: delegates of the citizens in the 1837 Municipal Governtment Act

Borgerskab: 1. Municipal license to trade and a precondition for political rights in the towns (only given to burghers). 2. The citizenry (the entire male population). 3. The burghers

Brogade: Pier Street

Brokvarterer: 'bridge neighbourhoods', Copenhagen (so named because of the bridges that cross the lakes between the old city and the new areas)

Budolphi Hospital: the Budolphi Foundation for Genteel Poor, Copenhagen

Byfoged: the town judge and chief of police

Bypræsident: town president

Bysser: two-masted ships

Børnehuset: 'the Children's House', the prison at Christianshavn, Copenhagen

Børsen: the Exchange, Copenhagen

Bøsseskytterpenge: a tax, 'money for maintenance of soldiers and boatmen'

Bådsmandsholdpenge: a tax, 'money for maintenance of soldiers and boatmen'

Bådsmandsudskrivningspenge: a tax, 'money for maintenance of soldiers and boatmen'

Christians Plejehus: hospital for the soldiers and the naval seamen, Eckernförde

Christianspflegehaus: state military nursing institution, Copenhagen

Corps de Gardes: guardhouses

Daler: see *Rigsdaler*

Danske Kancelli: the Danish Chancellery (was the ultimate authority for the courts, the clergy and the education system. The Chancellery also functioned as a cabinet office)

Danske Lov: 'Statute of the Danes', the codified statute-book dating back to 1683, issued by King Christian V

Danske skoler: Danish schools, i.e. national schools providing an elementary education

Den Store Skolekommission: the Commission for the Better Organisation of National Schools

Deputerede borger: delegated citizens

Det kongelige danske Landhusholdningsselskab: The Royal Danish Society of Agriculture

Det patriotiske Præmie-Selskab i Kalundborg: The Patriotic Prize Society in Kalundborg

Det patriotiske Selskab i Næstved: The Patriotic Society of Næstved

Det søsterlige Velgørenhedsselskab: The Sisterly Charity Society

Direktionen for Universitetet og de lærde Skoler: The Department for University and Grammar School Affairs

Direktionskommission: The Directions Commission, i.e. the board

Eligeret borger: trusted citizen, member of advisory town council

Embeds- og bestillingsmænd: civil servants and officials

Enevoldsarveregeringsakten: The Act of Hereditary and Sovereign Monarchy

Fabrikslister: annual factory records

Fald app.: a furlong (part of town field)

Fattigdirektionen: The Copenhagen poor relief board

Fattigforstandere: superintendents of the poor

Fattiggård: poor- and workhouse

Fattigkommissionen på Konventhuset: The Poor Commission at the Convent House

Fedel: fiddle

Flækker: small market towns, something in between regular villages and regular market towns

Folketinget: the Danish parliament

Forordning: ordinance

Forprang: trading outside the town gates and outside the fixed market hours

Forter: very broad grass paths which in addition to serving as roads were used for grazing, primarily for the livestock of visitors to the town

Fourer: the quartermaster sergeant

Frederiks Hospital: a hospital for the sick, Copenhagen

Frederiksstaden: Frederik's City (in Copenhagen), named after King Frederik V

Frifolk or *frimænd*: free men (soldiers)

Frimestre: free masters (artisans)

Fuldstændige skoler: 'finishing schools' with direct access to the university

Fuskere: dabblers

Fødselsstiftelsen: a birth clinic for the poor in Copenhagen

Gageringsplaner: the budgets according to which the army units had to order their affairs

Garnisonskirken: church for the Copenhagen garrison

Gehejmekabinetssekretær: The Privy Secretary

Gehejmeprokurøren/Generalprokurøren: was responsible for the implementation of the government's decrees and the supervision of the civil service

Generalitets- og Kommissariatskollegiet: The War Chancellery

Generalkrigsdirektoriet see *Generalitets- og Kommissariatskollegiet*

Generaltoldkammeret: the central administration of the customs duties, taxes and supervision of the Danish tropical colonies

Gige: fiddle

Gjethus: a building for casting metal, from the German 'giesen'

Grosserer-Societetet: The Society of Copenhagen Wholesale Dealers

Grundloven: the free liberal constitution 1849

Grundtakster: site valuations beginning in 1682

Guldhuset: The Gold House, a manufacture in Copenhagen

Gårde: 1. In towns: houses with outbuildings and a courtyard. 2. In the countryside: farms

Gårdsavlene: the town field parcels of the citizens

Harboes Jomfrukloster: Harboes Convent for Noble Maidens and Widows, Copenhagen

Hartkorn: taxes were chargeable on the individual farm on the basis of the hartkorn number. This number was an expression of the productivity of the land, as it took into consideration both the area and quality

Helligåndshospitalet: The Hospital of the Holy Spirit, Copenhagen, in daily speech called Vartov

Herred: the lowest legal district composed of a few parishes

Hittebørnsstiftelsen: an institution for foundlings, Copenhagen

Hof- og Statskalenderen: The Court and State Calendar

Hoftrompeterkorpset: The Royal Trumpeter Corps

Hosebinding: the proces of making knitted woollen socks

Hustakster: house valuations

Illustreret Tidende: Illustrated News, a gazelle

Islands Brygge: the Icelandic Wharf, Copenhagen

Kastellet: the Citadel in Copenhagen

Kastelskirken: church for the Citadel garrison, Copenhagen

Kommanderede: soldiers the regiment had supplied for other duties

Kommercekollegiet: a section of the central administration dealing with commerce and industry

Kommercelæster: the number of *kommercelæster* is an expression for the cargo carrying capacity of a ship.

Kongeloven Lex Regia: The Royal Law of 1665

Kongens Bryghus: The Royal Brewery, Copenhagen

Konsumtion: consumption tax, called the excise duty

Krejerter: three-masted ships

Krigsartiklerne: rules about the mutual relations between the troops and the officers, about the punishment for crimes committed and about the forms for enforcement of discipline in the army

Krigshospitalet på Ladegaarden: The War Hospital at the Barn House, Copenhagen

Krigskollegiet: the central administration for the army

Krigsretten: special military court

Kristendomsskoler: 'script-schools'

Kronarbejde: public work by soldiers

Kultusministeriet: The Ministry for Ecclesiastical and Educational Affairs

Kvæsthuset: The House for Maimed, Copenhagen

Kæmner: elected municipal servant in charge of the market town's municipal funds

Københavns Magistrat: the municipal corporation of Copenhagen

Købstad (sing.), *købstæder* (plur.): chartered towns, market towns

Landmilits: militia

Landprang: illegal selling and buying with peasants in the countryside

Landsoldater: national conscripted soldiers

Latinskoler: latin schools, i.e. grammar schools providing a preparatory education for university

Lav: guild

Len: fief

Lensmænd: noble holders of fiefs, from the 1660s replaced by the *amtmænd*

Livgarden: the military unit guarding the king

Livgarden til Fods: The Royal Life Guards Infantry

Lorchs Stiftelse for Unge Piger: orphanage for girls, Copenhagen

Lægeforeningens boliger: The Doctors' Union's dwellings, Copenhagen

Lært kunsten: learned the art

Læse- og arbejdsskole: literary and practical school

Læster: see kommercelæster

Magistraten: the town corporation or council (in towns where there was no council, the mayor in person of the *byfoged* made up the *magistrate* as well)

Manufaktur: pre-industrial production unit

Markjorderne: the field lands

Middelskoler: middle schools with the four lower forms and no direct access to the university

Nationalrekrutter: national recruits (conscripted soldiers with duties like those of the enlisted)

Nürnbergerkram: various small hardware products

Oldenborgske Infanteriregiment: The Oldenborg Infantry Regiment

Opfostringshuset: orphanage for boys and girls, Copenhagen

Ostindisk Kompagni: The Danish East Asia Company

Overretten: the provincial government and the high court of justice

Permitterede: soldiers on leave of absence

Petersens Jomfrukloster: Petersens Convent for Maidens, Copenhagen

Proviantgården: The Royal Provision Depot, Copenhagen

Præmieselskabet til at anføre den jødiske Ungdom til Kunstner og Haandværk: The Prize Society to Lead
    Jewish Youth into Arts and Crafts

Randers Amts Husholdningsselskab: The Society of Agriculture in Randers County

Realklasser: secondary school classes

Realskoler: secondary schools

Reces: body of laws

Rentekammeret: The Exchequer

Reskript: ordinance

Rigsbankdaler: the Danish currency 1813-1854

Rigsdagen: The Parliament

Rigsdaler: the Danish currency (1 *Rigsdaler* = 6 *Mark* or 96 *Skilling*)

Rigsrådet: i.e. a parliament comprising the Kingdom of Denmark and the Duchies of Schleswig,
    Holstein and Lauenburg

Ronde: special patrols

Rumlepotte: a kind of friction drum

Rådgivende stænderforsamlinger: advisory assemblies of Estates

Rådstueretten: the town court

Selskabet for Efterslægten paa Bornholm: The Society for Posterity in Bornholm

Selskabet for Norges Vel: The Society for the Well Being of Norway

Seminarium Pedagogicum: training college for grammar school teachers

Sjællandske Jægerkorps: The Zealand Chasseur Corps

Statkammerkollegiet: see *Rentekammeret*

Skatskillingslister: municipal tax lists based on valuations in *skilling*

Skib: ship

Skibstrompetere: trumpeters for The Royal Navy

Skilling: *see* Rigsdaler

Skoledirektionen: the county school board consisting of *amtmanden* and the dean

Skolekommissionen: the town's school board

Skude: craft

Skålpund: measuring unit (about 496 gr.)

Sletdaler: devaluated Danish currency in use 1618-1771. 1 *sletdaler* = 4 *mark* (2/3 of 1 *Rigsdaler*)

Soldateske: marine soldiery

St. Hans Hospital: a hospital for insane and syphilitic people, Copenhagen

Stadsmusikant: town musician employed by the town council

Statholder: royal governor

Stiftamtmand: the county governor

Storebælt: the Great Belt

Strømtolden: dues levied on vessels that passed through Storebælt (the Great Belt) and Lillebælt (the Little Belt) from the 15th century until 1857. They were a counterpart to the Sound Dues on Øresund

Stændermøde: assembly of the Estates

Subalterne: officers captains, first- and second-lieutenants

Søkvæsthuset: hospital for the soldiers and the naval seamen, Copenhagen

Toftejorder: corn gardens which lay alongside or close to the town ground

Tugt- og Børnehuset: a prison and orphanage, Copenhagen

Tugt-, Rasp- og Forbedringshuset: a prison for criminals and beggars, Copenhagen

Tyske Kancellli: The German Chancelly (dealt with relations to foreign countries and the administration of the Duchies)

Tøjhuset: The Royal Armoury, Copenhagen

Tønde land: unit area (1 = ca. 52,402 hectares)

Tårnblæsning: use of wind instruments in church and town hall towers

Udskiftning: division of land, app.: enclosure

Udstykning: division of a land area into plots which were then sold with full ownership and right of use to the buyers

Understaben: military term, see Karsten Skjold Petersens' article

Vaisenhuset: orphanage for boys and girls, Copenhagen

Vang: field

Vestindisk Kompagni: The Danish West India Company

Vestindisk Pakhus: West Indian Warehouse, Copenhagen

Øresund: the Sound (between Denmark and Sweden)

Illustrations

MICHAEL BREGNSBO

Fig. 1. Photo: The National Museum, Copenhagen.

Fig. 2. Photo: The National Museum, Copenhagen.

Fig. 3. E. Pontoppidan 1764. *Den Danske Atlas.* Vol. III, pp. 68 f.

Fig. 4. Photo: Scanpix.

LARS N. HENNINGSEN

Fig. 1. Map: Lisbeth Skjernov/The Danish Centre for Urban History, 2006.

Fig. 2. The Archives of the Danish Central Library of Southern Schleswig.

Fig. 3. E. Pontoppidan 1781. *Den danske Atlas.* Vol. VII.

Fig. 4a-b. The Provincial Archives for Southern Jutland, Aabenraa.

KARSTEN SKJOLD PETERSEN

Fig. 1. Photo: The Royal Library, Copenhagen.

Fig. 2. Photo: Øregaard Museum.

Fig. 3. Photo: The Royal Library, Copenhagen.

Fig. 4. Photo: The Royal Library, Copenhagen.

THOMAS BLOCH RAVN

Fig. 1. Drawing by Thomas Bloch Ravn, map by Lisbeth Skjernov, The Danish Centre for Urban History, 2006.

Fig. 2-6. Den Gamle By Open Air Museum, Aarhus. Photos: Knud Nielsen.

ANDERS MONRAD MØLLER

Fig. 1. Map: Lisbeth Skjernov, The Danish Centre for Urban History, 2006.

Fig. 2. J.P. Trap 1873. *Statistisk-topografisk Beskrivelse af Kongeriget Danmark.* Vol. 4, 2nd ed. Copenhagen, p. 289.

Fig. 3a-b-c. Georg Albrecht Koefoed 1993. *Forsøg til en Dansk Søe Ord-Bog med Beskrivelse på hver Ord og deres Benævning i det Frandske og Engelske Sprog.* Elsinore: The Danish Maritime Museum, fig. 115, 129 and 131.

Fig. 4. Photo: Museum of Svendborg. The Maritime Collection in Troense.

Fig. 5. Photo: The Danish Maritime Museum, Elsinore.

Fig. 6. Photo: The Danish Maritime Museum, Elsinore.

Fig. 7. Trap 1873 p. 164 f.

TRINE LOCHT ELKJÆR

Fig. 1+4. Maps by Trine Locht Elkjær, assisted by Lisbeth Skjernov, The Danish Centre for Urban History.

Fig. 2. Original map reproduced from: Povl v. Spreckelsen (ed.) 1952. *Randers Købstads historie*. Randers. Reconfigurated by Trine Locht Elkjær and Lisbeth Skjernov, The Danish Centre for Urban History.

Fig. 3. Original map in Skanderborg Local Archives. Reconfigurated by Trine Locht Elkjær.

HENRIK HARNOW

Fig. 1. Photo: Noury, Copenhagen City Museum.

Fig. 2. Photo: Odense City Museums.

Fig. 3. Map from Jens Toftgaard Jensen and Jeppe Norskov 2005. *Købstadens metamorfose. Byudvikling og byplanlægning i Århus 1800-1920*. Aarhus: Aarhus University Press.

Fig. 4. Photo: The Frederiks Værk Museum of Industry.

Fig. 5. Photo: Silkeborg Local History Archives.

PETER HENNINGSEN

Fig. 1. Reproduced by Peter Hansen, *Politivennen* 1904. Here reproduced from *Politihistorisk Selskab, Årsskrift* 1982, p. 77.

Fig. 2. Copperplate by Daniel Chodowiecki, in Basedow 1774. *Elementarwerk*. Reproducered from: Christoph Sachsse and Florian Tennstedt (eds.) 1983. *Bettler, Gauner und Proleten. Armut und Armenfürsorge in der deutschen Geschichte. Ein Bild-Lesebuch*. Reinbek: Rowohlt, fig. 54.

Fig. 3. Herslebs kortbog, Copenhagen City Archives.

Fig. 4. Photo: The Royal Library, Copenhagen.

Fig. 5. P. Klæstrup 1877. *Det forsvundne Kjøbenhavn. Tegninger af P. Klæstrup*. Copenhagen, XXXI.

JØRGEN MIKKELSEN

Fig. 1. Photo: Viborg Stiftsmuseum.

Fig. 2. Reproduced from Erich Pontoppidan 1768. *Den Danske Atlas*. Vol. IV, p. 532.

Fig. 3. Reproduced from Henrik Fangel 1975. *Haderslev bys historie 1800-1945*. Vol. I, p. 167.

Fig. 4. Photo: The National Museum, Copenhagen.

Fig. 5. Photo: Den Gamle By Open Air Museum, Aarhus.

Fig. 6. Photo: Den Gamle By Open Air Museum, Aarhus.

CHRISTIAN LARSEN

Fig. 1. Photo: The Old Town, Aarhus. Dias archives, VIII/E5S.

Fig. 2. Photo: Jørgen Mikkelsen.

Fig. 3. Drawing from 'Tegning fra Indbydelsesskrift til Indvielsen af Skolens nye Bygning den 23. October 1845'. Erik Nørr 1980. *Latinskolens programmer 1840-1903.* Copenhagen, p. 78.

Fig. 4. Map: Lisbeth Skjernov, The Danish Centre for Urban History, 2006.

JENS HENRIK KOUDAL

Fig. 1. Photo: The National Museum, Copenhagen, painted panel from the Grimstrup room. Photographer: Lennart Larsen.

Fig. 2. Jens Henrik Koudal 2000. *For borgere og bønder. Stadsmusikantvæsenet i Danmark ca. 1660-1800.* Copenhagen, p. 183.

Fig. 3. Photo: The National Museum, Copenhagen, skilderier, 7871/1952, 2nd Department 759.

Fig. 4. Peter Klæstrup: 'Flyttedagen. Et Laug flytter Skildt'. Engraving in Peter Klæstrup 1877. *Det forsvundne Kjøbenhavn.* Vol. 1. Copenhagen, X.

Fig. 5. Photo: Woodcut in The Royal Library, Copenhagen.

Fig. 6a-b. *'Fortid og Nutid'* 1833. Photo: Copenhagen City Museum.

JULIANE ENGELHARDT

Fig. 1. Map: Lisbeth Skjernov, The Danish Centre for Urban History, 2006.

Fig. 2. Drawing, 1863, Næstved Museum. Photo: Jens Olsen.

Fig. 3. Painting by Just Michael Hansen, 1833, Næstved Museum. Photo: Jens Olsen.

Fig. 4. Photo: Kalundborg Museum.

Fig. 5. The Old Town, Aarhus. Photo: Lorents Larsen.

The authors

MICHAEL BREGNSBO (B. 1962)

PhD, Ass. Professor of History, University of Southern Denmark. His major research fields are Danish Absolutism and Danish and international state formation history 1500-1900. International publications include: 'Denmark and the Westphalian Peace'. In H. Duchhardt (ed.), *Der Westfälische Friede. Diplomatie, politische Zäsur, kulturelles Umfeld, Rezeptionsgeschichte*. München: Oldenbourg 1998. 'Dänemark und 1848: Systemwechsel, Bürgerkrieg und Konsensus-Tradition'. In: H. Timmermann (ed.), *1848. Revolution in Europa. Verlauf, politische Programme, Folgen und Wirkungen*. Berlin: Duncker & Humblot 1999.

SØREN BITSCH CHRISTENSEN (B. 1969)

PhD, Ass. Professor at the Institute of History and Area Studies, University of Aarhus. Director of the Danish Centre for Urban History since 2001. Editor of the *Urban Studies* series (Danske Bystudier), vol. 1-3, and *Writings on Danish Urban History* (Skrifter om dansk byhistorie), vol. 1-4. His international publications include: Co-author of 'The Danish urban system pre-1800: a survey of recent research results'. In: *Urban History*, vol. 33, 3, 2006. Contributor to F.E Eliasen et al. (eds.), *Regional Integration in Early Modern Scandinavia*. Odense: Odense Universitetsforlag 2001, and S. Kroll et.al. (eds.), *Städtesystem und Urbanisierung im Ostseeraum in der frühen Neuzeit*. Berlin: LIT VERLAG, vol. 2-3.

OLE DEGN (B. 1937)

Dr. phil., ex-Senior Researcher and Archivist, The Danish National Archives (Landsarkivet for Nørrejylland). His life-long academic writing includes contributions to histories of Danish shipping and craft, editing ten volumes of *Kancelliets Brevbøger*, and three volumes of *Scandinavian Atlas of Historic towns*. International publications include: 'West Jutland, 1550-1900. Town, country and the surrounding world'. In: M. Guldberg et al. (eds.): *Facing the North Sea. West Jutland and the World. Proceedings of the Ribe conference April 6-8*. Esbjerg: Fiskeri- og Søfartsmuseet 1993. 'Small towns in Denmark in the sixteenth and seventeenth centuries'. In: A. Maczak & C. Smout (eds.), *Gründung und Bedeutung kleinerer Städte im nördlichen Europa der frühen Neuzeit*. (Wolfenbütteler Forschungen, 47). Wiesbaden 1991.

TRINE LOCHT ELKJÆR (B. 1954)

MA in history and music history, Audience Manager, Den Gamle By Open Air Museum of Urban History and Culture. Co-edited *Købstadens landbrug gennem 400 år: rapport fra seminar i Den Gamle By 21. september 1998*. Århus: Den Gamle By 2001, and several articles on the same subject.

JULIANE ENGELHARDT (B. 1968)

PhD, Post-doc fellow at the Saxo Institute, University of Copenhagen. Her primary research field is religious movement and reforms in Northern Europe 1675-1830 and the patriotic socities and Enlightenment in Denmark, Norway and the Schleswig-Holstein. Internationally, she has published 'Patriotism, nationalism and modernity: the patriotic societies in the Danish conglomerate state, 1769-1814'. In: *Nations and Nationalism*, 13 (2).

HENRIK HARNOW (B. 1961)

PhD, Curator, Odense City Museums. His research area is primarily industrial and technology history. He has written books and articles in Danish about the role of the engineer and the physical industrial environment and heritage as well as the book *Far and wide: the history of technical consultancy in Denmark – 1850 until today*. Copenhagen: Danish Association of Consulting Engineers 2004.

LARS N. HENNINGSEN (B. 1950)

Dr. phil., Director of the Archives and Study Centre of The Danish Central Library of the Duchy of Schleswig. His main research field is the history of the Danish minority and not least the 18th and 19th century social and economic history of Southern Schleswig, which includes the doctoral thesis *Provinsmatadorer fra 1700-årene. Reder-, købmands- og fabrikantfamilien Otte i Ekernførde i økonomi og politik 1700-1770*. Flensburg: Studieafdelingen og Arkivet ved Dansk Centralbibliotek for Sydslesvig 1985.

PETER HENNINGSEN (B. 1964)

Dr. phil., Archivist, Copenhagen City Archives. Being originally an rural and social historian, his main research field is peasant culture. Publications include 'Peasant Society and the Perception of a Moral Economy – Redistribution and Risk Aversion in Traditional Peasant Culture'. In: *Scandinavian Journal of History*, 2006/26, 4, pp. 271-96, and his doctoral thesis in 2006. Since 2003 editor of *Historiske Meddelelser om København*.

JENS HENRIK KOUDAL (B. 1951)

Dr. phil., Senior Researcher, the Danish Folklore Archives. His main research field is Danish and Scandinavian music and cultural history, c. 1600-1900. Among his publications with an urban history approach are 'Town Waits and Country Fiddlers in Denmark'. In: D. Stockmann & A. Erler (eds.), *Historische Volksmusikforschung. Studiengruppe zur Erforschung historischer Volksmusikquellen im ICTM*. Göttingen 1994. 'Mobility of Musicians in the Baltic in the 17th and 18th Century'. In: E. Ochs et.al. (eds.), *Musica Baltica. Interregionale musikkulturelle Beziehungen im Ostseeraum. Konferenzbericht Greifswald-Gdansk 28. November bis 3. Dezember 1993*. Sankt Augustin: Akademia Verlag 1996.

CHRISTIAN LARSEN (B. 1974)

MA in history, Archivist, the Danish National Archives (Rigsarkivet). His main research areas are education, poor relief, and church history and he has published a number of articles, source editions and bibliographies about these subjects.

JØRGEN MIKKELSEN (B. 1959)

PhD, Senior Researcher and Archivist, The Danish National Archives (Landsarkivet for Sjælland, Lolland-Falster & Bornholm). His primary research field is Danish and international urban history, c. 1700-1850, on which he has published a number of articles. Besides, he has a broad interest in administrative history. His international publications include: Co-author of 'The Danish urban system pre-1800: a survey of recent research results'. In: *Urban History*, vol. 33, 3, 2006. Co-editor of *Regional*

Integration in Early Modern Scandinavia. Odense: Odense Universitetsforlag 2001. Author of 'Märkte, Märktstädte und Marktwirtschaft: Das östliche Dänemark im späten 18. Jahrhundert als Beispiel'. In: H. Th. Gräf (Hrsg.): *Kleine Städte im neuzeitlichen Europa*. Berlin: Berliner Wissenschafts-Verlag 1997. Chairman of the Danish Committee of Urban History.

ANDERS MONRAD MØLLER (B. 1942)

Dr. phil, Part-time Lecturer at the Saxo Institute, University of Copenhagen. His main research field is maritime history and the history of tariffs and customs, on which he has published a great number of books. He has also published the letters and diaries of King Christian VIII. His urban studies include the industrial history of Odense.

KARSTEN SKJOLD PETERSEN (B. 1967)

PhD, Curator and Senior Researcher at Tøjhusmuseet (Royal Danish Arsenal Museum). His primary research interest is military history during Absolutism. A number of his works have an urban history approach, first of all *Husarer i Roskilde. En garnison og dens by 1778-1842*. Copenhagen: Roskilde Museum/Tøjhusmuseet 2003.

THOMAS BLOCH RAVN (B. 1954)

PhD, Director of Den Gamle By Open Air Museum of Urban History and Culture. Chairman of the Board of Directors of The Danish Centre for Urban History. His primary academic publications deal with the history of crafts and early modern urban culture and economics as well as a history of the town of Struer. He has also written *Den Gamle By – A Window into the Past*. Copenhagen: Gyldendal, 2002.

Index of towns and places

If no country is mentioned, the town or place belonged to The Kingdom of Denmark or the Duchies of Schleswig and Holstein.